Building Financial Models with Microsoft Excel

Founded in 1807, John Wiley & Sons is the oldest independent publishing company in the United States. With offices in North America, Europe, Australia, and Asia, Wiley is globally committed to developing and marketing print and electronic products and services for our customers' professional and personal knowledge and understanding.

The Wiley Finance series contains books written specifically for finance and investment professionals as well as sophisticated individual investors and their financial advisors. Book topics range from portfolio management to e-commerce, risk management, financial engineering, valuation and financial instrument analysis, as well as much more.

For a list of available titles, visit our Web site at www.WileyFinance.com.

Building Financial Models with Microsoft Excel

A Guide for Business Professionals

K. SCOTT PROCTOR

WILEY

John Wiley & Sons, Inc.

Published by John Wiley & Sons, Inc., Hoboken, New Jersey.
Published simultaneously in Canada.

For general information on our other products and services, or technical support, please contact our Customer Care Department within the United States at 800-762-2974, outside the United States at 317-572-3993 or fax 317-572-4002.

Wiley also publishes its books in a variety of electronic formats. Some content that appears in print may not be available in electronic books.

For more information about Wiley products, visit our web site at www.wiley.com.

Library of Congress Cataloging-in-Publication Data:
Proctor, K. Scott.
  Building financial models with Microsoft Excel : a guide for business professionals / K. Scott Proctor.
     p.   cm.
  ISBN 0-471-66103-1 (cloth/cd-rom)
  1. Corporations—Finance—Computer programs.   2. Microsoft Excel (Computer file)   I. Title.
  HG4012.5.P76   2005
  658.15'0285'554—dc22
                                                                          2004005515

Printed in the United States of America.

10   9   8   7   6   5   4

For Kimmell, Page, and Harris

Contents

Foreword

Before joining Microsoft, I spent a decade in consulting, focused primarily on helping customers implement financial and customer systems. These systems were the lifeblood of a company's financial modeling and decision support systems; they were responsible for ensuring quick and reliable business decisions, making the company more competitive while driving shareholder value. Given their importance to the business, we took great care in designing and delivering the analytical and reporting capabilities of these systems.

After implementing the modeling and reporting capabilities, I always enjoyed sitting down with the users to understand how they were utilizing their new tools. To my amazement, in almost every discussion with a user, the most noted feature of the reporting capabilities we delivered was the "Export to Excel" button. The robust capabilities that we had built for users were replaced by a tool that sat on every information worker's desktop that we could not match with any amount of effort—Microsoft Office Excel.

Financial modeling represents the practice of projecting a business's operating results. The process of building, maintaining, and using financial models involves many interrelated and complex steps. The extent to which the process of building financial models is made more straightforward through the use of Excel as a financial modeling tool is captured nicely in the title of this book, *Building Financial Models with Microsoft Excel*.

As one would expect, we use Excel for financial modeling inside Microsoft. In fact, when Microsoft deployed its financial, human resources, and customer systems, we started with Excel as the primary modeling, analytical, and reporting tool. We use financial models on a regular basis inside Microsoft to achieve business goals, and financial modeling has represented a key component of Microsoft's practice of planning for, and investing in, the future.

It is impressive to see employees at Microsoft model scenarios with Excel that are completely integrated with our back-end customer, product, and financial data. In addition, employees feel empowered in their ability to spend most of their time analyzing, modeling, and making business decisions, rather than hunting for data, crunching numbers, or making assumptions because of a lack of reliable data.

Watching employees collaborate between models, leverage the power of Excel, and run complex scenarios is very satisfying. It is especially satisfying to me, since as an information technology person I do not need to build many of the modeling capabilities that employees are using. Excel's capabilities go a long way in helping to make the process of building a financial model more straightforward.

The process of building financial models, which involves many integrated calculations, is made more manageable by Excel's ability to identify and track all of the points of linkage in calculations across financial models. Excel also enables users to test assumptions underlying financial models and run sensitivity analyses in real time with a high degree of accuracy—something that was not possible before the advent of the electronic spreadsheet.

As the world becomes increasingly connected from an electronic communications perspective, the ability to share and collaborate on financial models will increase. As more people use electronic spreadsheets such as Excel, the power to build complex financial models will extend to a wider audience. As standards underlying financial models emerge, such as XBRL (eXtensible Business Reporting Language), the ability to distribute and use clearly defined and well-understood elements of financial models will increase as well.

You can help ensure the success of your business through the use of financial models. Building a financial model helps to project a business's future operating results and allows for better business decision making. Microsoft has benefited in many ways through the efficient and effective use of financial models. This book will allow you to bolster your financial modeling skills and knowledge.

Building useful, accurate, and robust financial models can help ensure the success of your business. The opportunities have never been greater to use financial modeling tools such as Excel to make your company and your career more successful. The need for reliable modeling capabilities is stronger now than it has ever been. New features and functionality embedded in Excel 2003 offer users the ability to collaborate on, secure, and integrate financial models in new and exciting ways.

I highly recommend K. Scott Proctor's book as one of the best I have seen at providing the fundamental knowledge and insight for financial modeling in Excel. The book does a great job of walking through practical examples to help you build your financial modeling skills through the use of Excel—skills that will benefit you for years to come as financial modeling in Excel advances in this interconnected world.

—RON MARKEZICH
Chief Information Officer, Microsoft

Preface

PURPOSE OF THIS BOOK

Building Financial Models with Microsoft Excel is a step-by-step comprehensive guide to the process of building financial models using Microsoft Excel. I designed and wrote this book with the specific goal of making you an advanced financial model-builder using Excel. This is neither an accounting/finance textbook nor a "how to use Microsoft Excel" book. Rather, this book represents a real-world guide to using a powerful tool (Microsoft Excel) to accomplish a complex task (building a financial model). When you are finished reading this book, you should have a firm understanding of the steps involved in building financial models and you should know how to use Excel to put that understanding to work in the form of a working financial model.

A financial model is a quantitative representation of a company's past, present, and future business operations. Companies of all types and sizes use financial models every day to analyze and plan their business activities. Financial models serve as the foundation and basis of standard financial accounting reports, including the Balance Sheet, the Income Statement, and the Statement of Cash Flows.

This book contains step-by-step instructions for building a financial model. As such, this book can serve as either a tutorial or a reference. It is my hope that this book helps to demystify the process of building a financial model.

Microsoft Excel is a powerful application for the collection, analysis, and presentation of data in the business world. This book aims to build on the solid functionality and usability of Excel and extend these features into a specific and focused business application—that of building a working financial model. In so doing, this book extends the how-to nature of many Excel-oriented books to the subject matter of financial modeling.

Excel is an ideal tool for the design, construction, and maintenance of financial models. While many businesspeople are familiar with the output of financial models, namely the consolidated financial statements (Balance Sheet, Income Statement, and Statement of Cash Flows), few professionals are truly adept at building an accurate and effective financial model from the ground up. This book aims to endow you with the skills required to build a good financial model.

This book applies to several recent versions of Microsoft Excel (using a Microsoft Windows operating system), including Excel 2003, Excel XP, and Excel 2000. More recent versions of Excel provide additional features as compared to older versions, but these three versions of Excel provide the core functionality required through the course of this book. While Excel 2003 and Excel XP, for example, provide XML and Internet features and functions not found in Excel 2000, Excel 2000 offers sufficient functionality to build a financial model as outlined in this book (using a Microsoft operating system.) (Excel X for the Macintosh operating system also provides sufficient functionality—see "Minimum System Requirements" in the "About the CD-ROM" section of the book.)

NEED FOR THIS BOOK

While a number of books have been written on financial modeling with Microsoft Excel, the vast majority of these books are extremely advanced, often requiring extensive technical knowledge (such as the use of VBA—Visual Basic for Applications) and/or extensive corporate finance knowledge (including the mastery of topics such as efficient frontiers, variance–covariance matrices, Monte Carlo simulations, and Value-at-Risk). This book addresses the real, immediate, and significant need for a publication that covers how to build a financial model using Microsoft Excel from the perspective of a beginning- or intermediate-level computer user.

TARGET AUDIENCE FOR THIS BOOK

Building Financial Models with Microsoft Excel is for business professionals, entrepreneurs, and students who currently, or would like to, create or use financial models and/or statements as a part of their work. This book is targeted at individuals with a beginning to intermediate level of experience with both Microsoft Excel and finance/accounting.

While many business professionals and students have a working knowledge of Excel, few people possess the skill set required to build and maintain a financial model from the ground up. This is surprising, given the fact that several hundred thousand new businesses are launched and several hundred thousand business students graduate each year in the United States alone.

If any of these scenarios applies to you, this book is for you:

■ As a working professional, your job responsibilities include the analysis, use, and/or preparation of financial statements. Such responsibilities could include the preparation of a sales or departmental budget, the analysis of a division's financial performance compared to the rest of the company, or the valuation of a publicly traded company, among others. Examples of professionals in these scenarios could include: financial analysts, accounting managers, and vice presidents (and above) across all corporate divisions, among other professionals.

■ As an entrepreneur, or someone starting a new business, you are required to prepare and submit a set of financial statement projections to your bank or other source(s) of financing, such as a venture capital firm. Nearly all business plans associated with a new (or existing) company/business are required to have a set of "pro forma," or projected, financial statements.

■ As a business/management student at either the undergraduate or graduate level, you are required to build and analyze financial models. Financial literacy and skills are important in today's market; all business students should be well-versed in the use of financial models.

I have designed this book as a practical guide to get you started building a financial model quickly. As such, electronic copies of each of the examples and answers in the book are provided as Excel worksheets on a compact disc that is included with the book.

SUMMARY OF CONTENTS

Building a financial model is a step-by-step logical process—each component of the model builds on or feeds into another component of the model. This book, which is organized in a manner that follows this process, is divided into three major parts and includes an appendix that provides a general overview of Microsoft Excel's features and functionality.

Part One of the book introduces the concepts of budgets and financial models and covers the steps involved in building the Master Budget. You will learn about the various components of a Master Budget and how these components are related to one another. At the highest level of abstraction, the Master Budget contains two key components: the Operating Budget and the Financial Budget. The Master Budget template provided in this part of the book will serve as a roadmap for building each individual component of the financial model. This is the place to learn the fundamentals of the budgeting process and the nature of the relationships between the various components of the Master Budget.

Part One also covers the steps involved in building the Operating Budget, the first of the two key components of the Master Budget. Examples are provided for each of the steps described in this part of the book. It is important to work through this part of the book in detail, as the components of the Operating Budget are required elements of the overall financial model.

The steps involved in building the Financial Budget, the second of the two key components of the Master Budget, are also covered in Part One. As with the Operating Budget, examples are provided for each of the steps associated with building the Financial Budget. Each component of the Financial Budget is a required element of the overall financial model, so it is important to work through this part of the book in detail as well.

Part Two of the book deals with a company's consolidated financial statements and free cash flows. The consolidated financial statements include the Balance Sheet, the Income Statement, and the Statement of Cash Flows. This part of the book is built on data, calculations, and work from Part One. Many businesspeople are familiar with these consolidated financial statements—this part of the book provides a guide to building these statements from the ground up based on the Operating and the Financial Budgets for a company. Free cash flow calculations are covered in this part of the book as well to provide a cash-based perspective on a company's business operations and to provide a foundation for valuation calculations at a later point in the book.

Part Three deals with several topics, including various ways to analyze a financial model, the concept of valuation, and capitalization, or ownership, charts. The analytical techniques related to financial modeling include sensitivity analyses to test the assumptions underlying the financial model, contribution margin analyses to assess the fixed- and variable-cost elements of a company's cost structure, and financial ratios analyses to measure important financial ratios such as net income to sales (profit margin).

Valuation, covered in Part Three, is a complex issue—entire books are devoted to the subject. This part aims to cover some traditional valuation methodologies and link these techniques to the financial model built earlier in Parts One and Two. A capitalization chart provides a record of a company's ownership structure. Valuation and ownership are closely related (especially if a company raises any type of equity financing) and deceptively complex topics—this part of the book addresses how these topics relate to a financial model.

Finally, the book concludes with an appendix that provides a high-level overview of Microsoft Excel's features and functionality and detailed answers to all of the end-of-chapter questions. Note that you will often need to access the end-of-chapter question files on the accompanying CD-ROM to answer such questions.

A FINAL NOTE

While this book is written with United States GAAP (Generally Accepted Accounting Principles) in mind, the book's modular nature aims to help make the process of transitioning the modeling process to other accounting systems as straightforward as possible.

Acknowledgments

I would like to thank the editorial team at John Wiley & Sons for their support and assistance with this book. Special thanks to Bill Falloon, Melissa Scuereb, Jennifer MacDonald, and Todd Tedesco for helping to turn my ideas into a book.

I would also like to thank Gene Fife, Bob Coleman, and Dimitri Azar for their training, help, and guidance over the past several years. Thanks also to Bob Bruner for his role in inspiring my interest in, and pursuit of, the field of finance. Finally, thanks to my family for their support and understanding as I put this book together.

The Master Budget

CHAPTER 1

Overview of Budgets and Financial Models

BUDGETS

The *Cambridge Dictionary* defines a budget as "a plan to show how much money a person or organization will earn and how much they will need or be able to spend." Businesses use several different types of budgets to manage their operations. Whatever form various budgets may take, the primary goal of all budgets is to provide a tangible and quantifiable estimate of the receipt and allocation of resources. In the context of this book, a budget represents a core element of a financial model; financial models are discussed later in the chapter.

Businesses use several types of budgets for planning purposes. These budgets are typically categorized by the timeframe that they cover. A "long-range plan," one type of budget, typically forecasts financial statements out 5 to 10 years into the future. Long-range plans usually evolve from "strategic plans," which define the overall mission and goals for a business. These long-range plans are coordinated with Capital Budgets, which map out large monetary commitments for things such as facilities and large pieces of equipment.

From a budgeting perspective, this book is focused on the "Master Budget," which forecasts a business's complete operations over the medium-term (1–5 years). The Master Budget consists of many interrelated financial and operating schedules, including sales, purchases, and operating expenses, among many others. While some of the key outputs of a Master Budget are the consolidated financial statements (Balance Sheet, Income Statement, and Statement of Cash Flows), a vast array of supporting schedules are also part of the Master Budget. Figure 1.1 outlines the various components of the Master Budget.

As Figure 1.1 indicates, there are two key components of the Master Budget: the Operating Budget and the Financial Budget.

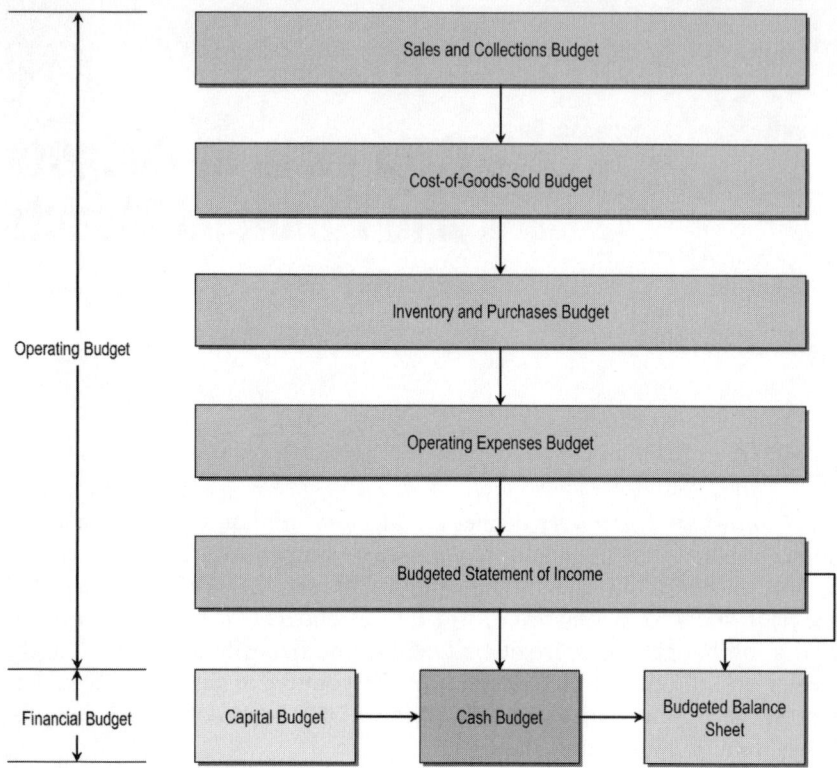

FIGURE 1.1 Components of the Master Budget

Operating Budget

The operating budget focuses on the Budgeted Income Statement and its supporting components and schedules—these items are described below.

Sales and Collections Budget The Sales and Collections Budget represents one of the first steps in the budgeting process, as items such as inventory levels and operating expenses are driven off of the Sales and Collections Budget. Effective sales budgeting is a key factor in building a useful and representative financial model for a business. Regardless of the nature of your business (for example, whether it is product- or service-based), this book takes a unit-based approach in which forecast sales are based on (1) projected unit sales and (2) projected unit prices. This topic is covered in detail later in the book.

Cost-of-Goods-Sold Budget The Cost-of-Goods-Sold Budget decomposes, or breaks down, the components of a business's cost of goods sold (in some cases referred to as the cost of revenues). This budget breaks out each separate factor underlying the cost of goods sold for a business.

Inventory and Purchases Budget   The Inventory and Purchases Budget, which represents what a business plans to buy and how much inventory it intends to hold over a given timeframe, is based on three factors: a business's desired ending inventory, cost of goods sold, and beginning inventory. A business's desired ending inventory will drive that business's budgeted purchases over a given period of time. A larger desired ending inventory will typically lead to a larger Purchases Budget and vice-versa. While the Purchases Budget, a component of the Inventory and Purchases Budget, represents an estimate of future purchases, this is an accrual-based accounting figure, and it is the Disbursements for Purchases Budget (another component of the Inventory and Purchases Budget) that drives a company's cash flows. This concept is discussed in detail later in the book.

Operating Expenses Budget   The Operating Expenses Budget forecasts all of the elements of a business's operating expenses, such as salaries, rent, depreciation, and others. Some of these expenses are fixed and some are variable (in other words, based on another metric, such as revenues); this concept of fixed versus variable costs is discussed in detail later in the book. While the Operating Expenses Budget represents an estimate of future expenses, this is an accrual-based accounting figure, and it is the Disbursements for Operating Expenses Budget, a component of the Operating Expenses Budget, that drives a company's cash flows. This concept is also discussed in detail later in the book.

Budgeted Statement of Income   The Budgeted Statement of Income (also referred to as the Budgeted Income Statement) integrates components of each of the other Operating Budget schedules. The Income Statement compares a business's revenues and costs for a given period of time and often serves as a benchmark for the performance of a business.

Financial Budget

The Financial Budget is focused on capital expenditures (large purchases of assets such as equipment and facilities) and on a business's budgeted cash position and Balance Sheet.

Capital Budget   A business's Capital Budget forecasts large expenditures for items such as machinery. Different companies set different thresholds for what qualifies as a capital expenditure (versus an expense). If the purchase of an item (such as a piece of machinery) is classified as a capital expenditure, it is then depreciated (or amortized in some cases) over a predetermined period of time. The Capital Budget covers Capital Expenditures, Disbursements for Capital Expenditures, and Depreciation Budgets.

Cash Budget   The Cash Budget tracks a business's anticipated cash receipts and disbursements. This is a very detailed and important schedule that draws on information in the Operating Budget.

Budgeted Balance Sheet   The budgeted Balance Sheet represents the final step in building the Master Budget as outlined in Figure 1.1. The budgeted Balance Sheet integrates components from both the Operating and the Financial Budgets.

FINANCIAL MODELS

A financial model is a quantitative representation of a company's past, present, and future business operations. This quantitative representation is expressed through the use of accounting—the language of business. Finance, which may be broadly defined as the science of managing money and other assets, is based on accounting. As such, it is important to recognize the central role accounting, or the enumeration of business transactions, plays in building financial models. While this book does not cover or address accounting concepts in any level of detail, it is worth noting that the consolidated financial statements (Balance Sheet, Income Statement, and Statement of Cash Flows) represent the product of a series of accounting transactions.

A financial model is a required component of any business plan. Anyone interested in starting a new business, starting a new line of business within an existing company, assessing the operations of an existing or proposed business, and/or comparing the operations of two or more businesses, among other tasks, should know how to build, use, and modify a financial model.

While there are a variety of approaches to building financial models, this book will focus on the inclusion of the following sections in a financial model: (1) a Master Budget (which is made up of an Operating Budget and a Financial Budget), (2) the consolidated financial statements (Balance Sheet, Income Statement, and Statement of Free Cash Flows), (3) a free cash flow analysis, (4) a sensitivity analysis of the model's outputs versus inputs, (5) a contribution margin analysis, (6) a financial ratios analysis, (7) a valuation analysis, and (8) a capitalization chart.

For the sake of illustration, sample templates for each of these sections are shown below. Please note that no numbers/values have been inserted into these templates—over the course of this book, I will walk through the process of filling in all of these templates one step at a time.

A financial model integrates all of the components of a Master Budget into a working model of a company's planned financial activities for a given time period. As this represents a significant amount of information, the components of a financial model are presented in several figures.

As discussed earlier, the components of the Master Budget are broken into the two primary budgets—the Operating Budget and the Financial Budget. Please note that the areas shaded in gray in the screenshots represent the areas in which I will fill in values to build a financial model over the course of this book. These figures are presented as a road map for the next several chapters of the book.

Master Budget—Operating Budget

The following figures represent components of the Operating Budget. Note the following convention used throughout the book for time periods: "1Q X4" is to be interpreted as "the first quarter of a year ending in the number 4." The use of "X4" for a year is a common practice in accounting and finance—it is meant to refer to a specific year without referring to an exact time period such as "94" or "04." I also use the following convention throughout the book: "X4" is to be interpreted as "the year X4." Again, this is meant to refer to a particular year without referring to an exact time period.

Sales and Collections Budget   The Sales and Collections Budget, shown in Figure 1.2, consists of a Sales Budget and a Collections Budget.

Cost-of-Goods-Sold Budget   The Cost-of-Goods-Sold Budget, shown in Figure 1.3, breaks out each component of a business's cost of goods sold.

Inventory and Purchases Budget   The Inventory and Purchases Budget, shown in Figure 1.4, consists of an Inventory Budget and a Purchases Budget.

Operating Expenses Budget   The Operating Expenses Budget, shown in Figure 1.5, consists of an Operating Expenses Budget and a Disbursements for Operating Expenses Budget.

Budgeted Statement of Income   The Budgeted Statement of Income, shown in Figure 1.6, compares a business's revenues and expenses.

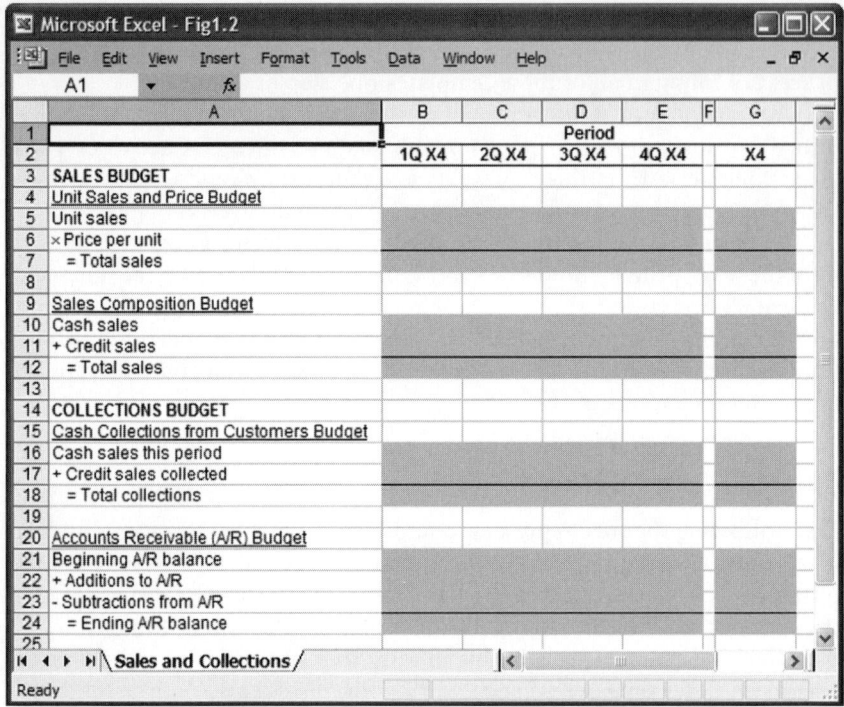

FIGURE 1.2   Sales and Collections Budget

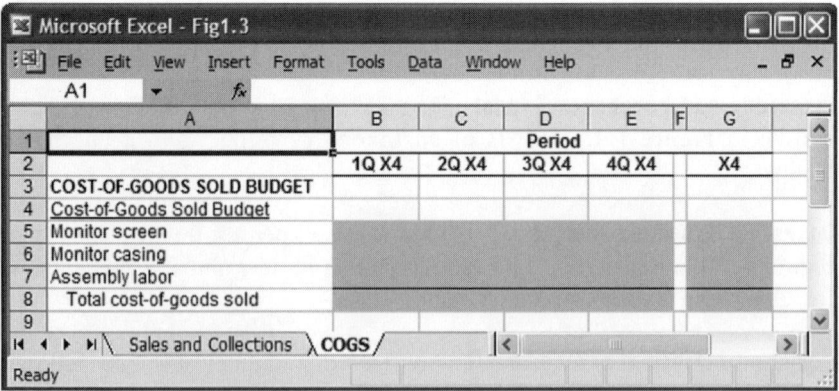

FIGURE 1.3   Cost-of-Goods-Sold Budget

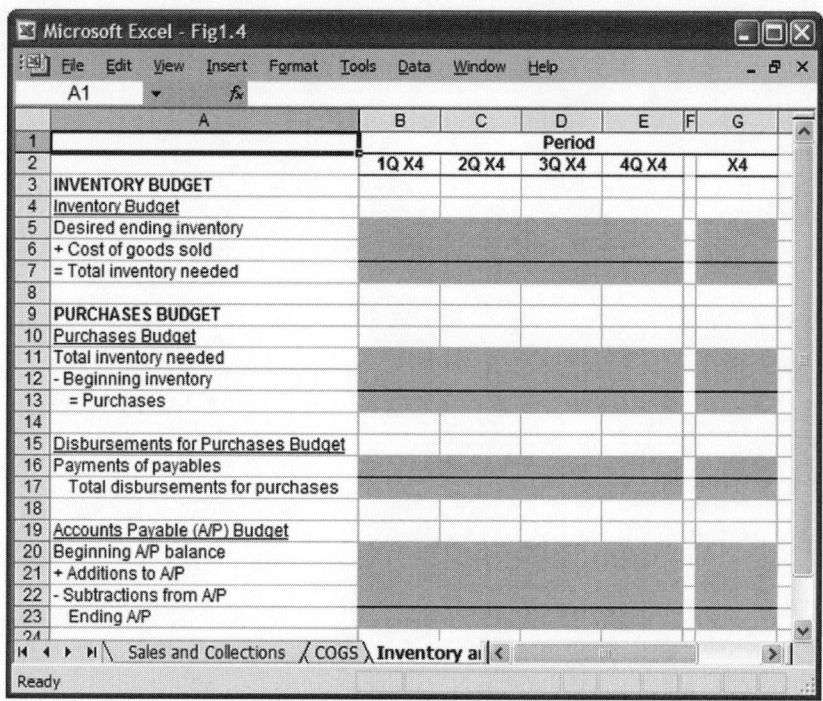

FIGURE 1.4 Inventory and Purchases Budget

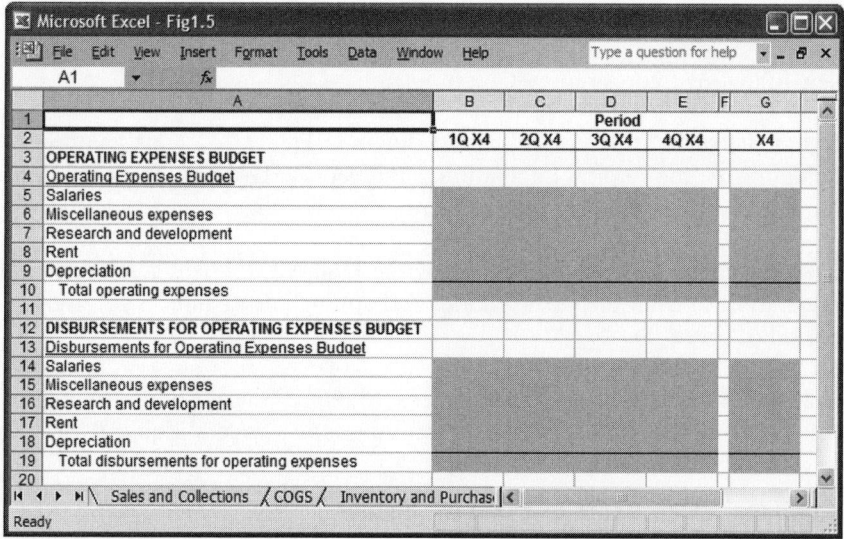

FIGURE 1.5 Operating Expenses Budget

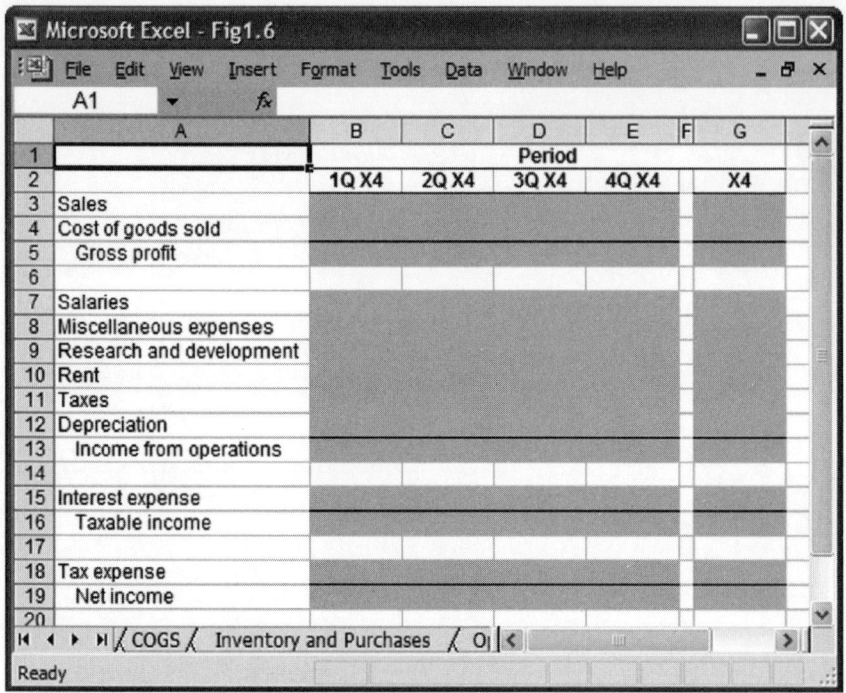

FIGURE 1.6   Budget Statement of Income

Master Budget—Financial Budget

The following figures represent components of the Financial Budget.

Capital Budget   The Capital Budget, shown in Figure 1.7, consists of three components: the Capital Expenditures Budget, the Disbursements for Capital Expenditures Budget, and the Depreciation Budget.

Cash Budget   The Cash Budget, shown in Figure 1.8, offers a detailed reconciliation of a business's beginning and ending cash balances for a given period of time.

Budgeted Balance Sheet   The Budgeted Balance Sheet, shown in Figure 1.9, compares a business's Assets, Liabilities, and Owners' Equity.

Additional Components of a Master Budget

A working financial model should include several additional schedules beyond those presented in Figures 1.2 through 1.9. These schedules include

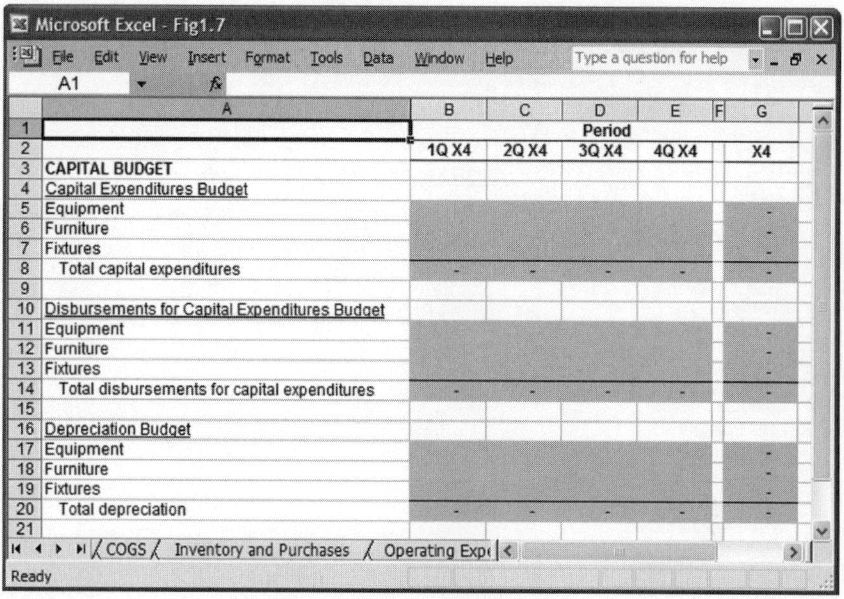

FIGURE 1.7 Capital Budget

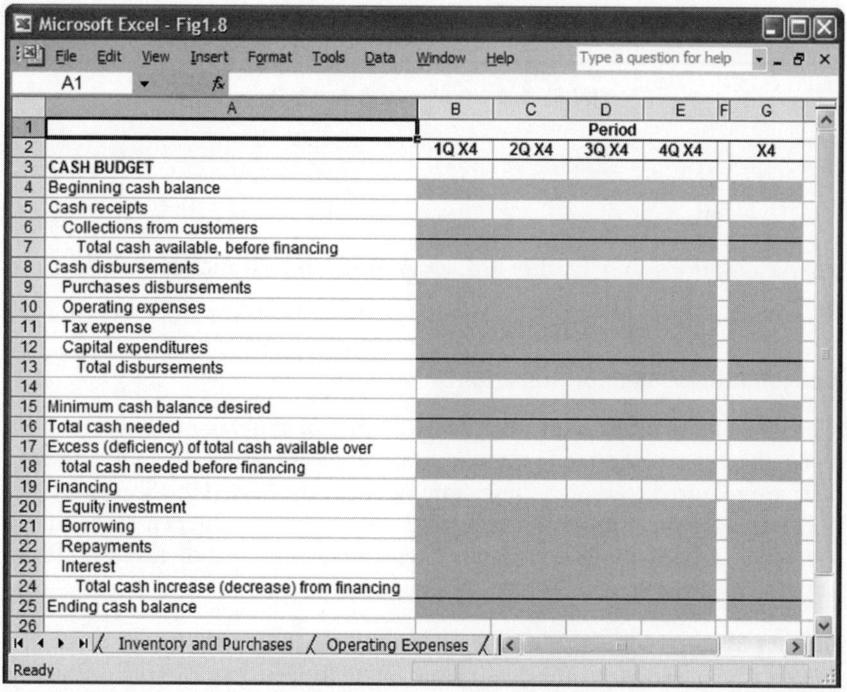

FIGURE 1.8 Cash Budget

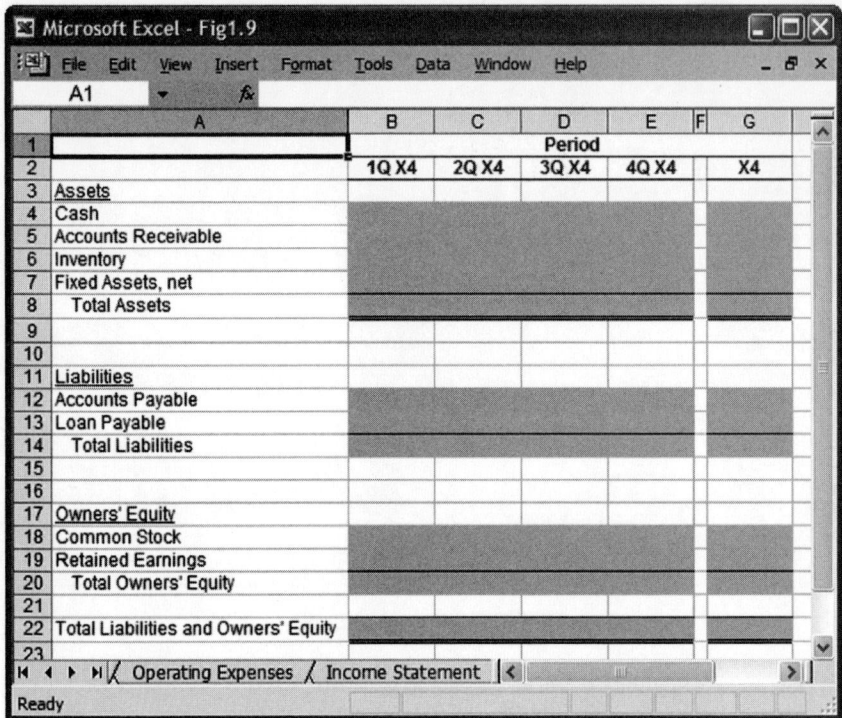

FIGURE 1.9   Budgeted Balance Sheet

an Assumptions and Dashboard worksheet and Headcount worksheets, among others.

Consolidated Financial Statements

The consolidated financial statements consist of the Balance Sheet, the Income Statement, and the Statement of Cash Flows. Publicly traded companies are required to report these statements to the SEC (U.S. Securities and Exchange Commission) on a regular basis, so many readers may be familiar with each of these statements. Templates for each of these financial statements are provided below.

Balance Sheet   A Balance Sheet, shown in Figure 1.10, offers a view of a business's financial position in terms of its Assets, Liabilities, and Owners' Equity.

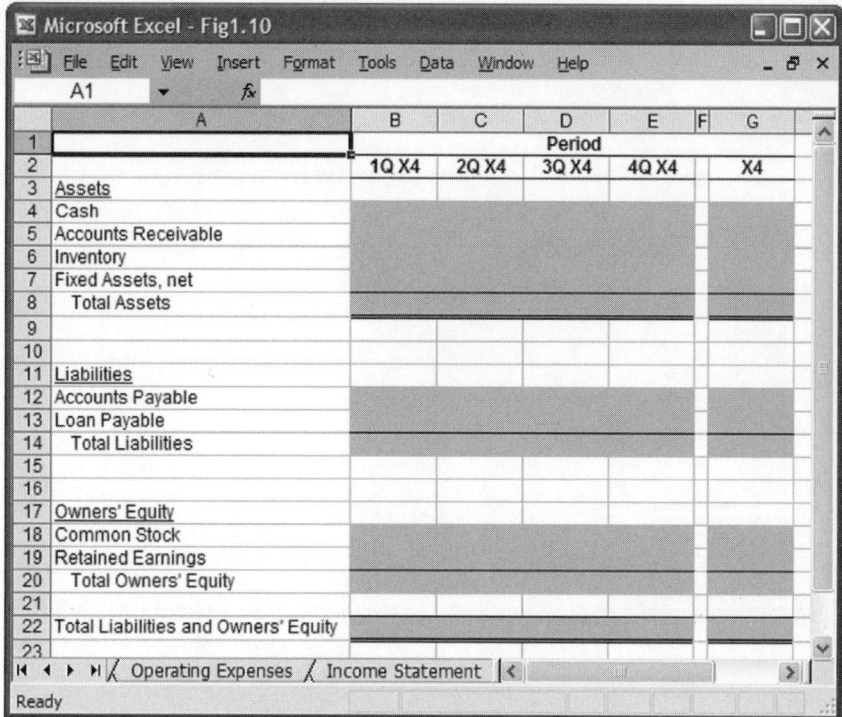

FIGURE 1.10 Balance Sheet

Income Statement An Income Statement, shown in Figure 1.11, presents a summary of a business's results of operations in terms of its revenues and expenses.

Statement of Cash Flows A Statement of Cash Flows, shown in Figure 1.12, reconciles a business's net income to its change in cash position over a given time period in terms of Cash Flows from Operating Activities, Cash Flows from Investing Activities, and Cash Flows from Financing Activities.

Free Cash Flow Analysis

The concept of free cash flows is central to modern finance. Broadly speaking, free cash flows represent the amount of cash a business generates (or, in some cases, consumes) over a given timeframe after paying all of its "required" costs for that period. I will discuss free cash flows in Chapter 9,

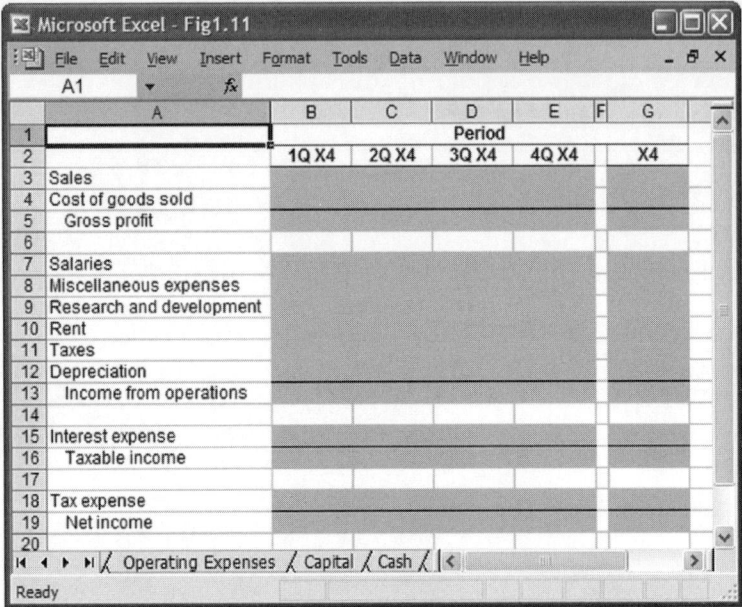

FIGURE 1.11   Income Statement

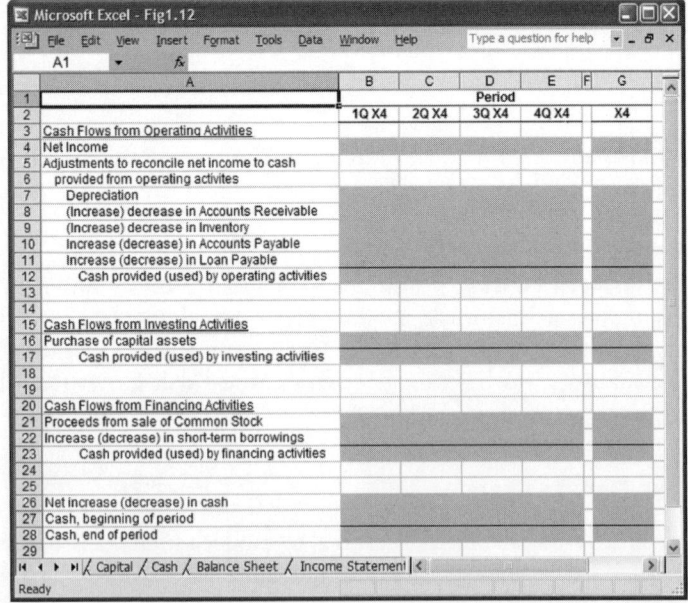

FIGURE 1.12   Statement of Cash Flows

but technically speaking, free cash flows represent the cash available to all providers of capital (providers of both debt and equity). Figure 1.13 presents a view of the free cash flows worksheet. All of the terms in this worksheet will be explained and discussed in Chapter 9.

Sensitivity Analysis

Sensitivity analyses are used to model the effect of changing input variables on some output of interest, such as net income or free cash flows. It is often helpful to build a series of sensitivity analyses to get a sense for what input variables will have a significant influence on your output metric of interest (for example, net income). Figure 1.14 shows a data table template that could be used to test the effect of varying the assumed growth rate in revenues on net income. Chapter 10 is devoted entirely to the coverage of sensitivity analyses.

Contribution Margin Analysis

Contribution margin is defined as the extent to which each unit sale contributes to a business's fixed cost base. This is calculated as unit price – variable costs per unit. Key operating metrics, such as operating leverage

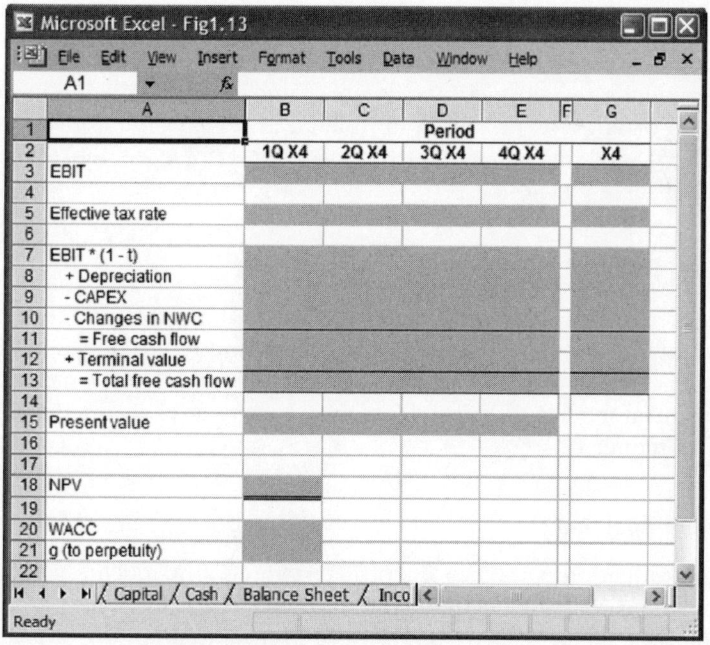

FIGURE 1.13 Free Cash Flows Worksheet

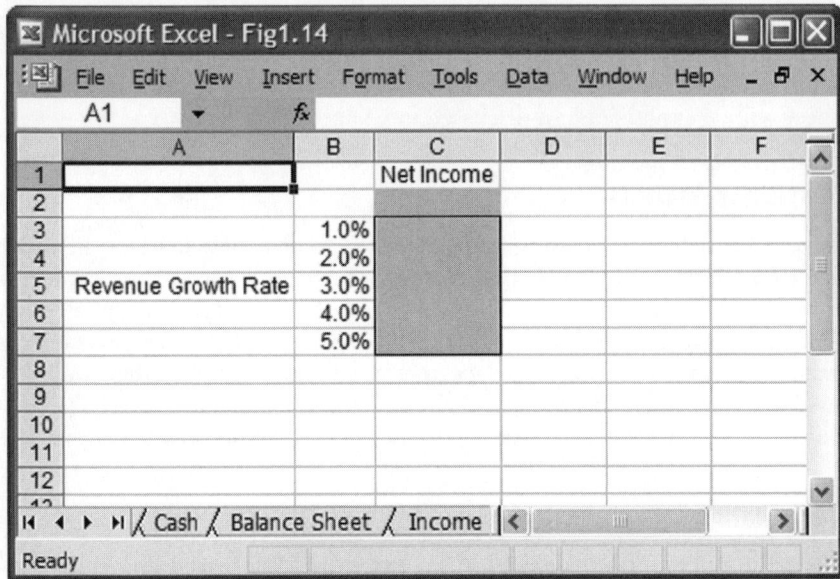

FIGURE 1.14   Data Table Template

(calculated as fixed costs/total costs), breakeven value in units (how many units must be sold before the business reaches "breakeven," or the point at which revenues cover all costs), and breakeven value in dollars (the level of sales, as measured in dollars, at which the business reaches breakeven), are covered in detail in Chapter 11. Figure 1.15 highlights several of these metrics.

Financial Ratios Analysis

Financial ratios, such as gross margin (calculated as gross profit/sales), net profit margin (calculated as net income/sales), and return on equity (calculated as net income/owners' equity), among others, are often used to analyze financial models. Figure 1.16 highlights several of the financial ratios used in Chapter 12.

Valuation Analysis

 Business valuation is the process of determining how much a company is worth—in other words, determining its value. The valuation of a business is a complex subject—many books have been written on this topic alone. This book will cover the concept of "triangulation," in which several well-

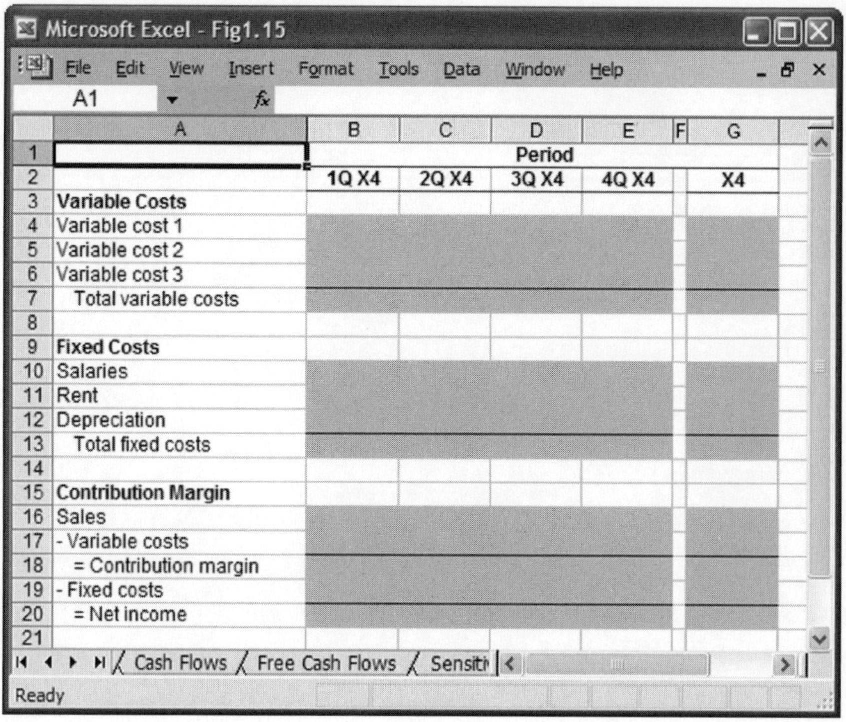

FIGURE 1.15 Examples of Contribution Margin Operating Metrics

known valuation techniques are used—and are weighed appropriately—to estimate the value of a business. Figure 1.17 highlights a model in which various valuation techniques are used to triangulate on the value of a business. Valuation is covered in detail in Chapter 13.

Capitalization Chart

A capitalization chart represents the ownership structure of a business. While this is one of a business's most important documents, few books on financial modeling cover this subject. Figure 1.18 demonstrates one approach to displaying a capitalization chart. I will build a set of capitalization charts in Chapter 14 to model the effects of an investment into a business over time.

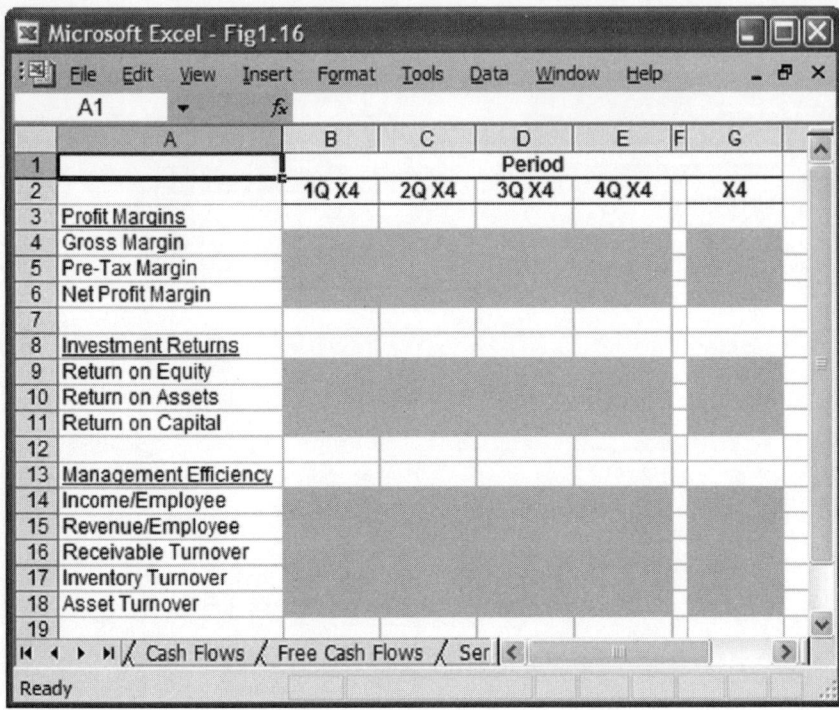

FIGURE 1.16 Financial Ratios Examples

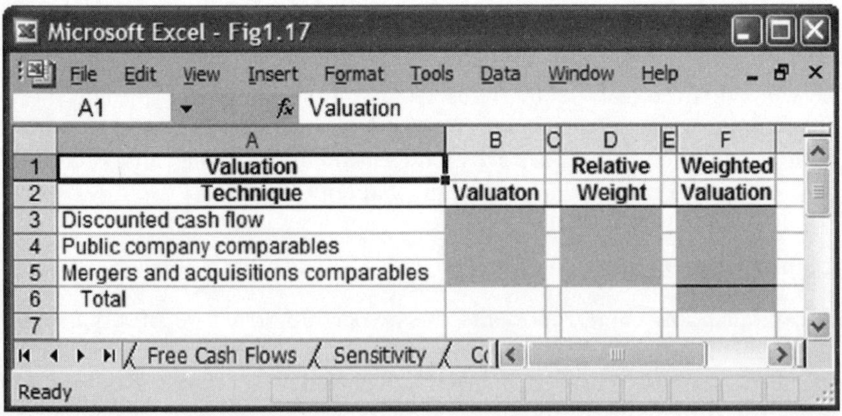

FIGURE 1.17 Valuation Model Example

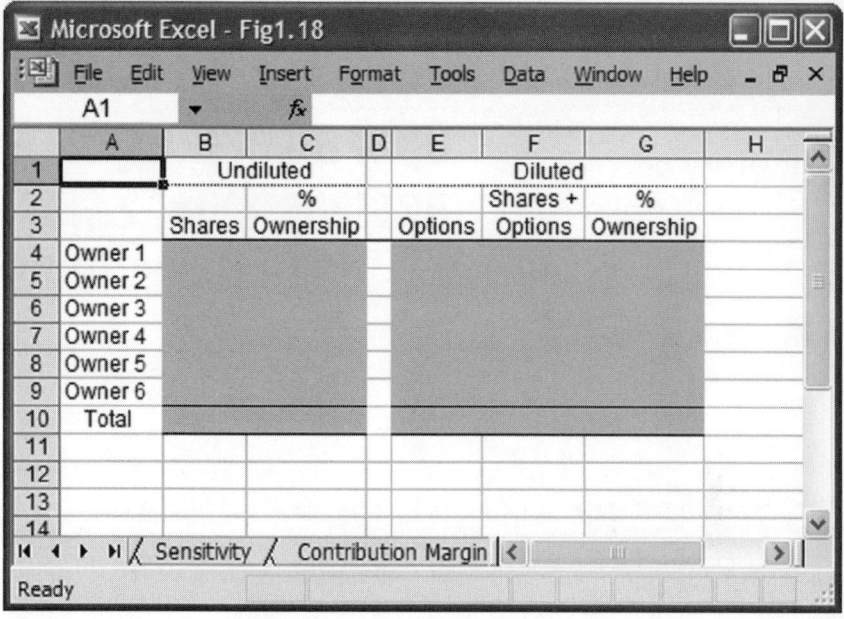

FIGURE 1.18   Capitalization Chart

QUESTIONS

1. What is the main goal of all budgets?
2. What are the two main components of a Master Budget?
3. What is a financial model?
4. What are the names of the three components of standard consolidated financial statements?
5. What do free cash flows represent for a business?
6. Why should a business use a sensitivity analysis? A contribution margin analysis? A financial ratios analysis?
7. What is valuation?
8. What is a capitalization chart?

CHAPTER 2

Operating Budget— Assumptions, Sales, and Collections

The Operating Budget, also known as a "profit plan," focuses on a company's Income Statement and its supporting components or "schedules." While Chapter 1 provides an overview of the concept of a Master Budget, this chapter covers the specific steps involved in building the sales components of an Operating Budget from the ground up. Chapters 3 and 4 provide detailed coverage of the steps involved in building the cost components of an Operating Budget. Figure 2.1 highlights the separate sales-oriented components of the Operating Budget.

Preparing an Operating Budget is the first step in the process of building a Master Budget. The preparation of an Operating Budget is a sequential process—it is critical to follow each step outlined below in the order presented. Moreover, the preparation of a financial budget in Chapters 6 and 7 and the consolidated financial statements in Chapter 8 build on the work in this chapter.

NAPAVALE—BACKGROUND INFORMATION ON EXAMPLE COMPANY

I will use a fictitious company named "Napavale" to illustrate the process of building a financial model. Napavale develops, markets, and sells advanced flat-screen computer monitors directly to consumers. These products are sold exclusively through a direct channel of distribution—the monitors are not sold through electronics stores or resellers, for example. Napavale offers customers several ways to purchase its monitors: through a mail-order catalog, over the telephone, or through Napavale's web site on the Internet.

STEP 1: Assumptions and Dashboard

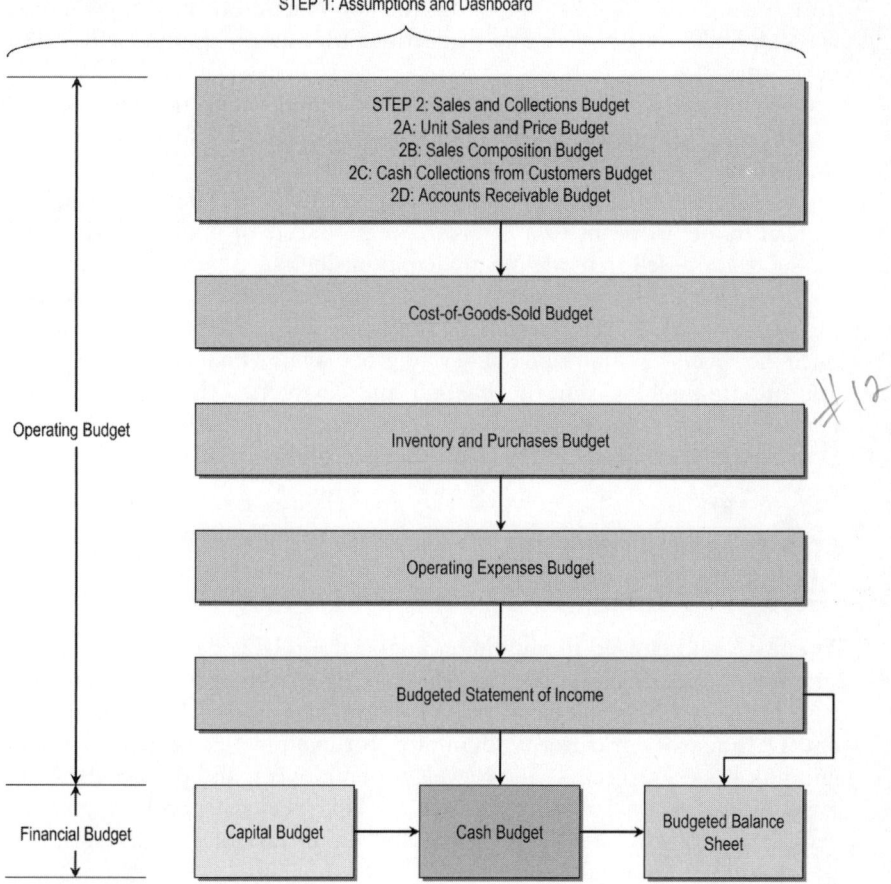

FIGURE 2.1   Sales-Oriented Components of the Operating Budget

Napavale's monitors, which are thin, lightweight, and offer excellent visibility and resolution, are sold on both cash and credit terms. Napavale's management prepares financial models so that they may run their business more efficiently and effectively.

Over the course of the next several chapters in which I will build a complete financial model for Napavale, I will project results out four quarters (one year) into the future. While most real-world budgets project results out three, and sometimes five years, the presentation of financial projections using Microsoft Excel screenshots in a book format is much more practical using four quarters of projections as opposed to using a three- or five-year time horizon. The process involved in building financial models is the same, however, for four quarters as it is for any other timeframe. Once you have a firm grasp of the process underlying the construction of financial models, you can build your models and projections for any timeframe, be it weeks or decades.

For the sake of presentation, I am assuming Napavale was founded and began operations in the first accounting period (quarter) covered throughout Napavale's financial model. While few businesses may be able to begin functioning operationally as quickly as Napavale, Napavale's financial model is meant to address the many facets of building a financial model (as opposed to modeling an actual business).

Any forward-looking financial model will be based on a set of underlying assumptions. In the interests of simplicity and readability, I will introduce the specific assumptions underlying Napavale's financial model at the appropriate points within this chapter and Chapters 3 through 7. The remainder of this chapter will cover the construction of the Assumptions and Dashboard worksheet and the sales elements of the Operating Budget.

STEP 1: ASSUMPTIONS AND DASHBOARD WORKSHEET

The first step involved in building a financial model is developing an "Assumptions and Dashboard" worksheet. This worksheet will contain the vast majority of the financial model's input variables. The Assumptions and Dashboard worksheet will contain, for example, projected unit sales and unit prices, projected salary levels for employees, and projected capital expenditures, among many other values. This worksheet will serve as the central point of reference for all of the input variables underlying Napavale's entire financial model.

By centralizing all of the input variables of a financial model into a single location (the Assumptions and Dashboard worksheet), users can easily test and evaluate the implications of changes in the values of input variables across all elements of a financial model, including the consolidated financial statements and other metrics of interest, such as free cash flows. The use of an Assumptions and Dashboard worksheet represents a core financial modeling concept: that of avoiding "hard coding," or entering specific input variables directly into a worksheet. Whenever possible, I represent input variables as values on a separate worksheet (or area of a worksheet). If you adhere to this technique in your own financial models, you stand to save yourself significant time and effort when you modify your financial models in the future.

The Assumptions and Dashboard worksheet includes an element that I refer to as the "Dashboard." The Dashboard offers a high-level gauge of a financial model's condition and state of health. A Dashboard can provide a synopsis of a financial model's key outputs, such as revenues and net income, and can also indicate, for example, whether the balance sheet is balanced. I will not cover the Dashboard, however, until Chapter 10. These are key features for all users of financial models, but especially for users that must present their financial models to audiences and executives that ask for changes in input variables in real time.

An Assumption and Dashboard worksheet allows you to, for example, change unit sales projections during a meeting and immediately evaluate the impact of this change and determine whether the model is still functioning properly—important and helpful features to have in a financial model. I refer to the Assumptions and Dashboard worksheet frequently over the course of this book.

For the sake of presentation, Figure 2.2 indicates the placeholders for some of the input variable assumptions that I will fill in with values over the next several chapters. As I work through each of the steps involved in building a financial model, I provide screenshots of the Assumptions worksheet with the relevant values indicated.

I use the following formatting convention for the remainder of the book: any input cells (those cells whose values/contents I can change) will be formatted in black with white numbers, and any output cells (those cells whose values are contingent on formulas and/or the values in other cells) will be formatted in gray with black numbers.

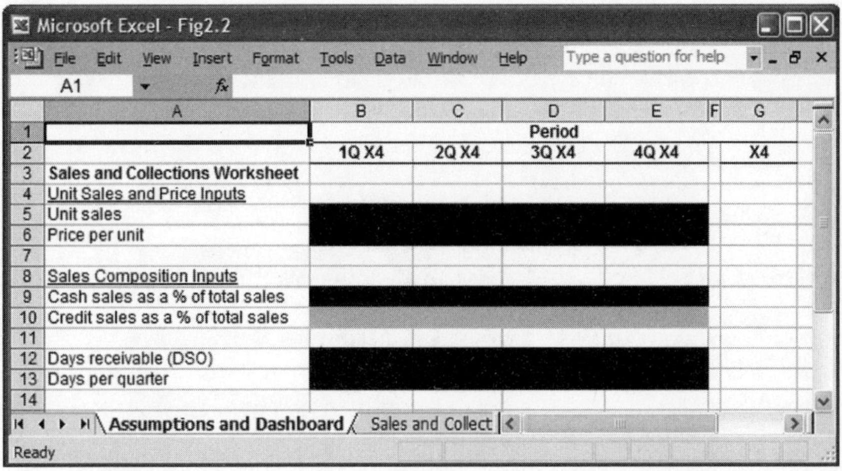

FIGURE 2.2 Placeholders for Several Input Variable Assumptions

STEP 2A: UNIT SALES AND PRICE BUDGET

The Unit Sales and Price Budget represents a central component of a financial model. Many other elements in the financial model, including inventory levels, operating expenses, and purchases, are often based off of projected sales levels.

The first step in building a sales budget is to project total sales levels for a time period, such as a fiscal quarter, or three months. An effective way in which to project these sales is on a per-unit basis. As Napavale, my fictitious company, sells computer monitors, I will project the number of monitors sold. Thus, "number of monitors sold" represents my unit of measure for sales projections. If you are modeling a service-oriented company, such as a consulting firm, you could just as easily use a metric such as "hours billed" as your unit for sales projections.

In addition to projecting unit sales of Napavale's product, I need to project the average selling price per unit over a period of time. While Napavale sells only one product, I could easily project sales levels in terms of units and selling price per unit for a range of products. I am using only one product for Napavale in the interest of ease of presentation for Excel screenshots.

Once the unit sales and the average selling price per unit are determined, I multiply these two values together for a time period (such as a quarter) to calculate the total sales figure in dollars for this time period.

Figure 2.3 indicates the assumptions underlying Napavale's unit sales projections (using the Assumptions and Dashboard worksheet). The Unit Sales and Price Budget is shown in Figure 2.4. Note that I have included a

Microsoft Excel - Fig2.3							
File Edit View Insert Format Tools Data Window Help					Type a question for help		
A1		fx					
	A	B	C	D	E	F	G
1				Period			
2		1Q X4	2Q X4	3Q X4	4Q X4		X4
3	Sales and Collections Worksheet						
4	Unit Sales and Price Inputs						
5	Unit sales	1,000	1,500	2,100	2,800		
6	Price per unit	$ 1,000	$ 960	$ 920	$ 900		
7							
8	Sales Composition Inputs						
9	Cash sales as a % of total sales						
10	Credit sales as a % of total sales						
11							
12	Days receivable (DSO)						
13	Days per quarter						
14							

Assumptions and Dashboard / Sales and Collecti

Ready

FIGURE 2.3 Assumptions Underlying Napavale's Unit Sales Projections

FORMATTING TIPS

As you can see in Figures 2.3 through 2.7, certain formatting techniques aid in the construction of a worksheet. Note the following uses of formatting (these formatting tips are also covered in the appendix):

1. *Bold headings.* To change text in a cell to a bold format, select the cell of interest, select the "Format" menu in Excel, select the "Cells" menu choice, and choose "Bold" in the "Font Style" selection box (found in the "Font" tab in Excel 2003).

2. *Center alignment.* To center text in a cell, select the cell of interest, select the "Format" menu in Excel, select the "Cells" menu choice, and choose "Center" from the horizontal text alignment drop-down menu (found in the "Alignment" tab in Excel 2003).

3. *Borders for cells.* To add a border to a cell, select the cell of interest, select the "Format" menu in Excel, select the "Cells" menu choice, and choose (a) the line style of interest in the "Line style" selection box and (b) the specific border(s) to which you would like to add a border from the "Border" selection box (both found in the "Border" tab in Excel 2003).

4. *Center text across columns.* To center text across a number of columns, select the columns of interest, select the "Format" menu in Excel, select the "Cells" menu choice, and choose "Merge cells" in the "Text control" section (found in the "Alignment" tab in Excel 2003).

5. *Indent text.* To indent text, select the cell of interest, select the "Format" menu in Excel, select the "Cells" menu choice, and click the up arrow once in the "Indent" box found in the "Text alignment" section (so that the value in the "Indent" box reflects the value of interest) (found in the "Alignment" tab in Excel 2003).

6. *Formatting numbers as currency.* To format numbers as currency, select the cell(s) of interest, select the "Format" menu in Excel, select the "Cells" menu choice, choose "Currency" from the "Category" selection box, click the appropriate arrow (up or down) in the "Decimal places" box to suit your specific needs, and select the "$" symbol, or the symbol for another currency from the "Symbol" drop-down menu (all found in the "Number" tab in Excel 2003).

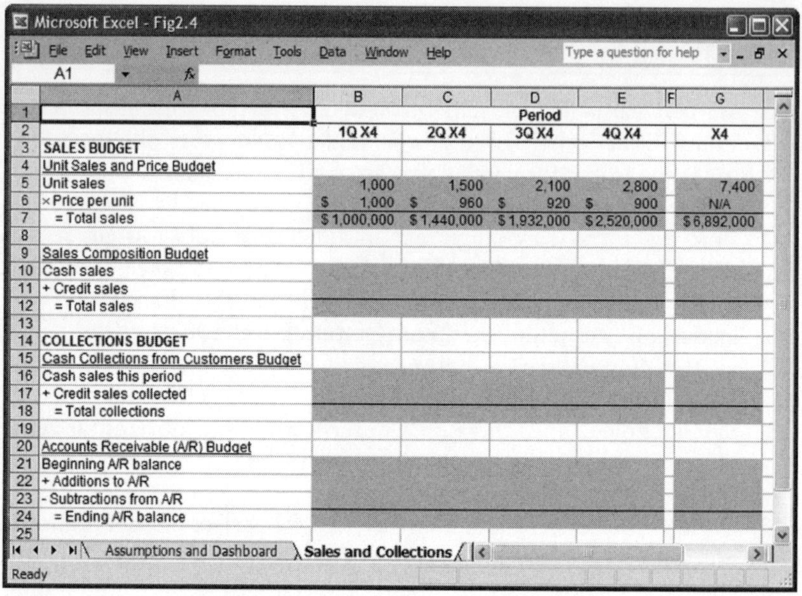

	A	B	C	D	E	F	G
1				Period			
2		1Q X4	2Q X4	3Q X4	4Q X4		X4
3	SALES BUDGET						
4	Unit Sales and Price Budget						
5	Unit sales	1,000	1,500	2,100	2,800		7,400
6	× Price per unit	$ 1,000	$ 960	$ 920	$ 900		N/A
7	= Total sales	$ 1,000,000	$ 1,440,000	$ 1,932,000	$ 2,520,000		$ 6,892,000
8							
9	Sales Composition Budget						
10	Cash sales						
11	+ Credit sales						
12	= Total sales						
13							
14	COLLECTIONS BUDGET						
15	Cash Collections from Customers Budget						
16	Cash sales this period						
17	+ Credit sales collected						
18	= Total collections						
19							
20	Accounts Receivable (A/R) Budget						
21	Beginning A/R balance						
22	+ Additions to A/R						
23	- Subtractions from A/R						
24	= Ending A/R balance						
25							

FIGURE 2.4 Unit Sales and Price Budget

row in Figure 2.4 to calculate sales in dollars for each accounting period. Dollar sales are calculated as unit sales * price per unit.

Please note that the projected price for each monitor decreases from quarter to quarter. As in many high-technology product-oriented companies such as Napavale, price competition is severe and it is often essential to remain competitive from a pricing perspective to maintain or increase market share.

Figure 2.5 presents an alternative view of the Unit Sales and Price Budget in which the values and formulas underlying each worksheet cell are exposed. You can always switch between the original and the alternative views in your worksheets by pressing and holding the Control (CTRL) key and then pressing the ~ key. In Figure 2.5, note that equations such as that found in cell B7 (= B5 * B6) are to be interpreted as follows: the value in cell B7 is equal to the value in B5 multiplied by the value in B6. For the sake of clarity, remember that the following symbols are used to represent arithmetic operators: + (plus/addition), – (minus/subtraction), * (times/multiplication), and / (divided by or division). I provide many of these alternative views of worksheets over the course of this book so that you can see the specific calculations underlying Napavale's financial model.

It is important to note that, over the course of building the financial model for Napavale, I will be naming many of the input and output cells

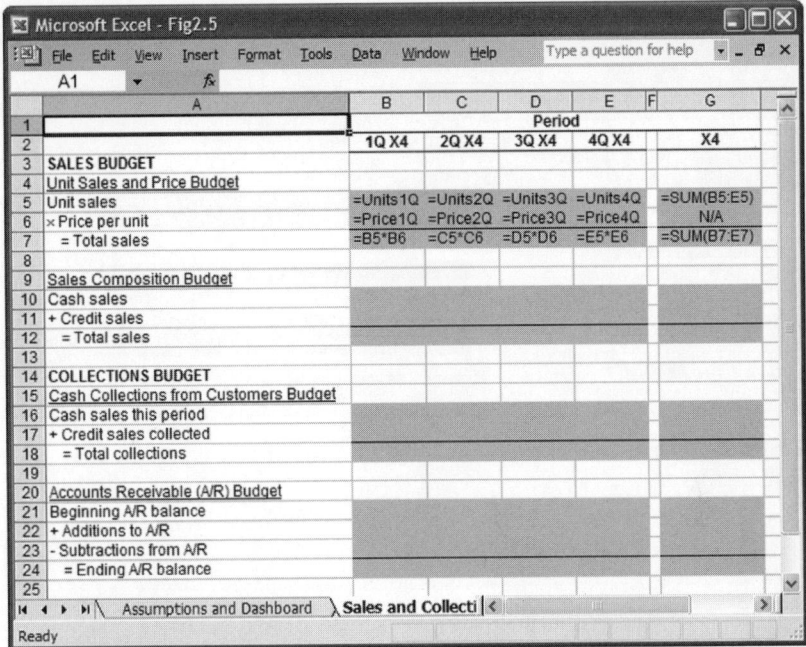

FIGURE 2.5   Alternative View of the Unit Sales and Price Budget

FEATURE TIP: NAMING CELLS AND CELL RANGES

The ability to name cells and cell ranges is a useful and powerful feature offered by Microsoft Excel. Cell references (discussed later in the appendix) are often used when building financial models—the use of names instead of obscure cell references, such as $AC165, makes it easier to build and modify models.

The easiest way to name a cell or a range of cells is to use the Name Box in Excel. The Name Box is typically found directly above the label for Column A in an open worksheet.

To name a cell or a range of cells, select the cell or range of cells that you would like to name and then click on the Name Box in your worksheet. Next, simply type in your desired name for the cell or range of cells. Note that you may not use any spaces in this name.

You may also name cells and ranges of cells by first selecting the cell or range of cells of interest and then selecting the "Insert" menu, choosing the "Name" option, and then selecting the "Define" option. You may then enter in your name of choice for the cell or range of cells.

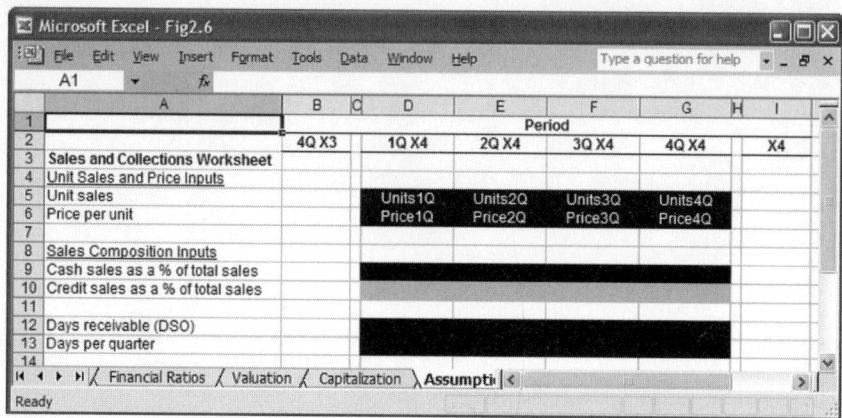

FIGURE 2.6 Names of the Input and Output Cells in the Assumptions and Dashboard Worksheet

Microsoft Excel - Fig2.7						
					Period	
	A	B	C	D	E	F	G
1							
2		1Q X4	2Q X4	3Q X4	4Q X4		X4
3	SALES BUDGET						
4	Unit Sales and Price Budget						
5	Unit sales						
6	× Price per unit						
7	= Total sales	Sales1Q	Sales2Q	Sales3Q	Sales4Q		SalesX4
8							
9	Sales Composition Budget						
10	Cash sales						
11	+ Credit sales						
12	= Total sales						
13							
14	COLLECTIONS BUDGET						
15	Cash Collections from Customers Budget						
16	Cash sales this period						
17	+ Credit sales collected						
18	= Total collections						
19							
20	Accounts Receivable (A/R) Budget						
21	Beginning A/R balance						
22	+ Additions to A/R						
23	- Subtractions from A/R						
24	= Ending A/R balance						
25							

FIGURE 2.7 Names of the Input and Output Cells in the Unit Sales and Price Budget

in Excel for Napavale. One of Microsoft Excel's more powerful features is the ability to refer to information across worksheets. I make frequent use of this feature throughout this book. The naming of cells and ranges of cells makes this ability to reference other worksheets and cells much easier.

The names of each input and output cell related to the Unit Sales and Price Budget are shown in Figure 2.6 from the Assumptions and Dashboard worksheet.

Figure 2.7 shows the names for each of the input and output cells in the Unit Sales and Price Budget itself. Note that all of the figures in which I show the names of the input and output cells are for display purposes only—no calculations actually take place in such figures. I clearly note when I am presenting worksheets for the purpose of showing the names of input and output cells over the course of the book.

For the sake of clear and consistent presentation of the steps involved in building each component of Napavale's Master Budget (covered in Chapters 2–7), I present the following figures related to each step in the Master Budget building process: (1) a view of the Assumptions and Dashboard worksheet, with the relevant areas shown, (2) a view of the specific budget worksheet I am describing (for example, the Unit Sales and Price Budget), (3) an alternative view of the specific budget worksheet I am discussing in which the values and formulas underlying the worksheet cells are exposed and visible, (4) a view of the Assumptions and Dashboard worksheet in which the names of all of the relevant cells are shown, and (5) a view of the specific budget worksheet I am discussing in which all of the names of the relevant cells are shown.

STEP 2B: SALES COMPOSITION BUDGET

Since a portion of Napavale's sales will be credit sales and a portion will be cash sales, I need to calculate the relative percentage of each type of sales in the financial model. Figure 2.8 highlights the assumptions underlying the Sales Composition Budget (using the Assumptions and Dashboard worksheet). Figure 2.9 presents the Sales Composition Budget itself.

Figure 2.10 represents an alternative view of the worksheet shown in Figure 2.9. This alternative view exposes all of the formulas used to calculate values such as Total Sales. All of the columns in this worksheet are not visible due to the length of the formulas underlying some of the worksheet cells.

Figure 2.11 shows all of the names for the input and output cells in the Assumptions and Dashboard worksheet. Figure 2.12 highlights all of the names for the input and output cells in the Sales Composition Budget itself.

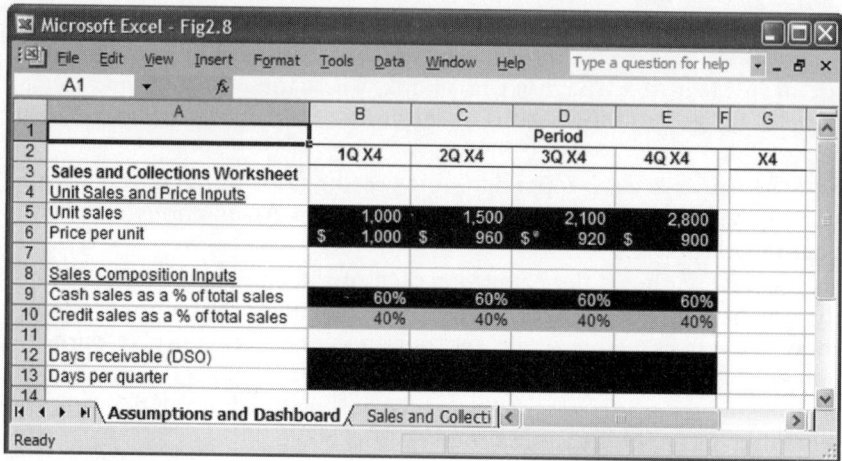

FIGURE 2.8   Assumptions Underlying the Sales Composition Budget

Microsoft Excel - Fig2.9

File   Edit   View   Insert   Format   Tools   Data   Window   Help   Type a question for help

A1

	A	B	C	D	E	F	G
1				Period			
2		1Q X4	2Q X4	3Q X4	4Q X4		X4
3	SALES BUDGET						
4	Unit Sales and Price Budget						
5	Unit sales	1,000	1,500	2,100	2,800		7,400
6	× Price per unit	$ 1,000	$ 960	$ 920	$ 900		N/A
7	= Total sales	$1,000,000	$1,440,000	$1,932,000	$2,520,000		$6,892,000
8							
9	Sales Composition Budget						
10	Cash sales	$ 600,000	$ 864,000	$1,159,200	$1,512,000		$4,135,200
11	+ Credit sales	400,000	576,000	772,800	1,008,000		2,756,800
12	= Total sales	$1,000,000	$1,440,000	$1,932,000	$2,520,000		$6,892,000
13							
14	COLLECTIONS BUDGET						
15	Cash Collections from Customers Budget						
16	Cash sales this period						
17	+ Credit sales collected						
18	= Total collections						
19							
20	Accounts Receivable (A/R) Budget						
21	Beginning A/R balance						
22	+ Additions to A/R						
23	- Subtractions from A/R						
24	= Ending A/R balance						
25							

Assumptions and Dashboard \ Sales and Collections /

Ready

FIGURE 2.9   Sales Composition Budget

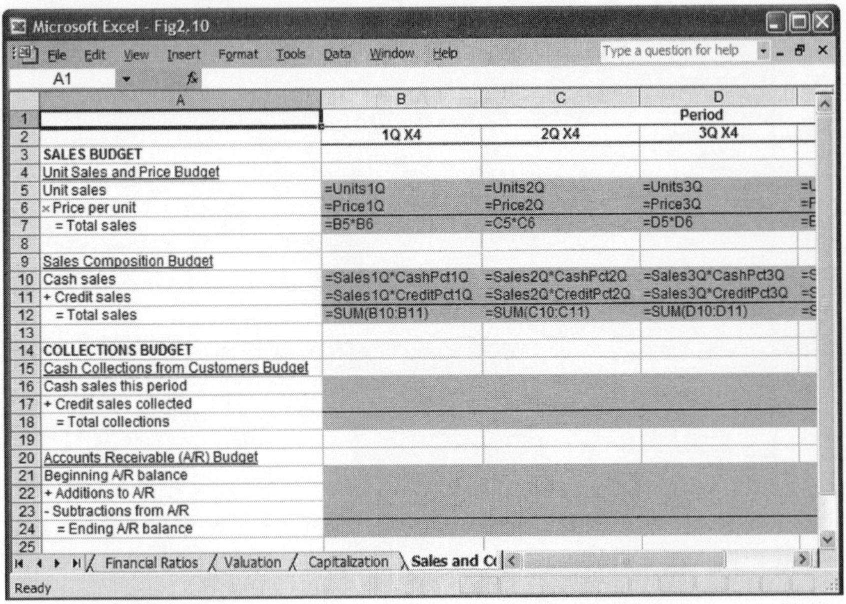

FIGURE 2.10 Alternative View of the Sales Composition Budget

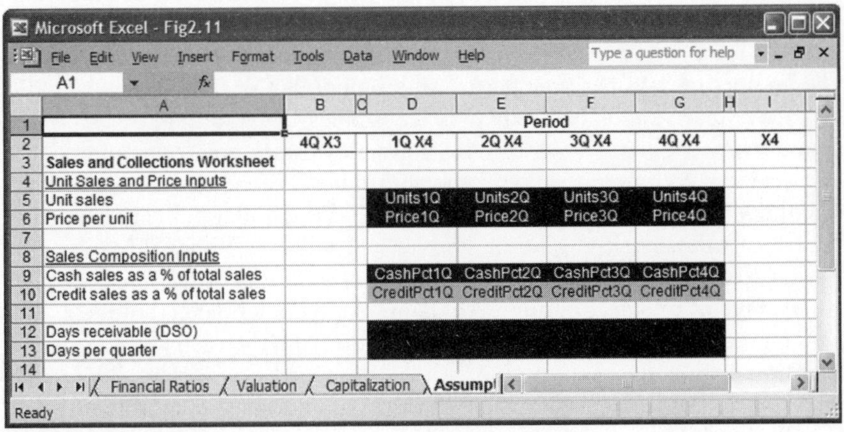

FIGURE 2.11 Names of the Input and Output Cells in the Assumptions and Dashboard Worksheet

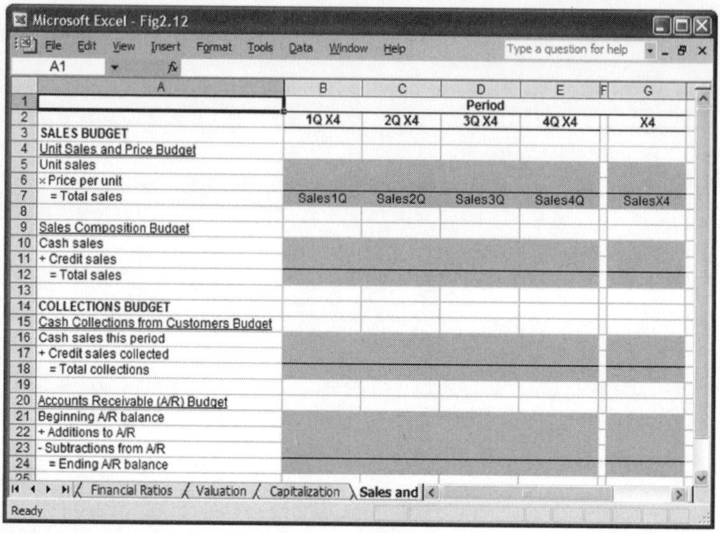

FIGURE 2.12   Names of the Input and Output Cells in the Sales Composition Budget

STEP 2C: CASH COLLECTIONS FROM CUSTOMERS BUDGET

The Cash Collections from Customers Budget calculates and tracks sales on a cash basis. Cash collections from customers are calculated as: cash sales for a given time period + credit sales for a given period collected in that same period + credit sales from a previous period collected during the given period. The credit sales collections amounts are based on two assumptions: the number of days per time period and the number of days receivable.

Days receivable (also known as Days Sales Outstanding, or DSO) is a financial metric that indicates how many days sales are "outstanding" or uncollected. A company's days receivable value is calculated as: the average accounts receivable balance for a time period/the dollar value of one day's worth of sales. For the sake of simplicity, I will use Napavale's Accounts Receivable balance at the end of specific accounting periods (as opposed to an average of two accounting periods) in Napavale's financial model.

Figure 2.13 shows the assumptions underlying the cash collections calculation (using the Assumptions and Dashboard worksheet). Note that Figure 2.13 presents another view of the assumptions shown in Figure 2.8.

Figure 2.14 shows the Cash Collections Budget worksheet itself. Note that the "credit sales collected" line in the Cash Collections Budget is not completed. This is because credit sales collections are driven off of Accounts Receivable calculations, which are shown in the next step.

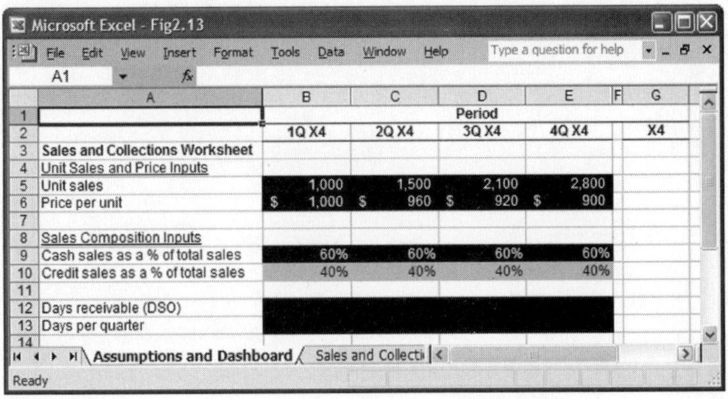

FIGURE 2.13 Assumptions Underlying the Cash Collections Calculation

Figure 2.15 represents an alternative view (in which all of the equations are exposed) of the Cash Collections Budget worksheet. Figure 2.16 shows the names of the input and output cells in the Assumptions and Dashboard worksheet. Figure 2.17 shows the names for the input and output cells from the Cash Collections from Customers Budget worksheet.

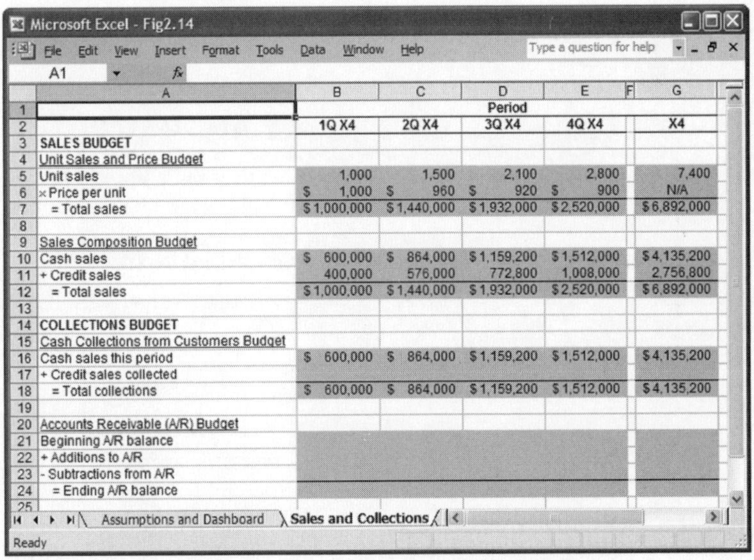

FIGURE 2.14 Cash Collections Budget

FIGURE 2.15 Alternative View of the Cash Collections Budget

	A	B (1Q X4)	C (2Q X4)	D (3Q X4)
1				Period
2		1Q X4	2Q X4	3Q X4
3	SALES BUDGET			
4	Unit Sales and Price Budget			
5	Unit sales	=Units1Q	=Units2Q	=Units3Q
6	×Price per unit	=Price1Q	=Price2Q	=Price3Q
7	= Total sales	=B5*B6	=C5*C6	=D5*D6
8				
9	Sales Composition Budget			
10	Cash sales	=Sales1Q*CashPct1Q	=Sales2Q*CashPct2Q	=Sales3Q*CashPct3Q
11	+ Credit sales	=Sales1Q*CreditPct1Q	=Sales2Q*CreditPct2Q	=Sales3Q*CreditPct3Q
12	= Total sales	=SUM(B10:B11)	=SUM(C10:C11)	=SUM(D10:D11)
13				
14	COLLECTIONS BUDGET			
15	Cash Collections from Customers Budget			
16	Cash sales this period	=CashSls1Q	=CashSls2Q	=CashSls3Q
17	+ Credit sales collected			
18	= Total collections	=SUM(B16:B17)	=SUM(C16:C17)	=SUM(D16:D17)
19				
20	Accounts Receivable (A/R) Budget			
21	Beginning A/R balance			
22	+ Additions to A/R			
23	- Subtractions from A/R			
24	= Ending A/R balance			
25				

Financial Ratios / Valuation / Capitalization \ Sales and C

FIGURE 2.16 Names of the Input and Output Cells in the Assumptions and Dashboard Worksheet

	A	B (4Q X3)	D (1Q X4)	E (2Q X4)	F (3Q X4)	G (4Q X4)	H (X4)
1				Period			
2		4Q X3	1Q X4	2Q X4	3Q X4	4Q X4	X4
3	Sales and Collections Worksheet						
4	Unit Sales and Price Inputs						
5	Unit sales		Units1Q	Units2Q	Units3Q	Units4Q	
6	Price per unit		Price1Q	Price2Q	Price3Q	Price4Q	
7							
8	Sales Composition Inputs						
9	Cash sales as a % of total sales		CashPct1Q	CashPct2Q	CashPct3Q	CashPct4Q	
10	Credit sales as a % of total sales		CreditPct1Q	CreditPct2Q	CreditPct3Q	CreditPct4Q	
11							
12	Days receivable (DSO)						
13	Days per quarter						
14							

Financial Ratios / Valuation / Capitalization \ Assumpt

FIGURE 2.17 Names of the Input and Output Cells in the Cash Collections from Customers Budget

	A	B (1Q X4)	C (2Q X4)	D (3Q X4)	E (4Q X4)	G (X4)
1				Period		
2		1Q X4	2Q X4	3Q X4	4Q X4	X4
3	SALES BUDGET					
4	Unit Sales and Price Budget					
5	Unit sales					
6	×Price per unit					
7	= Total sales	Sales1Q	Sales2Q	Sales3Q	Sales4Q	SalesX4
8						
9	Sales Composition Budget					
10	Cash sales	CashSls1Q	CashSls2Q	CashSls3Q	CashSls4Q	CashSlsX4
11	+ Credit sales	CreditSls1Q	CreditSls2Q	CreditSls3Q	CreditSls4Q	CreditSlsX4
12	= Total sales					
13						
14	COLLECTIONS BUDGET					
15	Cash Collections from Customers Budget					
16	Cash sales this period					
17	+ Credit sales collected					
18	= Total collections	Collections1Q	Collections2Q	Collections3Q	Collections4Q	CollectionsX4
19						
20	Accounts Receivable (A/R) Budget					
21	Beginning A/R balance					
22	+ Additions to A/R					
23	- Subtractions from A/R					
24	= Ending A/R balance					
25						

Financial Ratios / Valuation / Capitalization \ Sales and Collecti

STEP 2D: ACCOUNTS RECEIVABLE BUDGET

Napavale sells its monitors on both cash and credit terms. The Accounts Receivable Budget tracks Napavale's credit sales. As noted in Step 2C (Cash Collections from Customers Budget), credit sales collections are based on the assumptions underlying Napavale's days receivable and days per accounting period. Figure 2.18 highlights the assumptions underlying the Accounts Receivable calculation (using the Assumptions and Dashboard worksheet).

Figure 2.19 shows the Accounts Receivable Budget. Note that I am assuming Napavale began the year X4 with no (zero) accounts receivable. Also note that I am assuming Napavale's days receivable metric is always less than the days-per-quarter metric. While this is a simplifying assumption, as you will see below, the Accounts Receivable calculations are already detailed enough and I do not want to introduce excessive complications into the financial model at this point.

In the Accounts Receivable Budget calculations, note that the "Subtractions from Accounts Receivable" row in Figure 2.19 is always equal to the "Additions to Accounts Receivable" row from the immediately preceding quarter. This is because, as noted above, I am assuming the days receivable metric is always less than the days-per-quarter metric. Assuming this is the case, all the Accounts Receivables added during a given period will be collected in the subsequent period.

Figure 2.20 offers an alternative view of the Accounts Receivable calculations from the Accounts Receivable Budget in which the calculations within the worksheet cells are exposed. Only a portion of the columns of the worksheet are shown due to the length of the formulas associated with the underlying calculations.

Given the complex nature of some of the calculations underlying the

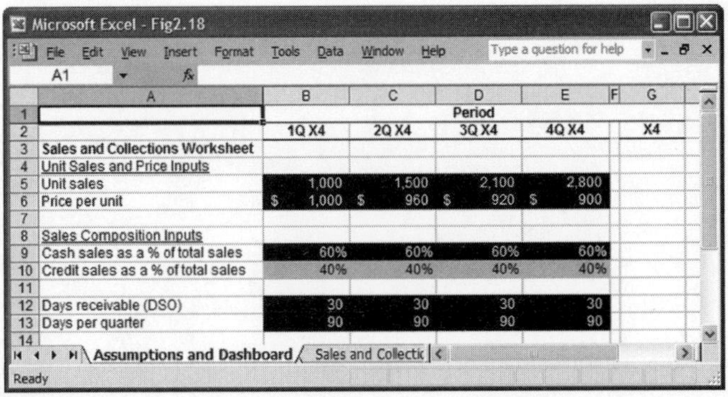

FIGURE 2.18 Assumptions Underlying the Accounts Receivable Calculation

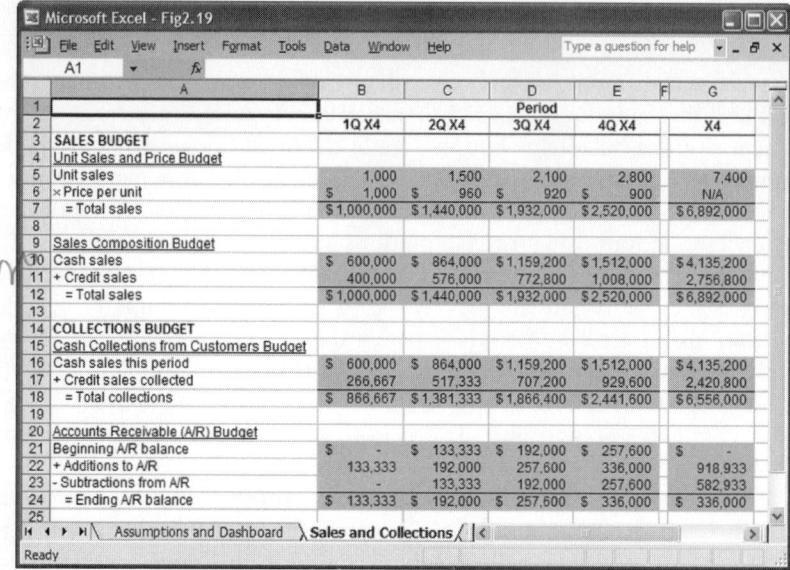

FIGURE 2.19   Accounts Receivable Budget

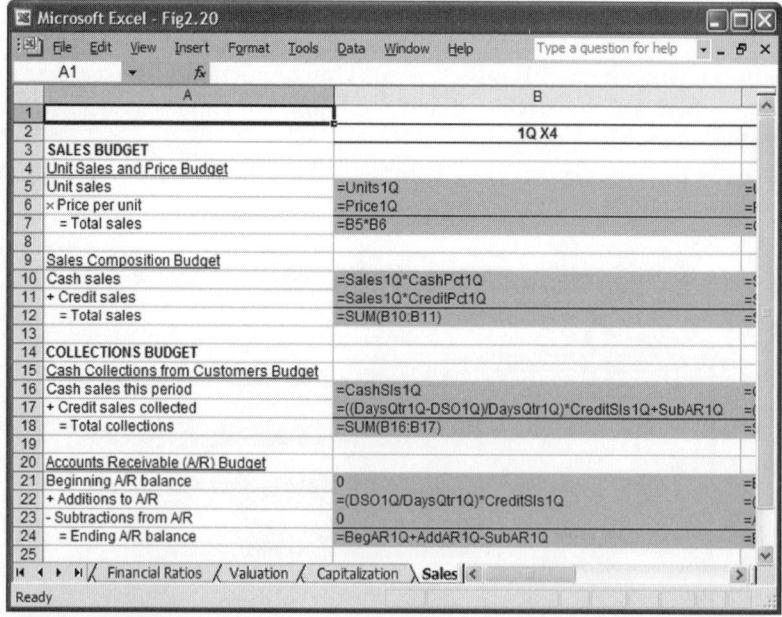

FIGURE 2.20   Alternative View of the Accounts Receivable Calculations

worksheet shown in Figure 2.20, I will walk through the logic behind the contents of two worksheet cells. The first cell that I will discuss, cell B17, calculates a value for "credit sales collected." This represents the dollar value of credit sales collected during the 1Q X4 time period. The general logic behind this calculation is as follows: credit sales collected for 1Q X4 are equal to: the percentage of credit sales from 1Q X4 that were collected in 1Q X4 + the subtractions from Napavale's Accounts Receivable.

Looking specifically at the formula underlying cell B17, note that the credit sales value for 1Q X4 is multiplied by: (days per quarter – days receivable)/(days per quarter). This formula will yield the dollar value of the credit sales that took place in 1Q X4 that were collected in 1Q X4. Also note in cell B17 that the result of this formula is added to the subtractions from Napavale's Accounts Receivable balance.

The second cell, cell B22, calculates a value for "Additions to A/R." This represents the dollar value of credit sales that took place in 1Q X4 that were not collected in 1Q X4. As the contents of cell B22 indicate, the credit sales value for 1Q X4 is multiplied by: (days receivable)/(days per quarter).

While these formulas may seem complex, their purpose is to divide up credit sales between different periods based on my assumptions regarding days receivable for Napavale. The approach that I am taking regarding Accounts Receivable and credit sales collections is one of many different ways to address the financial modeling of these topics; I am presenting this particular approach due to its utility and flexibility.

Figure 2.21 presents a view of the names of all of the input and output cells for the Accounts Receivable Budget in the Assumptions and Dashboard worksheet. Figure 2.22 offers a view of the input and output cells in the Accounts Receivable Budget itself.

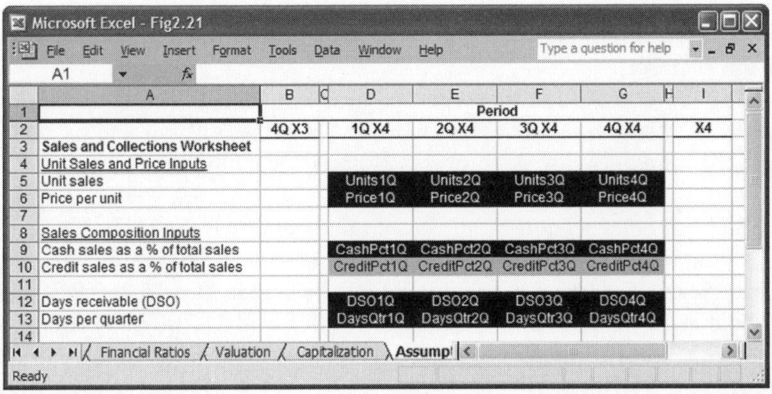

FIGURE 2.21 Names of the Input and Output Cells from the Assumptions and Dashboard Worksheet

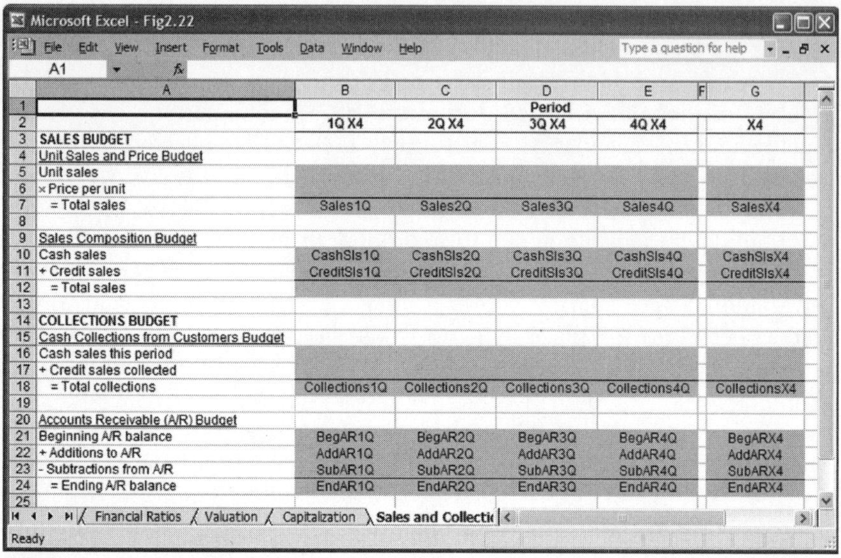

Row	A	B	C	D	E	G
1				Period		
2		1Q X4	2Q X4	3Q X4	4Q X4	X4
3	SALES BUDGET					
4	Unit Sales and Price Budget					
5	Unit sales					
6	× Price per unit					
7	= Total sales	Sales1Q	Sales2Q	Sales3Q	Sales4Q	SalesX4
8						
9	Sales Composition Budget					
10	Cash sales	CashSls1Q	CashSls2Q	CashSls3Q	CashSls4Q	CashSlsX4
11	+ Credit sales	CreditSls1Q	CreditSls2Q	CreditSls3Q	CreditSls4Q	CreditSlsX4
12	= Total sales					
13						
14	COLLECTIONS BUDGET					
15	Cash Collections from Customers Budget					
16	Cash sales this period					
17	+ Credit sales collected					
18	= Total collections	Collections1Q	Collections2Q	Collections3Q	Collections4Q	CollectionsX4
19						
20	Accounts Receivable (A/R) Budget					
21	Beginning A/R balance	BegAR1Q	BegAR2Q	BegAR3Q	BegAR4Q	BegARX4
22	+ Additions to A/R	AddAR1Q	AddAR2Q	AddAR3Q	AddAR4Q	AddARX4
23	- Subtractions from A/R	SubAR1Q	SubAR2Q	SubAR3Q	SubAR4Q	SubARX4
24	= Ending A/R balance	EndAR1Q	EndAR2Q	EndAR3Q	EndAR4Q	EndARX4

FIGURE 2.22 Names of the Input and Output Cells in the Accounts Receivable Budget

QUESTIONS

Each of the questions for this chapter relates to a hypothetical company named Company XYZ. Company XYZ sells "tablet" Personal Computers (PCs) to the consumer market. As such, Company XYZ is a product-oriented (as opposed to a service-oriented) business. The questions will address the fiscal year X5 on a quarterly basis (four specific quarters, 1Q–4Q for the year X5).

The following questions will test your knowledge of the material covered in this chapter in an applied manner—specifically, you will be asked to build the schedules discussed in this chapter for Company XYZ.

1. Build the first section of an Assumptions and Dashboard worksheet for Company XYZ given the following projections for the four quarters in the year X5: (i) 10,500 PCs (units) will be sold in 1Q, 15,250 PCs will be sold in 2Q, 25,000 units will be sold in 3Q, and 31,200 units will be sold in 4Q, and (ii) the selling price per PC (unit) will be as follows for each quarter: $3,100 in 1Q, $3,050 in 2Q, $3,000 in 3Q, and $2,910 in 4Q.
2. Build a Unit Sales and Price Budget based on the Assumptions and Dashboard worksheet that you built in Question 1.

3. Update the Assumptions and Dashboard worksheet for Company XYZ from Question 1 given the following projections for the breakdown between cash sales (as a percentage of total sales) and credit sales (as a percentage of total sales): (i) 100 percent cash sales and 0 percent credit sales in 1Q, (ii) 90 percent cash sales and 10 percent credit sales in 2Q, (iii) 70 percent cash sales and 30 percent credit sales in 3Q, and (iv) 50 percent cash sales and 50 percent credit sales in 4Q.

4. Build a Sales Composition Budget based on the updated Assumptions and Dashboard worksheet from Question 3.

5. Update the Assumptions and Dashboard worksheet for Company XYZ from Question 3 given the following projections for the Company's Days Receivable, otherwise known as Days Sales Outstanding (DSO), and the number of days per quarter: (i) 20 days receivable and 90 days per quarter for 1Q, (ii) 25 days receivable and 90 days per quarter for 2Q, (iii) 30 days receivable and 90 days per quarter in 3Q, and (iv) 30 days receivable and 90 days per quarter in 4Q.

6. Build a Cash Collections from Customers Budget based on your work in Questions 1–5. Note that you should not be able to complete the "credit sales collected" line in this Budget until the Accounts Receivable Budget is built (in Question 7).

7. Build an Accounts Receivable Budget based on your work in Questions 1–6 and complete the Cash Collections from Customers Budget from Question 6. Assume that Company XYZ had (i) a beginning Accounts Receivable value of 0 (zero) and (ii) 0 (zero) subtractions from Accounts Receivable for 1Q X5.

CHAPTER 3

Operating Budget—Cost of Goods Sold, Inventory, and Purchases

This chapter covers the first set of cost components for the Operating Budget, specifically the Cost-of-Goods-Sold Budget, the Inventory Budget, and the Purchases Budget. Whereas Chapter 2 addressed the sales components of the Operating Budget, this chapter, in conjunction with Chapters 4 and 5, addresses the budgets (in the Operating Budget) associated with planning for and purchasing the resources required to support a business's sales. Figure 3.1 highlights the separate Cost of Goods Sold, Inventory, and Purchases components of the Operating Budget in the context of the Master Budget.

As in Chapter 2, I use the Assumptions and Dashboard worksheet for Napavale to introduce and focus on important assumptions underlying Napavale's financial model. The remainder of this chapter will cover the steps involved in the continued construction of the Assumptions and Dashboard worksheet and the Cost of Goods Sold, Inventory, and Purchases elements of the Operating Budget.

STEP 3: COST-OF-GOODS-SOLD BUDGET

The first cost-oriented step in building Napavale's financial model, labeled Step 3 in Figure 3.1, is developing a Cost-of-Goods-Sold Budget. This budget is most applicable to product-oriented companies (as opposed to service-oriented companies), as service-oriented companies do not typically sell "goods." Some service-oriented companies refer to the cost of selling their service(s) as the "cost of revenues." In other cases, service-oriented companies may not even report a cost of revenues line item in their financial model.

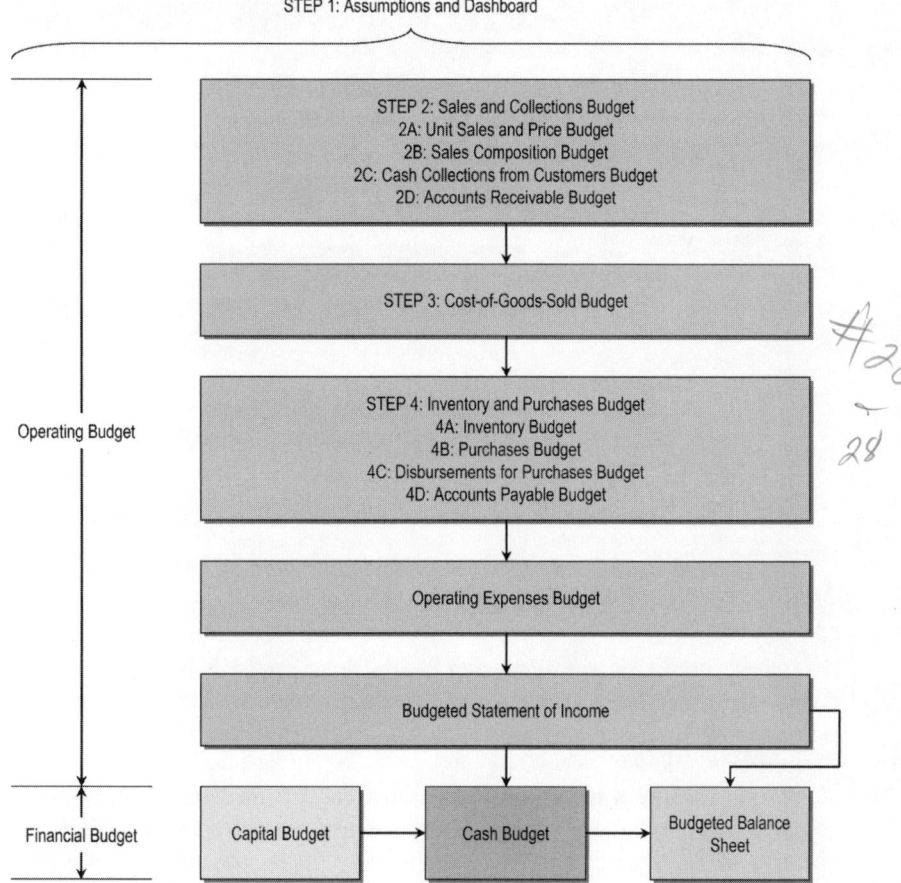

FIGURE 3.1 Cost of Goods Sold, Inventory, and Purchases Components of the Operating Budget in the Context of the Master Budget

As Napavale sells a specific product (a flat-screen computer monitor), I will be using a Cost-of-Goods-Sold Budget. If you are building a financial model for a service-oriented company, you may either identify and allocate the costs associated with service revenues to an account named "cost of revenues" or ignore this account altogether—it is up to you. It is essential, however, to account for all costs somewhere in your financial model.

Returning to my example company, Napavale has identified three specific cost components in the Cost-of-Goods-Sold Budget: monitor screen, monitor casing, and assembly labor. Figure 3.2 highlights each of these components on a per-unit basis in the Assumptions and Dashboard worksheet.

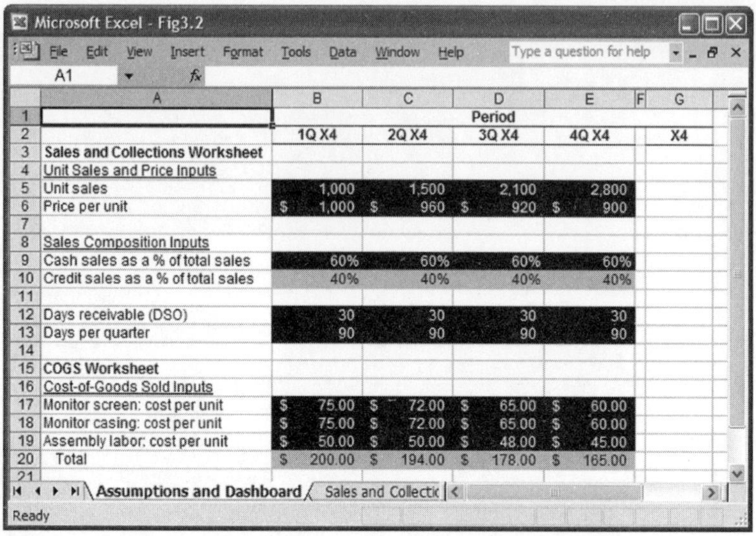

	A	B	C	D	E	F	G
1				Period			
2		1Q X4	2Q X4	3Q X4	4Q X4		X4
3	**Sales and Collections Worksheet**						
4	Unit Sales and Price Inputs						
5	Unit sales	1,000	1,500	2,100	2,800		
6	Price per unit	$ 1,000	$ 960	$ 920	$ 900		
7							
8	Sales Composition Inputs						
9	Cash sales as a % of total sales	60%	60%	60%	60%		
10	Credit sales as a % of total sales	40%	40%	40%	40%		
11							
12	Days receivable (DSO)	30	30	30	30		
13	Days per quarter	90	90	90	90		
14							
15	**COGS Worksheet**						
16	Cost-of-Goods Sold Inputs						
17	Monitor screen: cost per unit	$ 75.00	$ 72.00	$ 65.00	$ 60.00		
18	Monitor casing: cost per unit	$ 75.00	$ 72.00	$ 65.00	$ 60.00		
19	Assembly labor: cost per unit	$ 50.00	$ 50.00	$ 48.00	$ 45.00		
20	Total	$ 200.00	$ 194.00	$ 178.00	$ 165.00		

FIGURE 3.2 Cost Components in the Cost-of-Goods-Sold Budget from the Assumptions and Dashboard Worksheet

Please note that the projected cost values for each of the three cost components decreases from quarter to quarter. As in many high-technology product-oriented companies such as Napavale, the cost of materials often drops quickly.

These assumptions regarding the cost components of Napavale's cost of goods sold are fed directly from the Assumptions and Dashboard worksheet into the Cost-of-Goods-Sold Budget. The aggregate cost-of-goods-sold figure for each quarter is based on that quarter's projected unit sales. Figure 3.3 presents the Cost-of-Goods-Sold Budget.

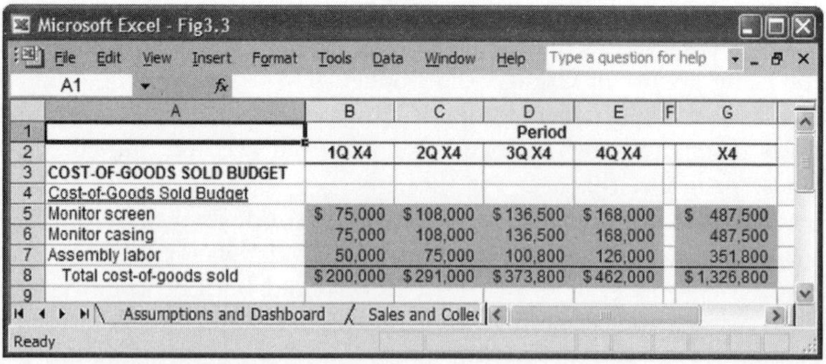

	A	B	C	D	E	F	G
1				Period			
2		1Q X4	2Q X4	3Q X4	4Q X4		X4
3	**COST-OF-GOODS SOLD BUDGET**						
4	Cost-of-Goods Sold Budget						
5	Monitor screen	$ 75,000	$ 108,000	$ 136,500	$ 168,000		$ 487,500
6	Monitor casing	75,000	108,000	136,500	168,000		487,500
7	Assembly labor	50,000	75,000	100,800	126,000		351,800
8	Total cost-of-goods sold	$ 200,000	$ 291,000	$ 373,800	$ 462,000		$ 1,326,800

FIGURE 3.3 Cost-of-Goods-Sold Budget

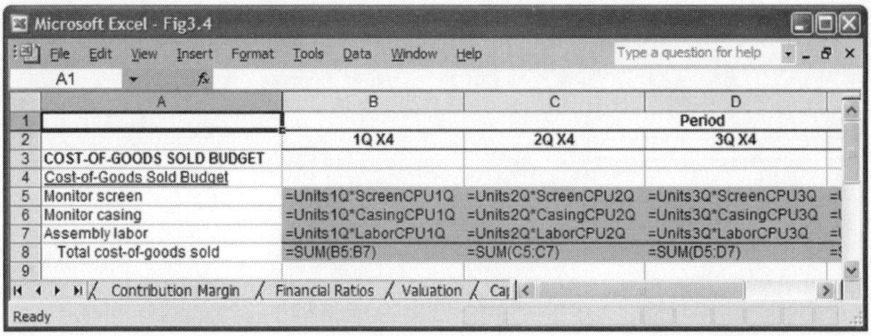

	A	B	C	D
1				Period
2		1Q X4	2Q X4	3Q X4
3	COST-OF-GOODS SOLD BUDGET			
4	Cost-of-Goods Sold Budget			
5	Monitor screen	=Units1Q*ScreenCPU1Q	=Units2Q*ScreenCPU2Q	=Units3Q*ScreenCPU3Q
6	Monitor casing	=Units1Q*CasingCPU1Q	=Units2Q*CasingCPU2Q	=Units3Q*CasingCPU3Q
7	Assembly labor	=Units1Q*LaborCPU1Q	=Units2Q*LaborCPU2Q	=Units3Q*LaborCPU3Q
8	Total cost-of-goods sold	=SUM(B5:B7)	=SUM(C5:C7)	=SUM(D5:D7)
9				

FIGURE 3.4 Alternative View of the Cost-of-Goods-Sold Budget

Figure 3.4 shows an alternative view of the Cost-of-Goods-Sold Budget in which the values and calculations underlying the worksheet cells are exposed.

Figure 3.5 presents a view of the Assumptions and Dashboard worksheet in which the names of the input and output cells are highlighted. I have used the acronym "CPU" in several of the names in this worksheet—CPU stands for "cost per unit" in this context.

Figure 3.6 offers a view of the Cost-of-Goods-Sold Budget in which the names of the input and output cells are shown. The acronym "COGS" is used in several of these names to stand for "Cost of Goods Sold."

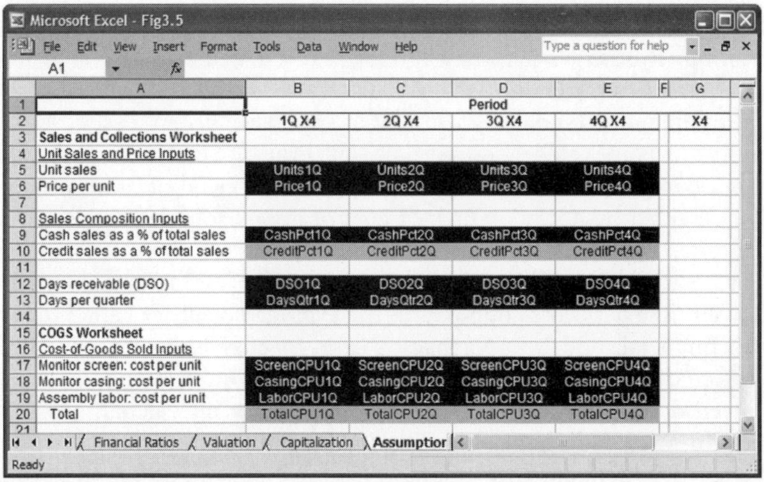

	A	B	C	D	E	F	G
1				Period			
2		1Q X4	2Q X4	3Q X4	4Q X4		X4
3	Sales and Collections Worksheet						
4	Unit Sales and Price Inputs						
5	Unit sales	Units1Q	Units2Q	Units3Q	Units4Q		
6	Price per unit	Price1Q	Price2Q	Price3Q	Price4Q		
7							
8	Sales Composition Inputs						
9	Cash sales as a % of total sales	CashPct1Q	CashPct2Q	CashPct3Q	CashPct4Q		
10	Credit sales as a % of total sales	CreditPct1Q	CreditPct2Q	CreditPct3Q	CreditPct4Q		
11							
12	Days receivable (DSO)	DSO1Q	DSO2Q	DSO3Q	DSO4Q		
13	Days per quarter	DaysQtr1Q	DaysQtr2Q	DaysQtr3Q	DaysQtr4Q		
14							
15	COGS Worksheet						
16	Cost-of-Goods Sold Inputs						
17	Monitor screen: cost per unit	ScreenCPU1Q	ScreenCPU2Q	ScreenCPU3Q	ScreenCPU4Q		
18	Monitor casing: cost per unit	CasingCPU1Q	CasingCPU2Q	CasingCPU3Q	CasingCPU4Q		
19	Assembly labor: cost per unit	LaborCPU1Q	LaborCPU2Q	LaborCPU3Q	LaborCPU4Q		
20	Total	TotalCPU1Q	TotalCPU2Q	TotalCPU3Q	TotalCPU4Q		

FIGURE 3.5 Names of the Input and Output Cells in the Assumptions and Dashboard Worksheet

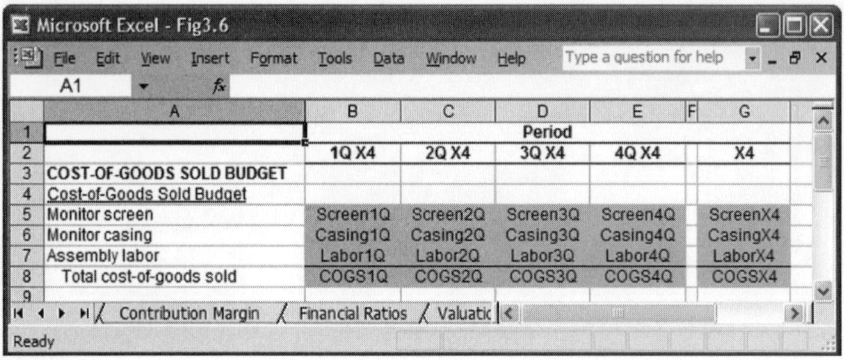

Microsoft Excel - Fig3.6

	A	B	C	D	E	F	G
1				Period			
2		1Q X4	2Q X4	3Q X4	4Q X4		X4
3	COST-OF-GOODS SOLD BUDGET						
4	Cost-of-Goods Sold Budget						
5	Monitor screen	Screen1Q	Screen2Q	Screen3Q	Screen4Q		ScreenX4
6	Monitor casing	Casing1Q	Casing2Q	Casing3Q	Casing4Q		CasingX4
7	Assembly labor	Labor1Q	Labor2Q	Labor3Q	Labor4Q		LaborX4
8	Total cost-of-goods sold	COGS1Q	COGS2Q	COGS3Q	COGS4Q		COGSX4

FIGURE 3.6 Names of the Input and Output Cells in the Cost-of-Goods-Sold Budget

STEP 4A: INVENTORY BUDGET

The Inventory Budget tracks Napavale's desired ending inventory for each of the four quarters covered in the financial model. Inventory represents goods that are, or will be, available for sale. Holding inventory has direct financial implications (specifically, it often costs money to purchase and hold inventory), so it is important to budget inventory levels appropriately. The budgeting process for inventory is often a balancing act, as a business does not want to hold too much inventory (because this often costs money), but it does want to have goods ready to sell and deliver when a customer makes a purchase.

In my financial model, I am basing a specific quarter's desired ending inventory on Napavale's "desired days inventory." Days inventory is defined as a company's average inventory level for a period of time (such as a quarter) divided by a day's worth of cost of goods sold for that same period of time.

For the sake of simplicity, I am going to use the ending inventory value for a given time period (as opposed to the average inventory value) for Napavale's financial model. In Napavale's case, for a given quarter, I will use the projected cost of goods sold for the subsequent quarter and the desired days inventory for that given quarter as the basis for my calculation of Napavale's "desired ending inventory" in the Inventory Budget.

Figure 3.7 highlights my assumptions for Napavale's desired days inventory in the Assumptions and Dashboard worksheet. Figure 3.8 below presents a view of the Inventory Budget itself.

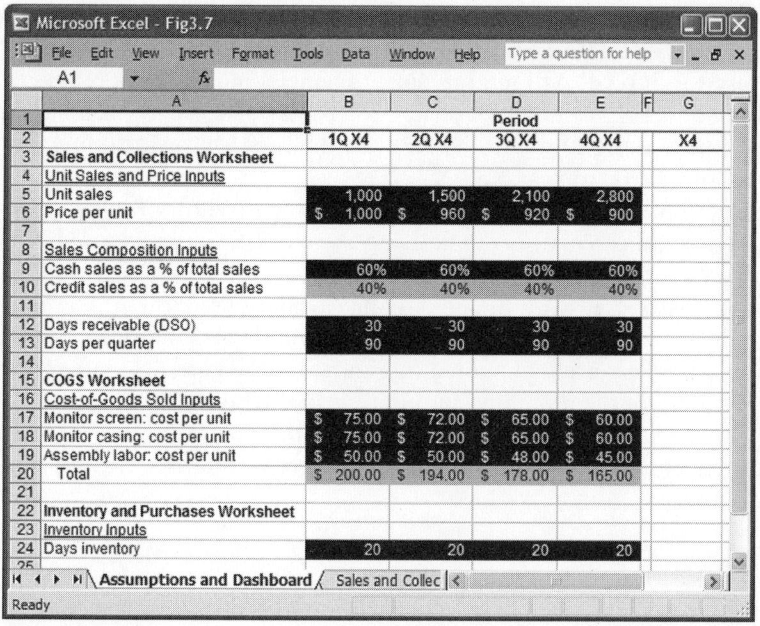

Microsoft Excel - Fig3.7

	A	B	C	D	E	F	G
1				Period			
2		1Q X4	2Q X4	3Q X4	4Q X4		X4
3	**Sales and Collections Worksheet**						
4	Unit Sales and Price Inputs						
5	Unit sales	1,000	1,500	2,100	2,800		
6	Price per unit	$ 1,000	$ 960	$ 920	$ 900		
7							
8	Sales Composition Inputs						
9	Cash sales as a % of total sales	60%	60%	60%	60%		
10	Credit sales as a % of total sales	40%	40%	40%	40%		
11							
12	Days receivable (DSO)	30	30	30	30		
13	Days per quarter	90	90	90	90		
14							
15	**COGS Worksheet**						
16	Cost-of-Goods Sold Inputs						
17	Monitor screen: cost per unit	$ 75.00	$ 72.00	$ 65.00	$ 60.00		
18	Monitor casing: cost per unit	$ 75.00	$ 72.00	$ 65.00	$ 60.00		
19	Assembly labor: cost per unit	$ 50.00	$ 50.00	$ 48.00	$ 45.00		
20	Total	$ 200.00	$ 194.00	$ 178.00	$ 165.00		
21							
22	**Inventory and Purchases Worksheet**						
23	Inventory Inputs						
24	Days inventory	20	20	20	20		

Assumptions and Dashboard / Sales and Collec

FIGURE 3.7 Assumptions for Desired Days Inventory in the Assumptions and Dashboard Worksheet

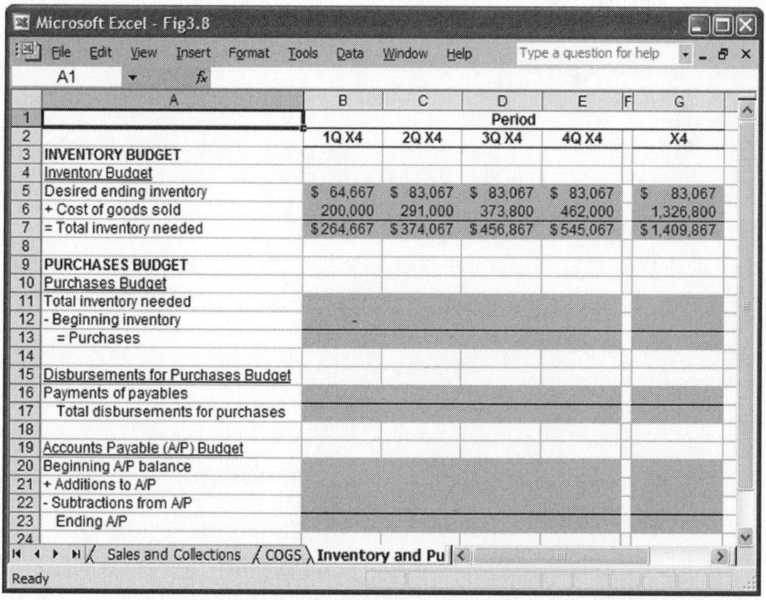

Microsoft Excel - Fig3.8

	A	B	C	D	E	F	G
1				Period			
2		1Q X4	2Q X4	3Q X4	4Q X4		X4
3	**INVENTORY BUDGET**						
4	Inventory Budget						
5	Desired ending inventory	$ 64,667	$ 83,067	$ 83,067	$ 83,067		$ 83,067
6	+ Cost of goods sold	200,000	291,000	373,800	462,000		1,326,800
7	= Total inventory needed	$264,667	$374,067	$456,867	$545,067		$1,409,867
8							
9	**PURCHASES BUDGET**						
10	Purchases Budget						
11	Total inventory needed						
12	- Beginning inventory						
13	= Purchases						
14							
15	Disbursements for Purchases Budget						
16	Payments of payables						
17	Total disbursements for purchases						
18							
19	Accounts Payable (A/P) Budget						
20	Beginning A/P balance						
21	+ Additions to A/P						
22	- Subtractions from A/P						
23	Ending A/P						

Sales and Collections / COGS / Inventory and Pu

FIGURE 3.8 Inventory Budget

Note the following assumption underlying Napavale's financial model: The desired ending inventory for 4Q X4 is equal to the desired ending inventory for 3Q X4. As I am building a financial model for only year X4, I will not address assumptions related to year X5. As such, this assumption represents a straightforward solution to the problem of including any information related to year X5.

Figure 3.9 offers an alternative view of the Inventory Budget in which the values and calculations underlying the worksheet are exposed. Only a portion of the columns of the worksheet are shown due to the length of the formulas associated with the underlying calculations.

The names of the input and output cells in the Assumptions and Dashboard worksheet are highlighted in Figure 3.10. Figure 3.11 offers a view of the names of the input and output cells in the Inventory Budget.

For the sake of reference, the cost of goods sold projections presented in the Inventory Budget are referenced directly from the Cost-of-Goods-Sold Budget.

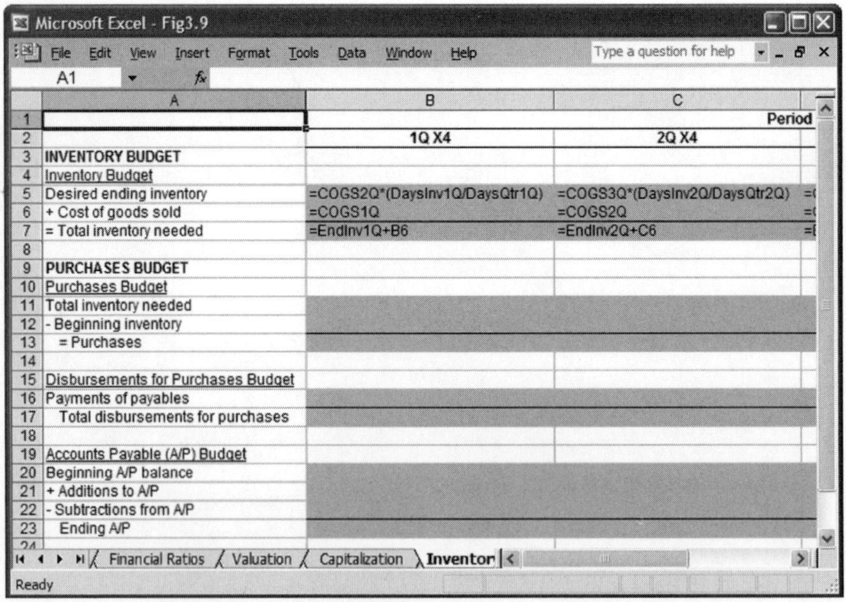

FIGURE 3.9 Alternative View of the Inventory Budget

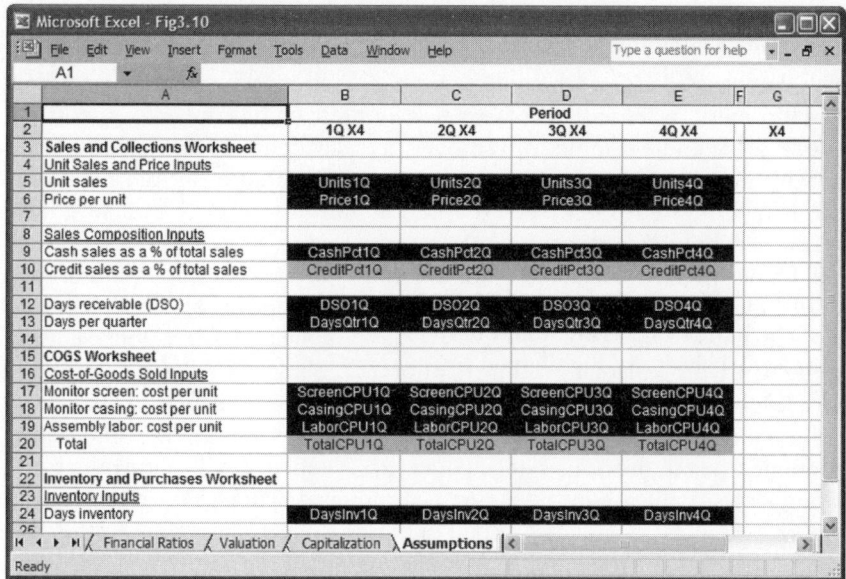

FIGURE 3.10 Names of the Input and Output Cells in the Assumptions and Dashboard Worksheet

Microsoft Excel - Fig3.11						
	B	C	D	E	F	G
1			Period			
2	1Q X4	2Q X4	3Q X4	4Q X4		X4
3 INVENTORY BUDGET						
4 Inventory Budget						
5 Desired ending inventory	EndInv1Q	EndInv2Q	EndInv3Q	EndInv4Q		EndInvX4
6 + Cost of goods sold						
7 = Total inventory needed	InvNeed1Q	InvNeed2Q	InvNeed3Q	InvNeed4Q		InvNeedX4
8						
9 PURCHASES BUDGET						
10 Purchases Budget						
11 Total inventory needed						
12 - Beginning inventory						
13 = Purchases						
14						
15 Disbursements for Purchases Budget						
16 Payments of payables						
17 Total disbursements for purchases						
18						
19 Accounts Payable (A/P) Budget						
20 Beginning A/P balance						
21 + Additions to A/P						
22 - Subtractions from A/P						
23 Ending A/P						
24						

FIGURE 3.11 Names of the Input and Output Cells in the Inventory Budget

STEP 4B: PURCHASES BUDGET

The Purchases Budget, which deals with goods that will eventually be sold to customers, is based on Napavale's desired ending inventory, cost of goods sold, and beginning inventory for each quarter. The specific budgeted purchases for a time period may be calculated using the following formula: Budgeted purchases = desired ending inventory + cost of goods sold – beginning inventory.

I have already calculated all of the input variables in this equation (desired ending inventory and cost of goods sold) except for Napavale's beginning inventory for each period, so the Purchases Budget represents a straightforward calculation. Furthermore, as Napavale's beginning inventory level for each accounting period is the result of a calculation, there are no unique assumptions underlying the Purchases Budget (beyond those contained in the previous budgeted steps). As such, I will not present another view of the Assumptions and Dashboard worksheet at this point. Figure 3.12 presents a view of the Purchases Budget. Figure 3.13 offers an alternative view of the Purchases Budget in which the values and formulas contained in the worksheet cells are exposed and visible.

The names of the input and output cells in the Assumptions and Dashboard worksheet are shown in Figure 3.14. Figure 3.15 offers a view of the names of the input and output cells in the Purchases Budget itself.

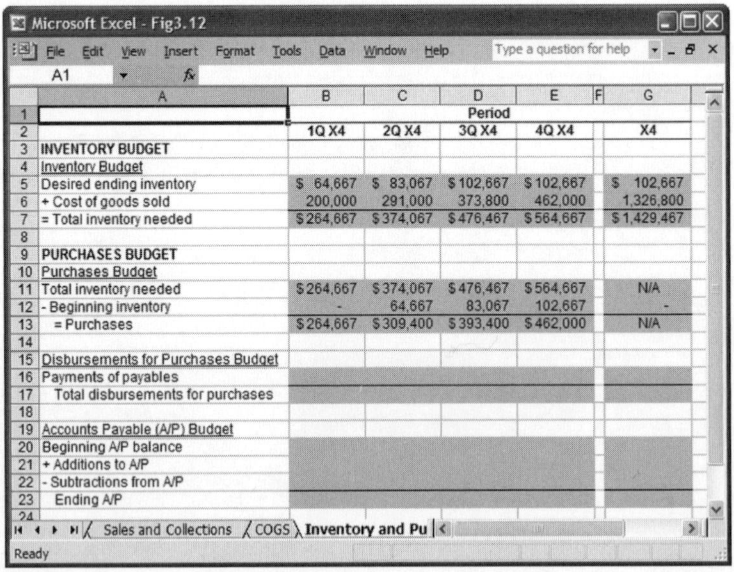

FIGURE 3.12   Purchases Budget

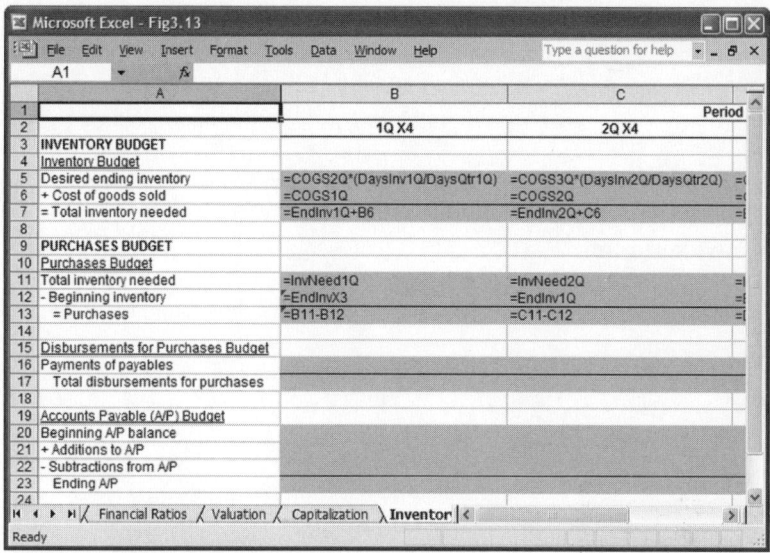

FIGURE 3.13 Alternative View of the Purchases Budget

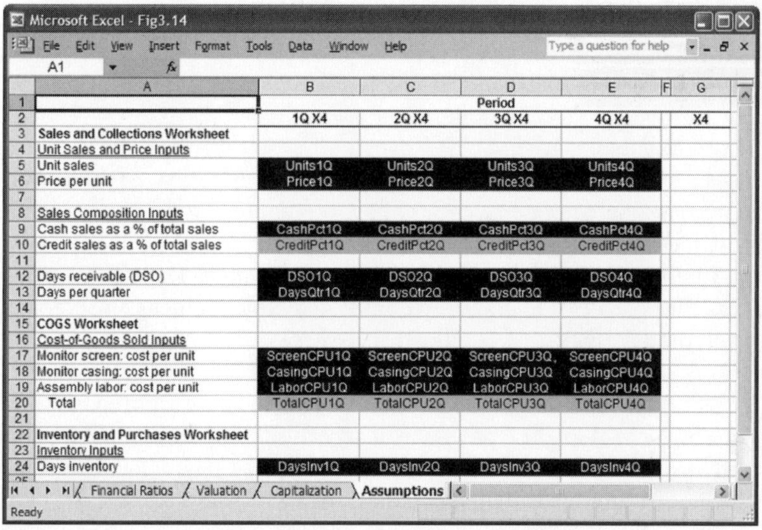

FIGURE 3.14 Names of the Input and Output Cells in the Assumptions and Dashboard Worksheet

Microsoft Excel - Fig3.15

	A	B	C	D	E	F	G
1				Period			
2		1Q X4	2Q X4	3Q X4	4Q X4		X4
3	INVENTORY BUDGET						
4	Inventory Budget						
5	Desired ending inventory	EndInv1Q	EndInv2Q	EndInv3Q	EndInv4Q		EndInvX4
6	+ Cost of goods sold						
7	= Total inventory needed	InvNeed1Q	InvNeed2Q	InvNeed3Q	InvNeed4Q		InvNeedX4
8							
9	PURCHASES BUDGET						
10	Purchases Budget						
11	Total inventory needed						
12	- Beginning inventory						
13	= Purchases	Purch1Q	Purch2Q	Purch3Q	Purch4Q		PurchX4
14							
15	Disbursements for Purchases Budget						
16	Payments of payables						
17	Total disbursements for purchases						
18							
19	Accounts Payable (A/P) Budget						
20	Beginning A/P balance						
21	+ Additions to A/P						
22	- Subtractions from A/P						
23	Ending A/P						
24							

Financial Ratios / Valuation / Capitalization \ Invent

Ready

FIGURE 3.15   Names of the Input and Output Cells in the Purchases Budget

STEP 4C: DISBURSEMENTS FOR PURCHASES BUDGET

The Disbursements for Purchases Budget reconciles the accrual values from Step 4B to cash figures. This schedule ties into the creation of the Cash Budget, which is covered in Chapter 6. This section of Napavale's financial model is based on two assumptions: the number of days per time period and the number of days payable.

Days payable is a financial metric that indicates how many days payables are "outstanding" or unpaid. A company's days payable value is calculated as: the average Accounts Payable balance for a time period/the dollar value of one day's worth of cost of goods sold. For the sake of simplicity, I will be using ending Accounts Payable values for a given time period (as opposed to average Accounts Payable values) in Napavale's financial model. Figure 3.16 illustrates these assumptions from the Assumptions and Dashboard worksheet.

Figure 3.17 presents a view of the Disbursements for Purchases Budget worksheet. Note that the "payment of payables" line in the disbursements for purchases is not completed. This is because the payment of payables is driven off of accounts payable calculations, which are shown in the next step (Step 4D).

An alternative view of the Disbursements for Purchases Budget, in which the values and calculations underlying the worksheet cells are ex-

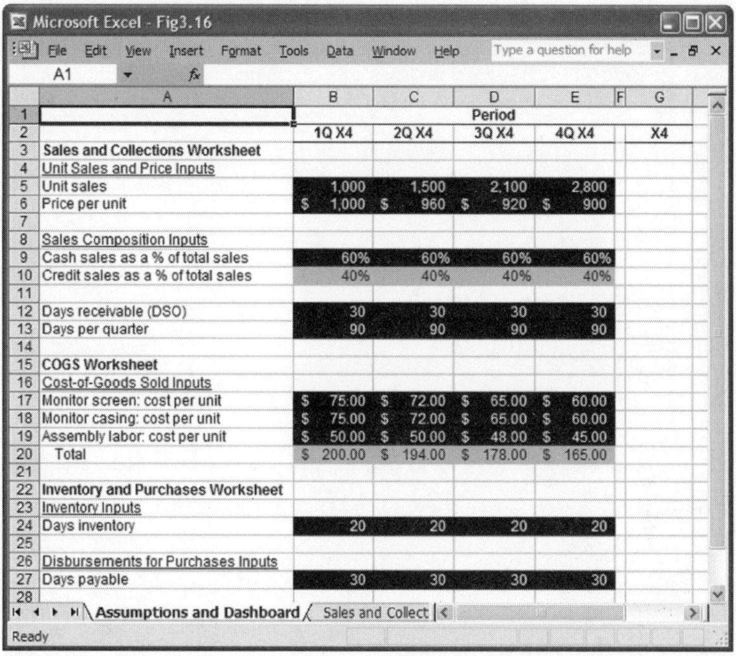

FIGURE 3.16 Assumptions in the Assumptions and Dashboard Worksheet

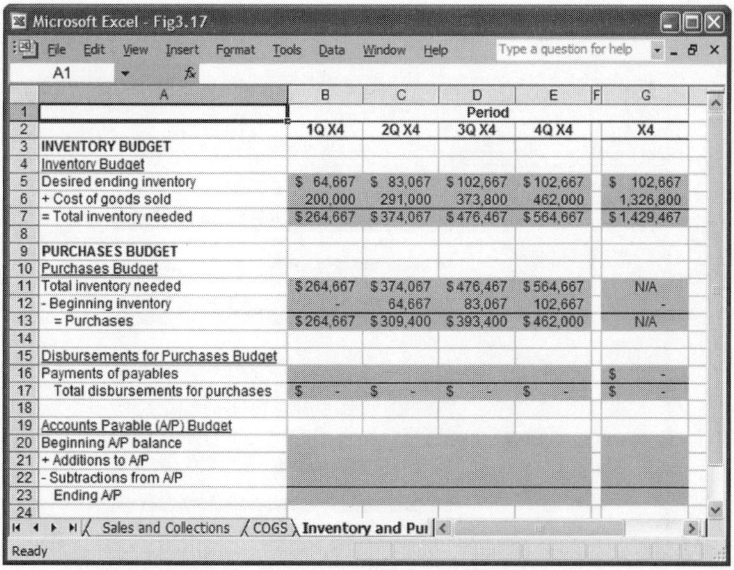

FIGURE 3.17 Disbursements for Purchases Budget

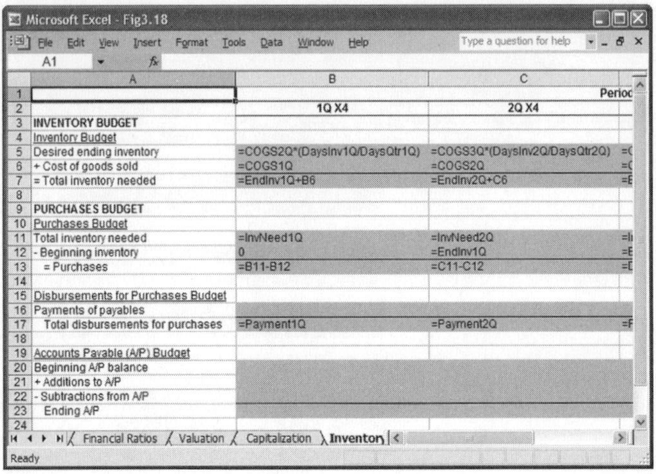

FIGURE 3.18 Alternative View of the Disbursements for Purchases Budget

posed and visible, is presented in Figure 3.18. Only a portion of the columns of the worksheet are shown due to the length of the formulas associated with the underlying calculations.

Figure 3.19 presents a view of the names of the input and output cells in the Assumptions and Dashboard worksheet. The names of the input and output cells in the Disbursements for Purchases Budget are shown in Figure 3.20.

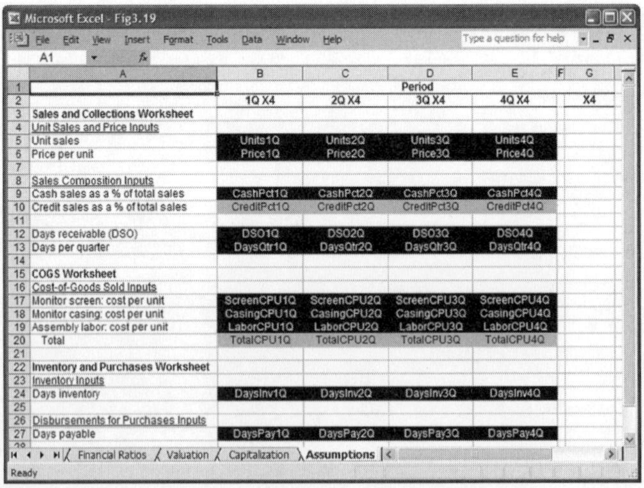

FIGURE 3.19 Names of the Input and Output Cells in the Assumptions and Dashboard Worksheet

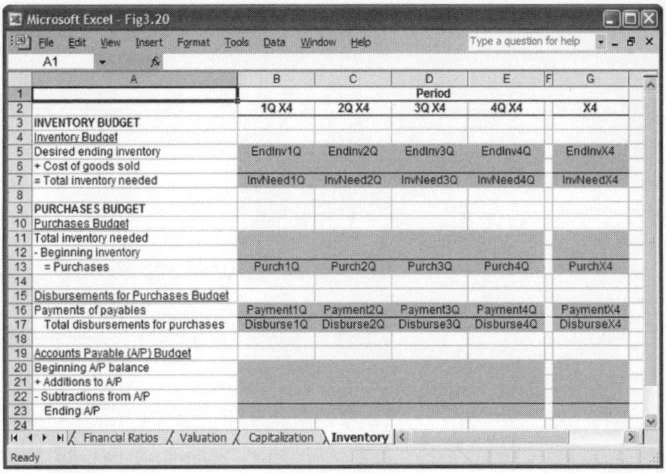

FIGURE 3.20 Names of the Input and Output Cells in the Disbursements for Purchases Budget

STEP 4D: ACCOUNTS PAYABLE BUDGET

Napavale pays for its inventory on both cash and credit terms. The Accounts Payable Budget tracks Napavale's credit purchases. As noted in Step 4C (Disbursements for Purchases Budget), payments of Accounts Payable are based on the assumptions underlying Napavale's days payable and days per accounting period. While there are no additional assumptions beyond those already mentioned associated with the Accounts Payable Budget, Figure 3.21 highlights the assumptions underlying the Accounts Payable calculation (using the Assumptions and Dashboard worksheet) for the sake of reference.

Figure 3.22 shows the Accounts Payable Budget worksheet. Note that I am assuming Napavale began the year X4 with no (zero) accounts payable. Also note that I am assuming Napavale's days payable metric is always less than the days-per-quarter metric. While this is a simplifying assumption, the Accounts Payable calculations are already detailed enough (as you will see below) and I do not want to introduce excessive complications to the model at this point.

Figure 3.23 offers an alternative view of the Accounts Payable calculations worksheet in which the calculations within the worksheet cells are exposed. Only a portion of the columns of the worksheet are shown due to the length of the formulas associated with the underlying calculations.

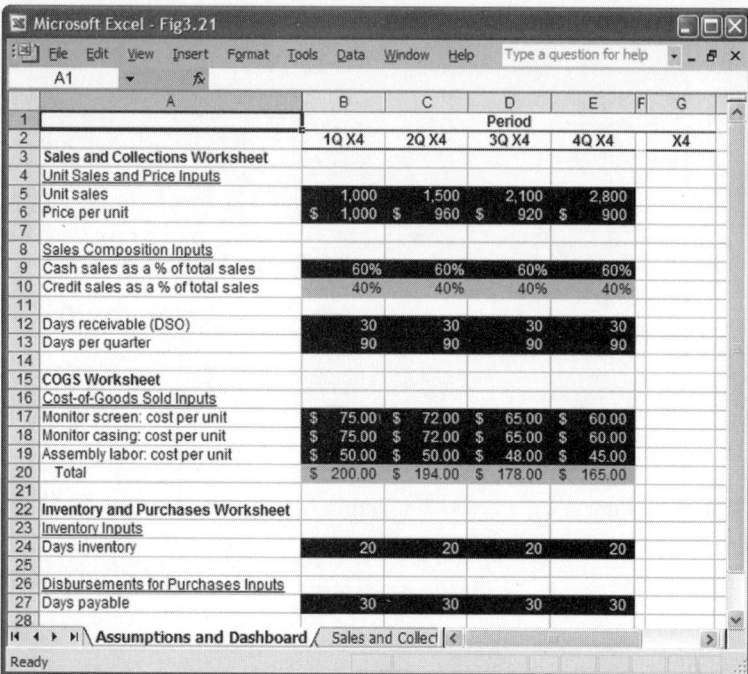

FIGURE 3.21   Assumptions Underlying the Accounts Payable Calculation

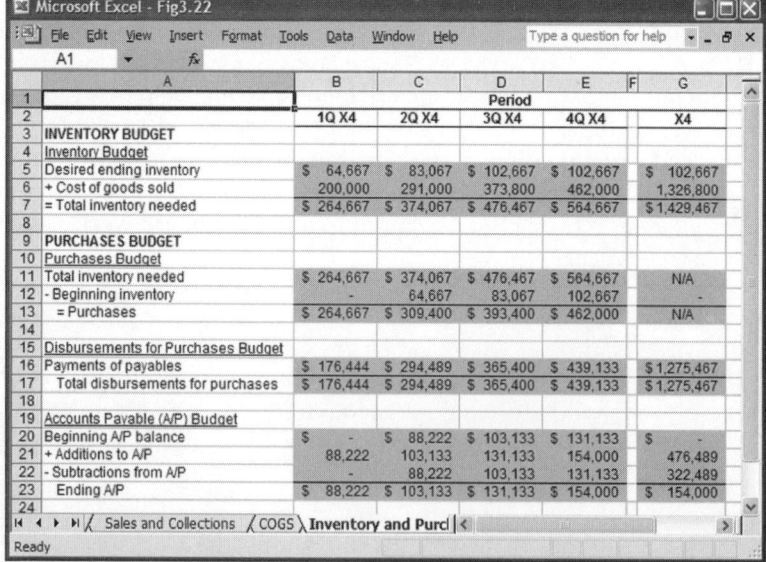

FIGURE 3.22   Accounts Payable Budget

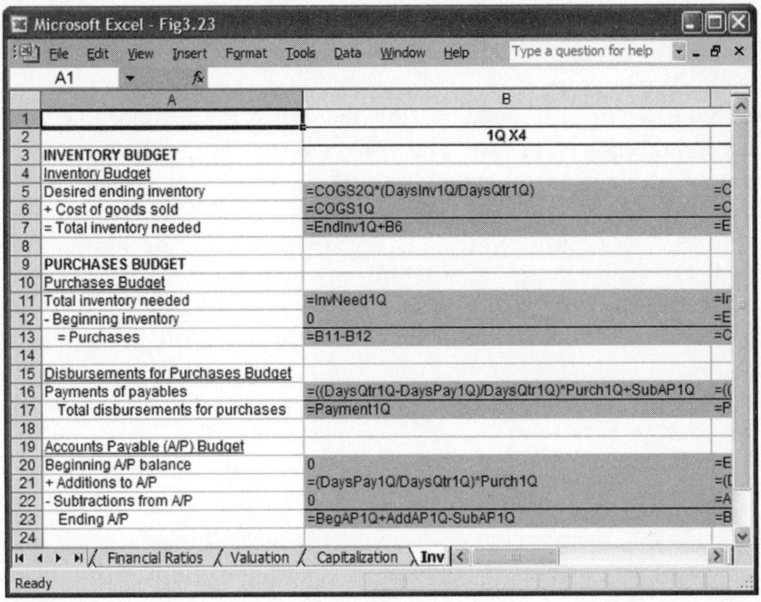

Microsoft Excel - Fig3.23

	A	B	
1			
2		1Q X4	
3	INVENTORY BUDGET		
4	Inventory Budget		
5	Desired ending inventory	=COGS2Q*(DaysInv1Q/DaysQtr1Q)	=C
6	+ Cost of goods sold	=COGS1Q	=C
7	= Total inventory needed	=EndInv1Q+B6	=E
8			
9	PURCHASES BUDGET		
10	Purchases Budget		
11	Total inventory needed	=InvNeed1Q	=Ir
12	- Beginning inventory	0	=E
13	= Purchases	=B11-B12	=C
14			
15	Disbursements for Purchases Budget		
16	Payments of payables	=((DaysQtr1Q-DaysPay1Q)/DaysQtr1Q)*Purch1Q+SubAP1Q	=((
17	Total disbursements for purchases	=Payment1Q	=P
18			
19	Accounts Payable (A/P) Budget		
20	Beginning A/P balance	0	=E
21	+ Additions to A/P	=(DaysPay1Q/DaysQtr1Q)*Purch1Q	=(I
22	- Subtractions from A/P	0	=A
23	Ending A/P	=BegAP1Q+AddAP1Q-SubAP1Q	=B
24			

FIGURE 3.23 Alternative View of the Accounts Payable Budget Worksheet

Given the complex nature of some of the calculations underlying the worksheet shown in Figure 3.23, I will walk through the logic behind the contents of two worksheet cells. The first cell that I will discuss, cell B16, calculates a value for "payment of payables." This represents the dollar value of purchases made during the 1Q X4 period that were paid for during 1Q X4. The general logic behind this calculation is as follows: The payment for purchases made during 1Q X4 is equal to: the percentage of purchases from 1Q X4 that were paid for in 1Q X4 + the subtractions from Napavale's Accounts Payable.

Looking specifically at the formula underlying cell B16, note that the purchases value for 1Q X4 is multiplied by: (days per quarter – days payable)/(days per quarter). This formula will yield the dollar value of the purchases that took place in 1Q X4 that were paid for in 1Q X4. Also note in cell B16 that the result of this formula is added to the subtractions from Napavale's Accounts Payable balance.

The second cell that I will discuss, cell B21, calculates a value for "additions to A/P." This represents the dollar value of purchases that took place in 1Q X4 that were not paid for in 1Q X4. As the contents of cell

B21 indicate, the purchases value for 1Q X4 is multiplied by: (days payable)/(days per quarter).

While these formulas may seem complex, their purpose is to divide up purchases between different periods based on my assumptions regarding days payable for Napavale. The approach that I am taking regarding Accounts Payable is one of many different ways to address the financial modeling of these topics—I am presenting this particular approach due to its utility and flexibility. Note that my approach for projecting Accounts Payable is similar to my approach for projecting Accounts Receivable, covered in Chapter 2.

The names of the input and output cells in the Assumptions and Dashboard worksheet are presented in Figure 3.24. Figure 3.25 offers a view of the names of the input and output cells in the Accounts Payable Budget.

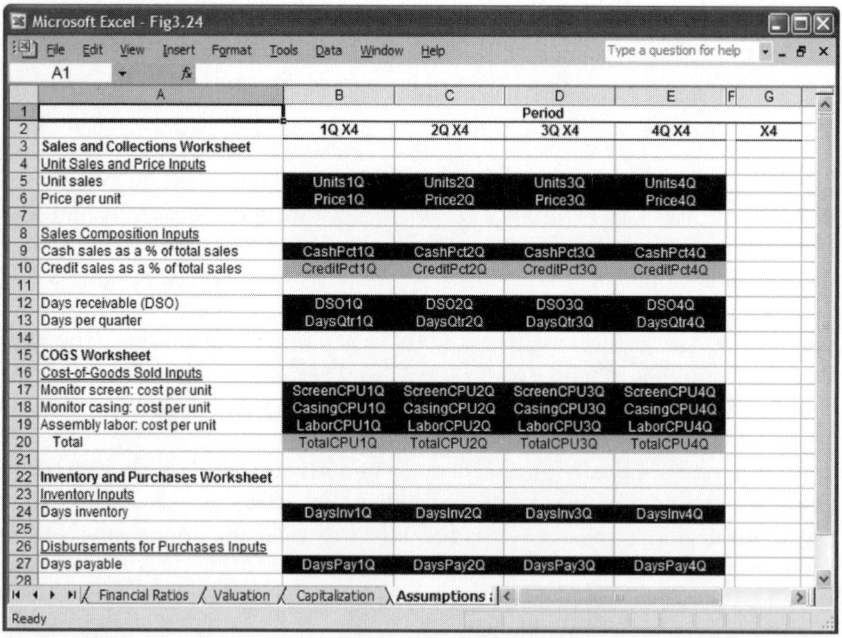

	A	B	C	D	E	F	G
1				Period			
2		1Q X4	2Q X4	3Q X4	4Q X4		X4
3	**Sales and Collections Worksheet**						
4	Unit Sales and Price Inputs						
5	Unit sales	Units1Q	Units2Q	Units3Q	Units4Q		
6	Price per unit	Price1Q	Price2Q	Price3Q	Price4Q		
7							
8	Sales Composition Inputs						
9	Cash sales as a % of total sales	CashPct1Q	CashPct2Q	CashPct3Q	CashPct4Q		
10	Credit sales as a % of total sales	CreditPct1Q	CreditPct2Q	CreditPct3Q	CreditPct4Q		
11							
12	Days receivable (DSO)	DSO1Q	DSO2Q	DSO3Q	DSO4Q		
13	Days per quarter	DaysQtr1Q	DaysQtr2Q	DaysQtr3Q	DaysQtr4Q		
14							
15	**COGS Worksheet**						
16	Cost-of-Goods Sold Inputs						
17	Monitor screen: cost per unit	ScreenCPU1Q	ScreenCPU2Q	ScreenCPU3Q	ScreenCPU4Q		
18	Monitor casing: cost per unit	CasingCPU1Q	CasingCPU2Q	CasingCPU3Q	CasingCPU4Q		
19	Assembly labor: cost per unit	LaborCPU1Q	LaborCPU2Q	LaborCPU3Q	LaborCPU4Q		
20	Total	TotalCPU1Q	TotalCPU2Q	TotalCPU3Q	TotalCPU4Q		
21							
22	**Inventory and Purchases Worksheet**						
23	Inventory Inputs						
24	Days inventory	DaysInv1Q	DaysInv2Q	DaysInv3Q	DaysInv4Q		
25							
26	Disbursements for Purchases Inputs						
27	Days payable	DaysPay1Q	DaysPay2Q	DaysPay3Q	DaysPay4Q		
28							

FIGURE 3.24 Names of the Input and Output Cells in the Assumptions and Dashboard Worksheet

	A	B	C	D	E	F	G
				Period			
1							
2		1Q X4	2Q X4	3Q X4	4Q X4		X4
3	**INVENTORY BUDGET**						
4	Inventory Budget						
5	Desired ending inventory	EndInv1Q	EndInv2Q	EndInv3Q	EndInv4Q		EndInvX4
6	+ Cost of goods sold						
7	= Total inventory needed	InvNeed1Q	InvNeed2Q	InvNeed3Q	InvNeed4Q		InvNeedX4
8							
9	**PURCHASES BUDGET**						
10	Purchases Budget						
11	Total inventory needed						
12	- Beginning inventory						
13	= Purchases	Purch1Q	Purch2Q	Purch3Q	Purch4Q		PurchX4
14							
15	Disbursements for Purchases Budget						
16	Payments of payables	Payment1Q	Payment2Q	Payment3Q	Payment4Q		PaymentX4
17	Total disbursements for purchases	Disburse1Q	Disburse2Q	Disburse3Q	Disburse4Q		DisburseX4
18							
19	Accounts Payable (A/P) Budget						
20	Beginning A/P balance	BegAP1Q	BegAP2Q	BegAP3Q	BegAP4Q		BegAPX4
21	+ Additions to A/P	AddAP1Q	AddAP2Q	AddAP3Q	AddAP4Q		AddAPX4
22	- Subtractions from A/P	SubAP1Q	SubAP2Q	SubAP3Q	SubAP4Q		SubAPX4
23	Ending A/P	EndAP1Q	EndAP2Q	EndAP3Q	EndAP4Q		EndAPX4
24							

FIGURE 3.25 Names of the Input and Output Cells in the Accounts Payable Budget

QUESTIONS

Each of the questions for this chapter relates to a hypothetical company named Company ABC. Company ABC sells functional desks to the business market. As such, Company ABC is a product-oriented (as opposed to a service-oriented) business. The questions for this chapter will address fiscal year X6 on a quarterly basis (four specific quarters, 1Q–4Q for the year X6).

The following questions will test your knowledge of the material covered in this chapter in an applied manner—specifically, you will be asked to build the schedules discussed in this chapter for Company ABC.

To prepare you for this chapter's questions, two figures provide background information related to Company ABC's operations. Figure Q3.1 offers a view of Company ABC's Assumptions and Dashboard worksheet. Note that there are three cost-of-goods-sold components for Company ABC's desks: (1) desk top, (2) desk body, and (3) assembly and labor. Figure Q3.2 presents a view of Company ABC's Unit Sales and Price Budget, Sales Composition Budget, Cash Collections from Customers Budget, and Accounts Receivable Budget.

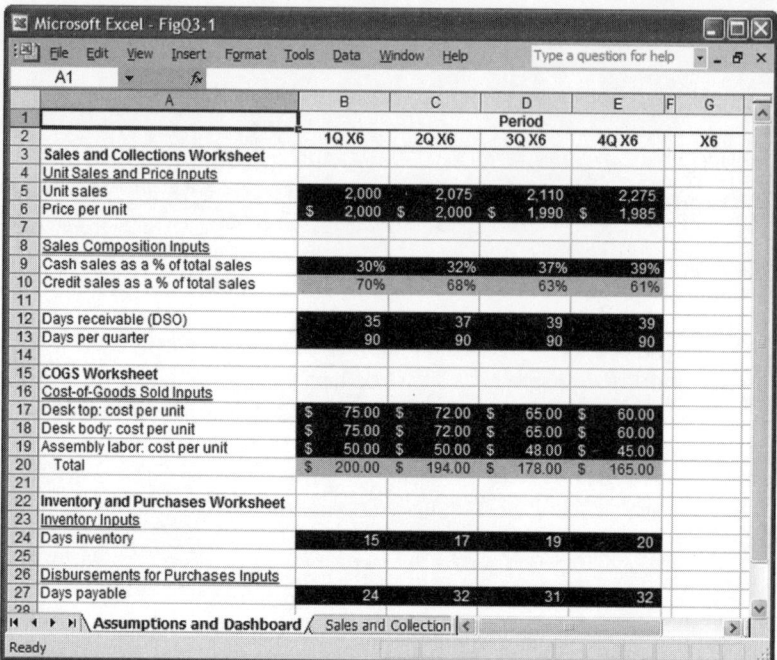

FIGURE Q3.1 Company ABC's Assumptions and Dashboard Worksheet

Microsoft Excel - FigQ3.1

	A	B	C	D	E	F	G
1				Period			
2		1Q X6	2Q X6	3Q X6	4Q X6		X6
3	**Sales and Collections Worksheet**						
4	Unit Sales and Price Inputs						
5	Unit sales	2,000	2,075	2,110	2,275		
6	Price per unit	$ 2,000	$ 2,000	$ 1,990	$ 1,985		
7							
8	Sales Composition Inputs						
9	Cash sales as a % of total sales	30%	32%	37%	39%		
10	Credit sales as a % of total sales	70%	68%	63%	61%		
11							
12	Days receivable (DSO)	35	37	39	39		
13	Days per quarter	90	90	90	90		
14							
15	**COGS Worksheet**						
16	Cost-of-Goods Sold Inputs						
17	Desk top: cost per unit	$ 75.00	$ 72.00	$ 65.00	$ 60.00		
18	Desk body: cost per unit	$ 75.00	$ 72.00	$ 65.00	$ 60.00		
19	Assembly labor: cost per unit	$ 50.00	$ 50.00	$ 48.00	$ 45.00		
20	Total	$ 200.00	$ 194.00	$ 178.00	$ 165.00		
21							
22	**Inventory and Purchases Worksheet**						
23	Inventory Inputs						
24	Days inventory	15	17	19	20		
25							
26	Disbursements for Purchases Inputs						
27	Days payable	24	32	31	32		

Assumptions and Dashboard / Sales and Collection

Ready

FIGURE Q3.2 Company ABC's Unit Sales and Price Budget

Microsoft Excel - FigQ3.2

	A	B	C	D	E	F	G
1				Period			
2		1Q X6	2Q X6	3Q X6	4Q X6		X6
3	**SALES BUDGET**						
4	Unit Sales and Price Budget						
5	Unit sales	2,000	2,075	2,110	2,275		8,460
6	× Price per unit	$ 2,000	$ 2,050	$ 2,100	$ 2,200		N/A
7	= Total sales	$4,000,000	$4,253,750	$4,431,000	$5,005,000		$17,689,750
8							
9	Sales Composition Budget						
10	Cash sales	$1,200,000	$1,361,200	$1,639,470	$1,951,950		$ 6,152,620
11	+ Credit sales	2,800,000	2,892,550	2,791,530	3,053,050		11,537,130
12	= Total sales	$4,000,000	$4,253,750	$4,431,000	$5,005,000		$17,689,750
13							
14	**COLLECTIONS BUDGET**						
15	Cash Collections from Customers Budget						
16	Cash sales this period	$1,200,000	$1,361,200	$1,639,470	$1,951,950		$ 6,152,620
17	+ Credit sales collected	1,711,111	2,792,279	2,771,026	2,939,725		10,214,142
18	= Total collections	$2,911,111	$4,153,479	$4,410,496	$4,891,675		$16,366,762
19							
20	Accounts Receivable (A/R) Budget						
21	Beginning A/R balance	$ -	$1,088,889	$1,189,159	$1,209,663		$ -
22	+ Additions to A/R	1,088,889	1,189,159	1,209,663	1,322,988		4,810,700
23	- Subtractions from A/R	-	1,088,889	1,189,159	1,209,663		3,487,711
24	= Ending A/R balance	$1,088,889	$1,189,159	$1,209,663	$1,322,988		$ 1,322,988

Assumptions and Dashboard \ Sales and Collections

Ready

1. Given the information regarding Company ABC, build a Cost-of-Goods-Sold Budget for Company ABC.
2. Based on the information presented and the Cost-of-Goods-Sold Budget that you built in Question 1, build an Inventory Budget for Company ABC. Use the days inventory approach outlined in this chapter and use the assumptions regarding days inventory shown in Figure Q3.1. Furthermore, assume that Company ABC's desired ending inventory for 4Q X6 is equal to the desired ending inventory for 3Q X6.
3. Build a Purchases Budget for Company ABC based on your work in Questions 1 and 2.
4. Build an Accounts Payable Budget for Company ABC based upon the Assumptions and Dashboard worksheet and your work in Questions 1–3. Assume that Company ABC started 1Q X6 with a beginning A/P balance of 0 (zero).
5. Based on your work in Questions 1–4 and the Assumptions and Dashboard worksheet, build a Disbursements for Purchases Budget for Company ABC.

CHAPTER 4

Operating Budget— Operating Expenses

This chapter covers the second set of cost components for the Operating Budget, specifically the Operating Expenses Budget. Operating expenses represent those expenses required to run, or operate, a business. These expenses typically include items such as salaries, research and development, and rent. Specific operating expenses vary from business to business and I will cover the operating expenses incurred by Napavale in the chapter. Figure 4.1 highlights the separate operating expense components of the Operating Budget in the context of the Master Budget.

Please note that operating expenses are different from the expenses listed in the Purchases budget from Step 4B in Chapter 3. It is helpful to divide operating expenses into two categories: variable and fixed. Variable operating expenses are those expenses that are directly influenced by other drivers, such as sales volume. Fixed operating expenses are those expenses that are not affected by drivers such as sales volume. I cover the concept of fixed versus variable expenses in Chapter 11.

As in Chapters 2 and 3, I will be using the Assumptions and Dashboard worksheet for Napavale to introduce and focus on important assumptions underlying Napavale's financial model. The remainder of this chapter will cover the steps involved in the continued construction of the Assumptions and Dashboard worksheet and the operating expense elements of the Operating Budget.

STEP 5A: HEADCOUNT BUDGET

The Headcount Budget tracks both the projected number of employees by position and the projected salary by position. This is a very important budget as the headcount expenses, which are otherwise known as

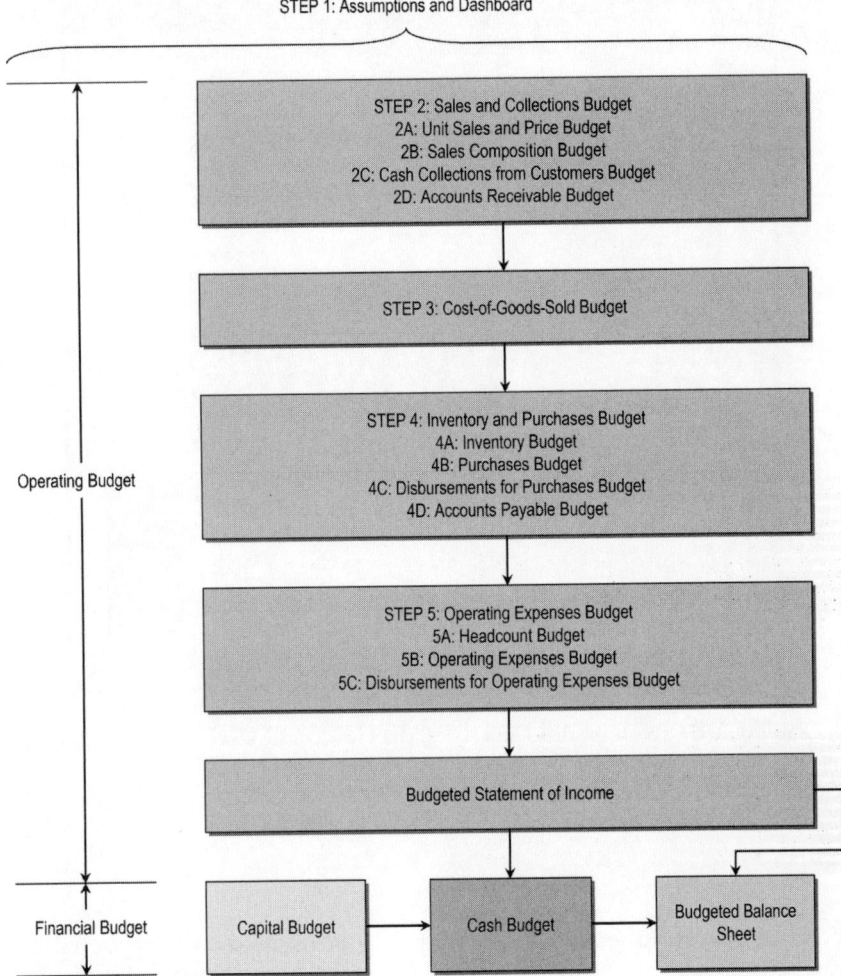

FIGURE 4.1 Separate Operating Expense Components of the Operating Budget in the Context of the Master Budget

"salaries," represent a significant portion of many business's overall operating expenses.

Headcount Overview Worksheet

Figure 4.2 presents the assumptions underlying the Headcount Overview worksheet, the first of two headcount worksheets for Napavale from the Assumptions and Dashboard worksheet. Note that Figure 4.2 highlights

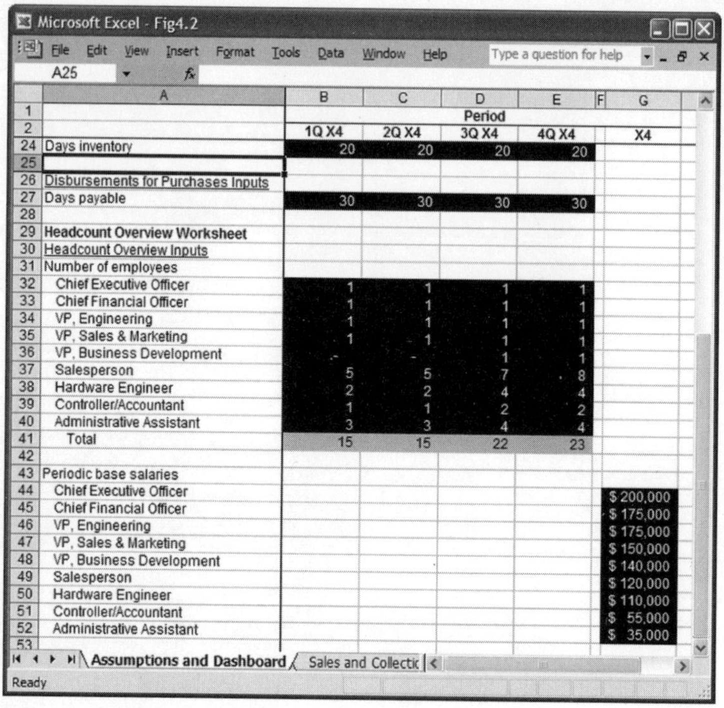

Microsoft Excel - Fig4.2

	A	B	C	D	E	F	G
1				Period			
2		1Q X4	2Q X4	3Q X4	4Q X4		X4
24	Days inventory	20	20	20	20		
25							
26	Disbursements for Purchases Inputs						
27	Days payable	30	30	30	30		
28							
29	**Headcount Overview Worksheet**						
30	Headcount Overview Inputs						
31	Number of employees						
32	Chief Executive Officer	1	1	1	1		
33	Chief Financial Officer	1	1	1	1		
34	VP, Engineering	1	1	1	1		
35	VP, Sales & Marketing	1	1	1	1		
36	VP, Business Development	-	-	1	1		
37	Salesperson	5	5	7	8		
38	Hardware Engineer	2	2	4	4		
39	Controller/Accountant	1	1	2	2		
40	Administrative Assistant	3	3	4	4		
41	Total	15	15	22	23		
42							
43	Periodic base salaries						
44	Chief Executive Officer						$ 200,000
45	Chief Financial Officer						$ 175,000
46	VP, Engineering						$ 175,000
47	VP, Sales & Marketing						$ 150,000
48	VP, Business Development						$ 140,000
49	Salesperson						$ 120,000
50	Hardware Engineer						$ 110,000
51	Controller/Accountant						$ 55,000
52	Administrative Assistant						$ 35,000

FIGURE 4.2 Assumptions Underlying the Headcount Overview Worksheet

both the number of employees projected by position and the projected annualized base salary by position. Figure 4.3 shows the Headcount Overview worksheet, which includes a separate table that calculates the periodic Headcount Cost based on the projected annualized base salary and the number of accounting periods per year. (In Napavale's case, this is four accounting periods per year as I am working with quarters as my accounting period.) Figure 4.4 offers an alternative view of the Headcount Overview worksheet in which the values and calculations underlying the worksheet are exposed and visible.

The names of the input and output cells in the Assumptions and Dashboard worksheet are highlighted in Figure 4.5. Figure 4.6 offers a view of the names of the input and output cells in the Headcount Overview worksheet.

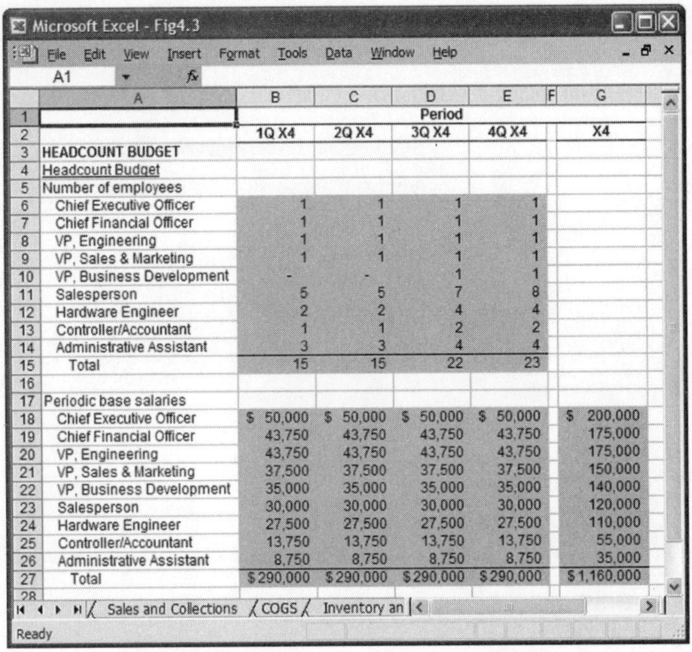

	A	B	C	D	E	G
1				Period		
2		1Q X4	2Q X4	3Q X4	4Q X4	X4
3	HEADCOUNT BUDGET					
4	Headcount Budget					
5	Number of employees					
6	Chief Executive Officer	1	1	1	1	
7	Chief Financial Officer	1	1	1	1	
8	VP, Engineering	1	1	1	1	
9	VP, Sales & Marketing	1	1	1	1	
10	VP, Business Development	-	-	1	1	
11	Salesperson	5	5	7	8	
12	Hardware Engineer	2	2	4	4	
13	Controller/Accountant	1	1	2	2	
14	Administrative Assistant	3	3	4	4	
15	Total	15	15	22	23	
16						
17	Periodic base salaries					
18	Chief Executive Officer	$ 50,000	$ 50,000	$ 50,000	$ 50,000	$ 200,000
19	Chief Financial Officer	43,750	43,750	43,750	43,750	175,000
20	VP, Engineering	43,750	43,750	43,750	43,750	175,000
21	VP, Sales & Marketing	37,500	37,500	37,500	37,500	150,000
22	VP, Business Development	35,000	35,000	35,000	35,000	140,000
23	Salesperson	30,000	30,000	30,000	30,000	120,000
24	Hardware Engineer	27,500	27,500	27,500	27,500	110,000
25	Controller/Accountant	13,750	13,750	13,750	13,750	55,000
26	Administrative Assistant	8,750	8,750	8,750	8,750	35,000
27	Total	$ 290,000	$ 290,000	$ 290,000	$ 290,000	$ 1,160,000

FIGURE 4.3 Headcount Overview Worksheet

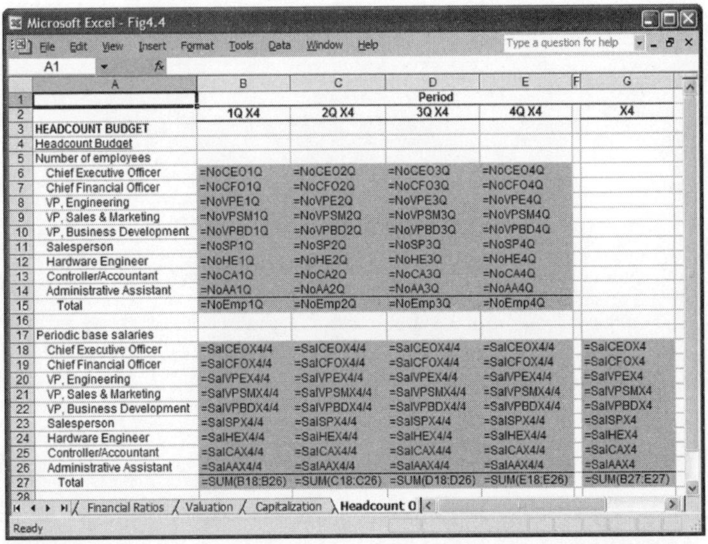

	A	B	C	D	E	G
1				Period		
2		1Q X4	2Q X4	3Q X4	4Q X4	X4
3	HEADCOUNT BUDGET					
4	Headcount Budget					
5	Number of employees					
6	Chief Executive Officer	=NoCEO1Q	=NoCEO2Q	=NoCEO3Q	=NoCEO4Q	
7	Chief Financial Officer	=NoCFO1Q	=NoCFO2Q	=NoCFO3Q	=NoCFO4Q	
8	VP, Engineering	=NoVPE1Q	=NoVPE2Q	=NoVPE3Q	=NoVPE4Q	
9	VP, Sales & Marketing	=NoVPSM1Q	=NoVPSM2Q	=NoVPSM3Q	=NoVPSM4Q	
10	VP, Business Development	=NoVPBD1Q	=NoVPBD2Q	=NoVPBD3Q	=NoVPBD4Q	
11	Salesperson	=NoSP1Q	=NoSP2Q	=NoSP3Q	=NoSP4Q	
12	Hardware Engineer	=NoHE1Q	=NoHE2Q	=NoHE3Q	=NoHE4Q	
13	Controller/Accountant	=NoCA1Q	=NoCA2Q	=NoCA3Q	=NoCA4Q	
14	Administrative Assistant	=NoAA1Q	=NoAA2Q	=NoAA3Q	=NoAA4Q	
15	Total	=NoEmp1Q	=NoEmp2Q	=NoEmp3Q	=NoEmp4Q	
16						
17	Periodic base salaries					
18	Chief Executive Officer	=SalCEOX4/4	=SalCEOX4/4	=SalCEOX4/4	=SalCEOX4/4	=SalCEOX4
19	Chief Financial Officer	=SalCFOX4/4	=SalCFOX4/4	=SalCFOX4/4	=SalCFOX4/4	=SalCFOX4
20	VP, Engineering	=SalVPEX4/4	=SalVPEX4/4	=SalVPEX4/4	=SalVPEX4/4	=SalVPEX4
21	VP, Sales & Marketing	=SalVPSMX4/4	=SalVPSMX4/4	=SalVPSMX4/4	=SalVPSMX4/4	=SalVPSMX4
22	VP, Business Development	=SalVPBDX4/4	=SalVPBDX4/4	=SalVPBDX4/4	=SalVPBDX4/4	=SalVPBDX4
23	Salesperson	=SalSPX4/4	=SalSPX4/4	=SalSPX4/4	=SalSPX4/4	=SalSPX4
24	Hardware Engineer	=SalHEX4/4	=SalHEX4/4	=SalHEX4/4	=SalHEX4/4	=SalHEX4
25	Controller/Accountant	=SalCAX4/4	=SalCAX4/4	=SalCAX4/4	=SalCAX4/4	=SalCAX4
26	Administrative Assistant	=SalAAX4/4	=SalAAX4/4	=SalAAX4/4	=SalAAX4/4	=SalAAX4
27	Total	=SUM(B18:B26)	=SUM(C18:C26)	=SUM(D18:D26)	=SUM(E18:E26)	=SUM(B27:E27)

FIGURE 4.4 Alternative View of the Headcount Overview Worksheet

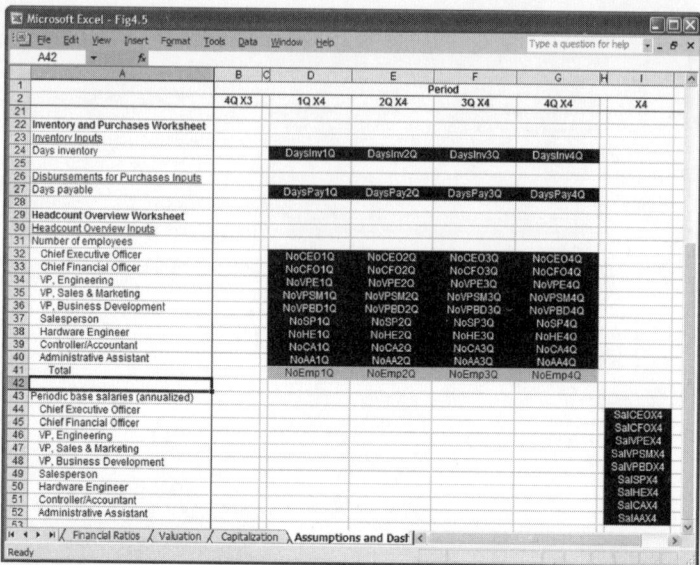

FIGURE 4.5   Names of the Input and Output Cells in the Assumptions and Dashboard Worksheet

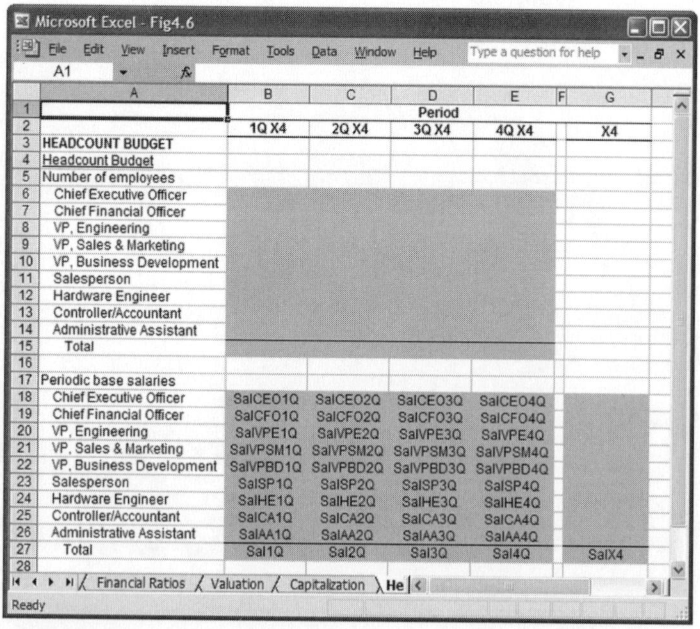

FIGURE 4.6   Names of the Input and Output Cells in the Headcount Overview Worksheet

Headcount Cost Worksheet

The Headcount Cost worksheet, which is the second worksheet included in the Headcount Budget, calculates the periodic Headcount Costs based on the projected number of employees by position and the projected periodic cost per position. The only new assumption underlying the Headcount Cost worksheet is that of Napavale's benefits rate. In addition to base salaries, companies often must pay taxes and employment benefit costs (such as health care costs). As such, I am modeling these benefits costs as an incremental percentage above the base salary projections for Napavale. Figure 4.7 highlights the benefits rate assumption using the Assumptions and Dashboard worksheet.

The Headcount Cost worksheet is presented in Figure 4.8. Figure 4.9 offers an alternative view of the Headcount Cost worksheet in which the values and calculations underlying the worksheet cells are exposed and visible.

The names of the input and output cells in the Assumptions and Dashboard worksheet are shown in Figure 4.10. The names of the input and output cells in the Headcount Cost worksheet are shown in Figure 4.11.

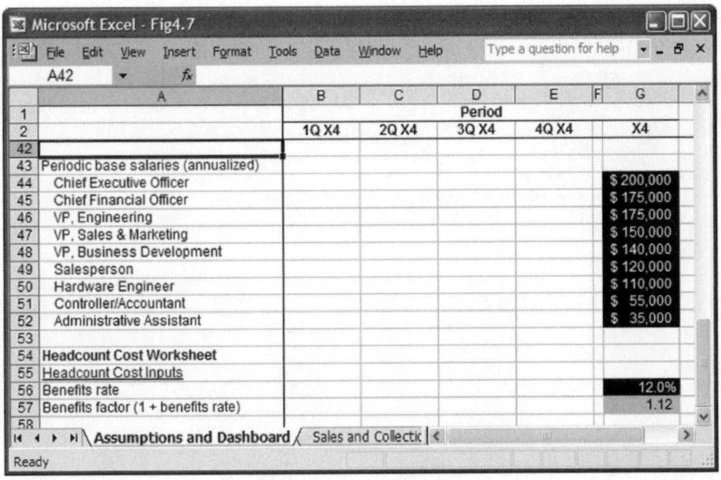

FIGURE 4.7 Benefits Rate Assumption in the Assumptions and Dashboard Worksheet

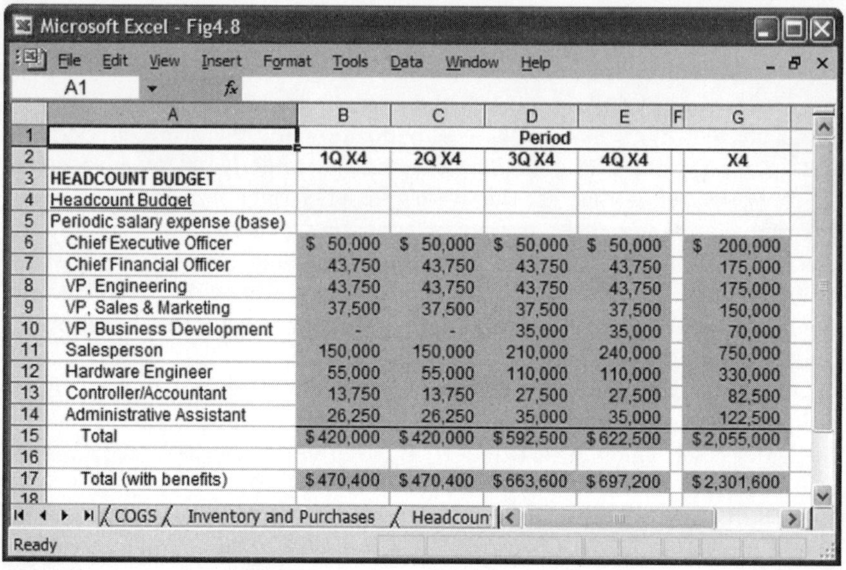

	A	B	C	D	E	G
1				Period		
2		1Q X4	2Q X4	3Q X4	4Q X4	X4
3	HEADCOUNT BUDGET					
4	Headcount Budget					
5	Periodic salary expense (base)					
6	Chief Executive Officer	$ 50,000	$ 50,000	$ 50,000	$ 50,000	$ 200,000
7	Chief Financial Officer	43,750	43,750	43,750	43,750	175,000
8	VP, Engineering	43,750	43,750	43,750	43,750	175,000
9	VP, Sales & Marketing	37,500	37,500	37,500	37,500	150,000
10	VP, Business Development	-	-	35,000	35,000	70,000
11	Salesperson	150,000	150,000	210,000	240,000	750,000
12	Hardware Engineer	55,000	55,000	110,000	110,000	330,000
13	Controller/Accountant	13,750	13,750	27,500	27,500	82,500
14	Administrative Assistant	26,250	26,250	35,000	35,000	122,500
15	Total	$ 420,000	$ 420,000	$ 592,500	$ 622,500	$ 2,055,000
16						
17	Total (with benefits)	$ 470,400	$ 470,400	$ 663,600	$ 697,200	$ 2,301,600

FIGURE 4.8 Headcount Cost Worksheet

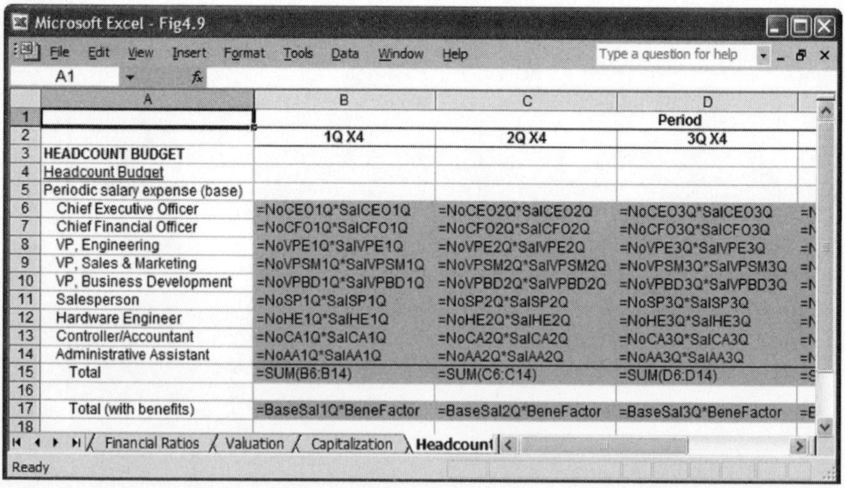

	A	B	C	D	
1				Period	
2		1Q X4	2Q X4	3Q X4	
3	HEADCOUNT BUDGET				
4	Headcount Budget				
5	Periodic salary expense (base)				
6	Chief Executive Officer	=NoCEO1Q*SalCEO1Q	=NoCEO2Q*SalCEO2Q	=NoCEO3Q*SalCEO3Q	=N
7	Chief Financial Officer	=NoCFO1Q*SalCFO1Q	=NoCFO2Q*SalCFO2Q	=NoCFO3Q*SalCFO3Q	=N
8	VP, Engineering	=NoVPE1Q*SalVPE1Q	=NoVPE2Q*SalVPE2Q	=NoVPE3Q*SalVPE3Q	=N
9	VP, Sales & Marketing	=NoVPSM1Q*SalVPSM1Q	=NoVPSM2Q*SalVPSM2Q	=NoVPSM3Q*SalVPSM3Q	=N
10	VP, Business Development	=NoVPBD1Q*SalVPBD1Q	=NoVPBD2Q*SalVPBD2Q	=NoVPBD3Q*SalVPBD3Q	=N
11	Salesperson	=NoSP1Q*SalSP1Q	=NoSP2Q*SalSP2Q	=NoSP3Q*SalSP3Q	=N
12	Hardware Engineer	=NoHE1Q*SalHE1Q	=NoHE2Q*SalHE2Q	=NoHE3Q*SalHE3Q	=N
13	Controller/Accountant	=NoCA1Q*SalCA1Q	=NoCA2Q*SalCA2Q	=NoCA3Q*SalCA3Q	=N
14	Administrative Assistant	=NoAA1Q*SalAA1Q	=NoAA2Q*SalAA2Q	=NoAA3Q*SalAA3Q	=N
15	Total	=SUM(B6:B14)	=SUM(C6:C14)	=SUM(D6:D14)	=S
16					
17	Total (with benefits)	=BaseSal1Q*BeneFactor	=BaseSal2Q*BeneFactor	=BaseSal3Q*BeneFactor	=E

FIGURE 4.9 Alternative View of the Headcount Cost Worksheet

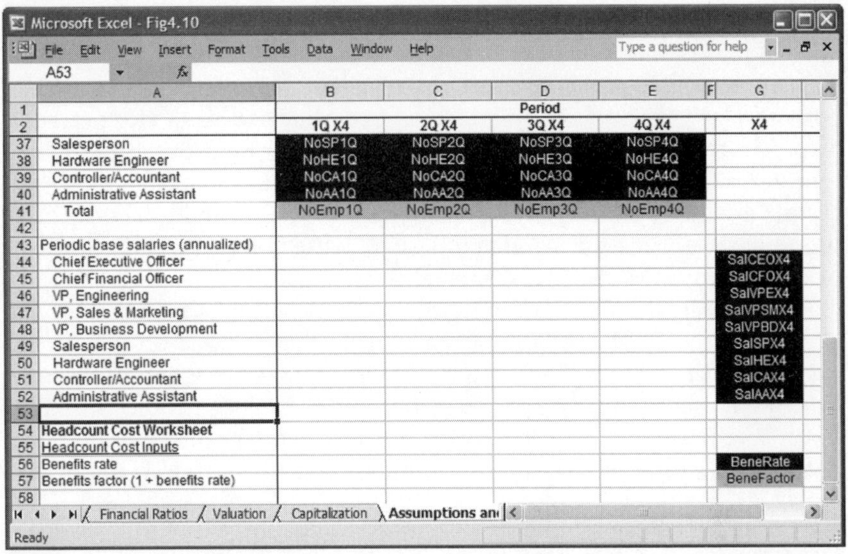

FIGURE 4.10 Names of the Input and Output Cells in the Assumptions and Dashboard Worksheet

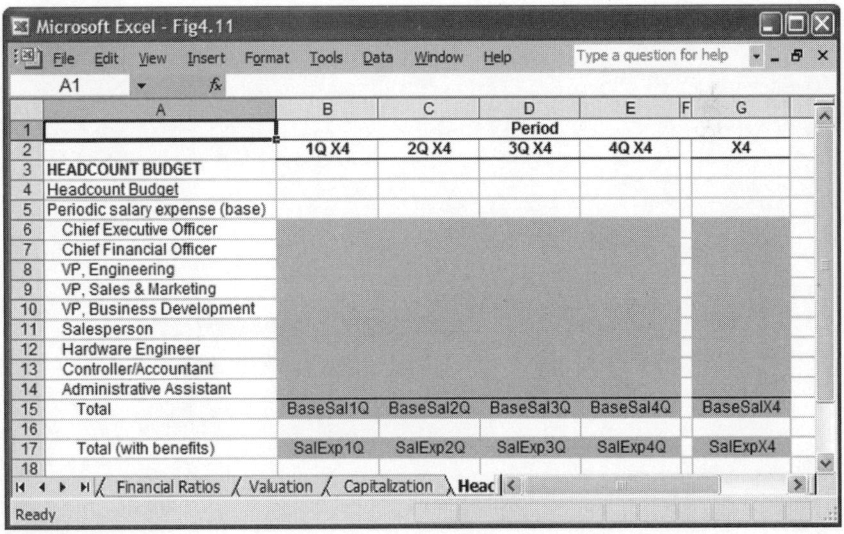

FIGURE 4.11 Names of the Input and Output Cells in the Headcount Cost Worksheet

STEP 5B: OPERATING EXPENSES BUDGET

The Operating Expenses Budget covers all of Napavale's operating expenses (salary expenses, a component of operating expenses, are covered in Step 5A: Headcount Budget). For Napavale, operating expenses include rent, research and development, depreciation, and miscellaneous expenses, among others. Specific operating expenses will vary from business to business, but the expenses covered in this Step 5B are fairly typical for product-oriented companies such as Napavale.

Please note that I am not entering any values into the depreciation line item at this point. Depreciation is an expense that is based on the Capital Budget, which is covered in Chapter 6. Once the depreciation projections have been calculated for Napavale in Chapter 6, I will revisit the Operating Expenses Budget with the inclusion of the depreciation expense projections.

Figure 4.12 highlights the assumptions underlying the operating ex-

	A	B	C	D	E	F	G
1				Period			
2		1Q X4	2Q X4	3Q X4	4Q X4		X4
43	Periodic base salaries (annualized)						
44	Chief Executive Officer						$ 200,000
45	Chief Financial Officer						$ 175,000
46	VP, Engineering						$ 175,000
47	VP, Sales & Marketing						$ 150,000
48	VP, Business Development						$ 140,000
49	Salesperson						$ 120,000
50	Hardware Engineer						$ 110,000
51	Controller/Accountant						$ 55,000
52	Administrative Assistant						$ 35,000
53							
54	Headcount Cost Worksheet						
55	Headcount Cost Inputs						
56	Benefits rate						12.0%
57	Benefits factor (1 + benefits rate)						1.12
58							
59	Operating Expenses Worksheet						
60	Operating Expenses Inputs						
61	Miscellaneous expenses as a % of sales	3.0%	3.0%	3.0%	3.0%		
62							
63	R&D expenses as a % of sales	7.0%	7.0%	8.0%	8.0%		
64							
65	Rent expense per square foot per quarter	$ 5.00	$ 5.00	$ 5.00	$ 5.00		
66	Square feet of space rented	4,000	4,000	4,000	4,000		
67	Total rent expense	$ 20,000	$ 20,000	$ 20,000	$ 20,000		
68							
69	Tax rate	35.0%	35.0%	35.0%	35.0%		

FIGURE 4.12 Assumptions Underlying the Operating Expenses from the Assumptions and Dashboard Worksheet

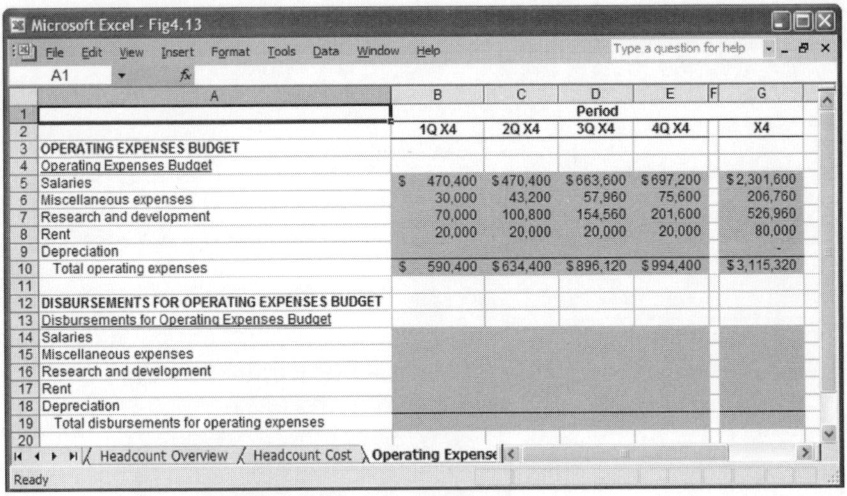

FIGURE 4.13 Operating Expenses Budget

penses for Napavale from the Assumptions and Dashboard worksheet. The Operating Expenses Budget is presented in Figure 4.13. Figure 4.14 offers an alternative view of the Operating Expenses Budget in which the values and formulas underlying the worksheet cells are exposed and visible.

The names of the input and output cells in the Assumptions and Dashboard worksheet are shown in Figure 4.15. Figure 4.16 offers a view of the names of the input and output cells in the Operating Expenses Budget.

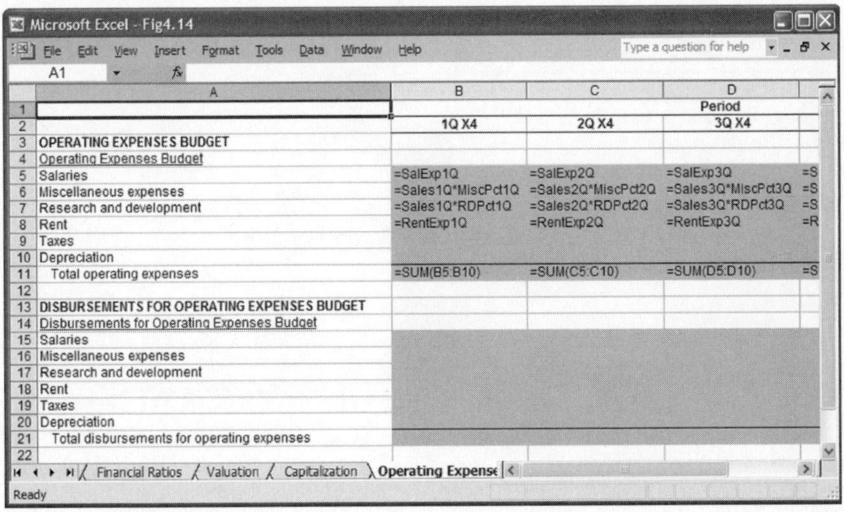

FIGURE 4.14 Alternative View of the Operating Expenses Budget

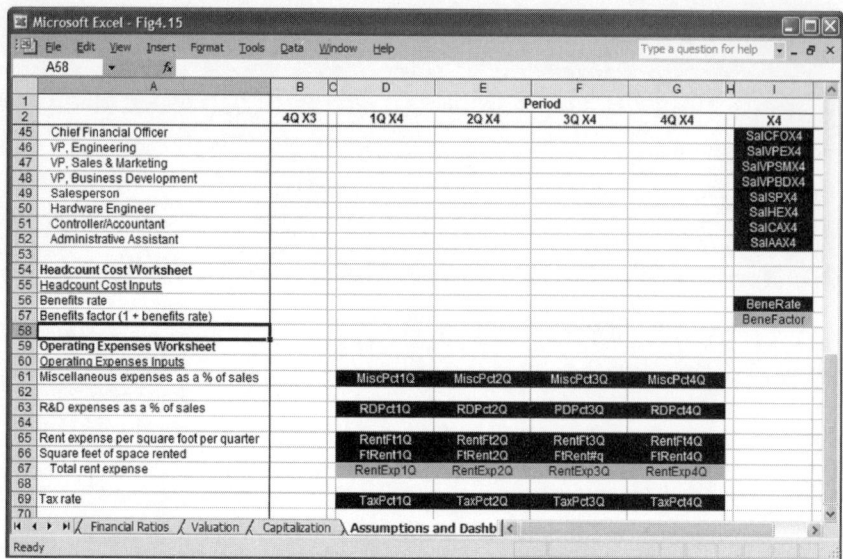

FIGURE 4.15 Names of the Input and Output Cells in the Assumptions and Dashboard Worksheet

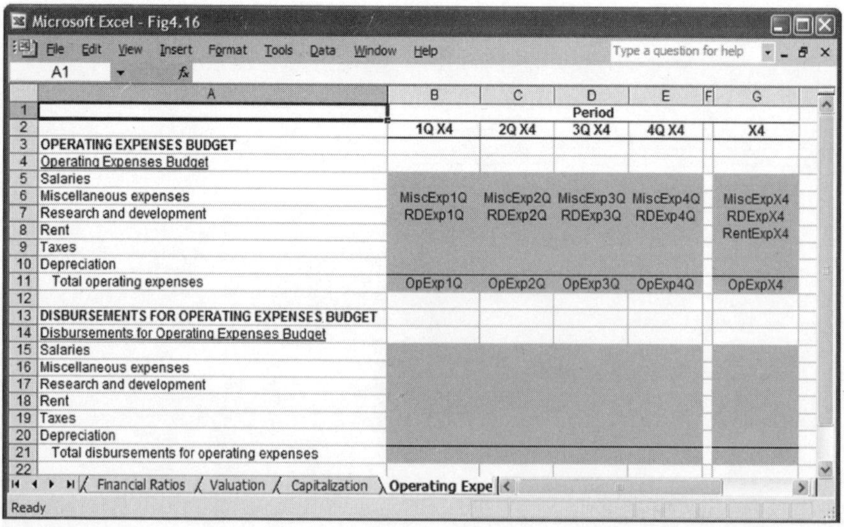

FIGURE 4.16 Names of the Input and Output Cells in the Operating Expenses Budget

STEP 5C: DISBURSEMENTS FOR OPERATING EXPENSES BUDGET

The Disbursements for Operating Expenses Budget reconciles the accrual-based values from Steps 5A and 5B to cash values. Remember that Napavale's operating expenses include both the headcount expenses calculated in Step 5A and the other operating expenses calculated in Step 5B. As there are no new assumptions underlying the Disbursements for Operating Expenses Budget, I will not present a view of the Assumptions and Dashboard worksheet at this point.

I am assuming Napavale disburses payments for its operating expenses in the periods in which such operating expenses occur. Note that I am treating disbursements for purchases (covered in Chapter 3) separately from disbursements for operating expenses. More specifically, my assumptions regarding days payable in Chapter 3 relate to purchases of goods that will eventually be sold to customers; my assumptions regarding the disbursement for operating expenses are treated as a separate category of disbursements.

As with the Disbursements for Purchases Budget covered in Step 4C in Chapter 3, the Disbursements for Operating Expenses Budget ties into the creation of the Cash Budget, which is covered in Chapter 6. I will assume that Napavale disburses 100 percent of its operating expenses in the period in which such expenses are incurred.

The Disbursements for Operating Expenses Budget is presented in Figure 4.17. Figure 4.18 presents an alternative view of the Disbursements for

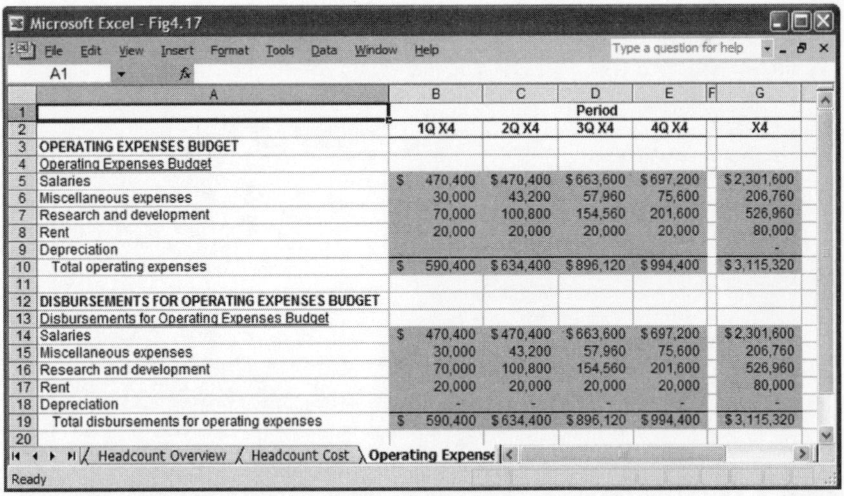

	A	B	C	D	E	F	G
1				Period			
2		1Q X4	2Q X4	3Q X4	4Q X4		X4
3	OPERATING EXPENSES BUDGET						
4	Operating Expenses Budget						
5	Salaries	$ 470,400	$ 470,400	$ 663,600	$ 697,200		$ 2,301,600
6	Miscellaneous expenses	30,000	43,200	57,960	75,600		206,760
7	Research and development	70,000	100,800	154,560	201,600		526,960
8	Rent	20,000	20,000	20,000	20,000		80,000
9	Depreciation						-
10	Total operating expenses	$ 590,400	$ 634,400	$ 896,120	$ 994,400		$ 3,115,320
11							
12	DISBURSEMENTS FOR OPERATING EXPENSES BUDGET						
13	Disbursements for Operating Expenses Budget						
14	Salaries	$ 470,400	$ 470,400	$ 663,600	$ 697,200		$ 2,301,600
15	Miscellaneous expenses	30,000	43,200	57,960	75,600		206,760
16	Research and development	70,000	100,800	154,560	201,600		526,960
17	Rent	20,000	20,000	20,000	20,000		80,000
18	Depreciation	-	-	-	-		-
19	Total disbursements for operating expenses	$ 590,400	$ 634,400	$ 896,120	$ 994,400		$ 3,115,320
20							

FIGURE 4.17 Disbursements for Operating Expenses Budget

	A	B	C	D	
1				Period	
2		1Q X4	2Q X4	3Q X4	
3	OPERATING EXPENSES BUDGET				
4	Operating Expenses Budget				
5	Salaries	=SalExp1Q	=SalExp2Q	=SalExp3Q	=S
6	Miscellaneous expenses	=Sales1Q*MiscPct1Q	=Sales2Q*MiscPct2Q	=Sales3Q*MiscPct3Q	=S
7	Research and development	=Sales1Q*RDPct1Q	=Sales2Q*RDPct2Q	=Sales3Q*RDPct3Q	=S
8	Rent	=RentExp1Q	=RentExp2Q	=RentExp3Q	=R
9	Taxes				
10	Depreciation				
11	Total operating expenses	=SUM(B5:B10)	=SUM(C5:C10)	=SUM(D5:D10)	=S
12					
13	DISBURSEMENTS FOR OPERATING EXPENSES BUDGET				
14	Disbursements for Operating Expenses Budget				
15	Salaries	=B5	=C5	=D5	=E
16	Miscellaneous expenses	=B6	=C6	=D6	=E
17	Research and development	=B7	=C7	=D7	=E
18	Rent	=B8	=C8	=D8	=E
19	Taxes	=B9	=C9	=D9	=E
20	Depreciation	=B10	=C10	=D10	=E
21	Total disbursements for operating expenses	=SUM(B15:B20)	=SUM(C15:C20)	=SUM(D15:D20)	=S
22					

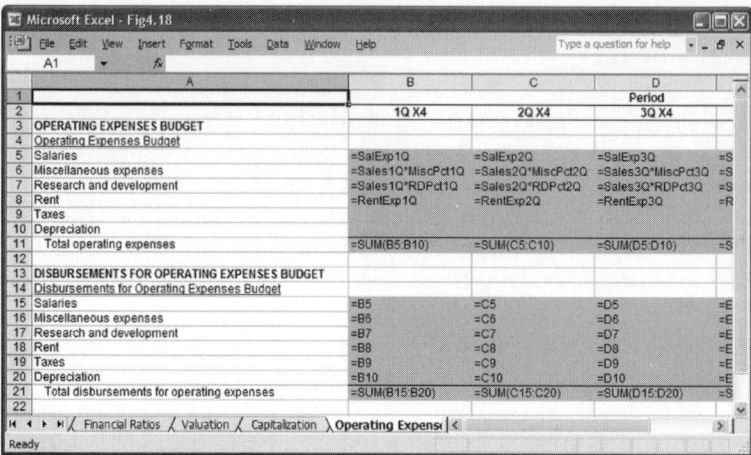

FIGURE 4.18 Alternative View of the Disbursements for Operating Expenses Budget

Operating Expenses Budget in which the formulas underlying the values are exposed. Figure 4.19 offers a view of the names of the input and output cells in the Disbursements for Operating Expenses Budget.

Steps 1 through 5C in the Master Budget building process, covered in Chapter 3 and this chapter, provide nearly all of the required information to build a budgeted Income Statement (from operations). I need to add another line item, interest expense, to complete this budgeted Income Statement, which I will cover in Chapter 6.

	A	B	C	D	E	F	G
1				Period			
2		1Q X4	2Q X4	3Q X4	4Q X4		X4
3	OPERATING EXPENSES BUDGET						
4	Operating Expenses Budget						
5	Salaries						
6	Miscellaneous expenses	MiscExp1Q	MiscExp2Q	MiscExp3Q	MiscExp4Q		MiscExpX4
7	Research and development	RDExp1Q	RDExp2Q	RDExp3Q	RDExp4Q		RDExpX4
8	Rent						RentExpX4
9	Depreciation						
10	Total operating expenses	OpExp1Q	OpExp2Q	OpExp3Q	OpExp4Q		OpExpX4
11							
12	DISBURSEMENTS FOR OPERATING EXPENSES BUDGET						
13	Disbursements for Operating Expenses Budget						
14	Salaries						
15	Miscellaneous expenses						
16	Research and development						
17	Rent						
18	Depreciation						
19	Total disbursements for operating expenses	DOE1Q	DOE2Q	DOE3Q	DOE4Q		DOEX4
20							

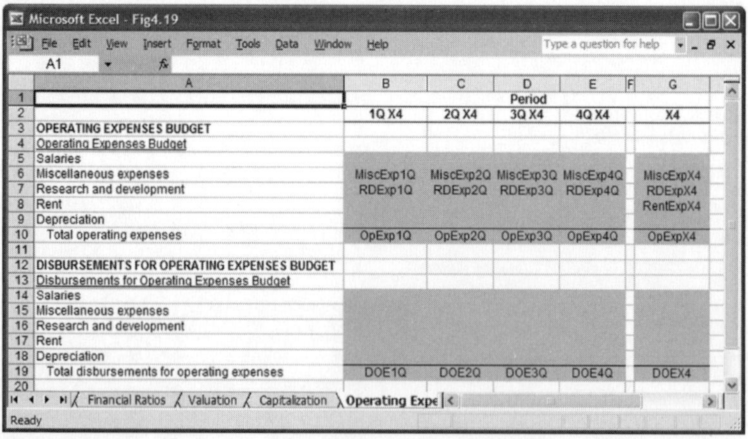

FIGURE 4.19 Names of the Input and Output Cells in the Disbursements for Operating Expenses Budget

QUESTIONS

Each of the questions for this chapter relates to a hypothetical company named Company DEF. Company DEF sells functional steering wheels to automobile manufacturers. As such, Company DEF is a product-oriented (as opposed to a service-oriented) business. Assume that company DEF disburses 100 percent of its operating expenses in the period in which such expenses are incurred. The questions for this chapter will address fiscal year X4 on a quarterly basis (four specific quarters, 1Q–4Q for year X4).

The following questions will test your knowledge of the material covered in this chapter in an applied manner—specifically, you will be asked to build the schedules discussed in this chapter for Company DEF.

To prepare you for this chapter's questions, several figures provide background information related to Company DEF's operations. Figure Q4.1 offers a view of a portion of Company DEF's Assumptions and Dash-

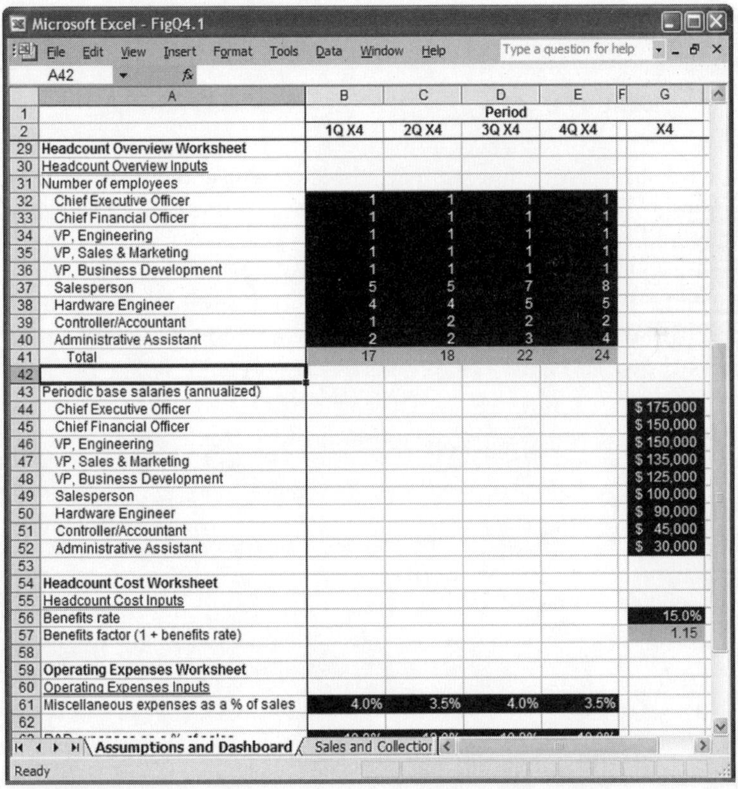

	A	B	C	D	E	F	G
1				Period			
2		1Q X4	2Q X4	3Q X4	4Q X4		X4
29	**Headcount Overview Worksheet**						
30	Headcount Overview Inputs						
31	Number of employees						
32	Chief Executive Officer	1	1	1	1		
33	Chief Financial Officer	1	1	1	1		
34	VP, Engineering	1	1	1	1		
35	VP, Sales & Marketing	1	1	1	1		
36	VP, Business Development	1	1	1	1		
37	Salesperson	5	5	7	8		
38	Hardware Engineer	4	4	5	5		
39	Controller/Accountant	1	2	2	2		
40	Administrative Assistant	2	2	3	4		
41	Total	17	18	22	24		
42							
43	Periodic base salaries (annualized)						
44	Chief Executive Officer						$ 175,000
45	Chief Financial Officer						$ 150,000
46	VP, Engineering						$ 150,000
47	VP, Sales & Marketing						$ 135,000
48	VP, Business Development						$ 125,000
49	Salesperson						$ 100,000
50	Hardware Engineer						$ 90,000
51	Controller/Accountant						$ 45,000
52	Administrative Assistant						$ 30,000
53							
54	**Headcount Cost Worksheet**						
55	Headcount Cost Inputs						
56	Benefits rate						15.0%
57	Benefits factor (1 + benefits rate)						1.15
58							
59	**Operating Expenses Worksheet**						
60	Operating Expenses Inputs						
61	Miscellaneous expenses as a % of sales	4.0%	3.5%	4.0%	3.5%		
62							

FIGURE Q4.1 Company DEF's Assumptions and Dashboard Worksheet

	A	B	C	D	E	F	G
1				Period			
2		1Q X4	2Q X4	3Q X4	4Q X4		X4
3	SALES BUDGET						
4	Unit Sales and Price Budget						
5	Unit sales	5,000	5,200	5,400	5,500		21,100
6	× Price per unit	$ 200	$ 200	$ 195	$ 190		N/A
7	= Total sales	$ 1,000,000	$ 1,040,000	$ 1,053,000	$ 1,045,000		$ 4,138,000
8							
9	Sales Composition Budget						
10	Cash sales	$ 500,000	$ 520,000	$ 526,500	$ 522,500		$ 2,069,000
11	+ Credit sales	500,000	520,000	526,500	522,500		2,069,000
12	= Total sales	$ 1,000,000	$ 1,040,000	$ 1,053,000	$ 1,045,000		$ 4,138,000
13							
14	COLLECTIONS BUDGET						
15	Cash Collections from Customers Budget						
16	Cash sales this period	$ 500,000	$ 520,000	$ 526,500	$ 522,500		$ 2,069,000
17	+ Credit sales collected	305,556	512,222	523,972	524,056		1,865,806
18	= Total collections	$ 805,556	$ 1,032,222	$ 1,050,472	$ 1,046,556		$ 3,934,806
19							
20	Accounts Receivable (A/R) Budget						
21	Beginning A/R balance	$ -	$ 194,444	$ 202,222	$ 204,750		$ -
22	+ Additions to A/R	194,444	202,222	204,750	203,194		804,611
23	- Subtractions from A/R	-	194,444	202,222	204,750		601,417
24	= Ending A/R balance	$ 194,444	$ 202,222	$ 204,750	$ 203,194		$ 203,194

FIGURE Q4.2 Company DEF's Unit Sales and Price Budget

board worksheet. Note that there are three cost-of-goods-sold components for Company DEF's steering wheels: (1) wheel frame, (2) air bag, and (3) assembly and labor.

Figure Q4.2 presents a view of Company DEF's Unit Sales and Price Budget, Sales Composition Budget, Cash Collections from Customers Budget, and Accounts Receivable Budget. Company DEF's Cost-of-Goods-Sold Budget is shown in Figure Q4.3. Figure Q4.4 presents a view of Company

	A	B	C	D	E	F	G
1				Period			
2		1Q X4	2Q X4	3Q X4	4Q X4		X4
3	COST-OF-GOODS SOLD BUDGET						
4	Cost-of-Goods Sold Budget						
5	Wheel frame	$ 275,000	$ 286,000	$ 286,200	$ 291,500		$ 1,138,700
6	Air bag	275,000	275,600	270,000	264,000		1,084,600
7	Assembly labor	200,000	202,800	189,000	181,500		773,300
8	Total cost-of-goods sold	$ 750,000	$ 764,400	$ 745,200	$ 737,000		$ 2,996,600

FIGURE Q4.3 Company DEF's Cost-of-Goods-Sold Budget

	Microsoft Excel - FigQ4.4							
	File Edit View Insert Format Tools Data Window Help				Type a question for help			
	A1 ▼ fx							
	A	B	C	D	E	F	G	
1				Period				
2		1Q X4	2Q X4	3Q X4	4Q X4		X4	
3	**INVENTORY BUDGET**							
4	Inventory Budget							
5	Desired ending inventory	$ 212,333	$ 207,000	$ 204,722	$ 204,722		$ 204,722	
6	+ Cost of goods sold	750,000	764,400	745,200	737,000		2,996,600	
7	= Total inventory needed	$ 962,333	$ 971,400	$ 949,922	$ 941,722		$3,201,322	
8								
9	**PURCHASES BUDGET**							
10	Purchases Budget							
11	Total inventory needed	$ 962,333	$ 971,400	$ 949,922	$ 941,722		N/A	
12	- Beginning inventory	-	212,333	207,000	204,722		-	
13	= Purchases	$ 962,333	$ 759,067	$ 742,922	$ 737,000		N/A	
14								
15	Disbursements for Purchases Budget							
16	Payments of payables	$ 641,556	$ 826,822	$ 748,304	$ 738,974		$2,955,656	
17	Total disbursements for purchases	$ 641,556	$ 826,822	$ 748,304	$ 738,974		$2,955,656	
18								
19	Accounts Payable (A/P) Budget							
20	Beginning A/P balance	$ -	$ 320,778	$ 253,022	$ 247,641		$ -	
21	+ Additions to A/P	320,778	253,022	247,641	245,667		1,067,107	
22	- Subtractions from A/P	-	320,778	253,022	247,641		821,441	
23	Ending A/P	$ 320,778	$ 253,022	$ 247,641	$ 245,667		$ 245,667	
24								

Sales and Collections / COGS \ **Inventory and Purc**

Ready

FIGURE Q4.4 Company DEF's Inventory Budget, Purchases Budget, Disbursements for Purchases Budget, and Accounts Payable Budget

DEF's Inventory Budget, Purchases Budget, Disbursements for Purchases Budget, and Accounts Payable Budget.

1. Given the information regarding Company DEF, build a Headcount Overview worksheet for Company DEF.
2. Based on the information presented and the headcount worksheet that you built in Question 1, build a Headcount Cost worksheet for Company DEF.
3. Build an Operating Expenses Budget for Company DEF based on the information presented and your work in Questions 1 and 2. Note that you will not be able to enter any values into the depreciation line item for the Operating Expenses Budget, as depreciation is based on the Capital Budget (which is not covered in this chapter or in the questions for this chapter).
4. Based on the information presented and your work in Questions 1–3, build a Disbursements for Operating Expenses Budget for Company DEF.

CHAPTER 5

Operating Budget—
Income Statement

This chapter covers the Budgeted Statement of Income, otherwise known as the Income Statement. The Income Statement (also called the "P&L" by financial professionals) is a central component of a financial model. The ultimate output of the Income Statement is known as "net income." Net income represents the difference between a business's revenues and a business's expenses. Figure 5.1 highlights the Budgeted Statement of Income and its relative position in the Master Budget hierarchy.

STEP 6: BUDGETED STATEMENT OF INCOME

The Budgeted Statement of Income combines elements from several different schedules on which I have worked thus far for Napavale. More specifically, the Income Statement draws from the Unit Sales Budget, Headcount Budget, and the Operating Expenses Budget.

Copying the sales and cost-of-goods-sold projections for Napavale into the Income Statement worksheet is the first step in building the Budgeted Statement of Income. Figure 5.2 shows the first section of the Income Statement, highlighting the sales and cost-of-goods-sold projections in addition to the resultant gross profit projections. Remember that gross profit is calculated as sales – cost of goods sold.

As I have indicated, the proper linking of information between worksheets is essential at all stages of building a financial model, and I am going to make frequent references to alternative views of worksheets in which the values and formulas contained within each cell are exposed for viewing and to views of the worksheets in which the names of the input and outputs cells are highlighted. In so doing, it should be easier to follow the extensive references and linkages between worksheets.

As I have discussed in previous chapters, I am naming all of the impor-

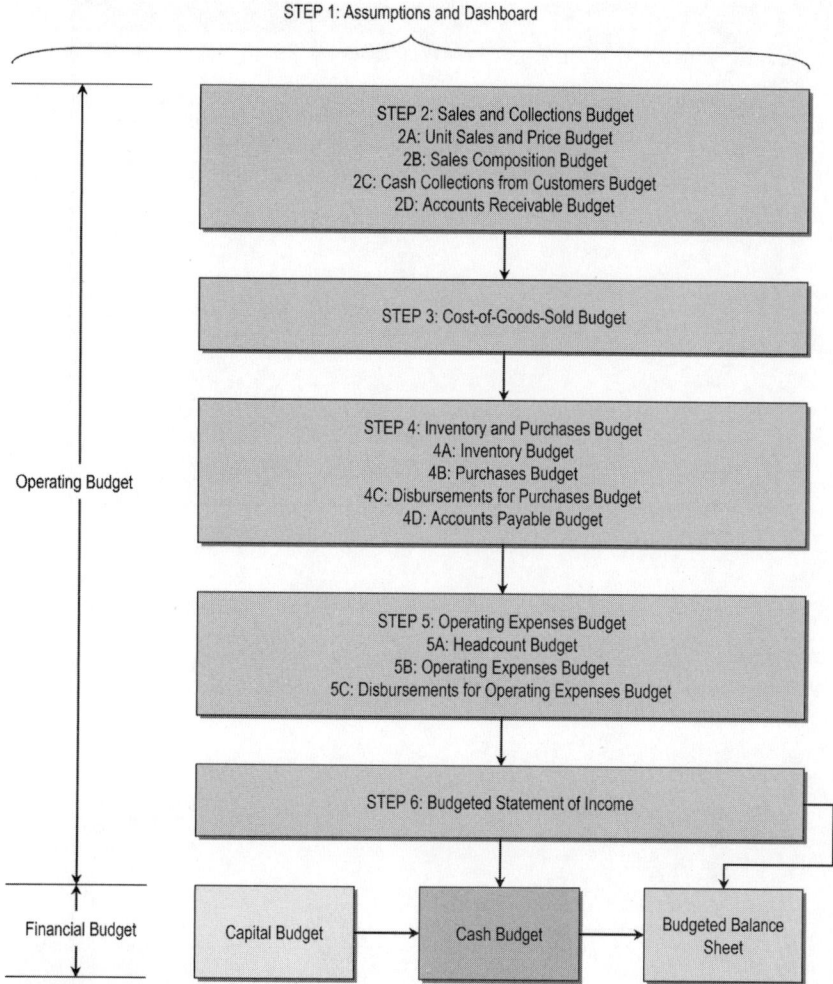

FIGURE 5.1 Budget Statement of Income and its Relative Position in the Master Budget Hierarchy

tant cells in Napavale's financial model. Each of these names is available across all worksheets—in other words, I am free to reference a cell named "Sales1Q" in any and all worksheets in my Napavale financial model workbook.

Figure 5.3 offers an alternative view of the first section of the Income Statement in which the values and formulas underlying the sales, cost-of-goods-sold, and gross margin projections are all exposed and visible. A view of the Income Statement in which the names of the input and output

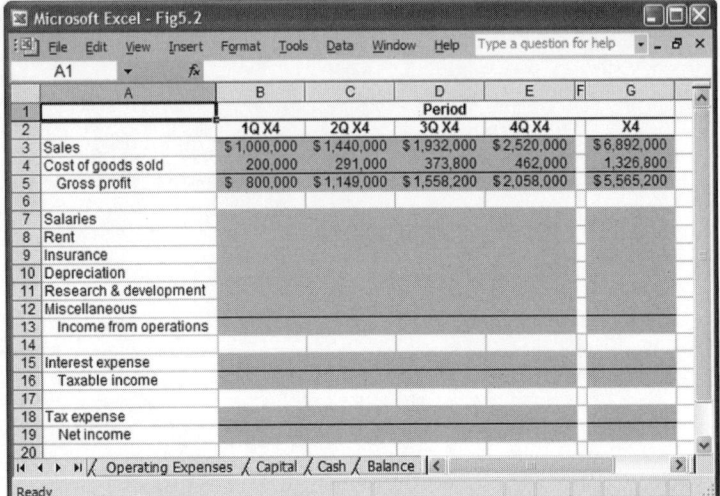

FIGURE 5.2   First Section of the Income Statement

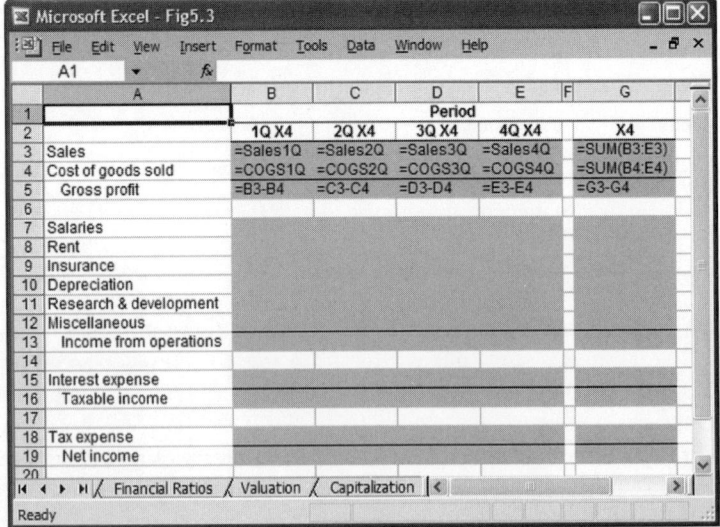

FIGURE 5.3   Alternative View of the First Section of the Income Statement

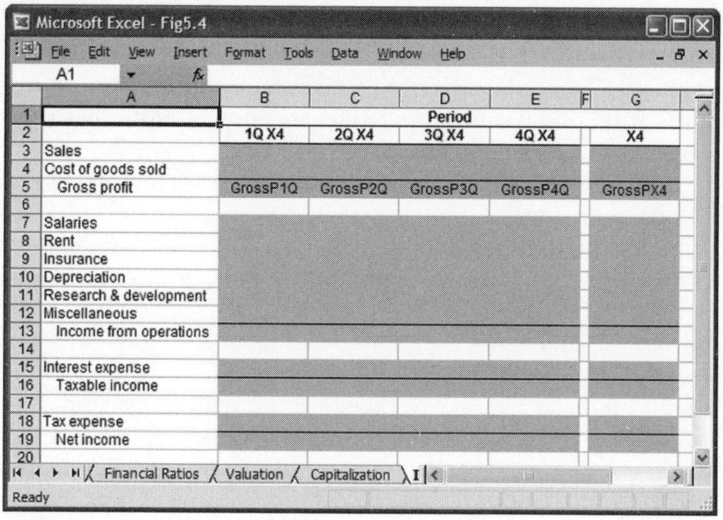

FIGURE 5.4 Names of the Input and Output Cells in the Income Statement

cells are shown is presented in Figure 5.4. "GrossP" is an abbreviation for "Gross Profit" in Figure 5.4.

Copying the salaries projections for Napavale into the Income State-ment worksheet is the next step in building the Budgeted Statement of In-come. The salaries projections flow out of the Headcount Cost worksheet that I built in Chapter 4. Figure 5.5 shows the inclusion of this line item in

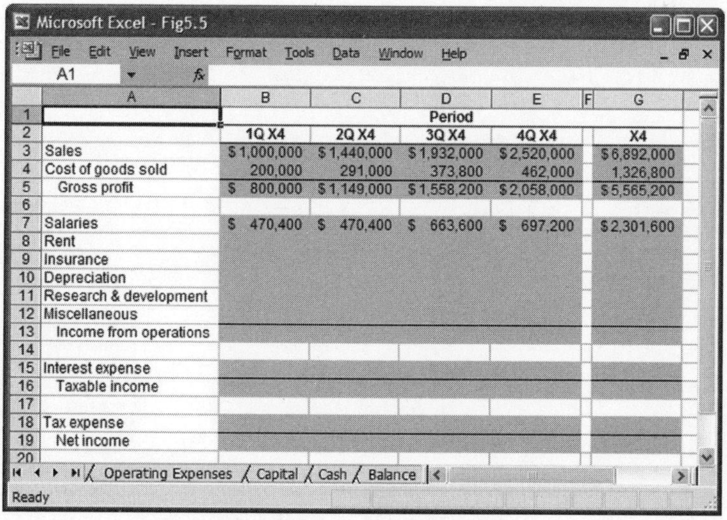

FIGURE 5.5 Income Statement

the Income Statement. An alternative view of the evolving Income Statement is presented in Figure 5.6. This view exposes the contents of the worksheet cells. Figure 5.7 offers a view of the Income Statement in which the names of the input and output cells are shown. Note that this is the same worksheet as presented in Figure 5.4.

The next step in building the Income Statement is to copy the remaining elements of the Operating Expenses Budget (other than (1) salaries, as I have just copied these values into the Income Statement as shown in Figures 5.5 through 5.7; (2) taxes, which I cover later in this chapter; and (3) depreciation, which I cover in Chapter 6) into the Income Statement worksheet. Figure 5.8 highlights the inclusion of these additional other operating expense items into the Income Statement.

As you can see in Figure 5.8, there is a line entitled "income from operations" in the Income Statement. Income from operations is calculated as gross profit – operating expenses. As discussed in Chapter 4, operating expenses represent the costs required to operate a business. Figure 5.9 offers an alternative view of the growing Income Statement worksheet in which the values and formulas underlying the worksheet cells are exposed and visible. Figure 5.10 shows the names of the input and output cells in the Income Statement worksheet.

	A	B	C	D	E	F	G
				Period			
		1Q X4	2Q X4	3Q X4	4Q X4		X4
3	Sales	=Sales1Q	=Sales2Q	=Sales3Q	=Sales4Q		=SUM(B3:E3)
4	Cost of goods sold	=COGS1Q	=COGS2Q	=COGS3Q	=COGS4Q		=SUM(B4:E4)
5	Gross profit	=B3-B4	=C3-C4	=D3-D4	=E3-E4		=G3-G4
6							
7	Salaries	=SalExp1Q	=SalExp2Q	=SalExp3Q	=SalExp4Q		=SUM(B7:E7)
8	Rent						
9	Insurance						
10	Depreciation						
11	Research & development						
12	Miscellaneous						
13	Income from operations						
14							
15	Interest expense						
16	Taxable income						
17							
18	Tax expense						
19	Net income						
20							

FIGURE 5.6   Alternative View of the Income Statement

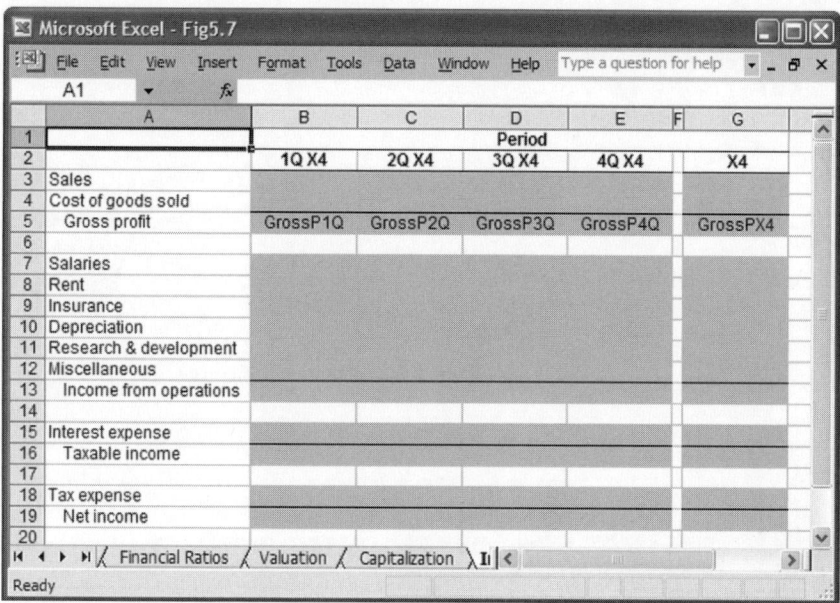

FIGURE 5.7 Names of the Input and Output Cells in the Income Statement

	A	B	C	D	E	F	G	
1				Period				
2		1Q X4	2Q X4	3Q X4	4Q X4		X4	
3	Sales	$1,000,000	$1,440,000	$1,932,000	$2,520,000		$6,892,000	
4	Cost of goods sold	200,000	291,000	373,800	462,000		1,326,800	
5	Gross profit	$ 800,000	$1,149,000	$1,558,200	$2,058,000		$5,565,200	
6								
7	Salaries	$ 470,400	$ 470,400	$ 663,600	$ 697,200		$2,301,600	
8	Miscellaneous expenses	30,000	43,200	57,960	75,600		206,760	
9	Research and development	70,000	100,800	154,560	201,600		526,960	
10	Rent	20,000	20,000	20,000	20,000		80,000	
11	Taxes							
12	Depreciation							
13	Income from operations	$ 209,600	$ 514,600	$ 662,080	$1,063,600		$2,449,880	
14								
15	Interest expense							
16	Taxable income							
17								
18	Tax expense							
19	Net income							
20								

FIGURE 5.8 Income Statement

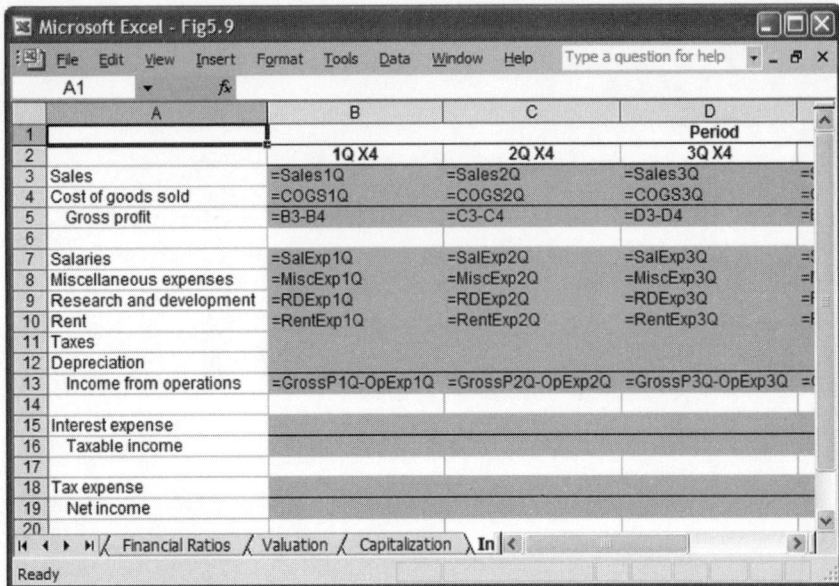

FIGURE 5.9   Alternative View of the Income Statement

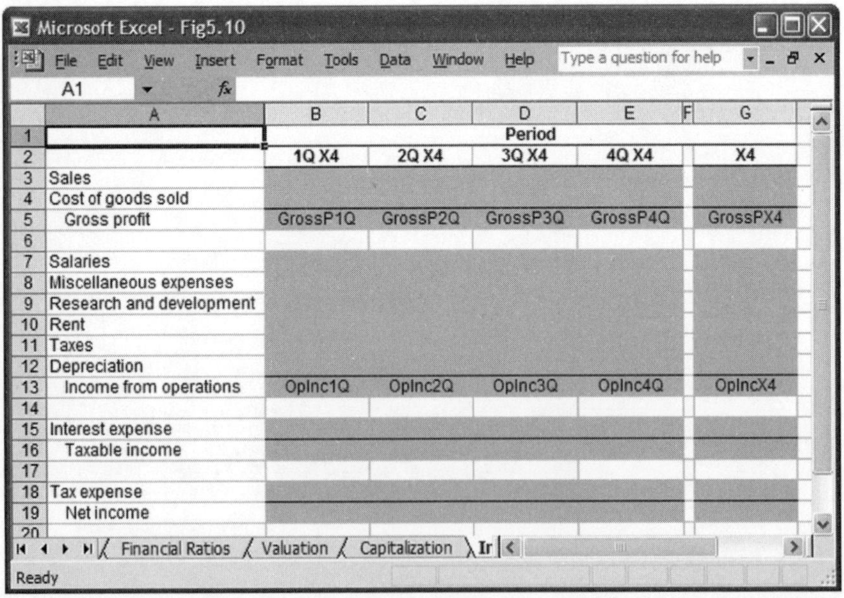

FIGURE 5.10   Name of the Input and Output Cells in the Income Statement

Please note that the depreciation line item does not contain any values yet. As discussed in Chapter 4, depreciation is an operating expense that is derived from the Capital Expenditures Budget, which is covered in Chapter 6. Financial models represent a set of highly integrated calculations—I am covering each of these calculations in as serial, or straightforward, a manner as possible. In this case, the vast majority of the elements of the Income Statement have been calculated. As I mentioned, I will cover the calculation of depreciation expense in Chapter 6. I will present a complete view of the Income Statement, including the depreciation figures, at the appropriate point in Chapter 6.

Interest expense, an item which I will also calculate in Chapter 6, represents expenses associated with borrowed funds. If a business borrows money, it is often required to pay periodic interest on these borrowed funds. Interest expense represents these expenses. I will cover interest expense in Chapter 6 as well.

Figure 5.11 shows the Income Statement with the addition of a calculation for an item entitled "taxable income." Taxable income is calculated as income from operations – interest expense. Figure 5.12 offers an alternative view of the Income Statement in which the values and underlying

	A	B	C	D	E	F	G
1				Period			
2		1Q X4	2Q X4	3Q X4	4Q X4		X4
3	Sales	$1,000,000	$1,440,000	$1,932,000	$2,520,000		$6,892,000
4	Cost of goods sold	200,000	291,000	373,800	462,000		1,326,800
5	Gross profit	$ 800,000	$1,149,000	$1,558,200	$2,058,000		$5,565,200
6							
7	Salaries	$ 470,400	$ 470,400	$ 663,600	$ 697,200		$2,301,600
8	Miscellaneous expenses	30,000	43,200	57,960	75,600		206,760
9	Research and development	70,000	100,800	154,560	201,600		526,960
10	Rent	20,000	20,000	20,000	20,000		80,000
11	Taxes						-
12	Depreciation						-
13	Income from operations	$ 209,600	$ 514,600	$ 662,080	$1,063,600		$2,449,880
14							
15	Interest expense						$ -
16	Taxable income	$ 209,600	$ 514,600	$ 662,080	$1,063,600		$2,449,880
17							
18	Tax expense						
19	Net income						
20							

FIGURE 5.11 Income Statement

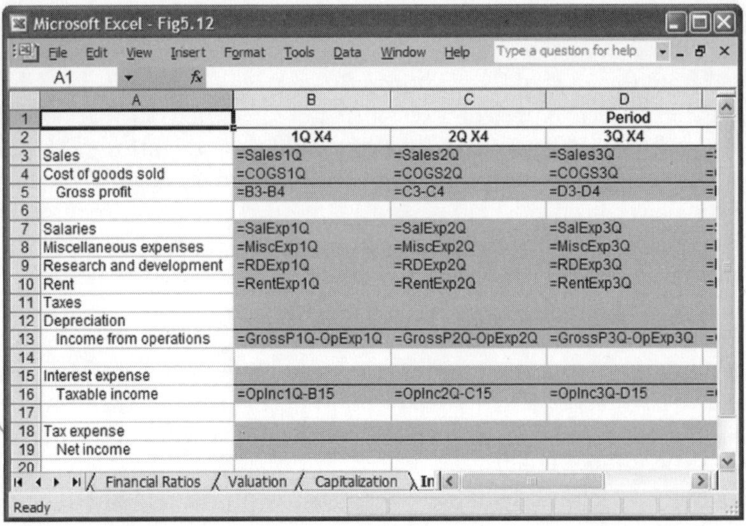

	A	B	C	D
1				Period
2		1Q X4	2Q X4	3Q X4
3	Sales	=Sales1Q	=Sales2Q	=Sales3Q
4	Cost of goods sold	=COGS1Q	=COGS2Q	=COGS3Q
5	Gross profit	=B3-B4	=C3-C4	=D3-D4
6				
7	Salaries	=SalExp1Q	=SalExp2Q	=SalExp3Q
8	Miscellaneous expenses	=MiscExp1Q	=MiscExp2Q	=MiscExp3Q
9	Research and development	=RDExp1Q	=RDExp2Q	=RDExp3Q
10	Rent	=RentExp1Q	=RentExp2Q	=RentExp3Q
11	Taxes			
12	Depreciation			
13	Income from operations	=GrossP1Q-OpExp1Q	=GrossP2Q-OpExp2Q	=GrossP3Q-OpExp3Q
14				
15	Interest expense			
16	Taxable income	=OpInc1Q-B15	=OpInc2Q-C15	=OpInc3Q-D15
17				
18	Tax expense			
19	Net income			

FIGURE 5.12 Alternative View of the Income Statement

formulas in the worksheet cells are exposed and visible. The names of the input and output cells in the Income Statement are shown in Figure 5.13.

Determining the periodic tax expense for Napavale represents the final calculation on the Income Statement. While calculating taxes may appear to be a simple exercise—multiply the taxable income by a tax rate—accounting for taxes is actually a complex exercise. Given the scope of this book, I am going to address the issue of taxes in a very simple and straightforward manner. Entire books have been written that address the issue of income taxes; this book is not meant to cover income taxes in any detail.

I am modeling Napavale's income taxes using the following formula: tax expense = taxable income * tax rate. Please note that this is a very simplistic approach to income taxes that does not address the reality facing corporations today. If, for instance, you project negative taxable income for a specific period in your own financial model, you should modify this calculation to indicate a tax expense of zero as opposed to a negative tax expense. As Napavale's taxable income is positive across all periods presented in the financial model presented in this book, negative taxable income is not an issue in this case.

Figure 5.14 shows the income tax rate assumption from the Assumptions and Dashboard worksheet. A view of the Income Statement, including the calculation of tax expense, is presented in Figure 5.15. Figure 5.16 presents an alternative view of the Income Statement in which the values and formulas underlying the worksheet cells are exposed and visible.

Microsoft Excel - Fig5.13

	A	B	C	D	E	F	G
1				Period			
2		1Q X4	2Q X4	3Q X4	4Q X4		X4
3	Sales						
4	Cost of goods sold						
5	Gross profit	GrossP1Q	GrossP2Q	GrossP3Q	GrossP4Q		GrossPX4
6							
7	Salaries						
8	Miscellaneous expenses						
9	Research and development						
10	Rent						
11	Taxes						
12	Depreciation						
13	Income from operations	OpInc1Q	OpInc2Q	OpInc3Q	OpInc4Q		OpIncX4
14							
15	Interest expense						
16	Taxable income	TaxInc1Q	TaxInc2Q	TaxInc3Q	TaxInc4Q		TaxIncX4
17							
18	Tax expense						
19	Net income						
20							

Financial Ratios / Valuation / Capitalization \ In

FIGURE 5.13   Names of the Input and Output Cells in the Income Statement

Microsoft Excel - Fig5.14

	A	B	C	D	E	F	G
1				Period			
2		1Q X4	2Q X4	3Q X4	4Q X4		X4
43	Periodic base salaries (annualized)						
44	Chief Executive Officer						$ 200,000
45	Chief Financial Officer						$ 175,000
46	VP, Engineering						$ 175,000
47	VP, Sales & Marketing						$ 150,000
48	VP, Business Development						$ 140,000
49	Salesperson						$ 120,000
50	Hardware Engineer						$ 110,000
51	Controller/Accountant						$ 55,000
52	Administrative Assistant						$ 35,000
53							
54	**Headcount Cost Worksheet**						
55	Headcount Cost Inputs						
56	Benefits rate						12.0%
57	Benefits factor (1 + benefits rate)						1.12
58							
59	**Operating Expenses Worksheet**						
60	Operating Expenses Inputs						
61	Miscellaneous expenses as a % of sales	3.0%	3.0%	3.0%	3.0%		
62							
63	R&D expenses as a % of sales	7.0%	7.0%	8.0%	8.0%		
64							
65	Rent expense per square foot per quarter	$ 5.00	$ 5.00	$ 5.00	$ 5.00		
66	Square feet of space rented	4,000	4,000	4,000	4,000		
67	Total rent expense	$ 20,000	$ 20,000	$ 20,000	$ 20,000		
68							
69	Tax rate	35.0%	35.0%	35.0%	35.0%		
70							

Assumptions and Dashboard / Sales and Collection

FIGURE 5.14   Income Tax Rate Assumptions from the Assumptions and Dashboard Worksheet

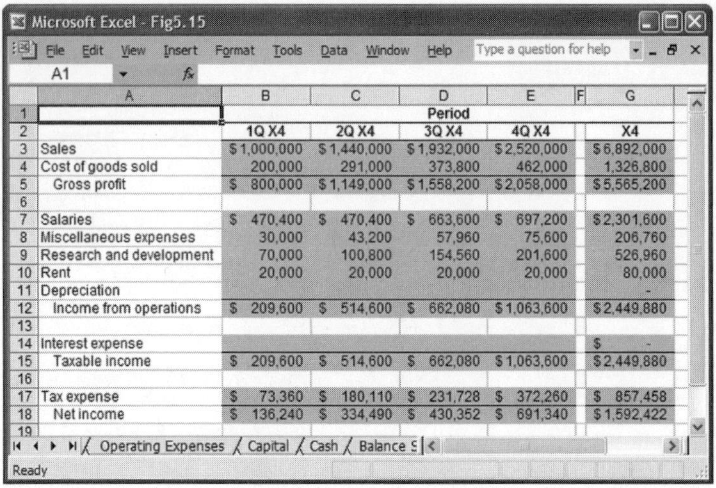

	1Q X4	2Q X4	3Q X4	4Q X4	X4
			Period		
Sales	$1,000,000	$1,440,000	$1,932,000	$2,520,000	$6,892,000
Cost of goods sold	200,000	291,000	373,800	462,000	1,326,800
Gross profit	$ 800,000	$1,149,000	$1,558,200	$2,058,000	$5,565,200
Salaries	$ 470,400	$ 470,400	$ 663,600	$ 697,200	$2,301,600
Miscellaneous expenses	30,000	43,200	57,960	75,600	206,760
Research and development	70,000	100,800	154,560	201,600	526,960
Rent	20,000	20,000	20,000	20,000	80,000
Depreciation					-
Income from operations	$ 209,600	$ 514,600	$ 662,080	$1,063,600	$2,449,880
Interest expense					$ -
Taxable income	$ 209,600	$ 514,600	$ 662,080	$1,063,600	$2,449,880
Tax expense	$ 73,360	$ 180,110	$ 231,728	$ 372,260	$ 857,458
Net income	$ 136,240	$ 334,490	$ 430,352	$ 691,340	$1,592,422

FIGURE 5.15 Income Statement

The names of the input and output cells from the Assumptions and Dashboard worksheet are shown in Figure 5.17. Figure 5.18 offers a view of the names of the input and output cells in the Income Statement.

The next step in building Napavale's financial model is to calculate the company's net income. Net income is defined as taxable income–tax expense. Figure 5.19 offers a view of the Income Statement, which is now

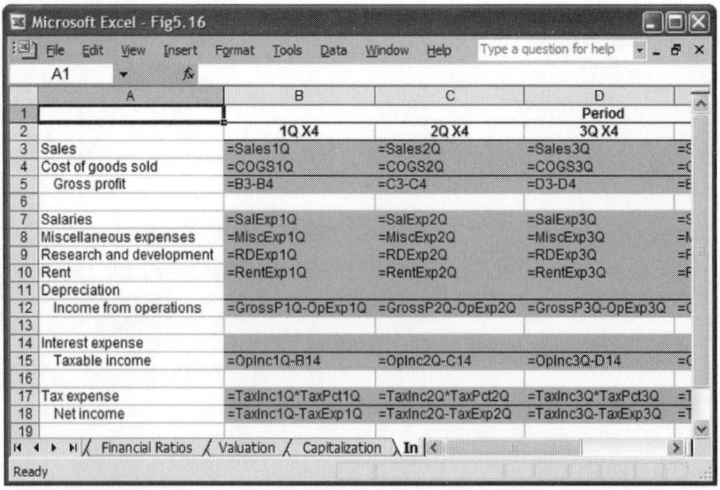

	1Q X4	2Q X4	3Q X4
			Period
Sales	=Sales1Q	=Sales2Q	=Sales3Q
Cost of goods sold	=COGS1Q	=COGS2Q	=COGS3Q
Gross profit	=B3-B4	=C3-C4	=D3-D4
Salaries	=SalExp1Q	=SalExp2Q	=SalExp3Q
Miscellaneous expenses	=MiscExp1Q	=MiscExp2Q	=MiscExp3Q
Research and development	=RDExp1Q	=RDExp2Q	=RDExp3Q
Rent	=RentExp1Q	=RentExp2Q	=RentExp3Q
Depreciation			
Income from operations	=GrossP1Q-OpExp1Q	=GrossP2Q-OpExp2Q	=GrossP3Q-OpExp3Q
Interest expense			
Taxable income	=OpInc1Q-B14	=OpInc2Q-C14	=OpInc3Q-D14
Tax expense	=TaxInc1Q*TaxPct1Q	=TaxInc2Q*TaxPct2Q	=TaxInc3Q*TaxPct3Q
Net income	=TaxInc1Q-TaxExp1Q	=TaxInc2Q-TaxExp2Q	=TaxInc3Q-TaxExp3Q

FIGURE 5.16 Alternative View of the Income Statement

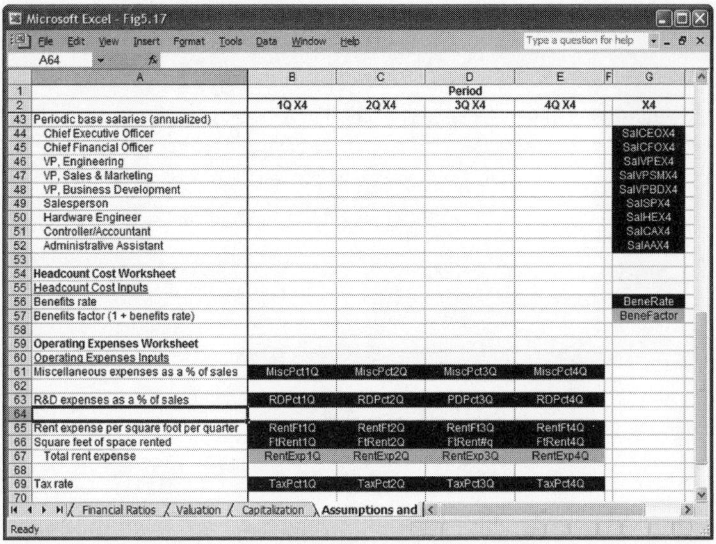

FIGURE 5.17 Names of the Input and Output Cells in the Assumptions and Dashboard Worksheet

complete except for the calculation of depreciation expense and interest expense, both of which are covered in Chapter 6.

Figure 5.20 offers an alternative view of the completed Income Statement in which the values and formulas in each cell are exposed and visible. The names associated with the input and outputs cells for the Assumptions and Dashboard worksheet are shown in Figure 5.21.

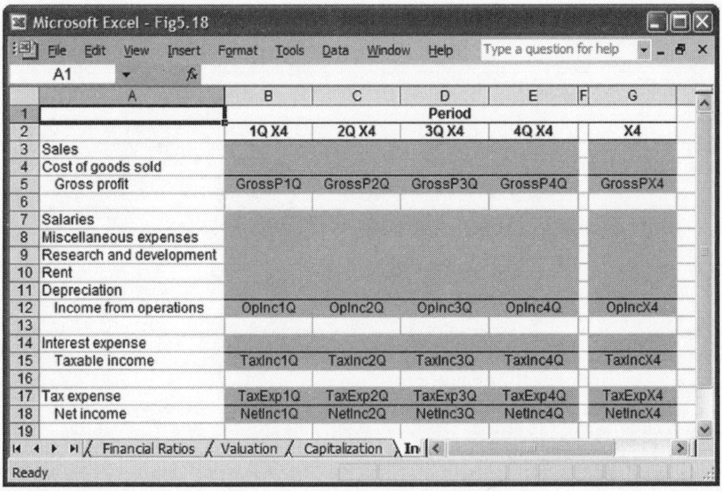

FIGURE 5.18 Names of the Input and Output Cells in the Income Statement

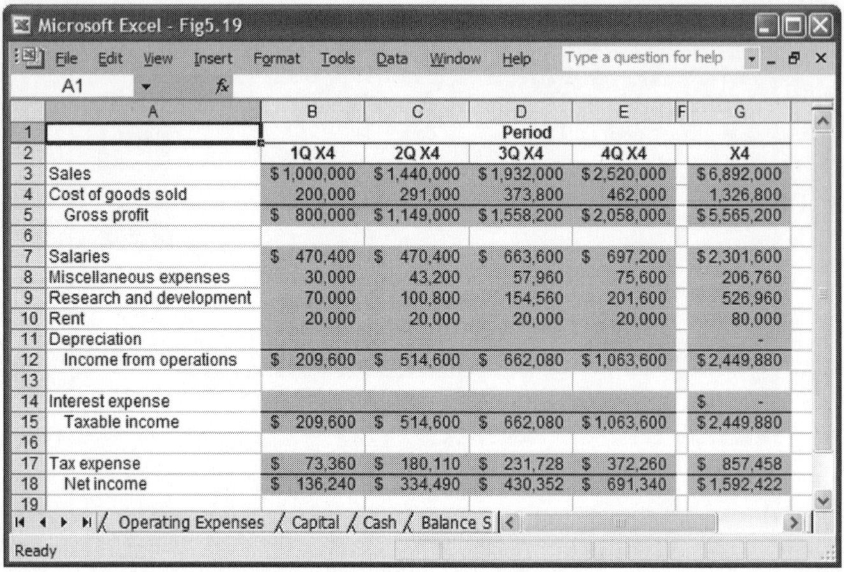

FIGURE 5.19   Income Statement

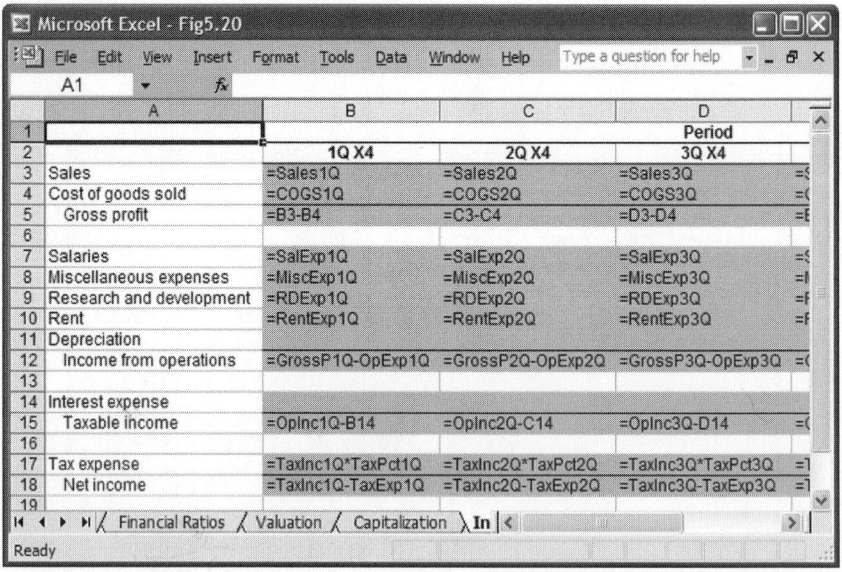

FIGURE 5.20   Alternative View of the Income Statement

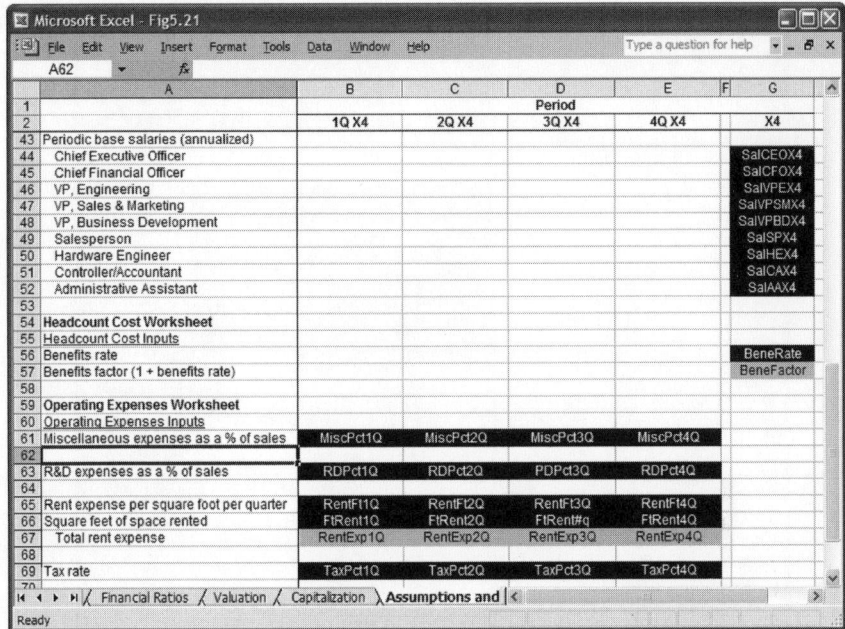

FIGURE 5.21   Names of the Input and Output Cells in the Assumptions and Dashboard Worksheet

QUESTIONS

Each of the questions for this chapter relates to a hypothetical company named Company GHI. Company GHI sells stethoscopes to physicians. As such, Company GHI is a product-oriented (as opposed to a service-oriented) business. The questions for this chapter will address fiscal year X4 on a quarterly basis (four specific quarters, 1Q–4Q for year X4).

The following questions will test your knowledge of the material covered in this chapter in an applied manner—specifically, you will be asked to build the schedules discussed in this chapter for Company GHI.

To prepare you for this chapter's questions, several figures provide background information related to Company GHI's operations. Figure Q5.1 offers a view of a portion of Company GHI's Assumptions and Dashboard worksheet. Note that there are three cost-of-goods-sold components for Company GHI's stethoscopes: (1) casing, (2) sensing element, and (3) assembly and labor.

Figure Q5.2 presents a view of Company GHI's Unit Sales and Price

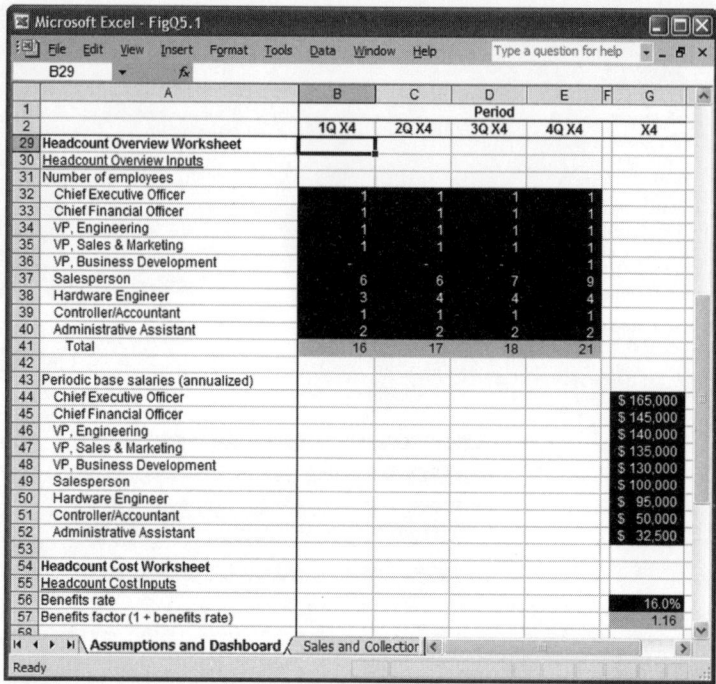

FIGURE Q5.1   Company GHI's Assumptions and Dashboard Worksheet

	A	B	C	D	E	F	G
1				Period			
2		1Q X4	2Q X4	3Q X4	4Q X4		X4
3	**SALES BUDGET**						
4	Unit Sales and Price Budget						
5	Unit sales	5,500	5,400	5,400	5,300		21,600
6	× Price per unit	$ 400	$ 400	$ 395	$ 395		N/A
7	= Total sales	$2,200,000	$2,160,000	$2,133,000	$2,093,500		$8,586,500
8							
9	Sales Composition Budget						
10	Cash sales	$1,760,000	$1,728,000	$1,706,400	$1,674,800		$6,869,200
11	+ Credit sales	440,000	432,000	426,600	418,700		1,717,300
12	= Total sales	$2,200,000	$2,160,000	$2,133,000	$2,093,500		$8,586,500
13							
14	**COLLECTIONS BUDGET**						
15	Cash Collections from Customers Budget						
16	Cash sales this period	$1,760,000	$1,728,000	$1,706,400	$1,674,800		$6,869,200
17	+ Credit sales collected	342,222	433,778	427,800	406,499		1,610,299
18	= Total collections	$2,102,222	$2,161,778	$2,134,200	$2,081,299		$8,479,499
19							
20	Accounts Receivable (A/R) Budget						
21	Beginning A/R balance	$ -	$ 97,778	$ 96,000	$ 94,800		$ -
22	+ Additions to A/R	97,778	96,000	94,800	107,001		395,579
23	- Subtractions from A/R	-	97,778	96,000	94,800		288,578
24	= Ending A/R balance	$ 97,778	$ 96,000	$ 94,800	$ 107,001		$ 107,001

FIGURE Q5.2   Company GHI's Unit Sales and Price Budget

	1Q X4	2Q X4	3Q X4	4Q X4	X4
COST-OF-GOODS SOLD BUDGET					
Cost-of-Goods Sold Budget					
Casing	$ 495,000	$ 475,200	$ 459,000	$ 450,500	$ 1,879,700
Sensing element	412,500	388,800	351,000	344,500	1,496,800
Assembly labor	165,000	162,000	140,400	132,500	599,900
Total cost-of-goods sold	$ 1,072,500	$ 1,026,000	$ 950,400	$ 927,500	$ 3,976,400

FIGURE Q5.3 Company GHI's Cost-of-Goods-Sold Budget

Budget, Sales Composition Budget, Cash Collections from Customers Budget, and Accounts Receivable Budget. Company GHI's Cost-of-Goods-Sold Budget is shown in Figure Q5.3. Figure Q5.4 presents a view of Company GHI's Inventory Budget, Purchases Budget, Disbursements for Purchases Budget, and Accounts Payable Budget. Company GHI's Headcount Overview worksheet is shown in Figure Q5.5. Company GHI's Headcount Cost worksheet is shown in Figure Q5.6. Figure Q5.7 offers a view of

	1Q X4	2Q X4	3Q X4	4Q X4	X4
INVENTORY BUDGET					
Inventory Budget					
Desired ending inventory	$ 228,000	$ 232,320	$ 226,722	$ 226,722	$ 226,722
+ Cost of goods sold	1,072,500	1,026,000	950,400	927,500	3,976,400
= Total inventory needed	$ 1,300,500	$ 1,258,320	$ 1,177,122	$ 1,154,222	$ 4,203,122
PURCHASES BUDGET					
Purchases Budget					
Total inventory needed	$ 1,300,500	$ 1,258,320	$ 1,177,122	$ 1,154,222	N/A
- Beginning inventory	-	228,000	232,320	226,722	-
= Purchases	$ 1,300,500	$ 1,030,320	$ 944,802	$ 927,500	N/A
Disbursements for Purchases Budget					
Payments of payables	$ 722,500	$ 1,150,400	$ 982,810	$ 935,190	$ 3,790,900
Total disbursements for purchases	$ 722,500	$ 1,150,400	$ 982,810	$ 935,190	$ 3,790,900
Accounts Payable (A/P) Budget					
Beginning A/P balance	$ -	$ 578,000	$ 457,920	$ 419,912	$ -
+ Additions to A/P	578,000	457,920	419,912	412,222	1,868,054
- Subtractions from A/P	-	578,000	457,920	419,912	1,455,832
Ending A/P	$ 578,000	$ 457,920	$ 419,912	$ 412,222	$ 412,222

FIGURE Q5.4 Company GHI's Inventory Budget, Purchases Budget, Disbursements for Purchases Budget, and Accounts Payable Budget

Microsoft Excel - FigQ5.5

File   Edit   View   Insert   Format   Tools   Data   Window   Help

A1

	A	B	C	D	E	F	G
1				Period			
2		1Q X4	2Q X4	3Q X4	4Q X4		X4
3	**HEADCOUNT BUDGET**						
4	Headcount Budget						
5	Number of employees						
6	Chief Executive Officer	1	1	1	1		
7	Chief Financial Officer	1	1	1	1		
8	VP, Engineering	1	1	1	1		
9	VP, Sales & Marketing	1	1	1	1		
10	VP, Business Development	-	-	-	1		
11	Salesperson	6	6	7	9		
12	Hardware Engineer	3	4	4	4		
13	Controller/Accountant	1	1	1	1		
14	Administrative Assistant	2	2	2	2		
15	Total	16	17	18	21		
16							
17	Periodic base salaries						
18	Chief Executive Officer	$ 41,250	$ 41,250	$ 41,250	$ 41,250		$ 165,000
19	Chief Financial Officer	36,250	36,250	36,250	36,250		145,000
20	VP, Engineering	35,000	35,000	35,000	35,000		140,000
21	VP, Sales & Marketing	33,750	33,750	33,750	33,750		135,000
22	VP, Business Development	32,500	32,500	32,500	32,500		130,000
23	Salesperson	25,000	25,000	25,000	25,000		100,000
24	Hardware Engineer	23,750	23,750	23,750	23,750		95,000
25	Controller/Accountant	12,500	12,500	12,500	12,500		50,000
26	Administrative Assistant	8,125	8,125	8,125	8,125		32,500
27	Total	$ 248,125	$ 248,125	$ 248,125	$ 248,125		$ 992,500

Headcount Overview / Headcount Cost / C

Ready

FIGURE Q5.5   Company GHI's Headcount Overview Worksheet

Microsoft Excel - FigQ5.6

File   Edit   View   Insert   Format   Tools   Data   Window   Help

A1

	A	B	C	D	E	F	G
1				Period			
2		1Q X4	2Q X4	3Q X4	4Q X4		X4
3	**HEADCOUNT BUDGET**						
4	Headcount Budget						
5	Periodic salary expense (base)						
6	Chief Executive Officer	$ 41,250	$ 41,250	$ 41,250	$ 41,250		$ 165,000
7	Chief Financial Officer	36,250	36,250	36,250	36,250		145,000
8	VP, Engineering	35,000	35,000	35,000	35,000		140,000
9	VP, Sales & Marketing	33,750	33,750	33,750	33,750		135,000
10	VP, Business Development	-	-	-	32,500		32,500
11	Salesperson	150,000	150,000	175,000	225,000		700,000
12	Hardware Engineer	71,250	95,000	95,000	95,000		356,250
13	Controller/Accountant	12,500	12,500	12,500	12,500		50,000
14	Administrative Assistant	16,250	16,250	16,250	16,250		65,000
15	Total	$ 396,250	$ 420,000	$ 445,000	$ 527,500		$ 1,788,750
16							
17	Total (with benefits)	$ 459,650	$ 487,200	$ 516,200	$ 611,900		$ 2,074,950

Headcount Overview / Headcount Cost / Or

Ready

FIGURE Q5.6   Company GHI's Headcount Cost Worksheet

		Period				
	1Q X4	2Q X4	3Q X4	4Q X4		X4
OPERATING EXPENSES BUDGET						
Operating Expenses Budget						
Salaries	$ 459,650	$487,200	$516,200	$611,900		$2,074,950
Miscellaneous expenses	88,000	97,200	106,650	94,208		386,058
Research and development	132,000	140,400	149,310	157,013		578,723
Rent	15,750	15,750	15,750	15,750		63,000
Depreciation						-
Total operating expenses	$ 695,400	$740,550	$787,910	$878,870		$3,102,730
DISBURSEMENTS FOR OPERATING EXPENSES BUDGET						
Disbursements for Operating Expenses Budget						
Salaries	$ 459,650	$487,200	$516,200	$611,900		$2,074,950
Miscellaneous expenses	88,000	97,200	106,650	94,208		386,058
Research and development	132,000	140,400	149,310	157,013		578,723
Rent	15,750	15,750	15,750	15,750		63,000
Depreciation	-	-	-	-		-
Total disbursements for operating expenses	$ 695,400	$740,550	$787,910	$878,870		$3,102,730

FIGURE Q5.7 Company GHI's Operating Expenses Budget and Disbursements for Operating Expenses Budget

Company GHI's Operating Expenses Budget and Disbursements for Operating Expenses Budget.

1. Given the information regarding Company GHI, build the first section of an Income Statement for Company GHI. This section should include sales, cost-of-goods-sold, and gross profit projections for Company GHI.
2. Given your work from Question 1 and the information presented, build an updated version of Company GHI's Income Statement by inserting the salaries projections for Company GHI into the Income Statement.
3. Build an updated version of Company GHI's Income Statement by adding in the projections for (i) miscellaneous expenses, (ii) research and development, and (iii) rent. Remember that the depreciation projections will not be added to the Income Statement until a Capital Budget is completed (which is not covered in the chapter or in the questions for this chapter). Be sure to calculate Company GHI's projected income from operations in the updated version of Company GHI's Income Statement.
4. Build another updated version of Company GHI's Income Statement by calculating the projected tax expenses for Company GHI. Assume

that Company GHI will pay taxes if it generates positive taxable income and will not pay taxes if it does not generate positive taxable income. Be sure to include line items for taxable income and for net income in your updated Income Statement. Remember that the interest expense projection will not be added to the Income Statement until Chapter 6.

CHAPTER 6

Financial Budget—
Capital Budget and Cash Budget

The Financial Budget represents the second of the two components of the Master Budget (the Operating Budget represents the first component) and includes the following components: the Capital Budget, the Cash Budget, and the budgeted Balance Sheet. In conjunction with the steps outlined in Chapters 2 through 5, this chapter represents the final step in building the Master Budget. Subsequent chapters in this book will cover topics such as the consolidated financial statements, free cash flows, and a variety of financial modeling tools and techniques. Figure 6.1 highlights the components of the Financial Budget and their relative position in the Master Budget hierarchy.

STEP 7A: CAPITAL EXPENDITURES BUDGET

The Capital Expenditures Budget (also know as the "CAPEX" budget) covers Napavale's projected purchases of large items such as equipment and furniture. When a business purchases something such as a computer or a desk for its own use, it must decide if it will expense or capitalize such an item. While many accounting regulations and pronouncements surround this issue of expensing versus capitalizing purchased goods, I will cover this topic in a very general fashion. In basic terms, Napavale's financial model assumes that large-value purchases, such as for furniture, are capitalized. When and if you build your own financial model, the issue of capitalization versus expensing is something you must address in a manner consistent with the business for which you are building a financial model. Figure 6.2 presents a view of the Assumptions and Dashboard worksheet in which my assumptions underlying Napavale's projected capital expenditures are shown.

Note that I am including three line items for Napavale's Capital Expen-

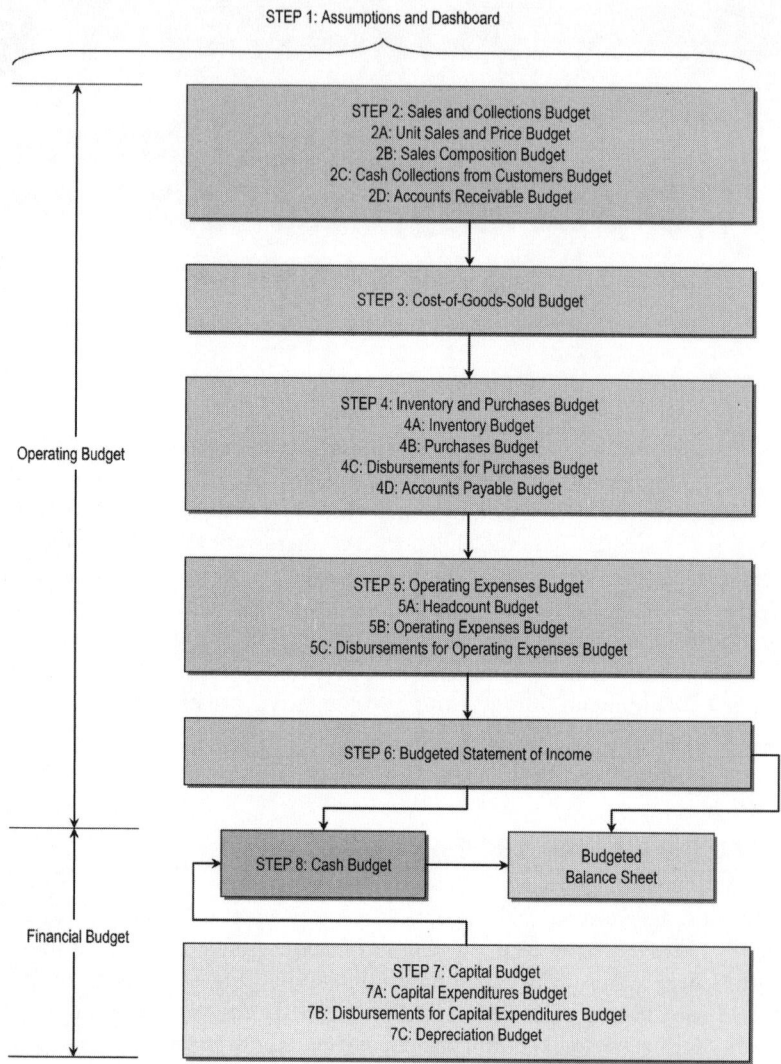

FIGURE 6.1 Components of the Financial Budget and Their Relative Position in the Master Budget

ditures Budget: equipment (used for manufacturing and assembling Napavale's products), furniture, and fixtures. These are broad categories for capital expenditures and you may choose to use different line items if and when you build your own financial model. Figure 6.3 presents a view of the Capital Expenditures Budget worksheet.

Figure 6.4 offers an alternative view of the Capital Expenditures Bud-

	A	B	C	D	E	F	G
				Period			
		1Q X4	2Q X4	3Q X4	4Q X4		X4
60	Operating Expenses Inputs						
61	Miscellaneous expenses as a % of sales	3.0%	3.0%	3.0%	3.0%		
62							
63	R&D expenses as a % of sales	7.0%	7.0%	8.0%	8.0%		
64							
65	Rent expense per square foot per quarter	$ 5.00	$ 5.00	$ 5.00	$ 5.00		
66	Square feet of space rented	4,000	4,000	4,000	4,000		
67	Total rent expense	$ 20,000	$ 20,000	$ 20,000	$ 20,000		
68							
69	Tax rate	35.0%	35.0%	35.0%	35.0%		
70							
71	**Capital Worksheet**						
72	Capital Expenditures (CAPEX) Inputs						
73	Equipment purchases	$ 30,000	$ 30,000	$ 30,000	$ 30,000		
74	Furniture purchases	$ 10,000	$ 10,000	$ 10,000	$ 10,000		
75	Fixtures purchases	$ 5,000	$ 5,000	$ 5,000	$ 5,000		
76	Total CAPEX purchases	$ 45,000	$ 45,000	$ 45,000	$ 45,000		
77							

FIGURE 6.2   Assumptions and Dashboard Worksheet

	A	B	C	D	E	F	G
				Period			
		1Q X4	2Q X4	3Q X4	4Q X4		X4
3	**CAPITAL BUDGET**						
4	Capital Expenditures Budget						
5	Equipment	$ 30,000	$ 30,000	$ 30,000	$ 30,000		$ 120,000
6	Furniture	10,000	10,000	10,000	10,000		40,000
7	Fixtures	5,000	5,000	5,000	5,000		20,000
8	Total capital expenditures	$ 45,000	$ 45,000	$ 45,000	$ 45,000		$ 180,000
9							
10	Disbursements for Capital Expenditures Budget						
11	Equipment						$ -
12	Furniture						-
13	Fixtures						-
14	Total disbursements for capital expenditures	$ -	$ -	$ -	$ -		$ -
15							
16	Depreciation Budget						
17	Equipment						$ -
18	Furniture						-
19	Fixtures						-
20	Total depreciation	$ -	$ -	$ -	$ -		$ -
21							

FIGURE 6.3   Capital Expenditures Budget

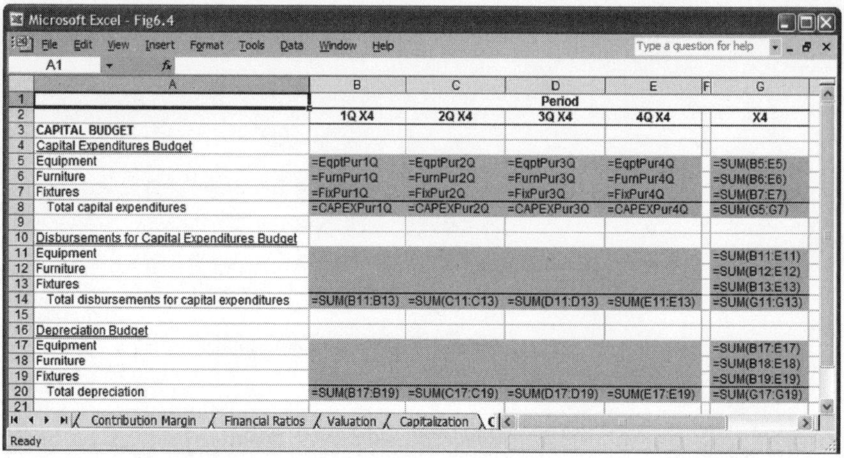

FIGURE 6.4   Alternative View of the Capital Expenditures Budget

get worksheet in which the values and formulas underlying the cells in the worksheet are exposed and visible. Note that I continue to name each cell that contains an important value for ease of reference.

The names of the input and output cells in the Assumptions and Dashboard worksheet are shown in Figure 6.5. Figure 6.6 offers a view of the names of the input and output cells in the Capital Expenditures Budget worksheet.

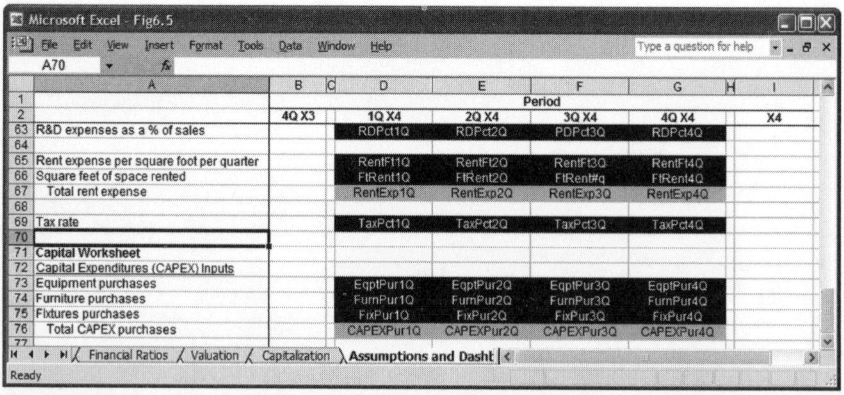

FIGURE 6.5   Names of the Input and Output Cells in the Assumptions and Dashboard Worksheet

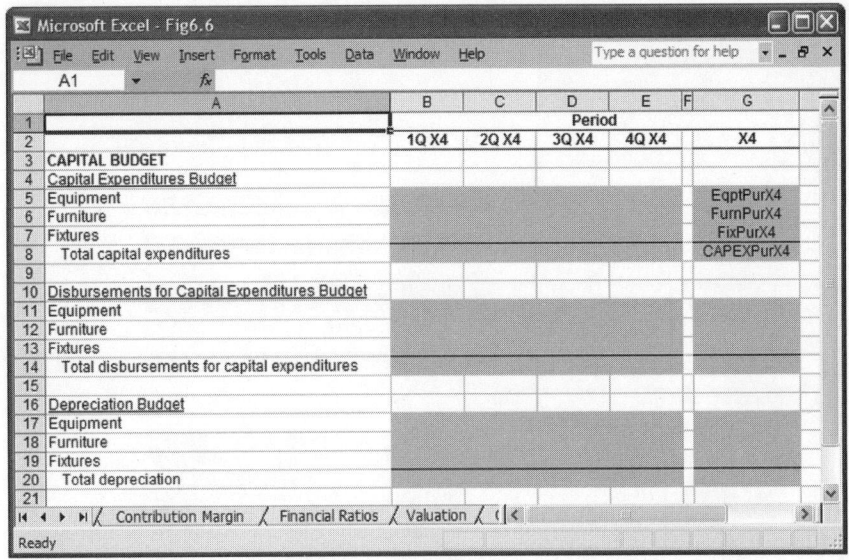

FIGURE 6.6 Names of the Input and Output Cells in the Capital Expenditures Budget

STEP 7B: DISBURSEMENTS FOR CAPITAL EXPENDITURES BUDGET

The Disbursements for Capital Expenditures Budget reconciles the accrual values from Step 7A to cash figures. This schedule ties into the creation of the Cash Budget, which is covered later in this chapter. My financial model makes the assumption that Napavale disburses, or pays for, 100 percent of the current period's capital expenditures purchases. This assumption is highlighted in the Assumptions and Dashboard worksheet in Figure 6.7. Note that I am treating the disbursements for capital expenditures in a fundamentally different way than I treated the disbursements for operating expenses in Chapter 4.

While I utilized the concept of "days payable" in Chapter 4 for the Disbursements for Operating Expenses Budget, I address the issue of linking disbursements for capital expenditures to the purchases projections for capital expenditures by assuming a certain percentage of a given period's purchases are paid for, or disbursed, in that same period.

It is important to note that I am assuming all capital expenditures will be paid for in either the period in which the item underlying the capital expenditure is bought or in the following period. As such, all capital expenditure purchases are either paid for in the period in which they were purchased or in the immediately subsequent period. This is not an issue in

	B	C	D	E	F	G
1			Period			
2	1Q X4	2Q X4	3Q X4	4Q X4		X4
59 Operating Expenses Worksheet						
60 Operating Expenses Inputs						
61 Miscellaneous expenses as a % of sales	3.0%	3.0%	3.0%	3.0%		
62						
63 R&D expenses as a % of sales	7.0%	7.0%	8.0%	8.0%		
64						
65 Rent expense per square foot per quarter	$ 5.00	$ 5.00	$ 5.00	$ 5.00		
66 Square feet of space rented	4,000	4,000	4,000	4,000		
67 Total rent expense	$ 20,000	$ 20,000	$ 20,000	$ 20,000		
68						
69 Tax rate	35.0%	35.0%	35.0%	35.0%		
70						
71 Capital Worksheet						
72 Capital Expenditures (CAPEX) Inputs						
73 Equipment purchases	$ 30,000	$ 30,000	$ 30,000	$ 30,000		
74 Furniture purchases	$ 10,000	$ 10,000	$ 10,000	$ 10,000		
75 Fixtures purchases	$ 5,000	$ 5,000	$ 5,000	$ 5,000		
76 Total CAPEX purchases	$ 45,000	$ 45,000	$ 45,000	$ 45,000		
77						
78 CAPEX Disbursements Inputs						
79 % of purchases paid for in purchase period	100%	100%	100%	100%		
80						

FIGURE 6.7   Assumptions and Dashboard Worksheet

my financial model for Napavale as I am assuming all capital expenditure purchases are paid for in the period incurred, but you can modify this style of financial model to account for different assumptions.

This "percentage paid for in a given period" approach to linking accrual-based budget figures and actual cash disbursements for those purchases represents another approach to building a financial model as compared to the days payable approach highlighted in Chapter 4. I am presenting this percentage approach for the sake of reference. You should feel free to use whichever approach is most appropriate for your own financial models.

Figure 6.8 presents the Capital Expenditures Budget worksheet, which now includes projections for the disbursements for capital expenditures.

Figure 6.9 offers an alternative view of the Capital Expenditures Budget worksheet in which the values and formulas contained within the worksheet's cells are exposed. Due to the length of several of the formulas in this worksheet, only a few of the columns are shown in Figure 6.9. Based on the manner in which the "percentage disbursement" approach for capital expenditures works, I need to account for the payment of capital expenditures incurred in prior periods using the formulas shown in the

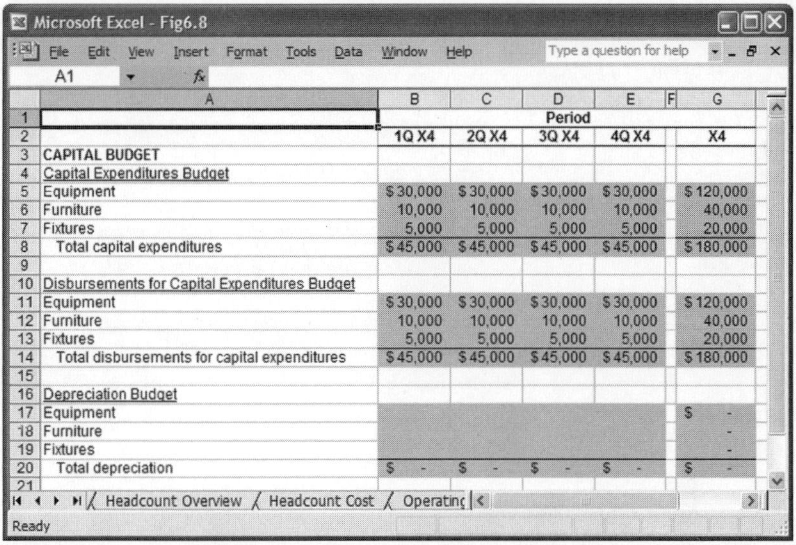

	A	B	C	D	E	F	G
1				Period			
2		1Q X4	2Q X4	3Q X4	4Q X4		X4
3	CAPITAL BUDGET						
4	Capital Expenditures Budget						
5	Equipment	$ 30,000	$ 30,000	$ 30,000	$ 30,000		$ 120,000
6	Furniture	10,000	10,000	10,000	10,000		40,000
7	Fixtures	5,000	5,000	5,000	5,000		20,000
8	Total capital expenditures	$ 45,000	$ 45,000	$ 45,000	$ 45,000		$ 180,000
9							
10	Disbursements for Capital Expenditures Budget						
11	Equipment	$ 30,000	$ 30,000	$ 30,000	$ 30,000		$ 120,000
12	Furniture	10,000	10,000	10,000	10,000		40,000
13	Fixtures	5,000	5,000	5,000	5,000		20,000
14	Total disbursements for capital expenditures	$ 45,000	$ 45,000	$ 45,000	$ 45,000		$ 180,000
15							
16	Depreciation Budget						
17	Equipment						$ -
18	Furniture						-
19	Fixtures						-
20	Total depreciation	$ -	$ -	$ -	$ -		$ -

FIGURE 6.8 Capital Expenditures Budget

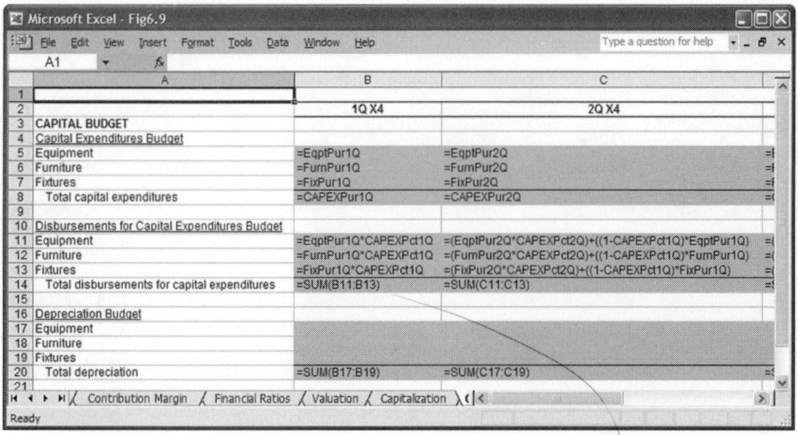

	A	B	C
1			
2		1Q X4	2Q X4
3	CAPITAL BUDGET		
4	Capital Expenditures Budget		
5	Equipment	=EqptPur1Q	=EqptPur2Q
6	Furniture	=FurnPur1Q	=FurnPur2Q
7	Fixtures	=FixPur1Q	=FixPur2Q
8	Total capital expenditures	=CAPEXPur1Q	=CAPEXPur2Q
9			
10	Disbursements for Capital Expenditures Budget		
11	Equipment	=EqptPur1Q*CAPEXPct1Q	=(EqptPur2Q*CAPEXPct2Q)+((1-CAPEXPct1Q)*EqptPur1Q)
12	Furniture	=FurnPur1Q*CAPEXPct1Q	=(FurnPur2Q*CAPEXPct2Q)+((1-CAPEXPct1Q)*FurnPur1Q)
13	Fixtures	=FixPur1Q*CAPEXPct1Q	=(FixPur2Q*CAPEXPct2Q)+((1-CAPEXPct1Q)*FixPur1Q)
14	Total disbursements for capital expenditures	=SUM(B11:B13)	=SUM(C11:C13)
15			
16	Depreciation Budget		
17	Equipment		
18	Furniture		
19	Fixtures		
20	Total depreciation	=SUM(B17:B19)	=SUM(C17:C19)

FIGURE 6.9 Alternative View of the Capital Expenditures Budget

rows in the worksheet under the "Disbursements for Capital Expenditures Budget" heading.

The names of the input and output cells in the Assumptions and Dashboard worksheet are presented in Figure 6.10. Figure 6.11 offers a view of the names of the input and output cells in the Disbursements for Capital Expenditures Budget worksheet.

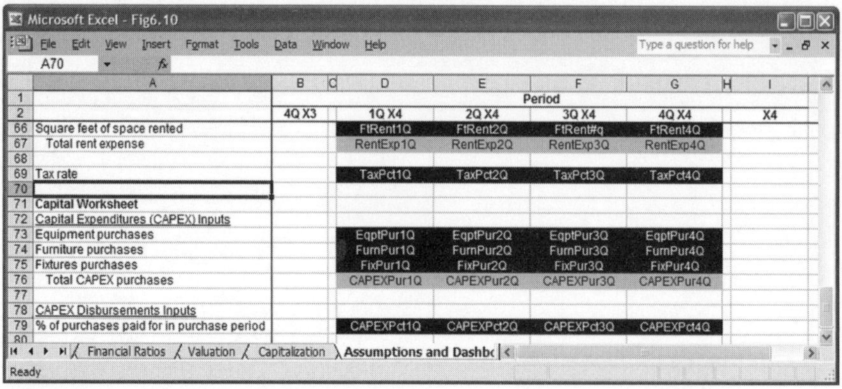

FIGURE 6.10 Names of the Input and Output Cells in the Assumptions and Dashboard Worksheet

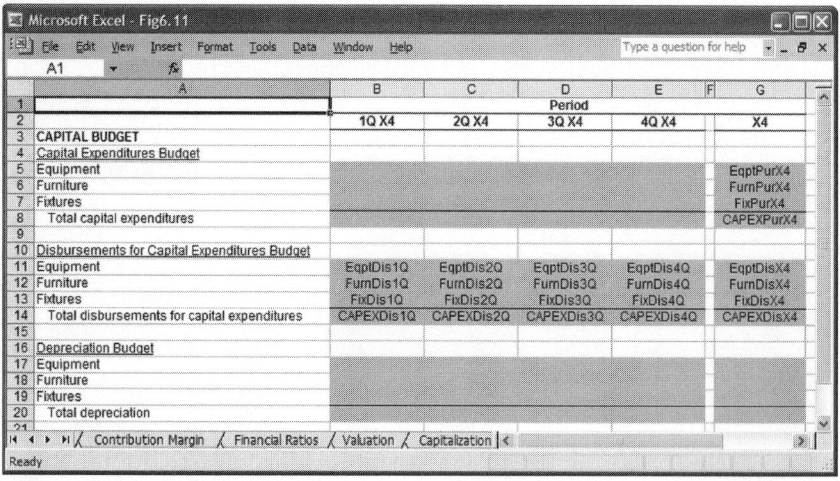

FIGURE 6.11 Names of the Input and Output Cells in the Disbursements for Capital Expenditures Budget

STEP 7C: DEPRECIATION BUDGET

The Depreciation Budget addresses projected depreciation expenses for Napavale. When a business accounts for the purchase of an item as a capital expenditure, that item must be depreciated. The philosophy underlying the concept of depreciation is this: If a company purchases and capitalizes an asset, the benefits that accrue from that asset will be recognized over a number of accounting periods in the future—that asset is depreciated over the expected period of benefit underlying the associated asset. Depreciation is an expense that appears as an operating expense in Napavale's Operating Budget.

Depreciation expenses, when calculated using the "straight line" method, are calculated in the following manner: the beginning value of an asset/the number of periods of expected benefit. So, for example, if a company capitalizes an asset with a value of $100 and the company believes it will receive benefit from that asset for five accounting periods, the depreciation expense for each accounting period will be equal to $100/5, or $20. Figure 6.12 presents a view of the Assumptions and Dashboard worksheet in which the assumptions underlying depreciation for Napavale's asset classes are shown.

The "depreciation multiplier" line items in Figure 6.12 represent the value by which capital expenditure purchases will be multiplied in each period over the purchases' depreciable life. The product of this multiplication will equal the depreciation expense for each line item for each period. This process is covered in greater detail over the course of this chapter.

Figure 6.13 offers a view of Napavale's Depreciation Budget and includes a line item that calculates the total depreciation expense for each period. Remember that this total depreciation expense flows directly into Napavale's Income Statement from Step 6.

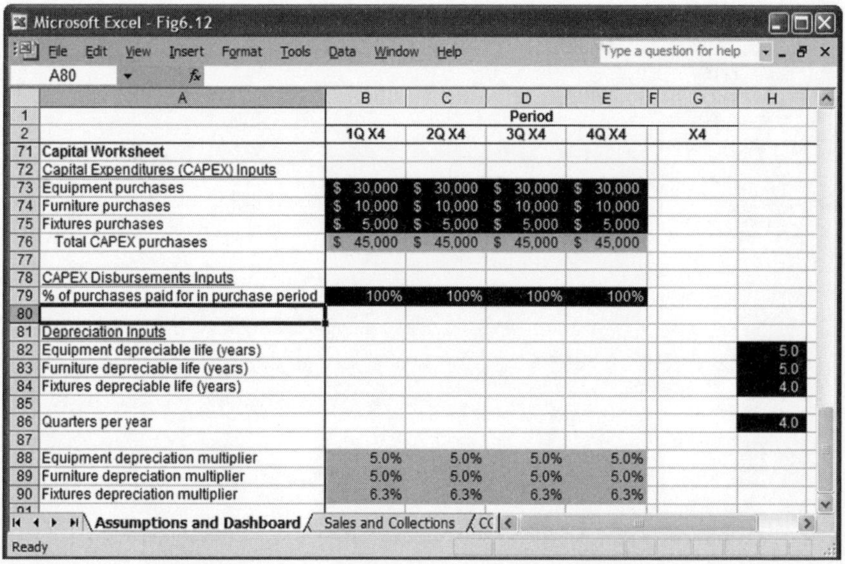

	A	B	C	D	E	F	G	H
1				Period				
2		1Q X4	2Q X4	3Q X4	4Q X4		X4	
71	Capital Worksheet							
72	Capital Expenditures (CAPEX) Inputs							
73	Equipment purchases	$ 30,000	$ 30,000	$ 30,000	$ 30,000			
74	Furniture purchases	$ 10,000	$ 10,000	$ 10,000	$ 10,000			
75	Fixtures purchases	$ 5,000	$ 5,000	$ 5,000	$ 5,000			
76	Total CAPEX purchases	$ 45,000	$ 45,000	$ 45,000	$ 45,000			
77								
78	CAPEX Disbursements Inputs							
79	% of purchases paid for in purchase period	100%	100%	100%	100%			
80								
81	Depreciation Inputs							
82	Equipment depreciable life (years)							5.0
83	Furniture depreciable life (years)							5.0
84	Fixtures depreciable life (years)							4.0
85								
86	Quarters per year							4.0
87								
88	Equipment depreciation multiplier	5.0%	5.0%	5.0%	5.0%			
89	Furniture depreciation multiplier	5.0%	5.0%	5.0%	5.0%			
90	Fixtures depreciation multiplier	6.3%	6.3%	6.3%	6.3%			

FIGURE 6.12 Assumptions and Dashboard Worksheet

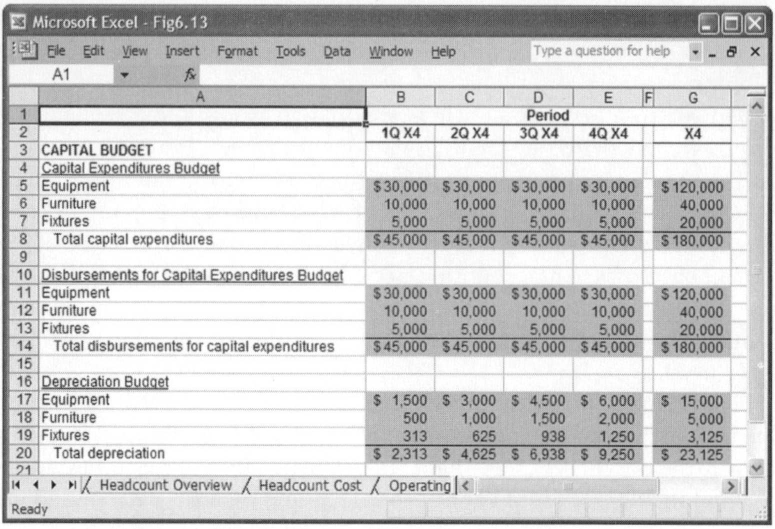

	Period				
	1Q X4	2Q X4	3Q X4	4Q X4	X4
CAPITAL BUDGET					
Capital Expenditures Budget					
Equipment	$ 30,000	$ 30,000	$ 30,000	$ 30,000	$ 120,000
Furniture	10,000	10,000	10,000	10,000	40,000
Fixtures	5,000	5,000	5,000	5,000	20,000
Total capital expenditures	$ 45,000	$ 45,000	$ 45,000	$ 45,000	$ 180,000
Disbursements for Capital Expenditures Budget					
Equipment	$ 30,000	$ 30,000	$ 30,000	$ 30,000	$ 120,000
Furniture	10,000	10,000	10,000	10,000	40,000
Fixtures	5,000	5,000	5,000	5,000	20,000
Total disbursements for capital expenditures	$ 45,000	$ 45,000	$ 45,000	$ 45,000	$ 180,000
Depreciation Budget					
Equipment	$ 1,500	$ 3,000	$ 4,500	$ 6,000	$ 15,000
Furniture	500	1,000	1,500	2,000	5,000
Fixtures	313	625	938	1,250	3,125
Total depreciation	$ 2,313	$ 4,625	$ 6,938	$ 9,250	$ 23,125

FIGURE 6.13 Depreciation Budget

An alternative view of Napavale's Depreciation Budget in which the values and formulas underlying the contents of each worksheet cell is presented in Figure 6.14. Note the references to the asset values and the depreciation multipliers in each calculation cell. Due to the length of some of the formulas in the worksheet shown in Figure 6.14, not all of the columns in the worksheet are visible.

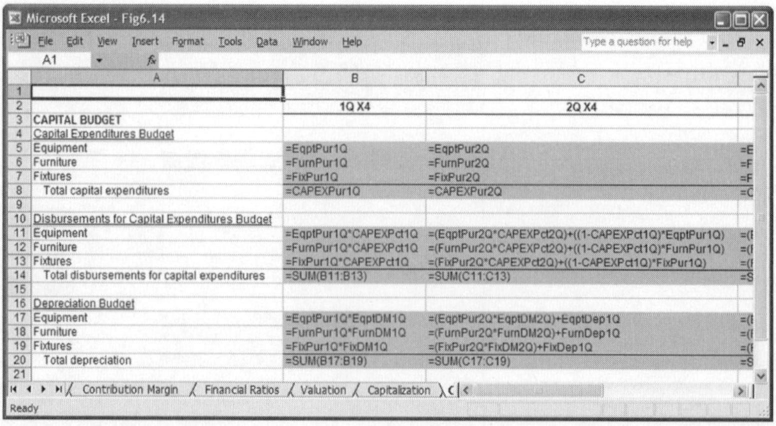

	1Q X4	2Q X4
CAPITAL BUDGET		
Capital Expenditures Budget		
Equipment	=EqptPur1Q	=EqptPur2Q
Furniture	=FurnPur1Q	=FurnPur2Q
Fixtures	=FixPur1Q	=FixPur2Q
Total capital expenditures	=CAPEXPur1Q	=CAPEXPur2Q
Disbursements for Capital Expenditures Budget		
Equipment	=EqptPur1Q*CAPEXPct1Q	=(EqptPur2Q*CAPEXPct2Q)+((1-CAPEXPct1Q)*EqptPur1Q)
Furniture	=FurnPur1Q*CAPEXPct1Q	=(FurnPur2Q*CAPEXPct2Q)+((1-CAPEXPct1Q)*FurnPur1Q)
Fixtures	=FixPur1Q*CAPEXPct1Q	=(FixPur2Q*CAPEXPct2Q)+((1-CAPEXPct1Q)*FixPur1Q)
Total disbursements for capital expenditures	=SUM(B11:B13)	=SUM(C11:C13)
Depreciation Budget		
Equipment	=EqptPur1Q*EqptDM1Q	=(EqptPur2Q*EqptDM2Q)+EqptDep1Q
Furniture	=FurnPur1Q*FurnDM1Q	=(FurnPur2Q*FurnDM2Q)+FurnDep1Q
Fixtures	=FixPur1Q*FixDM1Q	=(FixPur2Q*FixDM2Q)+FixDep1Q
Total depreciation	=SUM(B17:B19)	=SUM(C17:C19)

FIGURE 6.14 Alternative View of the Depreciation Budget

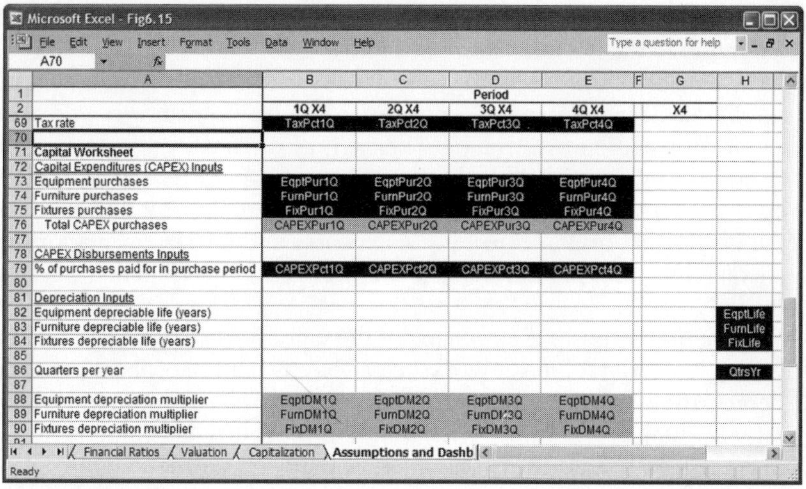

FIGURE 6.15 Names of the Input and Output Cells in the Assumptions and Dashboard Worksheet

Figure 6.15 shows the names of the input and output cells from the Assumptions and Dashboard worksheet. The names of the input and output cells in the Depreciation Budget worksheet are presented in Figure 6.16.

It is important to calculate the net effect (or total affect) of capitalized asset purchases and depreciation expenses on Napavale's base of fixed assets. Fixed assets, which are calculated net of depreciation (or after subtracting

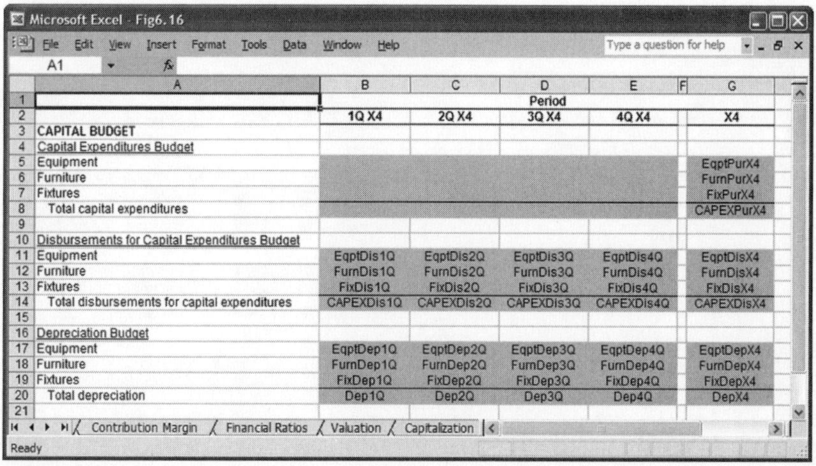

FIGURE 6.16 Names of the Input and Output Cells in the Depreciation Budget

depreciation expenses), appear on Napavale's Balance Sheet; I discuss the construction of the Balance Sheet in Chapter 7.

The calculation of Napavale's fixed assets net of depreciation incorporates two elements: Napavale's cumulative capital expenditures and accumulated depreciation over the time horizon of the financial model. Figure 6.17 offers a view of this calculation from the Capital Budget worksheet. Note that I have also added a calculation to determine any difference between Napavale's capital expenditure expenses and disbursements for capital expenditures. This calculation will influence the Balance Sheet in Chapter 7.

Figure 6.18 exposes the contents of the worksheet cells for this calculation from the Capital Budget worksheet. The calculation of fixed assets net of depreciation for each time period is equal to: the running total of Napavale's capital expenditures – the running total of Napavale's depreciation. Note that several of the columns in the worksheet shown in Figure 6.18 are not displayed due to the length of the formulas underlying the cells in the worksheet. The evolving list of names in the Depreciation Budget worksheet is shown in Figure 6.19.

Microsoft Excel - Fig6.17

	A	B	C	D	E	F	G
1				Period			
2		1Q X4	2Q X4	3Q X4	4Q X4		X4
3	CAPITAL BUDGET						
4	Capital Expenditures Budget						
5	Equipment	$30,000	$30,000	$ 30,000	$ 30,000		$120,000
6	Furniture	10,000	10,000	10,000	10,000		40,000
7	Fixtures	5,000	5,000	5,000	5,000		20,000
8	Total capital expenditures	$45,000	$45,000	$ 45,000	$ 45,000		$180,000
9							
10	Disbursements for Capital Expenditures Budget						
11	Equipment	$30,000	$30,000	$ 30,000	$ 30,000		$120,000
12	Furniture	10,000	10,000	10,000	10,000		40,000
13	Fixtures	5,000	5,000	5,000	5,000		20,000
14	Total disbursements for capital expenditures	$45,000	$45,000	$ 45,000	$ 45,000		$180,000
15							
16	Depreciation Budget						
17	Equipment	$ 1,500	$ 3,000	$ 4,500	$ 6,000		$ 15,000
18	Furniture	500	1,000	1,500	2,000		5,000
19	Fixtures	313	625	938	1,250		3,125
20	Total depreciation	$ 2,313	$ 4,625	$ 6,938	$ 9,250		$ 23,125
21							
22	Cumulative capital expenditures	$45,000	$90,000	$135,000	$180,000		
23	- Accumulated depreciation	2,313	6,938	13,875	23,125		
24	= Fixed assets, net of depreciation	$42,688	$83,063	$121,125	$156,875		
25							
26							
27	Cumulative disbursements for CAPEX	$45,000	$90,000	$135,000	$180,000		
28	Payables adjustment for CAPEX disbursements	$ -	$ -	$ -	$ -		

Headcount Overview / Headcount Cost / Operating I

Ready

FIGURE 6.17 Capital Budget Worksheet

	A	B
1		
2		1Q X4
3	CAPITAL BUDGET	
4	Capital Expenditures Budget	
5	Equipment	=EqptPur1Q
6	Furniture	=FurnPur1Q
7	Fixtures	=FixPur1Q
8	Total capital expenditures	=CAPEXPur1Q
9		
10	Disbursements for Capital Expenditures Budget	
11	Equipment	=EqptPur1Q*CAPEXPct1Q
12	Furniture	=FurnPur1Q*CAPEXPct1Q
13	Fixtures	=FixPur1Q*CAPEXPct1Q
14	Total disbursements for capital expenditures	=SUM(B11:B13)
15		
16	Depreciation Budget	
17	Equipment	=EqptPur1Q*EqptDM1Q
18	Furniture	=FurnPur1Q*FurnDM1Q
19	Fixtures	=FixPur1Q*FixDM1Q
20	Total depreciation	=SUM(B17:B19)
21		
22	Cumulative capital expenditures	=CAPEXPur1Q
23	- Accumulated depreciation	=Dep1Q
24	= Fixed assets, net of depreciation	=CumCAPEX1Q-AccDep1Q
25		
26		
27	Cumulative disbursements for CAPEX	=CAPEXDis1Q
28	Payables adjustment for CAPEX disbursements	=IF(CumCAPEX1Q>CDCAPEX1Q,CumCAPEX1Q-CDCAPEX1Q,0)
29		

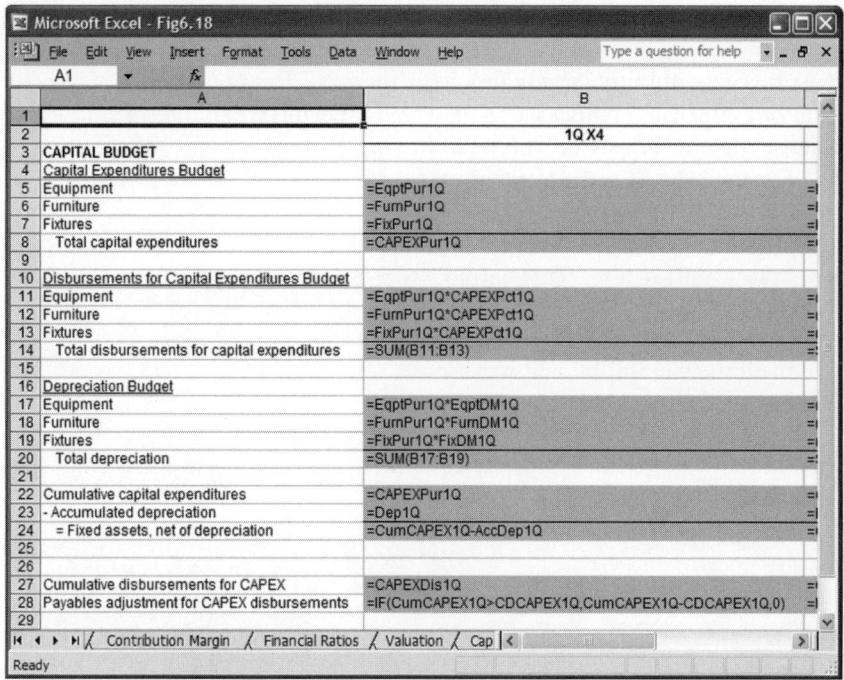

FIGURE 6.18 Alternative View of the Capital Budget

	A	B	C	D	E	G
1				Period		
2		1Q X4	2Q X4	3Q X4	4Q X4	X4
3	CAPITAL BUDGET					
4	Capital Expenditures Budget					
5	Equipment					EqptPurX4
6	Furniture					FurnPurX4
7	Fixtures					FixPurX4
8	Total capital expenditures					CAPEXPurX4
9						
10	Disbursements for Capital Expenditures Budget					
11	Equipment	EqptDis1Q	EqptDis2Q	EqptDis3Q	EqptDis4Q	EqptDisX4
12	Furniture	FurnDis1Q	FurnDis2Q	FurnDis3Q	FurnDis4Q	FurnDisX4
13	Fixtures	FixDis1Q	FixDis2Q	FixDis3Q	FixDis4Q	FixDisX4
14	Total disbursements for capital expenditures	CAPEXDis1Q	CAPEXDis2Q	CAPEXDis3Q	CAPEXDis4Q	CAPEXDisX4
15						
16	Depreciation Budget					
17	Equipment	EqptDep1Q	EqptDep2Q	EqptDep3Q	EqptDep4Q	EqptDepX4
18	Furniture	FurnDep1Q	FurnDep2Q	FurnDep3Q	FurnDep4Q	FurnDepX4
19	Fixtures	FixDep1Q	FixDep2Q	FixDep3Q	FixDep4Q	FixDepX4
20	Total depreciation	Dep1Q	Dep2Q	Dep3Q	Dep4Q	DepX4
21						
22	Cumulative capital expenditures	CumCAPEX1Q	CumCAPEX2Q	CumCAPEX3Q	CumCAPEX4Q	
23	- Accumulated depreciation	AccDep1Q	AccDep2Q	AccDep3Q	AccDep4Q	
24	= Fixed assets, net of depreciation	FixAssets1Q	FixAssets2Q	FixAssets3Q	FixAssets4Q	
25						
26						
27	Cumulative disbursements for CAPEX	CDCAPEX1Q	CDCAPEX2Q	CDCAPEX3Q	CDCAPEX4Q	
28	Payables adjustment for CAPEX disbursements	PACAPEX1Q	PACAPEX1Q	PACAPEX3Q	PACAPEX4Q	

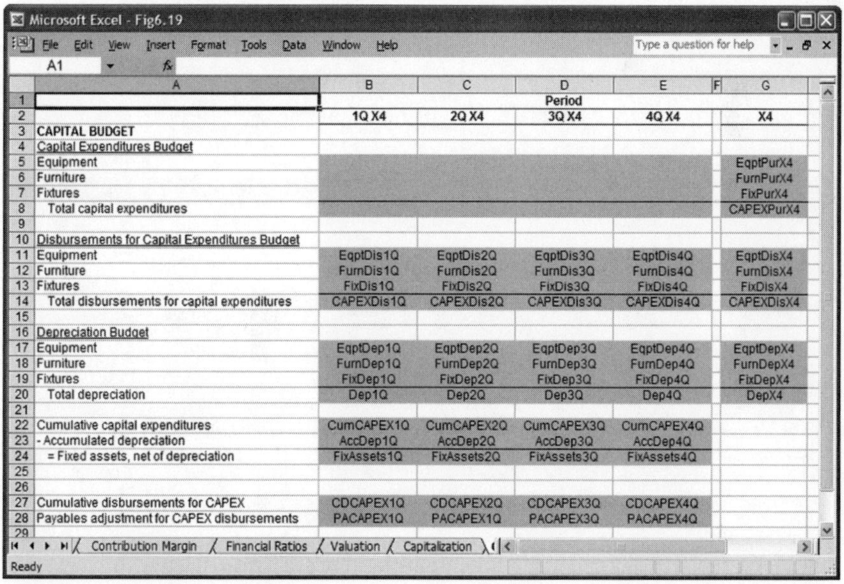

FIGURE 6.19 Names of the Input and Output Cells in the Depreciation Budget

As indicated in Chapter 5, I now present an updated view of Napavale's Income Statement, which now includes the line for depreciation expense. The only remaining line item that requires completion is that of "interest expense," which will be covered later in this chapter. Figure 6.20 offers a view of Napavale's updated Income Statement.

For the sake of reference, Figure 6.21 offers an alternative view of Na-

	A	B	C	D	E	F	G
1				Period			
2		1Q X4	2Q X4	3Q X4	4Q X4		X4
3	Sales	$1,000,000	$1,440,000	$1,932,000	$2,520,000		$6,892,000
4	Cost of goods sold	200,000	291,000	373,800	462,000		1,326,800
5	Gross profit	$ 800,000	$1,149,000	$1,558,200	$2,058,000		$5,565,200
6							
7	Salaries	$ 470,400	$ 470,400	$ 663,600	$ 697,200		$2,301,600
8	Miscellaneous expenses	30,000	43,200	57,960	75,600		206,760
9	Research and development	70,000	100,800	154,560	201,600		526,960
10	Rent	20,000	20,000	20,000	20,000		80,000
11	Depreciation	2,313	4,625	6,938	9,250		23,125
12	Income from operations	$ 209,600	$ 514,600	$ 662,080	$1,063,600		$2,449,880
13							
14	Interest expense						$ -
15	Taxable income	$ 209,600	$ 514,600	$ 662,080	$1,063,600		$2,449,880
16							
17	Tax expense	$ 73,360	$ 180,110	$ 231,728	$ 372,260		$ 857,458
18	Net income	$ 136,240	$ 334,490	$ 430,352	$ 691,340		$1,592,422
19							

FIGURE 6.20 Income Statement

	A	B	C	D	E	F	G
1				Period			
2		1Q X4	2Q X4	3Q X4	4Q X4		X4
3	Sales	=Sales1Q	=Sales2Q	=Sales3Q	=Sales4Q		=SUM(B3:E3)
4	Cost of goods sold	=COGS1Q	=COGS2Q	=COGS3Q	=COGS4Q		=SUM(B4:E4)
5	Gross profit	=B3-B4	=C3-C4	=D3-D4	=E3-E4		=G3-G4
6							
7	Salaries	=SalExp1Q	=SalExp2Q	=SalExp3Q	=SalExp4Q		=SUM(B7:E7)
8	Miscellaneous expenses	=MiscExp1Q	=MiscExp2Q	=MiscExp3Q	=MiscExp4Q		=SUM(B8:E8)
9	Research and development	=RDExp1Q	=RDExp2Q	=RDExp3Q	=RDExp4Q		=SUM(B9:E9)
10	Rent	=RentExp1Q	=RentExp2Q	=RentExp3Q	=RentExp4Q		=SUM(B10:E10)
11	Depreciation	=Dep1Q	=Dep2Q	=Dep3Q	=Dep4Q		=SUM(B11:E11)
12	Income from operations	=GrossP1Q-OpExp1Q	=GrossP2Q-OpExp2Q	=GrossP3Q-OpExp3Q	=GrossP4Q-OpExp4Q		=GrossPX4-OpExpX4
13							
14	Interest expense						=SUM(B14:E14)
15	Taxable income	=OpInc1Q-B14	=OpInc2Q-C14	=OpInc3Q-D14	=OpInc4Q-E14		=OpIncX4-G14
16							
17	Tax expense	=TaxInc1Q*TaxPct1Q	=TaxInc2Q*TaxPct2Q	=TaxInc3Q*TaxPct3Q	=TaxInc4Q*TaxPct4Q		=SUM(B17:E17)
18	Net income	=TaxInc1Q-TaxExp1Q	=TaxInc2Q-TaxExp2Q	=TaxInc3Q-TaxExp3Q	=TaxInc4Q-TaxExp4Q		=TaxIncX4-TaxExpX4
19							

FIGURE 6.21 Alternative View of the Income Statement

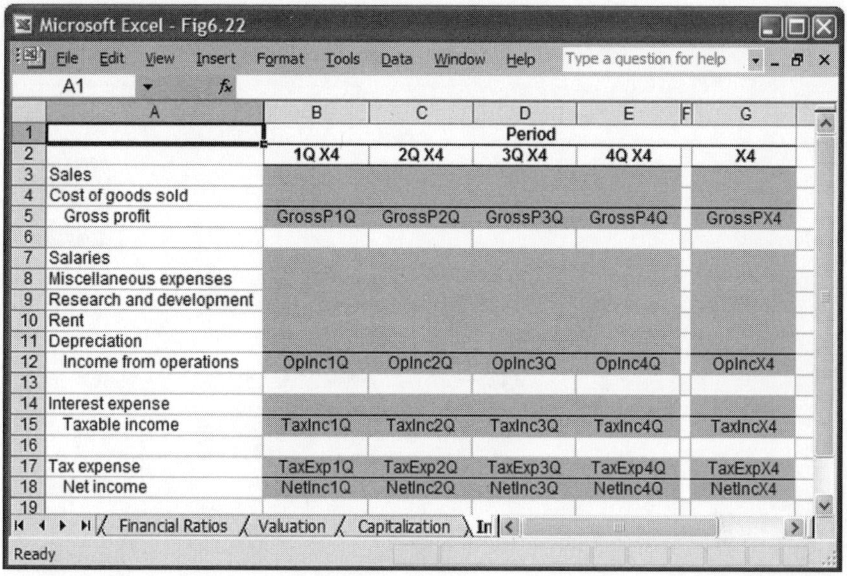

	A	B	C	D	E	F	G
1				Period			
2		1Q X4	2Q X4	3Q X4	4Q X4		X4
3	Sales						
4	Cost of goods sold						
5	Gross profit	GrossP1Q	GrossP2Q	GrossP3Q	GrossP4Q		GrossPX4
6							
7	Salaries						
8	Miscellaneous expenses						
9	Research and development						
10	Rent						
11	Depreciation						
12	Income from operations	OpInc1Q	OpInc2Q	OpInc3Q	OpInc4Q		OpIncX4
13							
14	Interest expense						
15	Taxable income	TaxInc1Q	TaxInc2Q	TaxInc3Q	TaxInc4Q		TaxIncX4
16							
17	Tax expense	TaxExp1Q	TaxExp2Q	TaxExp3Q	TaxExp4Q		TaxExpX4
18	Net income	NetInc1Q	NetInc2Q	NetInc3Q	NetInc4Q		NetIncX4
19							

FIGURE 6.22 Names of the Input and Output Cells in the Income Statement

pavale's updated Income Statement in which the values and formulas underlying each cell are exposed and visible. The names underlying the Income Statement worksheet are shown in Figure 6.22.

STEP 8: CASH BUDGET

The Cash Budget, which tracks Napavale's cash balance at the beginning and ending of each accounting period, is an important component of the Master Budget. As is often said in finance, "cash is king," and it is essential to maintain a detailed view of a company's cash balance.

The Cash Budget draws on information from several schedules, including the Income Statement and the Assumptions and Dashboard worksheet. Figure 6.23 presents several input variables from the Assumptions and Dashboard worksheet that I have not yet covered for Napavale; these variables will affect the Cash Budget.

As the Cash Budget consists of several sections, I will cover each section separately. Figure 6.24 shows the first section of the Cash Budget, which includes Napavale's beginning cash balance and cash collections for each period. Figure 6.25 offers another view of the Cash Budget in which the values of the worksheet's cells are exposed. The names underlying the input and output cells in the Assumptions and Dashboard worksheet are

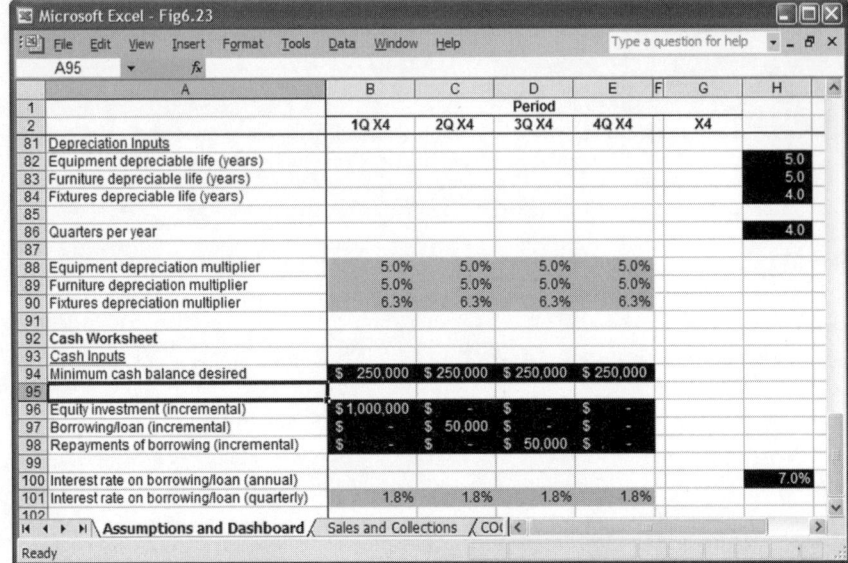

FIGURE 6.23   Assumptions and Dashboard Worksheet

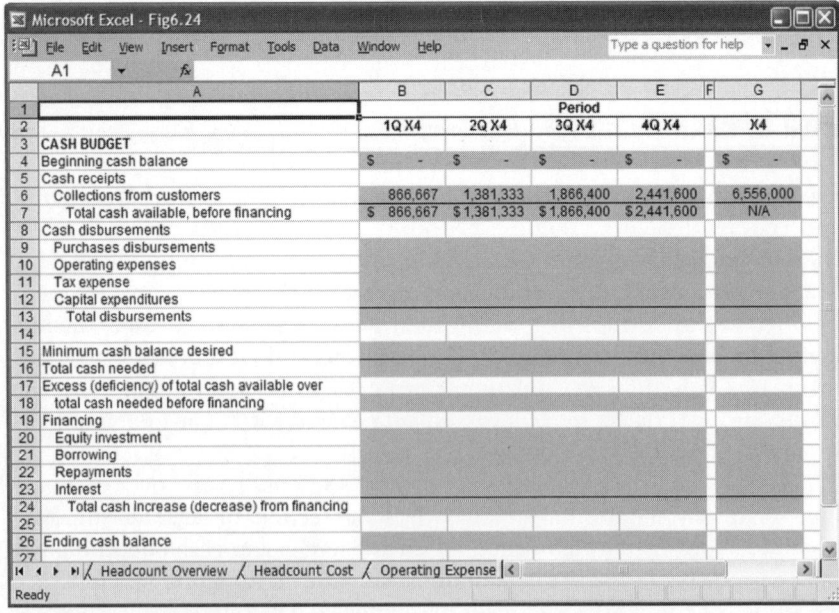

FIGURE 6.24   First Section of the Cash Budget

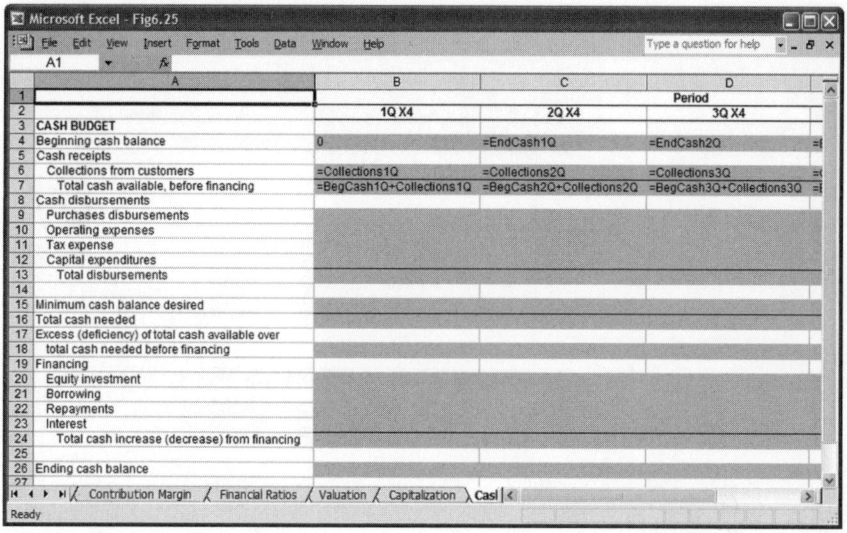
Microsoft Excel - Fig6.25

	A	B	C	D
1				Period
2		1Q X4	2Q X4	3Q X4
3	CASH BUDGET			
4	Beginning cash balance	0	=EndCash1Q	=EndCash2Q
5	Cash receipts			
6	Collections from customers	=Collections1Q	=Collections2Q	=Collections3Q
7	Total cash available, before financing	=BegCash1Q+Collections1Q	=BegCash2Q+Collections2Q	=BegCash3Q+Collections3Q
8	Cash disbursements			
9	Purchases disbursements			
10	Operating expenses			
11	Tax expense			
12	Capital expenditures			
13	Total disbursements			
14				
15	Minimum cash balance desired			
16	Total cash needed			
17	Excess (deficiency) of total cash available over			
18	total cash needed before financing			
19	Financing			
20	Equity investment			
21	Borrowing			
22	Repayments			
23	Interest			
24	Total cash increase (decrease) from financing			
25				
26	Ending cash balance			

FIGURE 6.25 Alternative View of the First Section of the Cash Budget

shown in Figure 6.26. Figure 6.27 highlights the names of the input and output cells from the Cash Budget itself.

The next section of the Cash Budget is presented in Figure 6.28. This section identifies Napavale's cash disbursements for each period and calculates the excess or deficiency of total cash available compared to the total cash required by the business (as stated on the Assumptions and Dashboard worksheet) before any financing takes place. Note that the "minimum cash balance" desired may be influenced by loan covenants if a company borrows money. Figure 6.29 offers an alternative view of the evolving Cash Budget in which the values and formulas in the worksheet cells are exposed and visible.

Note the formulas underlying the calculation of "total cash needed" and "excess (deficiency) of total cash available over total cash needed before financing." These calculations draw from both Napavale's projected cash receipts and cash disbursements as well as from the assumption underlying the "minimum cash balance desired." The evolving lists of names of the input and output cells in the Cash Budget are shown in Figure 6.30.

A final calculation to determine the "loan value used for interest calculations" in the Assumptions and Dashboard worksheet is shown in Figure 6.31. This calculation is used to simplify the calculation of periodic interest expenses associated with Napavale's borrowings (if any) for the Cash Budget. An alternative view of the Assumptions and Dashboard worksheet is

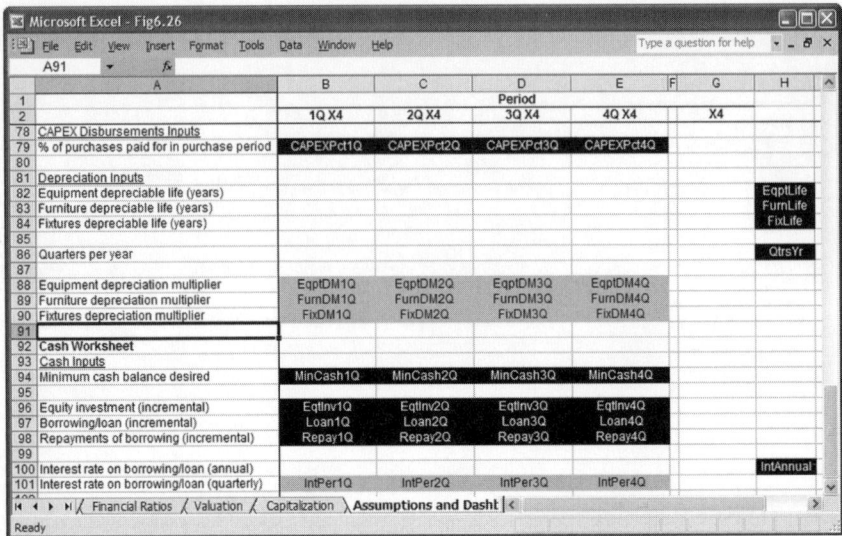

FIGURE 6.26 Names of the Input and Output Cells in the Assumptions and Dashboard Worksheet

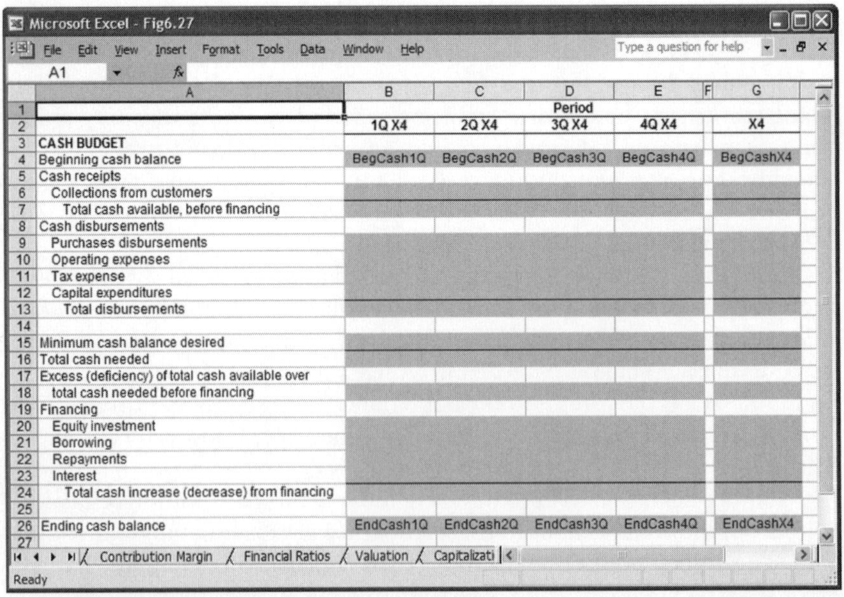

FIGURE 6.27 Names of the Input and Output Cells in the Cash Budget

FIGURE 6.28   Next Section of the Cash Budget

	A	B	C	D	E	F	G
1				Period			
2		1Q X4	2Q X4	3Q X4	4Q X4		X4
3	CASH BUDGET						
4	Beginning cash balance	$ -	$ -	$ -	$ -		$ -
5	Cash receipts						
6	Collections from customers	866,667	1,381,333	1,866,400	2,441,600		6,556,000
7	Total cash available, before financing	$ 866,667	$1,381,333	$1,866,400	$2,441,600		
8	Cash disbursements						
9	Purchases disbursements	$ 176,444	$ 294,489	$ 365,400	$ 439,133		$1,275,467
10	Operating expenses	590,400	634,400	896,120	994,400		3,115,320
11	Tax expense	73,360	180,110	231,728	372,260		857,458
12	Capital expenditures	45,000	45,000	45,000	45,000		180,000
13	Total disbursements	885,204	1,153,999	1,538,248	1,850,793		5,428,245
14							
15	Minimum cash balance desired	$ 250,000	$ 250,000	$ 250,000	$ 250,000		N/A
16	Total cash needed	$1,135,204	$1,403,999	$1,788,248	$2,100,793		N/A
17	Excess (deficiency) of total cash available over						
18	total cash needed before financing	$ (268,538)	$ (22,666)	$ 78,152	$ 340,807		N/A
19	Financing						
20	Equity investment						
21	Borrowing						
22	Repayments						
23	Interest						
24	Total cash increase (decrease) from financing						
25							
26	Ending cash balance						
27							

FIGURE 6.29   Alternative View of the Next Section of the Cash Budget

	A	B	C
1			
2		1Q X4	2Q X4
3	CASH BUDGET		
4	Beginning cash balance	0	=EndCash1Q
5	Cash receipts		
6	Collections from customers	=Collections1Q	=Collections2Q
7	Total cash available, before financing	=BegCash1Q+Collections1Q	=BegCash2Q+Collections2Q
8	Cash disbursements		
9	Purchases disbursements	=Disburse1Q	=Disburse2Q
10	Operating expenses	=DOE1Q	=DOE2Q
11	Tax Expense	=TaxExp1Q	=TaxExp2Q
12	Capital expenditures	=CAPEXDis1Q	=CAPEXDis2Q
13	Total disbursements	=SUM(B9:B12)	=SUM(C9:C12)
14			
15	Minimum cash balance desired	=MinCash1Q	=MinCash2Q
16	Total cash needed	=TotalDis1Q+MinCash1Q	=TotalDis2Q+MinCash2Q
17	Excess (deficiency) of total cash available over		
18	total cash needed before financing	=CBF1Q-TotalDis1Q-MinCash1Q	=CBF2Q-TotalDis2Q-MinCash2Q
19	Financing		
20	Equity investment		
21	Borrowing		
22	Repayments		
23	Interest		
24	Total cash increase (decrease) from financing		
25			
26	Ending cash balance		
27			

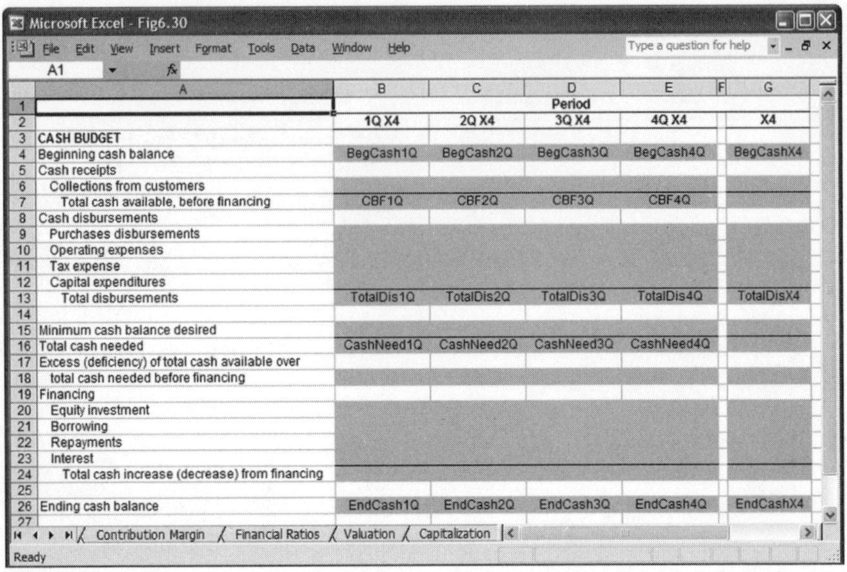

FIGURE 6.30   Names of the Input and Output Cells in the Cash Budget

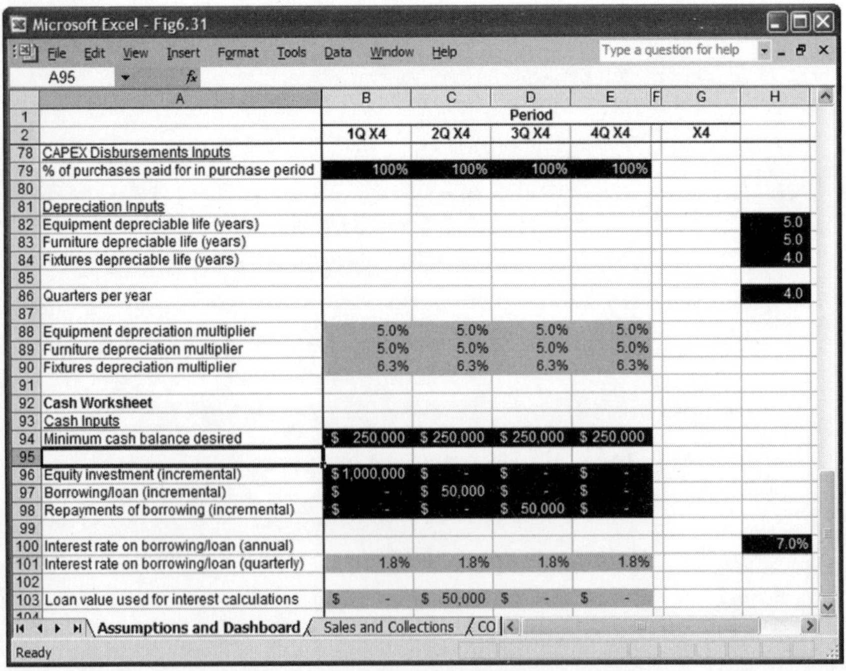

FIGURE 6.31   Assumptions and Dashboard Worksheet

presented in Figure 6.32 to highlight the calculations underlying the periodic interest expense figures mentioned in Figure 6.31.

The final section of the Cash Budget is presented in Figure 6.33. This section incorporates assumptions regarding the equity investments into Napavale, Napavale's borrowings, repayments, and interest payments. This section also calculates the change in Napavale's cash balance due to financing (including equity and debt activity) as well as Napavale's ending cash balance for each period.

Please note that for the calculation of interest on borrowings, Napavale's financial model calculates interest only if there is at least one period separating a borrowing and a repayment. If money is borrowed in one period and repaid in the subsequent period, one period of interest is computed for that borrowing. There are many ways to calculate interest on borrowings; my approach is simple and straightforward.

The ending cash balance is a very important figure that flows directly into Napavale's Balance Sheet, covered in Chapter 7. Figure 6.34 offers an alternative view of the Cash Budget in which the values and formulas contained within the cells in the worksheet are exposed and visible.

Figure 6.35 offers a view of the names of the input and output cells from the Assumptions and Dashboard worksheet. The final list of the

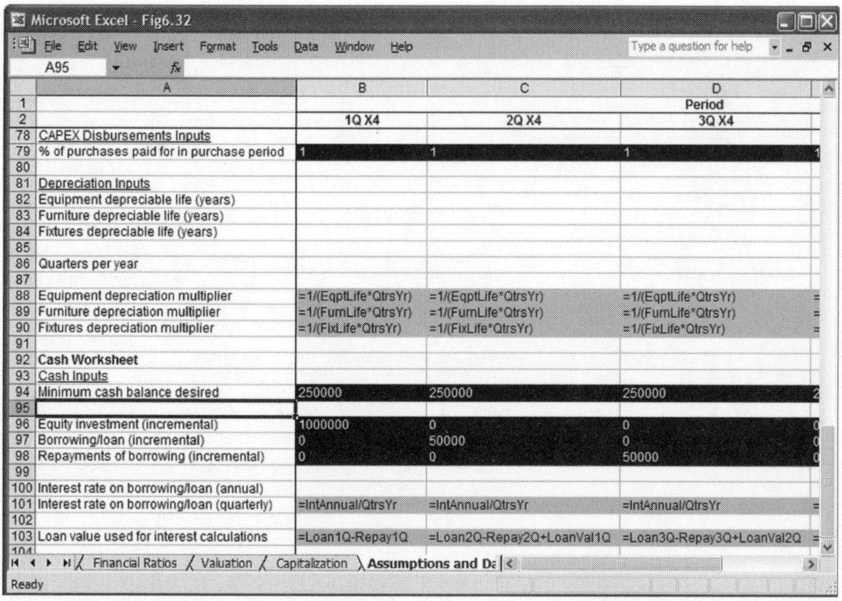

	A	B	C	D
1				Period
2		1Q X4	2Q X4	3Q X4
78	CAPEX Disbursements Inputs			
79	% of purchases paid for in purchase period	1	1	1
80				
81	Depreciation Inputs			
82	Equipment depreciable life (years)			
83	Furniture depreciable life (years)			
84	Fixtures depreciable life (years)			
85				
86	Quarters per year			
87				
88	Equipment depreciation multiplier	=1/(EqptLife*QtrsYr)	=1/(EqptLife*QtrsYr)	=1/(EqptLife*QtrsYr)
89	Furniture depreciation multiplier	=1/(FurnLife*QtrsYr)	=1/(FurnLife*QtrsYr)	=1/(FurnLife*QtrsYr)
90	Fixtures depreciation multiplier	=1/(FixLife*QtrsYr)	=1/(FixLife*QtrsYr)	=1/(FixLife*QtrsYr)
91				
92	Cash Worksheet			
93	Cash Inputs			
94	Minimum cash balance desired	250000	250000	250000
95				
96	Equity investment (incremental)	1000000	0	0
97	Borrowing/loan (incremental)	0	50000	0
98	Repayments of borrowing (incremental)	0	0	50000
99				
100	Interest rate on borrowing/loan (annual)			
101	Interest rate on borrowing/loan (quarterly)	=IntAnnual/QtrsYr	=IntAnnual/QtrsYr	=IntAnnual/QtrsYr
102				
103	Loan value used for interest calculations	=Loan1Q-Repay1Q	=Loan2Q-Repay2Q+LoanVal1Q	=Loan3Q-Repay3Q+LoanVal2Q

FIGURE 6.32 Alternative View of the Assumptions and Dashboard Worksheet

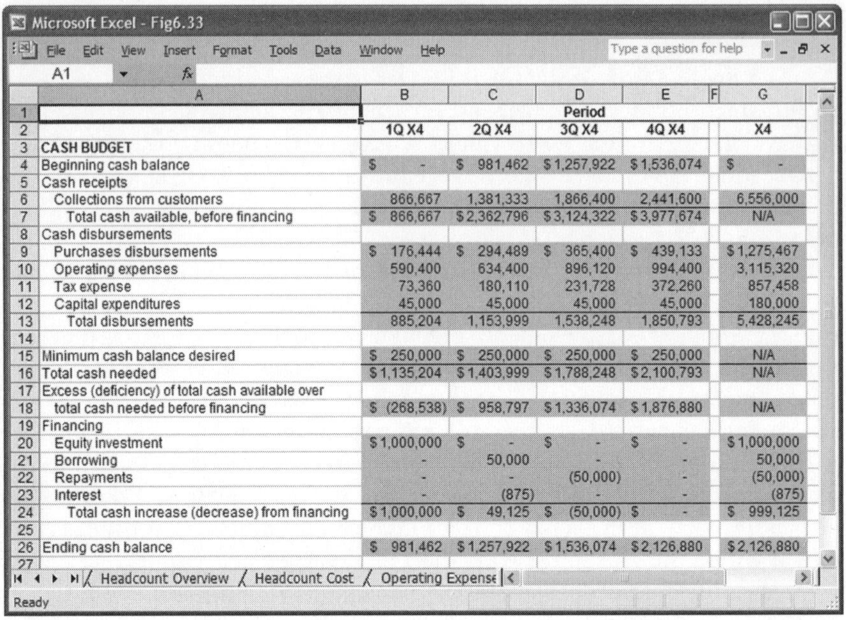

FIGURE 6.33 Final Section of the Cash Budget

FIGURE 6.34 Alternative View of the Final Section of the Cash Budget

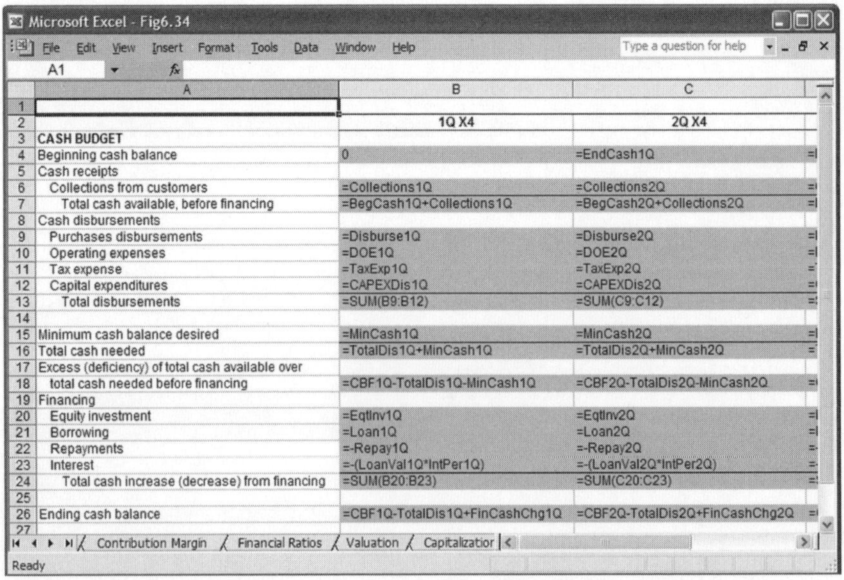

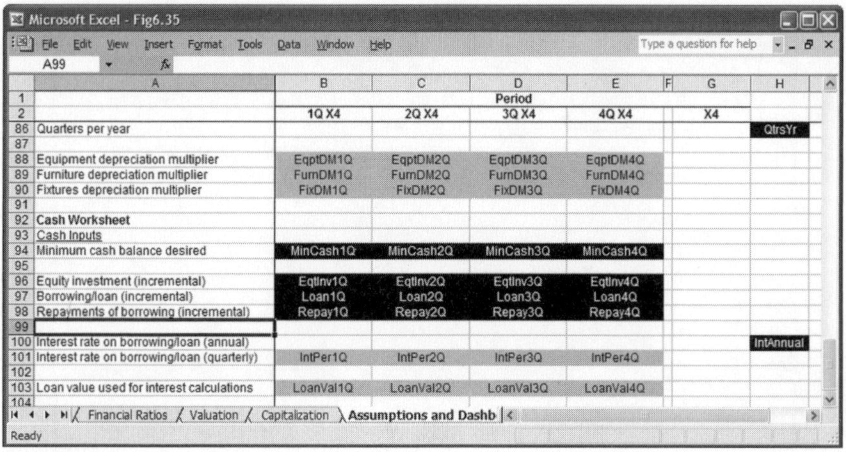

FIGURE 6.35 Names of the Input and Output Cells in the Assumptions and Dashboard Worksheet

names of the input and output cells from the Cash Budget is presented in Figure 6.36.

Now that I have calculated Napavale's periodic interest expenses, the last step in this chapter is to present the completed Income Statement. Figure 6.37 presents a view of the completed Income Statement, which now includes projections for interest expense.

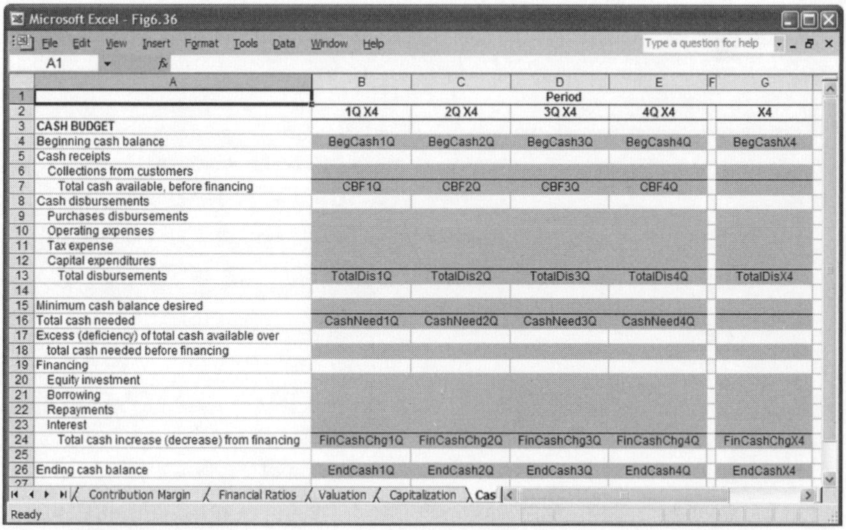

FIGURE 6.36 Names of the Input and Output Cells in the Cash Budget

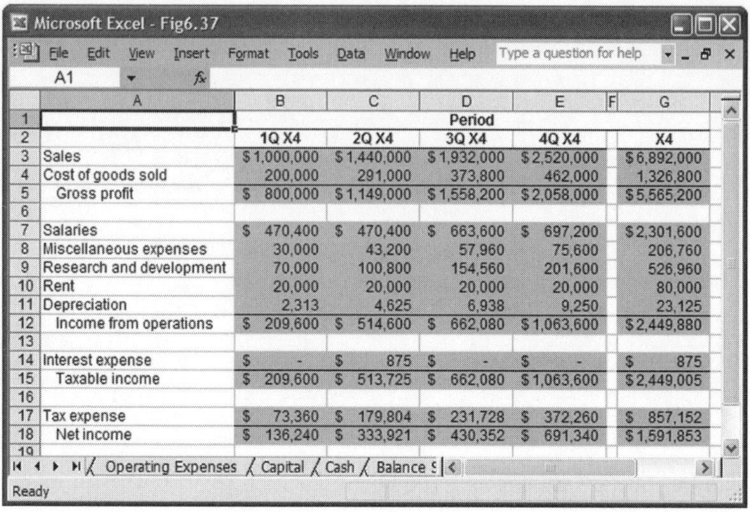

FIGURE 6.37 Income Statement

I named the cells associated with the periodic interest expense figures using the Cash Budget worksheet—these projections flow into the completed Income Statement. Take careful note of the fact that the "named" interest expense figures are negative values, so I have to place a negative sign in front of the referenced value in the Income Statement. Figure 6.38 presents a view of the Cash Budget worksheet with the names of the cells

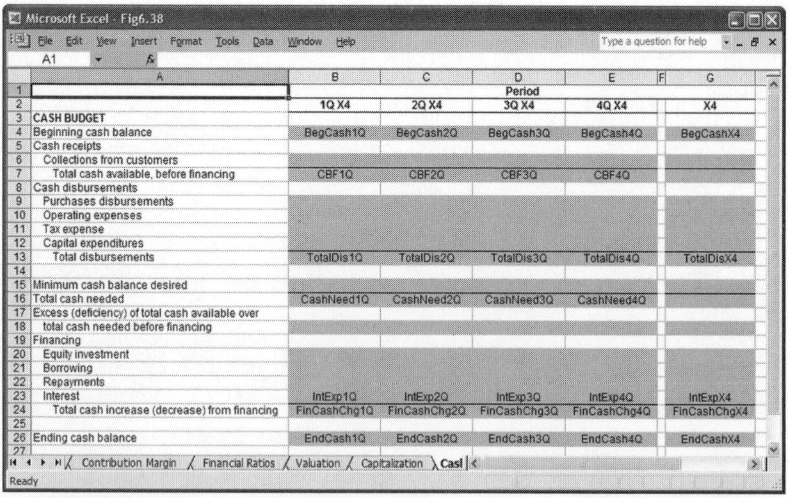

FIGURE 6.38 Names of the Input and Output Cells in the Cash Budget

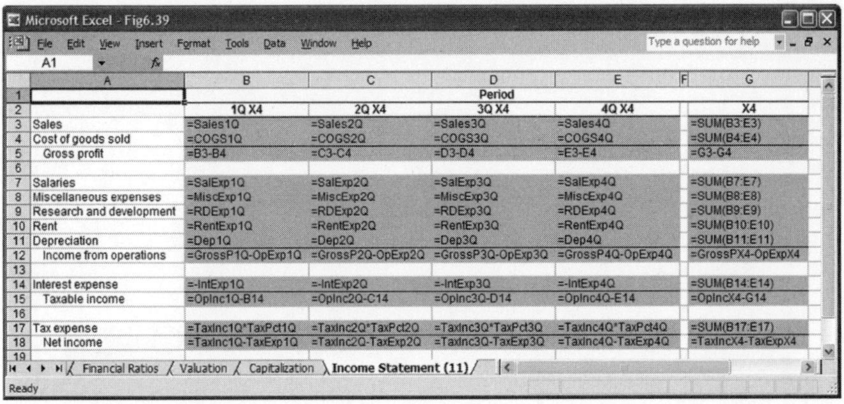

	A	B	C	D	E	F	G
1				Period			
2		1Q X4	2Q X4	3Q X4	4Q X4		X4
3	Sales	=Sales1Q	=Sales2Q	=Sales3Q	=Sales4Q		=SUM(B3:E3)
4	Cost of goods sold	=COGS1Q	=COGS2Q	=COGS3Q	=COGS4Q		=SUM(B4:E4)
5	Gross profit	=B3-B4	=C3-C4	=D3-D4	=E3-E4		=G3-G4
6							
7	Salaries	=SalExp1Q	=SalExp2Q	=SalExp3Q	=SalExp4Q		=SUM(B7:E7)
8	Miscellaneous expenses	=MiscExp1Q	=MiscExp2Q	=MiscExp3Q	=MiscExp4Q		=SUM(B8:E8)
9	Research and development	=RDExp1Q	=RDExp2Q	=RDExp3Q	=RDExp4Q		=SUM(B9:E9)
10	Rent	=RentExp1Q	=RentExp2Q	=RentExp3Q	=RentExp4Q		=SUM(B10:E10)
11	Depreciation	=Dep1Q	=Dep2Q	=Dep3Q	=Dep4Q		=SUM(B11:E11)
12	Income from operations	=GrossP1Q-OpExp1Q	=GrossP2Q-OpExp2Q	=GrossP3Q-OpExp3Q	=GrossP4Q-OpExp4Q		=GrossPX4-OpExpX4
13							
14	Interest expense	=-IntExp1Q	=-IntExp2Q	=-IntExp3Q	=-IntExp4Q		=SUM(B14:E14)
15	Taxable income	=OpInc1Q-B14	=OpInc2Q-C14	=OpInc3Q-D14	=OpInc4Q-E14		=OpIncX4-G14
16							
17	Tax expense	=TaxInc1Q*TaxPct1Q	=TaxInc2Q*TaxPct2Q	=TaxInc3Q*TaxPct3Q	=TaxInc4Q*TaxPct4Q		=SUM(B17:E17)
18	Net income	=TaxInc1Q-TaxExp1Q	=TaxInc2Q-TaxExp2Q	=TaxInc3Q-TaxExp3Q	=TaxInc4Q-TaxExp4Q		=TaxIncX4-TaxExpX4
19							

FIGURE 6.39 Alternative View of the Income Statement

indicated. An alternative view of the completed Income Statement is presented in Figure 6.39 in which the values and formulas underlying the worksheet cells are exposed and visible.

QUESTIONS

Each of the questions for this chapter relate to a hypothetical company named Company JKL. Company JKL sells rain jackets to consumers. As such, Company JKL is a product-oriented (as opposed to a service-oriented) business. The questions for this chapter will address fiscal year X4 on a quarterly basis (four specific quarters, 1Q–4Q for year X4).

The following questions will test your knowledge of the material covered in this chapter in an applied manner—specifically, you will be asked to build the schedules discussed in this chapter for Company JKL.

To prepare you for this chapter's questions, several figures provide background information related to Company JKL's operations. Figure Q6.1 offers a view of a portion of Company JKL's Assumptions and Dashboard worksheet. Note that there are three cost-of-goods-sold components for Company JKL's rain jackets: (1) exterior, (2) interior, and (3) assembly and labor.

Figure Q6.2 presents a view of Company JKL's Unit Sales and Price Budget, Sales Composition Budget, Cash Collections from Customers Budget, and Accounts Receivable Budget. Company JKL's Cost-of-Goods-Sold Budget is shown in Figure Q6.3. Figure Q6.4 presents a view of Company JKL's Inventory Budget, Purchases Budget, Disbursements for Purchases Budget, and Accounts Payable Budget. Company JKL's Headcount

A	B	C	D	E	F	G	H
1				Period			
2		1Q X4	2Q X4	3Q X4	4Q X4	X4	
70							
71 Capital Worksheet							
72 Capital Expenditures (CAPEX) Inputs							
73 Equipment purchases	$ 9,000	$ 5,000	$ 3,000	$ 3,000			
74 Furniture purchases	$ 2,500	$ 2,500	$ 2,500	$ 2,000			
75 Fixtures purchases	$ 1,500	$ 1,500	$ 1,500	$ 1,500			
76 Total CAPEX purchases	$ 13,000	$ 9,000	$ 7,000	$ 6,500			
77							
78 CAPEX Disbursements Inputs							
79 % of purchases paid for in purchase period	100%	100%	100%	100%			
80							
81 Depreciation Inputs							
82 Equipment depreciable life (years)							6.0
83 Furniture depreciable life (years)							5.0
84 Fixtures depreciable life (years)							5.0
85							
86 Quarters per year							4.0
87							
88 Equipment depreciation multiplier	4.2%	4.2%	4.2%	4.2%			
89 Furniture depreciation multiplier	5.0%	5.0%	5.0%	5.0%			
90 Fixtures depreciation multiplier	5.0%	5.0%	5.0%	5.0%			
91							
92 Cash Worksheet							
93 Cash Inputs							
94 Minimum cash balance desired	$ 100,000	$ 100,000	$ 100,000	$ 100,000			
95							
96 Equity investment (incremental)	$ 500,000	$ -	$ -	$ -			
97 Borrowing/loan (incremental)	$ -	$ -	$ 25,000	$ -			
98 Repayments of borrowing (incremental)	$ -	$ -	$ -	$ 25,000			

FIGURE Q6.1 Company JKL's Assumptions and Dashboard Worksheet

A	B	C	D	E	F	G
1				Period		
2		1Q X4	2Q X4	3Q X4	4Q X4	X4
3 SALES BUDGET						
4 Unit Sales and Price Budget						
5 Unit sales	10,000	10,400	10,900	11,100	42,400	
6 × Price per unit	$ 275	$ 270	$ 260	$ 260	N/A	
7 = Total sales	$2,750,000	$2,808,000	$2,834,000	$2,886,000	$11,278,000	
8						
9 Sales Composition Budget						
10 Cash sales	$1,650,000	$1,404,000	$1,700,400	$1,731,600	$ 6,486,000	
11 + Credit sales	1,100,000	1,404,000	1,133,600	1,154,400	4,792,000	
12 = Total sales	$2,750,000	$2,808,000	$2,834,000	$2,886,000	$11,278,000	
13						
14 COLLECTIONS BUDGET						
15 Cash Collections from Customers Budget						
16 Cash sales this period	$1,650,000	$1,404,000	$1,700,400	$1,731,600	$ 6,486,000	
17 + Credit sales collected	794,444	1,366,356	1,224,889	1,149,778	4,535,467	
18 = Total collections	$2,444,444	$2,770,356	$2,925,289	$2,881,378	$11,021,467	
19						
20 Accounts Receivable (A/R) Budget						
21 Beginning A/R balance	$ -	$ 305,556	$ 343,200	$ 251,911	$ -	
22 + Additions to A/R	305,556	343,200	251,911	256,533	1,157,200	
23 - Subtractions from A/R	-	305,556	343,200	251,911	900,667	
24 = Ending A/R balance	$ 305,556	$ 343,200	$ 251,911	$ 256,533	$ 256,533	

FIGURE Q6.2 Company JKL's Unit Sales and Price Budget

Microsoft Excel - FigQ6.3

	A	B	C	D	E	F	G
1				Period			
2		1Q X4	2Q X4	3Q X4	4Q X4		X4
3	COST-OF-GOODS SOLD BUDGET						
4	Cost-of-Goods Sold Budget						
5	Exterior	$ 750,000	$ 717,600	$ 708,500	$ 666,000		$ 2,842,100
6	Interior	750,000	728,000	708,500	666,000		2,852,500
7	Assembly labor	500,000	509,600	523,200	499,500		2,032,300
8	Total cost-of-goods sold	$ 2,000,000	$ 1,955,200	$ 1,940,200	$ 1,831,500		$ 7,726,900

Assumptions and Dashboard / Sales and Collection

FIGURE Q6.3 Company JKL's Cost-of-Goods-Sold Budget

Overview worksheet is shown in Figure Q6.5. Company JKL's Headcount Cost worksheet is shown in Figure Q6.6. Figure Q6.7 offers a view of Company JKL's Operating Expenses Budget and Disbursements for Operating Expenses Budget. Figure Q6.8 presents a view of Company JKL's Income Statement (except for the depreciation and interest expense calculations, both of which will be covered later in the questions for this chapter).

Microsoft Excel - FigQ6.4

	A	B	C	D	E	F	G
1				Period			
2		1Q X4	2Q X4	3Q X4	4Q X4		X4
3	INVENTORY BUDGET						
4	Inventory Budget						
5	Desired ending inventory	$ 325,867	$ 431,156	$ 386,650	$ 386,650		$ 386,650
6	+ Cost of goods sold	2,000,000	1,955,200	1,940,200	1,831,500		7,726,900
7	= Total inventory needed	$ 2,325,867	$ 2,386,356	$ 2,326,850	$ 2,218,150		$ 8,113,550
8							
9	PURCHASES BUDGET						
10	Purchases Budget						
11	Total inventory needed	$ 2,325,867	$ 2,386,356	$ 2,326,850	$ 2,218,150		N/A
12	- Beginning inventory	-	325,867	431,156	386,650		-
13	= Purchases	$ 2,325,867	$ 2,060,489	$ 1,895,694	$ 1,831,500		N/A
14							
15	Disbursements for Purchases Budget						
16	Payments of payables	$ 1,550,578	$ 2,217,631	$ 1,924,070	$ 1,810,772		$ 7,503,050
17	Total disbursements for purchases	$ 1,550,578	$ 2,217,631	$ 1,924,070	$ 1,810,772		$ 7,503,050
18							
19	Accounts Payable (A/P) Budget						
20	Beginning A/P balance	$ -	$ 775,289	$ 618,147	$ 589,772		$ -
21	+ Additions to A/P	775,289	618,147	589,772	610,500		2,593,707
22	- Subtractions from A/P	-	775,289	618,147	589,772		1,983,207
23	Ending A/P	$ 775,289	$ 618,147	$ 589,772	$ 610,500		$ 610,500

Sales and Collections / COGS / Inventory and Purch

FIGURE Q6.4 Company JKL's Inventory Budget, Purchases Budget, Disbursements for Purchases Budget, and Accounts Payable Budget

Microsoft Excel - FigQ6.5

File Edit View Insert Format Tools Data Window Help

A	B	C	D	E	F	G
1			Period			
2	1Q X4	2Q X4	3Q X4	4Q X4		X4
3 HEADCOUNT BUDGET						
4 Headcount Budget						
5 Number of employees						
6 Chief Executive Officer	1	1	1	1		
7 Chief Financial Officer	1	1	1	1		
8 VP, Engineering	1	1	1	1		
9 VP, Sales & Marketing	1	1	1	1		
10 VP, Business Development	-	-	1	1		
11 Salesperson	5	5	6	7		
12 Hardware Engineer	1	1	1	1		
13 Controller/Accountant	1	1	2	2		
14 Administrative Assistant	1	1	2	2		
15 Total	12	12	16	17		
16						
17 Periodic base salaries						
18 Chief Executive Officer	$ 47,500	$ 47,500	$ 47,500	$ 47,500		$ 190,000
19 Chief Financial Officer	42,500	42,500	42,500	42,500		170,000
20 VP, Engineering	42,500	42,500	42,500	42,500		170,000
21 VP, Sales & Marketing	36,250	36,250	36,250	36,250		145,000
22 VP, Business Development	32,500	32,500	32,500	32,500		130,000
23 Salesperson	27,500	27,500	27,500	27,500		110,000
24 Hardware Engineer	25,000	25,000	25,000	25,000		100,000
25 Controller/Accountant	12,500	12,500	12,500	12,500		50,000
26 Administrative Assistant	8,125	8,125	8,125	8,125		32,500
27 Total	$ 274,375	$ 274,375	$ 274,375	$ 274,375		$ 1,097,500

Sales and Collections / COGS / Inventory ar

Ready

FIGURE Q6.5   Company JKL's Headcount Overview Worksheet

Microsoft Excel - FigQ6.6

File Edit View Insert Format Tools Data Window Help

A	B	C	D	E	F	G
1			Period			
2	1Q X4	2Q X4	3Q X4	4Q X4		X4
3 HEADCOUNT BUDGET						
4 Headcount Budget						
5 Periodic salary expense (base)						
6 Chief Executive Officer	$ 47,500	$ 47,500	$ 47,500	$ 47,500		$ 190,000
7 Chief Financial Officer	42,500	42,500	42,500	42,500		170,000
8 VP, Engineering	42,500	42,500	42,500	42,500		170,000
9 VP, Sales & Marketing	36,250	36,250	36,250	36,250		145,000
10 VP, Business Development	-	-	32,500	32,500		65,000
11 Salesperson	137,500	137,500	165,000	192,500		632,500
12 Hardware Engineer	25,000	25,000	25,000	25,000		100,000
13 Controller/Accountant	12,500	12,500	25,000	25,000		75,000
14 Administrative Assistant	8,125	8,125	16,250	16,250		48,750
15 Total	$ 351,875	$ 351,875	$ 432,500	$ 460,000		$ 1,596,250
16						
17 Total (with benefits)	$ 399,378	$ 399,378	$ 490,888	$ 522,100		$ 1,811,744

COGS / Inventory and Purchases / Headcour

Ready

FIGURE Q6.6   Company JKL's Headcount Cost Worksheet

	Period				
	1Q X4	2Q X4	3Q X4	4Q X4	X4
OPERATING EXPENSES BUDGET					
Operating Expenses Budget					
Salaries	$ 399,378	$399,378	$490,888	$522,100	$1,811,744
Miscellaneous expenses	82,500	98,280	99,190	101,010	380,980
Research and development	137,500	140,400	141,700	144,300	563,900
Rent	16,500	16,500	16,500	16,500	66,000
Depreciation					-
Total operating expenses	$ 635,878	$654,558	$748,278	$783,910	$2,822,624
DISBURSEMENTS FOR OPERATING EXPENSES BUDGET					
Disbursements for Operating Expenses Budget					
Salaries	$ 399,378	$399,378	$490,888	$522,100	$1,811,744
Miscellaneous expenses	82,500	98,280	99,190	101,010	380,980
Research and development	137,500	140,400	141,700	144,300	563,900
Rent	16,500	16,500	16,500	16,500	66,000
Depreciation	-	-	-	-	-
Total disbursements for operating expenses	$ 635,878	$654,558	$748,278	$783,910	$2,822,624

FIGURE Q6.7 Company JKL's Operatiang Expenses Budget and Disbursements for Operating Expenses Budget

	Period				
	1Q X4	2Q X4	3Q X4	4Q X4	X4
Sales	$2,750,000	$2,808,000	$2,834,000	$2,886,000	$11,278,000
Cost of goods sold	2,000,000	1,955,200	1,940,200	1,831,500	7,726,900
Gross profit	$ 750,000	$ 852,800	$ 893,800	$1,054,500	$ 3,551,100
Salaries	$ 399,378	$ 399,378	$ 490,888	$ 522,100	$ 1,811,744
Miscellaneous expenses	82,500	98,280	99,190	101,010	380,980
Research and development	137,500	140,400	141,700	144,300	563,900
Rent	16,500	16,500	16,500	16,500	66,000
Depreciation	575	983	1,308	1,608	4,475
Income from operations	$ 114,122	$ 198,242	$ 145,523	$ 270,590	$ 728,476
Interest expense	$ -	$ -	$ 500	$ -	$ 500
Taxable income	$ 114,122	$ 198,242	$ 145,023	$ 270,590	$ 727,976
Tax expense	$ 37,090	$ 65,420	$ 47,132	$ 89,295	$ 238,936
Net income	$ 77,032	$ 132,822	$ 97,890	$ 181,295	$ 489,040

FIGURE Q6.8 Company JKL's Income Statement

1. Given the information regarding Company JKL, build the Capital Expenditures Budget for Company JKL. Note that this Capital Budget should include projections for three separate items: equipment, furniture, and fixtures.

2. Based on your work in Question 1 and the information presented, build a Disbursements for Capital Expenditures for Company JKL. Use the "percentage paid for a given period" approach as described in this chapter to project the disbursements associated with capital expenditures. The relevant assumptions related to these percentage assumptions are shown in Company JKL's Assumptions and Dashboard worksheet (Figure Q6.1).

3. Build a Depreciation Budget for Company JKL based on the information presented and your work in Questions 1 and 2. Use the same approach outlined in this chapter (using depreciation multipliers) to build the Depreciation Budget for Company JKL. Include a calculation of Company JKL's fixed assets, net of depreciation for each accounting period (quarter) in the Depreciation Budget.

4. Based on your work in Questions 1–3 and the information presented, build the first section of Company JKL's Cash Budget, which should include the beginning cash balance and cash collections for each accounting period (quarter) for Company JKL.

5. Build an updated Cash Budget for Company JKL in which the cash disbursements for each accounting period (quarter) and the excess or deficiency of total cash available compared to the total cash required before any financing takes place are calculated for Company JKL.

6. Build an updated Cash Budget for Company JKL in which the projections regarding equity investments, borrowings, repayment of borrowings, and interest expenses are included. Be sure to calculate the ending cash balance for Company JKL for each accounting period (quarter) as well.

7. Complete Company JKL's Income Statement by adding in the depreciation and interest expense projections for each accounting period (quarter).

CHAPTER 7

Financial Budget—Balance Sheet

This chapter covers the construction of Napavale's Balance Sheet. Building the Balance Sheet, which provides a view of Napavale's sources and uses of funds, represents the final step in the Master Budget framework. Figure 7.1 highlights the Budgeted Balance Sheet and its relative position in the Master Budget hierarchy.

STEP 9: BUDGETED BALANCE SHEET

The budgeted Balance Sheet incorporates components from several different schedules, including the Cash Budget, Accounts Receivable Budget, Inventory Budget, and Income Statement, among several others. While it is not a specific line item or account on the Balance Sheet, I also introduce and discuss the concept of "net working capital" later in this chapter. Net working capital calculations flow directly into the calculation of free cash flows, discussed in Chapter 9.

It is worth noting that a balance sheet offers a tangible representation of the central accounting identity: Assets = Liabilities + Owners' Equity. This equation will always balance; if it does not, there is an error in a calculation underlying the Balance Sheet. In general terms, there are two potential sources of funds for a business: Liabilities or Owners' Equity. Also in general terms, there is one use of funds for a business: Assets. While this book is not intended to cover (and does not cover) accounting concepts, I will try to point out major concepts at the appropriate points, such as the central accounting identity mentioned above.

As in previous chapters, I make frequent references to alternative views of worksheets in which the values and formulas contained within each cell are exposed for viewing and to the names of the input and output cells across various worksheets. In so doing, it should be easier to follow the extensive references and linkages between worksheets.

The first step in building the Balance Sheet is to identify and paste the

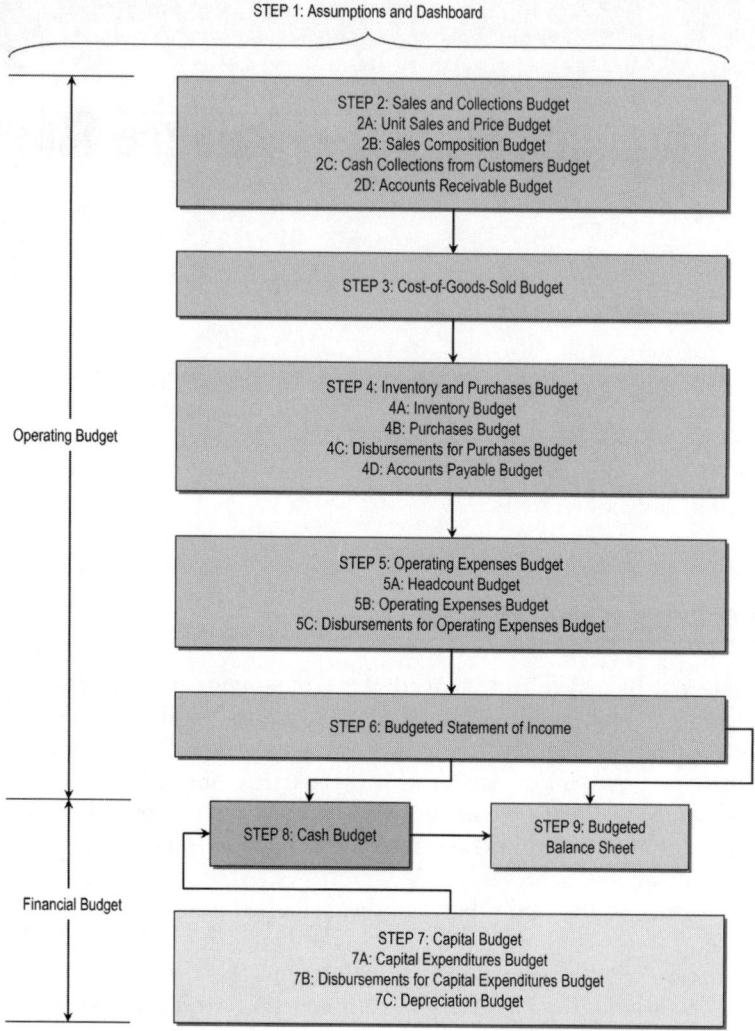

STEP 1: Assumptions and Dashboard

STEP 2: Sales and Collections Budget
2A: Unit Sales and Price Budget
2B: Sales Composition Budget
2C: Cash Collections from Customers Budget
2D: Accounts Receivable Budget

STEP 3: Cost-of-Goods-Sold Budget

STEP 4: Inventory and Purchases Budget
4A: Inventory Budget
4B: Purchases Budget
4C: Disbursements for Purchases Budget
4D: Accounts Payable Budget

STEP 5: Operating Expenses Budget
5A: Headcount Budget
5B: Operating Expenses Budget
5C: Disbursements for Operating Expenses Budget

STEP 6: Budgeted Statement of Income

Operating Budget

STEP 8: Cash Budget

STEP 9: Budgeted Balance Sheet

Financial Budget

STEP 7: Capital Budget
7A: Capital Expenditures Budget
7B: Disbursements for Capital Expenditures Budget
7C: Depreciation Budget

FIGURE 7.1   Budgeted Balance Sheet and the Master Budget

elements of the Asset side (also called the "left-hand side," as Assets are of-ten shown to the left of the Liabilities and Owners' Equity accounts of a balance sheet) of the Balance Sheet into a worksheet. In Napavale's case, I am including the following accounts in Assets: cash, accounts receivable, inventory, and fixed Assets, net. Depending on the nature of your business, the components of your Assets (and Liabilities and Owners' Equity for that

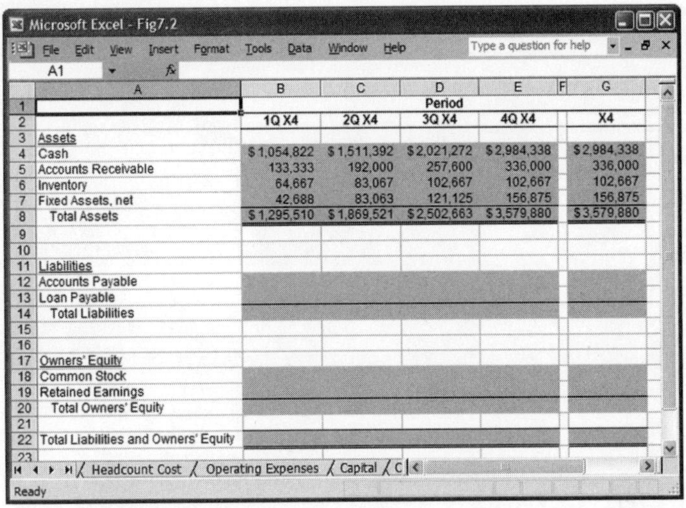

FIGURE 7.2 Asset Components of the Balance Sheet

matter) may vary. Figure 7.2 presents the Asset components of Napavale's Balance Sheet.

Figure 7.3 offers an alternative view of the asset components of the Balance Sheet in which the values and formulas in the worksheet cells are exposed and visible. I have calculated a total for the Asset components of the Balance Sheet in Figures 7.2 and 7.3. The names of the input and output cells underlying the Balance Sheet are shown in Figure 7.4.

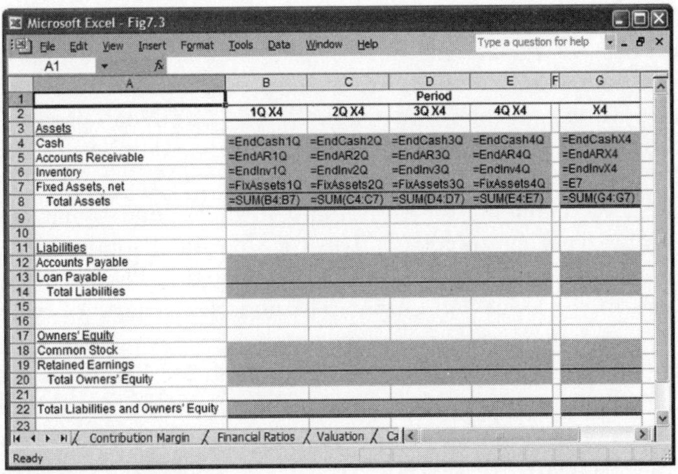

FIGURE 7.3 Alternative View of the Asset Components of the Balance Sheet

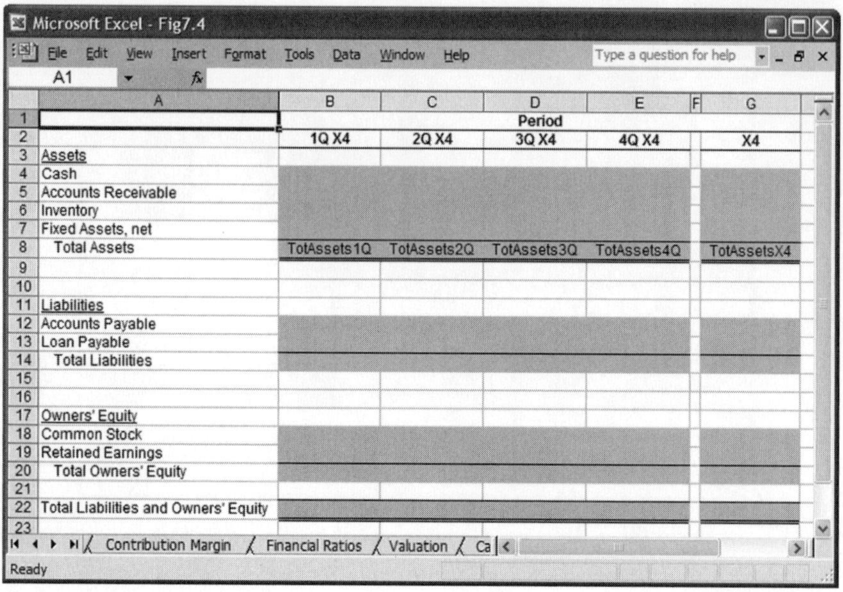

FIGURE 7.4   Names of the Input and Output Cells in the Balance Sheet

Note the various sources associated with each component of the Assets identified in Napavale's Balance Sheet: cash (Cash Budget), accounts receivable (Accounts Receivable Budget), inventory (Inventory Budget), and fixed Assets, net (Depreciation Budget).

Identifying and pasting the elements of the Liabilities section of the Balance Sheet represents the next step in building Napavale's Balance Sheet. The following Liabilities are included in Napavale's Balance Sheet: accounts payable, payables from Capital Budget, and loan payable. Figure 7.5 presents a view of the Balance Sheet with the addition of the components of the Liabilities section.

Figure 7.6 highlights the values and formulas underlying the worksheet cells by exposing the cell contents for viewing. A total for the Liabilities components of the Balance Sheet is calculated in Figures 7.5 and 7.6. The names of the input and output cells underlying the evolving Balance Sheet are shown in Figure 7.7.

Note the sources of each of the accounts in the Liabilities section of Napavale's Balance Sheet: accounts payable (Accounts Payable Budget), payables from capital budget (Capital Budget), and loan payable (Assumptions and Dashboard Worksheet).

	A	B	C	D	E	F	G
1				Period			
2		1Q X4	2Q X4	3Q X4	4Q X4		X4
3	Assets						
4	Cash	$1,054,822	$1,511,392	$2,021,272	$2,984,338		$2,984,338
5	Accounts Receivable	133,333	192,000	257,600	336,000		336,000
6	Inventory	64,667	83,067	102,667	102,667		102,667
7	Fixed Assets, net	42,688	83,063	121,125	156,875		156,875
8	Total Assets	$1,295,510	$1,869,521	$2,502,663	$3,579,880		$3,579,880
9							
10							
11	Liabilities						
12	Accounts Payable	$ 88,222	$ 103,133	$ 131,133	$ 154,000		$ 154,000
13	Payables from Capital Budget	-	-	-	-		-
14	Loan Payable	-	50,000	-	-		-
15	Total Liabilities	$ 88,222	$ 153,133	$ 131,133	$ 154,000		$ 154,000
16							
17							
18	Owners' Equity						
19	Common Stock						
20	Retained Earnings						
21	Total Owners' Equity						
22							
23	Total Liabilities and Owners' Equity						
24							

Sheet tabs: Headcount Cost / Operating Expenses / Capital / C

FIGURE 7.5 Liabilitites Components of the Balance Sheet

	A	B	C	D	E	F	G
1				Period			
2		1Q X4	2Q X4	3Q X4	4Q X4		X4
3	Assets						
4	Cash	=EndCash1Q	=EndCash2Q	=EndCash3Q	=EndCash4Q		=EndCashX4
5	Accounts Receivable	=EndAR1Q	=EndAR2Q	=EndAR3Q	=EndAR4Q		=EndARX4
6	Inventory	=EndInv1Q	=EndInv2Q	=EndInv3Q	=EndInv4Q		=EndInvX4
7	Fixed Assets, net	=FixAssets1Q	=FixAssets2Q	=FixAssets3Q	=FixAssets4Q		=E7
8	Total Assets	=SUM(B4:B7)	=SUM(C4:C7)	=SUM(D4:D7)	=SUM(E4:E7)		=SUM(G4:G7)
9							
10							
11	Liabilities						
12	Accounts Payable	=EndAP1Q	=EndAP2Q	=EndAP3Q	=EndAP4Q		=EndAPX4
13	Payables from Capital Budget	=PACAPEX1Q	=PACAPEX2Q	=PACAPEX3Q	=PACAPEX4Q		=PayCapB4Q
14	Loan Payable	=LoanVal1Q	=LoanVal2Q	=LoanVal3Q	=LoanVal4Q		=E14
15	Total Liabilities	=SUM(B12:B14)	=SUM(C12:C14)	=SUM(D12:D14)	=SUM(E12:E14)		=SUM(G12:G14)
16							
17							
18	Owners' Equity						
19	Common Stock						
20	Retained Earnings						
21	Total Owners' Equity						
22							
23	Total Liabilities and Owners' Equity						
24							

Sheet tabs: Contribution Margin / Financial Ratios / Valuation / Capitaliza

FIGURE 7.6 Alternative View of the Liabilities Components of the Balance Sheet

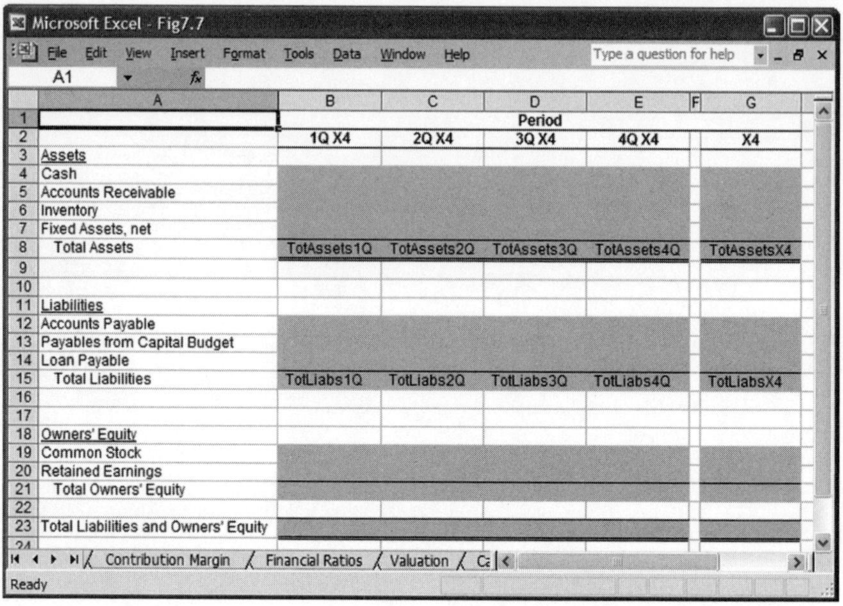

FIGURE 7.7   Names of the Input and Output Cells in the Balance Sheet

The final step in building Napavale's Balance Sheet is to identify and paste the elements of the Owners' Equity section of the Balance Sheet into the Balance Sheet worksheet. I have included a common stock and a retained earnings account in the Owners' Equity section of Napavale's Balance Sheet. The common stock account represents equity investments into Napavale and the retained earnings account represents, broadly speaking, a "running total" of Napavale's net income over time.

Figure 7.8 shows Napavale's Balance Sheet with the inclusion of the Owners' Equity section. Calculations for total Owners' Equity as well as a total for Liabilities + Owners' Equity are included in Figure 7.8 as well. Remember that in a "balanced" Balance Sheet, Assets = Liabilities + Owners' Equity. An alternative view of Napavale's completed Balance Sheet, in which the values and formulas contained within the worksheet cells are exposed for viewing, is presented in Figure 7.9. Figure 7.10 presents a view of the names of the input and output cells underlying the evolving Balance Sheet for Napavale.

Now that the Balance Sheet is completed, I will calculate an item known as "net working capital." Net working capital, which is defined as: current Assets – current Liabilities, represents a company's surplus

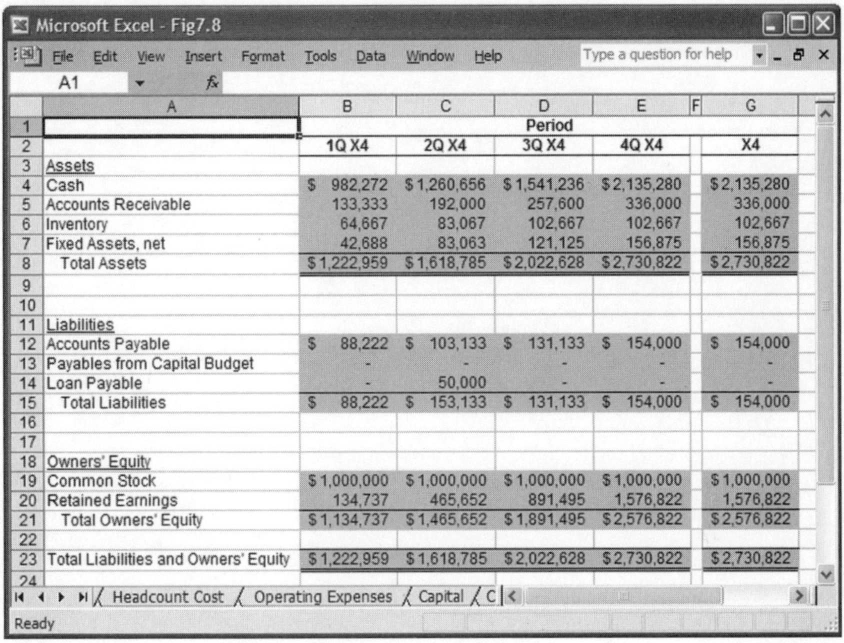

	Period				
	1Q X4	2Q X4	3Q X4	4Q X4	X4
Assets					
Cash	$ 982,272	$ 1,260,656	$ 1,541,236	$ 2,135,280	$ 2,135,280
Accounts Receivable	133,333	192,000	257,600	336,000	336,000
Inventory	64,667	83,067	102,667	102,667	102,667
Fixed Assets, net	42,688	83,063	121,125	156,875	156,875
Total Assets	$ 1,222,959	$ 1,618,785	$ 2,022,628	$ 2,730,822	$ 2,730,822
Liabilities					
Accounts Payable	$ 88,222	$ 103,133	$ 131,133	$ 154,000	$ 154,000
Payables from Capital Budget	-	-	-	-	-
Loan Payable	-	50,000	-	-	-
Total Liabilities	$ 88,222	$ 153,133	$ 131,133	$ 154,000	$ 154,000
Owners' Equity					
Common Stock	$ 1,000,000	$ 1,000,000	$ 1,000,000	$ 1,000,000	$ 1,000,000
Retained Earnings	134,737	465,652	891,495	1,576,822	1,576,822
Total Owners' Equity	$ 1,134,737	$ 1,465,652	$ 1,891,495	$ 2,576,822	$ 2,576,822
Total Liabilities and Owners' Equity	$ 1,222,959	$ 1,618,785	$ 2,022,628	$ 2,730,822	$ 2,730,822

FIGURE 7.8 Balance Sheet

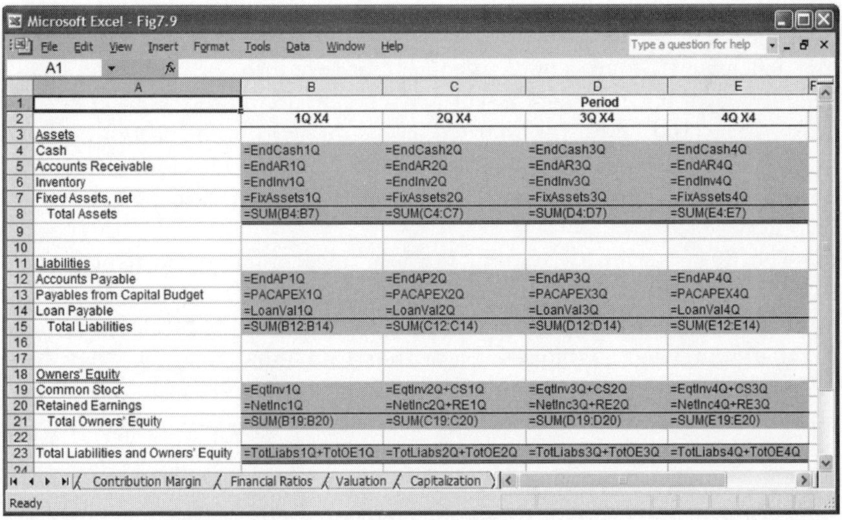

	Period			
	1Q X4	2Q X4	3Q X4	4Q X4
Assets				
Cash	=EndCash1Q	=EndCash2Q	=EndCash3Q	=EndCash4Q
Accounts Receivable	=EndAR1Q	=EndAR2Q	=EndAR3Q	=EndAR4Q
Inventory	=EndInv1Q	=EndInv2Q	=EndInv3Q	=EndInv4Q
Fixed Assets, net	=FixAssets1Q	=FixAssets2Q	=FixAssets3Q	=FixAssets4Q
Total Assets	=SUM(B4:B7)	=SUM(C4:C7)	=SUM(D4:D7)	=SUM(E4:E7)
Liabilities				
Accounts Payable	=EndAP1Q	=EndAP2Q	=EndAP3Q	=EndAP4Q
Payables from Capital Budget	=PACAPEX1Q	=PACAPEX2Q	=PACAPEX3Q	=PACAPEX4Q
Loan Payable	=LoanVal1Q	=LoanVal2Q	=LoanVal3Q	=LoanVal4Q
Total Liabilities	=SUM(B12:B14)	=SUM(C12:C14)	=SUM(D12:D14)	=SUM(E12:E14)
Owners' Equity				
Common Stock	=EqtInv1Q	=EqtInv2Q+CS1Q	=EqtInv3Q+CS2Q	=EqtInv4Q+CS3Q
Retained Earnings	=NetInc1Q	=NetInc2Q+RE1Q	=NetInc3Q+RE2Q	=NetInc4Q+RE3Q
Total Owners' Equity	=SUM(B19:B20)	=SUM(C19:C20)	=SUM(D19:D20)	=SUM(E19:E20)
Total Liabilities and Owners' Equity	=TotLiabs1Q+TotOE1Q	=TotLiabs2Q+TotOE2Q	=TotLiabs3Q+TotOE3Q	=TotLiabs4Q+TotOE4Q

FIGURE 7.9 Alternative View of the Balance Sheet

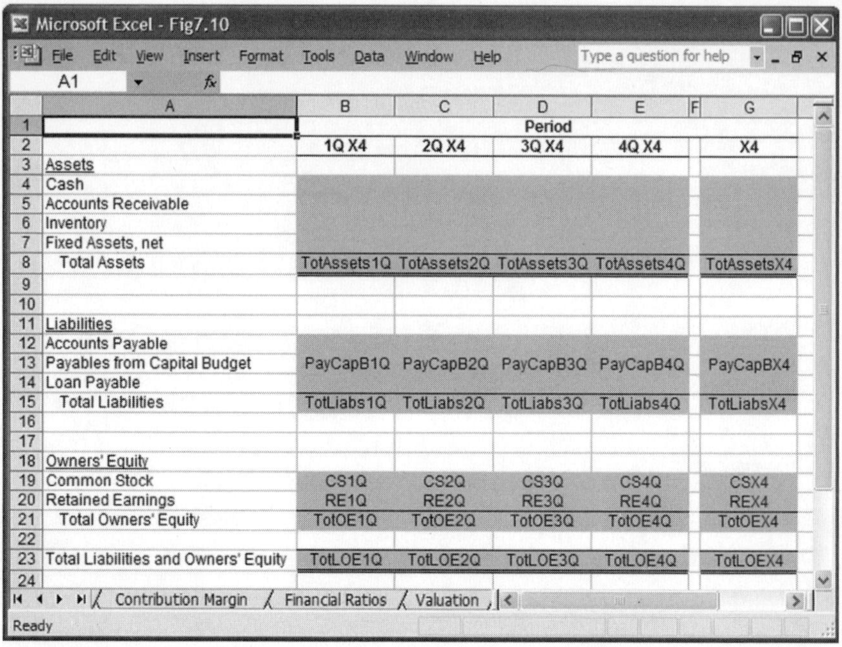

FIGURE 7.10   Names of the Input and Output Cells in the Balance Sheet

(or deficiency) of current Assets as compared to current Liabilities. Broadly speaking, current Assets and current Liabilities are defined as those Assets and Liabilities that will come due within the accounting period in which they are classified as current. Net working capital is an important metric that will come into play in Chapter 9 when I cover free cash flows.

The first step in calculating net working capital is to identify Napavale's current Assets and current Liabilities. For Napavale, I am defining accounts receivable and inventory as current Assets and accounts payable as current Liabilities. Note that I am not including "payables from capital budget" as a component of current Liabilities. My assumption is that any payables associated with capital purchases would represent longer-term liabilities, which typically are not included in net working capital calculations.

Different users often include different accounts in the calculation of net working capital. Many people often include the cash account in current Assets; I am not doing so here as Napavale is a recently formed business and its cash balance is a direct result of the formation capital that was invested into the business. For more stable and established businesses, including cash in a calculation of net working capital may indeed make sense.

Figure 7.11 presents a worksheet in which the components of net working capital are identified and net working capital itself is calculated as current Assets – current Liabilities. Note that net working capital can be either a positive or a negative number.

Figure 7.12 offers an alternative view of the worksheet presented in Figure 7.11 by exposing the values and formulas underlying the worksheet cells. The names of the input and output cells underlying the components of net working capital are presented in Figure 7.13.

As will be explained in Chapter 9 in the coverage of free cash flows,

Microsoft Excel - Fig7.11						
File Edit View Insert Format Tools Data Window Help		Type a question for help				
A1	fx					
A	B	C	D	E	F	G
1		Period				
2	1Q X4	2Q X4	3Q X4	4Q X4		X4
3 Assets						
4 Cash	$ 982,272	$1,260,656	$1,541,236	$2,135,280		$2,135,280
5 Accounts Receivable	133,333	192,000	257,600	336,000		336,000
6 Inventory	64,667	83,067	102,667	102,667		102,667
7 Fixed Assets, net	42,688	83,063	121,125	156,875		156,875
8 Total Assets	$1,222,959	$1,618,785	$2,022,628	$2,730,822		$2,730,822
9						
10						
11 Liabilities						
12 Accounts Payable	$ 88,222	$ 103,133	$ 131,133	$ 154,000		$ 154,000
13 Payables from Capital Budget	-	-	-	-		-
14 Loan Payable	-	50,000	-	-		-
15 Total Liabilities	$ 88,222	$ 153,133	$ 131,133	$ 154,000		$ 154,000
16						
17						
18 Owners' Equity						
19 Common Stock	$1,000,000	$1,000,000	$1,000,000	$1,000,000		$1,000,000
20 Retained Earnings	134,737	465,652	891,495	1,576,822		1,576,822
21 Total Owners' Equity	$1,134,737	$1,465,652	$1,891,495	$2,576,822		$2,576,822
22						
23 Total Liabilities and Owners' Equity	$1,222,959	$1,618,785	$2,022,628	$2,730,822		$2,730,822
24						
25						
26						
27 Net Working Capital						
28 Current assets	$ 198,000	$ 275,067	$ 360,267	$ 438,667		N/A
29 - Current liabilities	88,222	103,133	131,133	154,000		N/A
30 = Net working capital	$ 109,778	$ 171,933	$ 229,133	$ 284,667		N/A

Headcount Cost / Operating Expenses / Capital /

Ready

FIGURE 7.11 Calculation of Net Working Capital

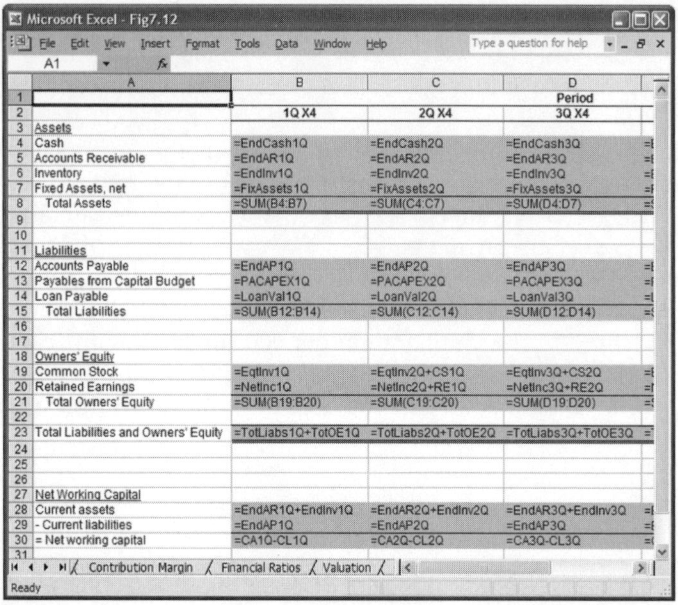

	A	B	C	D
1				Period
2		1Q X4	2Q X4	3Q X4
3	Assets			
4	Cash	=EndCash1Q	=EndCash2Q	=EndCash3Q
5	Accounts Receivable	=EndAR1Q	=EndAR2Q	=EndAR3Q
6	Inventory	=EndInv1Q	=EndInv2Q	=EndInv3Q
7	Fixed Assets, net	=FixAssets1Q	=FixAssets2Q	=FixAssets3Q
8	Total Assets	=SUM(B4:B7)	=SUM(C4:C7)	=SUM(D4:D7)
9				
10				
11	Liabilities			
12	Accounts Payable	=EndAP1Q	=EndAP2Q	=EndAP3Q
13	Payables from Capital Budget	=PACAPEX1Q	=PACAPEX2Q	=PACAPEX3Q
14	Loan Payable	=LoanVal1Q	=LoanVal2Q	=LoanVal3Q
15	Total Liabilities	=SUM(B12:B14)	=SUM(C12:C14)	=SUM(D12:D14)
16				
17				
18	Owners' Equity			
19	Common Stock	=EqtInv1Q	=EqtInv2Q+CS1Q	=EqtInv3Q+CS2Q
20	Retained Earnings	=NetInc1Q	=NetInc2Q+RE1Q	=NetInc3Q+RE2Q
21	Total Owners' Equity	=SUM(B19:B20)	=SUM(C19:C20)	=SUM(D19:D20)
22				
23	Total Liabilities and Owners' Equity	=TotLiabs1Q+TotOE1Q	=TotLiabs2Q+TotOE2Q	=TotLiabs3Q+TotOE3Q
24				
25				
26				
27	Net Working Capital			
28	Current assets	=EndAR1Q+EndInv1Q	=EndAR2Q+EndInv2Q	=EndAR3Q+EndInv3Q
29	- Current liabilities	=EndAP1Q	=EndAP2Q	=EndAP3Q
30	= Net working capital	=CA1Q-CL1Q	=CA2Q-CL2Q	=CA3Q-CL3Q

FIGURE 7.12 Alternative View of the Calculation of Net Working Capital

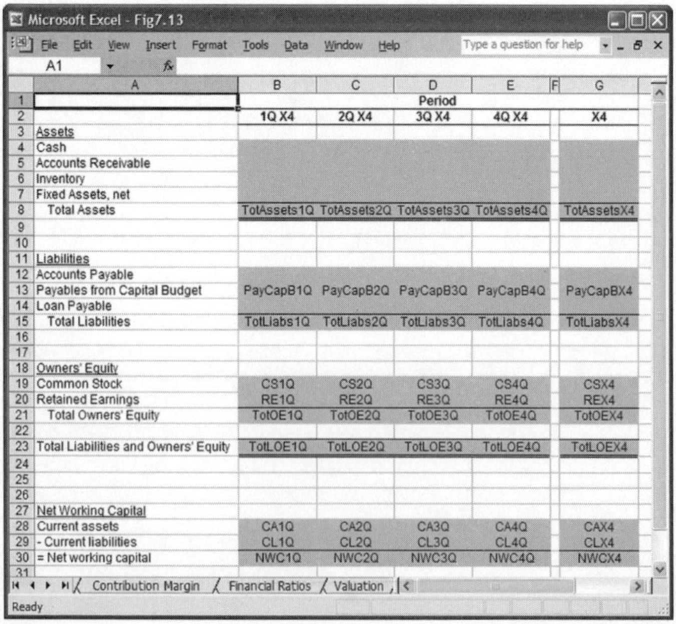

	A	B	C	D	E	F	G
1				Period			
2		1Q X4	2Q X4	3Q X4	4Q X4		X4
3	Assets						
4	Cash						
5	Accounts Receivable						
6	Inventory						
7	Fixed Assets, net						
8	Total Assets	TotAssets1Q	TotAssets2Q	TotAssets3Q	TotAssets4Q		TotAssetsX4
9							
10							
11	Liabilities						
12	Accounts Payable						
13	Payables from Capital Budget	PayCapB1Q	PayCapB2Q	PayCapB3Q	PayCapB4Q		PayCapBX4
14	Loan Payable						
15	Total Liabilities	TotLiabs1Q	TotLiabs2Q	TotLiabs3Q	TotLiabs4Q		TotLiabsX4
16							
17							
18	Owners' Equity						
19	Common Stock	CS1Q	CS2Q	CS3Q	CS4Q		CSX4
20	Retained Earnings	RE1Q	RE2Q	RE3Q	RE4Q		REX4
21	Total Owners' Equity	TotOE1Q	TotOE2Q	TotOE3Q	TotOE4Q		TotOEX4
22							
23	Total Liabilities and Owners' Equity	TotLOE1Q	TotLOE2Q	TotLOE3Q	TotLOE4Q		TotLOEX4
24							
25							
26							
27	Net Working Capital						
28	Current assets	CA1Q	CA2Q	CA3Q	CA4Q		CAX4
29	- Current liabilities	CL1Q	CL2Q	CL3Q	CL4Q		CLX4
30	= Net working capital	NWC1Q	NWC2Q	NWC3Q	NWC4Q		NWCX4

FIGURE 7.13 Names of the Input and Output Cells Underlying the Calculation of Net Working Capital

it is the change in net working capital across accounting periods that is of particular interest. As such, the change in net working capital across accounting periods is presented in Figure 7.14. An alternative view of the change in net working capital calculation, in which the values and formulas underlying the worksheet cells are exposed, is presented in Figure 7.15. Figure 7.16 offers a view of the names of the input and output cells underlying the calculation of the change in net working capital.

	1Q X4	2Q X4	3Q X4	4Q X4	X4
Assets					
Cash	$ 982,272	$1,260,656	$1,541,236	$2,135,280	$2,135,280
Accounts Receivable	133,333	192,000	257,600	336,000	336,000
Inventory	64,667	83,067	102,667	102,667	102,667
Fixed Assets, net	42,688	83,063	121,125	156,875	156,875
Total Assets	$ 1,222,959	$1,618,785	$2,022,628	$2,730,822	$2,730,822
Liabilities					
Accounts Payable	$ 88,222	$ 103,133	$ 131,133	$ 154,000	$ 154,000
Payables from Capital Budget	-	-	-	-	-
Loan Payable	-	50,000	-	-	-
Total Liabilities	$ 88,222	$ 153,133	$ 131,133	$ 154,000	$ 154,000
Owners' Equity					
Common Stock	$ 1,000,000	$1,000,000	$1,000,000	$1,000,000	$1,000,000
Retained Earnings	134,737	465,652	891,495	1,576,822	1,576,822
Total Owners' Equity	$ 1,134,737	$1,465,652	$1,891,495	$2,576,822	$2,576,822
Total Liabilities and Owners' Equity	$ 1,222,959	$1,618,785	$2,022,628	$2,730,822	$2,730,822
Net Working Capital (NWC)					
Current assets	$ 198,000	$ 275,067	$ 360,267	$ 438,667	N/A
- Current liabilities	88,222	103,133	131,133	154,000	N/A
= Net working capital	$ 109,778	$ 171,933	$ 229,133	$ 284,667	N/A
Beginning NWC	$ -	$ 109,778	$ 171,933	$ 229,133	N/A
- Ending NWC	109,778	171,933	229,133	284,667	N/A
= Change in NWC	$ (109,778)	$ (62,156)	$ (57,200)	$ (55,533)	N/A

FIGURE 7.14 Calculation of the Change in Net Working Capital

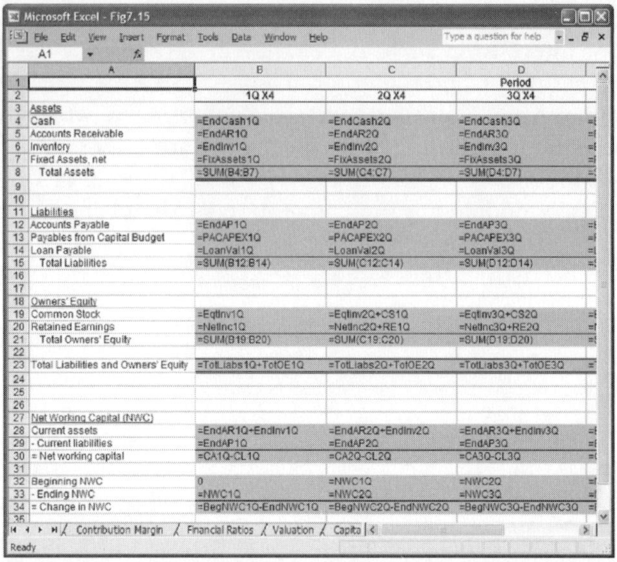

	A	B	C	D
1				Period
2		1Q X4	2Q X4	3Q X4
3	Assets			
4	Cash	=EndCash1Q	=EndCash2Q	=EndCash3Q
5	Accounts Receivable	=EndAR1Q	=EndAR2Q	=EndAR3Q
6	Inventory	=EndInv1Q	=EndInv2Q	=EndInv3Q
7	Fixed Assets, net	=FixAssets1Q	=FixAssets2Q	=FixAssets3Q
8	Total Assets	=SUM(B4:B7)	=SUM(C4:C7)	=SUM(D4:D7)
9				
10				
11	Liabilities			
12	Accounts Payable	=EndAP1Q	=EndAP2Q	=EndAP3Q
13	Payables from Capital Budget	=PACAPEX1Q	=PACAPEX2Q	=PACAPEX3Q
14	Loan Payable	=LoanVal1Q	=LoanVal2Q	=LoanVal3Q
15	Total Liabilities	=SUM(B12:B14)	=SUM(C12:C14)	=SUM(D12:D14)
16				
17				
18	Owners' Equity			
19	Common Stock	=EqtInv1Q	=EqtInv2Q+CS1Q	=EqtInv3Q+CS2Q
20	Retained Earnings	=NetInc1Q	=NetInc2Q+RE1Q	=NetInc3Q+RE2Q
21	Total Owners' Equity	=SUM(B19:B20)	=SUM(C19:C20)	=SUM(D19:D20)
22				
23	Total Liabilities and Owners' Equity	=TotLiabs1Q+TotOE1Q	=TotLiabs2Q+TotOE2Q	=TotLiabs3Q+TotOE3Q
24				
25				
26				
27	Net Working Capital (NWC)			
28	Current assets	=EndAR1Q+EndInv1Q	=EndAR2Q+EndInv2Q	=EndAR3Q+EndInv3Q
29	- Current liabilities	=EndAP1Q	=EndAP2Q	=EndAP3Q
30	= Net working capital	=CA1Q-CL1Q	=CA2Q-CL2Q	=CA3Q-CL3Q
31				
32	Beginning NWC	0	=NWC1Q	=NWC2Q
33	- Ending NWC	=NWC1Q	=NWC2Q	=NWC3Q
34	= Change in NWC	=BegNWC1Q-EndNWC1Q	=BegNWC2Q-EndNWC2Q	=BegNWC3Q-EndNWC3Q

FIGURE 7.15 Alternative View of the Calculation of the Change in Net Working Capital

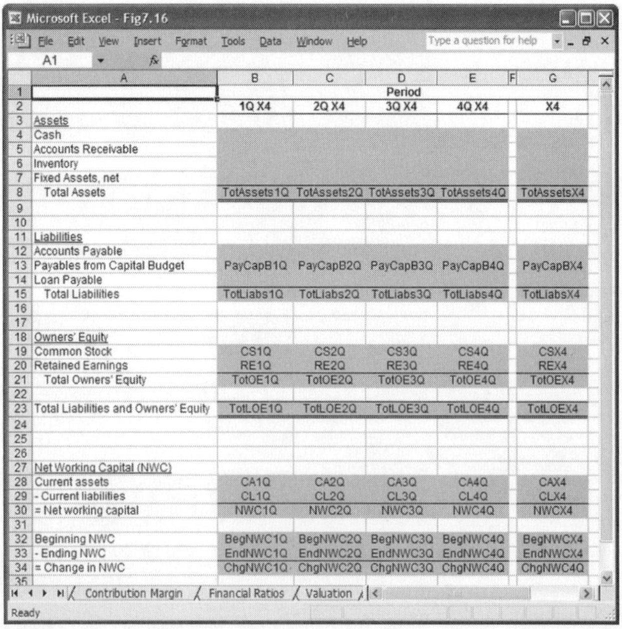

	A	B	C	D	E	F	G
1				Period			
2		1Q X4	2Q X4	3Q X4	4Q X4		X4
3	Assets						
4	Cash						
5	Accounts Receivable						
6	Inventory						
7	Fixed Assets, net						
8	Total Assets	TotAssets1Q	TotAssets2Q	TotAssets3Q	TotAssets4Q		TotAssetsX4
9							
10							
11	Liabilities						
12	Accounts Payable						
13	Payables from Capital Budget	PayCapB1Q	PayCapB2Q	PayCapB3Q	PayCapB4Q		PayCapBX4
14	Loan Payable						
15	Total Liabilities	TotLiabs1Q	TotLiabs2Q	TotLiabs3Q	TotLiabs4Q		TotLiabsX4
16							
17							
18	Owners' Equity						
19	Common Stock	CS1Q	CS2Q	CS3Q	CS4Q		CSX4
20	Retained Earnings	RE1Q	RE2Q	RE3Q	RE4Q		REX4
21	Total Owners' Equity	TotOE1Q	TotOE2Q	TotOE3Q	TotOE4Q		TotOEX4
22							
23	Total Liabilities and Owners' Equity	TotLOE1Q	TotLOE2Q	TotLOE3Q	TotLOE4Q		TotLOEX4
24							
25							
26							
27	Net Working Capital (NWC)						
28	Current assets	CA1Q	CA2Q	CA3Q	CA4Q		CAX4
29	- Current liabilities	CL1Q	CL2Q	CL3Q	CL4Q		CLX4
30	= Net working capital	NWC1Q	NWC2Q	NWC3Q	NWC4Q		NWCX4
31							
32	Beginning NWC	BegNWC1Q	BegNWC2Q	BegNWC3Q	BegNWC4Q		BegNWCX4
33	- Ending NWC	EndNWC1Q	EndNWC2Q	EndNWC3Q	EndNWC4Q		EndNWCX4
34	= Change in NWC	ChgNWC1Q	ChgNWC2Q	ChgNWC3Q	ChgNWC4Q		ChgNWC4Q

FIGURE 7.16 Names of the Input and Output Cells Underlying the Calculation of the Change in Net Working Capital

QUESTIONS

Each of the questions for this chapter relates to a hypothetical company named Company MNO. Company MNO sells coffee machines to businesses. As such, Company MNO is a product-oriented (as opposed to a service-oriented) business. The questions for this chapter will address fiscal year X4 on a quarterly basis (four specific quarters, 1Q–4Q for year X4).

The following questions will test your knowledge of the material covered in this chapter in an applied manner—specifically, you will be asked to build the schedules discussed in this chapter for Company MNO.

To prepare you for this chapter's questions, several figures provide background information related to Company MNO's operations. Figure Q7.1 offers a view of a portion of Company MNO's Assumptions and Dashboard worksheet. Note that there are three cost-of-goods-sold

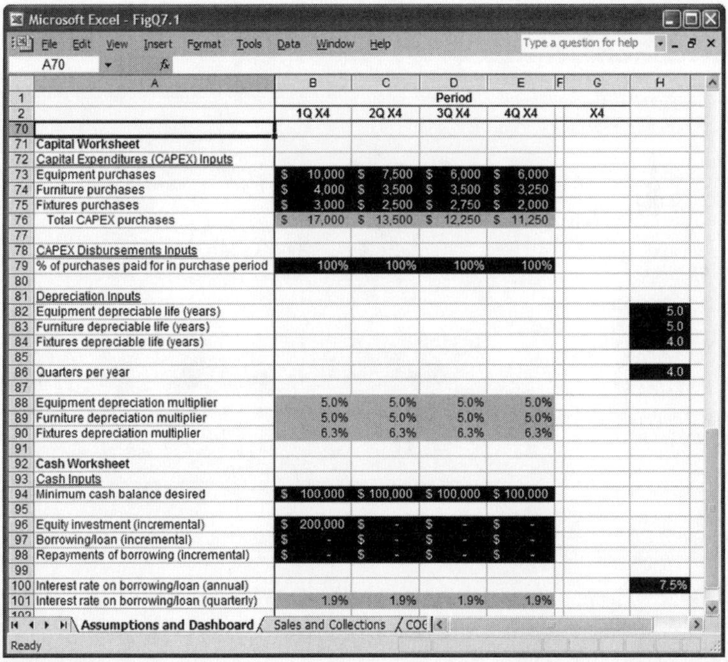

	A	B	C	D	E	F	G	H
1				Period				
2		1Q X4	2Q X4	3Q X4	4Q X4		X4	
70								
71	**Capital Worksheet**							
72	Capital Expenditures (CAPEX) Inputs							
73	Equipment purchases	$ 10,000	$ 7,500	$ 6,000	$ 6,000			
74	Furniture purchases	$ 4,000	$ 3,500	$ 3,500	$ 3,250			
75	Fixtures purchases	$ 3,000	$ 2,500	$ 2,750	$ 2,000			
76	Total CAPEX purchases	$ 17,000	$ 13,500	$ 12,250	$ 11,250			
77								
78	CAPEX Disbursements Inputs							
79	% of purchases paid for in purchase period	100%	100%	100%	100%			
80								
81	Depreciation Inputs							
82	Equipment depreciable life (years)							5.0
83	Furniture depreciable life (years)							5.0
84	Fixtures depreciable life (years)							4.0
85								
86	Quarters per year							4.0
87								
88	Equipment depreciation multiplier	5.0%	5.0%	5.0%	5.0%			
89	Furniture depreciation multiplier	5.0%	5.0%	5.0%	5.0%			
90	Fixtures depreciation multiplier	6.3%	6.3%	6.3%	6.3%			
91								
92	**Cash Worksheet**							
93	Cash Inputs							
94	Minimum cash balance desired	$ 100,000	$ 100,000	$ 100,000	$ 100,000			
95								
96	Equity investment (incremental)	$ 200,000	$ -	$ -	$ -			
97	Borrowing/loan (incremental)	$ -	$ -	$ -	$ -			
98	Repayments of borrowing (incremental)	$ -	$ -	$ -	$ -			
99								
100	Interest rate on borrowing/loan (annual)							7.5%
101	Interest rate on borrowing/loan (quarterly)	1.9%	1.9%	1.9%	1.9%			

FIGURE Q7.1 Company MNO's Assumptions and Dashboard Worksheet components for Company MNO's coffee machines: (1) exterior, (2) interior, and (3) assembly and labor.

Figure Q7.2 presents a view of Company MNO's Unit Sales and Price Budget, Sales Composition Budget, Cash Collections from Customers Budget, and Accounts Receivable Budget. Company MNO's Cost-of-Goods-Sold Budget is shown in Figure Q7.3. Figure Q7.4 presents a view of Company MNO's Inventory Budget, Purchases Budget, Disbursements for Purchases Budget, and Accounts Payable Budget. Company MNO's Headcount Overview worksheet is shown in Figure Q7.5. Company MNO's Headcount Cost worksheet is shown in Figure Q7.6. Figure Q7.7 offers a view of Company MNO's Operating Expenses Budget and Disbursements for Operating Expenses Budget. Figure Q7.8 presents a view of Company MNO's Income Statement. Company MNO's Capital Expenditures Budget, Disbursements for Capital Expenditures Budget, and Depreciation Budget are shown in Figure Q7.9. Figure Q7.10 offers a view of Company MNO's Cash Budget.

Microsoft Excel - FigQ7.2

	A	B	C	D	E	F	G
1				Period			
2		1Q X4	2Q X4	3Q X4	4Q X4		X4
3	**SALES BUDGET**						
4	Unit Sales and Price Budget						
5	Unit sales	11,500	11,700	12,000	11,900		47,100
6	× Price per unit	$ 300	$ 300	$ 300	$ 295		N/A
7	= Total sales	$3,450,000	$3,510,000	$3,600,000	$3,510,500		$14,070,500
8							
9	Sales Composition Budget						
10	Cash sales	$1,380,000	$1,579,500	$1,800,000	$1,755,250		$ 6,514,750
11	+ Credit sales	2,070,000	1,930,500	1,800,000	1,755,250		7,555,750
12	= Total sales	$3,450,000	$3,510,000	$3,600,000	$3,510,500		$14,070,500
13							
14	**COLLECTIONS BUDGET**						
15	Cash Collections from Customers Budget						
16	Cash sales this period	$1,380,000	$1,579,500	$1,800,000	$1,755,250		$ 6,514,750
17	+ Credit sales collected	1,035,000	2,043,150	1,822,350	1,875,139		6,775,639
18	= Total collections	$2,415,000	$3,622,650	$3,622,350	$3,630,389		$13,290,389
19							
20	Accounts Receivable (A/R) Budget						
21	Beginning A/R balance	$ -	$1,035,000	$ 922,350	$ 900,000		$ -
22	+ Additions to A/R	1,035,000	922,350	900,000	780,111		3,637,461
23	- Subtractions from A/R	-	1,035,000	922,350	900,000		2,857,350
24	= Ending A/R balance	$1,035,000	$ 922,350	$ 900,000	$ 780,111		$ 780,111

Assumptions and Dashboard | Sales and Collections

FIGURE Q7.2 Company MNO's Unit Sales and Price Budget, Sales Composition Budget, Cash Collections from Customers Budget, and Accounts Receivable Budget

			Period			
	A	B	C	D	E	F	G
		1Q X4	**2Q X4**	**3Q X4**	**4Q X4**		**X4**
3	COST-OF-GOODS SOLD BUDGET						
4	Cost-of-Goods Sold Budget						
5	Exterior	$ 747,500	$ 737,100	$ 756,000	$ 749,700		$2,990,300
6	Interior	690,000	655,200	660,000	654,500		2,659,700
7	Assembly labor	575,000	585,000	540,000	511,700		2,211,700
8	Total cost-of-goods sold	$2,012,500	$1,977,300	$1,956,000	$1,915,900		$7,861,700

Sheet tabs: Assumptions and Dashboard / Sales and Collection

FIGURE Q7.3 Company MNO's Cost-of-Goods-Sold Budget

			Period			
	A	B	C	D	E	F	G
		1Q X4	**2Q X4**	**3Q X4**	**4Q X4**		**X4**
3	INVENTORY BUDGET						
4	Inventory Budget						
5	Desired ending inventory	$ 461,370	$ 478,133	$ 468,331	$ 468,331		$ 468,331
6	+ Cost of goods sold	2,012,500	1,977,300	1,956,000	1,915,900		7,861,700
7	= Total inventory needed	$2,473,870	$2,455,433	$2,424,331	$2,384,231		$8,330,031
8							
9	PURCHASES BUDGET						
10	Purchases Budget						
11	Total inventory needed	$2,473,870	$2,455,433	$2,424,331	$2,384,231		N/A
12	- Beginning inventory	-	461,370	478,133	468,331		-
13	= Purchases	$2,473,870	$1,994,063	$1,946,198	$1,915,900		N/A
14							
15	Disbursements for Purchases Budget						
16	Payments of payables	$1,621,759	$2,070,705	$1,899,939	$1,886,117		$7,478,520
17	Total disbursements for purchases	$1,621,759	$2,070,705	$1,899,939	$1,886,117		$7,478,520
18							
19	Accounts Payable (A/P) Budget						
20	Beginning A/P balance	$ -	$ 852,111	$ 775,469	$ 821,728		$ -
21	+ Additions to A/P	852,111	775,469	821,728	851,511		3,300,819
22	- Subtractions from A/P	-	852,111	775,469	821,728		2,449,308
23	Ending A/P	$ 852,111	$ 775,469	$ 821,728	$ 851,511		$ 851,511

Sheet tabs: Sales and Collections / COGS \ **Inventory and Purcha**

FIGURE Q7.4 Company MNO's Inventory Budget, Purchases Budget,
Disbursements for Purchases Budget, and Accounts Payable Budget

Microsoft Excel - FigQ7.5

	A	B	C	D	E	F	G
1				Period			
2		1Q X4	2Q X4	3Q X4	4Q X4		X4
3	HEADCOUNT BUDGET						
4	Headcount Budget						
5	Number of employees						
6	Chief Executive Officer	1	1	1	1		
7	Chief Financial Officer	1	1	1	1		
8	VP, Engineering	1	1	1	1		
9	VP, Sales & Marketing	1	1	1	1		
10	VP, Business Development	-	-	-	1		
11	Salesperson	6	6	6	7		
12	Hardware Engineer	1	1	1	2		
13	Controller/Accountant	1	1	1	1		
14	Administrative Assistant	1	2	2	2		
15	Total	13	14	14	17		
16							
17	Periodic base salaries						
18	Chief Executive Officer	$ 37,500	$ 37,500	$ 37,500	$ 37,500		$ 150,000
19	Chief Financial Officer	31,250	31,250	31,250	31,250		125,000
20	VP, Engineering	27,500	27,500	27,500	27,500		110,000
21	VP, Sales & Marketing	25,000	25,000	25,000	25,000		100,000
22	VP, Business Development	22,500	22,500	22,500	22,500		90,000
23	Salesperson	22,500	22,500	22,500	22,500		90,000
24	Hardware Engineer	17,500	17,500	17,500	17,500		70,000
25	Controller/Accountant	11,250	11,250	11,250	11,250		45,000
26	Administrative Assistant	8,750	8,750	8,750	8,750		35,000
27	Total	$ 203,750	$ 203,750	$ 203,750	$ 203,750		$ 815,000

Sales and Collections / COGS / Inventory an |

Ready

FIGURE Q7.5 Company MNO's Headcount Overview Worksheet

Microsoft Excel - FigQ7.6

	A	B	C	D	E	F	G
1				Period			
2		1Q X4	2Q X4	3Q X4	4Q X4		X4
3	HEADCOUNT BUDGET						
4	Headcount Budget						
5	Periodic salary expense (base)						
6	Chief Executive Officer	$ 37,500	$ 37,500	$ 37,500	$ 37,500		$ 150,000
7	Chief Financial Officer	31,250	31,250	31,250	31,250		125,000
8	VP, Engineering	27,500	27,500	27,500	27,500		110,000
9	VP, Sales & Marketing	25,000	25,000	25,000	25,000		100,000
10	VP, Business Development	-	-	-	22,500		22,500
11	Salesperson	135,000	135,000	135,000	157,500		562,500
12	Hardware Engineer	17,500	17,500	17,500	35,000		87,500
13	Controller/Accountant	11,250	11,250	11,250	11,250		45,000
14	Administrative Assistant	8,750	17,500	17,500	17,500		61,250
15	Total	$ 293,750	$ 302,500	$ 302,500	$ 365,000		$ 1,263,750
16							
17	Total (with benefits)	$ 336,344	$ 346,363	$ 346,363	$ 417,925		$ 1,446,994

COGS / Inventory and Purchases / Headcoun |

Ready

FIGURE Q7.6 Company MNO's Headcount Cost Worksheet

Microsoft Excel - FigQ7.7

	A	B	C	D	E	G
1				Period		
2		1Q X4	2Q X4	3Q X4	4Q X4	X4
3	OPERATING EXPENSES BUDGET					
4	Operating Expenses Budget					
5	Salaries	$ 336,344	$346,363	$346,363	$417,925	$1,446,994
6	Miscellaneous expenses	86,250	105,300	108,000	105,315	404,865
7	Research and development	155,250	157,950	180,000	175,525	668,725
8	Rent	13,000	13,000	13,000	13,000	52,000
9	Depreciation	888	1,594	2,241	2,828	7,550
10	Total operating expenses	$ 591,731	$624,206	$649,603	$714,593	$2,580,134
11						
12	DISBURSEMENTS FOR OPERATING EXPENSES BUDGET					
13	Disbursements for Operating Expenses Budget					
14	Salaries	$ 336,344	$346,363	$346,363	$417,925	$1,446,994
15	Miscellaneous expenses	86,250	105,300	108,000	105,315	404,865
16	Research and development	155,250	157,950	180,000	175,525	668,725
17	Rent	13,000	13,000	13,000	13,000	52,000
18	Depreciation	-	-	-	-	-
19	Total disbursements for operating expenses	$ 590,844	$622,613	$647,363	$711,765	$2,572,584

Headcount Overview / Headcount Cost / Operating Expenses

FIGURE Q7.7 Company MNO's Operating Expenses Budget and Disbursements for Operating Expenses Budget

Microsoft Excel - FigQ7.8

	A	B	C	D	E	G
1				Period		
2		1Q X4	2Q X4	3Q X4	4Q X4	X4
3	Sales	$3,450,000	$3,510,000	$3,600,000	$3,510,500	$14,070,500
4	Cost of goods sold	2,012,500	1,977,300	1,956,000	1,915,900	7,861,700
5	Gross profit	$1,437,500	$1,532,700	$1,644,000	$1,594,600	$ 6,208,800
6						
7	Salaries	$ 336,344	$ 346,363	$ 346,363	$ 417,925	$ 1,446,994
8	Miscellaneous expenses	86,250	105,300	108,000	105,315	404,865
9	Research and development	155,250	157,950	180,000	175,525	668,725
10	Rent	13,000	13,000	13,000	13,000	52,000
11	Depreciation	888	1,594	2,241	2,828	7,550
12	Income from operations	$ 845,769	$ 908,494	$ 994,397	$ 880,007	$ 3,628,666
13						
14	Interest expense	$ -	$ -	$ -	$ -	$ -
15	Taxable income	$ 845,769	$ 908,494	$ 994,397	$ 880,007	$ 3,628,666
16						
17	Tax expense	$ 274,875	$ 299,803	$ 348,039	$ 308,002	$ 1,230,719
18	Net income	$ 570,894	$ 608,691	$ 646,358	$ 572,004	$ 2,397,947

Operating Expenses / Capital / Cash / Balance S

FIGURE Q7.8 Company MNO's Income Statement

	A	B	C	D	E	F	G
1				Period			
2		1Q X4	2Q X4	3Q X4	4Q X4		X4
3	CAPITAL BUDGET						
4	Capital Expenditures Budget						
5	Equipment	$ 10,000	$ 7,500	$ 6,000	$ 6,000		$ 29,500
6	Furniture	4,000	3,500	3,500	3,250		14,250
7	Fixtures	3,000	2,500	2,750	2,000		10,250
8	Total capital expenditures	$ 17,000	$ 13,500	$ 12,250	$ 11,250		$ 54,000
9							
10	Disbursements for Capital Expenditures Budget						
11	Equipment	$ 10,000	$ 7,500	$ 6,000	$ 6,000		$ 29,500
12	Furniture	4,000	3,500	3,500	3,250		14,250
13	Fixtures	3,000	2,500	2,750	2,000		10,250
14	Total disbursements for capital expenditures	$ 17,000	$ 13,500	$ 12,250	$ 11,250		$ 54,000
15							
16	Depreciation Budget						
17	Equipment	$ 500	$ 875	$ 1,175	$ 1,475		$ 4,025
18	Furniture	200	375	550	713		1,838
19	Fixtures	188	344	516	641		1,688
20	Total depreciation	$ 888	$ 1,594	$ 2,241	$ 2,828		$ 7,550
21							
22	Cumulative capital expenditures	$ 17,000	$ 30,500	$ 42,750	$ 54,000		
23	- Accumulated depreciation	888	2,481	4,722	7,550		
24	= Fixed assets, net of depreciation	$ 16,113	$ 28,019	$ 38,028	$ 46,450		
25							
26							
27	Cumulative disbursements for CAPEX	$ 17,000	$ 30,500	$ 42,750	$ 54,000		
28	Payables adjustment for CAPEX disbursements	$ -	$ -	$ -	$ -		

FIGURE Q7.9 Company MNO's Capital Expenditures Budget, Disbursements for Capital Expenditures Budget, and Depreciation Budget

	A	B	C	D	E	F	G
1				Period			
2		1Q X4	2Q X4	3Q X4	4Q X4		X4
3	CASH BUDGET						
4	Beginning cash balance	$ -	$ 110,522	$ 726,552	$ 1,441,311		$ -
5	Cash receipts						
6	Collections from customers	2,415,000	3,622,650	3,622,350	3,630,389		13,290,389
7	Total cash available, before financing	$ 2,415,000	$ 3,733,172	$ 4,348,902	$ 5,071,700		N/A
8	Cash disbursements						
9	Purchases disbursements	$ 1,621,759	$ 2,070,705	$ 1,899,939	$ 1,886,117		$ 7,478,520
10	Operating expenses	590,844	622,613	647,363	711,765		2,572,584
11	Tax expense	274,875	299,803	348,039	308,002		1,230,719
12	Capital expenditures	17,000	13,500	12,250	11,250		54,000
13	Total disbursements	2,504,478	3,006,620	2,907,590	2,917,134		11,335,823
14							
15	Minimum cash balance desired	$ 100,000	$ 100,000	$ 100,000	$ 100,000		N/A
16	Total cash needed	$ 2,604,478	$ 3,106,620	$ 3,007,590	$ 3,017,134		N/A
17	Excess (deficiency) of total cash available over						
18	total cash needed before financing	$ (189,478)	$ 626,552	$ 1,341,311	$ 2,054,566		N/A
19	Financing						
20	Equity investment	$ 200,000	$ -	$ -	$ -		$ 200,000
21	Borrowing (at beginning of quarter)	-	-	-	-		-
22	Repayments (at end of quarter)	-	-	-	-		-
23	Interest	-	-	-	-		-
24	Total cash increase (decrease) from financing	$ 200,000	$ -	$ -	$ -		$ 200,000
25							
26	Ending cash balance	$ 110,522	$ 726,552	$ 1,441,311	$ 2,154,566		$ 2,154,566

FIGURE Q7.10 Company MNO's Cash Budget

1. Given the information presented, build the Asset components of Company MNO's Balance Sheet.
2. Build the Liabilities components of Company MNO's Balance Sheet given the information provided.
3. Build the Owners' Equity components of Company MNO's Balance Sheet given the information provided.
4. Calculate the change in Company MNO's Net Working Capital using the information provided and your answers to Questions 1–3.

Financial Statements and Free Cash Flows

CHAPTER 8

Consolidated Financial Statements

This chapter covers Napavale's consolidated financial statements: the Balance Sheet, the Income Statement, and Statement of Cash Flows. Many readers may be familiar with these financial statements as they are widely used to assess a business's financial condition and the SEC (U.S. Securities and Exchange Commission) requires publicly traded companies to file these financial statements on a regular basis.

As I covered the Balance Sheet in Chapter 7 and the Income Statement in Chapter 5, the majority of this chapter will be focused on the Statement of Cash Flows. I will, however, provide a review of the source of each line item in Napavale's Balance Sheet and Income Statement. By identifying the budget from which values flow into the Balance Sheet and Income Statement, I hope to provide some perspective on the interrelated nature of financial statements (and financial models in general).

BALANCE SHEET

The Balance Sheet, as noted in Chapter 7, presents a business's Assets, Liabilities, and Owners' Equity accounts. To be correct, a Balance Sheet must always "balance"—in other words, the value of a business's Assets must be equal to the value of that business's Liabilities plus its Owners' Equity. This, as you may remember, is also referred to as the central accounting identity (Assets = Liabilities + Owners' Equity). Figure 8.1 offers a view of Napavale's Balance Sheet as of the end of Chapter 7.

Figure 8.2 presents another view of Napavale's Balance Sheet, in this case with the source of each line item labeled. More specifically, the budgets from which each element of the Balance Sheet comes are listed next to each of these elements in Figure 8.2.

A	B	C	D	E	F	G
			Period			
	1Q X4	2Q X4	3Q X4	4Q X4		X4
Assets						
Cash	$ 982,272	$ 1,260,656	$ 1,541,236	$ 2,135,280		$ 2,135,280
Accounts Receivable	133,333	192,000	257,600	336,000		336,000
Inventory	64,667	83,067	102,667	102,667		102,667
Fixed Assets, net	42,688	83,063	121,125	156,875		156,875
Total Assets	$ 1,222,959	$ 1,618,785	$ 2,022,628	$ 2,730,822		$ 2,730,822
Liabilities						
Accounts Payable	$ 88,222	$ 103,133	$ 131,133	$ 154,000		$ 154,000
Payables from Capital Budget	-	-	-	-		-
Loan Payable	-	50,000	-	-		-
Total Liabilities	$ 88,222	$ 153,133	$ 131,133	$ 154,000		$ 154,000
Owners' Equity						
Common Stock	$ 1,000,000	$ 1,000,000	$ 1,000,000	$ 1,000,000		$ 1,000,000
Retained Earnings	134,737	465,652	891,495	1,576,822		1,576,822
Total Owners' Equity	$ 1,134,737	$ 1,465,652	$ 1,891,495	$ 2,576,822		$ 2,576,822
Total Liabilities and Owners' Equity	$ 1,222,959	$ 1,618,785	$ 2,022,628	$ 2,730,822		$ 2,730,822
Net Working Capital (NWC)						
Current assets	$ 198,000	$ 275,067	$ 360,267	$ 438,667		N/A
- Current liabilities	88,222	103,133	131,133	154,000		N/A
= Net working capital	$ 109,778	$ 171,933	$ 229,133	$ 284,667		N/A
Beginning NWC	$ -	$ 109,778	$ 171,933	$ 229,133		N/A
- Ending NWC	109,778	171,933	229,133	284,667		N/A
= Change in NWC	$ (109,778)	$ (62,156)	$ (57,200)	$ (55,533)		N/A

FIGURE 8.1   Balance Sheet

INCOME STATEMENT

The Income Statement, discussed in Chapter 5, represents the difference between a business's revenues and a business's expenses. The "bottom line," or final output of the Income Statement, is the metric known as Net Income. As covered in Chapter 7, Net Income affects the Retained Earnings account in Napavale's Balance Sheet. The Income Statement also affects the Statement of Cash Flows. I will discuss the relationship between Napavale's Income Statement, Balance Sheet, and Statement of Cash Flows later in this chapter. Figure 8.3 offers a view of Napavale's Income Statement as of the end of Chapter 7. A view of Napavale's Income Statement in which the source of each line item is identified by budget is presented in Figure 8.4.

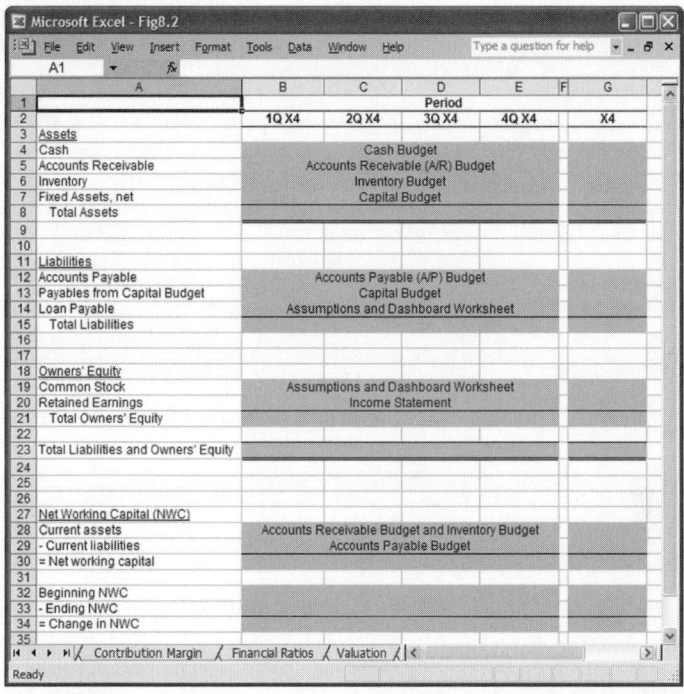

FIGURE 8.2 Source of Each Line Item in the Balance Sheet

	A	B	C	D	E	F	G
1				Period			
2		1Q X4	2Q X4	3Q X4	4Q X4		X4
3	Sales	$1,000,000	$1,440,000	$1,932,000	$2,520,000		$6,892,000
4	Cost of goods sold	200,000	291,000	373,800	462,000		1,326,800
5	Gross profit	$ 800,000	$1,149,000	$1,558,200	$2,058,000		$5,565,200
6							
7	Salaries	$ 470,400	$ 470,400	$ 663,600	$ 697,200		$2,301,600
8	Miscellaneous expenses	30,000	43,200	57,960	75,600		206,760
9	Research and development	70,000	100,800	154,560	201,600		526,960
10	Rent	20,000	20,000	20,000	20,000		80,000
11	Depreciation	2,313	4,625	6,938	9,250		23,125
12	Income from operations	$ 207,288	$ 509,975	$ 655,143	$1,054,350		$2,426,755
13							
14	Interest expense	$ -	$ 875	$ -	$ -		$ 875
15	Taxable income	$ 207,288	$ 509,100	$ 655,143	$1,054,350		$2,425,880
16							
17	Tax expense	$ 72,551	$ 178,185	$ 229,300	$ 369,023		$ 849,058
18	Net income	$ 134,737	$ 330,915	$ 425,843	$ 685,328		$1,576,822
19							

FIGURE 8.3 Income Statement

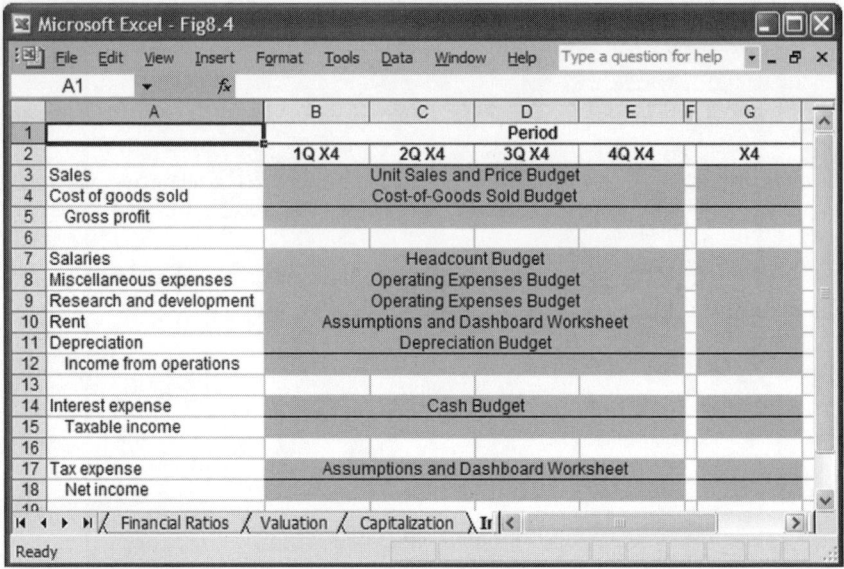

FIGURE 8.4   Source of Each Line Item in the Income Statement

STATEMENT OF CASH FLOWS

The Statement of Cash Flows, which is based on information contained in the Balance Sheet, Income Statement, and various other budgets and financial schedules, is an important financial statement. The goal of the Statement of Cash Flows is to reconcile Net Income, an accrual-based figure, with a business's changes in cash position.

The Statement of Cash Flows is divided into three sections: Cash Flows from Operating Activities, Cash Flows from Investing Activities, and Cash Flows from Financing Activities. This division of the Statement of Cash Flows into three separate sections identifies the sources and uses of cash across a variety of functions (operating activities, investing activities, and financing activities). I will cover the contents of each of these sections over the course of this chapter.

It is worth noting that there are two approaches to presenting a business's Statement of Cash Flows: the indirect method and the direct method. These methods are identical in structure for the Cash Flows from Investing Activities and Cash Flows from Financing Activities sections, but differ in the Cash Flows from Operating Activities section. The indirect method begins the Cash Flows from Operating Activities section with Net Income while the direct method compares "sources of cash" and "uses of cash" in the Cash Flows from Operating Activities section. I will use the indirect method throughout this book—this method is often used by publicly traded companies in their financial statements as filed with the SEC.

I will now walk through the process of building each of the three sections (Cash Flow from Operating Activities, Cash Flows from Investing Activities, and Cash Flows from Financing Activities) for Napavale. As in earlier chapters, I will make frequent references to alternative views of worksheets in which the values and formulas contained within each cell are exposed for viewing and to the names of the input and output cells across various worksheets. This should make it easier to follow the extensive references and linkages between worksheets.

Cash Flows from Operating Activities

The first section of the Statement of Cash Flows, Cash Flows from Operating Activities, reconciles Net Income to cash provided by operating activities. "Operating activities" include, in this context, those activities undertaken in the normal course of business operations. In the case of Napavale, these activities are captured through several Income Statement accounts and several Balance Sheet accounts.

As the Statement of Cash Flows is based entirely on information found in other budgets and schedules, I will not present views of Napavale's Assumptions and Dashboard worksheet in this Chapter. I will instead focus on (1) views of the Statement of Cash Flows, (2) alternative views of the Statement of Cash Flows in which the values and formulas underlying the worksheet cells are exposed and visible, and (3) views of the Statement of Cash Flows in which the names of the worksheet cells are shown.

Figure 8.5 presents a view of the Statement of Cash Flows in which the Net Income and depreciation values are shown. As the calculations associated with values that underly the remainder of the Cash Flows from Operating Activities section are more involved, I will discuss these accounts later in this section of the chapter. An alternative view of the Statement of Cash Flows is shown in Figure 8.6 in which the values and formulas underlying the worksheet are exposed and visible.

To calculate the increase or decrease in several Balance Sheet accounts for the Cash Flows from Operating Activities section of the Statement of Cash Flows, I am going to build an additional section in the Statement of Cash Flows. This section will paste the periodic (quarterly) values for each of the relevant accounts from the Balance Sheet into the Statement of Cash Flows. I will then calculate the increase or decrease in each of these accounts for use in the Cash Flows from Operating Activities section of the Statement of Cash Flows. Figure 8.7 presents a view of these calculations related to the relevant Balance Sheet accounts.

Note that "payables from capital budget" are not included in these

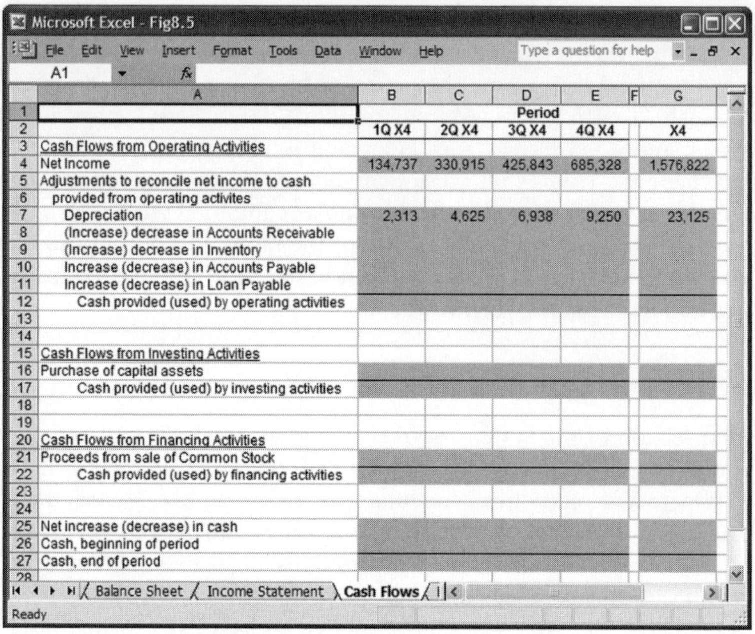

FIGURE 8.5 Statement of Cash Flows

FIGURE 8.6 Alternative View of the Statement of Cash Flows

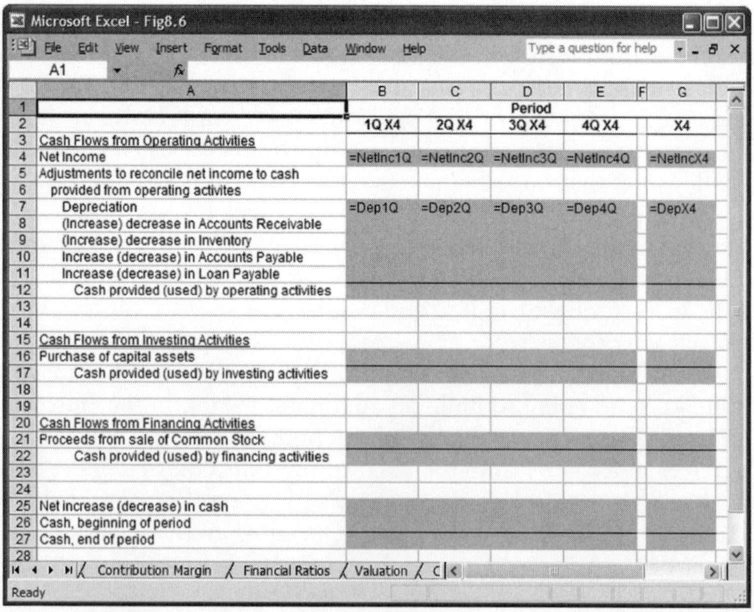

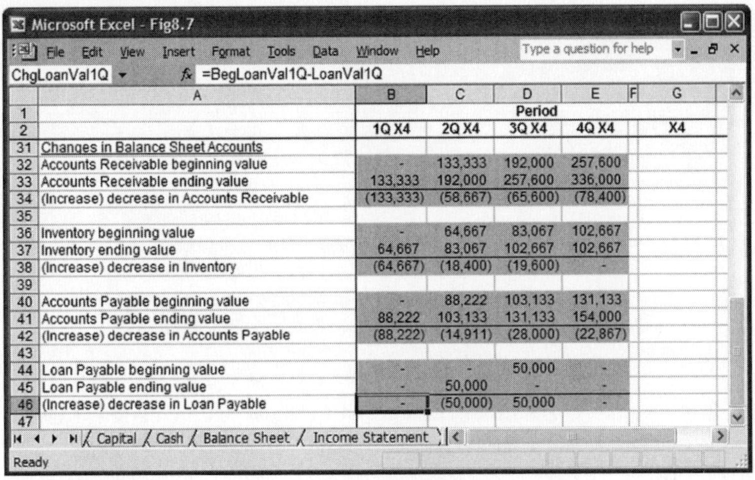

FIGURE 8.7 Calculations Related to Balance Sheet Accounts

calculations; as mentioned in Chapter 7, I am not including this account as a component of current liabilities. Also note that I am including changes in loan payable in cash flows from Operating Activities. I am assuming these cash flows are a part of Napavale's normal business operations. Changes in loan payable could alternatively be considered a part of financing cash flows.

An alternative view of the worksheet shown Figure 8.7 (in which the values and formulas underlying the worksheet cells are exposed and visible) is presented in Figure 8.8. Figure 8.9 offers a view of the names of the input and output cells underlying the calculations associated with the increase or decrease in the Balance Sheet accounts related to the Cash Flows from Operating Activities section of the Statement of Cash Flows.

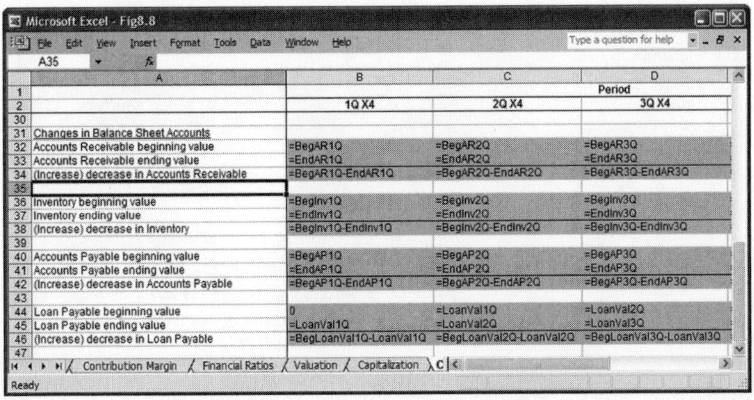

FIGURE 8.8 Alternative View of the Calculations Related to Balance Sheet Accounts

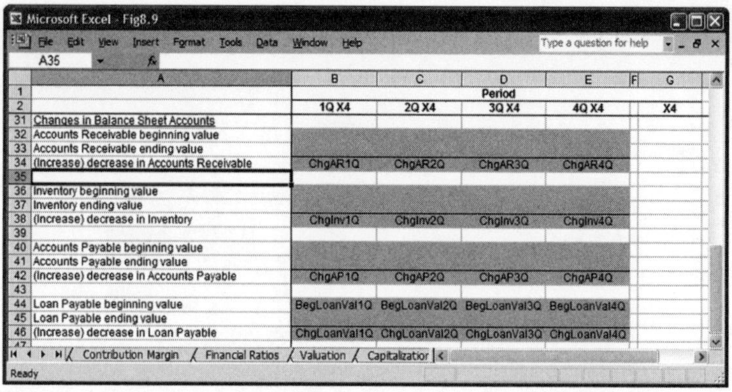

FIGURE 8.9 Names of the Input and Output Cells in the Calculations Related to Balance Sheet Accounts

As I added a set of names to several worksheet cells in the Inventory and Purchases Budget worksheet, Figure 8.10 presents an updated view of the names underlying the Inventory and Purchases worksheet. The completed Cash Flows from Operating Activities section of the Statement of Cash Flows is shown in Figure 8.11. A view of the values and formulas underlying the Cash Flows from Operating Activities section is presented in Figure 8.12. To summarize the Cash Flows from Operating Activities, a

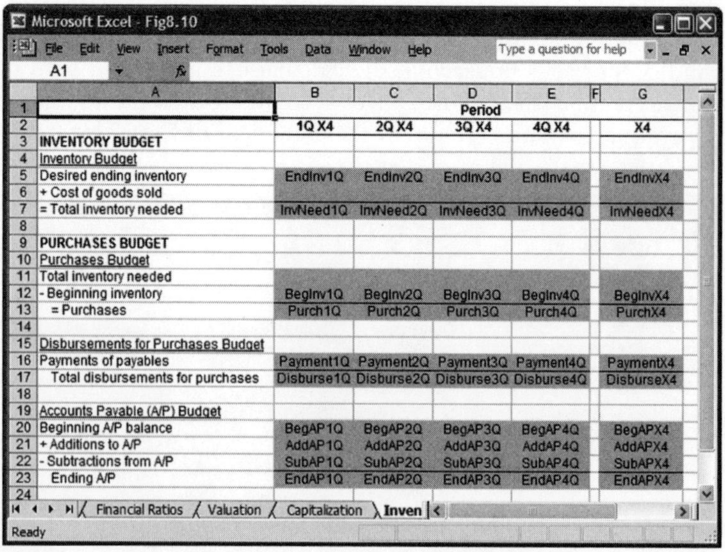

FIGURE 8.10 Names of the Input and Output Cells in the Inventory and Purchases Worksheet

	A	B	C	D	E	F	G
1				Period			
2		1Q X4	2Q X4	3Q X4	4Q X4		X4
3	Cash Flows from Operating Activities						
4	Net Income	134,737	330,915	425,843	685,328		1,576,822
5	Adjustments to reconcile net income to cash						
6	provided from operating activites						
7	Depreciation	2,313	4,625	6,938	9,250		23,125
8	(Increase) decrease in Accounts Receivable	(133,333)	(58,667)	(65,600)	(78,400)		(336,000)
9	(Increase) decrease in Inventory	(64,667)	(18,400)	(19,600)	-		(102,667)
10	Increase (decrease) in Accounts Payable	88,222	14,911	28,000	22,867		154,000
11	Increase (decrease) in Loan Payable	-	50,000	(50,000)	-		-
12	Cash provided (used) by operating activities	27,272	323,384	325,580	639,044		1,315,280
13							
14							
15	Cash Flows from Investing Activities						
16	Purchase of capital assets						
17	Cash provided (used) by investing activities						
18							
19							
20	Cash Flows from Financing Activities						
21	Proceeds from sale of Common Stock						
22	Cash provided (used) by financing activities						
23							
24							
25	Net increase (decrease) in cash						
26	Cash, beginning of period						
27	Cash, end of period						
28							

Income Statement \ **Cash Flows** / Free Cash Flows /

FIGURE 8.11   Cash Flows from Operating Activities

	A	B	C
1			
2		1Q X4	2Q X4
3	Cash Flows from Operating Activities		
4	Net Income	=NetInc1Q	=NetInc2Q
5	Adjustments to reconcile net income to cash		
6	provided from operating activites		
7	Depreciation	=Dep1Q	=Dep2Q
8	(Increase) decrease in Accounts Receivable	=ChgAR1Q	=ChgAR2Q
9	(Increase) decrease in Inventory	=ChgInv1Q	=ChgInv2Q
10	Increase (decrease) in Accounts Payable	=-ChgAP1Q	=-ChgAP2Q
11	Increase (decrease) in Loan Payable	=-ChgLoanVal1Q	=-ChgLoanVal2Q
12	Cash provided (used) by operating activities	=NetInc1Q+SUM(B7:B11)	=NetInc2Q+SUM(C7:C11)
13			
14			
15	Cash Flows from Investing Activities		
16	Purchase of capital assets		
17	Cash provided (used) by investing activities		
18			
19			
20	Cash Flows from Financing Activities		
21	Proceeds from sale of Common Stock		
22	Cash provided (used) by financing activities		
23			
24			
25	Net increase (decrease) in cash		
26	Cash, beginning of period		
27	Cash, end of period		
28			

Contribution Margin / Financial Ratios / Valuation /

FIGURE 8.12   Alternative View of the Cash Flows from Operating Activities view of the names underlying the input and output cells in this section is shown in Figure 8.13.

Cash Flows from Investing Activities

The second section of the Statement of Cash Flows, Cash Flows from Investing Activities, reflects Napavale's disbursements for and/or proceeds from capital assets. Capital assets include, in this context, large-value purchases such as furniture or equipment that are capitalized as opposed to expensed. This topic of capitalizing versus expensing was discussed in Chapter 6. Napavale's disbursements for capital expenditures are captured through the Disbursements for Capital Expenditures Budget.

Figure 8.14 presents a view of Napavale's Cash Flows from Investing Activities section of the Statement of Cash Flows. An alternative view of Napavale's Cash Flows from Investing Activities in which the values and formulas underlying the worksheet cells are exposed and visible is presented in Figure 8.15. The names of the input and output worksheet cells for the Cash Flows from Investing Activities are shown in Figure 8.16.

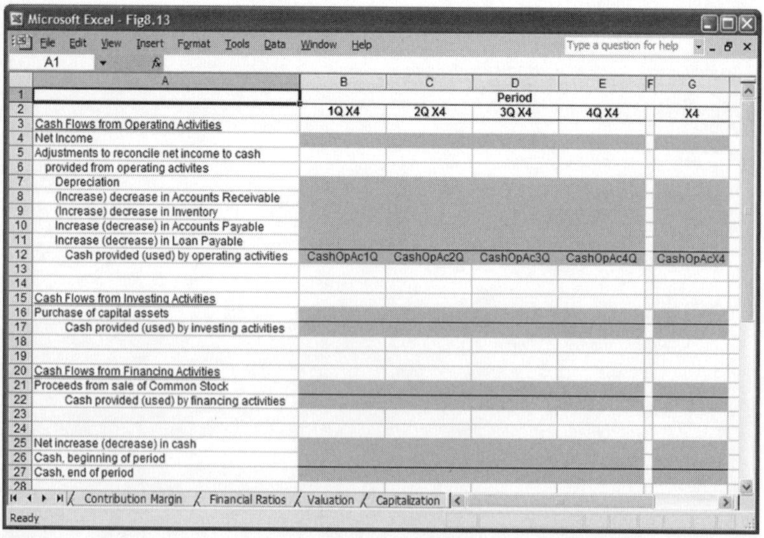

FIGURE 8.13   Names of the Input and Output Cells in the Cash Flows from Operating Activities

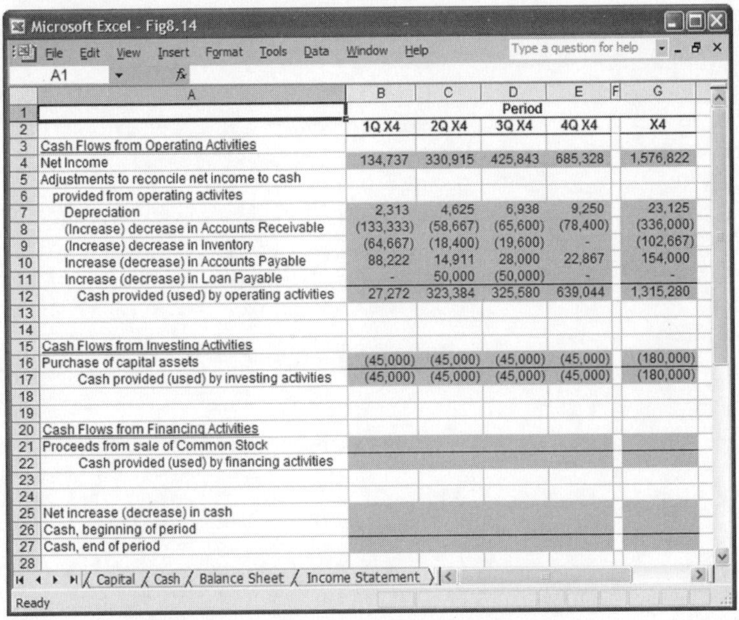

FIGURE 8.14 Cash Flows from Investing Activities

FIGURE 8.15 Alternative View of the Cash Flows from Investing Activities

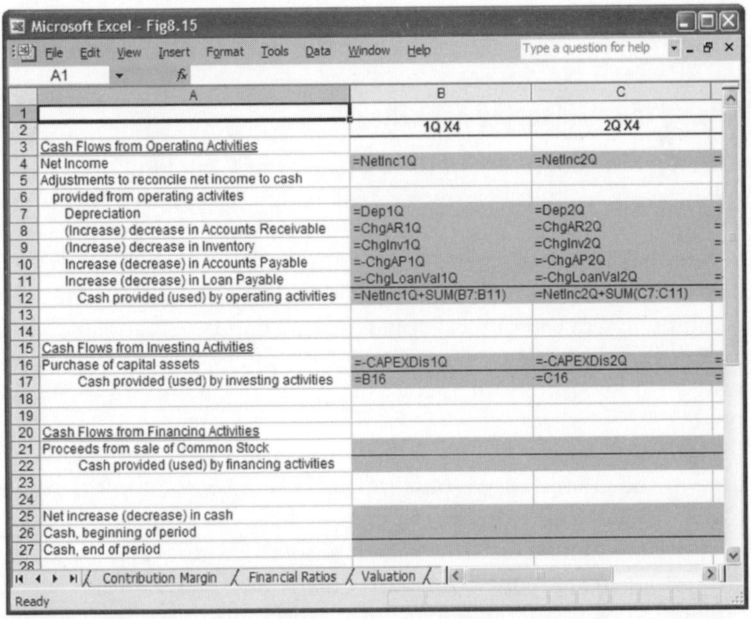

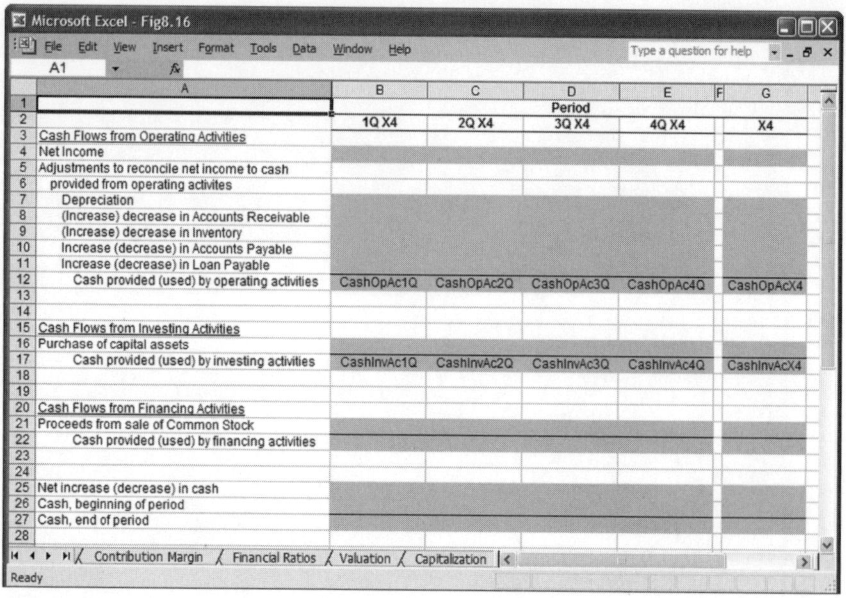

FIGURE 8.16 Names of the Input and Output Cells in the Cash Flows from Investing Activities

Cash Flows from Financing Activities

The third (and final) section of the Statement of Cash Flows, Cash Flows from Financing Activities, tracks Napavale's issuance(s) of common stock and borrowing and repayment of any short-term borrowings. Note that this section of the Statement of Cash Flows may include different and/or additional accounts for other companies. Specifically, some companies may issue several types of equity (stock) and/or debt (borrowings), in which case each class of equity and/or debt may be accounted for separately in the Cash Flows from Financing Activities section.

The values relevant to the Cash Flows from Financing Activities are captured in the Cash Budget (based directly on inputs from the Assumptions and Dashboard worksheet). Figure 8.17 presents a view of the Cash Flows from Financing Activities section for Napavale; as this is the final section of the Statement of Cash Flows, Figure 8.17 also represents a completed view of the Statement of Cash Flows. Note the calculation

	A	B	C	D	E	F	G	
				Period				
1								
2		1Q X4	2Q X4	3Q X4	4Q X4		X4	
3	Cash Flows from Operating Activities							
4	Net Income	134,737	330,915	425,843	685,328		1,576,822	
5	Adjustments to reconcile net income to cash							
6	provided from operating activites							
7	Depreciation	2,313	4,625	6,938	9,250		23,125	
8	(Increase) decrease in Accounts Receivable	(133,333)	(58,667)	(65,600)	(78,400)		(336,000)	
9	(Increase) decrease in Inventory	(64,667)	(18,400)	(19,600)	-		(102,667)	
10	Increase (decrease) in Accounts Payable	88,222	14,911	28,000	22,867		154,000	
11	Increase (decrease) in Loan Payable	-	50,000	(50,000)	-		-	
12	Cash provided (used) by operating activities	27,272	323,384	325,580	639,044		1,315,280	
13								
14								
15	Cash Flows from Investing Activities							
16	Purchase of capital assets	(45,000)	(45,000)	(45,000)	(45,000)		(180,000)	
17	Cash provided (used) by investing activities	(45,000)	(45,000)	(45,000)	(45,000)		(180,000)	
18								
19								
20	Cash Flows from Financing Activities							
21	Proceeds from sale of Common Stock	1,000,000	-	-	-		1,000,000	
22	Cash provided (used) by financing activities	1,000,000	-	-	-		1,000,000	
23								
24								
25	Net increase (decrease) in cash	982,272	278,384	280,580	594,044		2,135,280	
26	Cash, beginning of period	-	982,272	1,260,656	1,541,236		-	
27	Cash, end of period	982,272	1,260,656	1,541,236	2,135,280		2,135,280	

FIGURE 8.17 Cash Flows from Financing Activities and Completed Statement of Cash Flows

related to Napavale's net increase or decrease in cash for each period in Figure 8.17.

Napavale's Balance Sheet value for cash for each accounting period (quarter) must be equal to the "cash, end of period" value as calculated in Figure 8.17. If these values are not equal, there is an error in the financial model.

Figure 8.18 presents an alternative view of the completed Statement of Cash Flows (including the Cash Flows from Financing section) in which the values and formulas underlying the worksheet cells are exposed and visible. Finally, the names of the input and output cells in the completed Statement of Cash Flows (including the Cash Flows from Financing section) are shown in Figure 8.19.

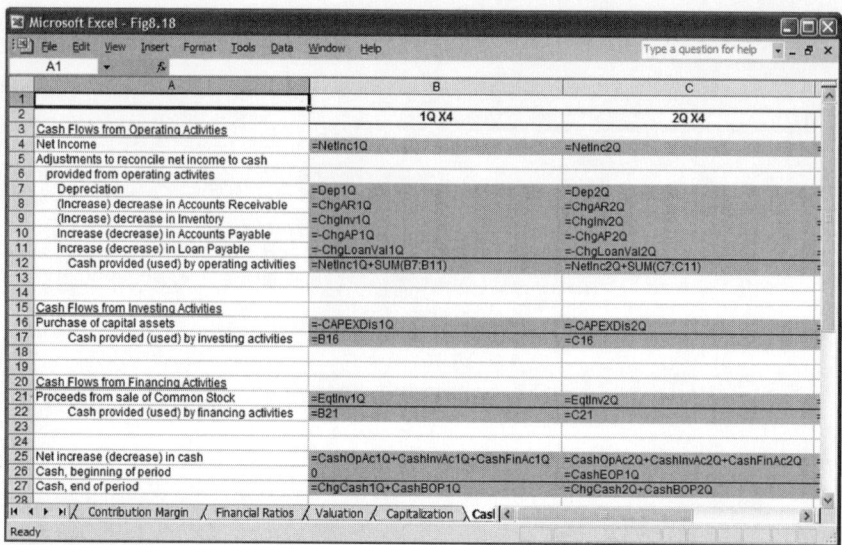

FIGURE 8.18　Alternative View of the Cash Flows from Financing Activities and Completed Statement of Cash Flows

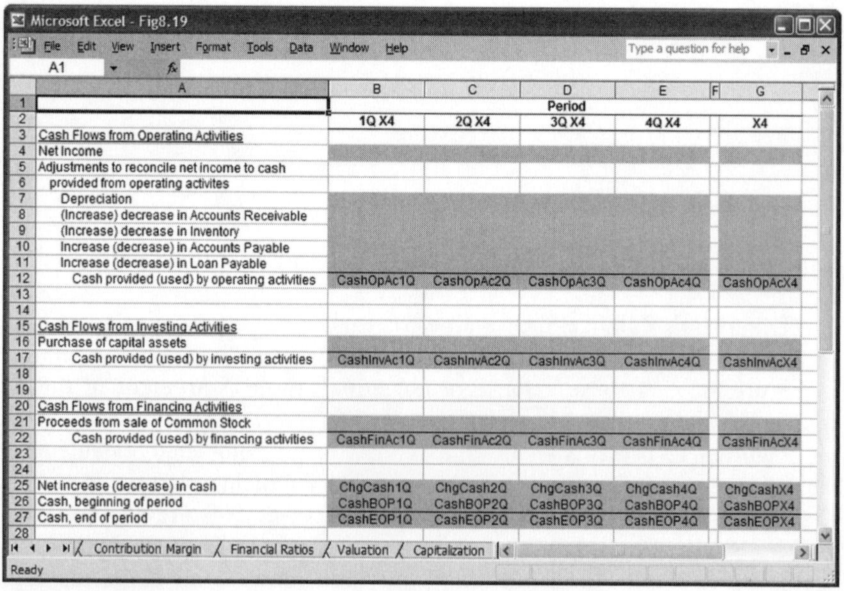

FIGURE 8.19　Names of the Input and Output Cells in the Cash Flows from Financing Activities and Completed Statement of Cash Flows

QUESTIONS

Each of the questions for this chapter relates to a hypothetical company named Company PQR. Company PQR sells camping tents to consumers. As such, Company PQR is a product-oriented (as opposed to a service-oriented) business. The questions for this chapter will address fiscal year X4 on a quarterly basis (four specific quarters, 1Q–4Q for year X4).

The following questions will test your knowledge of the material covered in this chapter in an applied manner—specifically, you will be asked to build Company PQR's Statement of Cash Flows.

To prepare you for this chapter's questions, several figures provide background information related to Company PQR's operations. Figure Q8.1 offers a view of Company PQR's Income Statement. Note that there are three cost-of-goods-sold components for Company PQR's camping tents: (1) fabric, (2) frame, and (3) assembly and labor.

Figure Q8.2 presents a view of Company PQR's Balance Sheet. Company PQR's Sales and Collections worksheet is presented in Figure Q8.3. Figure Q8.4 offers a view of Company PQR's Inventory and Purchases worksheet. A portion of Company PQR's Assumptions and Dashboard worksheet is presented in Figure Q8.5. The Capital Budget worksheet for Company PQR is shown in Figure Q8.6.

A	B	C	D	E	F	G
			Period			
	1Q X4	2Q X4	3Q X4	4Q X4		X4
Sales	$3,000,000	$3,171,250	$3,392,500	$3,480,000		$13,043,750
Cost of goods sold	1,300,000	1,397,500	1,437,500	1,500,000		5,635,000
Gross profit	$1,700,000	$1,773,750	$1,955,000	$1,980,000		$7,408,750
Salaries	$ 319,125	$ 356,500	$ 559,188	$ 587,938		$ 1,822,750
Miscellaneous expenses	90,000	95,138	101,775	104,400		391,313
Research and development	180,000	190,275	169,625	174,000		713,900
Rent	25,000	25,000	25,000	25,000		100,000
Depreciation	1,625	3,000	4,875	5,750		15,250
Income from operations	$1,084,250	$1,103,838	$1,094,538	$1,082,913		$ 4,365,538
Interest expense	$ 875	$ -	$ -	$ -		$ 875
Taxable income	$1,083,375	$1,103,838	$1,094,538	$1,082,913		$ 4,364,663
Tax expense	$ 379,181	$ 386,343	$ 383,088	$ 379,019		$ 1,527,632
Net income	$ 704,194	$ 717,494	$ 711,449	$ 703,893		$ 2,837,031

FIGURE Q8.1 Company PQR's Income Statement

Microsoft Excel - FigQ8.2

File   Edit   View   Insert   Format   Tools   Data   Window   Help   Type a question for help

A1

	A	B	C	D	E	F	G
1				Period			
2		1Q X4	2Q X4	3Q X4	4Q X4		X4
3	Assets						
4	Cash	$ 846,597	$1,344,153	$2,000,040	$2,699,281		$2,699,281
5	Accounts Receivable	250,000	264,271	282,708	290,000		290,000
6	Inventory	465,833	479,167	500,000	500,000		500,000
7	Fixed Assets, net	30,375	54,375	86,500	97,750		97,750
8	Total Assets	$ 1,592,805	$2,141,966	$2,869,249	$3,587,031		$3,587,031
9							
10							
11	Liabilities						
12	Accounts Payable	$ 588,611	$ 470,278	$ 486,111	$ 500,000		$ 500,000
13	Payables from Capital Budget	-	-	-	-		-
14	Loan Payable	50,000	-	-	-		-
15	Total Liabilities	$ 638,611	$ 470,278	$ 486,111	$ 500,000		$ 500,000
16							
17							
18	Owners' Equity						
19	Common Stock	$ 250,000	$ 250,000	$ 250,000	$ 250,000		$ 250,000
20	Retained Earnings	704,194	1,421,688	2,133,138	2,837,031		2,837,031
21	Total Owners' Equity	$ 954,194	$1,671,688	$2,383,138	$3,087,031		$3,087,031
22							
23	Total Liabilities and Owners' Equity	$ 1,592,805	$2,141,966	$2,869,249	$3,587,031		$3,587,031
24							
25							
26							
27	Net Working Capital (NWC)						
28	Current assets	$ 715,833	$ 743,438	$ 782,708	$ 790,000		N/A
29	- Current liabilities	588,611	470,278	486,111	500,000		N/A
30	= Net working capital	$ 127,222	$ 273,160	$ 296,597	$ 290,000		N/A
31							
32	Beginning NWC	$ -	$ 127,222	$ 273,160	$ 296,597		N/A
33	- Ending NWC	127,222	273,160	296,597	290,000		N/A
34	= Change in NWC	$ (127,222)	$ (145,938)	$ (23,437)	$ 6,597		N/A
35							

Headcount Cost / Operating Expenses / Capital / C

Ready

FIGURE Q8.2   Company PQR's Balance Sheet

Microsoft Excel - FigQ8.3

File   Edit   View   Insert   Format   Tools   Data   Window   Help   Type a question for help

A1

	A	B	C	D	E	F	G
1				Period			
2		1Q X4	2Q X4	3Q X4	4Q X4		X4
3	SALES BUDGET						
4	Unit Sales and Price Budget						
5	Unit sales	10,000	10,750	11,500	12,000		44,250
6	× Price per unit	$ 300	$ 295	$ 295	$ 290		N/A
7	= Total sales	$3,000,000	$3,171,250	$3,392,500	$3,480,000		$13,043,750
8							
9	Sales Composition Budget						
10	Cash sales	$2,250,000	$2,378,438	$2,544,375	$2,610,000		$ 9,782,813
11	+ Credit sales	750,000	792,813	848,125	870,000		3,260,938
12	= Total sales	$3,000,000	$3,171,250	$3,392,500	$3,480,000		$13,043,750
13							
14	COLLECTIONS BUDGET						
15	Cash Collections from Customers Budget						
16	Cash sales this period	$2,250,000	$2,378,438	$2,544,375	$2,610,000		$ 9,782,813
17	+ Credit sales collected	500,000	778,542	829,688	862,708		2,970,938
18	= Total collections	$2,750,000	$3,156,979	$3,374,063	$3,472,708		$12,753,750
19							
20	Accounts Receivable (A/R) Budget						
21	Beginning A/R balance	$ -	$ 250,000	$ 264,271	$ 282,708		$ -
22	+ Additions to A/R	250,000	264,271	282,708	290,000		1,086,979
23	- Subtractions from A/R	-	250,000	264,271	282,708		796,979
24	= Ending A/R balance	$ 250,000	$ 264,271	$ 282,708	$ 290,000		$ 290,000
25							

Sales and Collections / COGS / Inventory and Purchases

Ready

FIGURE Q8.3   Company PQR's Sales and Collections Worksheet

FIGURE Q8.4 Company PQR's Inventory and Purchases Worksheet

The first worksheet shown (FigQ8.4):

	A	B	C	D	E	F	G
1				Period			
2		1Q X4	2Q X4	3Q X4	4Q X4		X4
3	INVENTORY BUDGET						
4	Inventory Budget						
5	Desired ending inventory	$ 465,833	$ 479,167	$ 500,000	$ 500,000		$ 500,000
6	+ Cost of goods sold	1,300,000	1,397,500	1,437,500	1,500,000		5,635,000
7	= Total inventory needed	$1,765,833	$1,876,667	$1,937,500	$2,000,000		$6,135,000
8							
9	PURCHASES BUDGET						
10	Purchases Budget						
11	Total inventory needed	$1,765,833	$1,876,667	$1,937,500	$2,000,000		N/A
12	- Beginning inventory	-	465,833	479,167	500,000		-
13	= Purchases	$1,765,833	$1,410,833	$1,458,333	$1,500,000		N/A
14							
15	Disbursements for Purchases Budget						
16	Payments of payables	$1,177,222	$1,529,167	$1,442,500	$1,486,111		$5,635,000
17	Total disbursements for purchases	$1,177,222	$1,529,167	$1,442,500	$1,486,111		$5,635,000
18							
19	Accounts Payable (A/P) Budget						
20	Beginning A/P balance	$ -	$ 588,611	$ 470,278	$ 486,111		$ -
21	+ Additions to A/P	588,611	470,278	486,111	500,000		2,045,000
22	- Subtractions from A/P	-	588,611	470,278	486,111		1,545,000
23	Ending A/P	$ 588,611	$ 470,278	$ 486,111	$ 500,000		$ 500,000

Sheet tabs: Sales and Collections / COGS \ **Inventory and Purcha**

FIGURE Q8.5 Company PQR's Assumptions and Dashboard Worksheet

The second worksheet shown (FigQ8.5):

	A	B	C	D	E	F
1				Period		
2		1Q X4	2Q X4	3Q X4	4Q X4	
3	Sales and Collections Worksheet					
4	Unit Sales and Price Inputs					
5	Unit sales	10,000	10,750	11,500	12,000	
6	Price per unit	$ 300	$ 295	$ 295	$ 290	
7						
8	Sales Composition Inputs					
9	Cash sales as a % of total sales	75%	75%	75%	75%	
10	Credit sales as a % of total sales	25%	25%	25%	25%	
11						
12	Days receivable (DSO)	30	30	30	30	
13	Days per quarter	90	90	90	90	
14						
15	COGS Worksheet					
16	Cost-of-Goods Sold Inputs					
17	Fabric: cost per unit	$ 45.00	$ 45.00	$ 45.00	$ 45.00	
18	Frame: cost per unit	$ 45.00	$ 45.00	$ 40.00	$ 40.00	
19	Assembly labor: cost per unit	$ 40.00	$ 40.00	$ 40.00	$ 40.00	
20	Total	$ 130.00	$ 130.00	$ 125.00	$ 125.00	
21						
22	Inventory and Purchases Worksheet					
23	Inventory Inputs					
24	Days inventory	30	30	30	30	
25						
26	Disbursements for Purchases Inputs					
27	Days payable	30	30	30	30	

Sheet tabs: **Assumptions and Dashboard** / Sales and Coll

	Microsoft Excel - FigQ8.6							
	File Edit View Insert Format Tools Data Window Help				Type a question for help			
	A1							

	A	B	C	D	E	F	G
1				Period			
2		1Q X4	2Q X4	3Q X4	4Q X4		X4
3	**CAPITAL BUDGET**						
4	Capital Expenditures Budget						
5	Equipment	$ 25,000	$ 20,000	$ 30,000	$ 10,000		$ 85,000
6	Furniture	5,000	5,000	5,000	5,000		20,000
7	Fixtures	2,000	2,000	2,000	2,000		8,000
8	Total capital expenditures	$ 32,000	$ 27,000	$ 37,000	$ 17,000		$ 113,000
9							
10	Disbursements for Capital Expenditures Budget						
11	Equipment	$ 25,000	$ 20,000	$ 30,000	$ 10,000		$ 85,000
12	Furniture	5,000	5,000	5,000	5,000		20,000
13	Fixtures	2,000	2,000	2,000	2,000		8,000
14	Total disbursements for capital expenditures	$ 32,000	$ 27,000	$ 37,000	$ 17,000		$ 113,000
15							
16	Depreciation Budget						
17	Equipment	$ 1,250	$ 2,250	$ 3,750	$ 4,250		$ 11,500
18	Furniture	250	500	750	1,000		2,500
19	Fixtures	125	250	375	500		1,250
20	Total depreciation	$ 1,625	$ 3,000	$ 4,875	$ 5,750		$ 15,250
21							
22	Cumulative capital expenditures	$ 32,000	$ 59,000	$ 96,000	$ 113,000		
23	- Accumulated depreciation	1,625	4,625	9,500	15,250		
24	= Fixed assets, net of depreciation	$ 30,375	$ 54,375	$ 86,500	$ 97,750		
25							
26							
27	Cumulative disbursements for CAPEX	$ 32,000	$ 59,000	$ 96,000	$ 113,000		
28	Payables adjustment for CAPEX disbursements	$ -	$ -	$ -	$ -		

H ◀ ▶ H \ **Capital** / Cash / Balance Sheet / Income Statement /

Ready

FIGURE Q8.6   Company PQR's Capital Worksheet

1. Given the information presented, build the Cash Flows from Operating Activities section of Company PQR's Statement of Cash Flows.
2. Given the information presented, build the Cash Flows from Investing Activities section of Company PQR's Statement of Cash Flows.
3. Given the information presented, build the Cash Flows from Financing Activities section of Company PQR's Statement of Cash Flows.

CHAPTER 9

Free Cash Flows and Dashboard

While Chapters 2 through 8 covered the creation of Napavale's Master Budget, Operating Budget, Financial Budget, and Consolidated Financial Statements (Balance Sheet, Income Statement, and Statement of Cash Flows), this chapter is focused on Napavale's free cash flows and the Dashboard section of the Assumptions and Dashboard worksheet. The calculation of Napavale's projected free cash flows represents the final stage in building all of the components required for the analysis and evaluation of Napavale as a business. As such, after calculating Napavale's free cash flows, I will build the first Dashboard section of Napavale's Assumptions and Dashboard worksheet in which various outputs of the financial model are checked for consistency.

As mentioned briefly in Chapter 1, free cash flows represent the funds available to "all providers of capital"—a group that includes a company's equity (stock) owners and debt holders. The concept of free cash flows, which is a key component of all traditional MBA finance classes, is central to the modeling and analysis of any company's operations. In essence, free cash flows represent the cash left over after all of a company's expenses and obligations have been paid and fulfilled. I will revisit the concept of free cash flows later in the book when I cover the concept of valuation in Chapter 13.

The calculation and analysis of Napavale's free cash flows represent one way to assess and evaluate Napavale as a business. Note that the calculation of free cash flows is based largely on information that I have already calculated in previous chapters. I will present updated views of Napavale's Assumptions and Dashboard worksheet when new assumptions are introduced over the course of this chapter.

You may remember from Chapter 2 that the Dashboard offers a sense of a financial model's condition and "state of health." A Dashboard can provide both a synopsis of a financial model's key outputs, such as revenues and net income, and can also indicate, for example, whether the balance sheet is balanced. I will cover the synopsis of key outputs from the financial model in Chapter 10 and the indication of the financial model's accuracy and consistency later in this chapter.

CALCULATION OF FREE CASH FLOWS

There are several different ways to calculate free cash flows and the actual definition of free cash flows (and the components of free cash flows) can vary from person to person and from company to company. The definition and calculation of free cash flows that I present in this chapter are widely used in both academia and in industry. Do not be surprised, however, if you come across a different way of defining or calculating free cash flows as compared to the discussion of free cash flows in this book. The important thing to remember is the core meaning of free cash flows—namely, the funds available to all providers of capital after all required expenses have been paid.

The first step in calculating Napavale's free cash flows is to determine a metric known as EBIT (Earnings Before Interest and Taxes). In Napavale's case, EBIT is equivalent to "income from operations" on the Income Statement. For the sake of reference, Figure 9.1 presents a view of Napavale's Income Statement with the names of the worksheet cells indicated.

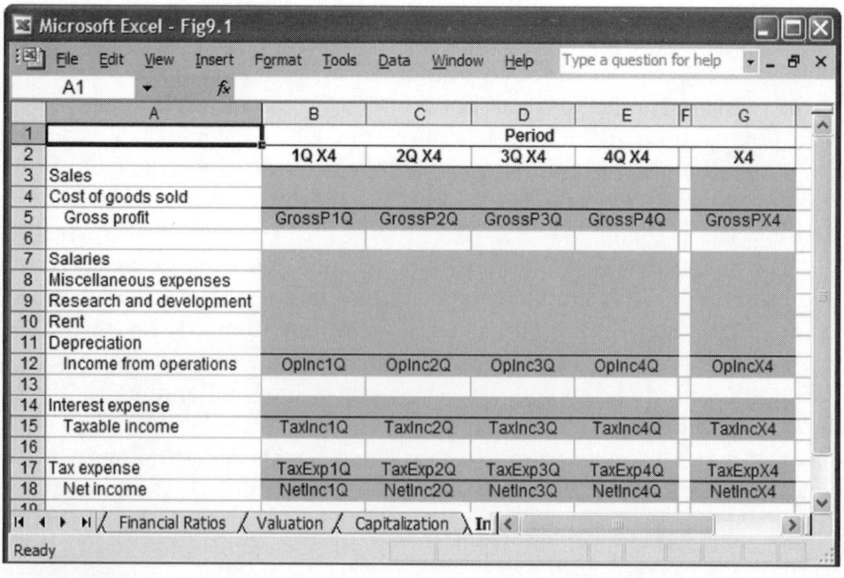

FIGURE 9.1   Names of the Input and Output Cells in the Income Statement

The next step in calculating Napavale's free cash flows is to adjust EBIT for any taxes that are paid. Taxes are expenses that must be paid to the tax authorities; interest payments are not removed from the EBIT figure because free cash flows represent the funds available to all providers of capital (including those providing debt, to whom interest payments are made). Figure 9.2 offers a view of the first section of Napavale's free cash flows worksheet in which "after-tax EBIT" is calculated. An alternative view of Napavale's free cash flows worksheet in which the values and formulas underlying the worksheet cells are exposed and visible is shown in Figure 9.3. The names of the input and output worksheet cells in Napavale's free cash flows worksheet are presented in Figure 9.4.

After calculating Napavale's "after-tax EBIT," several additional adjustments are required to determine the free cash flow projections for Napavale. Each of these adjustments reconciles the after-tax EBIT figure to a cash-based value. I will highlight each of these adjustments in the order in which I have included them in Napavale's free cash flows worksheet.

	A	B	C	D	E	F	G
1				Period			
2		1Q X4	2Q X4	3Q X4	4Q X4		X4
3	EBIT	207,288	509,975	655,143	1,054,350		2,426,755
4							
5	Effective tax rate	35.0%	35.0%	35.0%	35.0%		
6							
7	EBIT * (1 - t)	134,737	331,484	425,843	685,328		1,577,391
8	+ Depreciation						
9	- CAPEX						
10	- Changes in NWC						
11	= Free cash flow						
12	+ Terminal value						
13	= Total free cash flow						
14							
15	Present value						
16							
17							
18	NPV						
19							
20	WACC						
21	g (to perpetuity)						
22							

FIGURE 9.2 First Section of the Free Cash Flows Worksheet

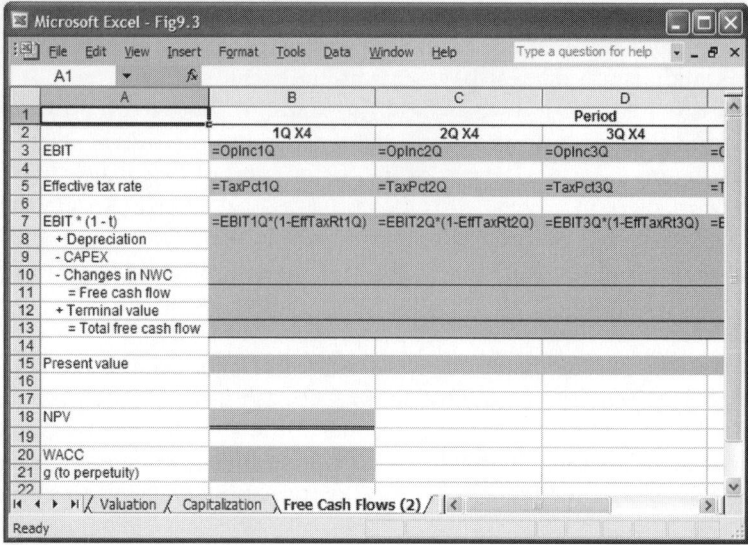

FIGURE 9.3 Alternative View of the First Section of the Free Cash
Flows Worksheet

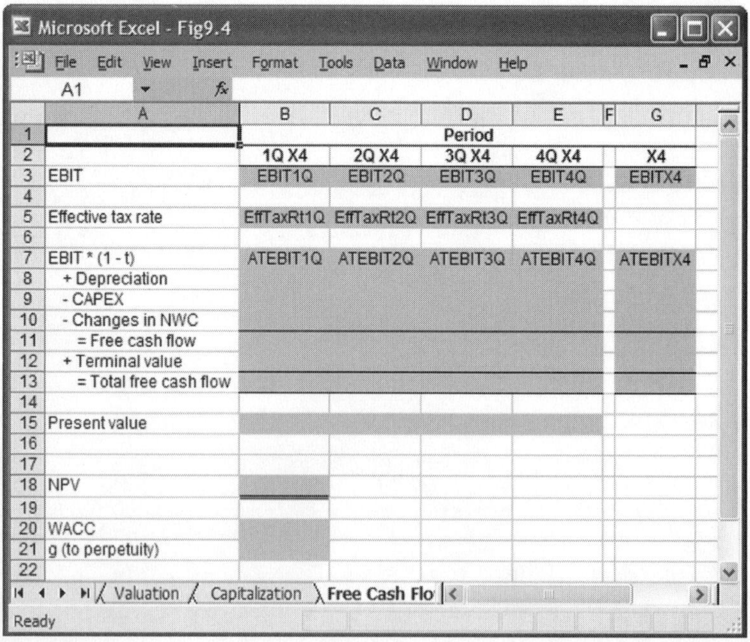

FIGURE 9.4 Names of the Input and Output Cells in the First Section of the Free
Cash Flows Worksheet

The first adjustment to after-tax EBIT is to add the depreciation expense for each accounting period (quarter) back into the after-tax EBIT. Depreciation is a non-cash expense and thus does not represent an outflow of cash from Napavale. Depreciation expense is a line item in Napavale's Income Statement; the names of the worksheet cells in Napavale's Income Statement are shown in Figure 9.1.

The second adjustment to after-tax EBIT is to subtract disbursements for capital expenditures for each accounting period (quarter) out of the after-tax EBIT. Capital expenditures do not appear directly as a component of EBIT (depreciation expenses related to capital expenditures, however, do show up in EBIT), so these disbursements must be accounted for as they represent cash outflows for Napavale. For the sake of reference, Figure 9.5 presents a view of Napavale's Statement of Cash Flows with the names of the worksheet cells indicated.

The final adjustment to after-tax EBIT is to subtract any positive changes in Napavale's net working capital for each accounting period (quarter) out of after-tax EBIT. The concept of net working capital and the calculations underlying the changes in Napavale's net working capital were covered in Chapter 7. An increase in net working capital represents a cash outflow for Napavale (and vice-versa), so any increase in net working capital must be accounted for as a cash outflow in the calculation of

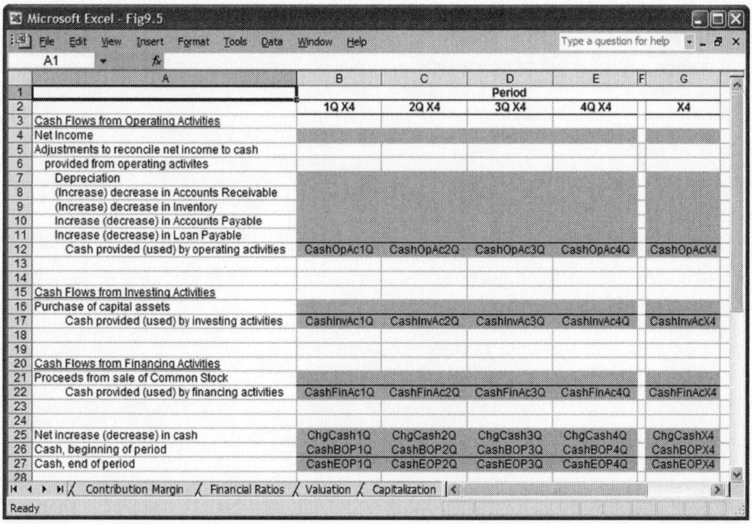

FIGURE 9.5 Names of the Input and Output Cells in the Statement of Cash Flows

Napavale's free cash flows. For the sake of reference, Figure 9.6 presents a view of Napavale's Balance Sheet with the names of the worksheet cells indicated.

Napavale's free cash flows worksheet is shown in Figure 9.7. Note that I have calculated the free cash flows for each accounting period (quarter) in Figure 9.7.

Napavale's free cash flows worksheet now includes adjustments for depreciation, capital expenditures, and changes in net working capital. An alternative view of Napavale's free cash flows worksheet in which the values and formulas underlying the worksheet cells are exposed and visible is presented in Figure 9.8. Figure 9.9 highlights the names of the input and output worksheet cells underlying Napavale's free cash flows worksheet.

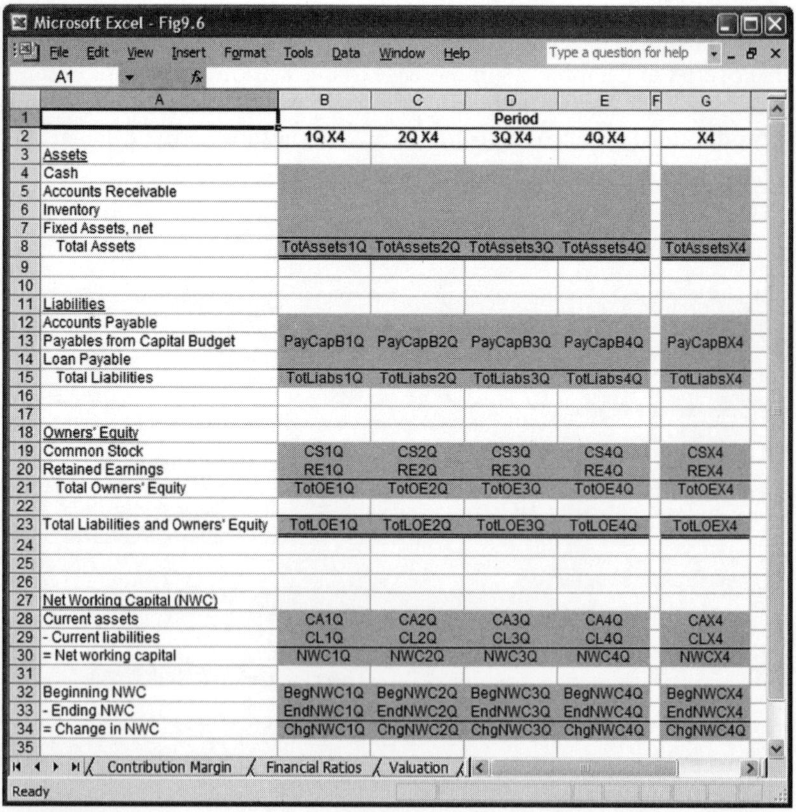

FIGURE 9.6 Names of the Input and Output Cells in the Balance Sheet

	A	B	C	D	E	F	G
1				Period			
2		1Q X4	2Q X4	3Q X4	4Q X4		X4
3	EBIT	207,288	509,975	655,143	1,054,350		2,426,755
4							
5	Effective tax rate	35.0%	35.0%	35.0%	35.0%		
6							
7	EBIT * (1 - t)	134,737	331,484	425,843	685,328		1,577,391
8	+ Depreciation	2,313	4,625	6,938	9,250		23,125
9	- CAPEX	45,000	45,000	45,000	45,000		180,000
10	- Changes in NWC	109,778	62,156	57,200	55,533		284,667
11	= Free cash flow	(17,728)	228,953	330,580	594,044		1,135,849
12	+ Terminal value						
13	= Total free cash flow						
14							
15	Present value						
16							
17							
18	NPV						
19							
20	WACC						
21	g (to perpetuity)						

Sheet tabs: Capital / Cash / Balance Sheet / Income

FIGURE 9.7 Free Cash Flows Worksheet

	A	B	C	D
1				Period
2		1Q X4	2Q X4	3Q X4
3	EBIT	=OpInc1Q	=OpInc2Q	=OpInc3Q
4				
5	Effective tax rate	=TaxPct1Q	=TaxPct2Q	=TaxPct3Q
6				
7	EBIT * (1 - t)	=EBIT1Q*(1-EffTaxRt1Q)	=EBIT2Q*(1-EffTaxRt2Q)	=EBIT3Q*(1-EffTaxRt3Q)
8	+ Depreciation	=Dep1Q	=Dep2Q	=Dep3Q
9	- CAPEX	=CAPEXDis1Q	=CAPEXDis2Q	=CAPEXDis3Q
10	- Changes in NWC	=-ChgNWC1Q	=-ChgNWC2Q	=-ChgNWC3Q
11	= Free cash flow	=ATEBIT1Q+B8-B9-B10	=ATEBIT2Q+C8-C9-C10	=ATEBIT3Q+D8-D9-D10
12	+ Terminal value			
13	= Total free cash flow			
14				
15	Present value			
16				
17				
18	NPV			
19				
20	WACC			
21	g (to perpetuity)			

Sheet tabs: Financial Ratios / Valuation / Capitalization / Free

FIGURE 9.8 Alternative View of the Free Cash Flows Worksheet

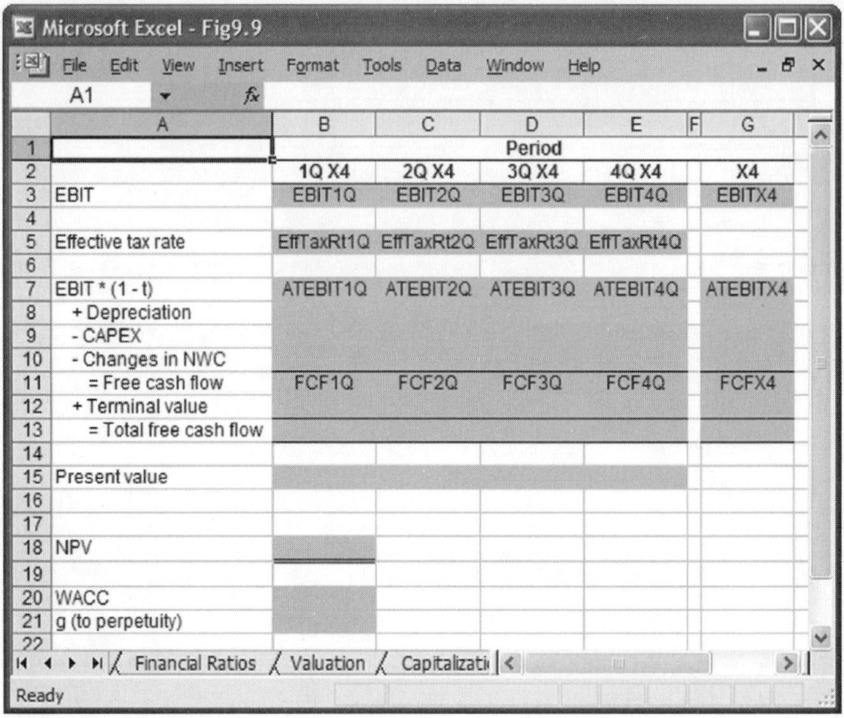

FIGURE 9.9   Names of the Input and Output Cells in the Free Cash Flows Worksheet

DASHBOARD

Now that I have calculated Napavale's projected free cash flows, I will build the first section of the Dashboard portion of the Assumptions and Dashboard worksheet. This section of the Dashboard, as mentioned at the beginning of this chapter, will give a sense of the accuracy and consistency of the internal workings of Napavale's financial model. Note that this will not give any indication of the reasonableness of the assumptions underlying Napavale's financial model. The Dashboard is simply meant to indicate whether the financial model is working properly.

The key metrics that I will use to determine if Napavale's financial model is working properly are (1) whether the Balance Sheet balances and (2) whether the "cash" values from the Balance Sheet equal the "cash, end of period" values from the Statement of Cash Flows. These two key metrics give a quick and good indication as to the inner workings of the financial model.

While you can always look at the Balance Sheet and/or the Statement of Cash Flows after any changes are made to a financial model to make sure the financial model is working properly, using a Dashboard makes this process more efficient and potentially less error-prone.

Balance Sheet Status

To determine whether the Balance Sheet balances, I must first add a calculation to the Balance Sheet itself. Remember that a Balance Sheet must always "balance" if it is working properly; in other words, a business's Assets must always equal its Liabilities + Owners' Equity. As such, I will calculate the differences between Napavale's Assets and Napavale's Liabilities and Owners' Equity. If this difference is any value other than zero, the model is not functioning properly. Figure 9.10 presents an updated view of

	A	B	C	D	E	F	G
1				Period			
2		1Q X4	2Q X4	3Q X4	4Q X4		X4
3	Assets						
4	Cash	$ 982,272	$1,260,656	$1,541,236	$2,135,280		$2,135,280
5	Accounts Receivable	133,333	192,000	257,600	336,000		336,000
6	Inventory	64,667	83,067	102,667	102,667		102,667
7	Fixed Assets, net	42,688	83,063	121,125	156,875		156,875
8	Total Assets	$ 1,222,959	$1,618,785	$2,022,628	$2,730,822		$2,730,822
9							
10							
11	Liabilities						
12	Accounts Payable	$ 88,222	$ 103,133	$ 131,133	$ 154,000		$ 154,000
13	Payables from Capital Budget	-	-	-	-		-
14	Loan Payable	-	50,000	-	-		-
15	Total Liabilities	$ 88,222	$ 153,133	$ 131,133	$ 154,000		$ 154,000
16							
17							
18	Owners' Equity						
19	Common Stock	$ 1,000,000	$1,000,000	$1,000,000	$1,000,000		$1,000,000
20	Retained Earnings	134,737	465,652	891,495	1,576,822		1,576,822
21	Total Owners' Equity	$ 1,134,737	$1,465,652	$1,891,495	$2,576,822		$2,576,822
22							
23	Total Liabilities and Owners' Equity	$ 1,222,959	$1,618,785	$2,022,628	$2,730,822		$2,730,822
24							
25	Balance Sheet calculation check	-	-	-	-		-
26							
27	Net Working Capital (NWC)						
28	Current assets	$ 198,000	$ 275,067	$ 360,267	$ 438,667		N/A
29	- Current liabilities	88,222	103,133	131,133	154,000		N/A
30	= Net working capital	$ 109,778	$ 171,933	$ 229,133	$ 284,667		N/A
31							
32	Beginning NWC	$ -	$ 109,778	$ 171,933	$ 229,133		N/A
33	- Ending NWC	109,778	171,933	229,133	284,667		N/A
34	= Change in NWC	$ (109,778)	$ (62,156)	$ (57,200)	$ (55,533)		N/A

FIGURE 9.10 Balance Sheet

Napavale's Balance Sheet in which the calculation that checks if the Balance Sheet balances is included.

An alternative view of Napavale's updated Balance Sheet in which the values and formulas underlying the worksheet cells are exposed and visible is presented in Figure 9.11. Figure 9.12 presents a view of the names of the worksheet cells in Napavale's updated Balance Sheet.

I now need to include an indicator in Napavale's Dashboard that displays the "status" of the Balance Sheet. Specifically, the Dashboard must display whether the Balance Sheet is balanced. To do so, I will reference the calculation highlighted in Figures 9.10 through 9.12 and I will use a function known as an "IF" in Excel. Figure 9.13 presents a view of the Dashboard from Napavale's Assumptions and Dashboard worksheet.

Note that the Balance Sheet status output cell contains the word "Yes." This is a result of the IF function, which I will discuss later in this

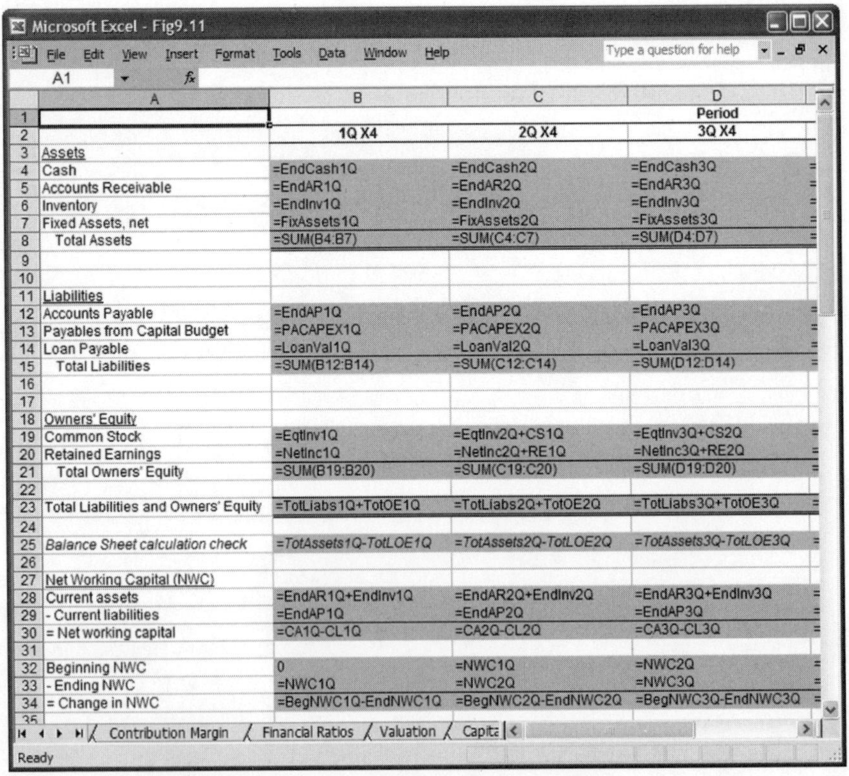

	A	B	C	D
1				Period
2		1Q X4	2Q X4	3Q X4
3	Assets			
4	Cash	=EndCash1Q	=EndCash2Q	=EndCash3Q
5	Accounts Receivable	=EndAR1Q	=EndAR2Q	=EndAR3Q
6	Inventory	=EndInv1Q	=EndInv2Q	=EndInv3Q
7	Fixed Assets, net	=FixAssets1Q	=FixAssets2Q	=FixAssets3Q
8	Total Assets	=SUM(B4:B7)	=SUM(C4:C7)	=SUM(D4:D7)
9				
10				
11	Liabilities			
12	Accounts Payable	=EndAP1Q	=EndAP2Q	=EndAP3Q
13	Payables from Capital Budget	=PACAPEX1Q	=PACAPEX2Q	=PACAPEX3Q
14	Loan Payable	=LoanVal1Q	=LoanVal2Q	=LoanVal3Q
15	Total Liabilities	=SUM(B12:B14)	=SUM(C12:C14)	=SUM(D12:D14)
16				
17				
18	Owners' Equity			
19	Common Stock	=EqtInv1Q	=EqtInv2Q+CS1Q	=EqtInv3Q+CS2Q
20	Retained Earnings	=NetInc1Q	=NetInc2Q+RE1Q	=NetInc3Q+RE2Q
21	Total Owners' Equity	=SUM(B19:B20)	=SUM(C19:C20)	=SUM(D19:D20)
22				
23	Total Liabilities and Owners' Equity	=TotLiabs1Q+TotOE1Q	=TotLiabs2Q+TotOE2Q	=TotLiabs3Q+TotOE3Q
24				
25	*Balance Sheet calculation check*	*=TotAssets1Q-TotLOE1Q*	*=TotAssets2Q-TotLOE2Q*	*=TotAssets3Q-TotLOE3Q*
26				
27	Net Working Capital (NWC)			
28	Current assets	=EndAR1Q+EndInv1Q	=EndAR2Q+EndInv2Q	=EndAR3Q+EndInv3Q
29	- Current liabilities	=EndAP1Q	=EndAP2Q	=EndAP3Q
30	= Net working capital	=CA1Q-CL1Q	=CA2Q-CL2Q	=CA3Q-CL3Q
31				
32	Beginning NWC	0	=NWC1Q	=NWC2Q
33	- Ending NWC	=NWC1Q	=NWC2Q	=NWC3Q
34	= Change in NWC	=BegNWC1Q-EndNWC1Q	=BegNWC2Q-EndNWC2Q	=BegNWC3Q-EndNWC3Q

FIGURE 9.11 Alternative View of the Balance Sheet

	A	B	C	D	E	F	G
				Period			
1							
2		1Q X4	2Q X4	3Q X4	4Q X4		X4
3	Assets						
4	Cash						
5	Accounts Receivable						
6	Inventory						
7	Fixed Assets, net						
8	Total Assets	TotAssets1Q	TotAssets2Q	TotAssets3Q	TotAssets4Q		TotAssetsX4
9							
10							
11	Liabilities						
12	Accounts Payable						
13	Payables from Capital Budget	PayCapB1Q	PayCapB2Q	PayCapB3Q	PayCapB4Q		PayCapBX4
14	Loan Payable						
15	Total Liabilities	TotLiabs1Q	TotLiabs2Q	TotLiabs3Q	TotLiabs4Q		TotLiabsX4
16							
17							
18	Owners' Equity						
19	Common Stock	CS1Q	CS2Q	CS3Q	CS4Q		CSX4
20	Retained Earnings	RE1Q	RE2Q	RE3Q	RE4Q		REX4
21	Total Owners' Equity	TotOE1Q	TotOE2Q	TotOE3Q	TotOE4Q		TotOEX4
22							
23	Total Liabilities and Owners' Equity	TotLOE1Q	TotLOE2Q	TotLOE3Q	TotLOE4Q		TotLOEX4
24							
25	*Balance Sheet calculation check*	BSCheck1Q	BSCheck2Q	BSCheck3Q	BSCheck4Q		BSCheckX4
26							
27	Net Working Capital (NWC)						
28	Current assets	CA1Q	CA2Q	CA3Q	CA4Q		CAX4
29	- Current liabilities	CL1Q	CL2Q	CL3Q	CL4Q		CLX4
30	= Net working capital	NWC1Q	NWC2Q	NWC3Q	NWC4Q		NWCX4
31							
32	Beginning NWC	BegNWC1Q	BegNWC2Q	BegNWC3Q	BegNWC4Q		BegNWCX4
33	- Ending NWC	EndNWC1Q	EndNWC2Q	EndNWC3Q	EndNWC4Q		EndNWCX4
34	= Change in NWC	ChgNWC1Q	ChgNWC2Q	ChgNWC3Q	ChgNWC4Q		ChgNWCX4

Tabs: Contribution Margin / Financial Ratios / Valuation

FIGURE 9.12   Names of the Input and Output Cells in the Balance Sheet

	A	B	C	D	E	F	G	H
1				Period				
2		1Q X4	2Q X4	3Q X4	4Q X4		X4	
111								
112								
113								
114	DASHBOARD							
115	Is the Balance Sheet balanced?							Yes
116	*Sum total of Balance Sheet differences*							$ -
117								

Tabs: Assumptions and Dashboard / Sales and Collections / COG

FIGURE 9.13   Dashboard

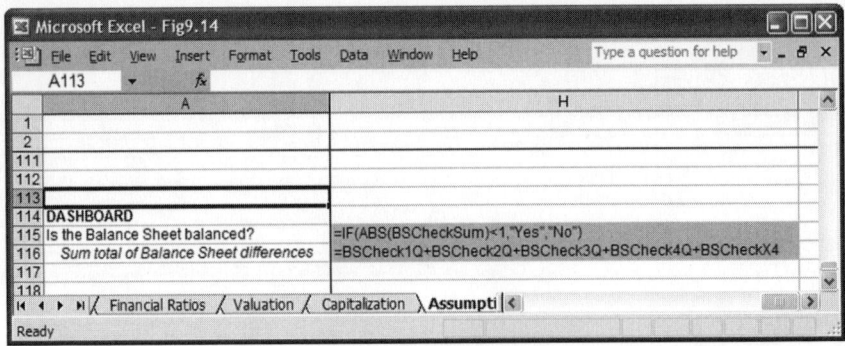

FIGURE 9.14 Alternative View of the Assumptions and Dashboard Worksheet

section. Figure 9.14 presents an alternative view of Napavale's Assumptions and Dashboard worksheet in which the values and formulas underlying the worksheet cells are exposed and visible. The names of the input and output cells in Napavale's Assumptions and Dashboard worksheet are shown in Figure 9.15.

The IF function shown in Figure 9.14 evaluates a condition, such as whether a variable is equal to a specified value, and then returns a result based on the evaluation of that condition. The specific syntax of the IF

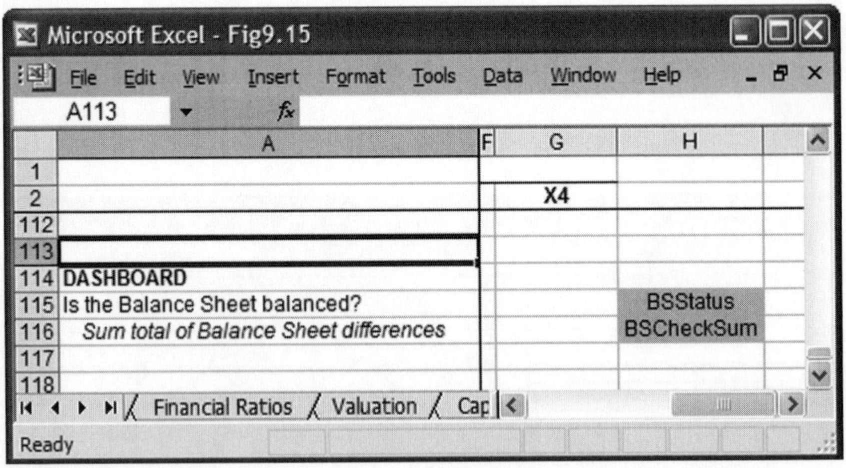

FIGURE 9.15 Names of the Input and Output Cells in the Assumptions and Dashboard Worksheet

function is as follows: = IF (Condition, True, False). "Condition" represents the condition to be evaluated, "true" represents the output of this function if the condition is true, and "false" represents the output of this function if the condition is false.

The IF function has many uses in financial modeling. In the context of Figures 9.13 through 9.15, the IF function determines if the absolute value (indicated by the use of the ABS, or absolute value, function) of the sum of the differences between Napavale's Assets and Napavale's Liabilities + Owners' Equity is less than 1 (I used "less than 1" instead of 0 here to account for any minor rounding errors). If the absolute value sum of these differences is greater than 1, Napavale's Balance Sheet is not balanced in some period (or periods).

The output of the IF function used in the Balance Sheet Status section of Napavale's Dashboard thus displays "Yes" if the Balance Sheet balances across all accounting periods (quarters) and "No" if the Balance Sheet is not balanced in one or more accounting periods (quarter(s)).

Statement of Cash Flows Status

To determine whether the "cash" values from the Balance Sheet equal the "cash, end of period" values from the Statement of Cash Flows, I will compare the cash values from the Balance Sheet with the cash values from the Statement of Cash Flows. This comparison of the cash figures from the Balance Sheet and the Statement of Cash Flows is meant to serve as a check on the internal consistency of Napavale's financial model. If the difference in cash values across these worksheets is any value other than zero, the model is not functioning properly.

Figure 9.16 presents an updated view of Napavale's Statement of Cash Flows in which the calculation that checks if the cash values are equal in both the Balance Sheet and the Statement of Cash Flows is included. An alternative view of Napavale's updated Statement of Cash Flows in which the values and formulas underlying the worksheet cells are exposed and visible is presented in Figure 9.17. Figure 9.18 presents a view of the names of the worksheet cells in Napavale's updated Statement of Cash Flows.

I now need to include an indicator in Napavale's Dashboard that displays the "status" of the Statement of Cash Flows. Specifically, the Dashboard must display whether the cash values in the Statement of Cash Flows are equal to the cash values in the Balance Sheet. To do so, I will reference the calculation highlighted in Figures 9.16 through 9.18 and I will use an IF function as I did in the Balance Sheet Status section of this

FIGURE 9.16   Statement of Cash Flows

FIGURE 9.17   Alternative View of the Statement of Cash Flows

		Period				
	1Q X4	2Q X4	3Q X4	4Q X4		X4
Cash Flows from Operating Activities						
Net Income						
Adjustments to reconcile net income to cash						
provided from operating activities						
Depreciation						
(Increase) decrease in Accounts Receivable						
(Increase) decrease in Inventory						
Increase (decrease) in Accounts Payable						
Increase (decrease) in Loan Payable						
Cash provided (used) by operating activities	CashOpAc1Q	CashOpAc2Q	CashOpAc3Q	CashOpAc4Q		CashOpAcX4
Cash Flows from Investing Activities						
Purchase of capital assets						
Cash provided (used) by investing activities	CashInvAc1Q	CashInvAc2Q	CashInvAc3Q	CashInvAc4Q		CashInvAcX4
Cash Flows from Financing Activities						
Proceeds from sale of Common Stock						
Cash provided (used) by financing activities	CashFinAc1Q	CashFinAc2Q	CashFinAc3Q	CashFinAc4Q		CashFinAcX4
Net increase (decrease) in cash	ChgCash1Q	ChgCash2Q	ChgCash3Q	ChgCash4Q		ChgCashX4
Cash, beginning of period	CashBOP1Q	CashBOP2Q	CashBOP3Q	CashBOP4Q		CashBOPX4
Cash, end of period	CashEOP1Q	CashEOP2Q	CashEOP3Q	CashEOP4Q		CashEOPX4
Cash Flows calculation check	CFCheck1Q	CFCheck2Q	CFCheck3Q	CFCheck4Q		CFCheckX4
Changes in Balance Sheet Accounts						
Accounts Receivable beginning value						
Accounts Receivable ending value						
(Increase) decrease in Accounts Receivable	ChgAR1Q	ChgAR2Q	ChgAR3Q	ChgAR4Q		
Inventory beginning value						
Inventory ending value						
(Increase) decrease in Inventory	ChgInv1Q	ChgInv2Q	ChgInv3Q	ChgInv4Q		

FIGURE 9.18 Names of the Input and Output Cells in the Statement of Cash Flows

chapter. Figure 9.19 presents a view of the Dashboard from Napavale's Assumptions and Dashboard worksheet.

Note that the Statement of Cash Flows Status output cell contains the word "Yes." This is a result of the IF function, which is covered in the Balance Sheet Status section of this chapter. Figure 9.20 presents an alternative view of Napavale's Assumptions and Dashboard worksheet in which the values and formulas underlying the worksheet cells are exposed and visible. The names of the input and output cells in Napavale's Assumptions and Dashboard worksheet are shown in Figure 9.21.

In the context of Figures 9.19 through 9.21, the IF function determines if the absolute value of the sum of the differences between Napavale's cash values from the Statement of Cash Flows and the Balance Sheet is greater than 1 (I used 1 instead of 0 here to account for any minor rounding errors). If the absolute value of the sum of these differences is greater than 1, there is an error somewhere in Napavale's financial model.

The output of the IF function used in the Statement of Cash Flows Status section of Napavale's Dashboard thus displays "Yes" if the cash values are equal between the Statement of Cash Flows and the Balance Sheet across all accounting periods (quarters) and "No" if the cash values are not equal in one or more accounting periods (quarter(s)).

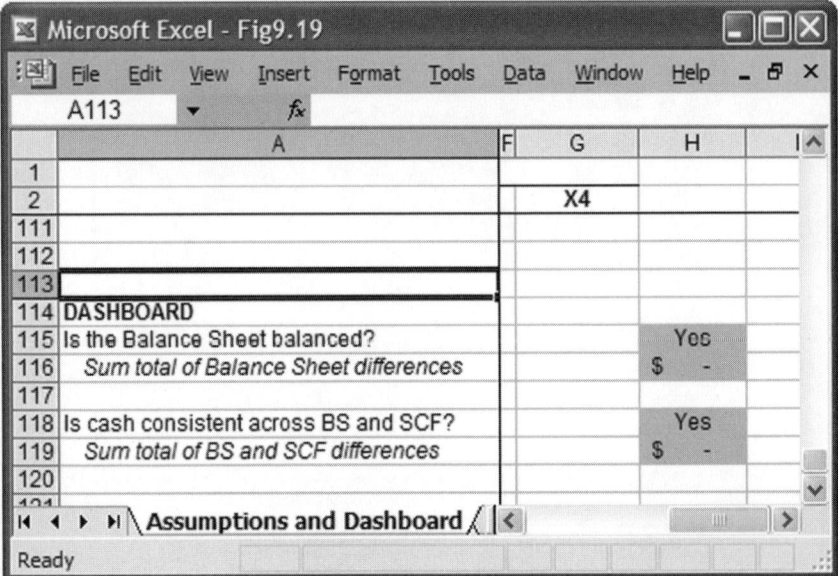

FIGURE 9.19   Dashboard

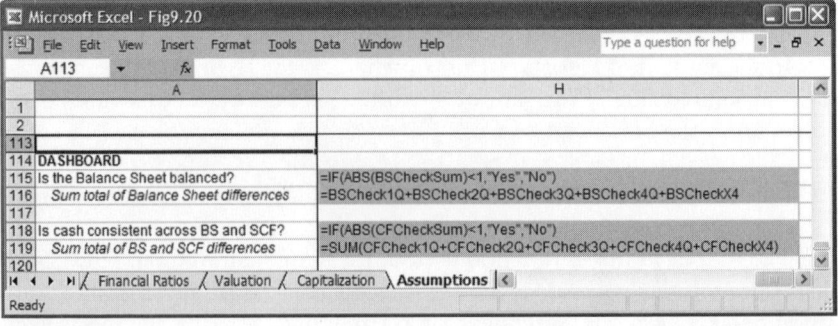

FIGURE 9.20   Alternative View of the Assumptions and Dashboard Worksheet

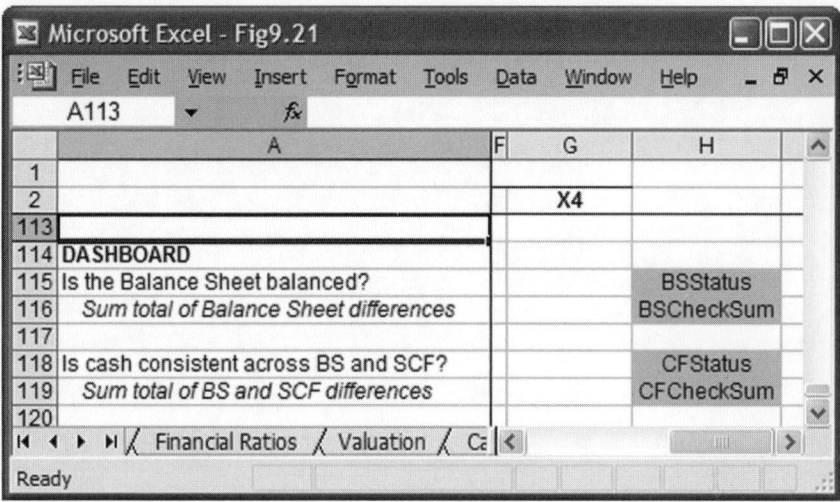

FIGURE 9.21   Names of the Input and Output Cells in the Assumptions and Dashboard Worksheet

QUESTIONS

Each of the questions for this chapter relates to a hypothetical company named Company STU. Company STU sells satellite radios to consumers. As such, Company STU is a product-oriented (as opposed to a service-oriented) business. The questions for this chapter will address fiscal year X4 on a quarterly basis (four specific quarters, 1Q–4Q for year X4).

The following questions will test your knowledge of the material covered in this chapter in an applied manner—specifically, you will be asked to calculate Company STU's free cash flows.

To prepare you for this chapter's questions, several figures provide background information related to Company STU's operations. Figure Q9.1 presents a view of Company STU's Income Statement. Note that there are three cost-of-goods-sold components for Company STU's satellite radios: (1) electronics, (2) casing, and (3) assembly and labor.

Figure Q9.2 presents a view of Company STU's Statement of Cash Flows. Company STU's Balance Sheet is shown in Figure Q9.3.

Microsoft Excel - FigQ9.1

File　Edit　View　Insert　Format　Tools　Data　Window　Help　　　Type a question for help

A1

A	B	C	D	E	F	G
1			Period			
2	1Q X4	2Q X4	3Q X4	4Q X4		X4
3 Sales	$ 20,000,000	$ 25,000,000	$ 29,250,000	$ 39,000,000		$ 113,250,000
4 Cost of goods sold	7,500,000	9,000,000	9,750,000	13,000,000		39,250,000
5　Gross profit	$ 12,500,000	$ 16,000,000	$ 19,500,000	$ 26,000,000		$ 74,000,000
6						
7 Salaries	$ 3,080,025	$ 3,379,838	$ 3,695,738	$ 3,995,550		$ 14,151,150
8 Miscellaneous expenses	1,000,000	1,250,000	1,462,500	1,950,000		5,662,500
9 Research and development	2,000,000	2,500,000	2,925,000	3,900,000		11,325,000
10 Rent	120,000	120,000	120,000	132,000		492,000
11 Depreciation	9,063	18,125	27,188	36,250		90,625
12　Income from operations	$ 6,290,913	$ 8,732,038	$ 11,269,575	$ 15,986,200		$ 42,278,725
13						
14 Interest expense	$　-	$　-	$　-	$　-		$　-
15　Taxable income	$ 6,290,913	$ 8,732,038	$ 11,269,575	$ 15,986,200		$ 42,278,725
16						
17 Tax expense	$ 2,201,819	$ 3,056,213	$ 3,944,351	$ 5,595,170		$ 14,797,554
18　Net income	$ 4,089,093	$ 5,675,824	$ 7,325,224	$ 10,391,030		$ 27,481,171

Capital ╱ Cash ╱ Balance Sheet ╲ Income Statement ╱

Ready

FIGURE Q9.1　Company STU's Income Statement

Microsoft Excel - FigQ9.2

File　Edit　View　Insert　Format　Tools　Data　Window　Help　　　Type a question for help

A1

A	B	C	D	E	F	G
1			Period			
2	1Q X4	2Q X4	3Q X4	4Q X4		X4
3 Cash Flows from Operating Activities						
4 Net Income	4,089,093	5,675,824	7,325,224	10,391,030		27,481,171
5 Adjustments to reconcile net income to cash						
6　provided from operating activites						
7　Depreciation	9,063	18,125	27,188	36,250		90,625
8　(Increase) decrease in Accounts Receivable	(2,666,667)	(666,667)	(647,917)	(1,327,083)		(5,308,333)
9　(Increase) decrease in Inventory	(3,000,000)	(250,000)	(1,805,556)	-		(5,055,556)
10　Increase (decrease) in Accounts Payable	4,083,333	(486,111)	896,605	561,728		5,055,556
11　Increase (decrease) in Loan Payable	-	-	-	-		-
12　Cash provided (used) by operating activities	2,514,822	4,291,172	5,795,544	9,661,925		22,263,463
13						
14						
15 Cash Flows from Investing Activities						
16 Purchase of capital assets	(175,000)	(175,000)	(175,000)	(175,000)		(700,000)
17　Cash provided (used) by investing activities	(175,000)	(175,000)	(175,000)	(175,000)		(700,000)
18						
19						
20 Cash Flows from Financing Activities						
21 Proceeds from sale of Common Stock	4,000,000	-	-	-		4,000,000
22　Cash provided (used) by financing activities	4,000,000	-	-	-		4,000,000
23						
24						
25 Net increase (decrease) in cash	6,339,822	4,116,172	5,620,544	9,486,925		25,563,463
26 Cash, beginning of period	-	6,339,822	10,455,994	16,076,538		-
27 Cash, end of period	6,339,822	10,455,994	16,076,538	25,563,463		25,563,463
28						
29 Cash Flows calculation check	-	-	-	-		-

Capital ╱ Cash ╱ Balance Sheet ╱ Income Statement ╲ Cash ╱

Ready

FIGURE Q9.2　Company STU's Statement of Cash Flows

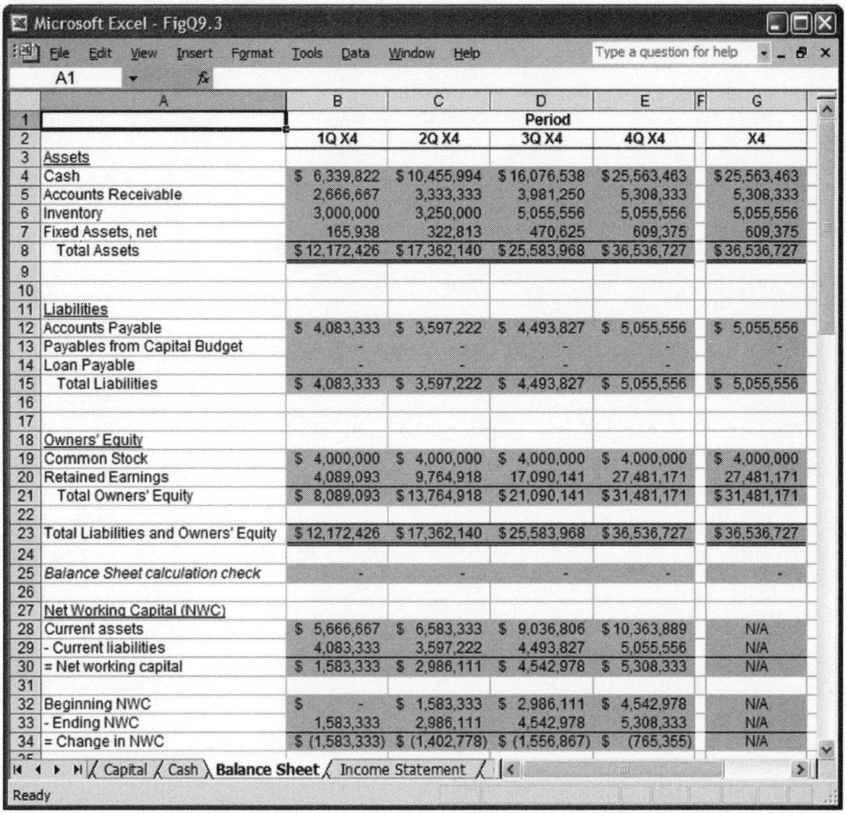

	A	B	C	D	E	G
1				Period		
2		1Q X4	2Q X4	3Q X4	4Q X4	X4
3	Assets					
4	Cash	$ 6,339,822	$ 10,455,994	$ 16,076,538	$ 25,563,463	$ 25,563,463
5	Accounts Receivable	2,666,667	3,333,333	3,981,250	5,308,333	5,308,333
6	Inventory	3,000,000	3,250,000	5,055,556	5,055,556	5,055,556
7	Fixed Assets, net	165,938	322,813	470,625	609,375	609,375
8	Total Assets	$ 12,172,426	$ 17,362,140	$ 25,583,968	$ 36,536,727	$ 36,536,727
9						
10						
11	Liabilities					
12	Accounts Payable	$ 4,083,333	$ 3,597,222	$ 4,493,827	$ 5,055,556	$ 5,055,556
13	Payables from Capital Budget	-	-	-	-	-
14	Loan Payable	-	-	-	-	-
15	Total Liabilities	$ 4,083,333	$ 3,597,222	$ 4,493,827	$ 5,055,556	$ 5,055,556
16						
17						
18	Owners' Equity					
19	Common Stock	$ 4,000,000	$ 4,000,000	$ 4,000,000	$ 4,000,000	$ 4,000,000
20	Retained Earnings	4,089,093	9,764,918	17,090,141	27,481,171	27,481,171
21	Total Owners' Equity	$ 8,089,093	$ 13,764,918	$ 21,090,141	$ 31,481,171	$ 31,481,171
22						
23	Total Liabilities and Owners' Equity	$ 12,172,426	$ 17,362,140	$ 25,583,968	$ 36,536,727	$ 36,536,727
24						
25	*Balance Sheet calculation check*	-	-	-	-	-
26						
27	Net Working Capital (NWC)					
28	Current assets	$ 5,666,667	$ 6,583,333	$ 9,036,806	$ 10,363,889	N/A
29	- Current liabilities	4,083,333	3,597,222	4,493,827	5,055,556	N/A
30	= Net working capital	$ 1,583,333	$ 2,986,111	$ 4,542,978	$ 5,308,333	N/A
31						
32	Beginning NWC	$ -	$ 1,583,333	$ 2,986,111	$ 4,542,978	N/A
33	- Ending NWC	1,583,333	2,986,111	4,542,978	5,308,333	N/A
34	= Change in NWC	$ (1,583,333)	$ (1,402,778)	$ (1,556,867)	$ (765,355)	N/A

FIGURE Q9.3 Company STU's Balance Sheet

1. Given the information presented, build a free cash flows worksheet for Napavale.
2. Given the information presented, build a Balance Sheet status indicator in Company STU's Assumptions and Dashboard worksheet.
3. Given the information presented, build a Statement of Cash Flows status indicator in Company STU's Assumptions and Dashboard worksheet.

Analysis of a Financial Model

CHAPTER 10

Sensitivity Analysis

After working through all of the steps in Chapters 2 through 9, I now have a financial model for Napavale that will generate consolidated projected financial statements (Balance Sheet, Income Statement, and Statement of Cash Flows) and free cash flows based on a series of assumptions and inputs (found in Napavale's Assumptions and Dashboard worksheet). Chapters 10 through 14 will cover ways in which I can evaluate and analyze Napavale as a business.

This chapter addresses an analytical technique known as "sensitivity analysis" in which I will evaluate the extent to which changes in assumptions and inputs affect various outputs of interest, such as revenues, net income, and free cash flows. In other words, a sensitivity analysis determines how sensitive an output variable is (or output variables are) to an input variable (or input variables). I will use the term "revenues" in place of "sales" (in dollars—not unit sales) throughout this chapter to avoid confusion. While revenues and sales may represent different meanings in some cases, I will use these terms interchangeably.

While there are a variety of ways to build sensitivity analyses in Microsoft Excel, one of the more efficient techniques is through the use of a tool known as a "data table." Data tables are well-suited to sensitivity analyses in that they enable the direct evaluation of how different values for an input variable would affect values for an output variable. To build data tables, however, I need to consolidate some information in Napavale's growing financial model into one Excel worksheet. I will consolidate this information in the Dashboard component of Napavale's Assumptions and Dashboard worksheet.

DASHBOARD

As I mentioned in Chapter 9, a Dashboard can provide a synopsis of a financial model's key outputs, such as revenues and net income, and can also indicate the accuracy and consistency of a financial model, such as whether the Balance Sheet is balanced. While I covered the use of the Dashboard to determine the accuracy and consistency of a financial model in Chapter 9, I discuss the synopsis of key outputs from the financial model in this chapter.

I am going to summarize several of Napavale's key financial metrics in the Dashboard section of the Assumptions and Dashboard worksheet. Specifically, I am going to consolidate Napavale's projected revenues, net income, and free cash flows for each accounting period (quarter). It is a matter of preference and relevance when it comes to choosing which financial metrics to include (if any) in the Dashboard. I chose these three metrics (revenues, net income, and free cash flows) for Napavale because I believe they are important determinants of the business's operational performance and because I am going to run sensitivity analyses on each of these metrics.

Figure 10.1 presents a view of the Dashboard section of Napavale's Assumptions and Dashboard worksheet. The Dashboard shown in Figure 10.1 now includes summary projections for revenues, net income, and free cash flows. An alternative view of the Dashboard in which the values and formulas underlying the worksheet cells are exposed is shown in Figure 10.2.

Figure 10.3 presents a view of the names of the worksheet cells in the Dashboard section of the Assumptions and Dashboard worksheet. Note that I am naming cells in the Dashboard that refer directly to other named cells (from the Income Statement and Free Cash Flows worksheet) so that the data tables presented later in this chapter are easier to understand.

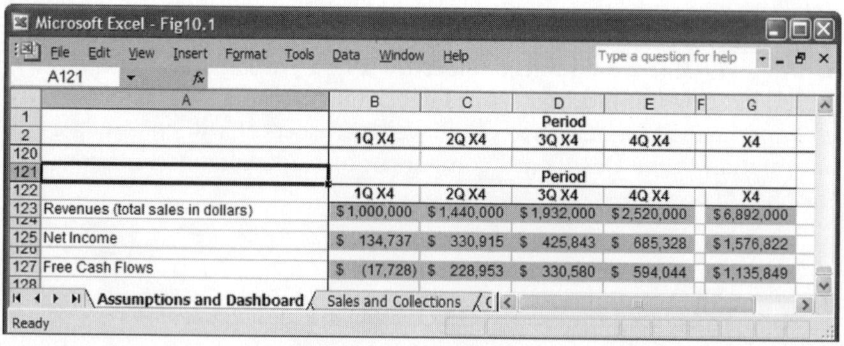

	A	B	C	D	E	F	G
1				Period			
2		1Q X4	2Q X4	3Q X4	4Q X4		X4
120							
121				Period			
122		1Q X4	2Q X4	3Q X4	4Q X4		X4
123	Revenues (total sales in dollars)	$1,000,000	$1,440,000	$1,932,000	$2,520,000		$6,892,000
125	Net Income	$ 134,737	$ 330,915	$ 425,843	$ 685,328		$1,576,822
127	Free Cash Flows	$ (17,728)	$ 228,953	$ 330,580	$ 594,044		$1,135,849

FIGURE 10.1 Dashboard

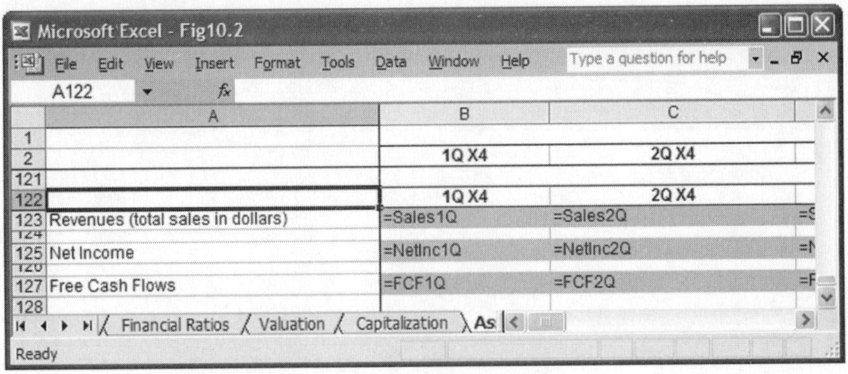

FIGURE 10.2 Alternative View of the Dashboard

The projections for Napavale's revenues and net income are drawn from the Income Statement. For the sake of reference, the names of the worksheet cells in the Income Statement are shown in Figure 10.4. Napavale's projected free cash flows figures are drawn from the Free Cash Flows worksheet, so the names of the cells in the Free Cash Flows worksheet are presented in Figure 10.5.

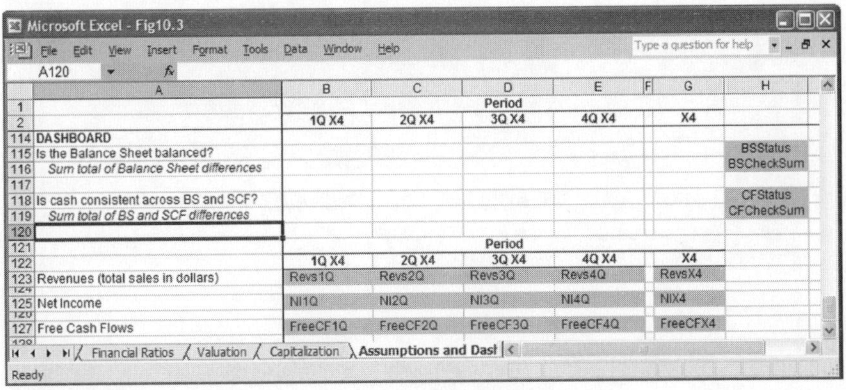

FIGURE 10.3 Names of the Input and Output Cells in the Assumptions and Dashboard Worksheet

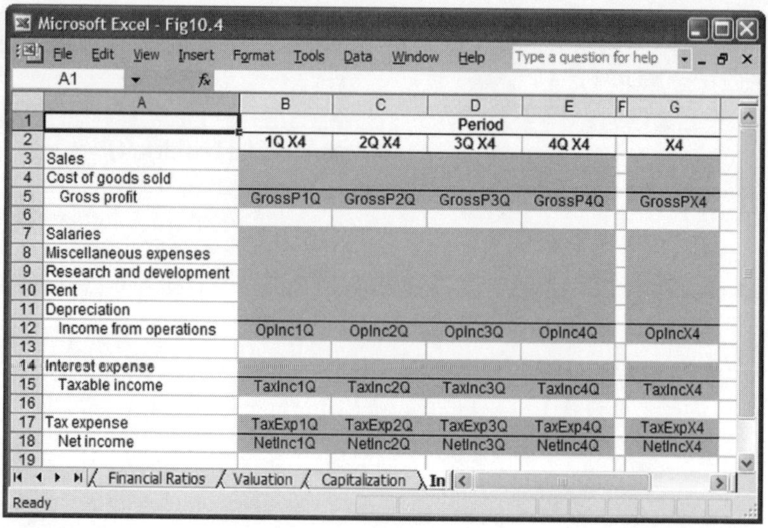

FIGURE 10.4 Names of the Input and Output Cells in the Income Statement

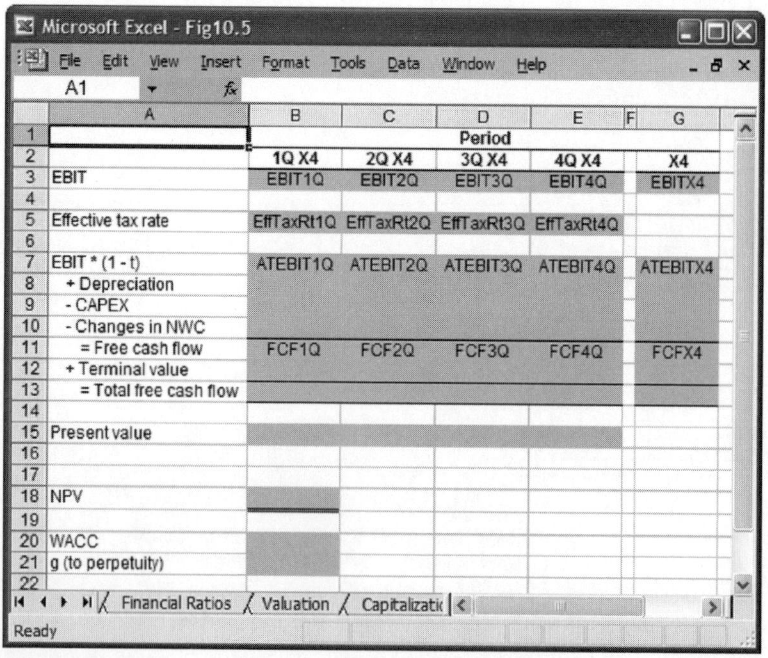

FIGURE 10.5 Names of the Input and Output Cells in the Free Cash Flows Worksheet

DATA TABLES

Now that I have incorporated the projections for Napavale's revenues, net income, and free cash flows into the Dashboard, I will run sensitivity analyses on each of these metrics through the use of data tables. Given the large number of variables involved in Napavale's financial model, there are many different types of sensitivity analyses that I could undertake. I am, however, going to focus on the sensitivity of one output variable (revenues for 1Q X4, for example) to one input variable (unit sales for 1Q X4, for example).

I hope to make the process of running sensitivity analyses using data tables as straightforward as possible by limiting the scope of input and output variables. If you build a financial model on your own, you may want to run sensitivity analyses on a wide array of input and output variables.

It is possible to build both one-variable and two-variable data tables in Microsoft Excel. One-variable data tables measure the change in one output variable based on a change in one input variable. Two-variable data tables measure the change in one output variable based on changes in two input variables. To keep things as simple as possible, I am going to discuss only one-variable data tables in this book. I will provide an overview of how to build data tables using revenues, net income, and free cash flows as separate output metrics of interest.

Revenues Data Table

To determine the sensitivity of Napavale's projected revenues to input variables in the financial model, I am going to vary the projected unit sales for 1Q X4 and measure the corresponding changes in revenues for 1Q X4. The first step in building a data table is to properly arrange both the output formula of interest (revenues for 1Q X4 in this case) and the various alternative values for the input variable of interest (unit sales for 1Q X4 in this case). While this may sound complex, it is actually fairly straightforward. Figure 10.6 presents a view of the properly arranged revenues data table for Napavale.

Note that I have arranged the data table in Figure 10.6 with the input values listed in a single column. It is also possible to list the input values in a single row. It is a matter of preference as to which format to use when building data tables. I will use "downward" formatted data tables in which the input values are listed in a single column throughout this chapter.

I hardcoded, or entered directly, the input values in Figure 10.6. You are free to choose whatever values may be of interest and you can even change these values after you have built a complete data table. I chose the specific input values in Figure 10.6 to get a sense of how moderate changes in Napavale's projected 1Q X4 unit sales will affect revenues for 1Q X4.

	A	B	C	D	E	F	G
1				Period			
2		1Q X4	2Q X4	3Q X4	4Q X4		X4
114	DASHBOARD						
115	Is the Balance Sheet balanced?						
116	*Sum total of Balance Sheet differences*						
117							
118	Is cash consistent across BS and SCF?						
119	*Sum total of BS and SCF differences*						
120							
121				Period			
122		1Q X4	2Q X4	3Q X4	4Q X4		X4
123	Revenues (total sales in dollars)	$1,000,000	$1,440,000	$1,932,000	$2,520,000		$6,892,000
124							
125	Net Income	$ 134,737	$ 330,915	$ 425,843	$ 685,328		$1,576,822
126							
127	Free Cash Flows	$ (17,728)	$ 228,953	$ 330,580	$ 594,044		$1,135,849
128							
129	Revenues Data Table						
130							
131			Revenues				
132			for 1Q X4				
133			$1,000,000				
133			800				
134			900				
135	Unit sales for 1Q X4		1,000				
136			1,100				
137			1,200				
138							

FIGURE 10.6   Revenues Data Table

The next step in building a data table is to select all of the input values and the formula of interest in Microsoft Excel. The selection of the appropriate cells for Napavale's revenues data table is shown in Figure 10.7

After the appropriate cells are selected in Excel, the next step is to select the "Data" menu in Excel and choose the "Table . . ." option from the drop-down menu. This will bring up a "Table" dialog box, into which I will enter the worksheet cell reference for the input variable (in the "Column input cell:" data entry box) that I would like to vary in the data table. Figure 10.8 presents a view of the Table dialog box along with the properly referenced input cell (cell B5 in this case) in front of the Assumptions and Dashboard worksheet. Cell B5 refers to the input cell for unit sales for 1Q X4 in the Assumptions and Dashboard worksheet.

After entering the proper cell reference into the Table dialog box, I will click "OK." Napavale's revenue data table is now complete. It is important to press the F9 key on the keyboard after the data table is complete; this ensures that the values in the data table are current and up-to-date (the F9 function key initiates a recalculation of all worksheet cells in an open workbook). Napavale's completed revenues data table is shown in Figure 10.9.

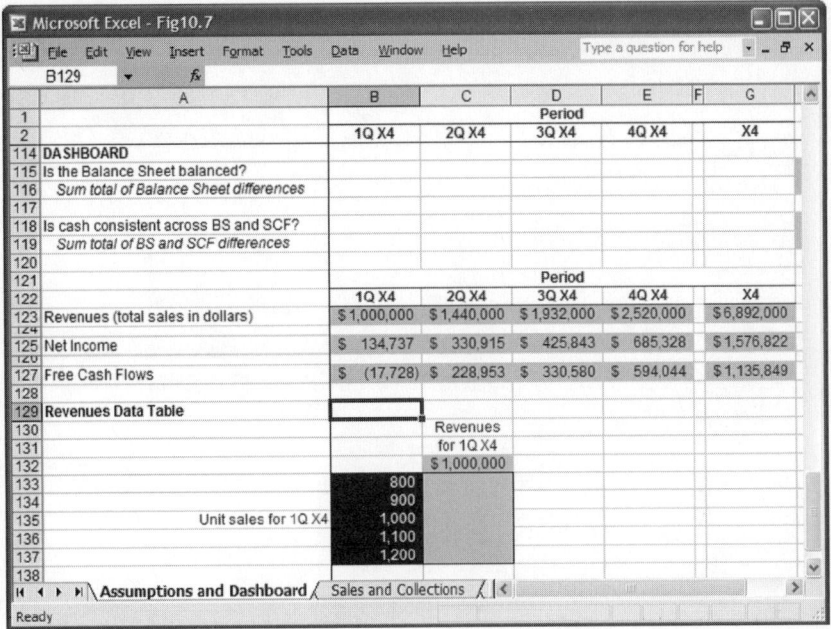

FIGURE 10.7   Revenues Data Table

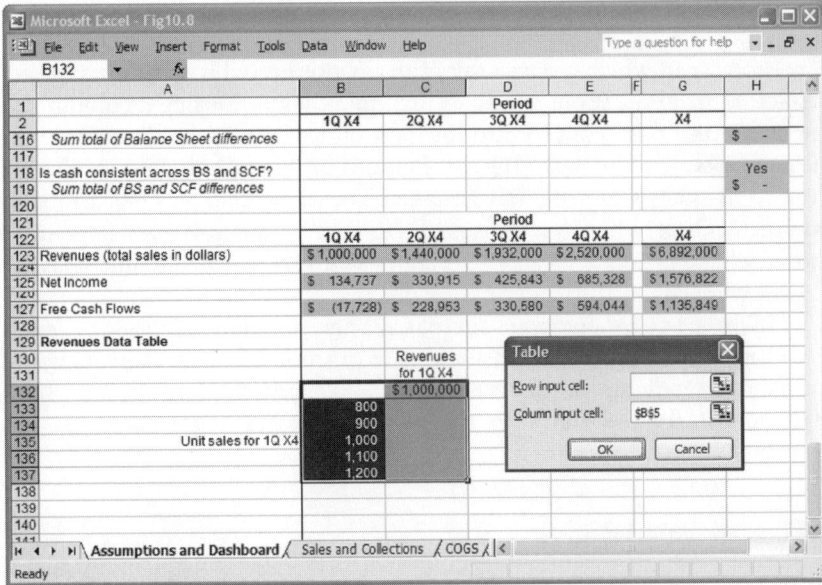

FIGURE 10.8   Data Table Dialog Box and the Assumptions and Dashboard Worksheet

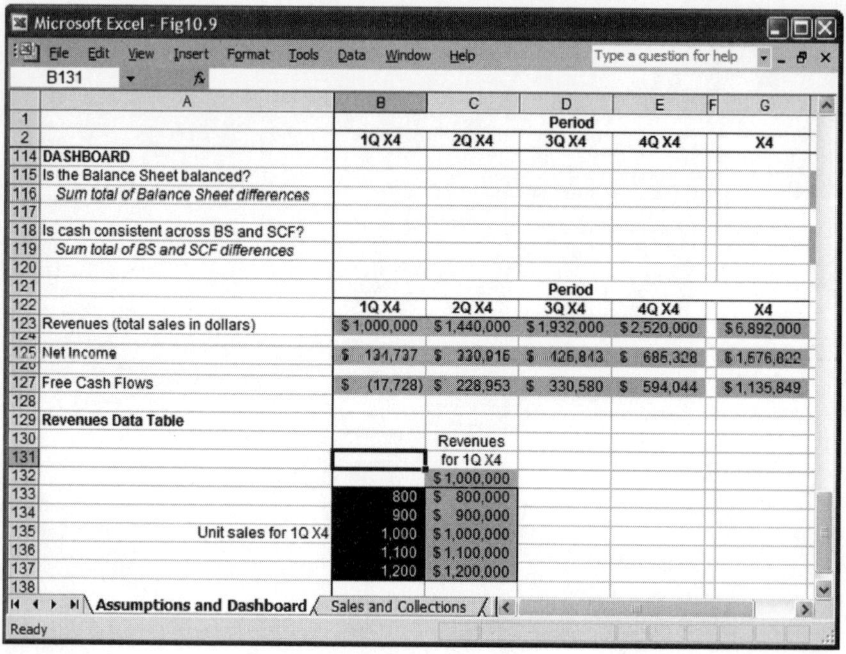

FIGURE 10.9   Revenues Data Table

The way in which a data table is to be interpreted is as follows: Reading across from the input variables (assuming you are using a column layout as I am in this chapter) into the data table itself, you will see how the output variable of interest (1Q X4 revenues in this case) would change for the various values of the input variable. The data table presents a tabular arrangement of what-if scenarios. In this case, the revenues data table shows what Napavale's 1Q X4 revenues would equal if the unit sales for 1Q X4 were changed to a different value.

Figure 10.10 presents an alternative view of the revenues data table from the Assumptions and Dashboard worksheet in which the values and formulas underlying the worksheet cells are exposed. Note the "TABLE" references in the revenues data table—this indicates that a data table has been used in Excel.

Net Income Data Table

To determine the sensitivity of Napavale's projected net income to input variables in the financial model, I am going to vary the projected price per

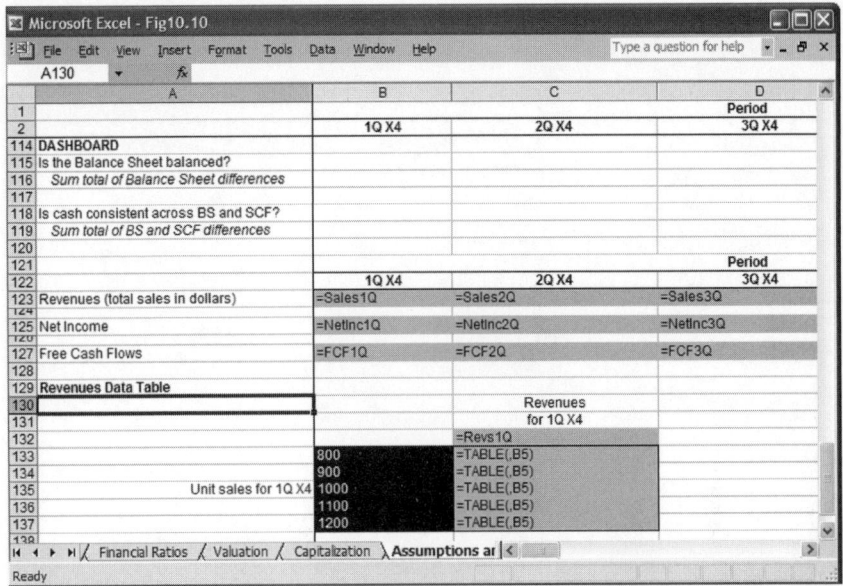

FIGURE 10.10   Alternative View of the Revenues Data Table

unit for 1Q X4 and measure the corresponding changes in net income for 1Q X4. As with the revenues data table, the first step in building the net income data table is to properly arrange both the output formula of interest (net income for 1Q X4 in this case) and the various alternative values for the input variable of interest (price per unit for 1Q X4 in this case). Figure 10.11 presents a view of the properly arranged net income data table for Napavale.

The subsequent steps involved in building the net income data table for Napavale are the same as those involved in building the revenues data table as outlined earlier in this chapter. Napavale's completed net income data table is presented in Figure 10.12.

In terms of interpreting Napavale's net income data table, the net income data table shows what Napavale's 1Q X4 net income would equal if the price per unit for 1Q X4 was changed to a different value. An alternative view of Napavale's net income data table, in which the values and formulas underlying the worksheet cells are exposed, is presented in Figure 10.13.

Microsoft Excel - Fig10.11

B129

	A	B	C	D	E	F	G	H
1				Period				
2		1Q X4	2Q X4	3Q X4	4Q X4		X4	
123	Revenues (total sales in dollars)	$ 1,000,000	$ 1,440,000	$ 1,932,000	$ 2,520,000		$ 6,892,000	
125	Net Income	$ 134,737	$ 330,915	$ 425,843	$ 685,328		$ 1,576,822	
127	Free Cash Flows	$ (17,728)	$ 228,953	$ 330,580	$ 594,044		$ 1,135,849	
128								
129	Revenues Data Table							
130			Revenues					
131			for 1Q X4					
132			$ 1,000,000					
133		800	$ 800,000					
134		900	$ 900,000					
135	Unit sales for 1Q X4	1,000	$ 1,000,000					
136		1,100	$ 1,100,000					
137		1,200	$ 1,200,000					
138								
139	Net Income Data Table							
140			Net Income					
141			for 1Q X4					
142			$ 134,737					
143		$ 700						
144		$ 850						
145	Price per unit for 1Q X4	$ 1,000						
146		$ 1,150						
147		$ 1,300						

Assumptions and Dashboard / Sales and Collections / COGS

Ready

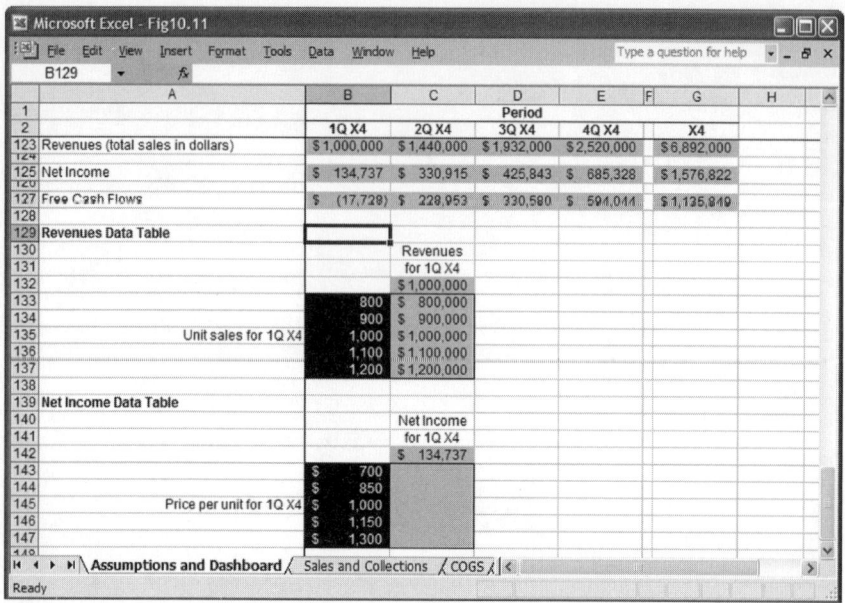

FIGURE 10.11 Net Income Data Table

Microsoft Excel - Fig10.12

A140

	A	B	C	D	E	F	G
1				Period			
2		1Q X4	2Q X4	3Q X4	4Q X4		X4
129	Revenues Data Table						
130			Revenues				
131			for 1Q X4				
132			$ 1,000,000				
133		800	$ 800,000				
134		900	$ 900,000				
135	Unit sales for 1Q X4	1,000	$ 1,000,000				
136		1,100	$ 1,100,000				
137		1,200	$ 1,200,000				
138							
139	Net Income Data Table						
140			Net Income				
141			for 1Q X4				
142			$ 134,737				
143		$ 700	$ (40,763)				
144		$ 850	$ 46,987				
145	Price per unit for 1Q X4	$ 1,000	$ 134,737				
146		$ 1,150	$ 222,487				
147		$ 1,300	$ 310,237				

Assumptions and Dashboard / Sales and Collections

Ready

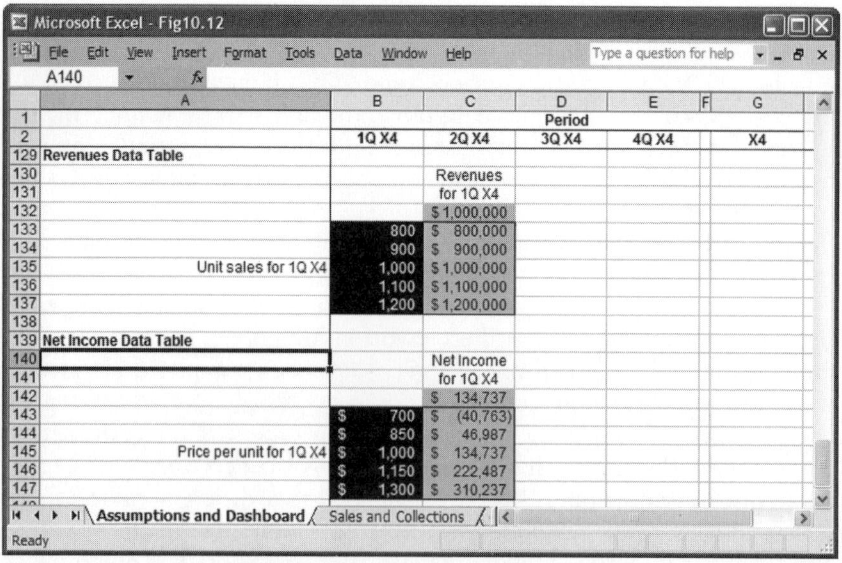

FIGURE 10.12 Net Income Data Table

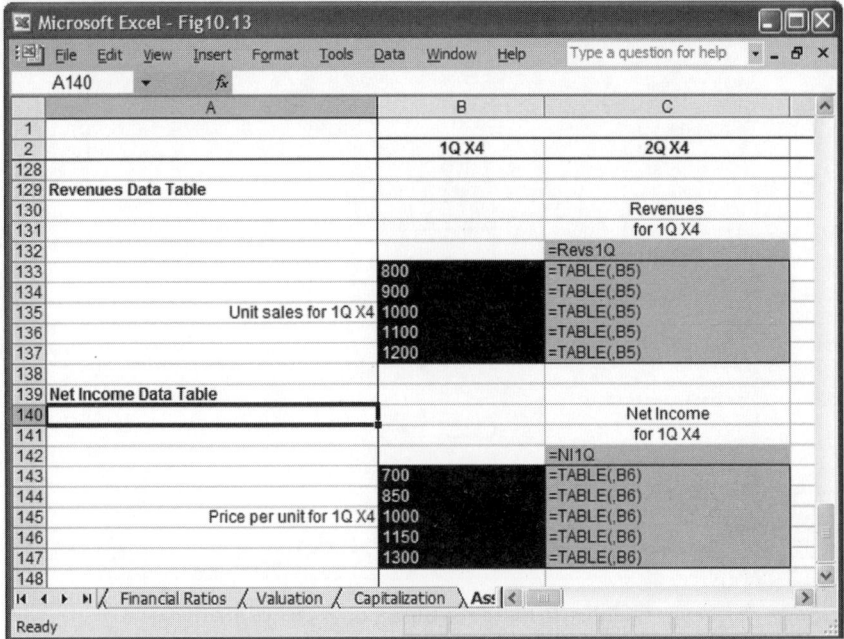

FIGURE 10.13   Alternative View of the Net Income Data Table

Free Cash Flows Data Table

To determine the sensitivity of Napavale's projected free cash flows to input variables in the financial model, I am going to vary the projected monitor screen: cost per unit for 1Q X4, and measure the corresponding changes in free cash flows for 1Q X4. As with the revenues data table and the net income data table, the first step in building the free cash flows data table is to properly arrange both the output formula of interest (free cash flows for 1Q X4 in this case) and the various alternative values for the input variable of interest (monitor screen: cost per unit for 1Q X4 in this case). Figure 10.14 presents a view of the properly arranged free cash flows data table for Napavale.

The subsequent steps involved in building the free cash flows data table for Napavale are the same as those involved in building the revenues data table and the net income data table as outlined earlier in this chapter. Napavale's completed free cash flows data table is presented in Figure 10.15.

In terms of interpreting Napavale's free cash flows data table, the free cash flows data table shows what Napavale's 1Q X4 free cash flows would

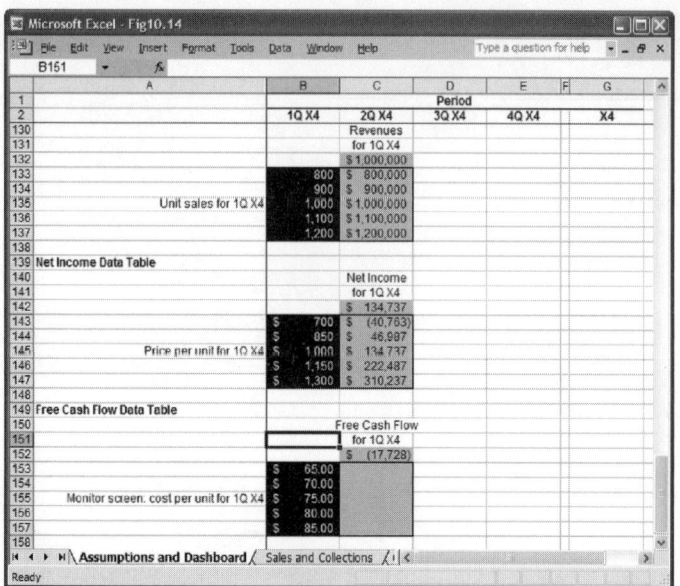

FIGURE 10.14 Free Cash Flows Data Table

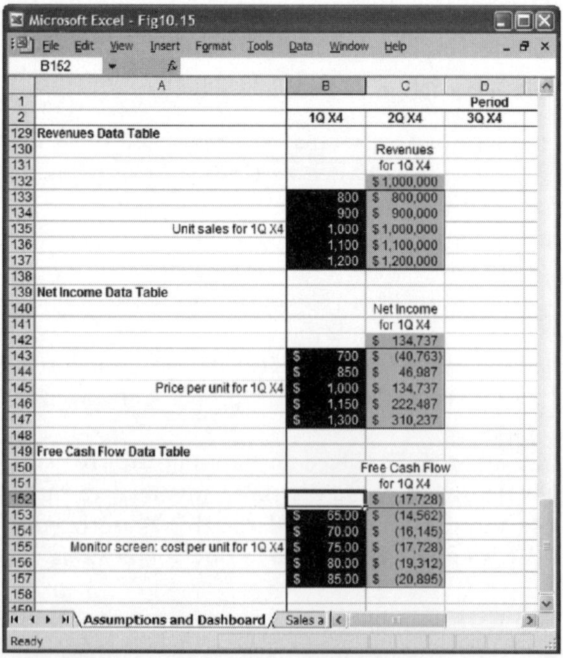

FIGURE 10.15 Free Cash Flows Data Table

equal if the monitor screen: cost per unit for 1Q X4 were changed to a different value. An alternative view of Napavale's free cash flows data table, in which the values and formulas underlying the worksheet cells are exposed, is presented in Figure 10.16.

QUESTIONS

Each of the questions for this chapter relates to a hypothetical company named Company VWX. Company VWX sells laser printers to consumers. As such, Company VWX is a product-oriented (as opposed to a service-oriented) business. Note that there are three cost-of-goods-sold components for Company VWX's laser printers: (1) electronics, (2) casing, and (3) assembly and labor.

The questions for this chapter will address fiscal year X4 on a quarterly basis (four specific quarters, 1Q–4Q for year X4). The following questions will test your knowledge of the material covered in this chapter

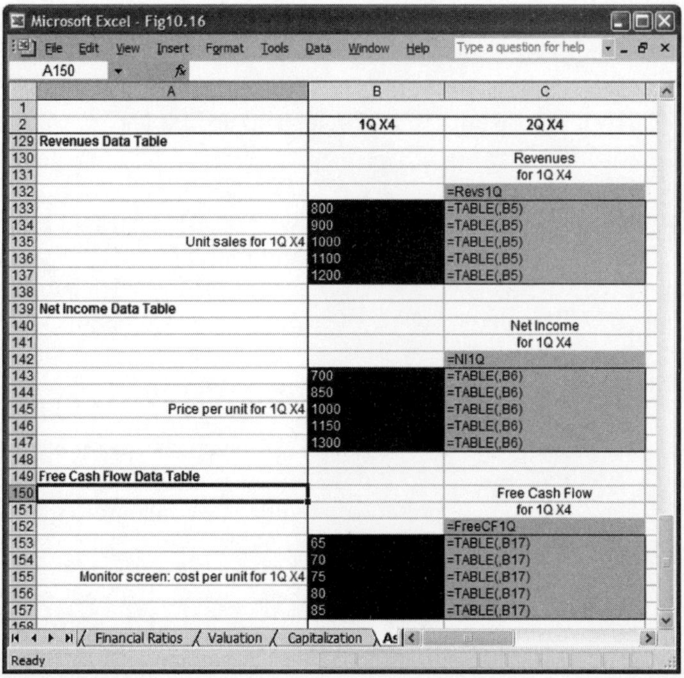

FIGURE 10.16 Alternative View of the Free Cash Flows Data Table

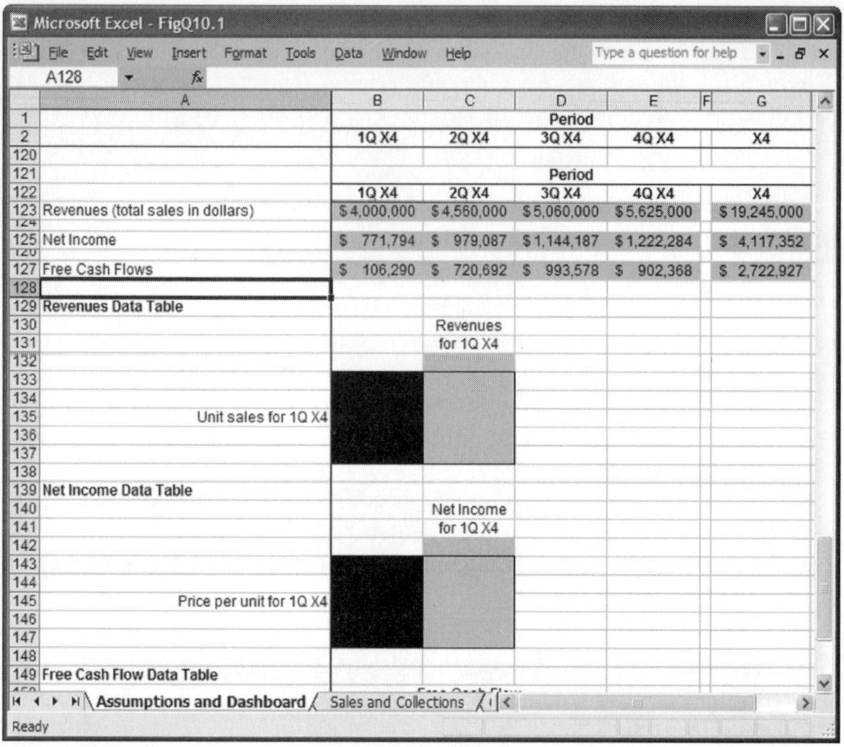

FIGURE Q10.1   Company VWX's Assumptions and Dashboard Worksheet

in an applied manner—specifically, you will be asked to build sensitivity analyses related to revenues, net income, and free cash flows, in the form of data tables, for Company VWX. To prepare you for this chapter's questions, Figure Q10.1 offers a view of a portion of Company VWX's Assumptions and Dashboard worksheet to provide some background information related to Company VWX's operations.

1. Given the information presented, build a revenues data table for Company VWX.
2. Given the information presented, build a net income data table for Company VWX.
3. Given the information presented, build a free cash flows data table for Company VWX.

CHAPTER 11

Contribution Margin Analysis

This chapter addresses an analytical metric known as "contribution margin." As noted in Chapter 1, contribution margin is defined as the extent to which each unit sale contributes to a business's fixed cost base. In other words, a business's contribution margin is equal to: unit price – variable costs per unit. Calculating a business's contribution margin enables the calculation of several important metrics such as operating leverage (fixed costs/total costs), breakeven value in units, and breakeven value in dollars. I will calculate each of these metrics for Napavale over the course of this chapter.

Using Napavale's financial model, I will cover the concept of fixed versus variable costs and I will calculate these costs for Napavale. After delineating Napavale's cost base between variable and fixed costs, I will then discuss the calculation of Napavale's contribution margin, operating leverage, and breakeven point in both units and dollars.

FIXED AND VARIABLE COSTS

In order to calculate Napavale's contribution margin, I must first determine which of Napavale's costs are fixed and which are variable. Fixed costs are defined as costs that are incurred regardless of anything else that may be happening at a company. Fixed costs are, in other words, fixed—they do not vary based on other factors. Examples of fixed costs may include salaries and rent.

Variable costs are defined as costs that vary in magnitude based on other factors, such as a company's level of revenues. Examples of variable costs may include cost of goods sold and miscellaneous expenses. There is an old saying, "In the long run, all costs are variable." While a company ultimately can vary all of its costs, fixed costs typically represent those costs that will not change based on other factors (such as the level of revenues) and variable costs typically represent those costs whose values depend on other factors (such as unit sales).

Figure 11.1 presents a view of Napavale's Contribution Margin worksheet in which I have identified Napavale's variable costs. An alternative view of the Contribution Margin worksheet in which the values and formulas underlying the worksheet cells are exposed and visible is presented in Figure 11.2. The names of the input and output cells in the Contribution Margin worksheet are shown in Figure 11.3. Napavale's fixed costs are identified and shown in the Contribution Margin worksheet in Figure 11.4. The values and formulas underlying the worksheet cells in the Contribution Margin worksheet are shown in Figure 11.5. Figure 11.6 presents a view of the names of the input and output cells underlying Napavale's Contribution Margin worksheet.

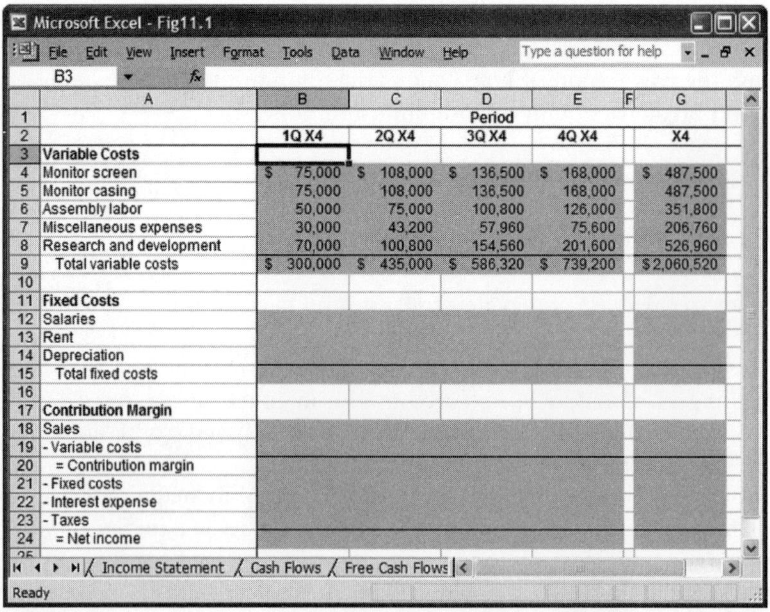

FIGURE 11.1 Contribution Margin Worksheet with Variable Costs Identified

Microsoft Excel - Fig11.2

File　Edit　View　Insert　Format　Tools　Data　Window　Help　　Type a question for help

B3

	A	B	C	D	E	F	G
1				Period			
2		1Q X4	2Q X4	3Q X4	4Q X4		X4
3	**Variable Costs**						
4	Monitor screen	=Screen1Q	=Screen2Q	=Screen3Q	=Screen4Q		=ScreenX4
5	Monitor casing	=Casing1Q	=Casing2Q	=Casing3Q	=Casing4Q		=CasingX4
6	Assembly labor	=Labor1Q	=Labor2Q	=Labor3Q	=Labor4Q		=LaborX4
7	Miscellaneous expenses	=MiscExp1Q	=MiscExp2Q	=MiscExp3Q	=MiscExp4Q		=MiscExpX4
8	Research and development	=RDExp1Q	=RDExp2Q	=RDExp3Q	=RDExp4Q		=RDExpX4
9	Total variable costs	=SUM(B4:B8)	=SUM(C4:C8)	=SUM(D4:D8)	=SUM(E4:E8)		=SUM(G4:G8)
10							
11	**Fixed Costs**						
12	Salaries						
13	Rent						
14	Depreciation						
15	Total fixed costs						
16							
17	**Contribution Margin**						
18	Sales						
19	- Variable costs						
20	= Contribution margin						
21	- Fixed costs						
22	- Interest expense						
23	- Taxes						
24	= Net income						
25							

Financial Ratios / Valuation / Capitalization \ Contr

Ready

FIGURE 11.2　Alternative View of the Contribution Margin Worksheet

Microsoft Excel - Fig11.3

File　Edit　View　Insert　Format　Tools　Data　Window　Help　　Type a question for help

B3

	A	B	C	D	E	F	G
1				Period			
2		1Q X4	2Q X4	3Q X4	4Q X4		X4
3	**Variable Costs**						
4	Monitor screen						
5	Monitor casing						
6	Assembly labor						
7	Miscellaneous expenses						
8	Research and development						
9	Total variable costs	VarCosts1Q	VarCosts2Q	VarCosts3Q	VarCosts4Q		VarCostsX4
10							
11	**Fixed Costs**						
12	Salaries						
13	Rent						
14	Depreciation						
15	Total fixed costs						
16							
17	**Contribution Margin**						
18	Sales						
19	- Variable costs						
20	= Contribution margin						
21	- Fixed costs						
22	- Interest expense						
23	- Taxes						
24	= Net income						
25							

Financial Ratios / Valuation / Capitalization \ Con

Ready

FIGURE 11.3　Names of the Input and Output Cells in the Contribution Margin Worksheet

	A	B	C	D	E	F	G
1				Period			
2		1Q X4	2Q X4	3Q X4	4Q X4		X4
3	**Variable Costs**						
4	Monitor screen	$ 75,000	$ 108,000	$ 136,500	$ 168,000		$ 487,500
5	Monitor casing	75,000	108,000	136,500	168,000		487,500
6	Assembly labor	50,000	75,000	100,800	126,000		351,800
7	Miscellaneous expenses	30,000	43,200	57,960	75,600		206,760
8	Research and development	70,000	100,800	154,560	201,600		526,960
9	Total variable costs	$ 300,000	$ 435,000	$ 586,320	$ 739,200		$ 2,060,520
10							
11	**Fixed Costs**						
12	Salaries	$ 470,400	$ 470,400	$ 663,600	$ 697,200		$ 2,301,600
13	Rent	20,000	20,000	20,000	20,000		80,000
14	Depreciation	2,313	4,625	6,938	9,250		23,125
15	Total fixed costs	$ 492,713	$ 495,025	$ 690,538	$ 726,450		$ 2,404,725
16							
17	**Contribution Margin**						
18	Sales						
19	- Variable costs						
20	= Contribution margin						
21	- Fixed costs						
22	- Interest expense						
23	- Taxes						
24	= Net income						

Income Statement / Cash Flows / Free Cash I

FIGURE 11.4   Contribution Margin Worksheet with Fixed Costs Identified

	A	B	C	D	E	F	G
1				Period			
2		1Q X4	2Q X4	3Q X4	4Q X4		X4
3	**Variable Costs**						
4	Monitor screen	=Screen1Q	=Screen2Q	=Screen3Q	=Screen4Q		=ScreenX4
5	Monitor casing	=Casing1Q	=Casing2Q	=Casing3Q	=Casing4Q		=CasingX4
6	Assembly labor	=Labor1Q	=Labor2Q	=Labor3Q	=Labor4Q		=LaborX4
7	Miscellaneous expenses	=MiscExp1Q	=MiscExp2Q	=MiscExp3Q	=MiscExp4Q		=MiscExpX4
8	Research and development	=RDExp1Q	=RDExp2Q	=RDExp3Q	=RDExp4Q		=RDExpX4
9	Total variable costs	=SUM(B4:B8)	=SUM(C4:C8)	=SUM(D4:D8)	=SUM(E4:E8)		=SUM(G4:G8)
10							
11	**Fixed Costs**						
12	Salaries	=SalExp1Q	=SalExp2Q	=SalExp3Q	=SalExp4Q		=SalExpX4
13	Rent	=RentExp1Q	=RentExp2Q	=RentExp3Q	=RentExp4Q		=RentExpX4
14	Depreciation	=Dep1Q	=Dep2Q	=Dep3Q	=Dep4Q		=DepX4
15	Total fixed costs	=SUM(B12:B14)	=SUM(C12:C14)	=SUM(D12:D14)	=SUM(E12:E14)		=SUM(G12:G14)
16							
17	**Contribution Margin**						
18	Sales						
19	- Variable costs						
20	= Contribution margin						
21	- Fixed costs						
22	- Interest expense						
23	- Taxes						
24	= Net income						

Financial Ratios / Valuation / Capitalization \ Contribution

FIGURE 11.5   Alternative View of the Contribution Margin Worksheet

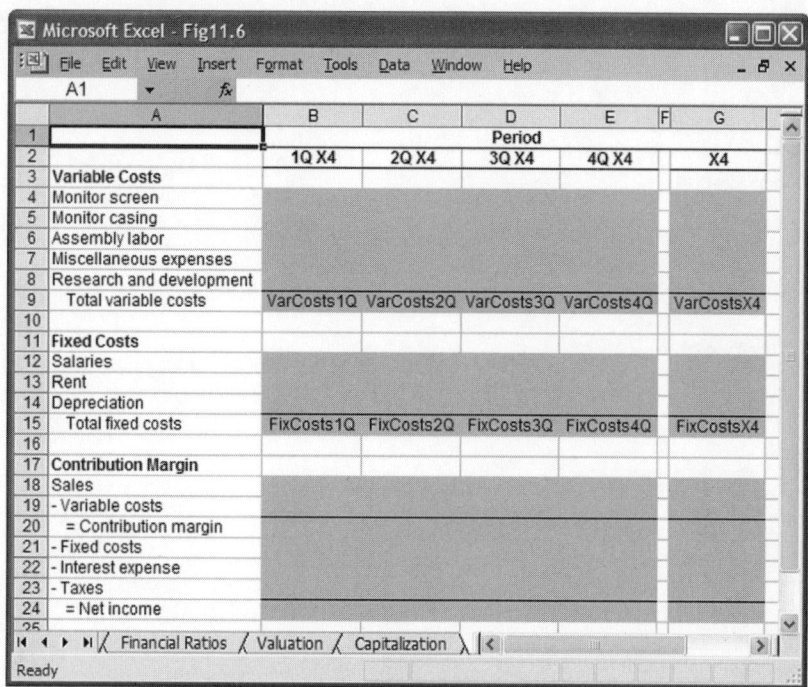

FIGURE 11.6   Names of the Input and Output Cells in the Contribution Margin Worksheet

CONTRIBUTION MARGIN

Napavale's contribution margin, which represents the amount that each unit sale contributes to the business's fixed cost base, is equal to: unit price – variable costs per unit. I am going to calculate Napavale's contribution margin at the "company" level as opposed to the unit level, so I calculate contribution margin as: sales (in dollars) – total variable costs (in dollars). The calculation of Napavale's contribution margin is presented in Figure 11.7.

An alternative view of the calculation of Napavale's contribution margin, in which the values and formulas underlying the worksheet cells are exposed and visible, is shown in Figure 11.8. The names of the input and output cells in Napavale's Contribution Margin worksheet are shown in Figure 11.9.

For the sake of reference, I reconcile Napavale's contribution margin

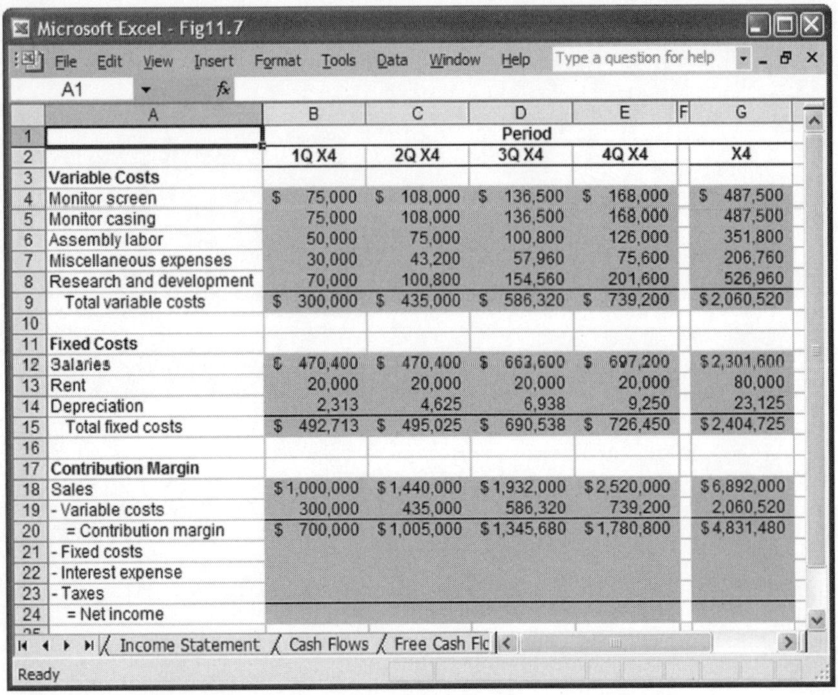

FIGURE 11.7   Calculation of the Contribution Margin

FIGURE 11.8   Alternative View of the Calculation of the Contribution Margin

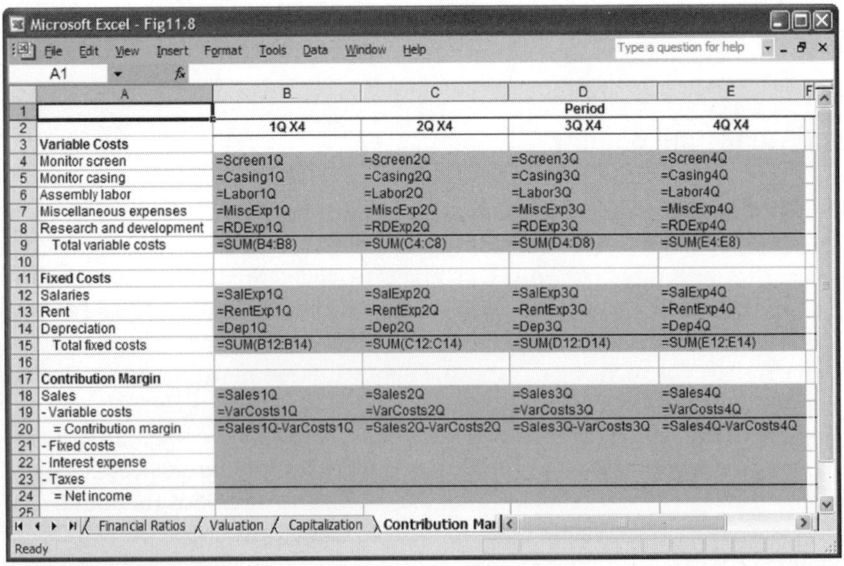

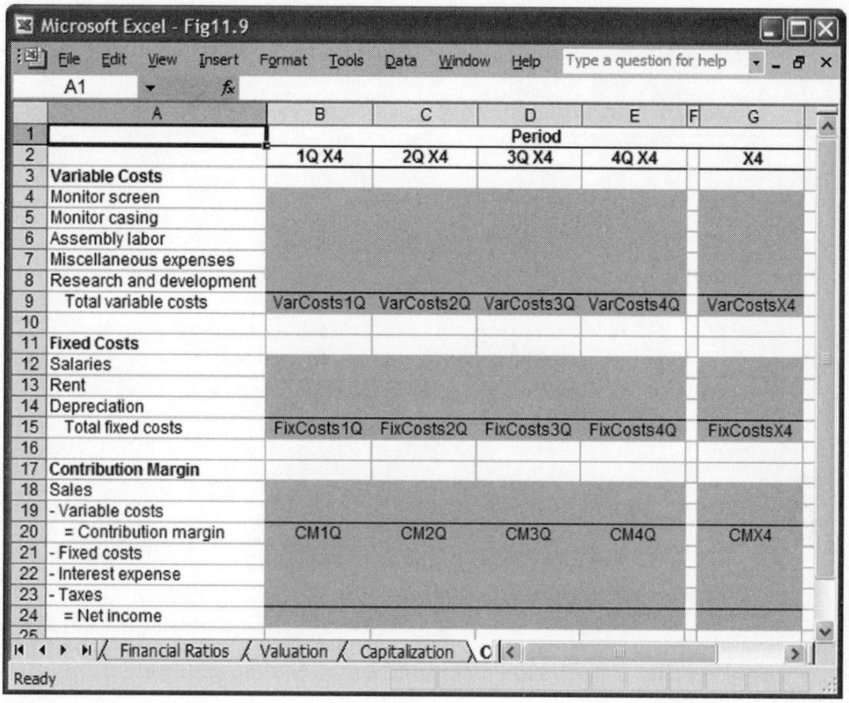

FIGURE 11.9 Names of the Input and Output Cells in the Contribution Margin Worksheet

with the business's net income. Napavale's operating cost base is made up of two different types of costs: fixed costs and variable costs. In addition to operating costs, Napavale is also projected to incur interest and tax expenses in the future. As such, if I subtract out fixed costs, variable costs, and interest and tax expenses from Napavale's total sales, I will have calculated net income. This calculation is presented in Figure 11.10. Figure 11.11 presents an alternative view of the Contribution Margin worksheet in which the values and formulas underlying the worksheet cells are exposed and visible.

As no new names have been added to the Contribution Margin worksheet since the calculation of Napavale's contribution margin, I will not present another view of the names of the input and output cells underlying Napavale's Contribution Margin worksheet at this point.

	A	B	C	D	E	F	G
1				Period			
2		1Q X4	2Q X4	3Q X4	4Q X4		X4
3	**Variable Costs**						
4	Monitor screen	$ 75,000	$ 108,000	$ 136,500	$ 168,000		$ 487,500
5	Monitor casing	75,000	108,000	136,500	168,000		487,500
6	Assembly labor	50,000	75,000	100,800	126,000		351,800
7	Miscellaneous expenses	30,000	43,200	57,960	75,600		206,760
8	Research and development	70,000	100,800	154,560	201,600		526,960
9	Total variable costs	$ 300,000	$ 435,000	$ 586,320	$ 739,200		$ 2,060,520
10							
11	**Fixed Costs**						
12	Salaries	$ 470,400	$ 470,400	$ 663,600	$ 697,200		$ 2,301,600
13	Rent	20,000	20,000	20,000	20,000		80,000
14	Depreciation	2,313	4,625	6,938	9,250		23,125
15	Total fixed costs	$ 492,713	$ 495,025	$ 690,538	$ 726,450		$ 2,404,725
16							
17	**Contribution Margin**						
18	Sales	$ 1,000,000	$ 1,440,000	$ 1,932,000	$ 2,520,000		$ 6,892,000
19	- Variable costs	300,000	435,000	586,320	739,200		2,060,520
20	= Contribution margin	$ 700,000	$ 1,005,000	$ 1,345,680	$ 1,780,800		$ 4,831,480
21	- Fixed costs	492,713	495,025	690,538	726,450		2,404,725
22	- Interest expense	-	875	-	-		875
23	- Taxes	72,551	178,185	229,300	369,023		849,058
24	= Net income	$ 134,737	$ 330,915	$ 425,843	$ 685,328		$ 1,576,822
25							

Income Statement / Cash Flows / Free Cash Flo

FIGURE 11.10   Reconciliation of Contribution Margin with Net Income

	A	B	C
1			
2		1Q X4	2Q X4
3	**Variable Costs**		
4	Monitor screen	=Screen1Q	=Screen2Q
5	Monitor casing	=Casing1Q	=Casing2Q
6	Assembly labor	=Labor1Q	=Labor2Q
7	Miscellaneous expenses	=MiscExp1Q	=MiscExp2Q
8	Research and development	=RDExp1Q	=RDExp2Q
9	Total variable costs	=SUM(B4:B8)	=SUM(C4:C8)
10			
11	**Fixed Costs**		
12	Salaries	=SalExp1Q	=SalExp2Q
13	Rent	=RentExp1Q	=RentExp2Q
14	Depreciation	=Dep1Q	=Dep2Q
15	Total fixed costs	=SUM(B12:B14)	=SUM(C12:C14)
16			
17	**Contribution Margin**		
18	Sales	=Sales1Q	=Sales2Q
19	- Variable costs	=VarCosts1Q	=VarCosts2Q
20	= Contribution margin	=Sales1Q-VarCosts1Q	=Sales2Q-VarCosts2Q
21	- Fixed costs	=FixCosts1Q	=FixCosts2Q
22	- Interest expense	=IntExp1Q	=IntExp2Q
23	- Taxes	=TaxExp1Q	=TaxExp2Q
24	= Net income	=CM1Q-FixCosts1Q+IntExp1Q-TaxExp1Q	=CM2Q-FixCosts2Q+IntExp2Q-TaxExp2Q
25			

Financial Ratios / Valuation / Capitalization / **Contribut**

FIGURE 11.11   Alternative View of the Reconciliation of Contribution Margin with Net Income

OPERATING LEVERAGE

Operating leverage is defined as the ratio of a company's fixed costs to #83 its overall costs. A company's level of operating leverage indicates what percentage of its total cost base is represented by fixed costs. Operating leverage is an important metric that indicates how leveraged a company is operationally. The calculation of Napavale's operating leverage is shown in Figure 11.12. The values and formulas underlying the worksheet cells related to the calculation of Napavale's operating leverage are shown in Figure 11.13. The names of the input and output cells associated with the calculation of Napavale's operating leverage are shown in Figure 11.14.

	A	B	C	D	E	F	G
1				Period			
2		1Q X4	2Q X4	3Q X4	4Q X4		X4
3	**Variable Costs**						
4	Monitor screen	$ 75,000	$ 108,000	$ 136,500	$ 168,000		$ 487,500
5	Monitor casing	75,000	108,000	136,500	168,000		487,500
6	Assembly labor	50,000	75,000	100,800	126,000		351,800
7	Miscellaneous expenses	30,000	43,200	57,960	75,600		206,760
8	Research and development	70,000	100,800	154,560	201,600		526,960
9	Total variable costs	$ 300,000	$ 435,000	$ 586,320	$ 739,200		$2,060,520
10							
11	**Fixed Costs**						
12	Salaries	$ 470,400	$ 470,400	$ 663,600	$ 697,200		$2,301,600
13	Rent	20,000	20,000	20,000	20,000		80,000
14	Depreciation	2,313	4,625	6,938	9,250		23,125
15	Total fixed costs	$ 492,713	$ 495,025	$ 690,538	$ 726,450		$2,404,725
16							
17	**Contribution Margin**						
18	Sales	$1,000,000	$1,440,000	$1,932,000	$2,520,000		$6,892,000
19	- Variable costs	300,000	435,000	586,320	739,200		2,060,520
20	= Contribution margin	$ 700,000	$1,005,000	$1,345,680	$1,780,800		$4,831,480
21	- Fixed costs	492,713	495,025	690,538	726,450		2,404,725
22	- Interest expense	-	875	-	-		875
23	- Taxes	72,551	178,185	229,300	369,023		849,058
24	= Net income	$ 134,737	$ 330,915	$ 425,843	$ 685,328		$1,576,822
25							
26	**Operating Leverage**						
27	Fixed costs	$ 492,713	$ 495,025	$ 690,538	$ 726,450		$2,404,725
28	Total costs (fixed + variable)	$ 792,713	$ 930,025	$1,276,858	$1,465,650		$4,465,245
29							
30	Operating leverage	62.2%	53.2%	54.1%	49.6%		53.9%
31							

FIGURE 11.12   Calculation of Operating Leverage

FIGURE 11.13 Alternative View of the Calculation of Operating Leverage

FIGURE 11.14 Names of the Input and Output Cells Underlying the Calculation of Operating Leverage

BREAKEVEN POINTS IN UNITS

A company's breakeven point is the point at which its revenues cover all of its costs. Breakeven point is an important metric that indicates how many units a company must sell, or the dollar value of revenues a company must generate, to cover all of its costs (both fixed and variable). A company's breakeven point in units is calculated as: (total fixed costs)/(contribution margin per unit). Note that I am calculating Napavale's breakeven point on an operating profit basis. In other words, I am not including interest expenses or taxes in my calculation of Napavale's breakeven point. This is because I am interested in assessing the operational dynamics of Napavale as a business; you may find it useful to include interest and tax expenses in your calculation of breakeven point. If you do decide to include such expenses in your calculation of a breakeven point, be sure to clearly note this fact in your calculation.

The calculations of Napavale's contribution margin per unit and breakeven point in units are shown in Figure 11.15. Note that Napavale's contribution margin per unit, and breakeven point, varies across accounting periods (quarters) due to the fluctuation in fixed costs, variable costs, and revenues over each of the accounting periods. An alternative view of Figure 11.15 in which the values and formulas underlying the worksheet cells are visible is shown in Figure 11.16. Figure 11.17 presents the names of the input and output cells associated with the calculation of Napavale's breakeven point in units.

FIGURE 11.15 Calculation of the Breakeven Point in Units

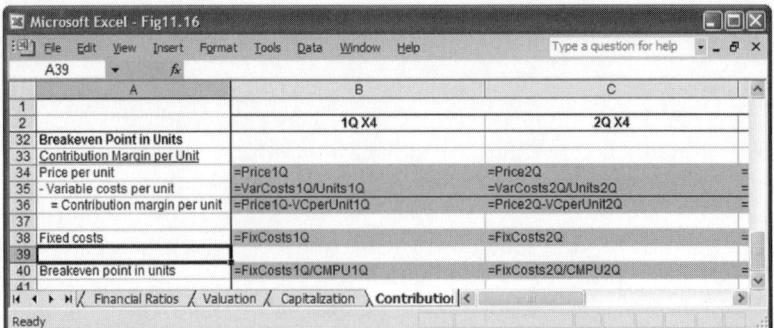

FIGURE 11.16   Alternative View of the Calculation of the Breakeven Point in Units

	Microsoft Excel - Fig11.17						
	File Edit View Insert Format Tools Data Window Help						
	A	B	C	D	E	F	G
1				Period			
2		1Q X4	2Q X4	3Q X4	4Q X4		X4
3	**Variable Costs**						
4	Monitor screen						
5	Monitor casing						
6	Assembly labor						
7	Miscellaneous expenses						
8	Research and development						
9	Total variable costs	VarCosts1Q	VarCosts2Q	VarCosts3Q	VarCosts4Q		VarCostsX4
10							
11	**Fixed Costs**						
12	Salaries						
13	Rent						
14	Depreciation						
15	Total fixed costs	FixCosts1Q	FixCosts2Q	FixCosts3Q	FixCosts4Q		FixCostsX4
16							
17	**Contribution Margin**						
18	Sales						
19	- Variable costs						
20	= Contribution margin	CM1Q	CM2Q	CM3Q	CM4Q		CMX4
21	- Fixed costs						
22	- Interest expense						
23	- Taxes						
24	= Net income						
25							
26	**Operating Leverage**						
27	Fixed costs						
28	Total costs (fixed + variable)	TotCosts1Q	TotCosts2Q	TotCosts3Q	TotCosts4Q		TotCostsX4
30	Operating leverage	OpLev1Q	OpLev2Q	OpLev3Q	OpLev4Q		OpLevX4
31							
32	**Breakeven Point in Units**						
33	Contribution Margin per Unit						
34	Price per unit						
35	- Variable costs per unit	VCperUnit1Q	VCperUnit2Q	VCperUnit3Q	VCperUnit4Q		
36	= Contribution margin per unit	CMPU1Q	CMPU2Q	CMPU3Q	CMPU4Q		
37							
38	Fixed costs						
39							
40	Breakeven point in units						

Financial Ratios / Valuation / Capitalization \ Con

FIGURE 11.17   Names of the Input and Output Cells Underlying the Calculation of the Breakeven Point in Units

BREAKEVEN POINT IN DOLLARS

Another way to calculate a company's breakeven point is in terms of dollars of revenues. Calculating Napavale's breakeven point in dollars of revenues does not change the breakeven point; it simply offers another metric (in addition to breakeven in units) by which Napavale may be analyzed and assessed. A company's breakeven point in dollars of revenues is equal to: (breakeven point in units) * (price per unit). The calculation of Napavale's breakeven point in dollars of revenue is presented in Figure 11.18. The values and formulas underlying the calculation of Napavale's breakeven point in dollars of revenue are shown in Figure 11.19. Figure 11.20 presents a view of the names of the input and output cells underlying the calculation of Napavale's breakeven point in dollars of revenues.

	A	B	C	D	E	F	G
1				Period			
2		1Q X4	2Q X4	3Q X4	4Q X4		X4
28	Total costs (fixed + variable)	$ 792,713	$ 930,025	$1,276,858	$1,465,650		$4,465,245
30	Operating leverage	62.2%	53.2%	54.1%	49.6%		53.9%
31							
32	**Breakeven Point in Units**						
33	Contribution Margin per Unit						
34	Price per unit	$ 1,000.00	$ 960.00	$ 920.00	$ 900.00		
35	- Variable costs per unit	300	290	279	264		
36	= Contribution margin per unit	$ 700.00	$ 670.00	$ 640.80	$ 636.00		
37							
38	Fixed costs	$ 492,713	$ 495,025	$ 690,538	$ 726,450		
39							
40	Breakeven point in units	704	739	1,078	1,142		
41							
42	**Breakeven Point in Dollars**						
43	Breakeven point in units	704	739	1,078	1,142		
44	* Price per unit	$ 1,000	$ 960	$ 920	$ 900		
45	= Breakeven point in dollars	$ 703,875	$ 709,290	$ 991,408	$1,027,995		

FIGURE 11.18 Calculation of the Breakeven Point in Dollars of Revenue

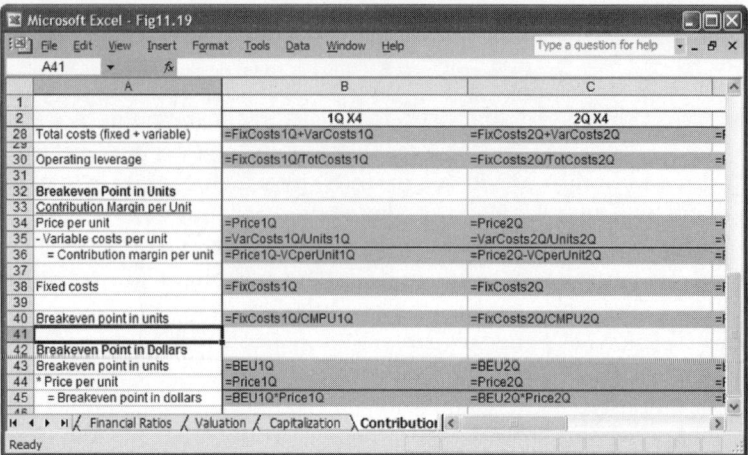

FIGURE 11.19   Alternative View of the Calculation of the Breakeven Point in Dollars of Revenue

	B	C	E	F	G
		1Q X4	2Q X4			

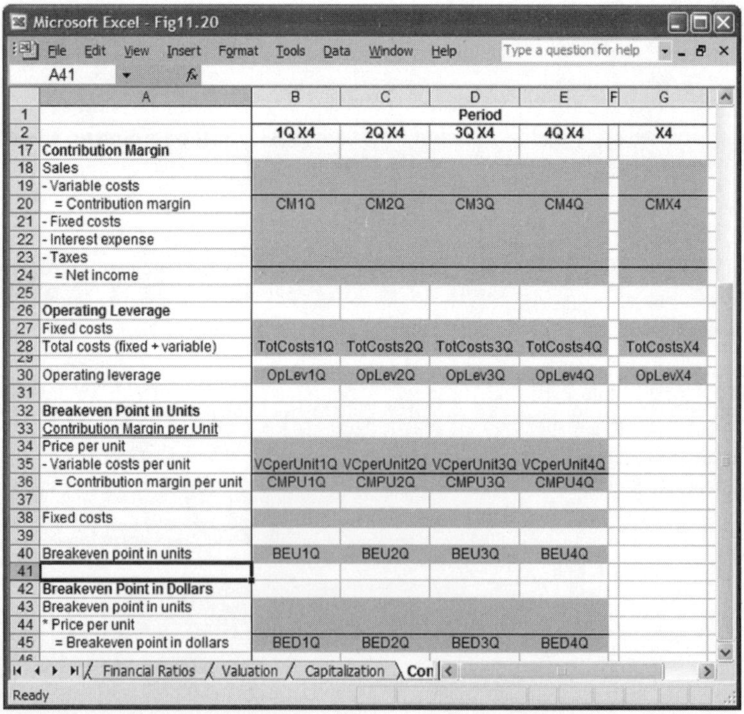

FIGURE 11.20   Names of the Input and Output Cells Underlying the Calculation of the Breakeven Point in Dollars of Revenue

QUESTIONS

Each of the questions for this chapter relates to a hypothetical company named Company 123. Company 123 sells GPS navigation systems to consumers. As such, Company 123 is a product-oriented (as opposed to a service-oriented) business. Note that there are three cost-of-goods-sold components for Company 123's GPS navigation systems: (1) electronics, (2) casing, and (3) assembly and labor.

The questions for this chapter will address fiscal year X4 on a quarterly basis (four specific quarters, 1Q–4Q for year X4). The following questions will test your knowledge of the material covered in this chapter in an applied manner—specifically, you will be asked to identify the fixed and variable costs, calculate the contribution margin, calculate the operating leverage, and calculate the breakeven point (in terms of both units and dollars) for Company 123.

To prepare you for this chapter's questions, Figure Q11.1 offers a view of Company 123's Cost-of-Goods-Sold Budget worksheet to provide some background information related to Company 123's operations. Figure Q11.2 provides a view of Company 123's Operating Expenses Budget. Company 123's Headcount Cost worksheet is shown in Figure Q11.3. Figure Q11.4 provides a view of a portion of Company 123's Assumptions and Dashboard worksheet. Company 123's Capital Budget worksheet is shown in Figure Q11.5. Company 123's Sales Budget is shown in Figure Q11.6. Figure Q11.7 provides a view of Company 123's Cash Budget. Figure Q11.8 provides a view of Company 123's Income Statement.

Note that I am assuming Company 123 generates a negative income tax expense in 1Q X4 and 2Q X4 to simplify these qustions. While this does not represent a real-world scenario, it should help to make these exercises easier to follow.

FIGURE Q11.1   Company 123's Cost-of-Goods-Sold Budget

FIGURE Q11.2 Company 123's Operating Expenses Budget

Microsoft Excel - FigQ11.2

	A	B	C	D	E	F	G
1				Period			
2		1Q X4	2Q X4	3Q X4	4Q X4		X4
3	OPERATING EXPENSES BUDGET						
4	Operating Expenses Budget						
5	Salaries	$ 447,063	$461,438	$526,125	$ 526,125		$1,960,750
6	Miscellaneous expenses	20,000	30,000	39,900	51,520		141,420
7	Research and development	25,000	37,500	49,875	64,400		176,775
8	Rent	18,000	18,000	18,000	18,000		72,000
9	Depreciation	1,375	3,000	4,575	5,950		14,900
10	Total operating expenses	$ 511,438	$549,938	$638,475	$ 665,995		$2,365,845
11							
12	DISBURSEMENTS FOR OPERATING EXPENSES BUDGET						
13	Disbursements for Operating Expenses Budget						
14	Salaries	$ 447,063	$461,438	$526,125	$ 526,125		$1,960,750
15	Miscellaneous expenses	20,000	30,000	39,900	51,520		141,420
16	Research and development	25,000	37,500	49,875	64,400		176,775
17	Rent	18,000	18,000	18,000	18,000		72,000
18	Depreciation	-	-	-	-		-
19	Total disbursements for operating expenses	$ 510,063	$546,938	$633,900	$ 660,045		$2,350,945

Headcount Overview / Headcount Cost / Operating Expense

FIGURE Q11.3 Company 123's Headcount Cost Worksheet

Microsoft Excel - FigQ11.3

	A	B	C	D	E	F	G
1				Period			
2		1Q X4	2Q X4	3Q X4	4Q X4		X4
3	HEADCOUNT BUDGET						
4	Headcount Budget						
5	Periodic salary expense (base)						
6	Chief Executive Officer	$ 45,000	$ 45,000	$ 45,000	$ 45,000		$ 180,000
7	Chief Financial Officer	41,250	41,250	41,250	41,250		165,000
8	VP, Engineering	40,000	40,000	40,000	40,000		160,000
9	VP, Sales & Marketing	35,000	35,000	35,000	35,000		140,000
10	VP, Business Development	30,000	30,000	30,000	30,000		120,000
11	Salesperson	100,000	100,000	125,000	125,000		450,000
12	Hardware Engineer	67,500	67,500	90,000	90,000		315,000
13	Controller/Accountant	12,500	25,000	25,000	25,000		87,500
14	Administrative Assistant	17,500	17,500	26,250	26,250		87,500
15	Total	$388,750	$401,250	$457,500	$457,500		$1,705,000
16							
17	Total (with benefits)	$447,063	$461,438	$526,125	$526,125		$1,960,750

COGS / Inventory and Purchases / Headcoun

Microsoft Excel - FigQ11.4

A59 | Operating Expenses Worksheet

	A	B	C	D	E	G	H
1				Period			
2		1Q X4	2Q X4	3Q X4	4Q X4	X4	
59	Operating Expenses Worksheet						
60	Operating Expenses Inputs						
61	Miscellaneous expenses as a % of sales	4.0%	4.0%	4.0%	4.0%		
62							
63	R&D expenses as a % of sales	5.0%	5.0%	5.0%	5.0%		
64							
65	Rent expense per square foot per quarter	$ 4.50	$ 4.50	$ 4.50	$ 4.50		
66	Square feet of space rented	4,000	4,000	4,000	4,000		
67	Total rent expense	$ 18,000	$ 18,000	$ 18,000	$ 18,000		
68							
69	Tax rate	30.0%	30.0%	35.0%	35.0%		
70							
71	Capital Worksheet						
72	Capital Expenditures (CAPEX) Inputs						
73	Equipment purchases	$ 20,000	$ 25,000	$ 25,000	$ 20,000		
74	Furniture purchases	$ 5,000	$ 5,000	$ 4,000	$ 5,000		
75	Fixtures purchases	$ 2,000	$ 2,000	$ 2,000	$ 2,000		
76	Total CAPEX purchases	$ 27,000	$ 32,000	$ 31,000	$ 27,000		
77							
78	CAPEX Disbursements Inputs						
79	% of purchases paid for in purchase period	100%	100%	100%	100%		
80							
81	Depreciation Inputs						
82	Equipment depreciable life (years)						5.0
83	Furniture depreciable life (years)						5.0
84	Fixtures depreciable life (years)						4.0
85							
86	Quarters per year						4.0
87							
88	Equipment depreciation multiplier	5.0%	5.0%	5.0%	5.0%		
89	Furniture depreciation multiplier	5.0%	5.0%	5.0%	5.0%		
90	Fixtures depreciation multiplier	6.3%	6.3%	6.3%	6.3%		

Assumptions and Dashboard / Sales and Collections / COGS

Ready

FIGURE Q11.4 Company 123's Assumptions and Dashboard Worksheet

Microsoft Excel - FigQ11.5

A1

	A	B	C	D	E	G
1				Period		
2		1Q X4	2Q X4	3Q X4	4Q X4	X4
3	CAPITAL BUDGET					
4	Capital Expenditures Budget					
5	Equipment	$ 20,000	$ 25,000	$ 25,000	$ 20,000	$ 90,000
6	Furniture	5,000	5,000	4,000	5,000	19,000
7	Fixtures	2,000	2,000	2,000	2,000	8,000
8	Total capital expenditures	$ 27,000	$ 32,000	$ 31,000	$ 27,000	$ 117,000
9						
10	Disbursements for Capital Expenditures Budget					
11	Equipment	$ 20,000	$ 25,000	$ 25,000	$ 20,000	$ 90,000
12	Furniture	5,000	5,000	4,000	5,000	19,000
13	Fixtures	2,000	2,000	2,000	2,000	8,000
14	Total disbursements for capital expenditures	$ 27,000	$ 32,000	$ 31,000	$ 27,000	$ 117,000
15						
16	Depreciation Budget					
17	Equipment	$ 1,000	$ 2,250	$ 3,500	$ 4,500	$ 11,250
18	Furniture	250	500	700	950	2,400
19	Fixtures	125	250	375	500	1,250
20	Total depreciation	$ 1,375	$ 3,000	$ 4,575	$ 5,950	$ 14,900
21						
22	Cumulative capital expenditures	$ 27,000	$ 59,000	$ 90,000	$ 117,000	
23	- Accumulated depreciation	1,375	4,375	8,950	14,900	
24	= Fixed assets, net of depreciation	$ 25,625	$ 54,625	$ 81,050	$ 102,100	
25						
26						
27	Cumulative disbursements for CAPEX	$ 27,000	$ 59,000	$ 90,000	$ 117,000	
28	Payables adjustment for CAPEX disbursements	$ -	$ -	$ -	$ -	

Headcount Overview / Headcount Cost / Operating

Ready

FIGURE Q11.5 Company 123's Capital Budget Worksheet

A	B	C	D	E	F	G
1			Period			
2	1Q X4	2Q X4	3Q X4	4Q X4		X4
3 SALES BUDGET						
4 Unit Sales and Price Budget						
5 Unit sales	1,000	1,500	2,100	2,800		7,400
6 × Price per unit	$ 500	$ 500	$ 475	$ 460		N/A
7 = Total sales	$ 500,000	$ 750,000	$ 997,500	$1,288,000		$3,535,500
8						
9 Sales Composition Budget						
10 Cash sales	$ 200,000	$ 300,000	$ 399,000	$ 515,200		$1,414,200
11 + Credit sales	300,000	450,000	598,500	772,800		2,121,300
12 = Total sales	$ 500,000	$ 750,000	$ 997,500	$1,288,000		$3,535,500
13						
14 COLLECTIONS BUDGET						
15 Cash Collections from Customers Budget						
16 Cash sales this period	$ 200,000	$ 300,000	$ 399,000	$ 515,200		$1,414,200
17 + Credit sales collected	216,667	413,333	552,250	724,383		1,906,633
18 = Total collections	$ 416,667	$ 713,333	$ 951,250	$1,239,583		$3,320,833
19						
20 Accounts Receivable (A/R) Budget						
21 Beginning A/R balance	$ -	$ 83,333	$ 120,000	$ 166,250		$ -
22 + Additions to A/R	83,333	120,000	166,250	214,667		584,250
23 - Subtractions from A/R	-	83,333	120,000	166,250		369,583
24 = Ending A/R balance	$ 83,333	$ 120,000	$ 166,250	$ 214,667		$ 214,667

Assumptions and Dashboard \ Sales and Collections

FIGURE Q11.6 Company 123's Sales Budget

A	B	C	D	E	F	G
1			Period			
2	1Q X4	2Q X4	3Q X4	4Q X4		X4
3 CASH BUDGET						
4 Beginning cash balance	$ -	$ 597,411	$ 439,838	$ 400,203		$ -
5 Cash receipts						
6 Collections from customers	416,667	713,333	951,250	1,239,583		3,320,833
7 Total cash available, before financing	$ 416,667	$1,310,744	$1,391,088	$1,639,787		N/A
8 Cash disbursements						
9 Purchases disbursements	$ 133,056	$ 253,500	$ 311,311	$ 383,600		$1,081,467
10 Operating expenses	510,063	546,938	633,900	660,045		2,350,945
11 Tax expense	(51,675)	(11,531)	14,674	73,642		25,109
12 Capital expenditures	27,000	32,000	31,000	27,000		117,000
13 Total disbursements	618,443	820,906	990,885	1,144,287		3,574,521
14						
15 Minimum cash balance desired	$ 250,000	$ 250,000	$ 250,000	$ 250,000		N/A
16 Total cash needed	$ 868,443	$1,070,906	$1,240,885	$1,394,287		N/A
17 Excess (deficiency) of total cash available over						
18 total cash needed before financing	$ (451,776)	$ 239,838	$ 150,203	$ 245,500		N/A
19 Financing						
20 Equity investment	$ 750,000	$ -	$ -	$ -		$ 750,000
21 Borrowing (at beginning of quarter)	50,000					50,000
22 Repayments (at end of quarter)	-	(50,000)	-	-		(50,000)
23 Interest	(813)	-	-	-		(813)
24 Total cash increase (decrease) from financing	$ 799,188	$ (50,000)	$ -	$ -		$ 749,188
25						
26 Ending cash balance	$ 597,411	$ 439,838	$ 400,203	$ 495,500		$ 495,500

Capital \ Cash \ Balance Sheet \ Income Statement \ Cash F

FIGURE Q11.7 Company 123's Cash Budget

Microsoft Excel - FigQ11.8

		Period				
	1Q X4	2Q X4	3Q X4	4Q X4		X4
Sales	$ 500,000	$ 750,000	$ 997,500	$ 1,288,000		$ 3,535,500
Cost of goods sold	160,000	238,500	317,100	411,600		1,127,200
Gross profit	$ 340,000	$ 511,500	$ 680,400	$ 876,400		$ 2,408,300
Salaries	$ 447,063	$ 461,438	$ 526,125	$ 526,125		$ 1,960,750
Miscellaneous expenses	20,000	30,000	39,900	51,520		141,420
Research and development	25,000	37,500	49,875	64,400		176,775
Rent	18,000	18,000	18,000	18,000		72,000
Depreciation	1,375	3,000	4,575	5,950		14,900
Income from operations	$ (171,438)	$ (38,438)	$ 41,925	$ 210,405		$ 42,455
Interest expense	$ 813	$ -	$ -	$ -		$ 813
Taxable income	$ (172,250)	$ (38,438)	$ 41,925	$ 210,405		$ 41,643
Tax expense	$ (51,675)	$ (11,531)	$ 14,674	$ 73,642		$ 25,109
Net income	$ (120,575)	$ (26,906)	$ 27,251	$ 136,763		$ 16,533

Income Statement / Cash Flows / Free Cash Flo

FIGURE Q11.8 Company 123's Income Statement

1. Given the information presented, identify Company 123's variable costs.
2. Using the information presented, identify Company 123's fixed costs.
3. Given the information presented, calculate Company 123's contribution margin and reconcile Company 123's contribution margin with its Net Income.
4. Calculate, using the information presented, Company 123's operating leverage.
5. Given the information presented, calculate Company 123's breakeven point in terms of units.
6. Calculate, using the information presented, Company 123's breakeven point in terms of dollars of revenues.

CHAPTER 12

Financial Ratios Analysis

This chapter covers the use of financial ratios to analyze and assess Napavale's operations. Financial ratios are metrics that compare various elements of a business's operations; one example would include Gross Margin, which is calculated as: (Gross Profit)/(Sales). Financial ratios are used in several productive ways: They enable the comparison of ratios for a specific company across various accounting periods and they enable the comparison of a specific company to competitors and/or a broad set of companies, such as those included in an index such as the S&P 500 (Standard & Poor's 500, which is an index used to track a set of companies), among other uses.

Using Napavale's financial model, I will calculate three sets of financial ratios: profit margins, investment returns and management efficiency. The ratios covered in this chapter represent a small subset of the range of ratios used in the financial community. Depending on the nature of your own financial model, you may find it useful to use different or additional ratios to analyze and assess the operations of your own company. Regardless of the ratios you use, the process described in this chapter should apply to a wide array of financial ratios calculations.

PROFIT MARGINS—FINANCIAL RATIOS

The first set of financial ratios that I cover in this chapter, those related to profit margins, measure Napavale's relative profitability in several different ways. The first ratio, Gross Margin, compares Napavale's Gross Profit (which is equal to Sales – Cost of Goods Sold) to Sales. Gross Margin is calculated as: (Gross Profit)/(Sales).

Figure 12.1 presents a view of the calculation of Napavale's Gross Margin. An alternative view of the calculation of Napavale's Gross Margin in which the values and formulas underlying the worksheet cells are revealed is shown in Figure 12.2. The names of the input and output cells underlying

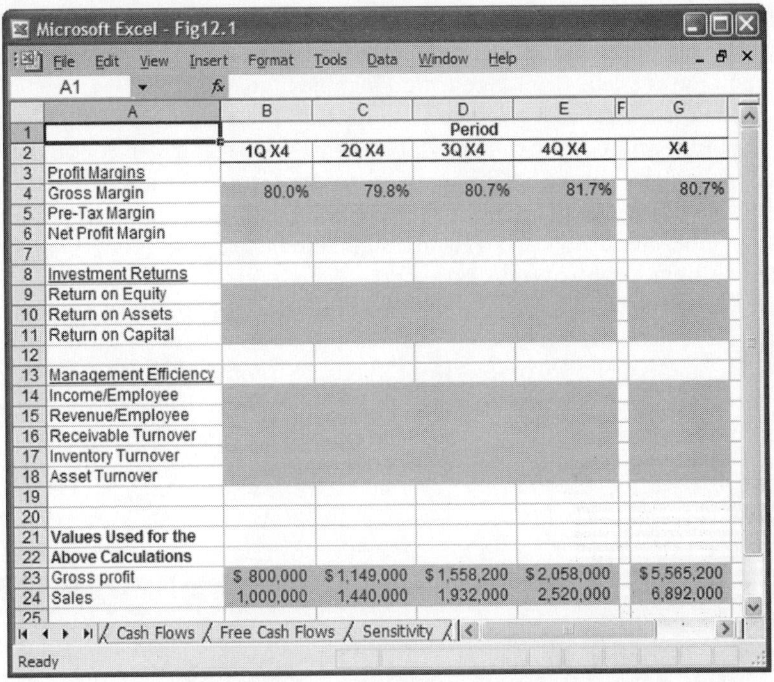

FIGURE 12.1 Calculation of Gross Margin

The spreadsheet shows:

A	B	C	D	E	F	G
			Period			
	1Q X4	2Q X4	3Q X4	4Q X4		X4
Profit Margins						
Gross Margin	80.0%	79.8%	80.7%	81.7%		80.7%
Pre-Tax Margin						
Net Profit Margin						
Investment Returns						
Return on Equity						
Return on Assets						
Return on Capital						
Management Efficiency						
Income/Employee						
Revenue/Employee						
Receivable Turnover						
Inventory Turnover						
Asset Turnover						
Values Used for the						
Above Calculations						
Gross profit	$ 800,000	$1,149,000	$1,558,200	$2,058,000		$5,565,200
Sales	1,000,000	1,440,000	1,932,000	2,520,000		6,892,000

FIGURE 12.2 Alternative View of the Calculation of Gross Margin

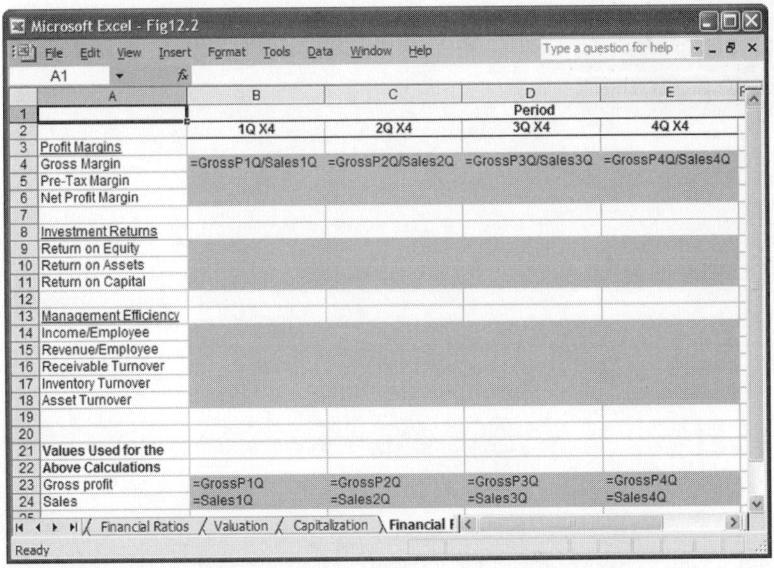

The spreadsheet shows:

A	B	C	D	E
			Period	
	1Q X4	2Q X4	3Q X4	4Q X4
Profit Margins				
Gross Margin	=GrossP1Q/Sales1Q	=GrossP2Q/Sales2Q	=GrossP3Q/Sales3Q	=GrossP4Q/Sales4Q
Pre-Tax Margin				
Net Profit Margin				
Investment Returns				
Return on Equity				
Return on Assets				
Return on Capital				
Management Efficiency				
Income/Employee				
Revenue/Employee				
Receivable Turnover				
Inventory Turnover				
Asset Turnover				
Values Used for the				
Above Calculations				
Gross profit	=GrossP1Q	=GrossP2Q	=GrossP3Q	=GrossP4Q
Sales	=Sales1Q	=Sales2Q	=Sales3Q	=Sales4Q

the calculation of Napavale's Gross Margin are presented in Figure 12.3. For the sake of reference, Figure 12.4 presents a view of the names of the input and output cells from Napavale's Income Statement.

Also for the sake of reference, Figure 12.5 presents a view of the names of the input and output cells from Napavale's Sales and Collections worksheet. Note the source of the inputs into the Gross Margin calculation—Sales values are drawn from the Sales and Collections worksheet and Gross Profit values are drawn from the Income Statement.

The next profit margin ratio, Pre-Tax Margin, compares Napavale's pre-tax income (also referred to as "Taxable Income") to Sales. I calculated Napavale's Taxable Income in Chapter 5—another way to think of Taxable Income is "Net Income + Tax Expense." In other words, the only difference between Taxable Income and Net Income is that Net Income incorporates the deduction of any tax expenses. As such, Pre-Tax Margin is calculated as: (Taxable Income)/(Sales). Figure 12.6 presents a view of

	A	B	C	D	E	F	G
1				Period			
2		1Q X4	2Q X4	3Q X4	4Q X4		X4
3	Profit Margins						
4	Gross Margin	GrMar1Q	GrMar2Q	GrMar3Q	GrMar4Q		GrMarX4
5	Pre-Tax Margin						
6	Net Profit Margin						
7							
8	Investment Returns						
9	Return on Equity						
10	Return on Assets						
11	Return on Capital						
12							
13	Management Efficiency						
14	Income/Employee						
15	Revenue/Employee						
16	Receivable Turnover						
17	Inventory Turnover						
18	Asset Turnover						
19							
20							
21	Values Used for the						
22	Above Calculations						
23	Gross profit						
24	Sales						
25							

Microsoft Excel - Fig12.3 — File Edit View Insert Format Tools Data Window Help — A1

Financial Ratios / Valuation / Capitalization

Ready

FIGURE 12.3 Names of the Input and Output Cells Underlying the Calculation of Gross Margin

	A	B	C	D	E	F	G
1				Period			
2		1Q X4	2Q X4	3Q X4	4Q X4		X4
3	Sales						
4	Cost of goods sold						
5	Gross profit	GrossP1Q	GrossP2Q	GrossP3Q	GrossP4Q		GrossPX4
6							
7	Salaries						
8	Miscellaneous expenses						
9	Research and development						
10	Rent						
11	Depreciation						
12	Income from operations	OpInc1Q	OpInc2Q	OpInc3Q	OpInc4Q		OpIncX4
13							
14	Interest expense						
15	Taxable income	TaxInc1Q	TaxInc2Q	TaxInc3Q	TaxInc4Q		TaxIncX4
16							
17	Tax expense	TaxExp1Q	TaxExp2Q	TaxExp3Q	TaxExp4Q		TaxExpX4
18	Net income	NetInc1Q	NetInc2Q	NetInc3Q	NetInc4Q		NetIncX4

Sheet tabs: Financial Ratios / Valuation / Capitalization / Ir

FIGURE 12.4 Names of the Input and Output Cells Underlying the Income Statement

	A	B	C	D	E	F	G
1				Period			
2		1Q X4	2Q X4	3Q X4	4Q X4		X4
3	SALES BUDGET						
4	Unit Sales and Price Budget						
5	Unit sales						
6	× Price per unit						
7	= Total sales	Sales1Q	Sales2Q	Sales3Q	Sales4Q		SalesX4
8							
9	Sales Composition Budget						
10	Cash sales	CashSls1Q	CashSls2Q	CashSls3Q	CashSls4Q		CashSlsX4
11	+ Credit sales	CreditSls1Q	CreditSls2Q	CreditSls3Q	CreditSls4Q		CreditSlsX4
12	= Total sales						
13							
14	COLLECTIONS BUDGET						
15	Cash Collections from Customers Budget						
16	Cash sales this period						
17	+ Credit sales collected						
18	= Total collections	Collections1Q	Collections2Q	Collections3Q	Collections4Q		CollectionsX4
19							
20	Accounts Receivable (A/R) Budget						
21	Beginning A/R balance	BegAR1Q	BegAR2Q	BegAR3Q	BegAR4Q		BegARX4
22	+ Additions to A/R	AddAR1Q	AddAR2Q	AddAR3Q	AddAR4Q		AddARX4
23	- Subtractions from A/R	SubAR1Q	SubAR2Q	SubAR3Q	SubAR4Q		SubARX4
24	= Ending A/R balance	EndAR1Q	EndAR2Q	EndAR3Q	EndAR4Q		EndARX4

Sheet tabs: Financial Ratios / Valuation / Capitalization / **Sales and Co**

FIGURE 12.5 Names of the Input and Output Cells Underlying the Sales and Collections Worksheet

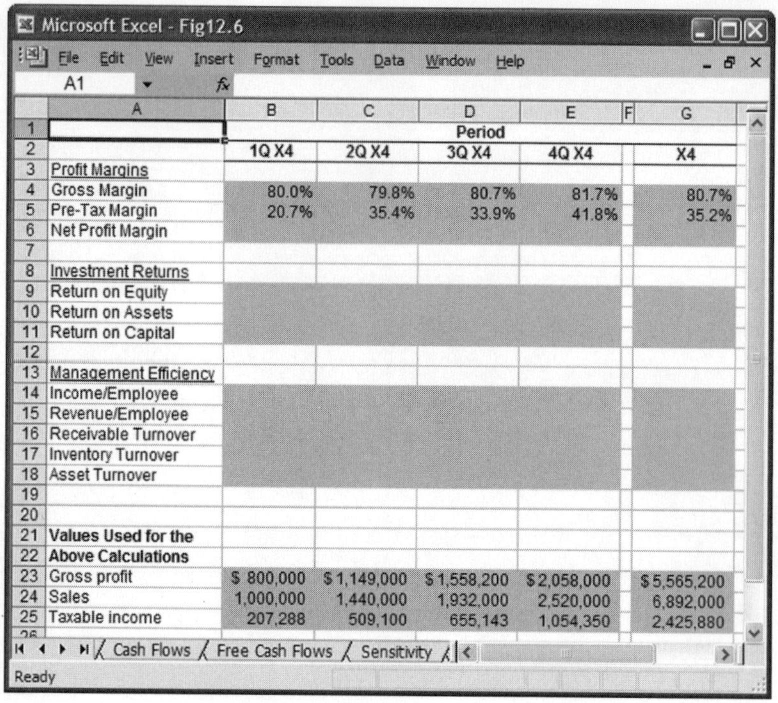

FIGURE 12.6   Calculation of Pre-Tax Margin

the calculation of Napavale's Pre-Tax Margin. Figure 12.7 presents a view of the values and formulas underlying the calculation of Napavale's Pre-Tax Margin.

The names of the input and output cells associated with the calculation of Napavale's Pre-Tax Margin are shown in Figure 12.8. Note the source of the input values in this calculation—Taxable Income values are drawn from the Income Statement and Sales values are drawn from the Sales and Collections worksheet.

Net Profit Margin, the third profit margin ratio, compares Napavale's Net Income to Sales. This is a widely used financial ratio that is also referred to as "Net Margin" or "Net Income Margin," among other names. Net Profit Margin is calculated as: (Net Income)/(Sales). Figure 12.9 presents a view of the calculation of Napavale's Net Profit Margin.

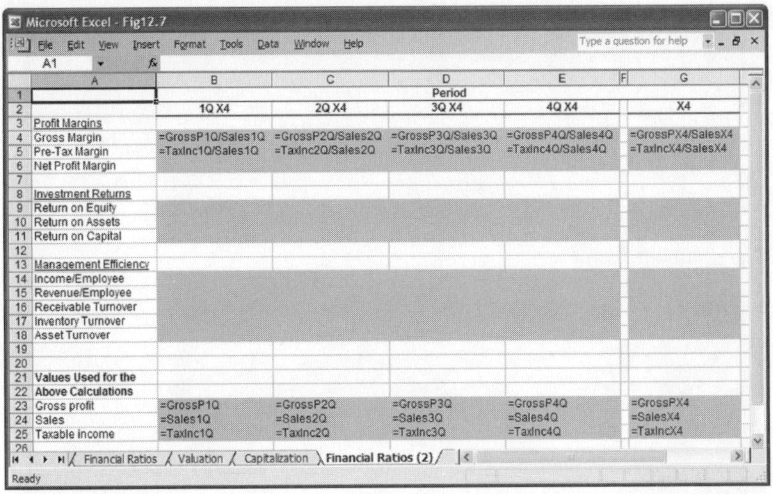

FIGURE 12.7 Alternative View of the Calculation of Pre-Tax Margin

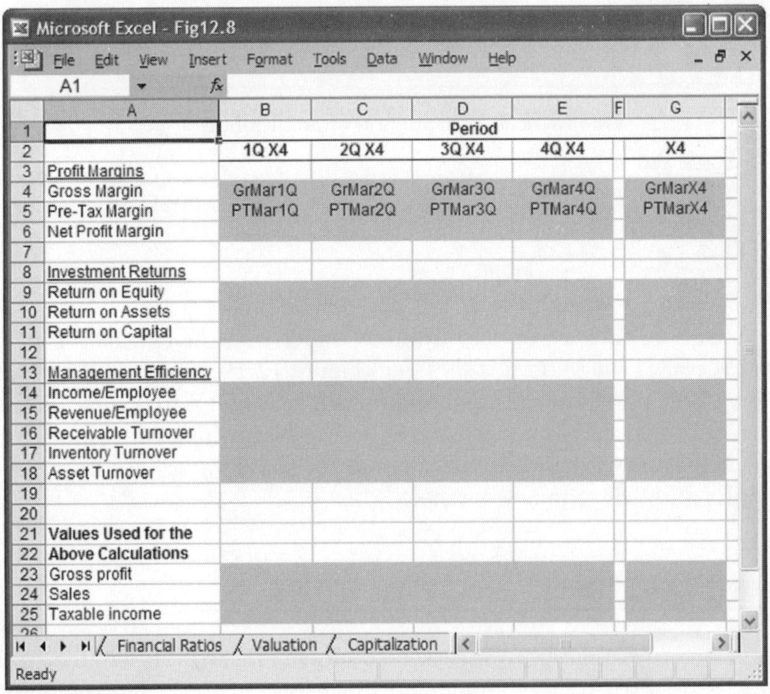

FIGURE 12.8 Names of the Input and Output Cells Underlying the Calculation of Pre-Tax Margin

	A	B	C	D	E	F	G	
1				Period				
2		1Q X4	2Q X4	3Q X4	4Q X4		X4	
3	Profit Margins							
4	Gross Margin	80.0%	79.8%	80.7%	81.7%		80.7%	
5	Pre-Tax Margin	20.7%	35.4%	33.9%	41.8%		35.2%	
6	Net Profit Margin	13.5%	23.0%	22.0%	27.2%		22.9%	
7								
8	Investment Returns							
9	Return on Equity							
10	Return on Assets							
11	Return on Capital							
12								
13	Management Efficiency							
14	Income/Employee							
15	Revenue/Employee							
16	Receivable Turnover							
17	Inventory Turnover							
18	Asset Turnover							
19								
20								
21	Values Used for the							
22	Above Calculations							
23	Gross profit	$ 800,000	$ 1,149,000	$ 1,558,200	$ 2,058,000		$ 5,565,200	
24	Sales	1,000,000	1,440,000	1,932,000	2,520,000		6,892,000	
25	Taxable income	207,288	509,100	655,143	1,054,350		2,425,880	
26	Net income	134,737	330,915	425,843	685,328		1,576,822	
27								

FIGURE 12.9   Calculation of Net Profit Margin

A view of the values and formulas underlying the calculation of Napavale's Net Profit Margin is shown in Figure 12.10. Figure 12.11 presents a view of the names of the input and output cells associated with the calculation of Napavale's Net Profit Margin. The Net Income values are drawn from Napavale's Income Statement and the Sales values are drawn from the Sales and Collections worksheet.

INVESTMENT RETURNS—FINANCIAL RATIOS

Financial ratios related to investment returns measure how efficiently a business uses (or used) its financial resources. In this context, financial resources may include equity, debt, or assets (remember that assets represent the use of funds and equity and debt represent the source of funds for a business). Investment returns ratios typically relate an Income

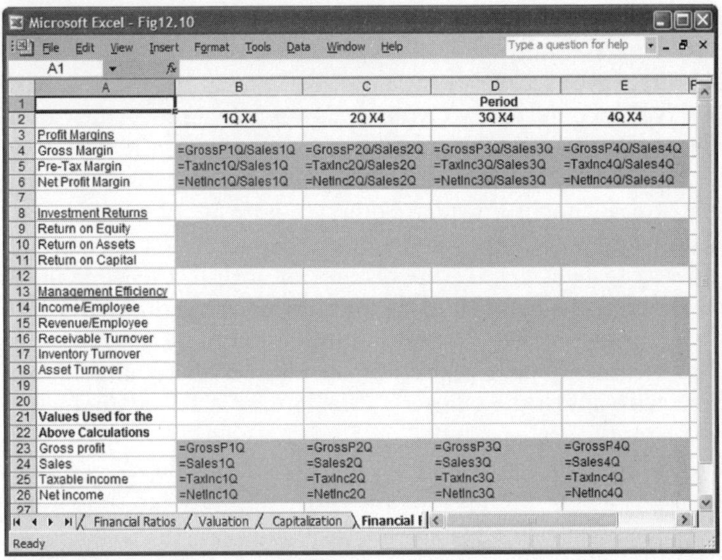

FIGURE 12.10 Alternative View of the Calculation of Net Profit Margin

FIGURE 12.11 Names of the Input and Output Cells Underlying the Calculation of Net Profit Margin

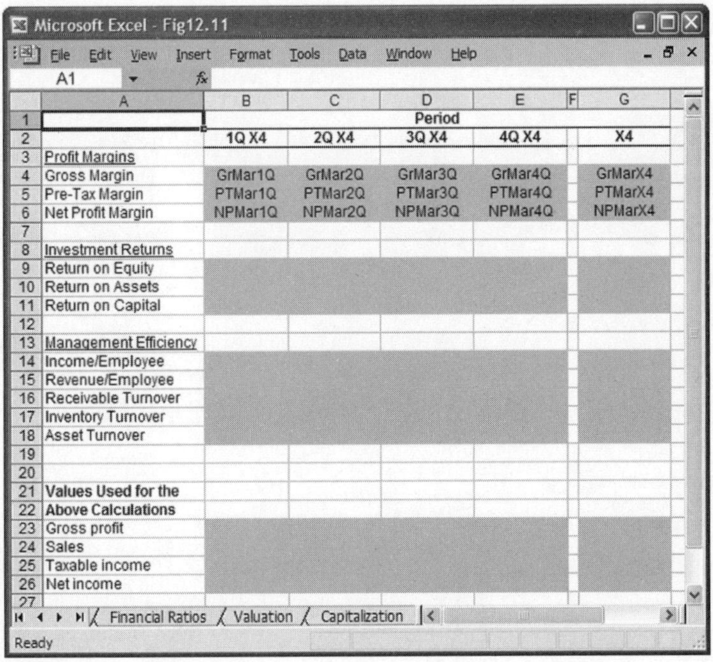

Statement account, such as Net Income, to a Balance Sheet account, such as Owners' Equity.

The first investment returns ratio, Return on Equity, compares Napavale's Net Income to its Owners' Equity account. Return on Equity provides a measure of how effectively Napavale used its equity base in terms of generating profits (or Net Income). Return on Equity is calculated as: (Net Income)/(Owners' Equity). Figure 12.12 presents the calculation of Napavale's Return on Equity. Note that I am "annualizing" each quarter's investment returns ratio (for each of the three investment returns covered in this section) by multiplying the ratio by four (as there are four quarters in each year). I am interested in measuring Napavale's investment returns, such as Return on Equity, on an annual basis. As such, I need to adjust the quarterly calculations to reflect my focus on annualized figures.

The values and formulas underlying the worksheet cells associated with the calculation of Napavale's Return on Equity are shown in Figure

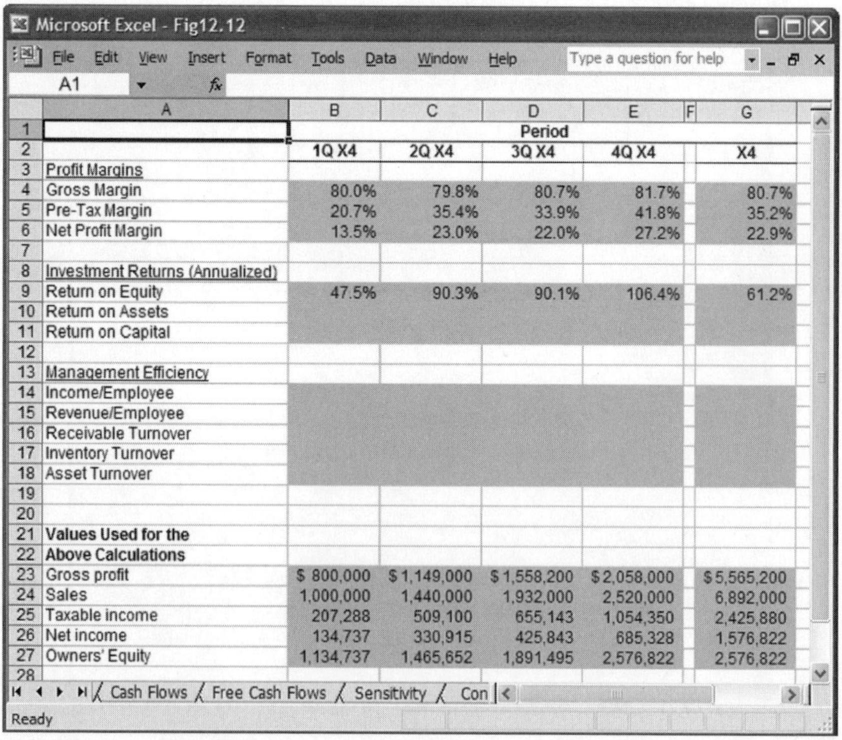

FIGURE 12.12   Calculation of Return on Equity

12.13. Figure 12.14 presents a view of the names of the input and output cells related to the calculation of Napavale's Return on Equity.

Note that the Net Income values are drawn from the Income Statement and the Owners' Equity values are drawn from the Balance Sheet. A view of the names of the input and output worksheet cells from Napavale's Balance Sheet is presented in Figure 12.15 for the sake of reference.

The next investment returns ratio, Return on Assets, compares Napavale's Net Income to its Assets. Return on Assets provides an indication of how effectively Napavale utilized its Assets in generating Net Income. Return on Assets is calculated as: (Net Income)/(Assets). Figure 12.16 presents a view of the calculation of Napavale's Return on Assets. An alternative view of the calculation of Napavale's Return on Assets in which the values and formulas underlying the worksheet cells are exposed and visible is presented in Figure 12.17. The names of the input and output cells related to the calculation of Napavale's Return on Assets are shown in Figure 12.18. The Net Income values are drawn from Napavale's Income Statement and the Assets values are drawn from Napavale's Balance Sheet.

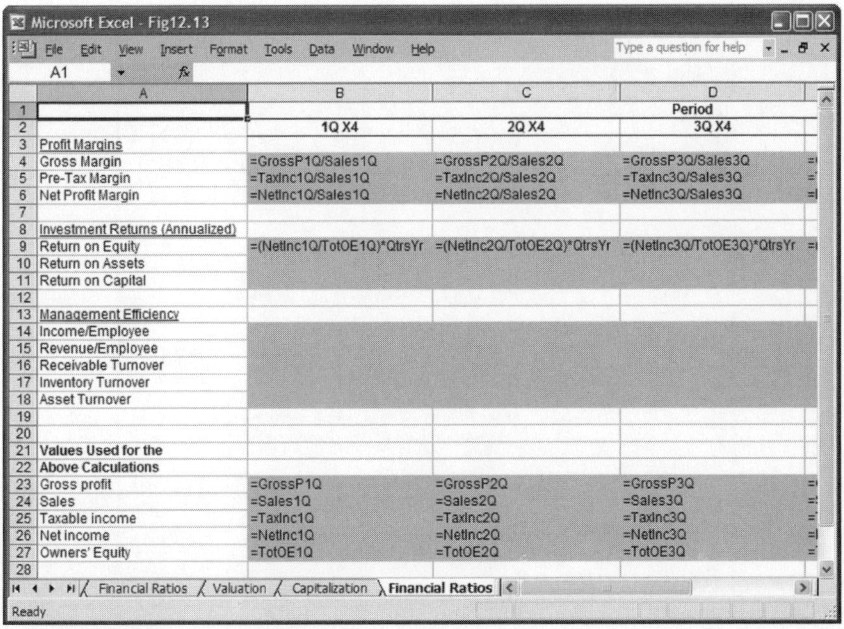

	A	B	C	D
1				Period
2		1Q X4	2Q X4	3Q X4
3	Profit Margins			
4	Gross Margin	=GrossP1Q/Sales1Q	=GrossP2Q/Sales2Q	=GrossP3Q/Sales3Q
5	Pre-Tax Margin	=TaxInc1Q/Sales1Q	=TaxInc2Q/Sales2Q	=TaxInc3Q/Sales3Q
6	Net Profit Margin	=NetInc1Q/Sales1Q	=NetInc2Q/Sales2Q	=NetInc3Q/Sales3Q
7				
8	Investment Returns (Annualized)			
9	Return on Equity	=(NetInc1Q/TotOE1Q)*QtrsYr	=(NetInc2Q/TotOE2Q)*QtrsYr	=(NetInc3Q/TotOE3Q)*QtrsYr
10	Return on Assets			
11	Return on Capital			
12				
13	Management Efficiency			
14	Income/Employee			
15	Revenue/Employee			
16	Receivable Turnover			
17	Inventory Turnover			
18	Asset Turnover			
19				
20				
21	Values Used for the			
22	Above Calculations			
23	Gross profit	=GrossP1Q	=GrossP2Q	=GrossP3Q
24	Sales	=Sales1Q	=Sales2Q	=Sales3Q
25	Taxable income	=TaxInc1Q	=TaxInc2Q	=TaxInc3Q
26	Net income	=NetInc1Q	=NetInc2Q	=NetInc3Q
27	Owners' Equity	=TotOE1Q	=TotOE2Q	=TotOE3Q
28				

FIGURE 12.13 Alternative View of the Calculation of Return on Equity

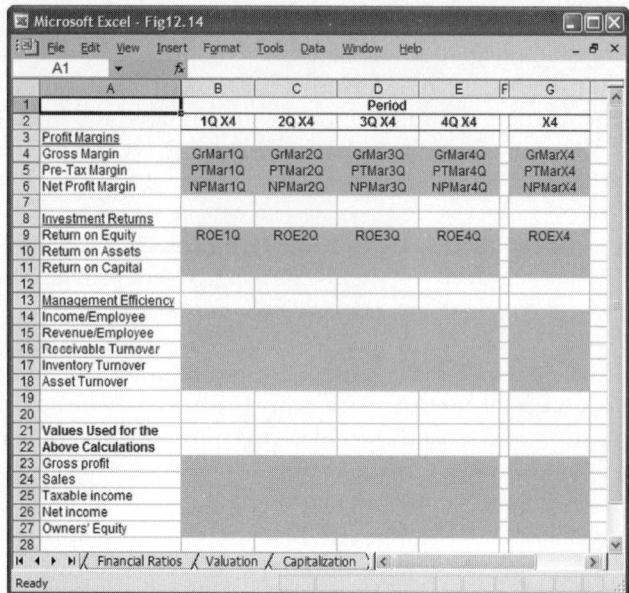

FIGURE 12.14   Names of the Input and Output Cells Underlying the Calculation of Return on Equity

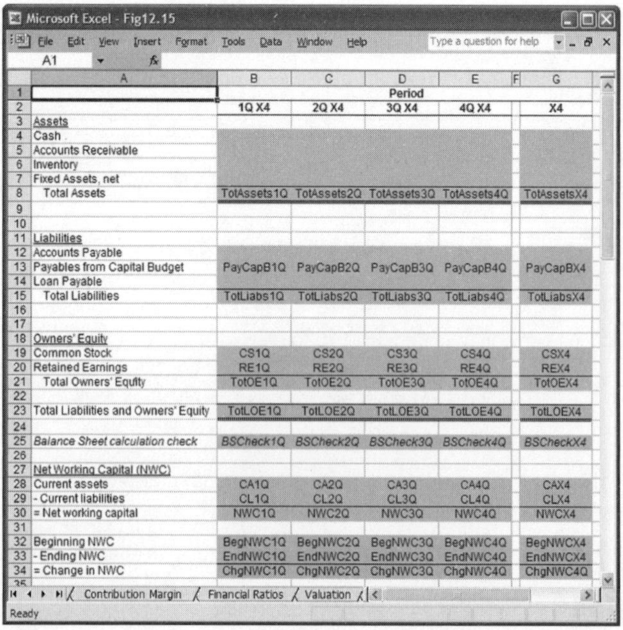

FIGURE 12.15   Names of the Input and Output Cells Underlying the Balance Sheet

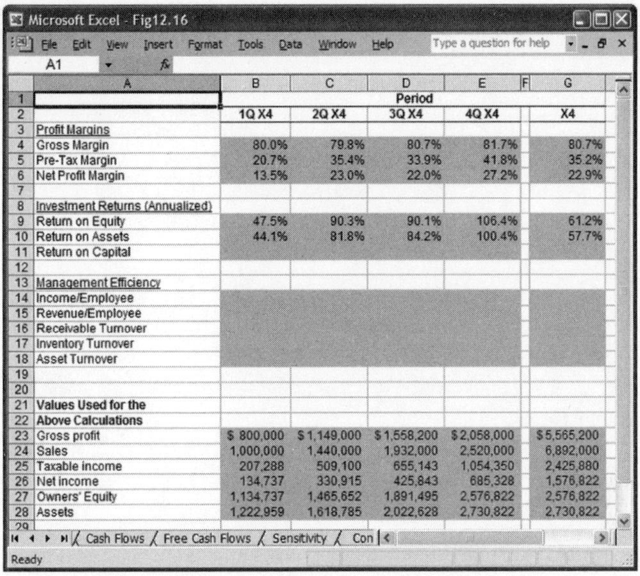

FIGURE 12.16 Calculation of Return on Assets

FIGURE 12.17 Alternative View of the Calculation of Return on Assets

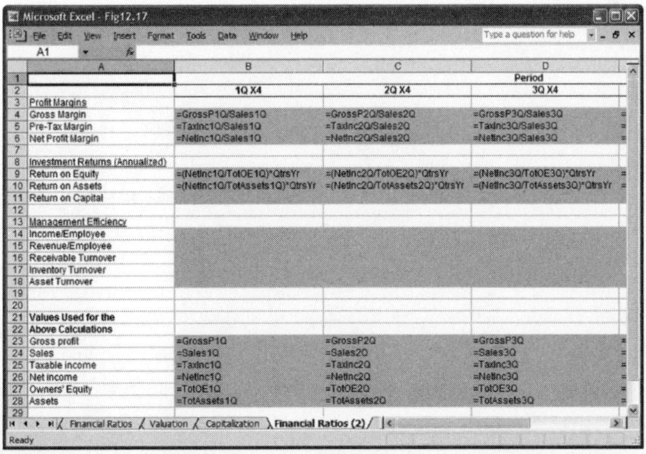

	A	B	C	D	E	F	G
1				Period			
2		1Q X4	2Q X4	3Q X4	4Q X4		X4
3	Profit Margins						
4	Gross Margin	GrMar1Q	GrMar2Q	GrMar3Q	GrMar4Q		GrMarX4
5	Pre-Tax Margin	PTMar1Q	PTMar2Q	PTMar3Q	PTMar4Q		PTMarX4
6	Net Profit Margin	NPMar1Q	NPMar2Q	NPMar3Q	NPMar4Q		NPMarX4
7							
8	Investment Returns						
9	Return on Equity	ROE1Q	ROE2Q	ROE3Q	ROE4Q		ROEX4
10	Return on Assets	ROA1Q	ROA2Q	ROA3Q	ROA4Q		ROAX4
11	Return on Capital						
12							
13	Management Efficiency						
14	Income/Employee						
15	Revenue/Employee						
16	Receivable Turnover						
17	Inventory Turnover						
18	Asset Turnover						
19							
20							
21	Values Used for the						
22	Above Calculations						
23	Gross profit						
24	Sales						
25	Taxable income						
26	Net income						
27	Owners' Equity						
28	Assets						
29							

Financial Ratios / Valuation / Capitalization

FIGURE 12.18   Names of the Input and Output Cells Underlying the Calculation of Return on Assets

Return on Capital, the third investment returns ratio, measures how effectively Napavale utilized its Capital (defined as equity + debt in this case) in generating Net Income. As Capital includes both equity and debt in this context, a specific company's Return on Equity may be very similar to or very different from its Return on Capital depending upon how much debt that company has in its capital structure. Return on Capital is calculated as: (Net Income)/(Owners' Equity + Debt). The calculation of Napavale's Return on Capital is shown in Figure 12.19. Figure 12.20 presents a view of the calculation of Napavale's Return on Capital in which the values and formulas underlying the calculation are visible. The names of the input and output cells related to the calculation of Napavale's Return on Capital are shown in Figure 12.21. Note that the Net Income values are

FIGURE 12.19 Calculation of Return on Capital

A	B	C	D	E	F	G
1			Period			
2	1Q X4	2Q X4	3Q X4	4Q X4		X4
3 Profit Margins						
4 Gross Margin	80.0%	79.8%	80.7%	81.7%		80.7%
5 Pre-Tax Margin	20.7%	35.4%	33.9%	41.8%		35.2%
6 Net Profit Margin	13.5%	23.0%	22.0%	27.2%		22.9%
7						
8 Investment Returns (Annualized)						
9 Return on Equity	47.5%	90.3%	90.1%	106.4%		61.2%
10 Return on Assets	44.1%	81.8%	84.2%	100.4%		57.7%
11 Return on Capital	47.5%	87.3%	90.1%	106.4%		61.2%
12						
13 Management Efficiency						
14 Income/Employee						
15 Revenue/Employee						
16 Receivable Turnover						
17 Inventory Turnover						
18 Asset Turnover						
19						
20						
21 Values Used for the						
22 Above Calculations						
23 Gross profit	$ 800,000	$1,149,000	$1,558,200	$2,058,000		$5,565,200
24 Sales	1,000,000	1,440,000	1,932,000	2,520,000		6,892,000
25 Taxable income	207,288	509,100	655,143	1,054,350		2,425,880
26 Net income	134,737	330,915	425,843	685,328		1,576,822
27 Owners' Equity	1,134,737	1,465,652	1,891,495	2,576,822		2,576,822
28 Assets	1,222,959	1,618,785	2,022,628	2,730,822		2,730,822
29 Capital	1,134,737	1,515,652	1,891,495	2,576,822		2,576,822

FIGURE 12.20 Alternative View of the Calculation of Return on Capital

A	B	C
1		
2	1Q X4	2Q X4
3 Profit Margins		
4 Gross Margin	=GrossP1Q/Sales1Q	=GrossP2Q/Sales2Q
5 Pre-Tax Margin	=TaxInc1Q/Sales1Q	=TaxInc2Q/Sales2Q
6 Net Profit Margin	=NetInc1Q/Sales1Q	=NetInc2Q/Sales2Q
7		
8 Investment Returns (Annualized)		
9 Return on Equity	=(NetInc1Q/TotOE1Q)*QtrsYr	=(NetInc2Q/TotOE2Q)*QtrsYr
10 Return on Assets	=(NetInc1Q/TotAssets1Q)*QtrsYr	=(NetInc2Q/TotAssets2Q)*QtrsYr
11 Return on Capital	=(NetInc1Q/(TotOE1Q+LoanVal1Q))*QtrsYr	=(NetInc2Q/(TotOE2Q+LoanVal2Q))*QtrsYr
12		
13 Management Efficiency		
14 Income/Employee		
15 Revenue/Employee		
16 Receivable Turnover		
17 Inventory Turnover		
18 Asset Turnover		
19		
20		
21 Values Used for the		
22 Above Calculations		
23 Gross profit	=GrossP1Q	=GrossP2Q
24 Sales	=Sales1Q	=Sales2Q
25 Taxable income	=TaxInc1Q	=TaxInc2Q
26 Net income	=NetInc1Q	=NetInc2Q
27 Owners' Equity	=TotOE1Q	=TotOE2Q
28 Assets	=TotAssets1Q	=TotAssets2Q
29 Capital	=TotOE1Q+LoanVal1Q	=TotOE2Q+LoanVal2Q

	A	B	C	D	E	F	G
1				Period			
2		1Q X4	2Q X4	3Q X4	4Q X4		X4
3	Profit Margins						
4	Gross Margin	GrMar1Q	GrMar2Q	GrMar3Q	GrMar4Q		GrMarX4
5	Pre-Tax Margin	PTMar1Q	PTMar2Q	PTMar3Q	PTMar4Q		PTMarX4
6	Net Profit Margin	NPMar1Q	NPMar2Q	NPMar3Q	NPMar4Q		NPMarX4
7							
8	Investment Returns (Annualized)						
9	Return on Equity	ROE1Q	ROE2Q	ROE3Q	ROE4Q		ROEX4
10	Return on Assets	ROA1Q	ROA2Q	ROA3Q	ROA4Q		ROAX4
11	Return on Capital	ROC1Q	ROC2Q	ROC3Q	ROC4Q		ROCX4
12							
13	Management Efficiency						
14	Income/Employee						
15	Revenue/Employee						
16	Receivable Turnover						
17	Inventory Turnover						
18	Asset Turnover						
19							
20							
21	Values Used for the						
22	Above Calculations						
23	Gross profit						
24	Sales						
25	Taxable income						
26	Net income						
27	Owners' Equity						
28	Assets						
29	Capital						
30							

FIGURE 12.21   Names of the Input and Output Cells Underlying the Calculation of Return on Capital

drawn from Napavale's Income Statement and the values underlying the calculation of Napavale's Capital are drawn from the Balance Sheet.

MANAGEMENT EFFICIENCY—FINANCIAL RATIOS

Financial ratios related to management efficiency measure how efficiently a business has been managed. While a wide array of management efficiency ratios are used, I focus on two types of ratios for Napavale: "per-employee" ratios and "turnover" ratios. Per-employee ratios compare operating metrics such as Net Income and Sales to the number of employees at Napavale. Turnover ratios compare various Balance Sheet accounts, such as Accounts Receivable and Inventory, to Sales (an Income Statement account).

As I did with the investment returns, I will annualize each of the quarterly calculations by multiplying the quarterly results by four (as there are four quarters in a year). Also, while some of these management efficiency ratios technically call for the use of an average value, such as the average number of employees over a given period of time (such as a year), I am going to use year-end figures for the sake of simplicity.

The two per-employee management efficiency ratios that I cover for Napavale are Income/Employee and Revenue/Employee. Income/Employee compares Napavale's Income (or Net Income) to the number of employees at Napavale—this ratio is calculated as: (Net Income)/(Number of Employees). Revenue/Employee compares Napavale's Revenue (or Sales) to the number of employees at Napavale—this ratio is calculated as (Sales)/(Number of Employees). Figure 12.22 presents a view of the calculation of Napavale's Income/Employee and Revenue/Employee.

	A	B	C	D	E	F	G
1				Period			
2		1Q X4	2Q X4	3Q X4	4Q X4		X4
3	Profit Margins						
4	Gross Margin	80.0%	79.8%	80.7%	81.7%		80.7%
5	Pre-Tax Margin	20.7%	35.4%	33.9%	41.8%		35.2%
6	Net Profit Margin	13.5%	23.0%	22.0%	27.2%		22.9%
7							
8	Investment Returns (Annualized)						
9	Return on Equity	47.5%	90.3%	90.1%	106.4%		61.2%
10	Return on Assets	44.1%	81.8%	84.2%	100.4%		57.7%
11	Return on Capital	47.5%	87.3%	90.1%	106.4%		61.2%
12							
13	Management Efficiency (Annualized)						
14	Income/Employee	$ 35,930	$ 88,244	$ 77,426	$ 119,187		$ 68,557
15	Revenue/Employee	$ 266,667	$ 384,000	$ 351,273	$ 438,261		$ 299,652
16	Receivable Turnover						
17	Inventory Turnover						
18	Asset Turnover						
19							
20							
21	Values Used for the						
22	Above Calculations						
23	Gross profit	$ 800,000	$1,149,000	$1,558,200	$2,058,000		$5,565,200
24	Sales	1,000,000	1,440,000	1,932,000	2,520,000		6,892,000
25	Taxable income	207,288	509,100	655,143	1,054,350		2,425,880
26	Net income	134,737	330,915	425,843	685,328		1,576,822
27	Owners' Equity	1,134,737	1,465,652	1,891,495	2,576,822		2,576,822
28	Assets	1,222,959	1,618,785	2,022,628	2,730,822		2,730,822
29	Capital	1,134,737	1,515,652	1,891,495	2,576,822		2,576,822
30	Employees	15	15	22	23		23
31							

FIGURE 12.22 Calculation of Income/Employee and Revenue/Employee

A view of the values and formulas underlying the worksheet cells associated with the calculation of Napavale's Income/Employee and Revenue/Employee is presented in Figure 12.23. Figure 12.24 offers a view of the input and output worksheet cells related to the calculation of Napavale's Income/Employee and Revenue/Employee.

Note that the Net Income values are drawn from Napavale's Income Statement, the Sales values are drawn from Napavale's Sales and Collections worksheet, and the Number of Employees values are drawn from Napavale's Headcount Overview worksheet. For the sake of reference, Figure 12.25 presents a view of the names of the worksheet cells underlying the Headcount Overview worksheet.

The three turnover management efficiency ratios that I cover for Napavale are Receivable Turnover, Inventory Turnover, and Asset Turnover. Receivable Turnover, which compares Napavale's Sales to its Accounts Receivable, is calculated as: (Sales)/(Accounts Receivable). Inventory Turnover, which compares Napavale's Cost of Goods Sold to its Inventory, is calculated as: (Cost of Goods Sold)/(Inventory). The third turnover

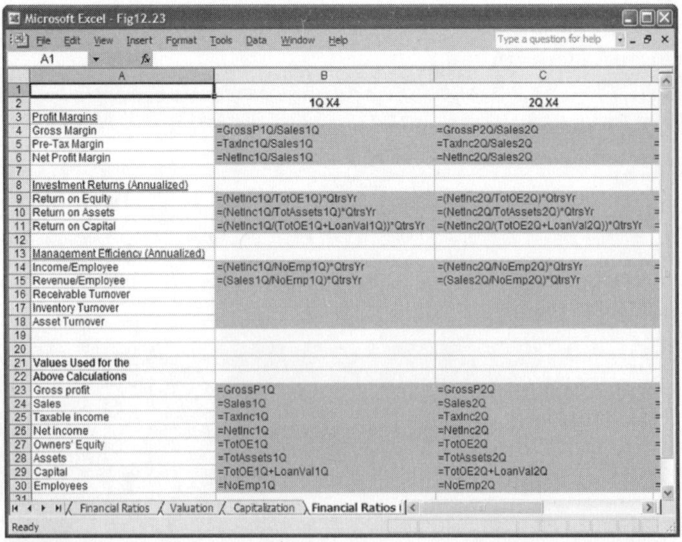

FIGURE 12.23 Alternative View of the Calculation of Income/Employee and Revenue/Employee

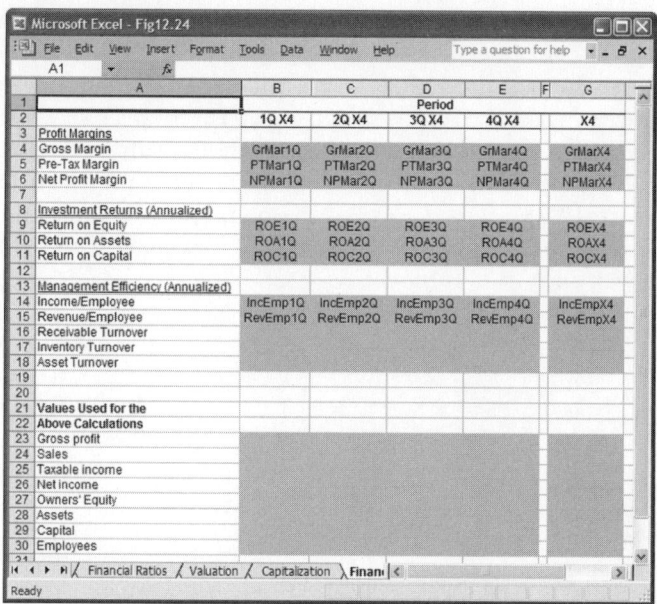

FIGURE 12.24   Names of the Input and Output Cells Underlying the Calculation of Income/Employee and Revenue/Employee

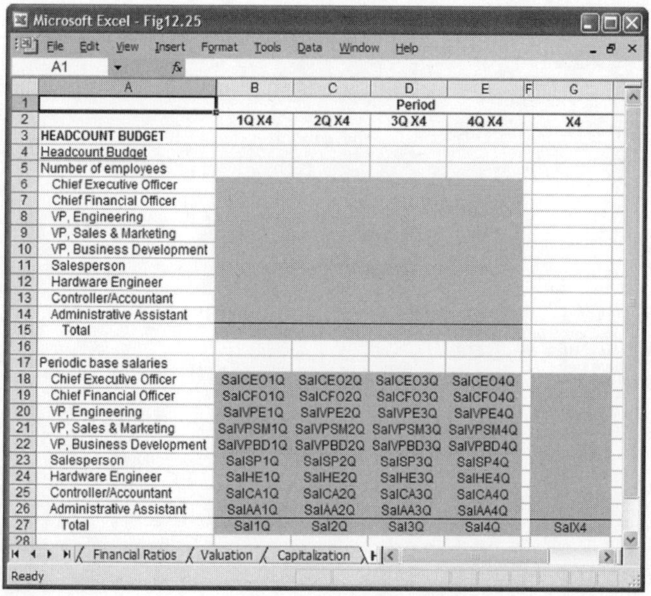

FIGURE 12.25   Names of the Input and Output Cells Underlying the Headcount Overview Worksheet

management efficiency ratio, Asset Turnover, compares Napavale's Sales to its Assets and is calculated as: (Sales)/(Assets).

Figure 12.26 presents a view of the calculation of Napavale's Receivable Turnover, Inventory Turnover, and Asset Turnover. A view of the values and formulas underlying the calculation of Napavale's Receivable Turnover, Inventory Turnover, and Asset Turnover is presented in Figure 12.27. Figure 12.28 offers a view of the names of the input and output cells underlying the calculation of Napavale's Receivable Turnover, Inventory Turnover, and Asset Turnover.

A	B	C	D	E	F	G
1			Period			
2	1Q X4	2Q X4	3Q X4	4Q X4		X4
3 Profit Margins						
4 Gross Margin	80.0%	79.8%	80.7%	81.7%		80.7%
5 Pre-Tax Margin	20.7%	35.4%	33.9%	41.8%		35.2%
6 Net Profit Margin	13.5%	23.0%	22.0%	27.2%		22.9%
7						
8 Investment Returns (Annualized)						
9 Return on Equity	47.5%	90.3%	90.1%	106.4%		61.2%
10 Return on Assets	44.1%	81.8%	84.2%	100.4%		57.7%
11 Return on Capital	47.5%	87.3%	90.1%	106.4%		61.2%
12						
13 Management Efficiency (Annualized)						
14 Income/Employee	$ 35,930	$ 88,244	$ 77,426	$ 119,187		$ 68,557
15 Revenue/Employee	$ 266,667	$ 384,000	$ 351,273	$ 438,261		$ 299,652
16 Receivable Turnover	30.0	30.0	30.0	30.0		20.5
17 Inventory Turnover	12.4	14.0	14.6	18.0		12.9
18 Asset Turnover	3.3	3.6	3.8	3.7		2.5
19						
20						
21 Values Used for the						
22 Above Calculations						
23 Gross profit	$ 800,000	$1,149,000	$1,558,200	$2,058,000		$5,565,200
24 Sales	1,000,000	1,440,000	1,932,000	2,520,000		6,892,000
25 Taxable income	207,288	509,100	655,143	1,054,350		2,425,880
26 Net income	134,737	330,915	425,843	685,328		1,576,822
27 Owners' Equity	1,134,737	1,465,652	1,891,495	2,576,822		2,576,822
28 Assets	1,222,959	1,618,785	2,022,628	2,730,822		2,730,822
29 Capital	1,134,737	1,515,652	1,891,495	2,576,822		2,576,822
30 Employees	15	15	22	23		23
31 Accounts Receivable	133,333	192,000	257,600	336,000		336,000
32 Cost-of-goods sold	200,000	291,000	373,800	462,000		1,326,800
33 Inventory	64,667	83,067	102,667	102,667		102,667

FIGURE 12.26   Calculation of Receivables Turnover, Inventory Turnover, and Asset Turnover

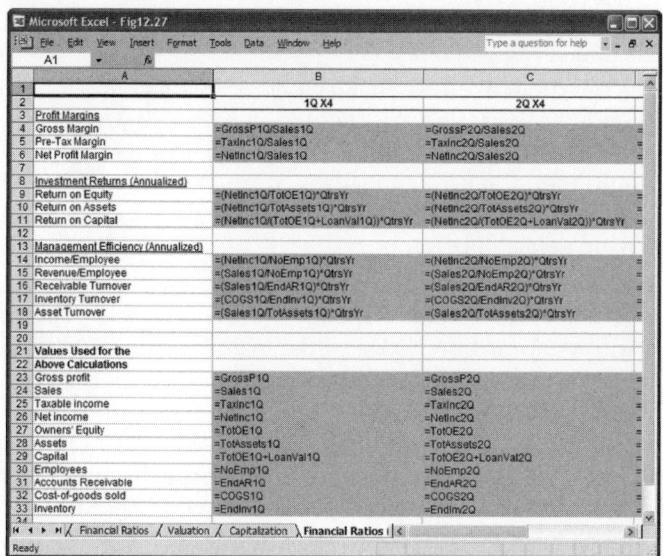

FIGURE 12.27 Alternative View of the Calculation of Receivables Turnover, Inventory Turnover, and Asset Turnover

	1Q X4	2Q X4
Profit Margins		
Gross Margin	GrMar1Q	GrMar2Q
Pre-Tax Margin	PTMar1Q	PTMar2Q
Net Profit Margin	NPMar1Q	NPMar2Q
Investment Returns (Annualized)		
Return on Equity	ROE1Q	ROE2Q
Return on Assets	ROA1Q	ROA2Q
Return on Capital	ROC1Q	ROC2Q
Management Efficiency (Annualized)		
Income/Employee	IncEmp1Q	IncEmp2Q
Revenue/Employee	RevEmp1Q	RevEmp2Q
Receivable Turnover	RecTurn1Q	RecTurn2Q
Inventory Turnover	InvTurn1Q	InvTurn2Q
Asset Turnover	AssetTurn1Q	AssetTurn2Q

(Figure 12.28 — Period columns: 1Q X4, 2Q X4, 3Q X4, 4Q X4, X4)

	1Q X4	2Q X4	3Q X4	4Q X4	X4
			Period		
Profit Margins					
Gross Margin	GrMar1Q	GrMar2Q	GrMar3Q	GrMar4Q	GrMarX4
Pre-Tax Margin	PTMar1Q	PTMar2Q	PTMar3Q	PTMar4Q	PTMarX4
Net Profit Margin	NPMar1Q	NPMar2Q	NPMar3Q	NPMar4Q	NPMarX4
Investment Returns (Annualized)					
Return on Equity	ROE1Q	ROE2Q	ROE3Q	ROE4Q	ROEX4
Return on Assets	ROA1Q	ROA2Q	ROA3Q	ROA4Q	ROAX4
Return on Capital	ROC1Q	ROC2Q	ROC3Q	ROC4Q	ROCX4
Management Efficiency (Annualized)					
Income/Employee	IncEmp1Q	IncEmp2Q	IncEmp3Q	IncEmp4Q	IncEmpX4
Revenue/Employee	RevEmp1Q	RevEmp2Q	RevEmp3Q	RevEmp4Q	RevEmpX4
Receivable Turnover	RecTurn1Q	RecTurn2Q	RecTurn3Q	RecTurn4Q	RecTurnX4
Inventory Turnover	InvTurn1Q	InvTurn2Q	InvTurn3Q	InvTurn4Q	InvTurnX4
Asset Turnover	AssetTurn1Q	AssetTurn2Q	AssetTurn3Q	AssetTurn4Q	AssetTurnX4
Values Used for the					
Above Calculations					
Gross profit					
Sales					
Taxable income					
Net income					
Owners' Equity					
Assets					
Capital					
Employees					
Accounts Receivable					
Cost-of-goods sold					
Inventory					

FIGURE 12.28 Names of the Input and Output Cells Underlying the Calculation of Receivables Turnover, Inventory Turnover, and Asset Turnover

QUESTIONS

Each of the questions for this chapter relates to a hypothetical company named Company 456. Company 456 sells display monitors to physicians. As such, Company 456 is a product-oriented (as opposed to a service-oriented) business. Note that there are three cost-of-goods-sold components for Company 456's display monitors: (1) monitor screen, (2) monitor casing, and (3) assembly and labor.

The questions for this chapter will address fiscal year X4 on a quarterly basis (four specific quarters, 1Q–4Q for year X4). The following questions will test your knowledge of the material covered in this chapter in an applied manner—specifically, you will be asked to calculate a set of financial ratios for Company 456.

To prepare you for this chapter's questions, Figure Q12.1 offers a view of Company 456's Income Statement to provide some background information related to Company 456's operations. Company 456's Sales and Collections worksheet is shown in Figure Q12.2. Figure Q12.3 offers a view of Company 456's Balance Sheet. A section of Company 456's Assumptions and Dashboard worksheet is shown in Figure Q12.4. Company 456's Cost-of-Goods Sold worksheet is shown in Figure Q12.5. Figure Q12.6 provides a view of Company 456's Inventory and Purchases worksheet.

A	B	C	D	E	F	G
1			Period			
2	1Q X4	2Q X4	3Q X4	4Q X4		X4
3 Sales	$7,500,000	$8,250,000	$8,625,000	$8,555,000		$32,930,000
4 Cost of goods sold	3,650,000	3,954,500	4,065,250	4,171,300		15,841,050
5 Gross profit	$3,850,000	$4,295,500	$4,559,750	$4,383,700		$17,088,950
6						
7 Salaries	$ 991,800	$ 991,800	$1,329,650	$1,407,950		$ 4,721,200
8 Miscellaneous expenses	300,000	330,000	258,750	256,650		1,145,400
9 Research and development	450,000	577,500	690,000	684,400		2,401,900
10 Rent	35,000	35,000	35,000	35,000		140,000
11 Depreciation	1,950	4,150	6,150	8,200		20,450
12 Income from operations	$2,071,250	$2,357,050	$2,240,200	$1,991,500		$ 8,660,000
13						
14 Interest expense	$ -	$ -	$ -	$ -		$ -
15 Taxable income	$2,071,250	$2,357,050	$2,240,200	$1,991,500		$ 8,660,000
16						
17 Tax expense	$ 724,938	$ 824,968	$ 784,070	$ 697,025		$ 3,031,000
18 Net income	$1,346,313	$1,532,083	$1,456,130	$1,294,475		$ 5,629,000
19						

FIGURE Q12.1   Company 456's Income Statement

A	B	C	D	E	F	G
1			Period			
2	1Q X4	2Q X4	3Q X4	4Q X4		X4
3 SALES BUDGET						
4 Unit Sales and Price Budget						
5 Unit sales	500	550	575	590		2,215
6 × Price per unit	$ 15,000	$ 15,000	$ 15,000	$ 14,500		N/A
7 = Total sales	$7,500,000	$8,250,000	$8,625,000	$8,555,000		$32,930,000
8						
9 Sales Composition Budget						
10 Cash sales	$3,750,000	$4,125,000	$4,312,500	$4,277,500		$16,465,000
11 + Credit sales	3,750,000	4,125,000	4,312,500	4,277,500		16,465,000
12 = Total sales	$7,500,000	$8,250,000	$8,625,000	$8,555,000		$32,930,000
13						
14 COLLECTIONS BUDGET						
15 Cash Collections from Customers Budget						
16 Cash sales this period	$3,750,000	$4,125,000	$4,312,500	$4,277,500		$16,465,000
17 + Credit sales collected	2,083,333	3,958,333	4,229,167	4,293,056		14,563,889
18 = Total collections	$5,833,333	$8,083,333	$8,541,667	$8,570,556		$31,028,889
19						
20 Accounts Receivable (A/R) Budget						
21 Beginning A/R balance	$ -	$1,666,667	$1,833,333	$1,916,667		$ -
22 + Additions to A/R	1,666,667	1,833,333	1,916,667	1,901,111		7,317,778
23 - Subtractions from A/R	-	1,666,667	1,833,333	1,916,667		5,416,667
24 = Ending A/R balance	$1,666,667	$1,833,333	$1,916,667	$1,901,111		$ 1,901,111

FIGURE Q12.2   Company 456's Sales and Collections Worksheet

A	B	C	D	E	F	G
1			Period			
2	1Q X4	2Q X4	3Q X4	4Q X4		X4
3 Assets						
4 Cash	$ 783,503	$1,639,041	$2,992,164	$4,301,817		$4,301,817
5 Accounts Receivable	1,666,667	1,833,333	1,916,667	1,901,111		1,901,111
6 Inventory	1,318,167	1,355,083	1,390,433	1,390,433		1,390,433
7 Fixed Assets, net	36,050	74,900	107,750	139,550		139,550
8 Total Assets	$ 3,804,387	$4,902,358	$6,407,014	$7,732,911		$7,732,911
9						
10						
11 Liabilities						
12 Accounts Payable	$ 2,208,074	$1,773,963	$1,822,489	$1,853,911		$1,853,911
13 Payables from Capital Budget	-	-	-	-		-
14 Loan Payable	-	-	-	-		-
15 Total Liabilities	$ 2,208,074	$1,773,963	$1,822,489	$1,853,911		$1,853,911
16						
17						
18 Owners' Equity						
19 Common Stock	$ 250,000	$ 250,000	$ 250,000	$ 250,000		$ 250,000
20 Retained Earnings	1,346,313	2,878,395	4,334,525	5,629,000		5,629,000
21 Total Owners' Equity	$ 1,596,313	$3,128,395	$4,584,525	$5,879,000		$5,879,000
22						
23 Total Liabilities and Owners' Equity	$ 3,804,387	$4,902,358	$6,407,014	$7,732,911		$7,732,911
24						
25 Balance Sheet calculation check	-	-	-	-		-
26						
27 Net Working Capital (NWC)						
28 Current assets	$ 2,984,833	$3,188,417	$3,307,100	$3,291,544		N/A
29 - Current liabilities	2,208,074	1,773,963	1,822,489	1,853,911		N/A
30 = Net working capital	$ 776,759	$1,414,454	$1,484,611	$1,437,633		N/A
31						
32 Beginning NWC	$ -	$ 776,759	$1,414,454	$1,484,611		N/A
33 - Ending NWC	776,759	1,414,454	1,484,611	1,437,633		N/A
34 = Change in NWC	$ (776,759)	$ (637,694)	$ (70,157)	$ 46,978		N/A

FIGURE Q12.3   Company 456's Balance Sheet

	A	B	C	D	E	F
				Period		
2		1Q X4	2Q X4	3Q X4	4Q X4	
3	Sales and Collections Worksheet					
4	Unit Sales and Price Inputs					
5	Unit sales	500	550	575	590	
6	Price per unit	$ 15,000	$ 15,000	$ 15,000	$ 14,500	
7						
8	Sales Composition Inputs					
9	Cash sales as a % of total sales	50%	50%	50%	50%	
10	Credit sales as a % of total sales	50%	50%	50%	50%	
11						
12	Days receivable (DSO)	40	40	40	40	
13	Days per quarter	90	90	90	90	
14						
15	COGS Worksheet					
16	Cost-of-Goods Sold Inputs					
17	Monitor screen: cost per unit	$ 7,000.00	$ 6,900.00	$ 6,800.00	$ 6,800.00	
18	Monitor casing: cost per unit	$ 200.00	$ 190.00	$ 180.00	$ 180.00	
19	Assembly labor: cost per unit	$ 100.00	$ 100.00	$ 90.00	$ 90.00	
20	Total	$ 7,300.00	$ 7,190.00	$ 7,070.00	$ 7,070.00	
21						
22	Inventory and Purchases Worksheet					
23	Inventory Inputs					
24	Days inventory	30	30	30	30	
25						
26	Disbursements for Purchases Inputs					
27	Days payable	40	40	40	40	
28						

FIGURE Q12.4   Company 456's Assumptions and Dashboard Worksheet

	A	B	C	D	E	F	G
1				Period			
2		1Q X4	2Q X4	3Q X4	4Q X4		X4
3	COST-OF-GOODS SOLD BUDGET						
4	Cost-of-Goods Sold Budget						
5	Monitor screen	$3,500,000	$3,795,000	$3,910,000	$4,012,000		$15,217,000
6	Monitor casing	100,000	104,500	103,500	106,200		414,200
7	Assembly labor	50,000	55,000	51,750	53,100		209,850
8	Total cost-of-goods sold	$3,650,000	$3,954,500	$4,065,250	$4,171,300		$15,841,050
9							

FIGURE Q12.5   Company 456's Cost-of-Goods-Sold Worksheet

	A	B	C	D	E	F	G
1				Period			
2		1Q X4	2Q X4	3Q X4	4Q X4		X4
3	**INVENTORY BUDGET**						
4	Inventory Budget						
5	Desired ending inventory	$ 1,318,167	$ 1,355,083	$ 1,390,433	$ 1,390,433		$ 1,390,433
6	+ Cost of goods sold	3,650,000	3,954,500	4,065,250	4,171,300		15,841,050
7	= Total inventory needed	$ 4,968,167	$ 5,309,583	$ 5,455,683	$ 5,561,733		$ 17,231,483
8							
9	**PURCHASES BUDGET**						
10	Purchases Budget						
11	Total inventory needed	$ 4,968,167	$ 5,309,583	$ 5,455,683	$ 5,561,733		N/A
12	- Beginning inventory	-	1,318,167	1,355,083	1,390,433		-
13	= Purchases	$ 4,968,167	$ 3,991,417	$ 4,100,600	$ 4,171,300		N/A
14							
15	Disbursements for Purchases Budget						
16	Payments of payables	$ 2,760,093	$ 4,425,528	$ 4,052,074	$ 4,139,878		$ 15,377,572
17	Total disbursements for purchases	$ 2,760,093	$ 4,425,528	$ 4,052,074	$ 4,139,878		$ 15,377,572
18							
19	Accounts Payable (A/P) Budget						
20	Beginning A/P balance	$ -	$ 2,208,074	$ 1,773,963	$ 1,822,489		$ -
21	+ Additions to A/P	2,208,074	1,773,963	1,822,489	1,853,911		7,658,437
22	- Subtractions from A/P	-	2,208,074	1,773,963	1,822,489		5,804,526
23	Ending A/P	$ 2,208,074	$ 1,773,963	$ 1,822,489	$ 1,853,911		$ 1,853,911

FIGURE Q12.6 Company 456's Inventory and Purchases Worksheet

1. Given the information presented, calculate Company 456's Gross Margin, Pre-Tax Margin, and Net Profit Margin.
2. Given the information presented, calculate Company 456's Return on Equity, Return on Assets, and Return on Capital.
3. Given the information presented, calculate Company 456's Income per Employee, Revenue per Employee, Receivables Turnover, Inventory Turnover, and Asset Turnover.

CHAPTER **13**

Valuation

This chapter covers the topic of valuation, or the practice of placing a value on a business. Valuation is a vast and complex topic—many books have been written on this subject alone. My goal in this chapter is to introduce several of the most commonly used valuation approaches, including discounted cash flow, public company comparables, and mergers and acquisitions comparables.

Beyond the coverage of specific valuation methodologies, a core concept of valuation is this: The best valuation approach is often a combination of approaches. In other words, it is often best to use several valuation techniques to assess the value of a business. In so doing, it is possible to triangulate on the value of a business by weighting various valuation approaches. I address the valuation of Napavale in this chapter by triangulating on the value of Napavale—by using and weighing several valuation methodologies.

I cover the discounted cash flow, public company comparables, and mergers and acquisitions comparables valuation methodologies separately and then discuss the concept of triangulation and weighing these various approaches at the end of the chapter.

DISCOUNTED CASH FLOW

The discounted cash flow (DCF) valuation approach is widely used and is covered in many undergraduate and graduate-level finance classes in the United States. In essence, the general premise of the DCF approach is this: The value of a business is equal to the present value of the cash flows generated by that business in the future. There are two key concepts in this definition—"present value" and "cash flows."

While various interpretations of the meaning of "cash flows" exist, I will use Napavale's free cash flows (as covered in Chapter 9) as the proxy for "cash flows" in this context. Using free cash flows in a DCF approach is a common practice and it builds on my work in Chapter 9 on the Free Cash Flows worksheet.

The concept of present value, which I have not yet covered in this book, is central to the discipline of finance. Present value and the related concept of future value both deal with the value of something at a particular point in time. While present value may seem like a simple concept, it is actually deceptively complex.

One way to think about the concept of present value is in terms of the value of a dollar now and the value of that same dollar in the future. Generally speaking, a dollar today is worth more than a dollar tomorrow. Please note, this is a broad and sweeping statement that incorporates a variety of assumptions and complex economic theories. My intent here is only to convey the essence of the concept of present value—nothing more. In an inflationary economic environment (meaning, among other things, one in which prices increase), a dollar's buying power will decrease over time. As such, if a dollar's buying power decreases over time, it is worth more today than it is in the future.

The equation that defines the relationship between present value and future value quantifies this concept of the changing value of a dollar (or any other good or service) over time. This equation is:

$$\text{Present Value} = \frac{\text{Future Value}}{(1 + \text{Discount Rate})\text{Time Period}}$$

Using this equation, it is possible to determine the present value of an asset given the following: its future value, a discount rate, and the time period (such as the number of years into the future) associated with the future value. The use of this equation should become clear as I walk through the DCF approach for Napavale.

The first step in building a DCF model for Napavale is to calculate the free cash flows for each of the accounting periods (quarters) covered in Napavale's financial model. I calculated the free cash flows in Chapter 9 and Figure 13.1 presents a view of the Free Cash Flows worksheet as I left it in Chapter 9.

Figure 13.2 presents a view of the values and formulas underlying the worksheet cells in Napavale's Free Cash Flows worksheet. The names of the input and output worksheet cells in Napavale's Free Cash Flows worksheet are shown in Figure 13.3. Please refer to the coverage of free cash flows in Chapter 9 if you need to review the elements of the Free Cash Flows worksheet.

Calculating something known as a "terminal value" for Napavale is the next step in building the DCF model. A terminal value represents the present value of all of a company's future free cash flows (until perpetuity, or the end of time) at some point in the future. Since I cannot build a financial

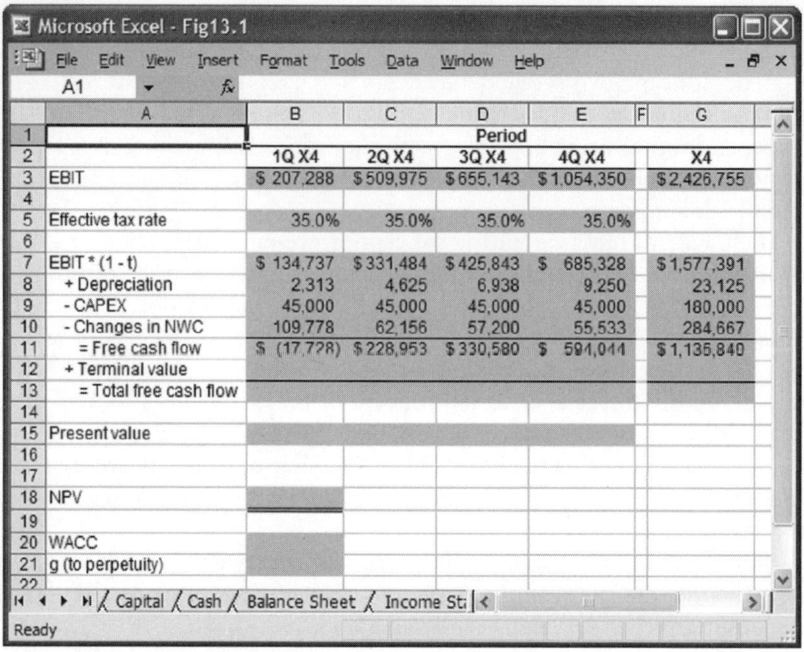

Microsoft Excel - Fig13.1

	A	B	C	D	E	F	G
1				Period			
2		1Q X4	2Q X4	3Q X4	4Q X4		X4
3	EBIT	$ 207,288	$ 509,975	$ 655,143	$ 1,054,350		$ 2,426,755
4							
5	Effective tax rate	35.0%	35.0%	35.0%	35.0%		
6							
7	EBIT * (1 - t)	$ 134,737	$ 331,484	$ 425,843	$ 685,328		$ 1,577,391
8	+ Depreciation	2,313	4,625	6,938	9,250		23,125
9	- CAPEX	45,000	45,000	45,000	45,000		180,000
10	- Changes in NWC	109,778	62,156	57,200	55,533		284,667
11	= Free cash flow	$ (17,728)	$ 228,953	$ 330,580	$ 594,044		$ 1,135,840
12	+ Terminal value						
13	= Total free cash flow						
14							
15	Present value						
16							
17							
18	NPV						
19							
20	WACC						
21	g (to perpetuity)						

Capital / Cash / Balance Sheet / Income St

FIGURE 13.1 Free Cash Flows Worksheet

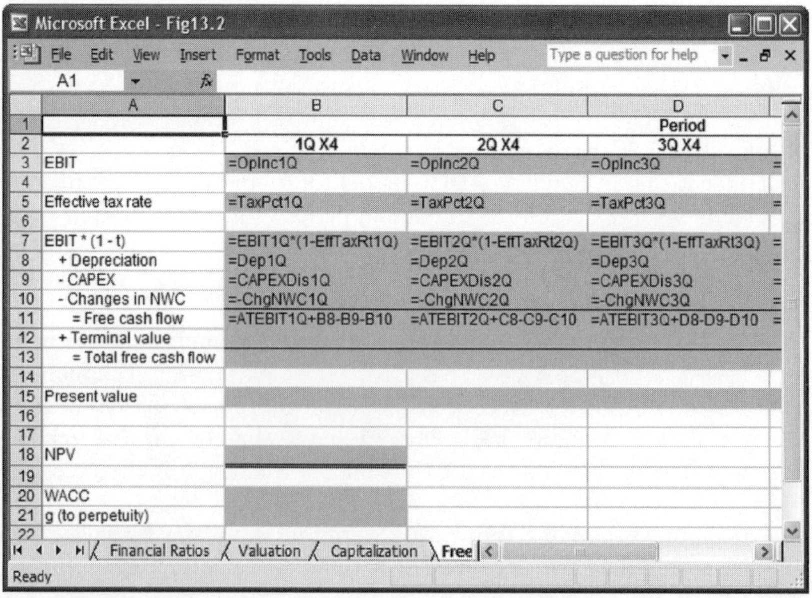

Microsoft Excel - Fig13.2

	A	B	C	D
1				Period
2		1Q X4	2Q X4	3Q X4
3	EBIT	=OpInc1Q	=OpInc2Q	=OpInc3Q
4				
5	Effective tax rate	=TaxPct1Q	=TaxPct2Q	=TaxPct3Q
6				
7	EBIT * (1 - t)	=EBIT1Q*(1-EffTaxRt1Q)	=EBIT2Q*(1-EffTaxRt2Q)	=EBIT3Q*(1-EffTaxRt3Q)
8	+ Depreciation	=Dep1Q	=Dep2Q	=Dep3Q
9	- CAPEX	=CAPEXDis1Q	=CAPEXDis2Q	=CAPEXDis3Q
10	- Changes in NWC	=-ChgNWC1Q	=-ChgNWC2Q	=-ChgNWC3Q
11	= Free cash flow	=ATEBIT1Q+B8-B9-B10	=ATEBIT2Q+C8-C9-C10	=ATEBIT3Q+D8-D9-D10
12	+ Terminal value			
13	= Total free cash flow			
14				
15	Present value			
16				
17				
18	NPV			
19				
20	WACC			
21	g (to perpetuity)			

Financial Ratios / Valuation / Capitalization / Free

FIGURE 13.2 Alternative View of the Free Cash Flows Worksheet

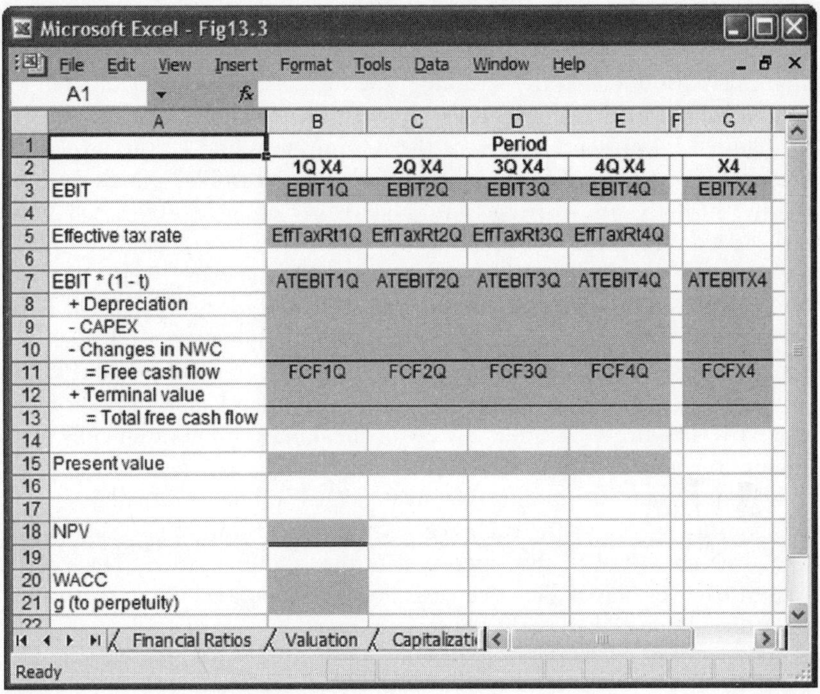

FIGURE 13.3 Names of the Input and Output Cells Underlying the Free Cash Flows Worksheet

model out indefinitely into time, a terminal value encapsulates assumptions regarding future free cash flows (beyond the timeframe covered by the financial model) in a single number. The terminal value is calculated for the final accounting period covered by the financial model. In essence, the terminal value represents the present value of Napavale's free cash flows into perpetuity at some point in the future.

I have calculated Napavale's terminal value using the following formula:

$$\text{Terminal Value} = \frac{(\text{Free Cash Flow for X4}) * (1 + \text{Growth Rate to Perpetuity})}{\text{Discount Rate} - \text{Growth Rate to Perpetuity}}$$

This is a well-known formula, but many different approaches may be used to calculate a terminal value. Please note that I am using free cash flow for X4 in this calculation. Technically speaking, this terminal value calculation is meant to project out free cash flow for the time period subsequent to the final period (typically a particular year) covered in the financial model. As such, I have based my terminal value calculation on the free cash flow that is generated in all of X4.

When you build your own financial models, it is important to be clear on how you are calculating free cash flow projections in your terminal value calculation, Generally speaking, the free cash flow value used in this terminal value calculation relates to a year time period.

Figure 13.4 presents a view of the Assumptions and Dashboard worksheet with the addition of the assumptions related to Napavale's discount rate and growth rate to perpetuity. Napavale's updated Free Cash Flows worksheet is presented in Figure 13.5. Note that I have calculated Napavale's total free cash flows by adding the terminal value to the free cash flows calculated in Chapter 9. An alternative view of the Free Cash Flows worksheet in which the values and formulas underlying the worksheet cells are exposed is presented in Figure 13.6. The names of the input and output worksheet cells in Napavale's Free Cash Flows worksheet are shown in Figure 13.7. Figure 13.8 offers a view of the names of the input cells in the Assumptions and Dashboard worksheet.

The final step in building Napavale's DCF model is to calculate and add the present values for each accounting period (quarter) based on the "total free cash flows" that incorporate the terminal value. The present value of each of Napavale's free cash flows is calculated using the present value formula described earlier in this chapter:

$$\text{Present Value} = \frac{\text{Future Value}}{(1 + \text{Discount Rate})\ \hat{}\ \text{Time Period}}$$

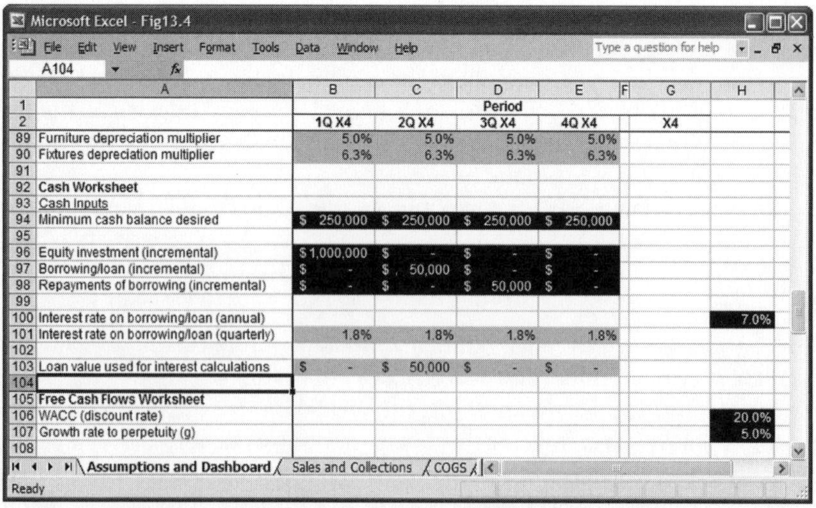

	A	B	C	D	E	F	G	H
1				Period				
2		1Q X4	2Q X4	3Q X4	4Q X4		X4	
89	Furniture depreciation multiplier	5.0%	5.0%	5.0%	5.0%			
90	Fixtures depreciation multiplier	6.3%	6.3%	6.3%	6.3%			
91								
92	**Cash Worksheet**							
93	Cash Inputs							
94	Minimum cash balance desired	$ 250,000	$ 250,000	$ 250,000	$ 250,000			
95								
96	Equity investment (incremental)	$1,000,000	$ -	$ -	$ -			
97	Borrowing/loan (incremental)	$ -	$ 50,000	$ -	$ -			
98	Repayments of borrowing (incremental)	$ -	$ -	$ 50,000	$ -			
99								
100	Interest rate on borrowing/loan (annual)							7.0%
101	Interest rate on borrowing/loan (quarterly)	1.8%	1.8%	1.8%	1.8%			
102								
103	Loan value used for interest calculations	$ -	$ 50,000	$ -	$ -			
104								
105	**Free Cash Flows Worksheet**							
106	WACC (discount rate)							20.0%
107	Growth rate to perpetuity (g)							5.0%
108								

FIGURE 13.4 Assumptions and Dashboard Worksheet

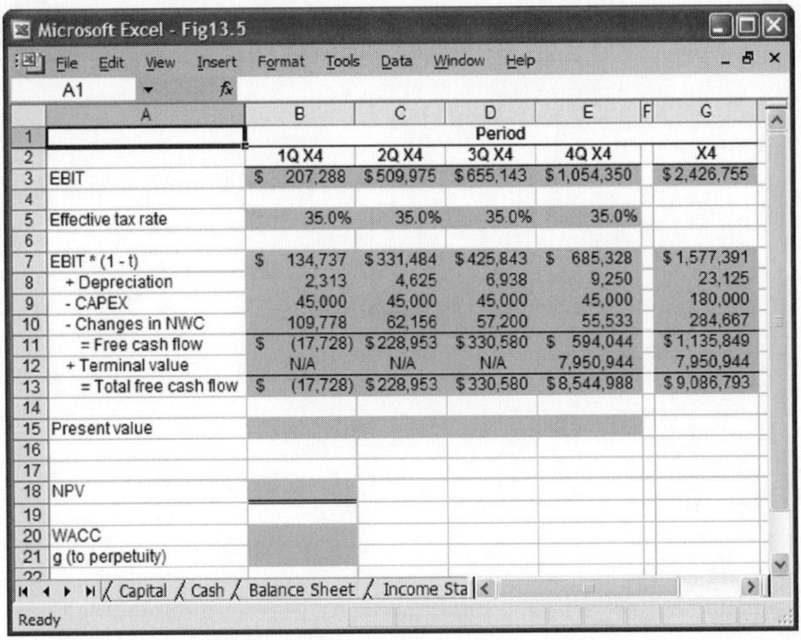

	A	B	C	D	E	F	G
1				Period			
2		1Q X4	2Q X4	3Q X4	4Q X4		X4
3	EBIT	$ 207,288	$509,975	$655,143	$1,054,350		$2,426,755
4							
5	Effective tax rate	35.0%	35.0%	35.0%	35.0%		
6							
7	EBIT * (1 - t)	$ 134,737	$331,484	$425,843	$ 685,328		$1,577,391
8	+ Depreciation	2,313	4,625	6,938	9,250		23,125
9	- CAPEX	45,000	45,000	45,000	45,000		180,000
10	- Changes in NWC	109,778	62,156	57,200	55,533		284,667
11	= Free cash flow	$ (17,728)	$228,953	$330,580	$ 594,044		$1,135,849
12	+ Terminal value	N/A	N/A	N/A	7,950,944		7,950,944
13	= Total free cash flow	$ (17,728)	$228,953	$330,580	$8,544,988		$9,086,793
14							
15	Present value						
16							
17							
18	NPV						
19							
20	WACC						
21	g (to perpetuity)						

FIGURE 13.5 Updated Free Cash Flows Worksheet

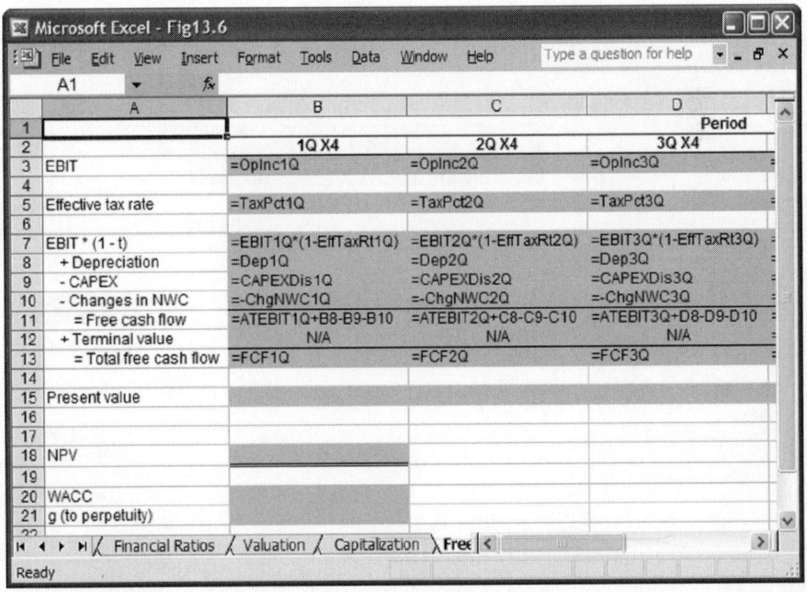

	A	B	C	D
1				Period
2		1Q X4	2Q X4	3Q X4
3	EBIT	=OpInc1Q	=OpInc2Q	=OpInc3Q
4				
5	Effective tax rate	=TaxPct1Q	=TaxPct2Q	=TaxPct3Q
6				
7	EBIT * (1 - t)	=EBIT1Q*(1-EffTaxRt1Q)	=EBIT2Q*(1-EffTaxRt2Q)	=EBIT3Q*(1-EffTaxRt3Q)
8	+ Depreciation	=Dep1Q	=Dep2Q	=Dep3Q
9	- CAPEX	=CAPEXDis1Q	=CAPEXDis2Q	=CAPEXDis3Q
10	- Changes in NWC	=-ChgNWC1Q	=-ChgNWC2Q	=-ChgNWC3Q
11	= Free cash flow	=ATEBIT1Q+B8-B9-B10	=ATEBIT2Q+C8-C9-C10	=ATEBIT3Q+D8-D9-D10
12	+ Terminal value	N/A	N/A	N/A
13	= Total free cash flow	=FCF1Q	=FCF2Q	=FCF3Q
14				
15	Present value			
16				
17				
18	NPV			
19				
20	WACC			
21	g (to perpetuity)			

FIGURE 13.6 Alternative View of the Free Cash Flows Worksheet

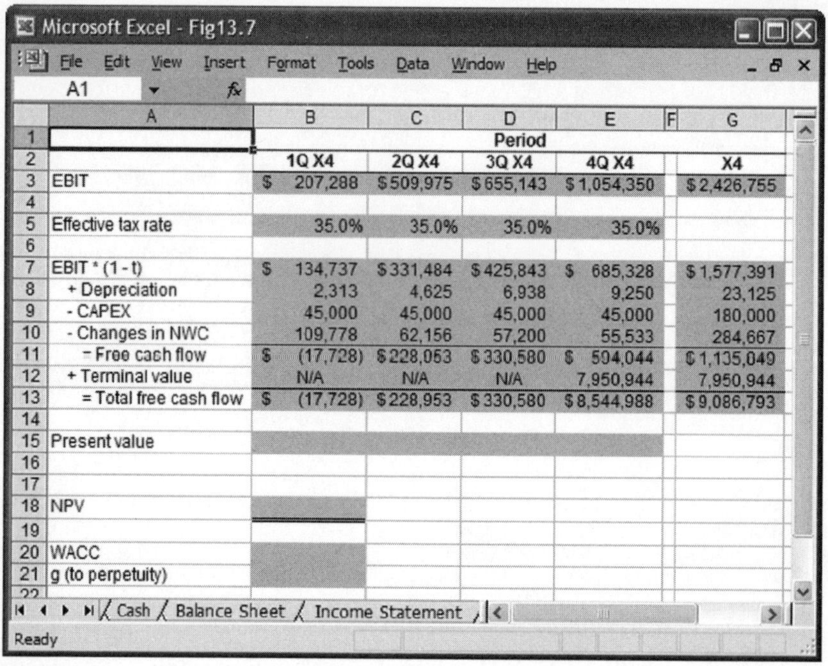

FIGURE 13.7 Names of the Input and Output Cells Underlying the Free Cash Flows Worksheet

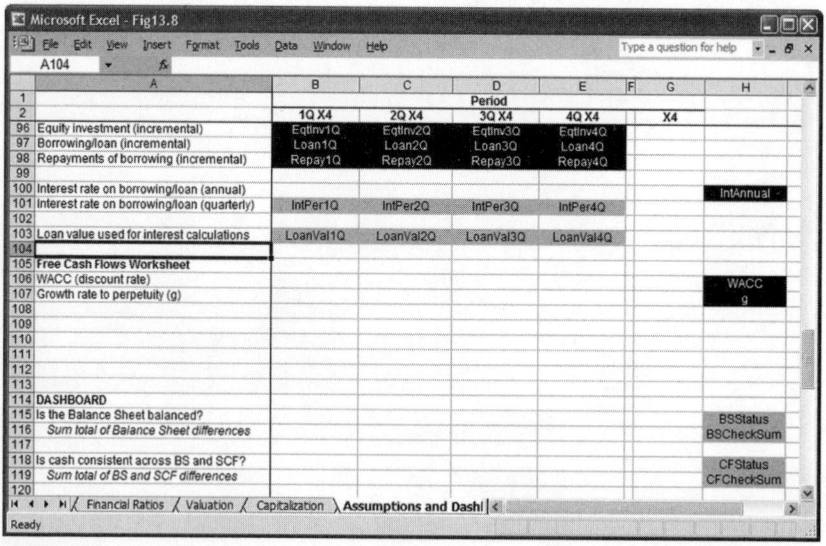

FIGURE 13.8 Names of the Input and Output Cells Underlying the Assumptions and Dashboard Worksheet

Using the assumption that today is the first day of 1Q X4 and each accounting period (quarter) represents one quarter (0.25) of a year, Figure 13.9 presents Napavale's updated Free Cash Flows worksheet in which the present value of each accounting period's (quarter's) free cash flow is calculated. Note that Napavale's NPV—in other words, Napavale's "value" as determined by the DCF model—is equal to the sum of all of the present values of each of the accounting period's (quarter's) free cash flows.

Figure 13.10 presents a view of Napavale's updated Free Cash Flows worksheet in which the values and formulas underlying the worksheet cells are visible. The names of the input and output worksheet cells in Napavale's updated Free Cash Flows worksheet are shown in Figure 13.11.

	1Q X4	2Q X4	3Q X4	4Q X4	X4
			Period		
EBIT	$ 207,288	$509,975	$655,143	$1,054,350	$2,426,755
Effective tax rate	35.0%	35.0%	35.0%	35.0%	
EBIT * (1 - t)	$ 134,737	$331,484	$425,843	$ 685,328	$1,577,391
+ Depreciation	2,313	4,625	6,938	9,250	23,125
- CAPEX	45,000	45,000	45,000	45,000	180,000
- Changes in NWC	109,778	62,156	57,200	55,533	284,667
= Free cash flow	$ (17,728)	$228,953	$330,580	$ 594,044	$1,135,849
+ Terminal value	N/A	N/A	N/A	7,950,944	7,950,944
= Total free cash flow	$ (17,728)	$228,953	$330,580	$8,544,988	$9,086,793
Present value	$ (16,938)	$209,005	$288,331	$7,120,823	
NPV	$ 7,601,220				
WACC	20.0%				
g (to perpetuity)	5.0%				

FIGURE 13.9 Updated Free Cash Flows Worksheet

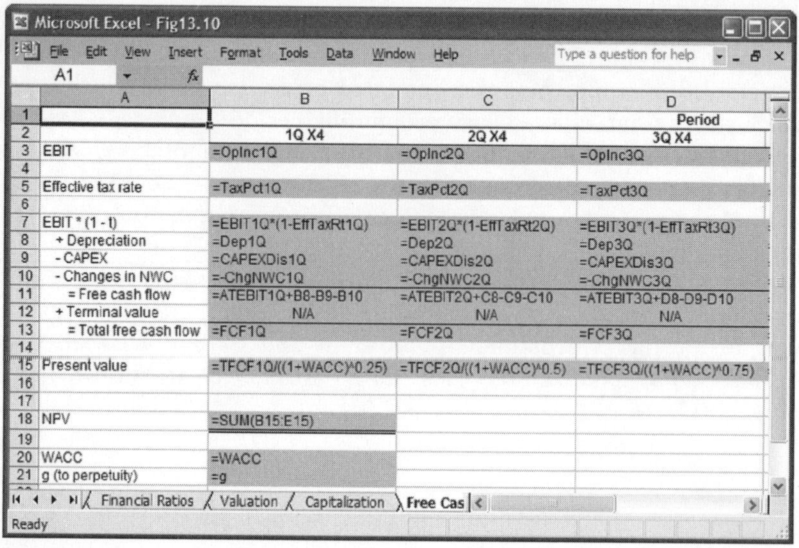

	A	B	C	D
1				Period
2		1Q X4	2Q X4	3Q X4
3	EBIT	=OpInc1Q	=OpInc2Q	=OpInc3Q
4				
5	Effective tax rate	=TaxPct1Q	=TaxPct2Q	=TaxPct3Q
6				
7	EBIT * (1 - t)	=EBIT1Q*(1-EffTaxRt1Q)	=EBIT2Q*(1-EffTaxRt2Q)	=EBIT3Q*(1-EffTaxRt3Q)
8	+ Depreciation	=Dep1Q	=Dep2Q	=Dep3Q
9	- CAPEX	=CAPEXDis1Q	=CAPEXDis2Q	=CAPEXDis3Q
10	- Changes in NWC	=-ChgNWC1Q	=-ChgNWC2Q	=-ChgNWC3Q
11	= Free cash flow	=ATEBIT1Q+B8-B9-B10	=ATEBIT2Q+C8-C9-C10	=ATEBIT3Q+D8-D9-D10
12	+ Terminal value	N/A	N/A	N/A
13	= Total free cash flow	=FCF1Q	=FCF2Q	=FCF3Q
14				
15	Present value	=TFCF1Q/((1+WACC)^0.25)	=TFCF2Q/((1+WACC)^0.5)	=TFCF3Q/((1+WACC)^0.75)
16				
17				
18	NPV	=SUM(B15:E15)		
19				
20	WACC	=WACC		
21	g (to perpetuity)	=g		

FIGURE 13.10 Alternative View of the Updated Free Cash Flows Worksheet

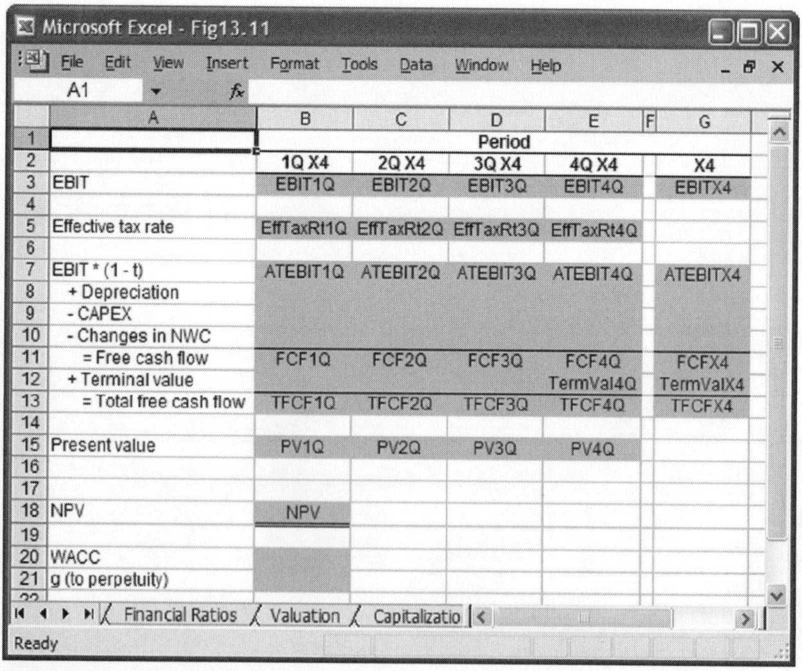

	A	B	C	D	E	F	G
1				Period			
2		1Q X4	2Q X4	3Q X4	4Q X4		X4
3	EBIT	EBIT1Q	EBIT2Q	EBIT3Q	EBIT4Q		EBITX4
4							
5	Effective tax rate	EffTaxRt1Q	EffTaxRt2Q	EffTaxRt3Q	EffTaxRt4Q		
6							
7	EBIT * (1 - t)	ATEBIT1Q	ATEBIT2Q	ATEBIT3Q	ATEBIT4Q		ATEBITX4
8	+ Depreciation						
9	- CAPEX						
10	- Changes in NWC						
11	= Free cash flow	FCF1Q	FCF2Q	FCF3Q	FCF4Q		FCFX4
12	+ Terminal value				TermVal4Q		TermValX4
13	= Total free cash flow	TFCF1Q	TFCF2Q	TFCF3Q	TFCF4Q		TFCFX4
14							
15	Present value	PV1Q	PV2Q	PV3Q	PV4Q		
16							
17							
18	NPV	NPV					
19							
20	WACC						
21	g (to perpetuity)						

FIGURE 13.11 Names of the Input and Output Cells Underlying the Updated Free Cash Flows Worksheet

PUBLIC COMPANY COMPARABLES

The public company comparables valuation approach is a comparative methodology in which the values of publicly traded companies are used as proxies for Napavale's valuation. More specifically, the manner in which publicly traded companies' valuations are related to certain metrics, such as sales, net income, or free cash flows, is used to estimate a value for Napavale as a company.

I am going to use fictitious companies and numbers in this analysis, but the methodology outlined in this section of the book may be easily applied to the use of actual market-based numbers as well. I will use two types of fictitious public companies for the public company comparables approach: direct competitors to Napavale and companies included in a fictitious index similar to the S&P 500. Using direct competitors should give a sense of how investors value companies in Napavale's industry and using an index of stocks should provide some perspective on how investors value the market as a whole.

The first step in building a public companies comparables analysis is to collect relevant data for the public companies against which Napavale will be compared. I am going to collect data on companies' valuations, sales, net income, and free cash flows. Note that this data will represent projections for each of these companies' next 12 months (four quarters) of operations. Using this data will allow a more direct comparison of Napavale with the competitors and the stock index. Figure 13.12 provides a

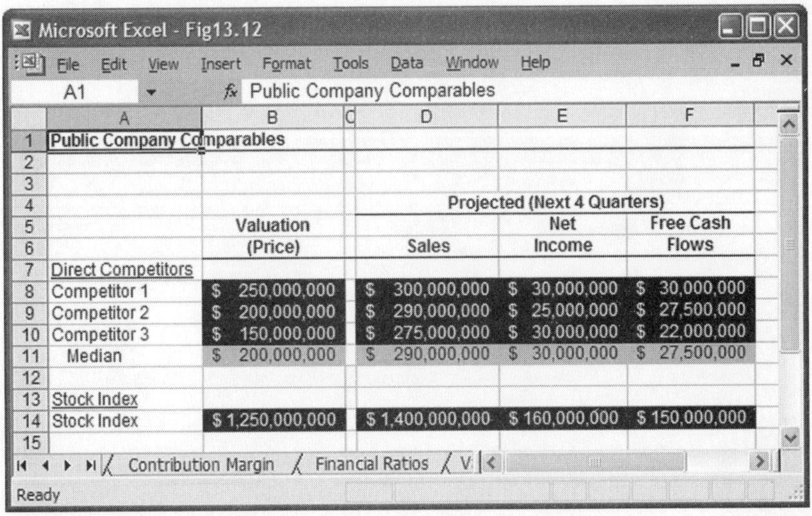

	A	B	D	E	F
1	Public Company Comparables				
2					
3					
4			Projected (Next 4 Quarters)		
5		Valuation		Net	Free Cash
6		(Price)	Sales	Income	Flows
7	Direct Competitors				
8	Competitor 1	$ 250,000,000	$ 300,000,000	$ 30,000,000	$ 30,000,000
9	Competitor 2	$ 200,000,000	$ 290,000,000	$ 25,000,000	$ 27,500,000
10	Competitor 3	$ 150,000,000	$ 275,000,000	$ 30,000,000	$ 22,000,000
11	Median	$ 200,000,000	$ 290,000,000	$ 30,000,000	$ 27,500,000
12					
13	Stock Index				
14	Stock Index	$ 1,250,000,000	$ 1,400,000,000	$ 160,000,000	$ 150,000,000
15					

FIGURE 13.12 Data for Fictitious Companies and Fictitious Index of Stocks

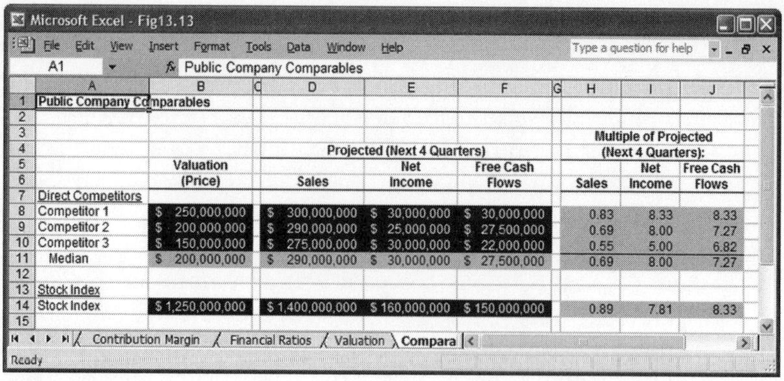
Microsoft Excel - Fig13.13

A1 | Public Company Comparables

	A	B	D	E	F	H	I	J
1	Public Company Comparables							
2								
3						Multiple of Projected		
4			Projected (Next 4 Quarters)			(Next 4 Quarters):		
5		Valuation		Net	Free Cash		Net	Free Cash
6		(Price)	Sales	Income	Flows	Sales	Income	Flows
7	Direct Competitors							
8	Competitor 1	$ 250,000,000	$ 300,000,000	$ 30,000,000	$ 30,000,000	0.83	8.33	8.33
9	Competitor 2	$ 200,000,000	$ 290,000,000	$ 25,000,000	$ 27,500,000	0.69	8.00	7.27
10	Competitor 3	$ 150,000,000	$ 275,000,000	$ 30,000,000	$ 22,000,000	0.55	5.00	6.82
11	Median	$ 200,000,000	$ 290,000,000	$ 30,000,000	$ 27,500,000	0.69	8.00	7.27
12								
13	Stock Index							
14	Stock Index	$ 1,250,000,000	$ 1,400,000,000	$ 160,000,000	$ 150,000,000	0.89	7.81	8.33
15								

Contribution Margin / Financial Ratios / Valuation / Compara

Ready

FIGURE 13.13 Calculations of Multiples of Various Operational Measures

view of this data for the fictitious companies and the fictitious index of stocks that I use in my valuation of Napavale.

The next step involved in building a public company comparables valuation model is to calculate what "multiple" each of these operational measures (sales, net income, and free cash flows) is represented by each of the competitor company's and stock index's valuation. Figure 13.13 provides a view of these calculations. Note that I have also included a calculation of the median for each of the respective multiple calculations—I will use these median figures to value Napavale using the public company comparables methodology later in this chapter.

A view of the values and formulas underlying the worksheet cells associated with the multiple calculations is shown in Figure 13.14. Figure 13.15 provides a view of the names of the input and output cells associated with the calculation of the "multiple" values.

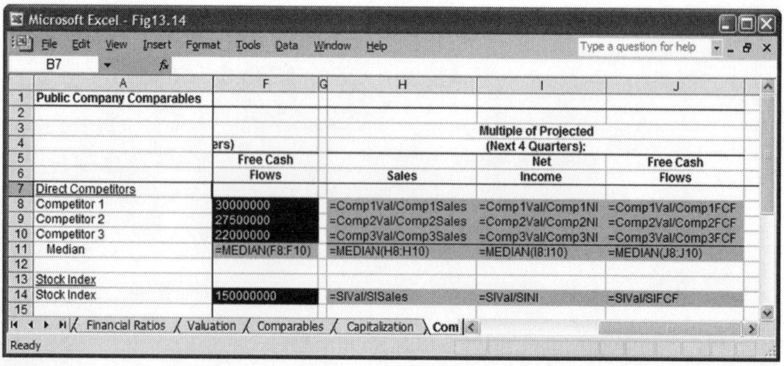
Microsoft Excel - Fig13.14

B7

	A	F	H	I	J
1	Public Company Comparables				
2					
3				Multiple of Projected	
4		ers)		(Next 4 Quarters):	
5		Free Cash		Net	Free Cash
6		Flows	Sales	Income	Flows
7	Direct Competitors				
8	Competitor 1	30000000	=Comp1Val/Comp1Sales	=Comp1Val/Comp1NI	=Comp1Val/Comp1FCF
9	Competitor 2	27500000	=Comp2Val/Comp2Sales	=Comp2Val/Comp2NI	=Comp2Val/Comp2FCF
10	Competitor 3	22000000	=Comp3Val/Comp3Sales	=Comp3Val/Comp3NI	=Comp3Val/Comp3FCF
11	Median	=MEDIAN(F8:F10)	=MEDIAN(H8:H10)	=MEDIAN(I8:I10)	=MEDIAN(J8:J10)
12					
13	Stock Index				
14	Stock Index	150000000	=SIVal/SISales	=SIVal/SINI	=SIVal/SIFCF
15					

Financial Ratios / Valuation / Comparables / Capitalization / Com

Ready

FIGURE 13.14 Alternative View of the Calculations of Multiples of Various Operational Measures

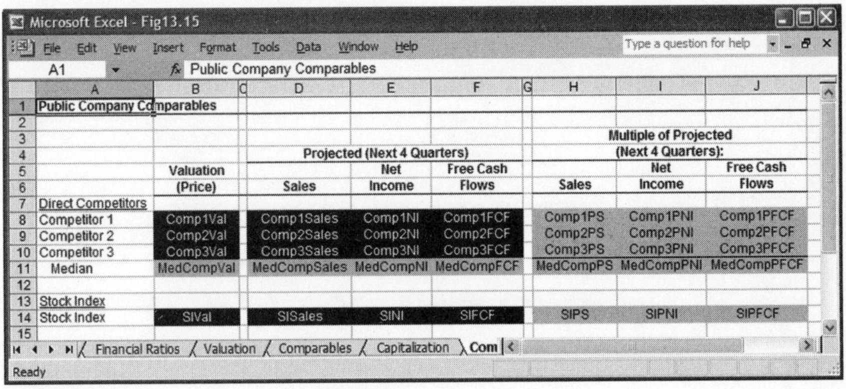

FIGURE 13.15 Names of the Input and Output Cells Underlying the Calculations of Multiples of Various Operational Measures

The final step in the public company comparables valuation approach is to apply the appropriate multiples of chosen metrics (sales, net income, and free cash flows in this case) to Napavale. I use the median multiples that I calculated for Napavale's competitors and the value that I calculated for the stock index to value Napavale using the public comparables valuation approach. Figure 13.16 shows the completed public company comparables valuation worksheet. The values and formulas underlying the worksheet cells in the public company comparables valuation worksheet are shown in Figure 13.17. Figure 13.18 offers a view of the names underlying the public company comparables valuation worksheet.

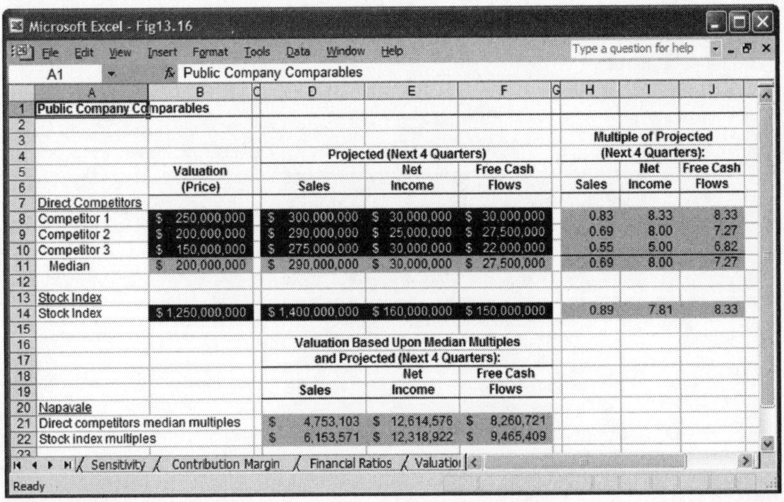

FIGURE 13.16 Completed Public Company Comparables Valuation Worksheet

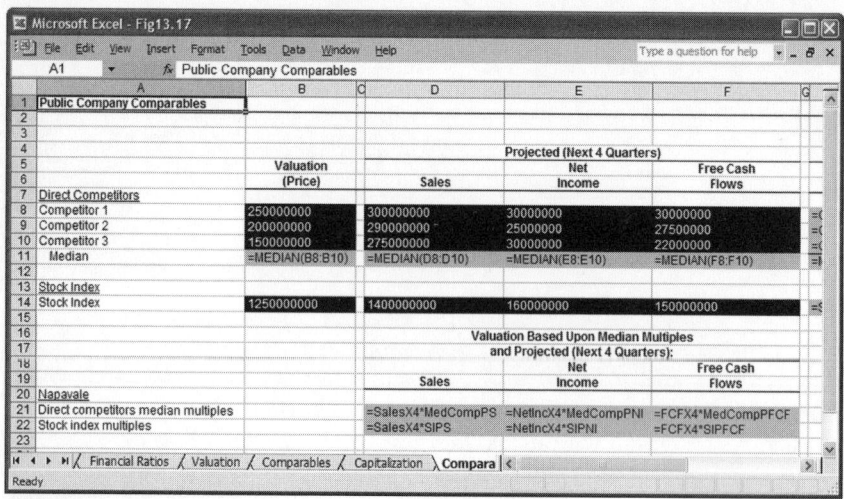

FIGURE 13.17 Alternative View of the Completed Public Company Comparables Valuation Worksheet

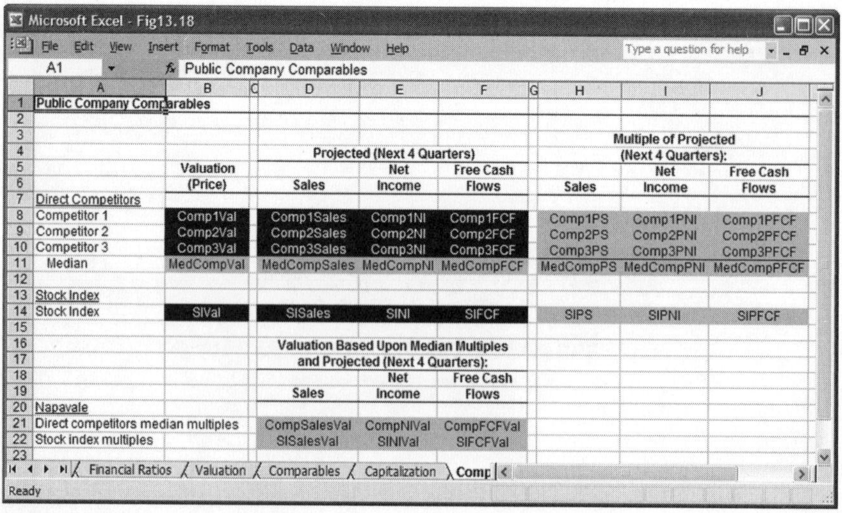

FIGURE 13.18 Names of the Input and Output Cells Underlying the Completed Public Company Comparables Valuation Worksheet

Note that when I triangulate on a value for Napavale later in this chapter, I use the value derived for Napavale's direct competitors using the public company comparables valuation approach and not the value derived for the stock index. I believe Napavale's direct competitors provides a better sense of how the market would value Napavale than does the stock index value—I calculated the stock index value for the sake of reference only.

MERGERS AND ACQUISITIONS COMPARABLES

The mergers and acquisitions comparables valuation approach, like the public company comparables valuation approach, is a comparative methodology. In the case of the mergers and acquisitions valuation approach, data from recent mergers and acquisitions in Napavale's market is used to estimate a value for Napavale as a company. The term "mergers and acquisitions" refers to the combination or acquisition of businesses.

As with the public company comparables approach, I am going to use fictitious companies and numbers in this analysis, but the methodology outlined in this section of the book may be easily applied to the use of actual market-based numbers as well. I will use data related to fictitious mergers and acquisitions within Napavale's market (also called "industry").

The first step in building a mergers and acquisitions comparables analysis is to collect relevant data for mergers and acquisitions transactions in Napavale's market. I am going to collect data on companies' valuations (as determined by mergers and acquisitions "prices"), sales, net income, and asset values. Note that this data will represent projections for each of these companies' next 12 months (four quarters) of operations. Using this data will allow a more direct comparison of Napavale with its competitors. Figure 13.19 provides a view of this data for the fictitious mergers and acquisitions transactions that I use in my valuation of Napavale.

The second step involved in building a mergers and acquisitions comparables valuation model is to calculate what multiple each of these operational measures (sales, net income, and asset values) is represented by each of the transactions' prices (which is the same idea as their valuations). Figure 13.20 provides a view of these calculations. Note that I have also included a calculation of the median for each of the respective multiple calculations—I will use these median figures to value Napavale using the mergers and acquisitions comparables methodology later in this chapter.

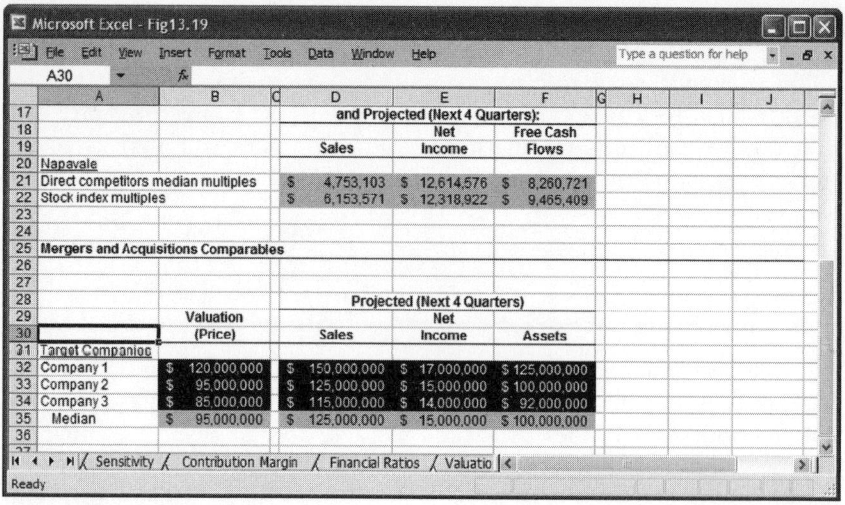

	A	B	D	E	F
17			and Projected (Next 4 Quarters):		
18				Net	Free Cash
19			Sales	Income	Flows
20	Napavale				
21	Direct competitors median multiples		$ 4,753,103	$ 12,614,576	$ 8,260,721
22	Stock index multiples		$ 6,153,571	$ 12,318,922	$ 9,465,409
23					
24					
25	Mergers and Acquisitions Comparables				
26					
27					
28			Projected (Next 4 Quarters)		
29		Valuation		Net	
30		(Price)	Sales	Income	Assets
31	Target Companies				
32	Company 1	$ 120,000,000	$ 150,000,000	$ 17,000,000	$ 125,000,000
33	Company 2	$ 95,000,000	$ 125,000,000	$ 15,000,000	$ 100,000,000
34	Company 3	$ 85,000,000	$ 115,000,000	$ 14,000,000	$ 92,000,000
35	Median	$ 95,000,000	$ 125,000,000	$ 15,000,000	$ 100,000,000
36					

FIGURE 13.19 Data for Fictitious Mergers and Acquisitions Transactions

A view of the values and formulas underlying the worksheet cells associated with the multiple calculations is shown in Figure 13.21. Figure 13.22 provides a view of the names of the input and output cells associated with the calculation of the multiple values.

The final step in the mergers and acquisitions comparables valuation approach is to apply the appropriate multiples of chosen metrics (sales, net

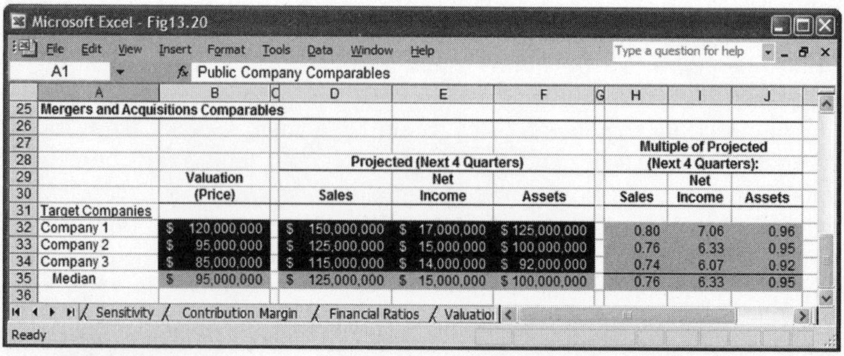

	A	B	D	E	F	H	I	J
25	Mergers and Acquisitions Comparables							
26								
27						Multiple of Projected		
28			Projected (Next 4 Quarters)			(Next 4 Quarters):		
29		Valuation		Net			Net	
30		(Price)	Sales	Income	Assets	Sales	Income	Assets
31	Target Companies							
32	Company 1	$ 120,000,000	$ 150,000,000	$ 17,000,000	$ 125,000,000	0.80	7.06	0.96
33	Company 2	$ 95,000,000	$ 125,000,000	$ 15,000,000	$ 100,000,000	0.76	6.33	0.95
34	Company 3	$ 85,000,000	$ 115,000,000	$ 14,000,000	$ 92,000,000	0.74	6.07	0.92
35	Median	$ 95,000,000	$ 125,000,000	$ 15,000,000	$ 100,000,000	0.76	6.33	0.95
36								

FIGURE 13.20 Calculations of Multiples of Various Operational Measures

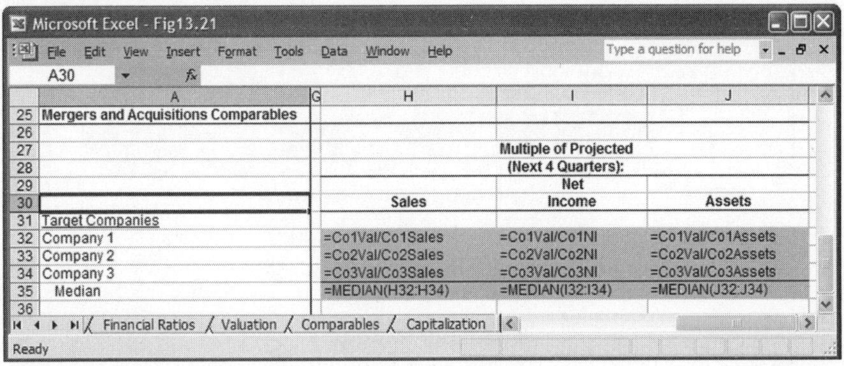

	A	H	I	J
25	Mergers and Acquisitions Comparables			
26				
27			Multiple of Projected	
28			(Next 4 Quarters):	
29			Net	
30		Sales	Income	Assets
31	Target Companies			
32	Company 1	=Co1Val/Co1Sales	=Co1Val/Co1NI	=Co1Val/Co1Assets
33	Company 2	=Co2Val/Co2Sales	=Co2Val/Co2NI	=Co2Val/Co2Assets
34	Company 3	=Co3Val/Co3Sales	=Co3Val/Co3NI	=Co3Val/Co3Assets
35	Median	=MEDIAN(H32:H34)	=MEDIAN(I32:I34)	=MEDIAN(J32:J34)
36				

FIGURE 13.21 Alternative View of the Calculations of Multiples of Various Operational Measures

income, and asset values in this case) to Napavale. I use the median multiples that I calculated for the mergers and acquisitions transactions to value Napavale in this case. Figure 13.23 shows the completed mergers and acquisitions comparables valuation worksheet.

The values and formulas underlying the worksheet cells in the mergers and acquisitions comparables valuation worksheet are shown in Figure 13.24. Figure 13.25 offers a view of the names underlying the mergers and acquisitions comparables valuation worksheet.

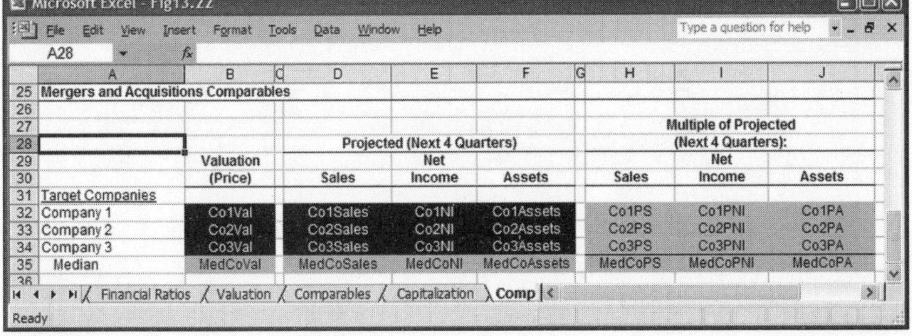

	A	B	D	E	F	H	I	J
25	Mergers and Acquisitions Comparables							
26								
27							Multiple of Projected	
28				Projected (Next 4 Quarters)			(Next 4 Quarters):	
29		Valuation		Net			Net	
30		(Price)	Sales	Income	Assets	Sales	Income	Assets
31	Target Companies							
32	Company 1	Co1Val	Co1Sales	Co1NI	Co1Assets	Co1PS	Co1PNI	Co1PA
33	Company 2	Co2Val	Co2Sales	Co2NI	Co2Assets	Co2PS	Co2PNI	Co2PA
34	Company 3	Co3Val	Co3Sales	Co3NI	Co3Assets	Co3PS	Co3PNI	Co3PA
35	Median	MedCoVal	MedCoSales	MedCoNI	MedCoAssets	MedCoPS	MedCoPNI	MedCoPA

FIGURE 13.22 Names of the Input and Output Cells Underlying the Calculations of Multiples of Various Operational Measures

Microsoft Excel - Fig13.23

Row	A	B	D	E	F	H	I	J
25	Mergers and Acquisitions Comparables							
27						Multiple of Projected		
28			Projected (Next 4 Quarters)			(Next 4 Quarters):		
29		Valuation		Net			Net	
30		(Price)	Sales	Income	Assets	Sales	Income	Assets
31	Target Companies							
32	Company 1	$ 120,000,000	$ 150,000,000	$ 17,000,000	$ 125,000,000	0.80	7.06	0.96
33	Company 2	$ 95,000,000	$ 125,000,000	$ 15,000,000	$ 100,000,000	0.76	6.33	0.95
34	Company 3	$ 85,000,000	$ 115,000,000	$ 14,000,000	$ 92,000,000	0.74	6.07	0.92
35	Median	$ 95,000,000	$ 125,000,000	$ 15,000,000	$ 100,000,000	0.76	6.33	0.95
37			Valuation Based Upon Median Multiples					
38			and Projected (Next 4 Quarters):					
39				Net				
40			Sales	Income	Assets			
41	Napavale							
42	Target companies median multiples		$ 5,237,920	$ 9,986,539	$ 2,594,281			

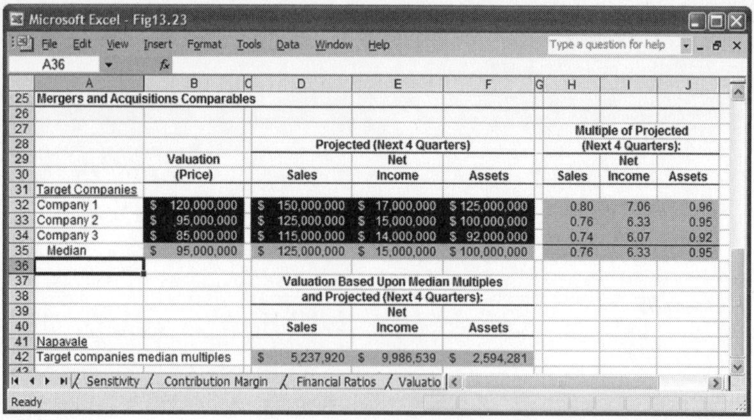

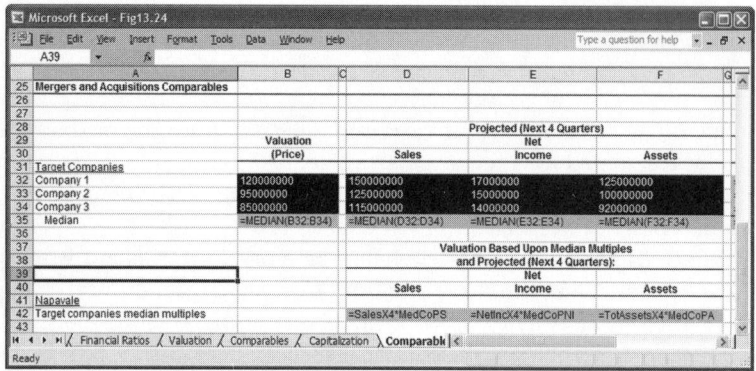

FIGURE 13.23 Completed Mergers and Acquisitions Comparables Valuation Worksheet

Microsoft Excel - Fig13.24

Row	A	B	D	E	F
25	Mergers and Acquisitions Comparables				
28			Projected (Next 4 Quarters)		
29		Valuation		Net	
30		(Price)	Sales	Income	Assets
31	Target Companies				
32	Company 1	120000000	150000000	17000000	125000000
33	Company 2	95000000	125000000	15000000	100000000
34	Company 3	85000000	115000000	14000000	92000000
35	Median	=MEDIAN(B32:B34)	=MEDIAN(D32:D34)	=MEDIAN(E32:E34)	=MEDIAN(F32:F34)
37			Valuation Based Upon Median Multiples		
38			and Projected (Next 4 Quarters):		
39				Net	
40			Sales	Income	Assets
41	Napavale				
42	Target companies median multiples		=SalesX4*MedCoPS	=NetIncX4*MedCoPNI	=TotAssetsX4*MedCoPA

FIGURE 13.24 Alternative View of the Completed Mergers and Acquistions Comparables Valuation Worksheet

Microsoft Excel - Fig13.25

Row	A	B	D	E	F	H	I	J
25	Mergers and Acquisitions Comparables							
27						Multiple of Projected		
28			Projected (Next 4 Quarters)			(Next 4 Quarters):		
29		Valuation		Net			Net	
30		(Price)	Sales	Income	Assets	Sales	Income	Assets
31	Target Companies							
32	Company 1	Co1Val	Co1Sales	Co1NI	Co1Assets	Co1PS	Co1PNI	Co1PA
33	Company 2	Co2Val	Co2Sales	Co2NI	Co2Assets	Co2PS	Co2PNI	Co2PA
34	Company 3	Co3Val	Co3Sales	Co3NI	Co3Assets	Co3PS	Co3PNI	Co3PA
35	Median	MedCoVal	MedCoSales	MedCoNI	MedCoAssets	MedCoPS	MedCoPNI	MedCoPA
37			Valuation Based Upon Median Multiples					
38			and Projected (Next 4 Quarters):					
39				Net				
40			Sales	Income	Assets			
41	Napavale							
42	Target companies median multiples		CoSalesVal	CoNIVal	CoAssetsVal			

FIGURE 13.25 Names of the Input and Output Cells Underlying the Completed Mergers and Acquisitions Comparables Valuation Worksheet

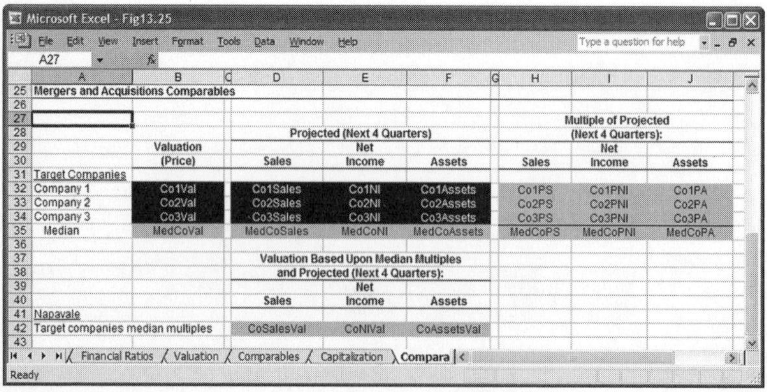

WEIGHTED VALUATION

Now that I have calculated Napavale's estimated valuation using the discounted cash flow technique, public company comparables approach, and mergers and acquisitions comparables approach, I apply a relative weight to each of these valuation methodologies to triangulate on an overall valuation for Napavale. Determining the appropriate weighting for each of these valuation methodologies is a matter of judgment—the weightings that I apply to the methodologies reflect my bias as to the relative importance of each valuation approach. You should use whatever relative weightings seem most appropriate for your own company.

Figure 13.26 presents a view of Napavale's Valuation worksheet in which the valuation results of each of the three valuation approaches covered in this chapter are shown. I have chosen to use the Price to Sales median multiple value for Napavale's direct competitors for the "public company comparables" valuation and the Price to Sales median multiple value for the "mergers and acquisitions comparables" valuation. This is only a matter of preference and you are free to choose which multiples to use in the valuations of your own companies. I have also included relative weights and "weighted valuations" for each of these valuation approaches. The weighted valuations are calculated as: (Weighted Valuation) = (Valuation) * (Relative Weight). Note that I have also totaled the weighted valuation figures to determine a total or final valuation for Napavale as a business.

The values and formulas underlying Napavale's Valuation worksheet are exposed in Figure 13.27. Figure 13.28 offers a view of the names of the worksheet cells underlying Napavale's Valuation worksheet.

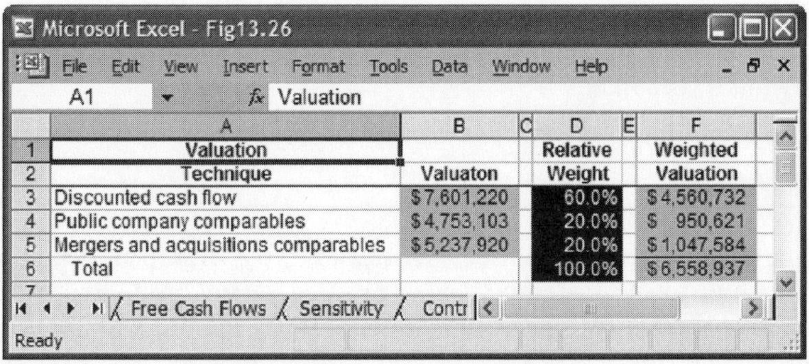

	A	B	C	D	E	F
1	Valuation			Relative		Weighted
2	Technique	Valuaton		Weight		Valuation
3	Discounted cash flow	$7,601,220		60.0%		$4,560,732
4	Public company comparables	$4,753,103		20.0%		$ 950,621
5	Mergers and acquisitions comparables	$5,237,920		20.0%		$1,047,584
6	Total			100.0%		$6,558,937

FIGURE 13.26 Valuation Worksheet

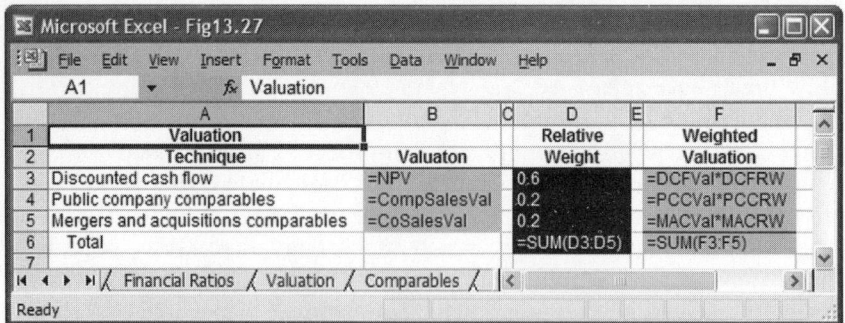

FIGURE 13.27 Alternative View of the Valuation Worksheet

Microsoft Excel - Fig13.28

File Edit View Insert Format Tools Data Window Help

A1 ▼ *fx* Valuation

	A	B	C	D	E	F
1	Valuation			Relative		Weighted
2	Technique	Valuaton		Weight		Valuation
3	Discounted cash flow	DCFVal		DCFRW		DCFWV
4	Public company comparables	PCCVal		PCCRW		PCCWV
5	Mergers and acquisitions comparables	MACVal		MACRW		MACWV
6	Total			TotRW		TotWV
7						

Financial Ratios / Valuation / Compara

Ready

FIGURE 13.28 Names of the Input and Output Cells Underlying the Valuation Worksheet

Please note that the "total" valuation shown in Figure 13.26 represents my estimate of Napavale's valuation. This value represents a weighted total of the three valuation approaches (discounted cash flow, public company comparables, and mergers and acquisitions comparables) covered in this chapter.

QUESTIONS

Each of the questions for this chapter relates to the hypothetical company named Company 456—this company was used in the Questions section of Chapter 12. To review, Company 456 sells display monitors to physicians. As such, Company 456 is a product-oriented (as opposed to a service-oriented) business.

The questions for this chapter will address fiscal year X4 on a quarterly basis (four specific quarters, 1Q–4Q for year X4). The following questions will test your knowledge of the material covered in this chapter in an applied manner—specifically, you will be asked to triangulate on a valuation for Company 456 using discounted cash flow, public company comparables, and mergers and acquisitions valuation methodologies.

To prepare you for this chapter's questions, Figure Q13.1 offers a view of Company 456's Free Cash Flows worksheet to provide some background information related to Company 456's operations. A portion of Company 456's Assumptions and Dashboard worksheet is shown in Figure Q13.2. Figure Q13.3 presents a view of the data associated with fictitious companies and fictitious stock index that will be used in the public company comparables valuation for Company 456. Data associated with fictitious mergers and acquisitions transactions that will be used in the mergers and acquisitions comparables valuation for Company 456 is presented in Figure Q13.4. The relative weightings to be used in Chapter 13's questions for each of the valuation approaches are shown in Figure Q13.5.

Microsoft Excel - FigQ13.1

	A	B	C	D	E	F	G
1				Period			
2		1Q X4	2Q X4	3Q X4	4Q X4		X4
3	EBIT	$ 2,071,250	$2,357,050	$2,240,200	$1,991,500		$8,660,000
4							
5	Effective tax rate	35.0%	35.0%	35.0%	35.0%		
6							
7	EBIT * (1 - t)	$ 1,346,313	$1,532,083	$1,456,130	$1,294,475		$5,629,000
8	+ Depreciation	1,950	4,150	6,150	8,200		20,450
9	- CAPEX	38,000	43,000	39,000	40,000		160,000
10	- Changes in NWC	776,759	637,694	70,157	(46,978)		1,437,633
11	= Free cash flow	$ 533,503	$ 855,538	$1,353,123	$1,309,653		$4,051,817
12	+ Terminal value						
13	= Total free cash flow						
14							
15	Present value						
16							
17							
18	NPV						
19							
20	WACC	25.0%					
21	g (to perpetuity)	5.0%					

Capital / Cash / Balance Sheet / Income State

FIGURE Q13.1 Company 456's Free Cash Flows Worksheet

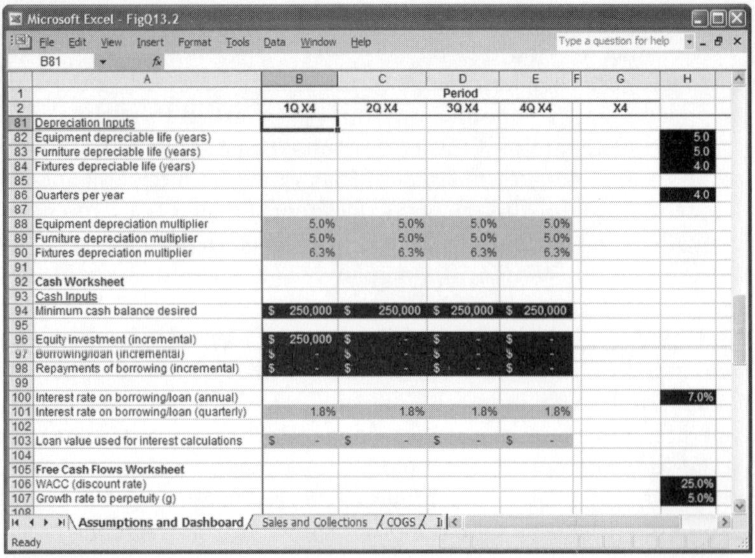

FIGURE Q13.2 Company 456's Assumptions and Dashboard Worksheet

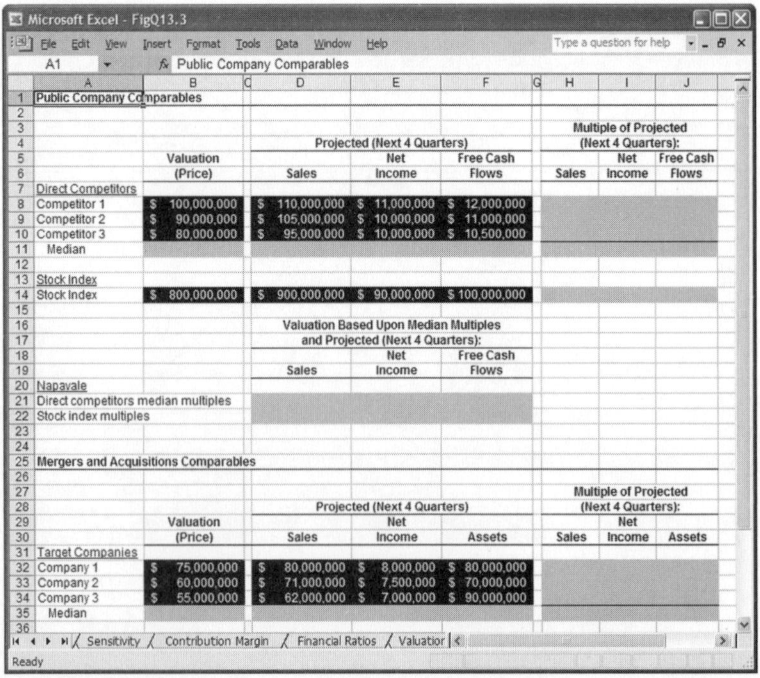

FIGURE Q13.3 Data for Fictitious Companies and Fictitious Index of Stocks

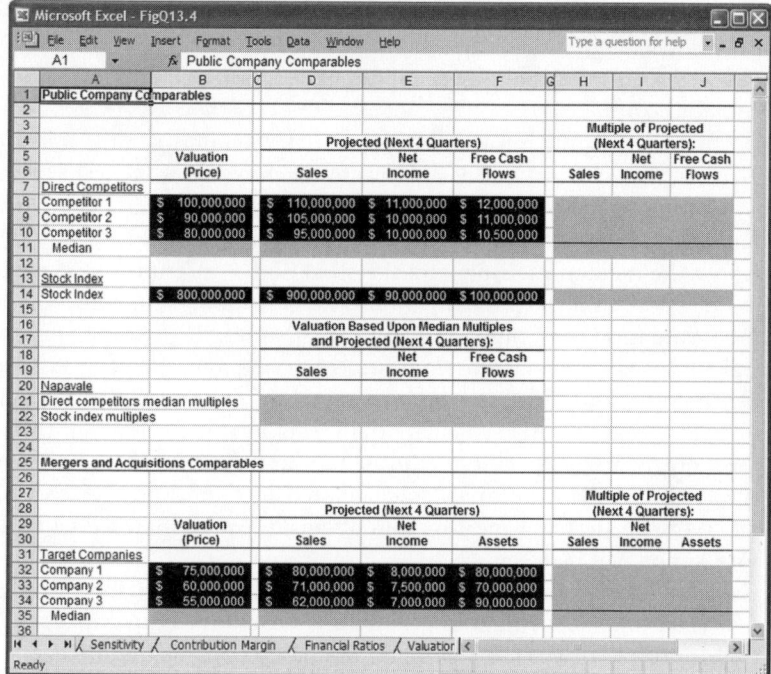

FIGURE Q13.4   Data for Fictitious Mergers and Acquisitions Transactions

	A	B	C	D	E	F	G	H	I	J
1	Public Company Comparables									
2										
3									Multiple of Projected	
4					Projected (Next 4 Quarters)				(Next 4 Quarters):	
5		Valuation			Net	Free Cash			Net	Free Cash
6		(Price)		Sales	Income	Flows		Sales	Income	Flows
7	Direct Competitors									
8	Competitor 1	$ 100,000,000		$ 110,000,000	$ 11,000,000	$ 12,000,000				
9	Competitor 2	$ 90,000,000		$ 105,000,000	$ 10,000,000	$ 11,000,000				
10	Competitor 3	$ 80,000,000		$ 95,000,000	$ 10,000,000	$ 10,500,000				
11	Median									
12										
13	Stock Index									
14	Stock Index	$ 800,000,000		$ 900,000,000	$ 90,000,000	$ 100,000,000				
15										
16				Valuation Based Upon Median Multiples						
17				and Projected (Next 4 Quarters):						
18					Net	Free Cash				
19				Sales	Income	Flows				
20	Napavale									
21	Direct competitors median multiples									
22	Stock index multiples									
23										
24										
25	Mergers and Acquisitions Comparables									
26										
27									Multiple of Projected	
28					Projected (Next 4 Quarters)				(Next 4 Quarters):	
29		Valuation			Net				Net	
30		(Price)		Sales	Income	Assets		Sales	Income	Assets
31	Target Companies									
32	Company 1	$ 75,000,000		$ 80,000,000	$ 8,000,000	$ 80,000,000				
33	Company 2	$ 60,000,000		$ 71,000,000	$ 7,500,000	$ 70,000,000				
34	Company 3	$ 55,000,000		$ 62,000,000	$ 7,000,000	$ 90,000,000				
35	Median									
36										

FIGURE Q13.5   Relative Weightings for Each Valuation Approach

	A	B	C	D	E	F
1	Valuation			Relative		Weighted
2	Technique	Valuaton		Weight		Valuation
3	Discounted cash flow			60.0%		$ -
4	Public company comparables			20.0%		$ -
5	Mergers and acquisitions comparables			20.0%		$ -
6	Total			100.0%		$ -
7						

1. Given the information presented, calculate Company 456's total free cash flows.
2. Given the information presented, calculate Company 456's net present value.
3. Calculate, using the information presented, the multiple of (i) sales, (ii) Net Income, and (iii) free cash flows for each of the comparable public companies and the stock index. Also calculate the median value for the multiples of the public company comparables as a group.
4. Apply the median multiple and the stock index multiple as calculated in Question 13.3 to Company 456 to derive a public company comparable valuation for Company 456.
5. Calculate, using the information presented, the multiple of (i) sales, (ii) Net Income, and (iii) Asset values for each of the mergers and acquisitions transactions. Also calculate the median value for the multiples of the mergers and acquisitions transactions as a group.
6. Apply the median multiples as calculated in Question 13.5 to Company 456 to derive a mergers and acquisitions comparable valuation for Company 456.
7. Calculate the weighted valuations and total valuation for Company 456 using the DCF valuation, the public company comparables valuation (multiple of sales for competitors method), and the mergers and acquisitions valuation (multiple of sales for competitors method).

CHAPTER 14

Capitalization Chart

This chapter covers the topic of a Capitalization Chart, which is a schedule that tracks the ownership structure of a company. A Capitalization Chart (also referred to as a "Cap Chart") is an important, and deceptively complex, schedule that has traditionally received little attention in finance-oriented books and textbooks. As such, I will cover this subject using the financial and valuation models developed over the course of this book.

I address the following specific issues related to Napavale's Cap Chart in this chapter: the "founding" Cap Chart, the effect of an equity investment into Napavale on the Cap Chart and the effect of issuing stock options to employees on Napavale's Cap Chart.

FOUNDING CAPITALIZATION CHART

As discussed in Chapter 2, Napavale was founded and began operations in the first accounting period (1Q X4) covered by the financial model used in this book. Upon its formation, the founders of Napavale determined their initial ownership percentages in Napavale. This initial ownership structure is captured and described in the founding Cap Chart.

I am assuming that Napavale was founded by three individuals and that each of these individuals received an identical allocation of stock in Napavale upon its formation. As such, each of the three founders received 33.3 percent of Napavale's equity upon the formation of the company. I am also assuming that there was an initial pool of 100,000 shares of "founder's stock." Thus, each of the three founders received 33,333 shares of stock in Napavale. Napavale's founding Cap Chart is shown in Figure 14.1.

Figure 14.2 offers a view of the values and formulas underlying

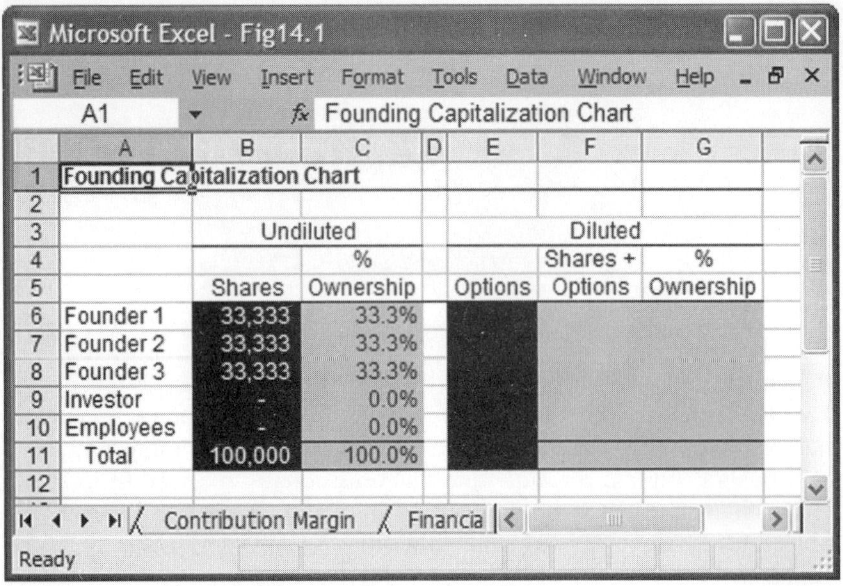

	A	B	C	D	E	F	G
1	Founding Capitalization Chart						
2							
3		Undiluted				Diluted	
4			%			Shares +	%
5		Shares	Ownership		Options	Options	Ownership
6	Founder 1	33,333	33.3%				
7	Founder 2	33,333	33.3%				
8	Founder 3	33,333	33.3%				
9	Investor	-	0.0%				
10	Employees	-	0.0%				
11	Total	100,000	100.0%				
12							

FIGURE 14.1 Founding Cap Chart

Napavale's founding Cap Chart. Note that I have included a section in the founding Cap Chart to account for any issued and outstanding stock options. While no stock options were issued upon Napavale's formation, the inclusion of stock options in Napavale's capital structure will be covered later in this chapter. The names of the input and output cells associated with Napavale's founding Cap Chart are shown in Figure 14.3.

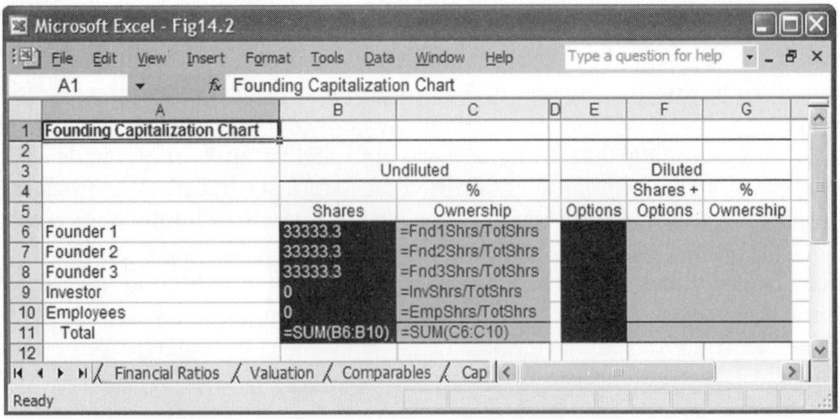

	A	B	C	D	E	F	G
1	Founding Capitalization Chart						
2							
3		Undiluted				Diluted	
4			%			Shares +	%
5		Shares	Ownership		Options	Options	Ownership
6	Founder 1	33333.3	=Fnd1Shrs/TotShrs				
7	Founder 2	33333.3	=Fnd2Shrs/TotShrs				
8	Founder 3	33333.3	=Fnd3Shrs/TotShrs				
9	Investor	0	=InvShrs/TotShrs				
10	Employees	0	=EmpShrs/TotShrs				
11	Total	=SUM(B6:B10)	=SUM(C6:C10)				
12							

FIGURE 14.2 Alternative View of the Founding Cap Chart

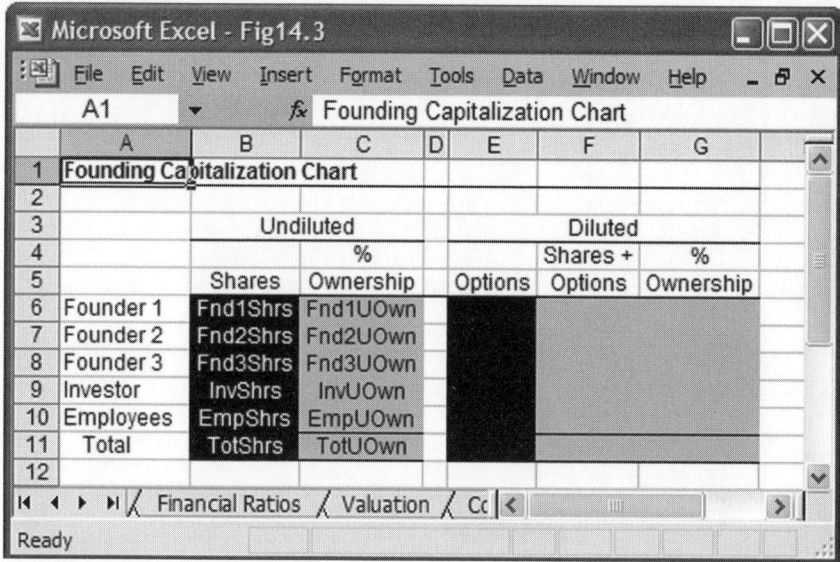

FIGURE 14.3 Names of the Input and Output Cells Underlying the Founding Cap Chart

EQUITY INVESTMENT'S EFFECT ON CAPITALIZATION CHART

Now that Napavale's founding Cap Chart is complete, I will cover the effect of an equity investment into Napavale on Napavale's Cap Chart. You may remember that I covered an equity investment into Napavale in Chapter 6 while discussing Napavale's Cash Budget. Specifically, $1 million was invested into Napavale in 1Q X4. Figure 14.4 provides a view of Napavale's Cash Budget for the sake of reference.

When an equity investment is made into a company, the ownership structure (and the Cap Chart) changes as well. In order to determine how Napavale's Cap Chart will change after the projected equity investment of $1 million in 1Q X4, I must calculate how much of Napavale as a company was "sold" to the investor providing this $1 million of equity capital. To do this, I must know Napavale's value when this investor will make this equity investment into Napavale.

Napavale's value was determined in Chapter 13; Figure 14.5 offers a view of Napavale's Valuation worksheet for the sake of reference.

You may remember that the valuation of Napavale as covered in Chapter 13 incorporated the assumption that a $1 million investment was made into the company. As such, the value of Napavale as shown in Figure

	Period				
	1Q X4	2Q X4	3Q X4	4Q X4	X4
CASH BUDGET					
Beginning cash balance	$ -	$ 982,272	$1,260,656	$1,541,236	$ -
Cash receipts					
Collections from customers	866,667	1,381,333	1,866,400	2,441,600	6,556,000
Total cash available, before financing	$ 866,667	$2,363,605	$3,127,056	$3,982,836	N/A
Cash disbursements					
Purchases disbursements	$ 176,444	$ 294,489	$ 365,400	$ 439,133	$1,275,467
Operating expenses	590,400	634,400	896,120	994,400	3,115,320
Tax expense	72,551	178,185	229,300	369,023	849,058
Capital expenditures	45,000	45,000	45,000	45,000	180,000
Total disbursements	884,395	1,152,074	1,535,820	1,847,556	5,419,845
Minimum cash balance desired	$ 250,000	$ 250,000	$ 250,000	$ 250,000	N/A
Total cash needed	$1,134,395	$1,402,074	$1,785,820	$2,097,556	N/A
Excess (deficiency) of total cash available over					
total cash needed before financing	$ (267,728)	$ 961,531	$1,341,236	$1,885,280	N/A
Financing					
Equity investment	$1,000,000	$ -	$ -	$ -	$1,000,000
Borrowing (at beginning of quarter)	-	50,000	-	-	50,000
Repayments (at end of quarter)	-	-	(50,000)	-	(50,000)
Interest	-	(875)	-	-	(875)
Total cash increase (decrease) from financing	$1,000,000	$ 49,125	$ (50,000)	$ -	$ 999,125
Ending cash balance	$ 982,272	$1,260,656	$1,541,236	$2,135,280	$2,135,280

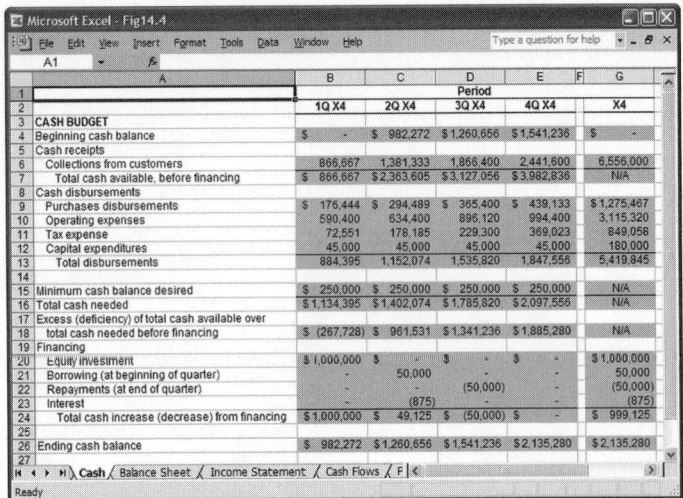

FIGURE 14.4 Cash Budget

14.5 represents what is known as the "post-money valuation." In other words, the valuation of Napavale as covered in Chapter 13 includes the value of the $1 million equity investment.

Thus, the percentage of Napavale purchased by the $1 million equity investment is calculated by answering the following question: What percentage of Napavale's post-money valuation does $1 million represent?

Valuation Technique	Valuaton	Relative Weight	Weighted Valuation
Discounted cash flow	$7,601,220	60.0%	$4,560,732
Public company comparables	$4,753,103	20.0%	$ 950,621
Mergers and acquisitions comparables	$5,237,920	20.0%	$1,047,584
Total		100.0%	$6,558,937

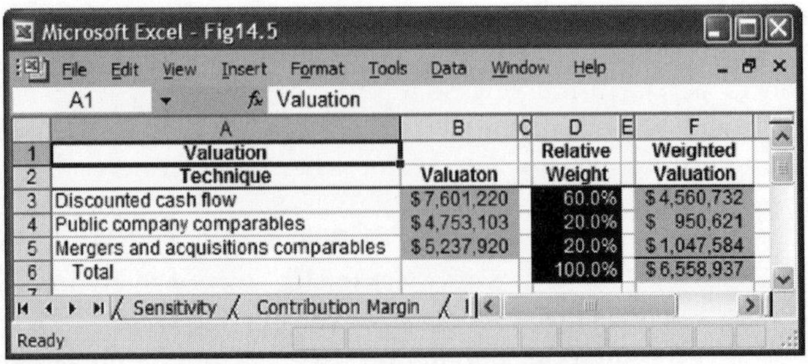

FIGURE 14.5 Valuation Worksheet

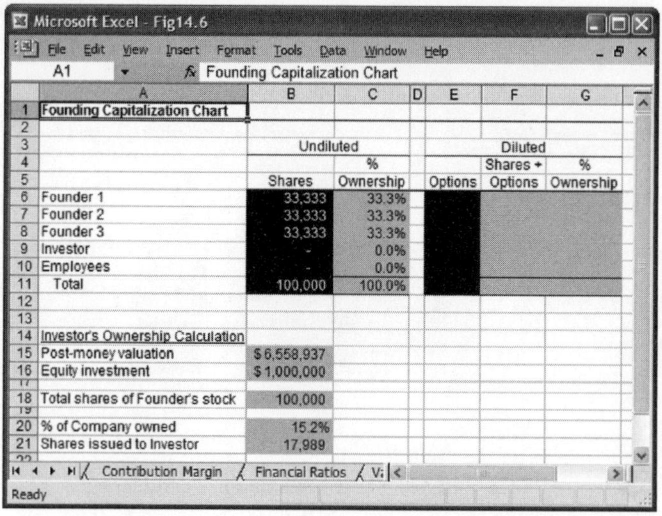

FIGURE 14.6   Calculation Related to Post-Money Valuation

This calculation, in addition to a related calculation that yields the number of shares issued to the equity investor and Napavale's updated Cap Chart, are all shown in Figure 14.6. The values and formulas underlying the calculation shown in Figure 14.6 are revealed in Figure 14.7. Figure 14.8 offers a view of the names of the input and output cells underlying the calculation shown in Figure 14.6.

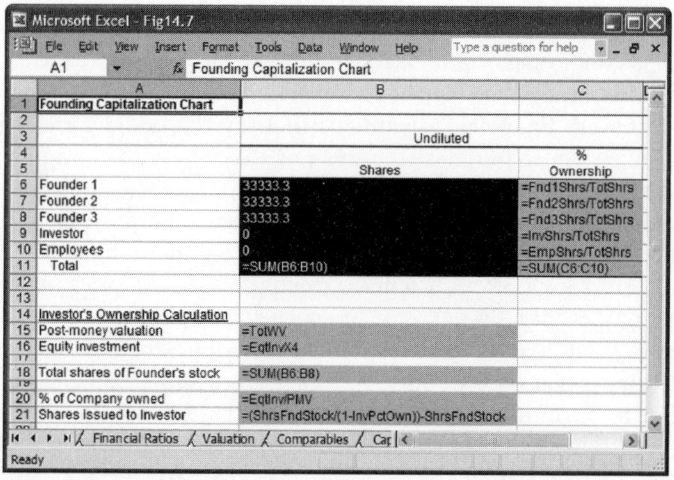

FIGURE 14.7   Alternative View of the Calculation Related to Post-Money Valuation

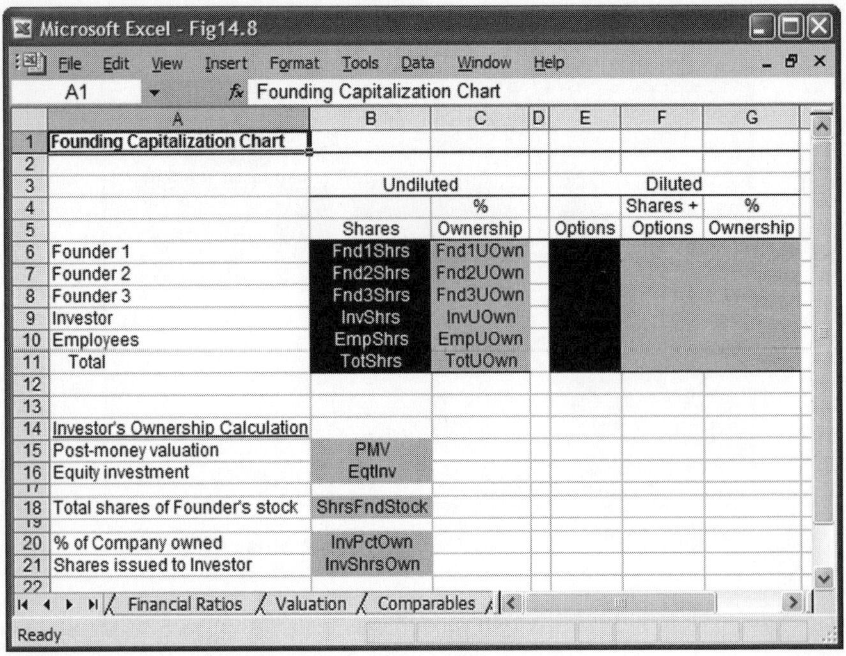

FIGURE 14.8   Names of the Input and Output Cells Underlying the Calculation Related to Post-Money Valuation

STOCK OPTIONS' EFFECT ON CAPITALIZATION CHART

The final step in building Napavale's Cap Chart is to track and reflect the effect of issuing stock options to employees on Napavale's Cap Chart. Stock options, a popular form of equity-based compensation in many companies, represent financial instruments that give the holder the right, but not the obligation, to purchase the stock of a company at a given price during a specified period of time.

Stock options are often "granted," or given to employees, at an exercise price equal to the then-market value of the underlying stock. In other words, when stock options are given to employees, the price at which the recipient may eventually purchase stock of the company is often equal to the then-current market price of the underlying stock. Accounting for stock options is a complex and somewhat controversial topic. This book is not meant to cover any of the issues surrounding the accounting for stock options and this section of the book does not affect any other sections of Napavale's financial model (except for the Cap Chart).

Many stock options "vest" over time, which means they are not "exercisable" until some point in the future. This is another way of saying that option holders may not use their options until a specified period of time has elapsed since they were granted the options (often 2 to 3 years from the date of option grant). As such, while stock options may be issued and outstanding, generally speaking, stock options do not count toward a company's number of shares outstanding and thus do not affect a company's Cap Chart using "issued and outstanding" stock as a basis for measuring the ownership structure of a company.

To account for this issue of stock options and a company's ownership, I have measured Napavale's ownership on both an undiluted and a diluted basis. Undiluted means the ownership of Napavale taking into account only issued and outstanding stock in the company. Diluted ownership means the ownership of Napavale taking into account outstanding future potential claims on equity of the company (such as stock options).

Figure 14.9 presents a view of Napavale's updated Cap Chart that incorporates the assumption that 20,000 stock options have been issued to employees. The values and formulas underlying Napavale's updated Cap Chart are shown in Figure 14.10. Figure 14.11 presents a view of the names of the input and output cells underlying Napavale's updated Cap Chart.

	Microsoft Excel - Fig14.9						
	A1 ▼ *fx* Founding Capitalization Chart						
	A	B	C	D	E	F	G
1	Founding Capitalization Chart						
2							
3			Undiluted			Diluted	
4			%			Shares +	%
5		Shares	Ownership		Options	Options	Ownership
6	Founder 1	33,333	28.3%		-	33,333	24.2%
7	Founder 2	33,333	28.3%		-	33,333	24.2%
8	Founder 3	33,333	28.3%		-	33,333	24.2%
9	Investor	17,989	15.2%		-	17,989	13.0%
10	Employees	-	0.0%		20,000	20,000	14.5%
11	Total	117,989	100.0%		20,000	137,989	100.0%
12							
13							
14	Investor's Ownership Calculation						
15	Post-money valuation	$6,558,937					
16	Equity investment	$1,000,000					
18	Total shares of Founder's stock	100,000					
20	% of Company owned	15.2%					
21	Shares issued to Investor	17,989					

FIGURE 14.9 Updated Cap Chart

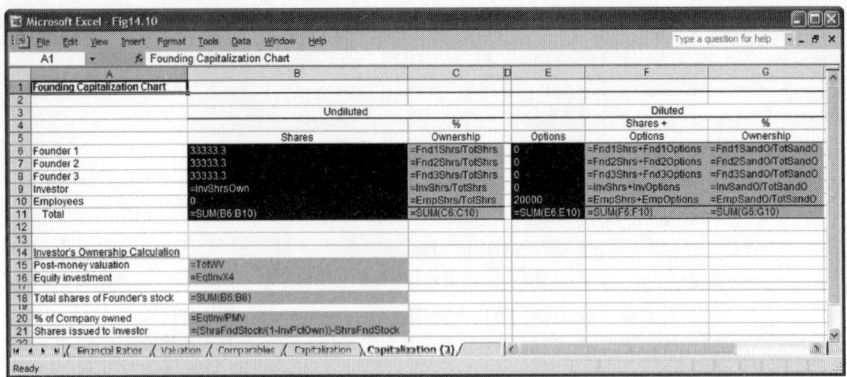

FIGURE 14.10 Alternative View of the Updated Cap Chart

	A	B	C	D	E	F	G
1	**Founding Capitalization Chart**						
2							
3			Undiluted			Diluted	
4				%		Shares +	%
5		Shares	Ownership	Options	Options	Ownership	
6	Founder 1	Fnd1Shrs	Fnd1UOwn	Fnd1Options	Fnd1SandO	Fnd1DOwn	
7	Founder 2	Fnd2Shrs	Fnd2UOwn	Fnd2Options	Fnd2SandO	Fnd2DOwn	
8	Founder 3	Fnd3Shrs	Fnd3UOwn	Fnd3Options	Fnd3SandO	Fnd3DOwn	
9	Investor	InvShrs	InvUOwn	InvOptions	InvSandO	InvDOwn	
10	Employees	EmpShrs	EmpUOwn	EmpOptions	EmpSandO	EmpDOwn	
11	Total	TotShrs	TotUOwn	TotOptions	TotSandO	TotDOwn	
12							
13							
14	Investor's Ownership Calculation						
15	Post-money valuation	PMV					
16	Equity investment	EqtInv					
17							
18	Total shares of Founder's stock	ShrsFndStock					
19							
20	% of Company owned	InvPctOwn					
21	Shares issued to Investor	InvShrsOwn					

FIGURE 14.11 Names of the Input and Output Cells Underlying the Updated Cap Chart

QUESTIONS

Each of the questions for this chapter relates to the hypothetical company named Company 456—this company was used in the Questions section of Chapters 12 and 13. To review, Company 456 sells display monitors to physicians. As such, Company 456 is a product-oriented (as opposed to a service-oriented) business.

The questions for this chapter address fiscal year X4 on a quarterly basis (four specific quarters, 1Q–4Q for year X4). The following questions will test your knowledge of the material covered in this chapter in an applied manner—specifically, you will be asked to build a founding Capitalization Chart for Company 456, calculate the effect of an equity investment into Company 456 on Company 456's Capitalization Chart, and calculate the effect of the issuance of stock options on Company 456's Capitalization Chart.

To prepare you for this chapter's questions, please assume that Company 456 was founded by three individuals and that (1) the first founder received 50.0 percent of the founding equity and (2) the second and third founders each received 25.0 percent of the founding equity in Company 456. More specifically, please assume that (1) the first founder received 500,000 shares of stock and (2) the second and third founders each received 250,000 shares of stock upon Company 456's founding.

In terms of stock options, please assume that 200,000 stock options (all of which are unvested) are issued to employees at Company 456 following the equity investment of $250,000 into Company 456 in Q1 X4. This equity investment is shown in Figure Q14.1, Company 456's Assumptions and Dashboard worksheet. Figure Q14.2 offers a view of Company 456's Cash Budget. Company 456's Valuation worksheet is shown in Figure Q14.3.

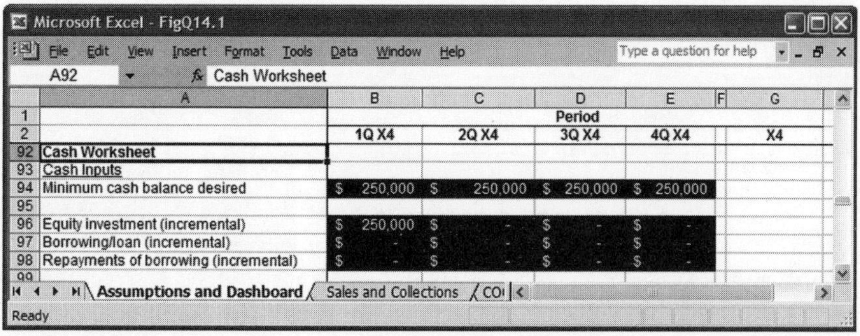

FIGURE Q14.1 Company 456's Assumptions and Dashboard Worksheet

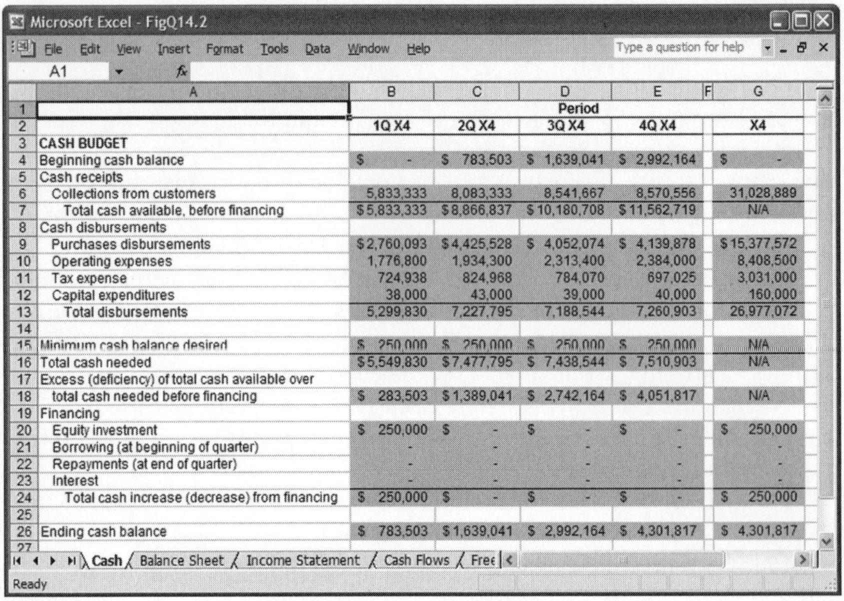

	A	B	C	D	E	G
1		Period				
2		1Q X4	2Q X4	3Q X4	4Q X4	X4
3	CASH BUDGET					
4	Beginning cash balance	$ -	$ 783,503	$ 1,639,041	$ 2,992,164	$ -
5	Cash receipts					
6	Collections from customers	5,833,333	8,083,333	8,541,667	8,570,556	31,028,889
7	Total cash available, before financing	$5,833,333	$8,866,837	$10,180,708	$11,562,719	N/A
8	Cash disbursements					
9	Purchases disbursements	$2,760,093	$4,425,528	$ 4,052,074	$ 4,139,878	$15,377,572
10	Operating expenses	1,776,800	1,934,300	2,313,400	2,384,000	8,408,500
11	Tax expense	724,938	824,968	784,070	697,025	3,031,000
12	Capital expenditures	38,000	43,000	39,000	40,000	160,000
13	Total disbursements	5,299,830	7,227,795	7,188,544	7,260,903	26,977,072
14						
15	Minimum cash balance desired	$ 250,000	$ 250,000	$ 250,000	$ 250,000	N/A
16	Total cash needed	$5,549,830	$7,477,795	$ 7,438,544	$ 7,510,903	N/A
17	Excess (deficiency) of total cash available over					
18	total cash needed before financing	$ 283,503	$1,389,041	$ 2,742,164	$ 4,051,817	N/A
19	Financing					
20	Equity investment	$ 250,000	$ -	$ -	$ -	$ 250,000
21	Borrowing (at beginning of quarter)	-	-	-	-	-
22	Repayments (at end of quarter)	-	-	-	-	-
23	Interest	-	-	-	-	-
24	Total cash increase (decrease) from financing	$ 250,000	$ -	$ -	$ -	$ 250,000
25						
26	Ending cash balance	$ 783,503	$1,639,041	$ 2,992,164	$ 4,301,817	$ 4,301,817

FIGURE Q14.2 Company 456's Cash Budget

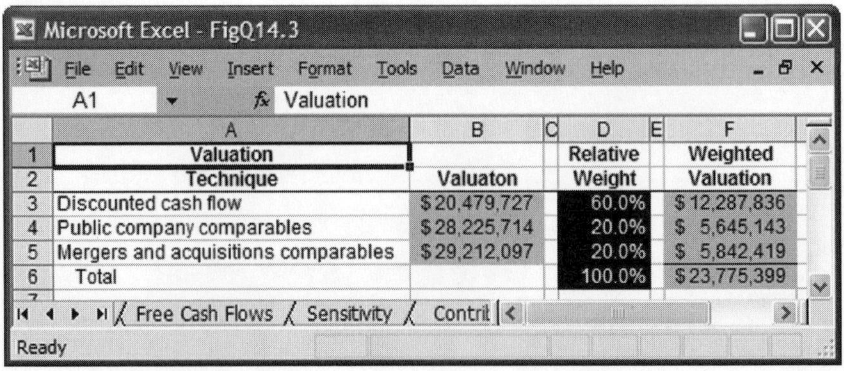

	A	B	D	F
1	Valuation		Relative	Weighted
2	Technique	Valuaton	Weight	Valuation
3	Discounted cash flow	$20,479,727	60.0%	$12,287,836
4	Public company comparables	$28,225,714	20.0%	$ 5,645,143
5	Mergers and acquisitions comparables	$29,212,097	20.0%	$ 5,842,419
6	Total		100.0%	$23,775,399

FIGURE Q14.3 Company 456's Valuation Worksheet

1. Given the information presented, build a founding Capitalization Chart for Company 456.
2. Given the information presented, build a Capitalization Chart for Company 456 to reflect the equity investment into Company 456 in 1Q X4 based on the valuation shown in Figure Q14.3.
3. Given the information presented, build a Capitalization Chart for Company 456 to reflect the issuance of stock options to employees of Company 456.

Answers to Chapter Questions

CHAPTER 1 Overview of Budgets and Financial Models

1. The main goal of all budgets is to provide a tangible and quantifiable estimate of the receipt and allocation of resources. A budget represents a core element of a financial model.
2. The two main components of a Master Budget are an Operating Budget and a Financial Budget.
3. A financial model is a quantitative representation of a company's past, present, and future business operations.
4. The three components of standard consolidated financial statements are the Balance Sheet, the Income Statement, and the Statement of Cash Flows.
5. Free cash flows represent the cash available to all providers of capital (providers of both debt and equity)—in other words, the amount of cash a business generates (or, conversely, consumes) over a given timeframe after paying all of its "required" costs for that period.
6. A business should use sensitivity analyses to model the effect of changing input variables on some output of interest, such as net income. Contribution margin analyses should be used to determine a business's operating leverage and breakeven point (both in terms of units and in terms of dollars). A business should use financial analyses to assess financial performance using metrics such as gross margin, net profit margin, and return on equity, among others.
7. Valuation is the process of determining how much a company is worth.
8. A capitalization chart represents, or tabulates, the ownership structure of a business.

CHAPTER 2 Operating Budget—Assumptions, Sales, and Collections

1. The first portion of an Assumptions and Dashboard worksheet for Company XYZ is shown in Figure A2.1.
2. A Unit Sales and Price Budget for Company XYZ is shown in Figure A2.2.

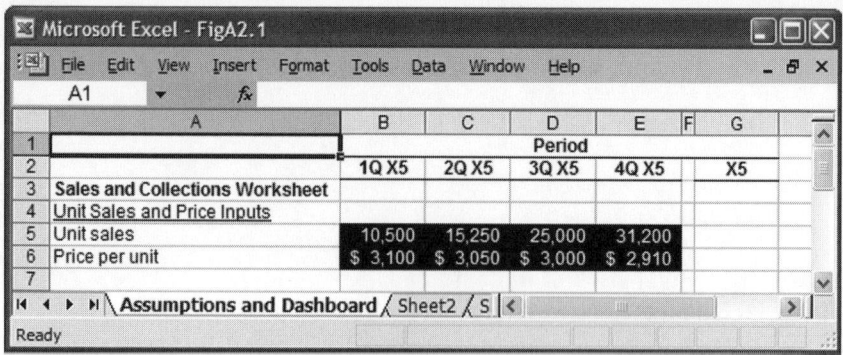

FIGURE A2.1   Assumptions and Dashboard Worksheet for Company XYZ

3. The updated Assumptions and Dashboard worksheet for Company XYZ is shown in Figure A2.3.
4. The Sales Composition Budget for Company XYZ is shown in Figure A2.4.
5. The updated Assumptions and Dashboard worksheet for Company XYZ is shown in Figure A2.5.
6. The Cash Collections from Customers Budget for Company XYZ is shown in Figure A2.6.
7. The Accounts Receivable Budget and updated Cash Collections from Customers Budget for Company XYZ is shown in Figure A2.7.

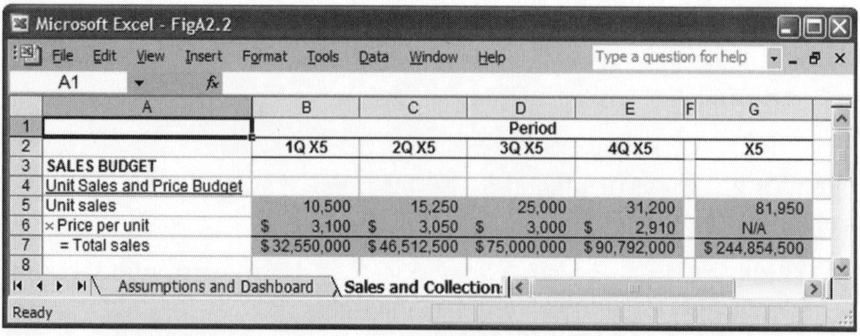

FIGURE A2.2   Unit Sales and Price Budget for Company XYZ

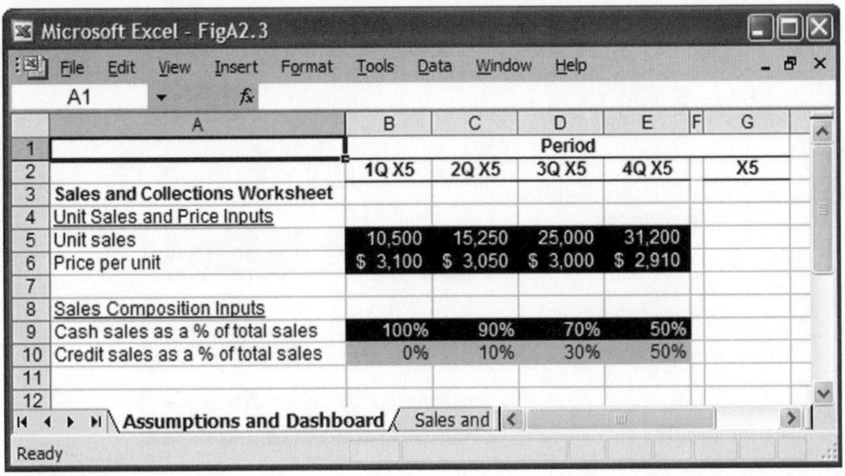

FIGURE A2.3 Updated Assumptions and Dashboard Worksheet for Company XYZ

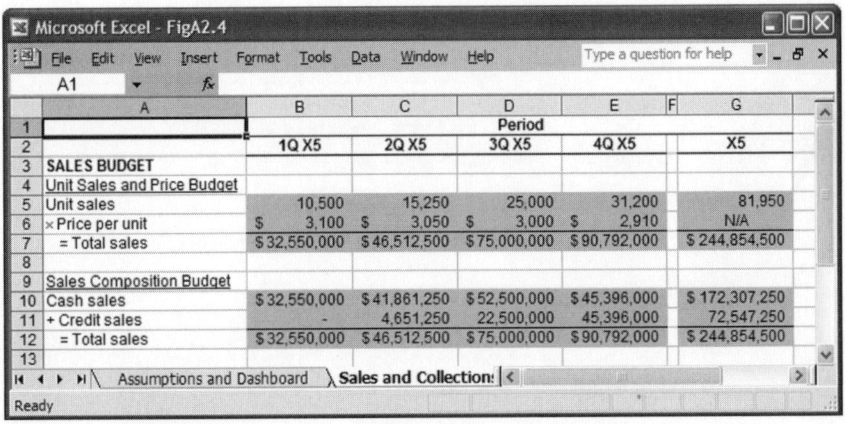

FIGURE A2.4 Sales Composition Budget for Company XYZ

FIGURE A2.5 Updated Assumptions and Dashboard Worksheet for Company XYZ

The spreadsheet in Figure A2.5 contains:

	A	B	C	D	E	F	G
1			Period				
2		1Q X5	2Q X5	3Q X5	4Q X5		X5
3	Sales and Collections Worksheet						
4	Unit Sales and Price Inputs						
5	Unit sales	10,500	15,250	25,000	31,200		
6	Price per unit	$ 3,100	$ 3,050	$ 3,000	$ 2,910		
7							
8	Sales Composition Inputs						
9	Cash sales as a % of total sales	100%	90%	70%	50%		
10	Credit sales as a % of total sales	0%	10%	30%	50%		
11							
12	Days receivable (DSO)	20	25	30	30		
13	Days per quarter	90	90	90	90		
14							

FIGURE A2.6 Cash Collections from Customers Budget for Company XYZ

The spreadsheet in Figure A2.6 contains:

	A	B	C	D	E	F	G
1			Period				
2		1Q X5	2Q X5	3Q X5	4Q X5		X5
3	SALES BUDGET						
4	Unit Sales and Price Budget						
5	Unit sales	10,500	15,250	25,000	31,200		81,950
6	×Price per unit	$ 3,100	$ 3,050	$ 3,000	$ 2,910		N/A
7	= Total sales	$ 32,550,000	$ 46,512,500	$ 75,000,000	$ 90,792,000		$ 244,854,500
8							
9	Sales Composition Budget						
10	Cash sales	$ 32,550,000	$ 41,861,250	$ 52,500,000	$ 45,396,000		$ 172,307,250
11	+ Credit sales	-	4,651,250	22,500,000	45,396,000		72,547,250
12	= Total sales	$ 32,550,000	$ 46,512,500	$ 75,000,000	$ 90,792,000		$ 244,854,500
13							
14	COLLECTIONS BUDGET						
15	Cash Collections from Customers Budget						
16	Cash sales this period	$ 32,550,000	$ 41,861,250	$ 52,500,000	$ 45,396,000		$ 172,307,250
17	+ Credit sales collected						
18	= Total collections	$ 32,550,000	$ 41,861,250	$ 52,500,000	$ 45,396,000		$ 172,307,250
19							

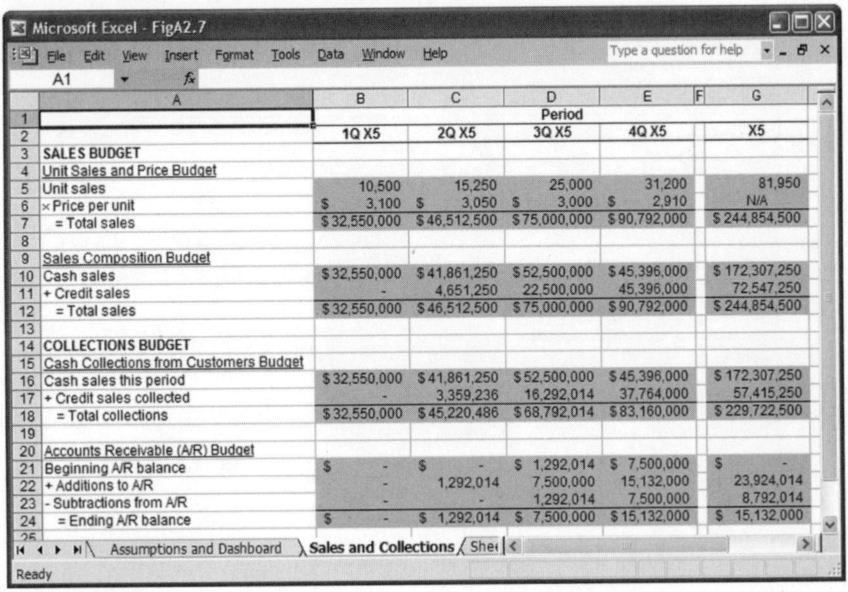

FIGURE A2.7   Accounts Receivable Budget and Updated Cash Collections from Customers Budget for Company XYZ

CHAPTER 3   Operating Budget—Cost of Goods Sold, Inventory, and Purchases

1. The Cost-of-Goods-Sold Budget for Company ABC is shown in Figure A3.1.
2. The Inventory Budget for Company ABC is shown in Figure A3.2.
3. The Purchases Budget for Company ABC is shown in Figure A3.3.

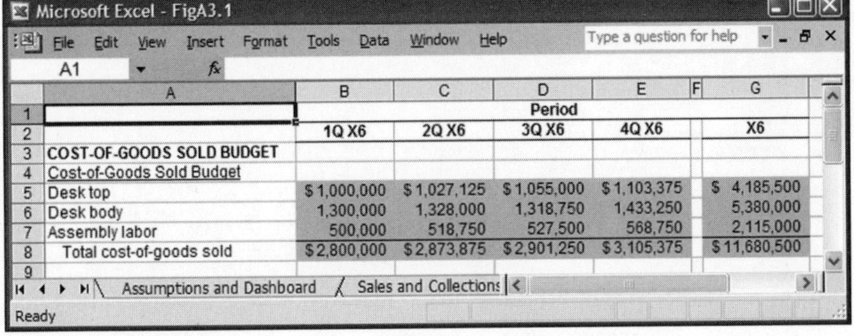

FIGURE A3.1   Cost-of-Goods-Sold Budget for Company ABC

	A	B	C	D	E	F	G
1				Period			
2		1Q X6	2Q X6	3Q X6	4Q X6		X6
3	**INVENTORY BUDGET**						
4	Inventory Budget						
5	Desired ending inventory	$ 478,979	$ 548,014	$ 655,579	$ 655,579		N/A
6	+ Cost of goods sold	2,800,000	2,873,875	2,901,250	3,105,375		11,680,500
7	= Total inventory needed	$3,278,979	$3,421,889	$3,556,829	$3,760,954		N/A
8							
9	**PURCHASES BUDGET**						
10	Purchases Budget						
11	Total inventory needed						
12	- Beginning inventory	-					
13	= Purchases						
14							
15	Disbursements for Purchases Budget						
16	Payments of payables						
17	Total disbursements for purchases						
18							
19	Accounts Payable (A/P) Budget						
20	Beginning A/P balance						
21	+ Additions to A/P						
22	- Subtractions from A/P						
23	Ending A/P						

FIGURE A3.2 Inventory Budget for Company ABC

	A	B	C	D	E	F	G
1				Period			
2		1Q X6	2Q X6	3Q X6	4Q X6		X6
3	**INVENTORY BUDGET**						
4	Inventory Budget						
5	Desired ending inventory	$ 478,979	$ 548,014	$ 655,579	$ 655,579		N/A
6	+ Cost of goods sold	2,800,000	2,873,875	2,901,250	3,105,375		11,680,500
7	= Total inventory needed	$3,278,979	$3,421,889	$3,556,829	$3,760,954		N/A
8							
9	**PURCHASES BUDGET**						
10	Purchases Budget						
11	Total inventory needed	$3,278,979	$3,421,889	$3,556,829	$3,760,954		N/A
12	- Beginning inventory	-	478,979	548,014	655,579		-
13	= Purchases	$3,278,979	$2,942,910	$3,008,815	$3,105,375		N/A
14							
15	Disbursements for Purchases Budget						
16	Payments of payables						
17	Total disbursements for purchases						
18							
19	Accounts Payable (A/P) Budget						
20	Beginning A/P balance						
21	+ Additions to A/P						
22	- Subtractions from A/P						
23	Ending A/P						

FIGURE A3.3 Purchases Budget for Company ABC

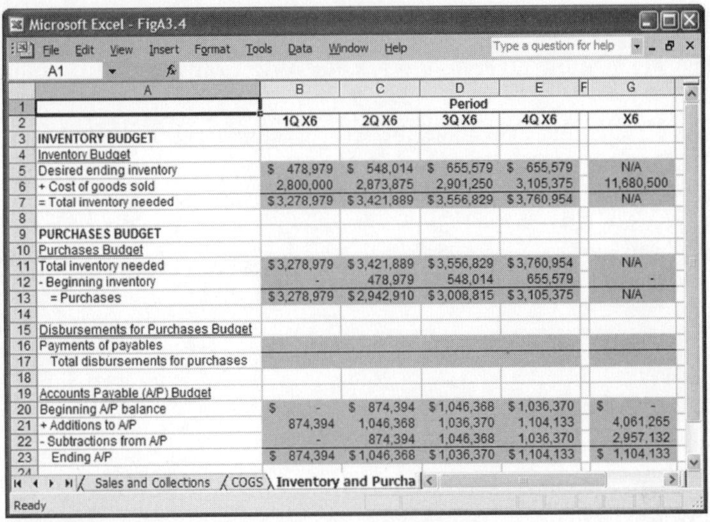

FIGURE A3.4 Accounts Payable Budget for Company ABC

4. The Accounts Payable Budget for Company ABC is shown in Figure A3.4.
5. The Disbursements for Purchases Budget for Company ABC is shown in Figure A3.5.

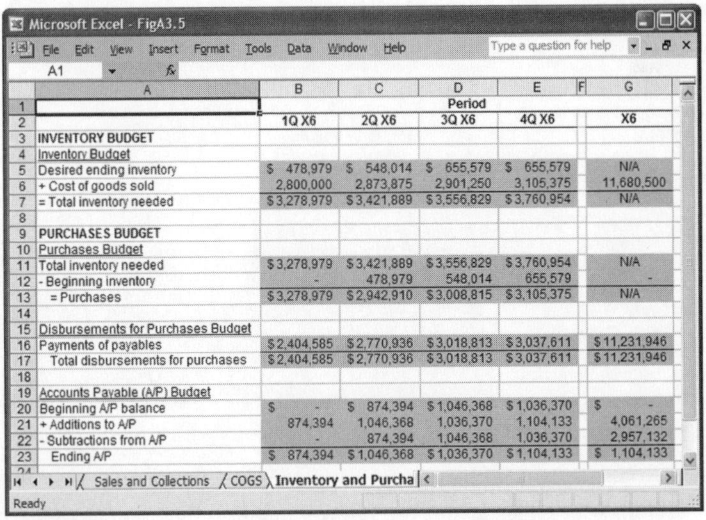

FIGURE A3.5 Disbursements for Purchases Budget for Company ABC

CHAPTER 4   Operating Budget—Operating Expenses

1. The Headcount Overview worksheet for Company DEF is shown in Figure A4.1.
2. The Headcount Cost worksheet for Company DEF is shown in Figure A4.2.
3. The Operating Expenses Budget for Company DEF is shown in Figure A4.3.
4. The Disbursements for Operating Expenses Budget for Company DEF is shown in Figure A4.4.

	A	B	C	D	E	F	G
1				Period			
2		1Q X4	2Q X4	3Q X4	4Q X4		X4
3	HEADCOUNT BUDGET						
4	Headcount Budget						
5	Number of employees						
6	Chief Executive Officer	1	1	1	1		
7	Chief Financial Officer	1	1	1	1		
8	VP, Engineering	1	1	1	1		
9	VP, Sales & Marketing	1	1	1	1		
10	VP, Business Development	1	1	1	1		
11	Salesperson	5	5	7	8		
12	Hardware Engineer	4	4	5	5		
13	Controller/Accountant	1	2	2	2		
14	Administrative Assistant	2	2	3	4		
15	Total	17	18	22	24		
16							
17	Periodic base salaries						
18	Chief Executive Officer	$ 43,750	$ 43,750	$ 43,750	$ 43,750		$ 175,000
19	Chief Financial Officer	37,500	37,500	37,500	37,500		150,000
20	VP, Engineering	37,500	37,500	37,500	37,500		150,000
21	VP, Sales & Marketing	33,750	33,750	33,750	33,750		135,000
22	VP, Business Development	31,250	31,250	31,250	31,250		125,000
23	Salesperson	25,000	25,000	25,000	25,000		100,000
24	Hardware Engineer	22,500	22,500	22,500	22,500		90,000
25	Controller/Accountant	11,250	11,250	11,250	11,250		45,000
26	Administrative Assistant	7,500	7,500	7,500	7,500		30,000
27	Total	$250,000	$250,000	$250,000	$250,000		$1,000,000

Headcount Overview / Headcount Cost / C

FIGURE A4.1   Headcount Overview Worksheet for Company DEF

	A	B	C	D	E	F	G
				Period			
1		1Q X4	2Q X4	3Q X4	4Q X4		X4
2							
3	HEADCOUNT BUDGET						
4	Headcount Budget						
5	Periodic salary expense (base)						
6	Chief Executive Officer	$ 43,750	$ 43,750	$ 43,750	$ 43,750		$ 175,000
7	Chief Financial Officer	37,500	37,500	37,500	37,500		150,000
8	VP, Engineering	37,500	37,500	37,500	37,500		150,000
9	VP, Sales & Marketing	33,750	33,750	33,750	33,750		135,000
10	VP, Business Development	31,250	31,250	31,250	31,250		125,000
11	Salesperson	125,000	125,000	175,000	200,000		625,000
12	Hardware Engineer	90,000	90,000	112,500	112,500		405,000
13	Controller/Accountant	11,250	22,500	22,500	22,500		78,750
14	Administrative Assistant	15,000	15,000	22,500	30,000		82,500
15	Total	$425,000	$436,250	$516,250	$548,750		$1,926,250
16							
17	Total (with benefits)	$488,750	$501,688	$593,688	$631,063		$2,215,188

Sheets: Headcount Overview \ **Headcount Cost** / Op

FIGURE A4.2   Headcount Cost Worksheet for Company DEF

	A	B	C	D	E	F	G
				Period			
1		1Q X4	2Q X4	3Q X4	4Q X4		X4
2							
3	OPERATING EXPENSES BUDGET						
4	Operating Expenses Budget						
5	Salaries	$ 488,750	$501,688	$593,688	$631,063		$2,215,188
6	Miscellaneous expenses	40,000	36,400	42,120	36,575		155,095
7	Research and development	100,000	104,000	105,300	104,500		413,800
8	Rent	20,250	20,250	20,250	20,250		81,000
9	Depreciation						-
10	Total operating expenses	$ 649,000	$662,338	$761,358	$792,388		$2,865,083
11							
12	DISBURSEMENTS FOR OPERATING EXPENSES BUDGET						
13	Disbursements for Operating Expenses Budget						
14	Salaries						
15	Miscellaneous expenses						
16	Research and development						
17	Rent						
18	Depreciation						
19	Total disbursements for operating expenses						

Sheets: Headcount Overview / Headcount Cost \ **Operating Expens**

FIGURE A4.3   Operating Expenses Budget for Company DEF

FIGURE A4.4 Disbursements for Operating Expenses Budget for Company DEF

CHAPTER 5 Operating Budget—Income Statement

1. The first section of the Income Statement for Company GHI is shown in Figure A5.1.
2. The updated Income Statement for Company GHI is shown in Figure A5.2.

FIGURE A5.1 First Section of the Income Statement for Company GHI

FIGURE A5.2 Updated Income Statement for Company GHI

3. The updated Income Statement for Company GHI is shown in Figure A5.3.
4. The updated Income Statement for Company GHI is shown in Figure A5.4.

FIGURE A5.3 Updated Income Statement for Company GHI

Microsoft Excel - FigA5.4

File Edit View Insert Format Tools Data Window Help   Type a question for help

A1

	A	B	C	D	E	F	G
1				Period			
2		1Q X4	2Q X4	3Q X4	4Q X4		X4
3	Sales	$2,200,000	$2,160,000	$2,133,000	$2,093,500		$8,586,500
4	Cost of goods sold	1,072,500	1,026,000	950,400	927,500		3,976,400
5	Gross profit	$1,127,500	$1,134,000	$1,182,600	$1,166,000		$4,610,100
6							
7	Salaries	$ 459,650	$ 487,200	$ 516,200	$ 611,900		$2,074,950
8	Miscellaneous expenses	88,000	97,200	106,650	94,208		386,058
9	Research and development	132,000	140,400	149,310	157,013		578,723
10	Rent	15,750	15,750	15,750	15,750		63,000
11	Depreciation						-
12	Income from operations	$ 432,100	$ 393,450	$ 394,690	$ 287,130		$1,507,370
13							
14	Interest expense						$ -
15	Taxable income	$ 432,100	$ 393,450	$ 394,690	$ 287,130		$1,507,370
16							
17	Tax expense	$ 138,272	$ 125,904	$ 130,248	$ 94,753		$ 489,177
18	Net income	$ 293,828	$ 267,546	$ 264,442	$ 192,377		$1,018,193
19							

Operating Expenses / Capital / Cash / Balance S

Ready

FIGURE A5.4 Updated Income Statement for Company GHI

CHAPTER 6 Financial Budget—Capital Budget and Cash Budget

1. The Capital Expenditures Budget for Company JKL is shown in Figure A6.1.
2. The Disbursements for Capital Expenditures Budget for Company JKL is shown in Figure A6.2.
3. The Depreciation Budget for Company JKL is shown in Figure A6.3.
4. The first section of Company JKL's Cash Budget is shown in Figure A6.4.
5. The updated Cash Budget for Company JKL is shown in Figure A6.5.
6. The updated Cash Budget for Company JKL is shown in Figure A6.6.
7. The completed Income Statement for Company JKL is shown in Figure A6.7.

FIGURE A6.1 Capital Expenditures Budget for Company JKL

FIGURE A6.2 Disbursements for Capital Expenditures Budget for Company JKL

Microsoft Excel - FigA6.3						
File Edit View Insert Format Tools Data Window Help				Type a question for help		
A1 ▼ fx						

	A	B	C	D	E	F	G
1				Period			
2		1Q X4	2Q X4	3Q X4	4Q X4		X4
3	CAPITAL BUDGET						
4	Capital Expenditures Budget						
5	Equipment	$ 9,000	$ 5,000	$ 3,000	$ 3,000		$ 20,000
6	Furniture	2,500	2,500	2,500	2,000		9,500
7	Fixtures	1,500	1,500	1,500	1,500		6,000
8	Total capital expenditures	$13,000	$ 9,000	$ 7,000	$ 6,500		$ 35,500
9							
10	Disbursements for Capital Expenditures Budget						
11	Equipment	$ 9,000	$ 5,000	$ 3,000	$ 3,000		$ 20,000
12	Furniture	2,500	2,500	2,500	2,000		9,500
13	Fixtures	1,500	1,500	1,500	1,500		6,000
14	Total disbursements for capital expenditures	$13,000	$ 9,000	$ 7,000	$ 6,500		$ 35,500
15							
16	Depreciation Budget						
17	Equipment	$ 375	$ 583	$ 708	$ 833		$ 2,500
18	Furniture	125	250	375	475		1,225
19	Fixtures	75	150	225	300		750
20	Total depreciation	$ 575	$ 983	$ 1,308	$ 1,608		$ 4,475
21							
22	Cumulative capital expenditures	$13,000	$22,000	$ 29,000	$ 35,500		
23	- Accumulated depreciation	575	1,558	2,867	4,475		
24	= Fixed assets, net of depreciation	$12,425	$20,442	$ 26,133	$ 31,025		
25							

H ◄ ► H \ Headcount Overview / Headcount Cost / Operating |◄

Ready

FIGURE A6.3 Depreciation Budget for Company JKL

Microsoft Excel - FigA6.4						
File Edit View Insert Format Tools Data Window Help				Type a question for help		
A1 ▼ fx						

	A	B	C	D	E	F	G
1				Period			
2		1Q X4	2Q X4	3Q X4	4Q X4		X4
3	CASH BUDGET						
4	Beginning cash balance	$ -	$2,444,444	$5,214,800	$ 8,140,089		$ -
5	Cash receipts						
6	Collections from customers	2,444,444	2,770,356	2,925,289	2,881,378		11,021,467
7	Total cash available, before financing	$2,444,444	$5,214,800	$8,140,089	$11,021,467		N/A
8	Cash disbursements						
9	Purchases disbursements						
10	Operating expenses						
11	Capital expenditures						
12	Total disbursements	-	-	-	-		-
13							
14	Minimum cash balance desired						
15	Total cash needed						
16	Excess (deficiency) of total cash available over						
17	total cash needed before financing						
18	Financing						
19	Equity investment						
20	Borrowing (at beginning of quarter)						
21	Repayments (at end of quarter)						
22	Interest						
23	Total cash increase (decrease) from financing						
24							
25	Ending cash balance	$2,444,444	$5,214,800	$8,140,089	$11,021,467		$11,021,467
26							

H ◄ ► H \ Headcount Overview / Headcount Cost / Operating Expenses |◄

Ready

FIGURE A6.4 First Section of Company JKL's Cash Budget

FIGURE A6.5 Updated Cash Budget for Company JKL

	A	B	C	D	E	F	G
1				Period			
2		1Q X4	2Q X4	3Q X4	4Q X4		X4
3	CASH BUDGET						
4	Beginning cash balance	$ -	$ 54,822	$ 462,267	$ 1,022,147		$ -
5	Cash receipts						
6	Collections from customers	866,667	1,381,333	1,866,400	2,441,600		6,556,000
7	Total cash available, before financing	$ 866,667	$1,436,156	$2,328,667	$3,463,747		N/A
8	Cash disbursements						
9	Purchases disbursements	$ 176,444	$ 294,489	$ 365,400	$ 439,133		$1,275,467
10	Operating expenses	590,400	634,400	896,120	994,400		3,115,320
11	Capital expenditures	45,000	45,000	45,000	45,000		180,000
12	Total disbursements	811,844	973,889	1,306,520	1,478,533		4,570,787
13							
14	Minimum cash balance desired	$ 250,000	$ 250,000	$ 250,000	$ 250,000		N/A
15	Total cash needed	$1,061,844	$1,223,889	$1,556,520	$1,728,533		N/A
16	Excess (deficiency) of total cash available over						
17	total cash needed before financing	$ (195,178)	$ 212,267	$ 772,147	$1,735,213		N/A
18	Financing						
19	Equity investment						
20	Borrowing (at beginning of quarter)						
21	Repayments (at end of quarter)						
22	Interest						
23	Total cash increase (decrease) from financing						
24							
25	Ending cash balance	$ 54,822	$ 462,267	$1,022,147	$1,985,213		$1,985,213

FIGURE A6.6 Updated Cash Budget for Company JKL Including Projections Regarding Equity Investments, Borrowings, Repayment of Borrowings, and Interest Expenses

	A	B	C	D	E	F	G
1				Period			
2		1Q X4	2Q X4	3Q X4	4Q X4		X4
3	CASH BUDGET						
4	Beginning cash balance	$ -	$ 744,989	$ 634,155	$ 904,597		$ -
5	Cash receipts						
6	Collections from customers	2,444,444	2,770,356	2,925,289	2,881,378		11,021,467
7	Total cash available, before financing	$2,444,444	$3,515,344	$3,559,444	$3,785,975		N/A
8	Cash disbursements						
9	Purchases disbursements	$1,550,578	$2,217,631	$1,924,070	$1,810,772		$7,503,050
10	Operating expenses	635,878	654,558	748,278	783,910		2,822,624
11	Capital expenditures	13,000	9,000	7,000	6,500		35,500
12	Total disbursements	2,199,456	2,881,189	2,679,347	2,601,182		10,361,174
13							
14	Minimum cash balance desired	$ 100,000	$ 100,000	$ 100,000	$ 100,000		N/A
15	Total cash needed	$2,299,456	$2,981,189	$2,779,347	$2,701,182		N/A
16	Excess (deficiency) of total cash available over						
17	total cash needed before financing	$ 144,989	$ 534,155	$ 780,097	$1,084,793		N/A
18	Financing						
19	Equity investment	$ 500,000	$ -	$ -	$ -		$ 500,000
20	Borrowing (at beginning of quarter)	-	-	25,000			25,000
21	Repayments (at end of quarter)	-	-		(25,000)		(25,000)
22	Interest	-	-	(500)	-		(500)
23	Total cash increase (decrease) from financing	$ 500,000	$ -	$ 24,500	$ (25,000)		$ 499,500
24							
25	Ending cash balance	$ 744,989	$ 634,155	$ 904,597	$1,159,793		$1,159,793

	A	B	C	D	E	F	G
	Microsoft Excel - FigA6.7						
	File Edit View Insert Format Tools Data Window Help				Type a question for help		
	A1 ▼ _fx_						
1				Period			
2		1Q X4	2Q X4	3Q X4	4Q X4		X4
3	Sales	$2,750,000	$2,808,000	$2,834,000	$2,886,000		$11,278,000
4	Cost of goods sold	2,000,000	1,955,200	1,940,200	1,831,500		7,726,900
5	Gross profit	$ 750,000	$ 852,800	$ 893,800	$1,054,500		$ 3,551,100
6							
7	Salaries	$ 399,378	$ 399,378	$ 490,888	$ 522,100		$ 1,811,744
8	Miscellaneous expenses	82,500	98,280	99,190	101,010		380,980
9	Research and development	137,500	140,400	141,700	144,300		563,900
10	Rent	16,500	16,500	16,500	16,500		66,000
11	Depreciation	575	983	1,308	1,608		4,475
12	Income from operations	$ 114,122	$ 198,242	$ 145,523	$ 270,590		$ 728,476
13							
14	Interest expense	$ -	$ -	$ 500	$ -		$ 500
15	Taxable income	$ 114,122	$ 198,242	$ 145,023	$ 270,590		$ 727,976
16							
17	Tax expense	$ 37,090	$ 65,420	$ 47,132	$ 89,295		$ 238,936
18	Net income	$ 77,032	$ 132,822	$ 97,890	$ 181,295		$ 489,040
19							

Operating Expenses / Capital / Cash / Balance Sl

Ready

FIGURE A6.7 Completed Income Statement for Company JKL

CHAPTER 7   Financial Budget—Balance Sheet

1. The Asset components of Company MNO's Balance Sheet are shown in Figure A7.1.
2. The Liabilities components of Company MNO's Balance Sheet are shown in Figure A7.2.
3. The Owners' Equity components of Company MNO's Balance Sheet are shown in Figure A7.3.
4. The changes in Company MNO's Net Working Capital are shown in Figure A7.4.

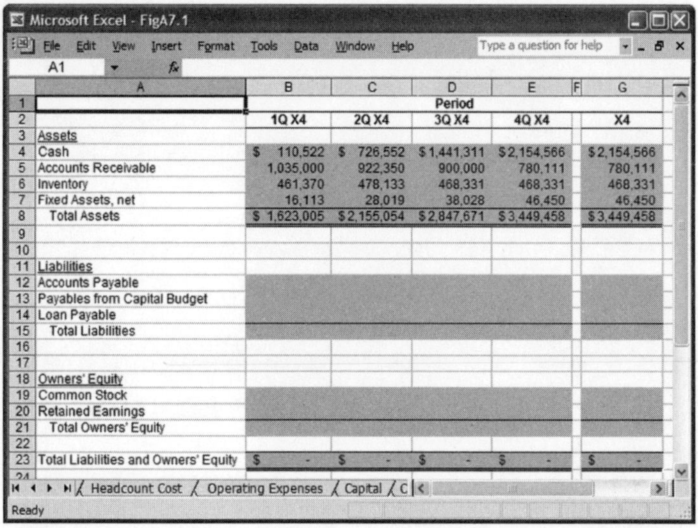

Microsoft Excel - FigA7.1

	A	B	C	D	E	F	G
1				Period			
2		1Q X4	2Q X4	3Q X4	4Q X4		X4
3	Assets						
4	Cash	$ 110,522	$ 726,552	$1,441,311	$2,154,566		$2,154,566
5	Accounts Receivable	1,035,000	922,350	900,000	780,111		780,111
6	Inventory	461,370	478,133	468,331	468,331		468,331
7	Fixed Assets, net	16,113	28,019	38,028	46,450		46,450
8	Total Assets	$ 1,623,005	$2,155,054	$2,847,671	$3,449,458		$3,449,458
9							
10							
11	Liabilities						
12	Accounts Payable						
13	Payables from Capital Budget						
14	Loan Payable						
15	Total Liabilities						
16							
17							
18	Owners' Equity						
19	Common Stock						
20	Retained Earnings						
21	Total Owners' Equity						
22							
23	Total Liabilities and Owners' Equity	$ -	$ -	$ -	$ -		$ -

Headcount Cost / Operating Expenses / Capital / C

Ready

FIGURE A7.1 Asset Components of Company MNO's Balance Sheet

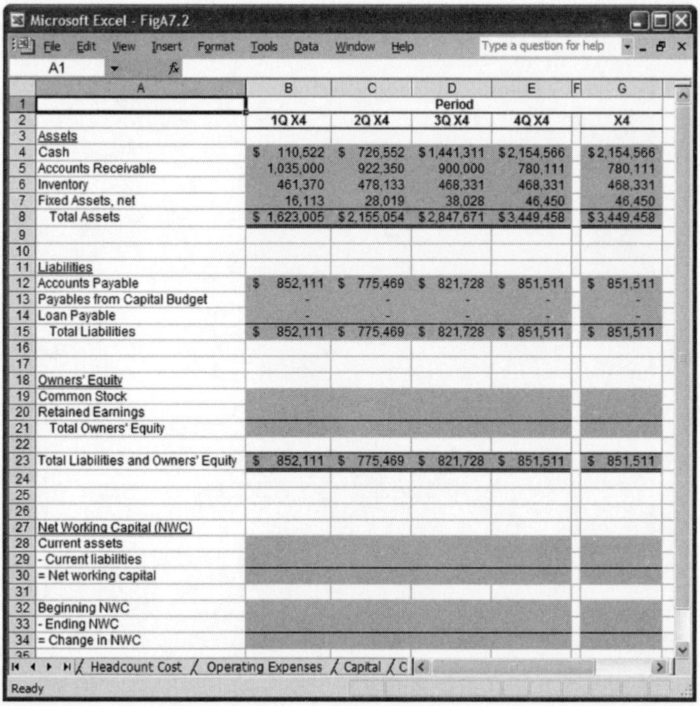

Microsoft Excel - FigA7.2

	A	B	C	D	E	F	G
1				Period			
2		1Q X4	2Q X4	3Q X4	4Q X4		X4
3	Assets						
4	Cash	$ 110,522	$ 726,552	$1,441,311	$2,154,566		$2,154,566
5	Accounts Receivable	1,035,000	922,350	900,000	780,111		780,111
6	Inventory	461,370	478,133	468,331	468,331		468,331
7	Fixed Assets, net	16,113	28,019	38,028	46,450		46,450
8	Total Assets	$ 1,623,005	$2,155,054	$2,847,671	$3,449,458		$3,449,458
9							
10							
11	Liabilities						
12	Accounts Payable	$ 852,111	$ 775,469	$ 821,728	$ 851,511		$ 851,511
13	Payables from Capital Budget	-	-	-	-		-
14	Loan Payable	-	-	-	-		-
15	Total Liabilities	$ 852,111	$ 775,469	$ 821,728	$ 851,511		$ 851,511
16							
17							
18	Owners' Equity						
19	Common Stock						
20	Retained Earnings						
21	Total Owners' Equity						
22							
23	Total Liabilities and Owners' Equity	$ 852,111	$ 775,469	$ 821,728	$ 851,511		$ 851,511
24							
25							
26							
27	Net Working Capital (NWC)						
28	Current assets						
29	- Current liabilities						
30	= Net working capital						
31							
32	Beginning NWC						
33	- Ending NWC						
34	= Change in NWC						

Headcount Cost / Operating Expenses / Capital / C

Ready

FIGURE A7.2 Liabilities Components of Company MNO's Balance Sheet

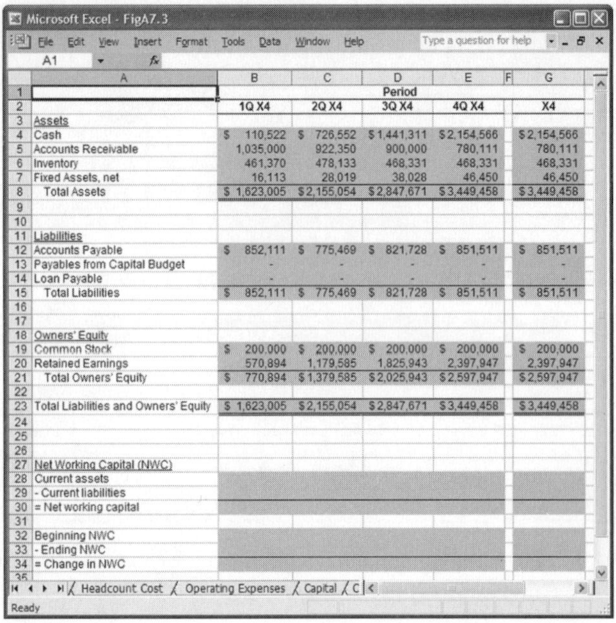

FIGURE A7.3   Owners' Equity Components of Company MNO's Balance Sheet

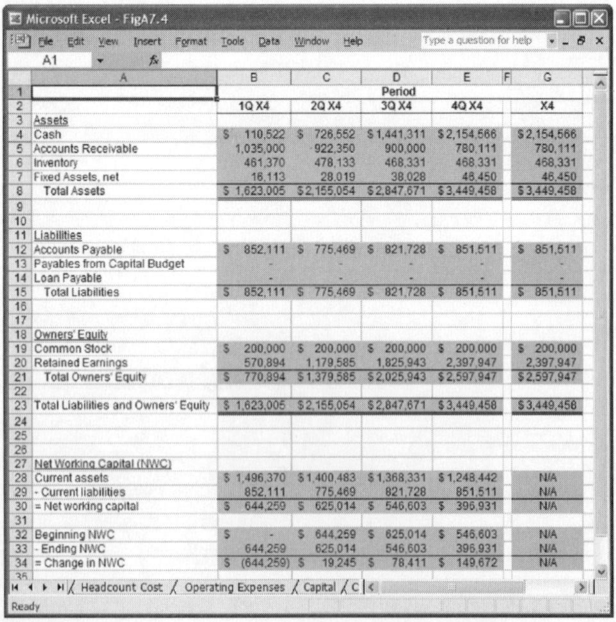

FIGURE A7.4   Changes in Company MNO's Net Working Capital

CHAPTER 8   Consolidated Financial Statements

1. The Cash Flows from Operating Activities in Company PQR's Statement of Cash Flows are shown in Figure A8.1.
2. The Cash Flows from Investing Activities in Company PQR's Statement of Cash Flows are shown in Figure A8.2.
3. The Cash Flows from Financing Activities in Company PQR's Statement of Cash Flows are shown in Figure A8.3.

FIGURE A8.1   Cash Flows from Operating Activities in Company PQR's Statement of Cash Flows

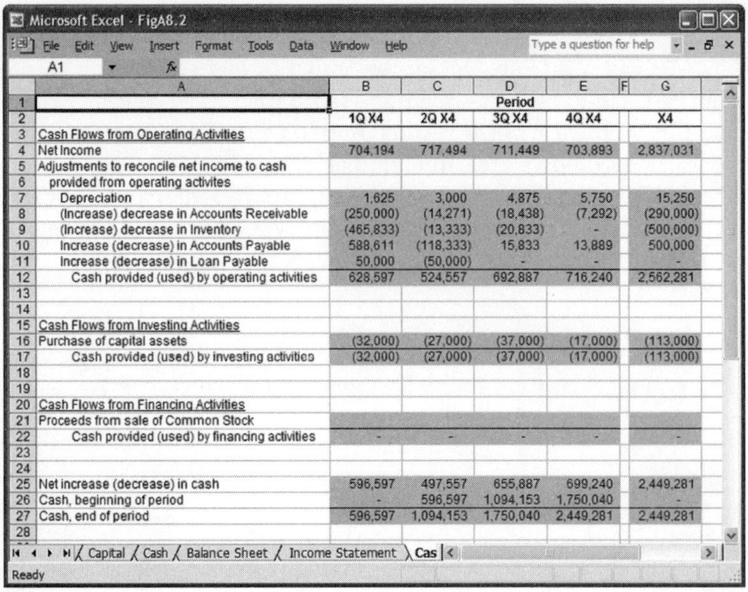

FIGURE A8.2   Cash Flows from Investing Activities in Company PQR's Statement of Cash Flows

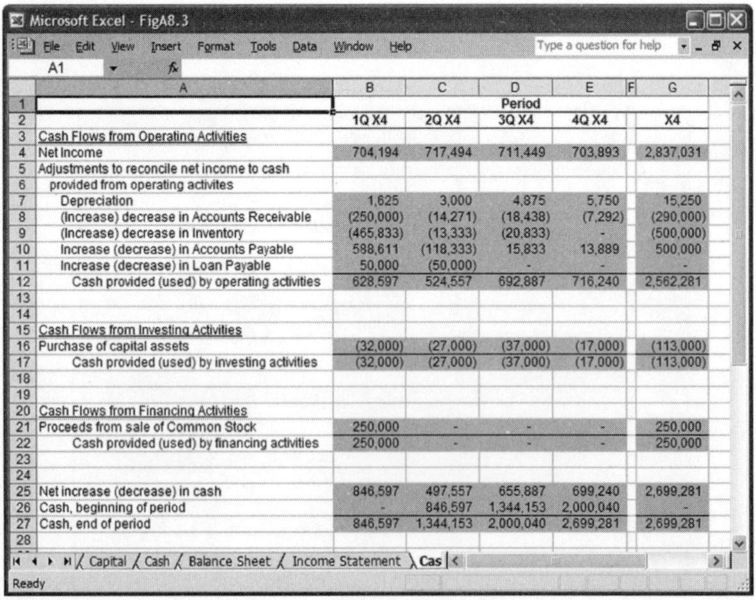

FIGURE A8.3   Cash Flows from Financing Activities in Company PQR's Statement of Cash Flows

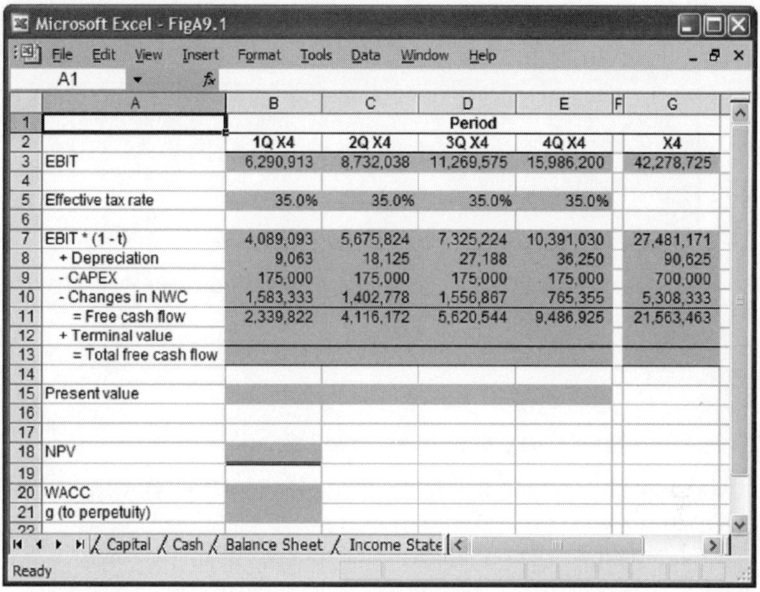

	A	B	C	D	E	G
1				Period		
2		1Q X4	2Q X4	3Q X4	4Q X4	X4
3	EBIT	6,290,913	8,732,038	11,269,575	15,986,200	42,278,725
4						
5	Effective tax rate	35.0%	35.0%	35.0%	35.0%	
6						
7	EBIT * (1 - t)	4,089,093	5,675,824	7,325,224	10,391,030	27,481,171
8	+ Depreciation	9,063	18,125	27,188	36,250	90,625
9	- CAPEX	175,000	175,000	175,000	175,000	700,000
10	- Changes in NWC	1,583,333	1,402,778	1,556,867	765,355	5,308,333
11	= Free cash flow	2,339,822	4,116,172	5,620,544	9,486,925	21,563,463
12	+ Terminal value					
13	= Total free cash flow					
14						
15	Present value					
16						
17						
18	NPV					
19						
20	WACC					
21	g (to perpetuity)					

FIGURE A9.1 Company STU's Free Cash Flows Worksheet

CHAPTER 9 Free Cash Flows and Dashboard

1. Company STU's free cash flows worksheet is shown in Figure A9.1.
2. The Balance Sheet status indicator in Company STU's Assumptions and Dashboard worksheet is shown in Figure A9.2.
3. The Statement of Cash Flows status indicator in Company STU's Assumptions and Dashboard worksheet is shown in Figure A9.3

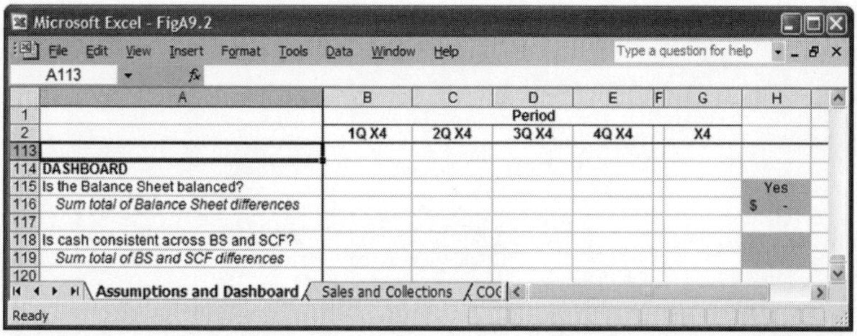

	A	B	C	D	E	G	H
1				Period			
2		1Q X4	2Q X4	3Q X4	4Q X4	X4	
113							
114	DASHBOARD						
115	Is the Balance Sheet balanced?						Yes
116	*Sum total of Balance Sheet differences*						$ -
117							
118	Is cash consistent across BS and SCF?						
119	*Sum total of BS and SCF differences*						

FIGURE A9.2 Balance Sheet Status Indicator in Company STU's Assumptions and Dashboard Worksheet

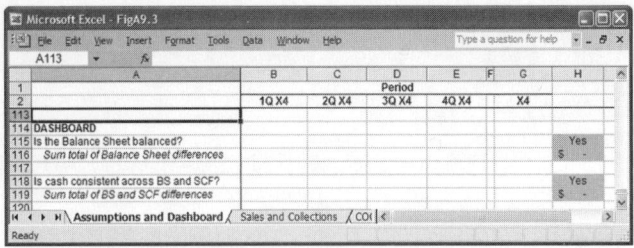

FIGURE A9.3 Statement of Cash Flows Status Indicator in Company STU's Assumptions and Dashboard Worksheet

CHAPTER 10 Sensitivity Analysis

1. The Revenues data table for Company VWX is shown in Figure A10.1.
2. The Net Income data table for Company VWX is shown in Figure A10.2.
3. The Free Cash Flows data table for Company VWX is shown in Figure A10.3.

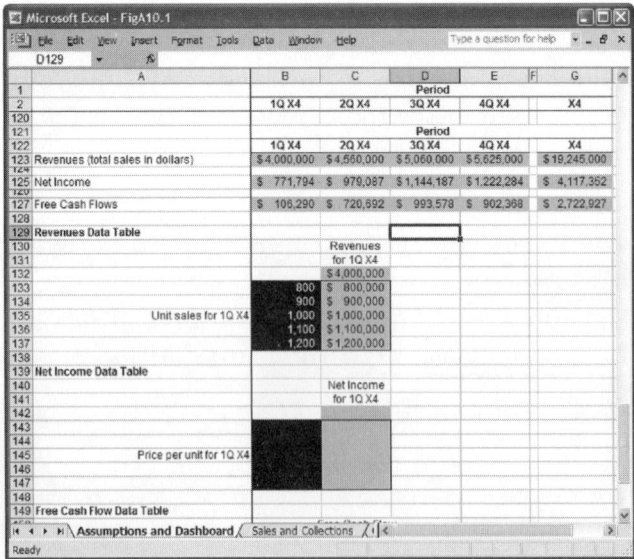

FIGURE A10.1 Revenues Data Table for Company VWX

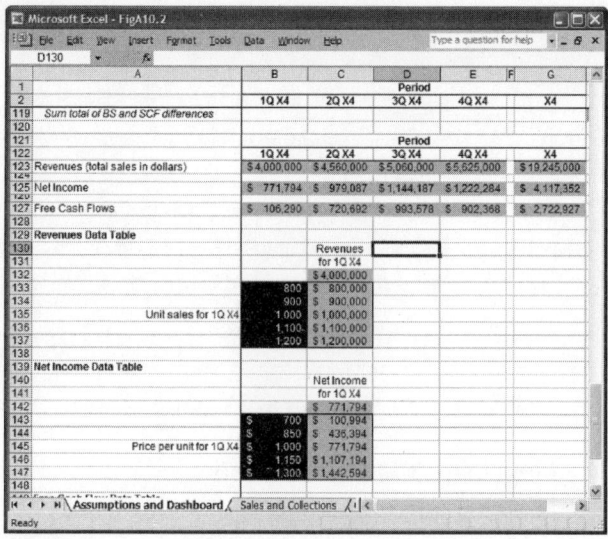

FIGURE A10.2 Net Income Data Table for Company VWX

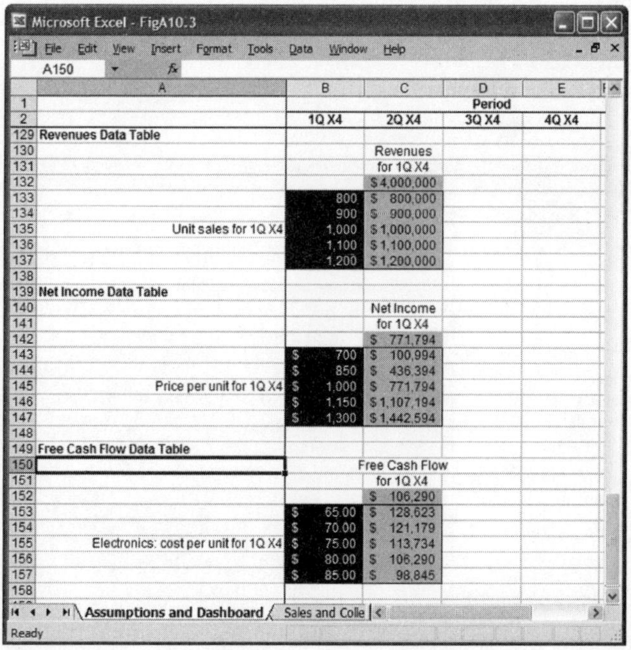

FIGURE A10.3 Free Cash Flows Data Table for Company VWX

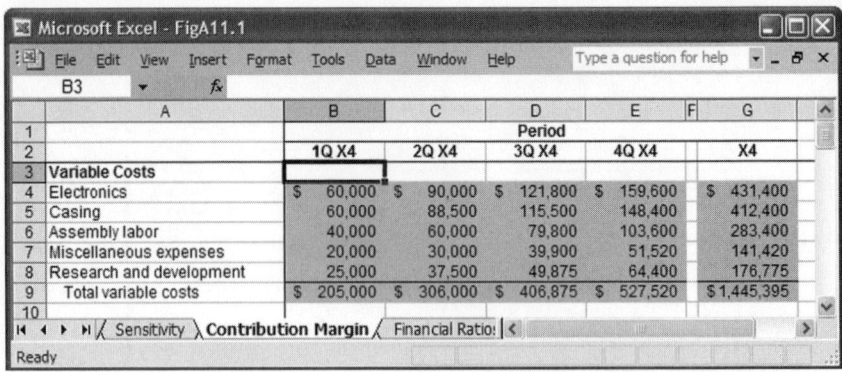

FIGURE A11.1   Company 123's Variable Costs

CHAPTER 11   Contribution Margin Analysis

1. Company 123's variable costs are identified in Figure A11.1.
2. Company 123's fixed costs are identified in Figure A11.2
3. Company 123's contribution margin is calculated and reconciled with Company 123's Net Income in Figure A11.3.
4. Company 123's operating leverage is calculated in Figure A11.4.
5. Company 123's breakeven point in terms of units is calculated in Figure A11.5.
6. Company 123's breakeven point in terms of dollars of revenue is calculated in Figure A11.6.

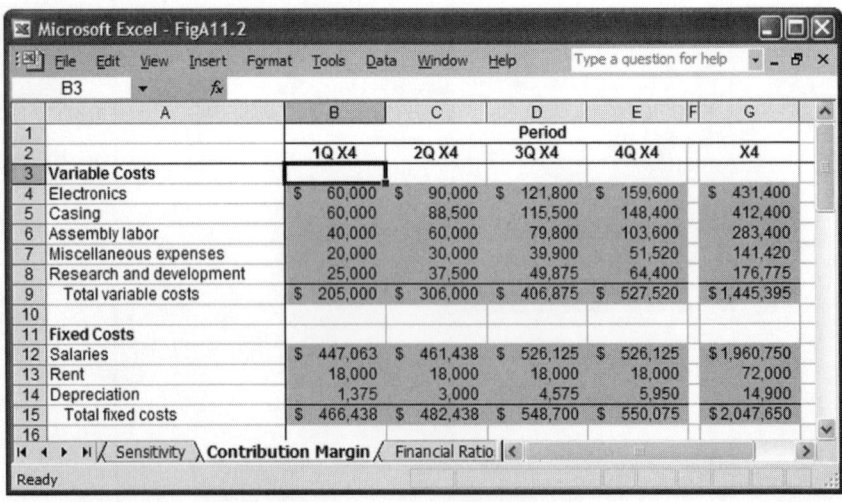

FIGURE A11.2   Company 123's Fixed Costs

	A	B	C	D	E	F	G
1				Period			
2		1Q X4	2Q X4	3Q X4	4Q X4		X4
3	**Variable Costs**						
4	Electronics	$ 60,000	$ 90,000	$ 121,800	$ 159,600		$ 431,400
5	Casing	60,000	88,500	115,500	148,400		412,400
6	Assembly labor	40,000	60,000	79,800	103,600		283,400
7	Miscellaneous expenses	20,000	30,000	39,900	51,520		141,420
8	Research and development	25,000	37,500	49,875	64,400		176,775
9	Total variable costs	$ 205,000	$ 306,000	$ 406,875	$ 527,520		$ 1,445,395
10							
11	**Fixed Costs**						
12	Salaries	$ 447,063	$ 461,438	$ 526,125	$ 526,125		$ 1,960,750
13	Rent	18,000	18,000	18,000	18,000		72,000
14	Depreciation	1,375	3,000	4,575	5,950		14,900
15	Total fixed costs	$ 466,438	$ 482,438	$ 548,700	$ 550,075		$ 2,047,650
16							
17	**Contribution Margin**						
18	Sales	$ 500,000	$ 750,000	$ 997,500	$ 1,288,000		$ 3,535,500
19	- Variable costs	205,000	306,000	406,875	527,520		1,445,395
20	= Contribution margin	$ 295,000	$ 444,000	$ 590,625	$ 760,480		$ 2,090,105
21	- Fixed costs	466,438	482,438	548,700	550,075		2,047,650
22	- Interest expense	813	-	-	-		813
23	- Taxes	(51,675)	(11,531)	14,674	73,642		25,109
24	= Net income	$ (120,575)	$ (26,906)	$ 27,251	$ 136,763		$ 16,533

FIGURE A11.3 Company 123's Contribution Margin and Reconciliation with Net Income

	A	B	C	D	E	F	G
1				Period			
2		1Q X4	2Q X4	3Q X4	4Q X4		X4
17	**Contribution Margin**						
18	Sales	$ 500,000	$ 750,000	$ 997,500	$ 1,288,000		$ 3,535,500
19	- Variable costs	205,000	306,000	406,875	527,520		1,445,395
20	= Contribution margin	$ 295,000	$ 444,000	$ 590,625	$ 760,480		$ 2,090,105
21	- Fixed costs	466,438	482,438	548,700	550,075		2,047,650
22	- Interest expense	813	-	-	-		813
23	- Taxes	(51,675)	(11,531)	14,674	73,642		25,109
24	= Net income	$ (120,575)	$ (26,906)	$ 27,251	$ 136,763		$ 16,533
25							
26	**Operating Leverage**						
27	Fixed costs	$ 466,438	$ 482,438	$ 548,700	$ 550,075		$ 2,047,650
28	Total costs (fixed + variable)	$ 671,438	$ 788,438	$ 955,575	$ 1,077,595		$ 3,493,045
30	Operating leverage	69.5%	61.2%	57.4%	51.0%		58.6%

FIGURE A11.4 Company 123's Operating Leverage

FIGURE A11.5 Company 123's Breakeven Point in Terms of Units

FIGURE A11.6 Company 123's Breakeven Point in Terms of Dollars of Revenue

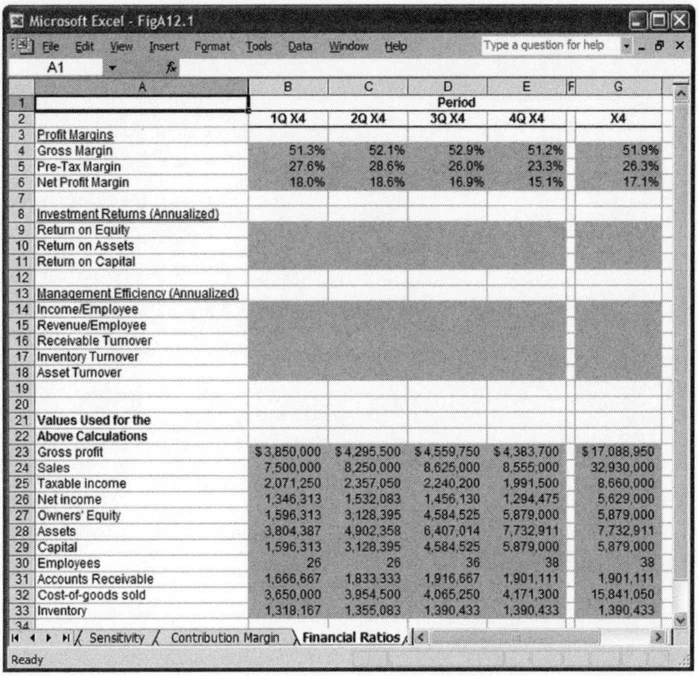

	Period				
	1Q X4	2Q X4	3Q X4	4Q X4	X4
Profit Margins					
Gross Margin	51.3%	52.1%	52.9%	51.2%	51.9%
Pre-Tax Margin	27.6%	28.6%	26.0%	23.3%	26.3%
Net Profit Margin	18.0%	18.6%	16.9%	15.1%	17.1%
Investment Returns (Annualized)					
Return on Equity					
Return on Assets					
Return on Capital					
Management Efficiency (Annualized)					
Income/Employee					
Revenue/Employee					
Receivable Turnover					
Inventory Turnover					
Asset Turnover					
Values Used for the					
Above Calculations					
Gross profit	$3,850,000	$4,295,500	$4,559,750	$4,383,700	$17,088,950
Sales	7,500,000	8,250,000	8,625,000	8,555,000	32,930,000
Taxable income	2,071,250	2,357,050	2,240,200	1,991,500	8,660,000
Net income	1,346,313	1,532,083	1,456,130	1,294,475	5,629,000
Owners' Equity	1,596,313	3,128,395	4,584,525	5,879,000	5,879,000
Assets	3,804,387	4,902,358	6,407,014	7,732,911	7,732,911
Capital	1,596,313	3,128,395	4,584,525	5,879,000	5,879,000
Employees	26	26	36	38	38
Accounts Receivable	1,666,667	1,833,333	1,916,667	1,901,111	1,901,111
Cost-of-goods sold	3,650,000	3,954,500	4,065,250	4,171,300	15,841,050
Inventory	1,318,167	1,355,083	1,390,433	1,390,433	1,390,433

FIGURE A12.1 Company 456's Gross Margin, Pre-Tax Margin, and Net Profit Margin

CHAPTER 12 Financial Ratios Analysis

1. Company 456's Gross Margin, Pre-Tax Margin, and Net Profit Margin are calculated in Figure A12.1.
2. Company 456's Return on Equity, Return on Assets, and Return on Capital are calculated in Figure A12.2.
3. Company 456's Income per Employee, Revenue per Employee, Receivable Turnover, Inventory Turnover, and Asset Turnover are calculated in Figure A12.3.

	1Q X4	2Q X4	3Q X4	4Q X4	X4
Profit Margins					
Gross Margin	51.3%	52.1%	52.9%	51.2%	51.9%
Pre-Tax Margin	27.6%	28.6%	26.0%	23.3%	26.3%
Net Profit Margin	18.0%	18.6%	16.9%	15.1%	17.1%
Investment Returns (Annualized)					
Return on Equity	337.4%	195.9%	127.0%	88.1%	95.7%
Return on Assets	141.6%	125.0%	90.9%	67.0%	72.8%
Return on Capital	337.4%	195.9%	127.0%	88.1%	95.7%
Management Efficiency (Annualized)					
Income/Employee					
Revenue/Employee					
Receivable Turnover					
Inventory Turnover					
Asset Turnover					
Values Used for the Above Calculations					
Gross profit	$3,850,000	$4,295,500	$4,559,750	$4,383,700	$17,088,950
Sales	7,500,000	8,250,000	8,625,000	8,555,000	32,930,000
Taxable income	2,071,250	2,357,050	2,240,200	1,991,500	8,660,000
Net income	1,346,313	1,532,083	1,456,130	1,294,475	5,629,000
Owners' Equity	1,596,313	3,128,395	4,584,525	5,879,000	5,879,000
Assets	3,804,387	4,902,358	6,407,014	7,732,911	7,732,911
Capital	1,596,313	3,128,395	4,584,525	5,879,000	5,879,000
Employees	26	26	36	38	38
Accounts Receivable	1,666,667	1,833,333	1,916,667	1,901,111	1,901,111
Cost-of-goods sold	3,650,000	3,954,500	4,065,250	4,171,300	15,841,050
Inventory	1,318,167	1,355,083	1,390,433	1,390,433	1,390,433

FIGURE A12.2 Company 456's Return on Equity, Return on Assets, and Return on Capital

	1Q X4	2Q X4	3Q X4	4Q X4	X4
Profit Margins					
Gross Margin	51.3%	52.1%	52.9%	51.2%	51.9%
Pre-Tax Margin	27.6%	28.6%	26.0%	23.3%	26.3%
Net Profit Margin	18.0%	18.6%	16.9%	15.1%	17.1%
Investment Returns (Annualized)					
Return on Equity	337.4%	195.9%	127.0%	88.1%	95.7%
Return on Assets	141.6%	125.0%	90.9%	67.0%	72.8%
Return on Capital	337.4%	195.9%	127.0%	88.1%	95.7%
Management Efficiency (Annualized)					
Income/Employee	$ 207,125	$ 235,705	$ 161,792	$ 136,261	$ 148,132
Revenue/Employee	$1,153,846	$1,269,231	$ 958,333	$ 900,526	$ 866,579
Receivable Turnover	18.0	18.0	18.0	18.0	17.3
Inventory Turnover	11.1	11.7	11.7	12.0	11.4
Asset Turnover	7.9	6.7	5.4	4.4	4.3
Values Used for the Above Calculations					
Gross profit	$3,850,000	$4,295,500	$4,559,750	$4,383,700	$17,088,950
Sales	7,500,000	8,250,000	8,625,000	8,555,000	32,930,000
Taxable income	2,071,250	2,357,050	2,240,200	1,991,500	8,660,000
Net income	1,346,313	1,532,083	1,456,130	1,294,475	5,629,000
Owners' Equity	1,596,313	3,128,395	4,584,525	5,879,000	5,879,000
Assets	3,804,387	4,902,358	6,407,014	7,732,911	7,732,911
Capital	1,596,313	3,128,395	4,584,525	5,879,000	5,879,000
Employees	26	26	36	38	38
Accounts Receivable	1,666,667	1,833,333	1,916,667	1,901,111	1,901,111
Cost-of-goods sold	3,650,000	3,954,500	4,065,250	4,171,300	15,841,050
Inventory	1,318,167	1,355,083	1,390,433	1,390,433	1,390,433

FIGURE A12.3 Company 456's Income Per Employee, Revenue Per Employee, Receivables Turnover, Inventory Turnover, and Asset Turnover

CHAPTER 13   Valuation

1. Company 456's total free cash flows are calculated in Figure A13.1.
2. Company 456's Net Present Value is calculated in Figure A13.2.
3. The multiples of (i) sales, (ii) Net Income, and (iii) free cash flows for each of the comparable public companies, along with a calculation for median values associated with these metrics, are calculated in Figure A13.3.
4. Company 456's public company comparable valuation is calculated in Figure A13.4.
5. The multiples of (i) sales, (ii) Net Income, and (iii) Asset values for each of the mergers and acquisitions transactions, along with a calculation for median values associated with these metrics, and the fictitious stock index, are calculated in Figure A13.5.
6. Company 456's mergers and acquisitions comparable valuation is calculated in Figure A13.6.
7. Company 456's weighted valuations and total valuation are calculated in Figure A13.7.

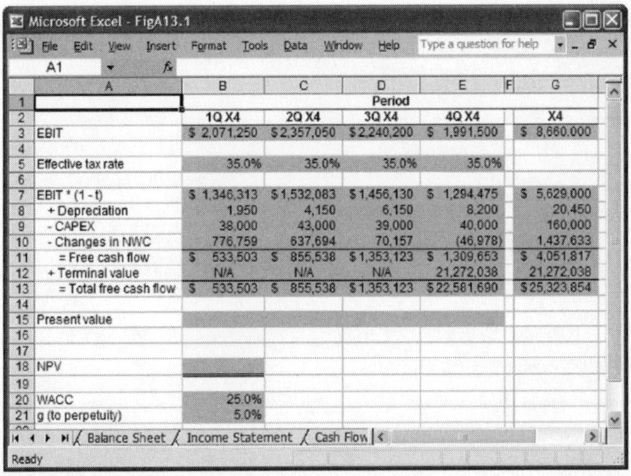

FIGURE A13.1   Company 456's Total Free Cash Flows

	A	B	C	D	E	F	G
1				Period			
2		1Q X4	2Q X4	3Q X4	4Q X4		X4
3	EBIT	$ 2,071,250	$ 2,357,050	$ 2,240,200	$ 1,991,500		$ 8,660,000
4							
5	Effective tax rate	35.0%	35.0%	35.0%	35.0%		
6							
7	EBIT * (1 - t)	$ 1,346,313	$ 1,532,083	$ 1,456,130	$ 1,294,475		$ 5,629,000
8	+ Depreciation	1,950	4,150	6,150	8,200		20,450
9	- CAPEX	38,000	43,000	39,000	40,000		160,000
10	- Changes in NWC	776,759	637,694	70,157	(46,978)		1,437,633
11	= Free cash flow	$ 533,503	$ 855,538	$ 1,353,123	$ 1,309,653		$ 4,051,817
12	+ Terminal value	N/A	N/A	N/A	21,272,038		21,272,038
13	= Total free cash flow	$ 533,503	$ 855,538	$ 1,353,123	$ 22,581,690		$ 25,323,854
14							
15	Present value	$ 504,556	$ 765,216	$ 1,144,602	$ 18,065,352		
16							
17							
18	NPV	$ 20,479,727					
19							
20	WACC	25.0%					
21	g (to perpetuity)	5.0%					

FIGURE A13.2 Company 456's Net Present Value

	A	B	C	D	E	F	G	H	I	J
1	Public Company Comparables									
2										
3								Multiple of Projected		
4				Projected (Next 4 Quarters)				(Next 4 Quarters):		
5		Valuation			Net	Free Cash			Net	Free Cash
6		(Price)		Sales	Income	Flows		Sales	Income	Flows
7	Direct Competitors									
8	Competitor 1	$ 100,000,000		$ 110,000,000	$ 11,000,000	$ 12,000,000		0.91	9.09	8.33
9	Competitor 2	$ 90,000,000		$ 105,000,000	$ 10,000,000	$ 11,000,000		0.86	9.00	8.18
10	Competitor 3	$ 80,000,000		$ 95,000,000	$ 10,000,000	$ 10,500,000		0.84	8.00	7.62
11	Median	$ 90,000,000		$ 105,000,000	$ 10,000,000	$ 11,000,000		0.86	9.00	8.18
12										
13	Stock Index									
14	Stock Index	$ 800,000,000		$ 900,000,000	$ 90,000,000	$ 100,000,000		0.89	8.89	8.00

FIGURE A13.3 Multiple and Median Calculations For Public Company Comparables

Answers to Chapter Questions

FIGURE A13.4   Company 456's Public Company Comparable Valuation

Microsoft Excel - FigA13.4

File Edit View Insert Format Tools Data Window Help

A1   *fx* Public Company Comparables

	A	B	C	D	E	F	G	H	I	J
1	Public Company Comparables									
2										
3									Multiple of Projected	
4					Projected (Next 4 Quarters)				(Next 4 Quarters):	
5		Valuation			Net	Free Cash			Net	Free Cash
6		(Price)		Sales	Income	Flows		Sales	Income	Flows
7	Direct Competitors									
8	Competitor 1	$ 100,000,000		$ 110,000,000	$ 11,000,000	$ 12,000,000		0.91	9.09	8.33
9	Competitor 2	$ 90,000,000		$ 105,000,000	$ 10,000,000	$ 11,000,000		0.86	9.00	8.18
10	Competitor 3	$ 80,000,000		$ 95,000,000	$ 10,000,000	$ 10,500,000		0.84	8.00	7.62
11	Median	$ 90,000,000		$ 105,000,000	$ 10,000,000	$ 11,000,000		0.86	9.00	8.18
12										
13	Stock Index									
14	Stock Index	$ 800,000,000		$ 900,000,000	$ 90,000,000	$ 100,000,000		0.89	8.89	8.00
15										
16				Valuation Based Upon Median Multiples						
17				and Projected (Next 4 Quarters):						
18					Net	Free Cash				
19				Sales	Income	Flows				
20	Napavale									
21	Direct competitors median multiples			$ 28,225,714	$ 50,661,000	$ 33,151,227				
22	Stock index multiples			$ 29,271,111	$ 50,035,556	$ 32,414,533				
23										

|◄ ◄ ► ►|\ Sensitivity / Contribution Margin / Financial Ratios / Valuatio |<

Ready

FIGURE A13.5   Multiple and Median Calculations for Mergers and Acquisitions

Microsoft Excel - FigA13.5

File Edit View Insert Format Tools Data Window Help

A25   *fx* Mergers and Acquisitions Comparables

	A	B	C	D	E	F	G	H	I	J
25	Mergers and Acquisitions Comparables									
26										
27									Multiple of Projected	
28					Projected (Next 4 Quarters)				(Next 4 Quarters):	
29		Valuation			Net				Net	
30		(Price)		Sales	Income	Assets		Sales	Income	Assets
31	Target Companies									
32	Company 1	$ 75,000,000		$ 80,000,000	$ 8,000,000	$ 80,000,000		0.94	9.38	0.94
33	Company 2	$ 60,000,000		$ 71,000,000	$ 7,500,000	$ 70,000,000		0.85	8.00	0.86
34	Company 3	$ 55,000,000		$ 62,000,000	$ 7,000,000	$ 90,000,000		0.89	7.86	0.61
35	Median	$ 60,000,000		$ 71,000,000	$ 7,500,000	$ 80,000,000		0.89	8.00	0.86
36										
37				Valuation Based Upon Median Multiples						
38				and Projected (Next 4 Quarters):						
39					Net					
40				Sales	Income	Assets				
41	Napavale									
42	Target companies median multiples									
43										

|◄ ◄ ► ►|\ Contribution Margin / Financial Ratios / Valuation \Compara |<

Ready

FIGURE A13.6   Company 456's Mergers and Acquisitions Comparable Valuation

FIGURE A13.7   Company 456's Weighted Valuations and Total Valuation

CHAPTER 14   Capitalization Chart

1. Company 456's founding Capitalization Chart is shown in Figure A14.1.

2. Company 456's post–equity investment Capitalization Chart is shown in Figure A14.2.

3. Company 456's post–stock options issuance Capitalization Chart is shown in Figure A14.3.

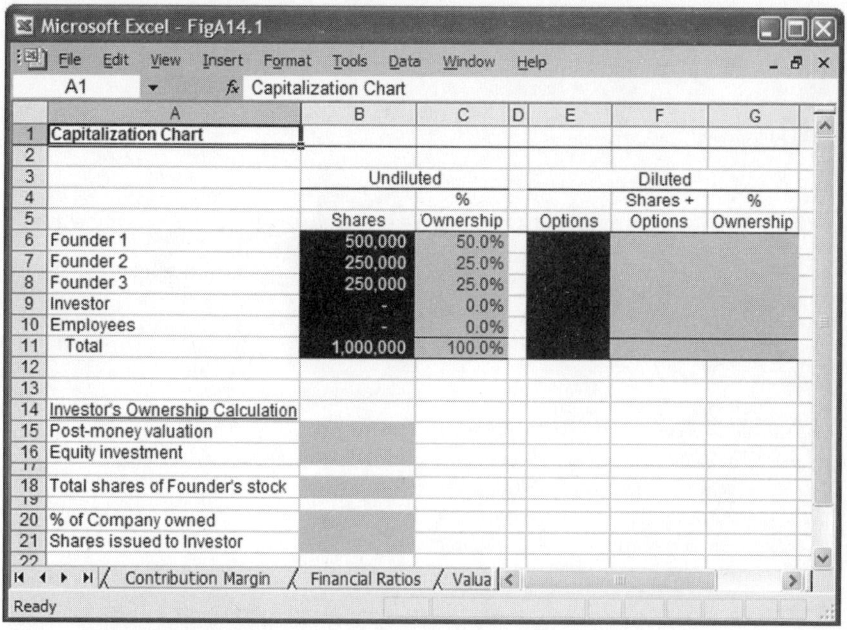

FIGURE A14.1   Company 456's Founding Capitalization Chart

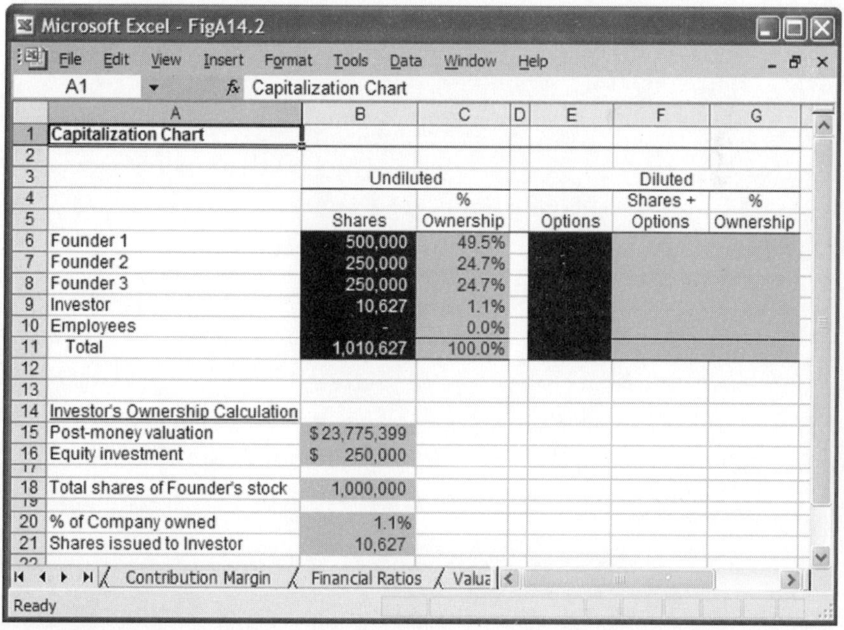

FIGURE A14.2   Company 456's Post–Equity Investment Capitalization Chart

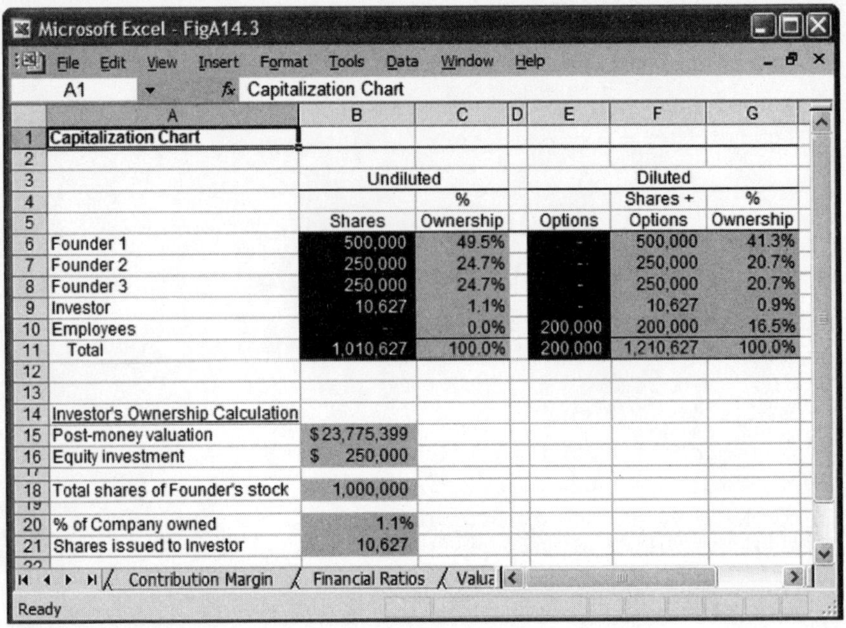

Microsoft Excel - FigA14.3

File Edit View Insert Format Tools Data Window Help

A1 ▼ ƒx Capitalization Chart

	A	B	C	D	E	F	G
1	**Capitalization Chart**						
2							
3		Undiluted				Diluted	
4			%			Shares +	%
5		Shares	Ownership		Options	Options	Ownership
6	Founder 1	500,000	49.5%		-	500,000	41.3%
7	Founder 2	250,000	24.7%		--	250,000	20.7%
8	Founder 3	250,000	24.7%		-	250,000	20.7%
9	Investor	10,627	1.1%		-	10,627	0.9%
10	Employees	-	0.0%		200,000	200,000	16.5%
11	Total	1,010,627	100.0%		200,000	1,210,627	100.0%
12							
13							
14	Investor's Ownership Calculation						
15	Post-money valuation	$ 23,775,399					
16	Equity investment	$ 250,000					
17							
18	Total shares of Founder's stock	1,000,000					
19							
20	% of Company owned	1.1%					
21	Shares issued to Investor	10,627					
22							

◄ ► ►◄ Contribution Margin ╱ Financial Ratios ╱ Valua ◄

Ready

FIGURE A14.3 Company 456's Post–Stock Options Issuance Capitalization Chart

General Overview of Microsoft Excel Features and Functionality

This appendix provides a targeted overview of Microsoft Excel features and functionality related to building financial models. While many full-length books on the market today cover each feature of Microsoft Excel in detail, this appendix covers the most frequently used features of Excel at a general level. As this book assumes a basic level of understanding of Microsoft Excel, this appendix should serve as a reference and/or starting point from which you can delve more deeply into the vast capabilities of Excel.

This appendix is divided into four sections: (1) Basic Functionality, (2) Formatting, (3) Formulas and Functions, and (4) Advanced Features. While I use Excel 2003 throughout this appendix to demonstrate Excel's features and functionality, the vast majority of these features and functions are available in earlier versions of Excel, such as Excel 2000 and Excel XP.

BASIC FUNCTIONALITY

Microsoft Excel files are also referred to as "workbooks." These files, which end with the ".xls" extension, store and organize information. Microsoft Excel's basic functionality includes creating, modifying, viewing, and saving information.

Keyboard Shortcuts

Microsoft Excel offers many keyboard shortcuts to execute certain tasks. Navigating menus and executing commands using these shortcuts can save you time and effort as you build financial models in Excel.

The menu bar in Excel lists a series of drop-down menus—the specific menus that appear in your version of Excel will depend on a number of factors, such as your version of Excel and your operating system. Figure AP1 shows the menu bar for Microsoft Excel 2003 running in Microsoft Windows XP Home Edition.

The menu bar runs across the top of the screenshot and contains selections such as "File" and "Edit." Each of the menus in Figure AP1 has one letter underlined—"File" has the *F* underlined and "Edit" has the *E* underlined, for example. By pressing the ALT key on your keyboard and then the underlined letter for the menu of interest (e.g. pressing ALT + F for "File"), a drop-down menu will appear. Figure AP2 presents a view of this File drop-down menu.

Many of the options that appear in the drop-down menu will also have a letter underlined. You may simply type the letter of interest and that option will execute. Using the File menu above, for example, once the drop-down menu appears, you can type the letter *N* on your keyboard to start a new document (because the new document command appears as "<u>N</u>ew . . ." in the File drop-down menu).

New, Open, Close, and Save

Once the Microsoft Excel application is open on your computer, you may (among many other tasks) create a new workbook, open an existing workbook, close any open workbooks, and save any open workbooks. Each of these tasks may be accomplished using the File menu.

Click on the File menu (or use the keyboard shortcut technique mentioned above) and then select the option of interest. Selecting "New" allows you to start a new workbook. Selecting "Open" allows to you open an existing workbook—a dialog box will appear after you select "Open" through which you can navigate to the file of interest. If you select "Close," the workbook on which you are working will close. Be sure to

FIGURE AP1   Menu Bar for Excel 2003

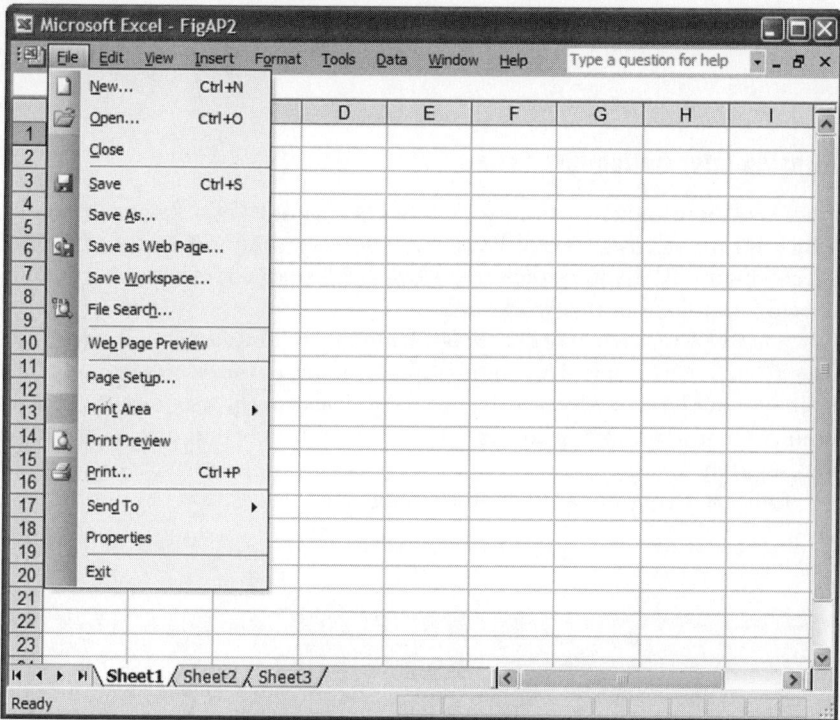

FIGURE AP2   File Drop-Down Menu

save any desired changes to your workbook before closing the file if you would like to save the changes you have made since you last saved the file.

Selecting "Save" from the File drop-down menu will save the workbook on which you are working. If you have not saved the workbook previously, a dialog box will appear asking you to name the file and select the location in which you would like to save the file. You may also select "Save As" from the File drop-down menu—this allows you to save your workbook in another format or in another location.

Viewing Information

Excel allows you to "zoom," or change the size/magnification, into or out of workbooks. Given the wide range of monitor resolutions that people use today, it is often helpful to change the zoom settings of a workbook. To change the zoom settings within Excel, select the "View" menu and choose the "Zoom . . ." option. A dialog box will appear listing a variety of zoom settings—choose the setting that best suits your preferences. Figure AP3 shows a typical zoom dialog box (with 75% selected for the magnification).

Entering Information into Cells

Each cell in an Excel workbook represents a unique location, or place, in which information is stored. Excel workbooks contain at least one worksheet—Figure AP4 shows the three worksheets (named Sheet1, Sheet2, and Sheet3) contained in this workbook.

Each cell in each worksheet is identified by a column and row "address" such as cell A1. The address of the active (or selected) cell appears in the "name box," which in Figure AP4 is shown directly above the column A identifier and appears as "A1." This indicates that cell A1 is active and selected.

Cells may contain, among other things, numeric values, text, formulas,

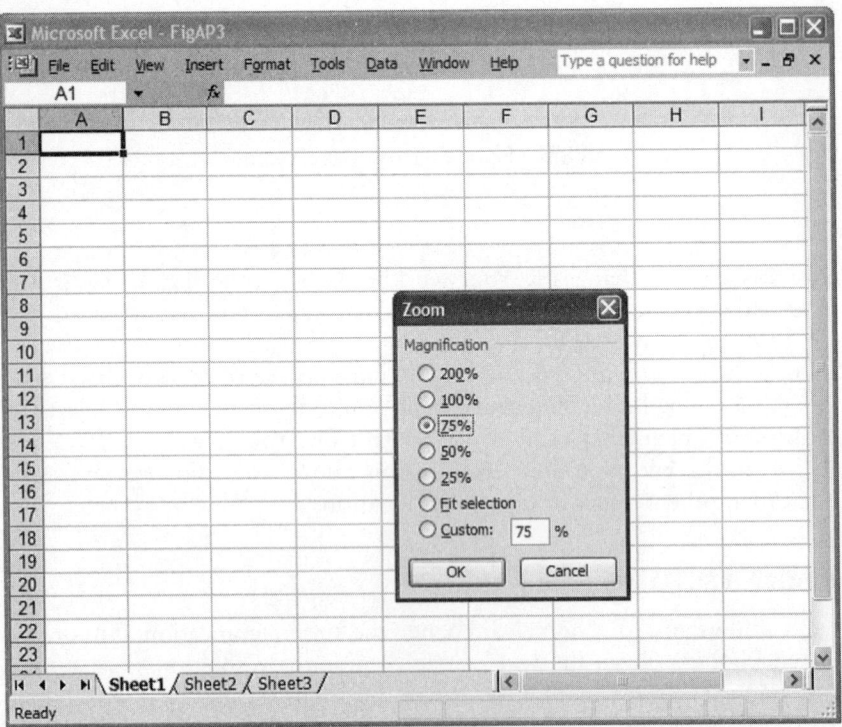

FIGURE AP3   Zoom Dialog Box

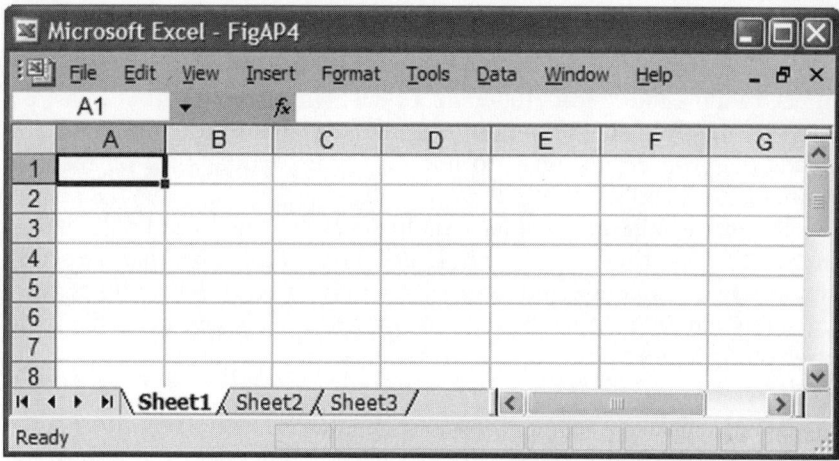

FIGURE AP4   Worksheets in Excel Workbook

functions, or hyperlinks, or they may be empty. Entering information into cells is an important and straightforward task. Information is entered into cells by first selecting the cell of interest (by clicking on that cell). You may then either type the information directly into the active cell or first click in the "formula bar," which is shown in Figure AP4 as the empty white box directly to the right of "fx."

How you enter information in a cell is determined by the type of information that you are entering. You may enter a number directly—for example, to enter the number 211, you may type 211 directly into a cell. You may also type text directly into cells. Entering formulas and functions requires that you first type in the "=" sign—additional information regarding the use of formulas and functions is provided later in this appendix.

Copy, Cut, and Paste

Copying, cutting, and pasting information in Excel are common tasks. Copying information leaves the source data intact, while cutting information removes the source data. You may access all of these features through the Edit menu in Excel or you can use several well-known keyboard shortcuts. The shortcuts are as follows: (1) cut = CTRL + X, (2) copy = CTRL + C, and (3) paste = CTRL + V. CTRL stands for the "Control" key on your keyboard and the "+" indicates that you should press the CTRL key and the subsequent letter in the above examples while holding down the CTRL key.

Undo and Redo

It is easy to make mistakes in Microsoft Excel. Thankfully, the application offers "undo" and "redo" functions to deal with mistakes. If you make a mistake, simply click on the Edit menu in Excel and select "Undo." If you decide that you do not want to undo a certain action, click on the Edit menu in Excel and select "Redo."

Recent versions of Excel have multiple levels of undo and redo, meaning you can undo and redo a number of actions. Please note that the action steps that you can undo and redo are reset after you save a file. In essence, the undo and redo memory is erased anytime a file is saved (the file itself, however, will be saved).

Insert, Remove, and Move Columns and Rows

You may insert, remove, and move columns and rows in Microsoft Excel. To insert a column or row, select the "Insert" menu and choose either column or row from the drop-down menu.

To remove or move columns or rows, you must first select the column or row of interest. To do so, click on the column or row header of interest. Figure AP5 shows row 3 as selected—this is evident as the entire row is highlighted. Click on the row number itself ("3" in Figure AP5) to select an entire row (and click on a column number to select an entire column).

You may also select several columns or several rows at the same time

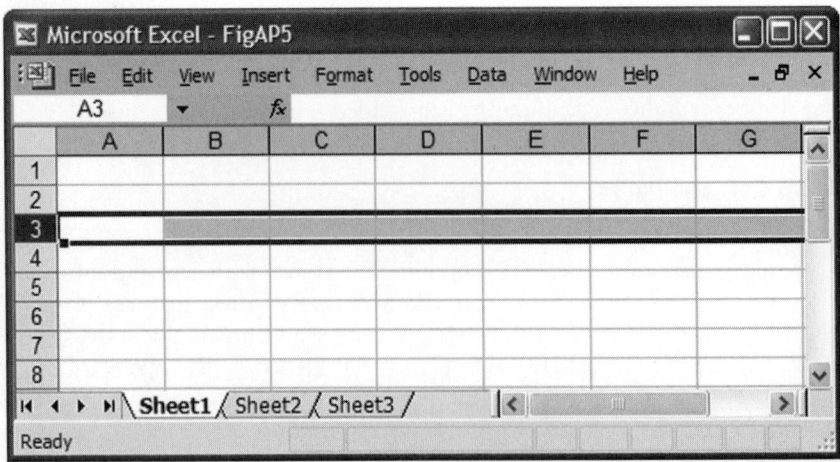

FIGURE AP5   Row 3 Selected

by clicking on the first column or row and then, while holding the left mouse button down, dragging the cursor over the other columns or rows of interest. You can select noncontiguous columns or rows simultaneously by clicking on the first column or row of interest and then, while holding down the CTRL key, selecting the other columns or rows of interest. Holding down the SHIFT key while doing this selects all of the columns or rows between the last column or row selected and the column or row on which you subsequently click.

Naming Worksheets

It is often helpful to name the worksheets in a workbook. To do so, double-click on the worksheet tab at the bottom of the Excel window. This will highlight the current name of the selected worksheet. You may then type in a new name for the worksheet. The three worksheets in Figure AP6 have been renamed "Monday," "Tuesday," and "Wednesday."

FIGURE AP6   Three Named Worksheets

Naming Cells and Cell Ranges

The ability to name cells and cell ranges is a useful and powerful feature embedded in Excel. Cell references (discussed later in this appendix) are used regularly when building financial models—the use of names instead of obscure cell references, such as $AC165, makes it easier to build and modify models.

The easiest way to name a cell or a range of cells is to use the Name Box in Excel. The Name Box is typically found directly above the label for Column A in the worksheet.

To name a cell or a range of cells, select the cell or range of cells that you would like to name and then click on the Name Box in your worksheet. Next, simply type in your desired name for the cell or range of cells. Note that you may not use any spaces in this name. Figure AP7 shows that cell A1 has now been named "Home"—you can see the name "Home" in the name box.

You may also name cells and ranges of cells by first selecting the cell or

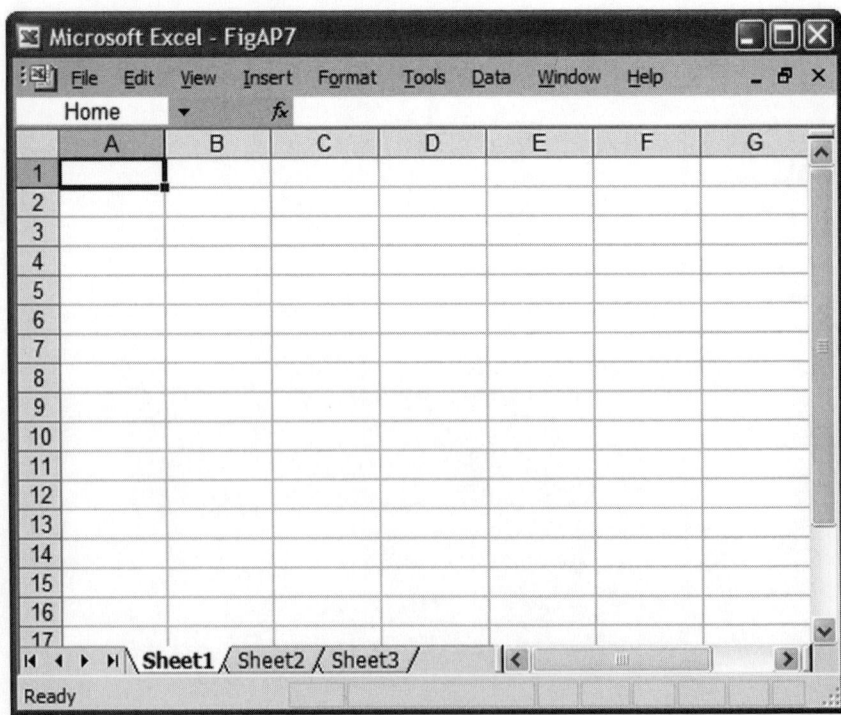

FIGURE AP7   Named Worksheet Cell

range of cells of interest and then selecting the Insert menu, choosing the "Name" option and then selecting the "Define" option. You may then enter in your name of choice for the cell or range of cells.

FORMATTING

Excel offers a wide range of formatting options for worksheets and for information within cells.

Cell Height and Width

You may change the height and width of any cell within Excel. To change the height of a cell, you can either click and drag the line separating the row numbers at the left side of the worksheet or select the "Format" menu and choose "Row" and then choose "Height"—enter your desired height setting into the dialog box that appears. To "auto-fit" a row to include all of the contents in the row, double-click on the bottom of the line separating the row of interest from the subsequent row (click beneath the row number label).

To change the width of a cell, you can either click and drag the line separating the column numbers on the top of the worksheet or select the Format menu and choose "Column" and then choose "Width"—enter your desired width setting into the dialog box that appears. To auto-fit a column to include all of the contents in the column, double-click on the line to the right of the column of interest (click to the right of the column letter label).

Alignment

You can align the contents of a cell in many different ways. To see the alignment options for a cell, select the Format menu and choose "Cells . . ." from the drop-down menu. Next, click on the "Alignment" tab in the dialog box that appears. Figure AP8 shows the alignment options.

As Figure AP8 indicates, you have the ability to control (1) the horizontal alignment of the cell's contents, (2) the vertical alignment of the cell's contents, (3) the orientation (e.g. horizontal versus vertical) of the cell's contents, and (4) text control options, among other features.

Number Format

The ability to alter the numerical format of a cell's contents is one of Excel's more powerful formatting features. This feature allows you to specify

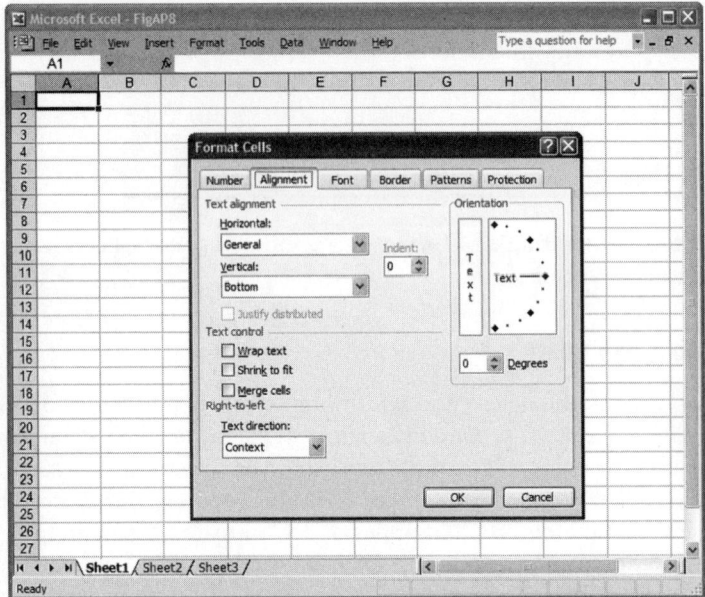

FIGURE AP8   Alignment Options

if, for example, a cell contains a date, a percentage, a dollar figure, or a basic number, among several other formats.

To see the number formatting options for a cell, select the Format menu and choose "Cells . . ." from the drop-down menu. Next, click on the "Number" tab in the dialog box that appears. Figure AP9 shows the number format options. The available number formats are listed in the "Category:" section of this dialog box. You can see the formatting choices available within each of these categories by selecting a specific category. Figure AP10 highlights the suboptions available for formatting a number in "Currency" format.

Font Format

Excel also provides for a wide range of font formatting options. These options control how the font within a selected cell (or selected cells) appears. To see the font formatting options for a cell, select the Format menu and choose "Cells . . ." from the drop-down menu. Next, click on the "Font"

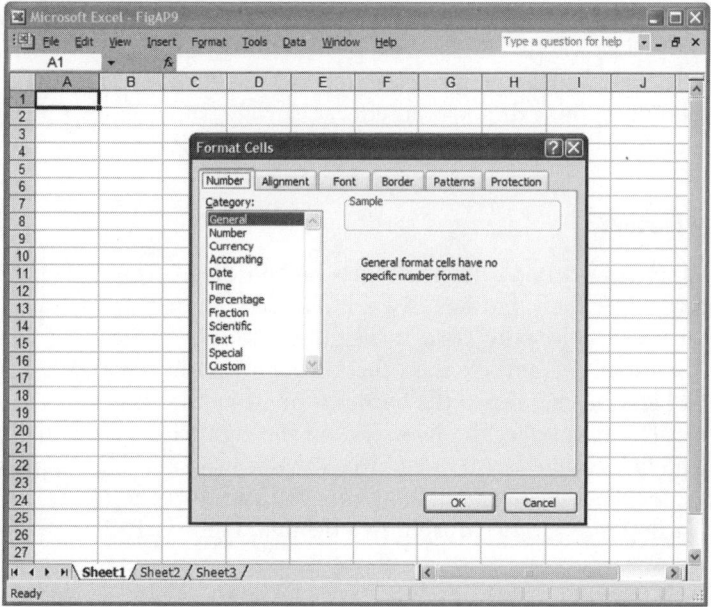

FIGURE AP9   Formatting Options

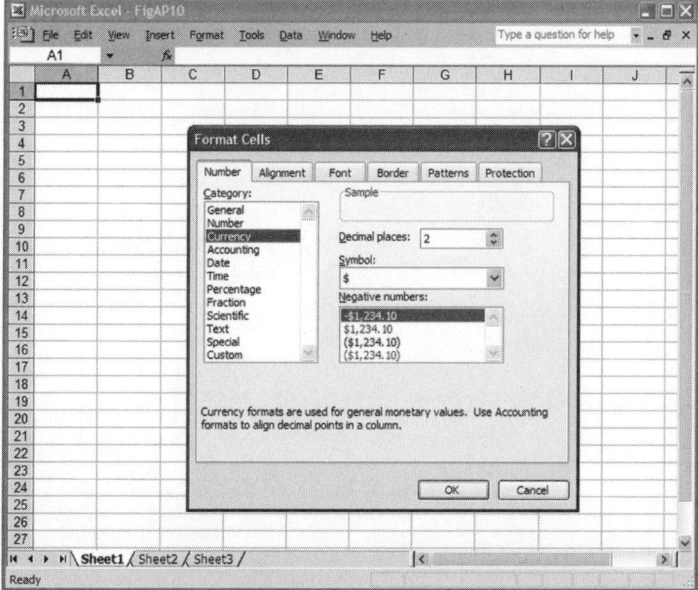

FIGURE AP10   Formatting Suboptions

tab in the dialog box that appears. Figure AP11 shows the font formatting dialog box. The "Font" dialog box provides a way for you to change the font, style, size, and color of the selected cell or cells. You can also control the underline options and special effects, such as super- and subscripts in this dialog box.

Border Format

Each cell in a workbook has four sides or "borders." You can change the format of all of these borders in Excel. To see the border formatting options for a cell, select the Format menu and choose "Cells . . ." from the drop-down menu. Next, click on the "Border" tab in the dialog box that appears. Figure AP12 shows the border formatting dialog box. To format a cell's borders, first select the line style on the right side of the dialog box and then click on the border or borders that you would like to modify in the "Border" section of the dialog box. You can also change the color of borders using the "Color" drop-down menu in Figure AP12.

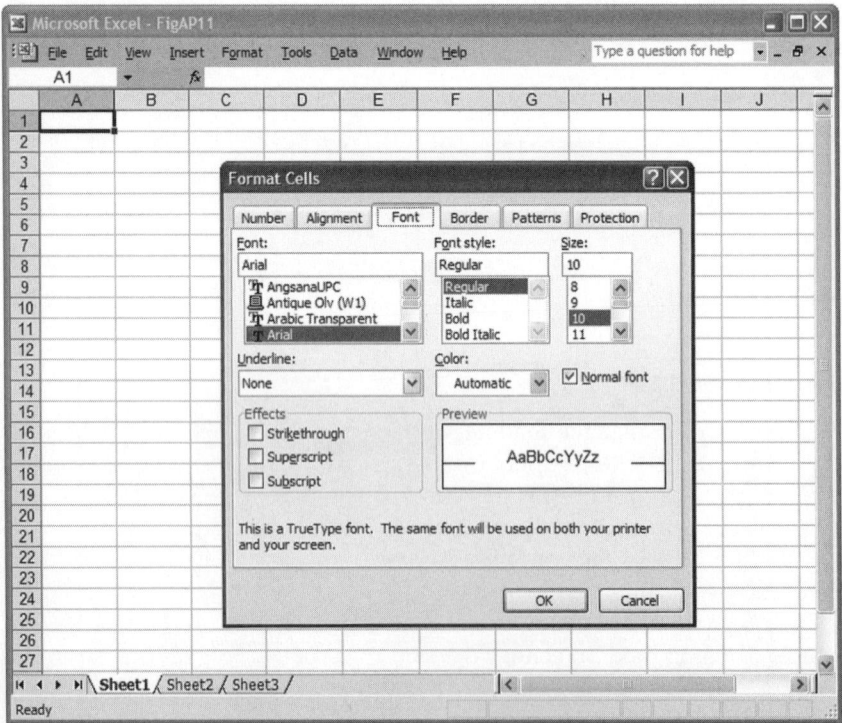

FIGURE AP11   Font Formatting Options

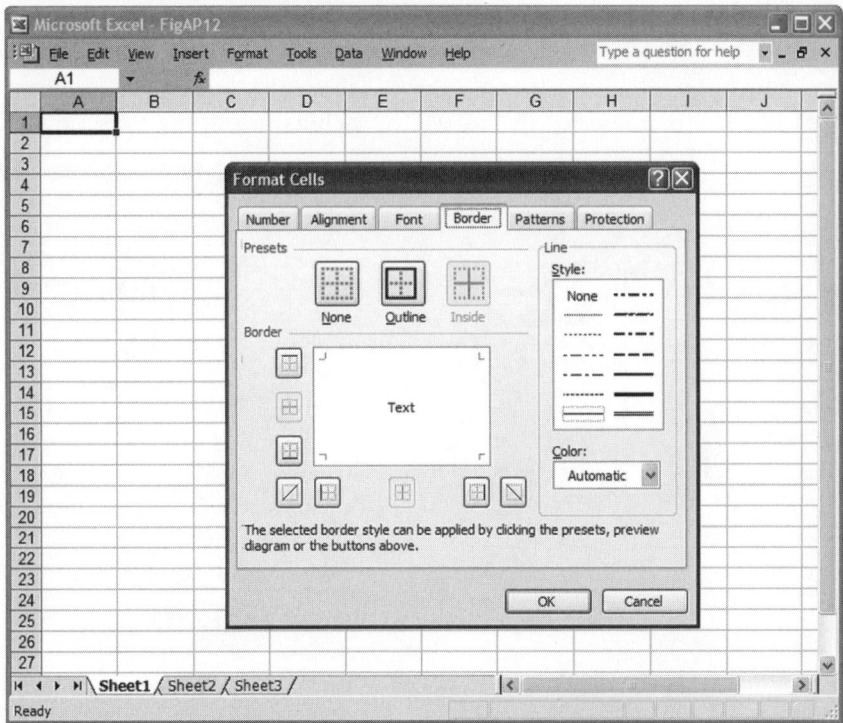

FIGURE AP12 Border Formatting Options

Patterns Format

The ability to change the shading, or pattern, color of cells is another powerful formatting feature offered by Excel. Using this feature, you can, for example, make several cells of interest yellow while leaving the rest of a worksheet's cells clear (or without any special colors).

To see the pattern formatting options for a cell, select the Format menu and choose "Cells . . ." from the drop-down menu. Next, click on the "Patterns" tab in the dialog box that appears. Figure AP13 shows the cell patterns dialog box. To change the shading of a cell (or cells), click on the color of your choice as shown in Figure AP13. This action will alter the color of the cell or cells that were selected in Excel before you opened this dialog box.

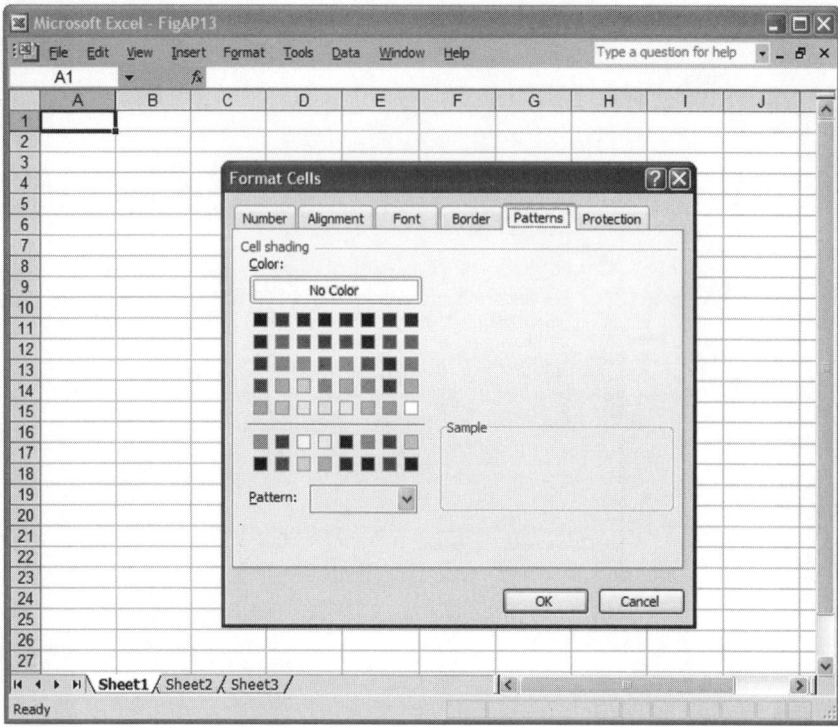

FIGURE AP13 Patterns Dialog Box

Copy Formatting

It is possible to copy the format of a cell (or group of cells) in Excel. This feature is quite helpful when, for instance, you would like one column in a financial model to look like another column from that same model.

To copy formatting, select the cell or cells whose format you would like to copy. Select the Edit menu and choose "Copy" from the drop-down menu. Next, select the cell or cells whose format you would like to change to match the format of the cell or cells that you copied above. Select the Edit menu again and now choose "Paste Special" from the drop-down menu. The dialog box offering several options will then appear—choose the "Formats" option in the "Paste" section and then click OK. A screenshot of the "Paste Special" dialog box is shown in Figure AP14. Using the "Paste Special" dialog box allows you to copy the format of one cell (or set of cells) and paste this formatting to a new cell (or set of cells).

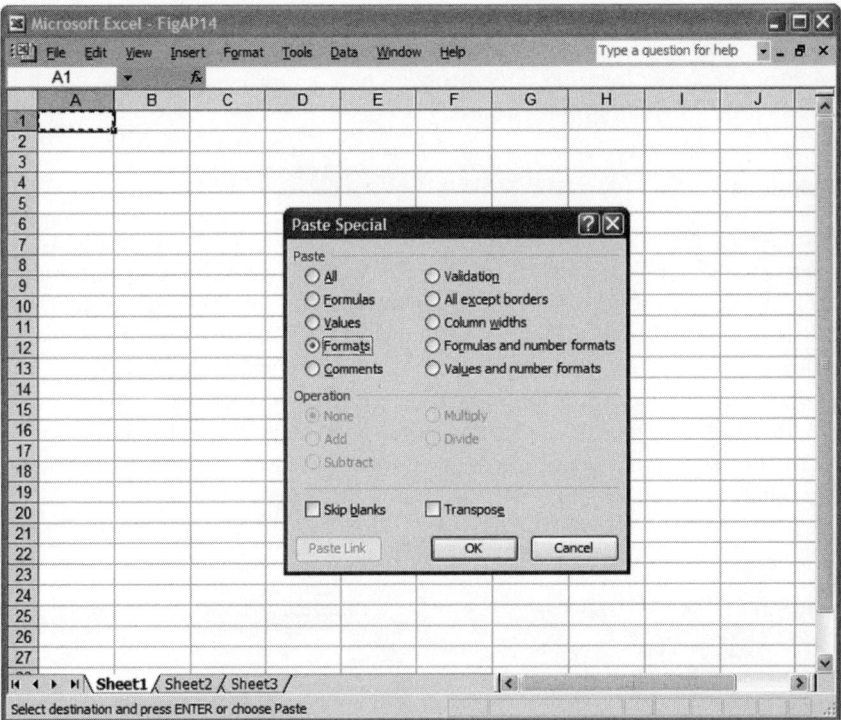

FIGURE AP14 "Paste Special" Dialog Box

FORMULAS AND FUNCTIONS

Microsoft Excel's powerful formulas and functions make it an ideal tool for building financial models.

Formulas

Formulas are statements, or equations, that perform operations on information in your worksheets. A formula, which always begins with an equals (=) sign in a cell in Excel, can contain any or all of the following: functions, references, operators, and/or constants.

Functions, which are described in more detail below, are predefined formulas. References identify a cell or group of cells into which Excel should look to find a value (or values). As such, references are essentially "pointers" to other cells that hold values of interest. Operators specify that a particular type of calculation should be performed on the elements of a formula. Excel has a set and predefined order in which operators are evaluated (or used) in a formula. Operators include + (add), – (subtract), * (multiply), and / (divide), among others.

Functions

Functions are predefined formulas that perform calculations by using arguments, which are specific values, in a particular order. Excel offers many useful built-in functions—an easy way to view the available functions for a cell is to press SHIFT + F3 (the key marked "F3" at the top of your keyboard). Alternatively, you can click on the "fx" button, which typically appears directly above the column headings in your worksheet.

In terms of structure, functions begin with an equals (=) sign, followed by the function name (e.g., SUM), an opening parenthesis, the arguments for the function separating by commas, and a closing parenthesis. Figure AP15

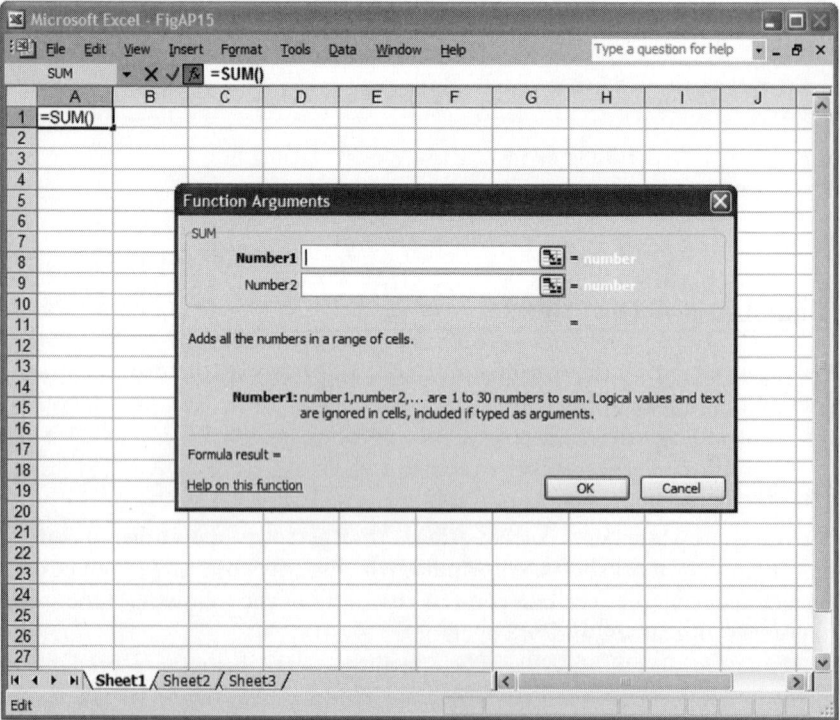

FIGURE AP15   Function Arguments Dialog Box

shows a "Function Arguments" dialog box for the SUM function (which adds a series of values together).

You can always click on the "Help on this function" hyperlink in the dialog box for additional help, but the tips shown in the dialog box usually do a good job of indicating how to use a particular function.

When you are entering arguments for the function into the "Function Arguments" dialog box, you can click on the small worksheet icons at the right edge of the input cells for the arguments (i.e., Number1 and Number2 in Figure AP15). Doing so will collapse the dialog box so that you can see more of the workbook on which you are working. Simply click on the same worksheet icon again to expand the dialog box to its original size and format.

Referencing Other Cells

When using formulas and functions in Excel, it is common to refer to, or reference, other cells. Using cell (and cell range) references offers a great deal of flexibility when building financial models. By using a "dashboard," or master input sheet, for a financial model, you can change one assumption on that one dashboard sheet and the rest of the financial model (e.g., Balance Sheet, Income Statement, and/or Statement of Cash Flows) will automatically reflect the change.

A reference identifies a cell or a range of cells and tells Excel where to look for the data that you want to use in a formula. References to cells in other worksheets are called "links." The three key types of references are called "relative references," "absolute references," and "mixed references."

Relative references are based on the relative position of the cell in which the formula resides and the cell to which the reference refers. If the position of the cell containing the formula changes, the reference changes as well. If you copy the formula across rows or down columns, the reference automatically adjusts. In Excel, new formulas use relative references by default. Relative cell references take the form of "A1."

Absolute references always refer to a cell in a specific location. If the position of the cell containing the formula changes, the absolute reference remains the same. If you copy the formula across rows or down columns, the reference does not adjust. Absolute cell references take the form of "A1."

Mixed cell references have either absolute columns and relative rows or relative columns and absolute rows. An absolute column reference takes the form of "$A1" or "$B1" and an absolute row reference takes the form of "A$1" or "B$1." If the position of the cell containing the formula changes, the absolute reference remains the same and the relative reference changes. If you copy the formula across rows or down columns, the absolute reference does not adjust but the relative reference automatically adjusts.

Another important feature of Excel is the ability to reference information in other worksheets using formulas. An easy way to refer to information in another worksheet is to create a new formula (this can be as simple as entering "=") and then click on another worksheet of interest. Next, click on the cell or range of cells in this worksheet of interest and finally hit the "Enter" or "Return" key on your keyboard. Figure AP16 shows a reference to another worksheet (in this case, cell A1 in Sheet3).

Please note that relative, absolute, and mixed references apply when referencing other worksheets—Figure AP16 shows a relative reference, as it is in the form of "A1." You can also reference separate Excel files, but this can become complicated if you do not have access to all of the referenced files when sharing workbooks.

ADVANCED FEATURES

Among the many advanced features offered by Microsoft Excel, one in particular is worth noting as it relates to building financial models: data tables. This feature is useful in building and analyzing business case scenarios.

Data Tables

The data tables feature in Excel is especially useful when running sensitivity analyses. Specifically, if you are interested in evaluating the impact of

FIGURE AP16   Reference to Another Worksheet

one or more variables on an output of interest, such as free cash flow, data tables make this task quite manageable.

It is possible to build both one-variable and two-variable data tables in Excel. While a one-variable data table allows you to vary one independent variable, a two-variable data table allows you to evaluate the impact of changing two independent variables on an outcome of interest.

For the sake of simplicity, the example below discusses a one-variable data table. To build a data table, first identify your output of interest. This output must be found in a single cell—in other words, you want to see how a single output is affected by changing an input variable. Figure AP17 shows a properly arranged data table—its components will be described later in this appendix.

The output of interest in Figure AP17 is Z. Z is equal to X plus Y. The

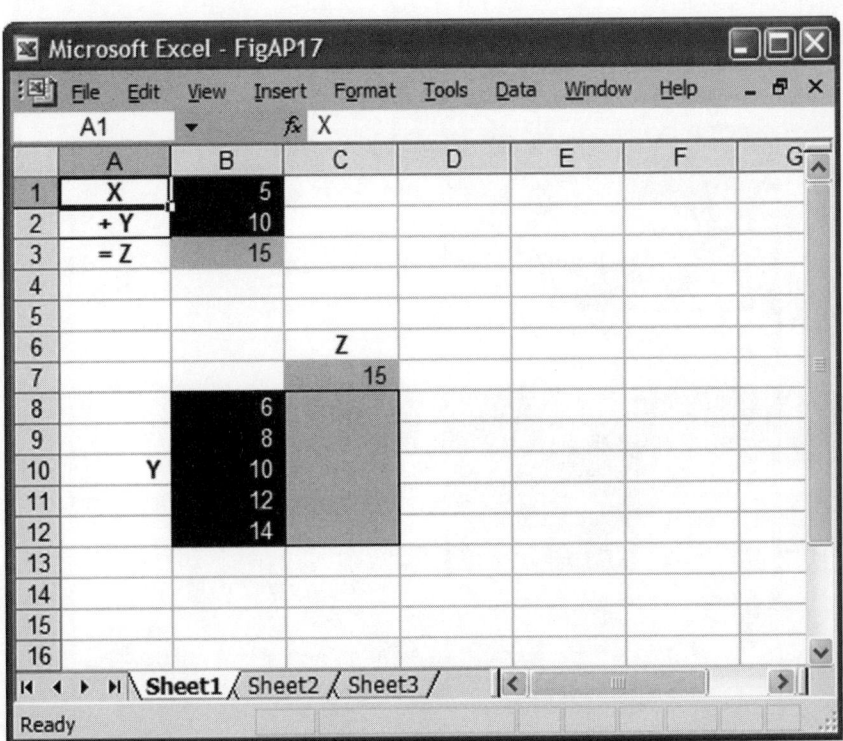

FIGURE AP17 Completed Data Table

data table in this screenshot calculates what happens to Z if Y is changed. To build this data table, first reference the output cell of the calculation (cell B3 in Figure AP17)—this reference is placed in cell C7 in Figure AP17. Next, enter in potential values of Y that you would like to evaluate—this must be done one column to the left of and one row down from the referenced cell. These potential values of Y are found in cells B8 through B12 in Figure AP17. Figure AP18 highlights the reference to the output of interest (cell B3, which has been named Z).

Next highlight the referenced cell (cell C7 in Figures AP17 and AP18) and the cells containing the input values that you would like to evaluate. In this case, you would highlight cells B7 through C12 as shown in Figure AP19. Next, select the "Data" menu and click on the "Table . . ." option—Figure AP20 shows the dialog box that will appear. Since we have entered in the input values that we would like to evaluate in a column, click in the "Column input cell" data input box and refer to cell B2 as shown in Figure AP21. Cell B2 contains the initial

FIGURE AP18   Reference to Output of Interest (Cell B3)

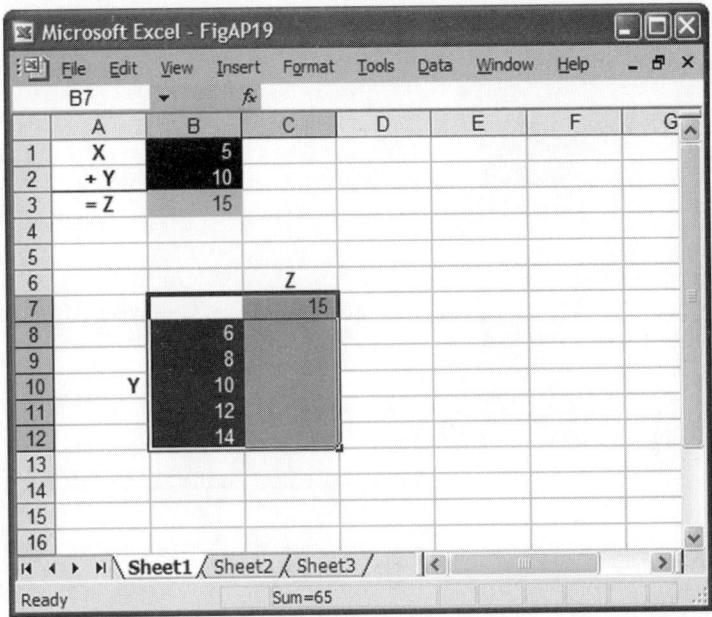

FIGURE AP19   Highlighted Cells

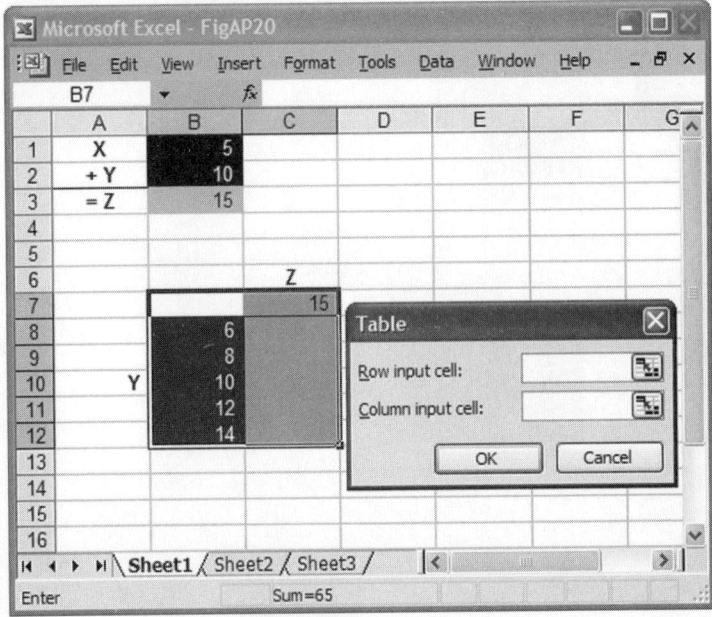

FIGURE AP20   Dialog Box

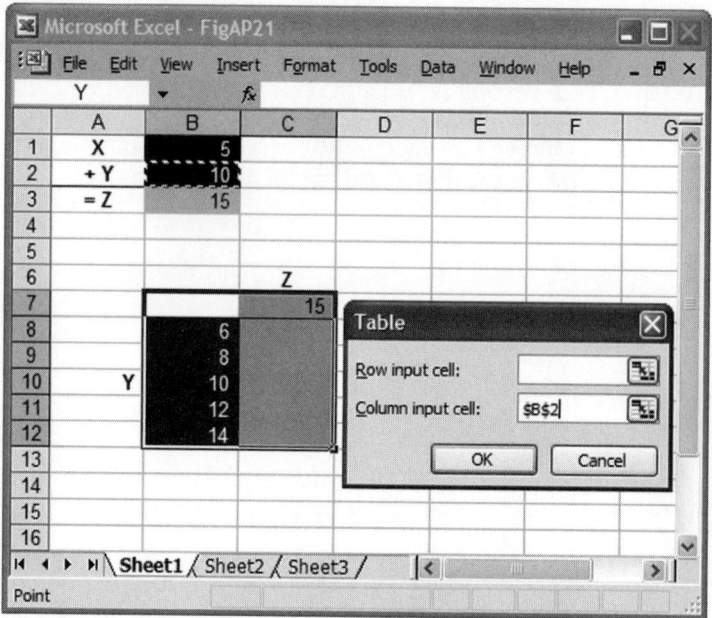

FIGURE AP21   Cell Reference

FIGURE AP22   Data Table

value of the Y variable. By selecting cell B2 as the column input cell, the data table feature will build a table that evaluates the Z variable under different Y values. Figure AP22 shows the resultant data table. As suggested by the annotations in Figure AP22, this data table may be used to evaluate Z under varying conditions of Y. For example, referring to Figure AP22, we can see that Z will equal 19 if Y equals 14.

About the CD-ROM

INTRODUCTION

This CD contains each of the Excel worksheets that are presented as figures in *Building Financial Models with Microsoft Excel*. These worksheets are provided for your reference so that you may track the course of the book using Microsoft Excel and so that you may build financial models of your own using these worksheets as templates. When opening a file on this CD, the worksheet corresponding to the relevant figure in the book will appear. Note that each file on this CD, however, typically contains additional information in different worksheets within that file.

CD-ROM TABLE OF CONTENTS

FigQ11.1.xls–FigQ11.8.xls   FigQ13.1.xls–FigQ13.5.xls

FigA11.1.xls–FigA11.6.xls   FigA13.1.xls–FigA13.7.xls

Folder: Chapter 12   Folder: Chapter 14

Fig12.1.xls–Fig12.28.xls   Fig14.1.xls–Fig14.11.xls

FigQ12.1.xls–FigQ12.6.xls   FigQ14.1.xls–FigQ14.3.xls

FigA12.1.xls–FigA12.3.xls   FigA14.1.xls–FigA14.3.xls

Folder: Chapter 13   Folder: Appendix

Fig13.1.xls–Fig13.28.xls   FigAP1.xls–FigAP22.xls

MINIMUM SYSTEM REQUIREMENTS

Make sure that your computer meets the minimum system requirements listed in this section. If your computer doesn't match up to most of these requirements, you may have a problem using the contents of the CD.

For Windows 9x, Windows 2000, Windows NT4 (with SP 4 or later), Windows Me, or Windows XP:

- PC with a Pentium processor running at 120 Mhz or faster.
- At least 32 MB of total RAM installed on your computer; for best performance, we recommend at least 64 MB.
- Ethernet network interface card (NIC) or modem with a speed of at least 28,800 bps.
- A CD-ROM drive.
- Microsoft Excel, Version 2000 or later.

For Macintosh:

- Mac OS computer with a 68040 of faster processor running OS 7.6 or later.
- At least 32 MB of total RAM installed on your computer; for best performance, we recommend at least 64 MB.
- Microsoft Excel, Version X or later.
- PC exchange must be installed.

USING THE CD WITH WINDOWS

To use the files on the CD, follow these steps:

1. Insert the CD into your computer's CD-ROM drive.
2. A window appears with the contents of the CD-ROM listed in their directory structure.

If you do not have autorun enabled, or if the autorun window does not appear, follow these steps to access the CD:

1. Click Start and select Run.
2. In the dialog box that appears, type *d:* where *d* is the letter of your CD-ROM drive. This brings up the autorun window described in the preceding set of steps.

USING THE CD WITH THE MAC OS

To use the items from the CD to your hard drive, follow these steps:

1. Insert the CD into your CD-ROM drive.
2. Double-click the icon for the CD after it appears on the desktop.

TROUBLESHOOTING

If you have difficulty installing or using any of the materials on the companion CD, try the following solutions:

- **Turn of any antivirus software that you may have running.** Installers sometimes mimic virus activity and can make your computer incorrectly believe that it is being infected by a virus. (Be sure to turn the antivirus software back on later.)
- **Close all running programs.** The more programs you're running, the less memory is available to other programs. Installers also typically update files and programs; if you keep other programs running, installation may not work properly.
- **Reference the ReadMe.** Please refer to the ReadMe file located at the root of the CD-ROM for the latest product information at the time of publication.

If you still have trouble with the CD-ROM, please call the Wiley Product Technical Support phone number: (800) 762-2974. Outside the United States, call (317) 572-3994. You can also contact Wiley Product Technical Support at www. wiley.com/techsupport. Wiley Publishing will provide technical support only for installation and other general quality control items; for technical support on the application themselves, consult the program's vendor or author.

To place additional orders or to request information about other Wiley products, please call (800) 225-5945.

USING THE SOFTWARE

Please refer to the readme.txt file on the CD for more information.

USER ASSISTANCE

If you need assistance or have a damaged disk, please contact Wiley Technical Support at:

Phone: (201) 748-6753
Fax: (201) 748-6800 (Attention: Wiley Technical Support)
E-mail: techhelp@wiley.com

To place additional orders or to request information about Wiley products, please call (800) 225-5945.

Index

For information about the CD-ROM see the About the CD-ROM section on page 337.